Super Baby Food ®

your complete guide to what, when, and how to feed your baby and toddler

OVER 350 YUMMY RECIPES · GREEN-BABY INFO
MONEY-SAVING TIPS · AND MUCH MORE

RUTH YARON

*"**Super Baby Food** is the first book I've seen with a simple, organized and specific menu for how to feed your baby fresh healthy foods. I love the charts, and time saving tips. What first may seem daunting, is really quite do-able."*

— Debbie Lillard, author of *A Mom's Guide to Home Organization*

"I'm a busy mom with two kids and thought I knew all there was to know about feeding my infant since I just did all of this with my 4-year old. After reading **Super Baby Food**, I discovered many new methods, recipes, tips, and facts that I can use for my infant and preschooler, too! Busy moms have a tough time keeping up with the daily routine. I love the idea of having a baby food guide that is easily laid out and cuts right to the chase. This one is staying in the kitchen next to the other recipe books!"

— Nicole from MamaNYC.net

"More than just a collection of recipes, **Super Baby Food** offers parents a comprehensive lesson in nutrition; the month-by-month food introduction schedule and easy preparation instructions make this book a must-have for any parent or caregiver."

— Stefanie Coughlen, NecessaryStrangeness.com

"**Super Baby Food** is a complete guide to teach parents how to feed their baby right from the start. I love the reliable resource to know when to start my baby on a certain food and ideas for how to feed those foods to baby. It includes detailed, healthy extras (quickie ways to add nutrition to meals), easy-to-follow charts, schedules, recipes, and never-ending baby and toddler-feeding ideas!"

— Valerie Plowman, *Chronicles of a Babywise Mom*
www.babywisemom.com

What parents and others are saying . . .

"*Super Baby Food* is a fantastic guide for introducing your baby to delicious and wholesome homemade foods."

— Martha Stewart

"Ruth Yaron has done it again! The original **Super Baby Food** was a monumental breakthrough; this major update is a treasure. Babies are built out of food, and Yaron has made it simple for parents to give their children food they can feel great about: easy, inexpensive, safe, tasty, and fabulous for their kids."

— Alan Greene, MD
Pediatrician, Founder DrGreene.com and author of *Feeding Baby Green*

"**Super Baby Food** is the bible of infant feeding. Ruth is obsessed with babies, nutrition and health. She has done all the research, so busy parents like you, don't have to. Packed with tips, recipes, and important information, this comprehensive guide will help you through the first few years."

— Dr. Jenn Berman, author of *SuperBaby:*
12 Ways to Give Your Child a Head Start in the First 3 Years

"There is nothing more important to a parent than their child's health and well-being. Ruth Yaron's Super Baby Food, Third Edition, is a useful and easy-to-read tool that helps parents learn how to feed their children the very best wholesome, nutritious and tasty food right from the start."

— Elizabeth Pantley, author of the award-winning 'No-Cry Solution'
books series, including *The No-Cry Picky Eater Solution:*
Gentle Ways to Encourage Your Child to Eat–and Eat Healthy

"I dreamed of making my own baby food but when I found myself a mom to a micro-preemie I was daunted by her intense dietary needs. I am so thankful to Ruth Yaron for writing a book that helped me become confident in taking charge of my daughter's nutrition. I constantly recommend *Super Baby Food* to my mommy friends because it is my number one go-to resource when it comes to preparing healthy meals for my child, from making my own baby food to creating tempting treats for my now toddler!"

— Kayla Aimee, mom to Scarlette and writer at www.kaylaaimee.com

Super Baby Food

Your complete guide to what, when and how to feed your baby and toddler

Ruth Yaron

Third Edition

F. J. Roberts Publishing Company
Peckville, Pennsylvania

Printing Number 3.03

Third Edition 2013
Completely Revised and Updated

Published by:
F. J. Roberts Publishing, LLC
20 Blythe Drive
Peckville, PA 18452 US
(815) 425-8942
www.SuperBabyFood.com

Publisher's Cataloging-In-Publication Data
(Prepared by The Donohue Group, Inc.)

Yaron, Ruth.
  Super baby food : your complete guide to what, when and how to feed your baby and toddler / Ruth Yaron. — 3rd ed.

  p. : ill. ; cm.

First published in 1996.
Includes bibliographical references and index.
ISBN: 978-0-9652603-2-9

1. Baby foods. 2. Infants—Nutrition. I. Title.

RJ206 .Y37 2013
641.3/00083

Printed in the United States of America

This book is dedicated to God,
who blesses me much more than I deserve,
and to Pastor Ernest and Louise Drost,
my twins' other parents.

Acknowledgements

I would like to thank my wonderful husband, Bob, who is always there whenever I need him. Sweetie, thanks for your support throughout the years of work on this project and for knowing just the right things to say when I was tired and unsure. My appreciation to the best boys in the world: Fred and John and Bobby, my grown-up Super Babies, for all of their patience and understanding throughout this project. I love you guys. You are great! My appreciation to my dear friend and ex-sister-in-law, Terri, who suffered through a half-written draft of this manuscript throughout her baby's first year. And thanks to my mother-in-law, Helen ("Meme"), and my ex-mother-in-law, ("Grandma Leona"), who kept me fed when I was working, and to my lovely daugher-in-law, Katie. Love to my siblings, Linda, John, and David, who are too much like their big sister.

My sincere thanks to the folks at the Valley Community Library, who allowed me to take out hundreds of books and dozens of interlibrary loans without complaint. (At least they didn't complain to me!) Thanks so much for your help: Mary Barna, Karen Slachta, Lisa Kozlowski, Kim Scritchfield, Garren Levi, Rivkah Peller, Art Fuller, Beverly Elvidge, Henry Heflin, Barbara Melodia, Paula Melesky, Donna Simpson, Kevin Kozlowski, and Amy Simpson.

My gratitude to April Rudat, R.D., M.S., my Maternal and Infant Nutrition Professor at Marywood University, and to the poor graduate students in our classes who had to suffer through my unending questions, which sometimes made the three-hour classes run late.

Also, thanks to our *Super Baby Food* team: Claudine Wolk, Julie Murkette, Stacey Hurley, Sharon Castlen, Kate Bandos, Rosemary Bert, and so many others that made this book possible.

I would especially like to thank all of the Moms, Dads, and friends of young babies who have written to me with very kind compliments and helpful criticisms—you have really helped to improve the third edition!

Disclaimer

This book is designed to provide information on the care and feeding of babies and toddlers. It is sold with the understanding that neither F. J. Roberts Publishing, LLC, F. J. Roberts Holdings LLC, nor Ruth Yaron is engaged in rendering professional opinions or advice. If professional assistance is needed, the services of a competent healthcare provider, pediatrician, or registered dietitian should be sought. F. J. Roberts Publishing, LLC, F. J. Roberts Holdings LLC and/or Ruth Yaron shall have neither liability nor responsibility to any parent, person, or entity with respect to any illness, disability, injury, loss, or damage caused, or alleged to be caused, directly or indirectly by the information contained in this book.

The book should be used only as a supplement to your baby's professional healthcare provider's advice, not as a substitute for it. Be sure to discuss with him or her any food or drink before you feed it to your baby. It is not the purpose of this book to replace the regular care of, or contradict the advice from the American Academy of Pediatrics, the American Dietetic Association, or any pediatrician, nutritionist, registered dietitian, or other professional person or organization. This text should be used only as a general guide and should not be considered an ultimate source of child care, child feeding, food preparation, food storing, or other information. You are urged to read other professional books and information and learn as much as possible about child care, safe methods of food preparation and storage, and the nutrition and feeding of young children.

Every reasonable effort has been made to make this book as complete and accurate as possible. However, there may be mistakes both typographical and in content. Therefore, this text should be used only as a general guide. You should discuss with your baby's professional healthcare provider the information contained in this book before applying it. This book contains information available only up to the copyright date. New information, or information contradicting that which is found in this book, should be actively sought from your child's competent healthcare professionals.

A note from Ruth Yaron
Before you pick up the spoon. . .

. . . check with your Healthcare Provider. I cannot stress this enough and I actually do mention it quite a few times throughout the book. Here are some questions you want to ask your pediatrician before you get started feeding solid foods:

- How old your baby should be before starting solid foods
- Which foods should be the first solid foods to feed your baby
- How much liquid should your baby drink
- Ask about Iron and other nutritional supplements
- Ask about food allergies and about your baby's family history of allergies

Hot New Baby Feeding Topics

What is "correct" in the world of baby feeding changes daily, or so it seems. In the third edition of *Super Baby Food*, I have included the most up-to-date guidelines available when we went to press. From the first edition of *Super Baby Food* to the third edition, as you can guess, there have been many changes in those guidelines. I include here some of the "Hot Topics" where guidelines have most dramatically changed.

Plastic Wrap: I do not recommend using plastic wrap or plastic bags. Recent studies have shown a potential danger from transference of plastic onto food that is wrapped or stored or frozen in plastic. I suggest the use of glass containers and 100% stainless steel ice cube trays and containers. An alternative idea is to wrap food in organic, unbleached wax paper and THEN place in a plastic bag (for refrigeration) or plastic freezer bag (for freezing). This solution means that the food does not touch the plastic directly.

Aluminum Foil: I do not recommend using aluminum foil to wrap food when it is in direct contact with the food for cooking or storage. Aluminum can be toxic.

Microwave: Recent studies have shown that microwaving destroys phyto-nutrients in food. Throughout this edition I do not include microwave use.

Allergies: The American Academy of Pediatrics (AAP) has determined that late introduction of highly allergenic foods may actually boost an allergic reaction in babies. I have included this latest development throughout the text of *Super Baby Food*. I highly suggest you discuss this development with your pediatrician, though, and decide together when to introduce highly allergenic foods to your baby.

Eggs: The AAP has also changed its recommendation on feeding eggs. Where egg whites were avoided due to allergy concerns, it is now suggested to feed baby the whole egg at the appropriate time, some say 6 months.

The Dirty Dozen Plus™: Although I suggest buying only certified organic food to prepare your baby food, I realize that this may not always be possible. With that in mind, you should be aware of the foods determined to have the most chance of pesticide danger. The Environmental Working Group (www.ewg.org) put a list together of *The Dirty Dozen* for you. The Dirty Dozen includes: apples, celery, cherry tomatoes, cucumbers, grapes, hot peppers, imported nectarines, peaches, potatoes, spinach, strawberries, sweet bell peppers, summer squash, kale/collard greens.

The Clean 15™: Conversely there are foods that have the least pesticide danger. Introducing *The Clean 15*: asparagus, avocado, cabbage, cantaloupe, sweet corn, eggplant, grapefruit, kiwi, mangoes, mushrooms, onions, papaya, pineapple, sweet peas (frozen), sweet potatoes.

I hope you enjoy reading this edition of *Super Baby Food* as much as I enjoyed writing it. Please feel free to contact me on Facebook or Twitter with questions or feedback. You'll find the links in the Resources section.

Enjoy the ride!
Ruth Yaron
June 2013

Contents

Part I

The Super Baby Food System

1

Overview of the Super Baby Food System

Introduction to Super Baby Food

Congratulations on the birth of your new little one! Only those of us who have experienced parenthood understand the joy that comes from watching a child grow. You feel that you want to give the world to your baby. The most important things you can give your baby are not toys or a college fund, but YOU—your time and your love. You've heard it a million times, but I'll say it again: Enjoy them while they're young. They do grow so very fast.

You want the best of everything for your new baby, including the most nutritious food possible. The best food for your baby comes out of your kitchen, not from an industrial food plant. Making your own baby food gives you the power to ensure that only healthy, whole foods are used as ingredients. Homemade food is more natural, tastier, and much more economical.

The easiest way to feed your baby homemade food is to feed her along with the rest of the family. Take some of their unseasoned plain food, purée it, and feed it to her. However, if your household is like mine, the family doesn't always eat together. Most of the time I end up feeding my baby with no one else around. I don't think I'd ever go through the trouble of cooking and puréeing a few ounces of fresh vegetables each time I gave my baby a meal—I'd be much too tempted to pop open a jar instead. Using the *Super Baby Food System*, baby-sized portions of vegetables, fruits, and cereals are at the ready. In literally two minutes, you can whip up an entire home-cooked baby meal, complete with cereal, two vegetables, and a fruit or juice. This amazing feat is done by grabbing pre-measured, pre-cooked foods out of the freezer and refrigerator and thawing them on the stove top.

The Commercial Baby Food Industry

Advertising works. It worked a few decades ago, when mothers didn't even consider breastfeeding because advertisers convinced them that commercial infant formula was somehow better than mother's milk and more convenient. It's working now. How else would generations of parents be convinced to pay exorbitant prices for nutritionally inferior baby foods? Modern society has come so far from nature that we sometimes forget where real food comes from. I can remember once feeding my baby orange juice and my husband asked me where I had gotten it (because we had finished our last carton the day before). When I said that I squeezed it out of an orange from our refrigerator, he joked that he thought orange juice came from cartons.

Orange juice comes from fresh, whole oranges. Baby cereal should come from whole brown rice and other whole grains, with all their nutrients intact and not processed out during refinement. All baby food should come from fresh, whole, minimally-processed food—and you can make it easily and cheaply in your own kitchen.

Myth: Commercial baby food is superior to homemade baby food.

The food that you make at home from fresh whole vegetables and fruits is nutritionally superior to any jarred commercial variety on your grocer's shelf. The cereals you can quickly and easily make at home from brown rice (and other whole grains) cannot be compared to the processed, refined white rice commercial baby cereals.

Myth: It takes too much time to make homemade baby food.

Making homemade baby food is much easier than you think. Yes, I agree that popping open a jar is less work than preparing a fresh fruit for your baby, but not by much. Aren't the benefits worth a little extra time?

Myth: Homemade baby food may cause my baby to get sick or get food poisoning.

Some parents think that there's something magical that goes into the preparation of commercial baby food that cannot be done at home, which somehow makes it the only food suitable and safe for their baby. I hope this book will dispel that notion.

Myth: The convenience of commercial baby food is worth the price.
On the next two pages I compare the costs of commercial baby food and homemade baby food. I think most parents, once they realize how much the convenience of commercial baby food actually costs, will choose to make at least some of their own baby food at home.

You Don't Have to Go "All the Way"

There's no rule that says that you cannot have some jars of commercial baby food in your cabinet and still be a good parent. Yes, even I confess to keeping a few jars on hand for emergencies, like when I run out of homemade, or for long-distance travel. I suggest organic brands that use whole grain cereal.

The Super Baby Food System

The *Super Baby Food System* is a method of preparing and storing extremely nutritious homemade baby food. The method saves time, energy, and money. Once you get the system down, it becomes part of your routine. The system is so easy that, if you spend any time at all in the kitchen, you will be able to prepare baby food simultaneously while doing your other kitchen tasks. Preparing homemade baby food will take only a few extra minutes in the kitchen each day.

You don't need to be a good cook to use the *Super Baby Food System*. I hate to cook—that's why I came up with such a quick and easy system. When I told my friends I was writing a baby food cookbook, they rolled on the floor laughing. If you are concerned that you need advanced (or even average!) kitchen knowledge to use the system, fear not. I assume you know practically nothing about cooking. Did you worry that you wouldn't know how to take care of your baby after you brought her home? We all did. Within days, we knew how to give better care to our new little one than anyone else in the world. Give the *Super Baby Food System* the same time, and you'll be a pro after only a couple batches of cooked vegetables!

Super Baby Food is Better

The *Super Baby Food Diet* is based on the fact that anything the commercial baby food manufacturers can do, you can do better in your own kitchen. When you prepare your own baby foods, you can be sure that only wholesome ingredients, with no additives or fillers, are used.

Instead of these commercial baby foods	Feed your baby these homemade Super Baby Foods
Baby fruits in jars	Fresh ripe fruits
Baby vegetables in jars	Fresh cooked and puréed vegetables
Refined, processed baby rice and other cereals in boxes	*Super Porridge*, a super healthy homemade cereal made from whole grains, and when your baby is 9 months old, from whole grains and legumes for complete protein
Commercial dinners: mixed junior dinners in jars, high-sodium frozen dinners marketed for children, canned pasta dinners	Homemade and frozen toddler TV dinners made from whole, healthy foods with no added salt or preservatives

How Much Time Is This Going To Take?

The answer is: as much time as you want. You don't have to feed your baby the entire diet. For instance, you could choose to use just the idea of adding a teaspoon of wheat germ to commercial baby cereal for a nutritional boost. Time: 30 seconds. Or you can choose to peel and fork-mash a fresh ripe peach instead of buying the commercial jarred baby peaches. Time: 2 minutes. Or you can go all the way and do the whole diet. Time: average of less than a few minutes per meal—guaranteed! The keyword here is "average." You may put in an hour making a month's supply of broccoli, or you may put in 12 minutes making 6 servings of cooked brown rice cereal, but it all averages out to only a few minutes per meal.

The *Super Baby Food System* works this way: You spend some time preparing and refrigerating/freezing batches of baby food. The secret is batch cooking—cooking large batches of food at once. Just as you would not prepare a single bottle of formula at a time, you should not prepare one baby-sized food portion or meal at a time. When mealtime comes, you pull out already-prepared baby-sized portions of food, thaw or reheat and—*voilá*—fast food for baby. If you're willing to spend an hour or two a month to prepare cooked veggies, and a few minutes every two or three days preparing cereal, you can prepare a whole diet of extremely nutritious, natural *Super Baby Food*.

How Do I Do This Preparation?

Each type of food is prepared and stored using a different method. For example, vegetables are cooked, puréed, and frozen in ice cube trays—the perfect size for baby portions. Brown rice and other grains or cereals are ground to a coarse powder in the blender, cooked, and refrigerated. Or, just as easy, brown rice or other grains can be cooked first, then puréed, and refrigerated or frozen. The table on page 9 gives a summary of how each type of *Super Baby Food* is prepared and stored, and the time necessary for preparation.

Detailed step-by-step instructions for each category of food in the table are given in Part III of this book.

It's Like Making Money At Home

Let's figure out how much more you pay for commercial baby food by analyzing a very common jarred commercial baby food—carrots. At the time this book was published, my local supermarket was selling a four-ounce jar of brand name puréed baby carrots for $1.00. That works out to $4.00 a pound ($1.00 for four ounces or ¼ pound, times 4). However, there are less than 4 ounces of carrots in each jar, because water is added during processing, and your actual cost is more than $4.00 per pound.

How much water is added to commercial jarred baby vegetables and fruits? I called two major baby food manufacturers to try to find out. They would not tell me exactly. In both cases, after I told them the information was for my book, the supervisor was called to the phone. One hinted that it was about 15%. Assuming this is true, the price of commercial baby carrots is more like $4.71 a pound ($4.00 divided by 85%).

Fresh carrots at my local supermarket cost about 79¢ per pound. Therefore, commercial baby carrots at $4.71 a pound is almost six times the cost of fresh carrots! Maybe you think that it's worth the extra cost for the convenience of commercial baby food. After all, you just pop open a jar. But it is not difficult or very time consuming to make your own baby food using the *Super Baby Food System*. Following the method described in this book, you can make a month's supply of vegetables for your baby in about an hour. If your baby eats three jars of veggies a day, and you're paying $1.00 per jar, that's $3.00 a day or about $90 a month. If you make your own baby food, it will cost you only 20% of that or $18 a month.

In approximately one hour, by making your own carrots, you're saving $72—and that's tax free! In fact, if you get fresh veggies on sale at the supermarket, it is possible to make healthy homemade *Super Baby Food* for less than 20 cents a serving!

If that's not enough to motivate you to make homemade baby food, remember that you're making food that is nutritionally superior for your precious baby. I always feel great after feeding my baby homemade food—it's another way I have to give him my love.

I have done the same analysis with rice and barley cereals and oatmeal, and the difference in price is even greater. The difference in nutritional quality between commercial baby cereals and the whole grain cereals you can easily prepare at home is, in my opinion, shocking. The typical baby rice cereal on the market today is made from processed white rice, which has most of its natural nutrients and fiber removed during refinement. Then, one nutrient, iron, is put back into the cereal, and it may be in a form that is not as well assimilated by your baby as the iron found in whole, natural food. Brown rice is much healthier for your growing baby, and you can make two or three days' worth in minutes.

Add up the savings from feeding your baby homemade vegetables, fruits, and cereals, instead of the overpriced, nutritionally inferior commercial variety, and you'll find that making homemade baby food is well worth your time. You literally save **hundreds of dollars!**

MONEY SAVER: Sometimes busy parents need the convenience of commercial baby foods. You can save money by buying food products that are essentially equivalent to commercial baby foods. Buy unsweetened regular applesauce instead of commercial baby food applesauce—they are essentially equivalent and the regular applesauce is much cheaper. Buy regular canned fruits packed in juice (not syrups) and no-salt-added canned vegetables instead of toddler diced fruits and vegetables and dice them yourself. Instead of baby fruit juices, buy regular, pasteurized, vitamin C-fortified, no-sugar-added 100% juice and dilute. Be sure to follow instructions for safe handling of baby food and leftovers in Part IV.

Preparation and Storage of Super Baby Foods

Food	Preparation Method	Time Needed for Preparation	Frequency of Preparation
Vegetables	Cook in large batches, purée, and freeze	1-2 hours	Once every month or two
Fruits	Fork-mash or purée, then feed immediately or freeze	A few minutes	Once or twice a day
Grains and Cereals	Grind large batches, cook two days' supply (4 to 6 servings), and refrigerate	Several minutes to grind a large batch; 10-minute wait while cooking	Grind a large batch once a month; cook every 2-3 days, and refrigerate
	Brown rice cereal and other whole grain cereals can also be cooked and puréed in batches and refrigerated or frozen. Waiting time to cook a batch of any size is about 45 minutes. Puréeing takes several extra minutes.		
Lentils, split peas, soybeans, and other legumes	Add dried beans and other legumes to the grains and cereals above and prepare them together to make high-protein whole grain baby cereals. Requires no additional time.		
Eggs	Hard cook and refrigerate	15 minutes to cook	Once a week
Nuts and Seeds	Grind and feed immediately	2 minutes	Once a day
Miscellaneous foods: yogurt, tofu, wheat germ, and many more	None	A few seconds to add to foods as nutritional enhancers	As often as once a meal

Why Doesn't Every Parent Make Homemade?

I imagine there are many reasons, perhaps the most common one being that they just never thought of it; the image of those little glass jars of baby food are ingrained in us. Or maybe they think they don't have a choice and just assume that you must feed a baby commercial baby food. They may think it takes too much work to make homemade, or maybe they even think it's dangerous. Our society still tends to trust manufactured products more than homemade natural products.

Pressure from Parents and In-Laws

If your family is pressuring you to feed your baby jarred foods, believe me, I know what you're going through. When I was making baby food for my own twins, I was practically accused of abusing them. One day, I was so upset that I was ready to quit and buy commercial baby food. Luckily, on that very day, I just so happened to have a pediatrician's appointment. She told me that she had never seen such healthy babies, which was amazing because they were born 10 weeks early and were very sick when they were born. That did it!

I had forgotten about all this pressure until I received a letter from a young mother saying that her mother was insisting that she use a popular commercial brand of baby food. It is interesting. Somehow people feel they have the right to give unwanted advice to a new mother. My advice is to politely listen to them and try not to get angry. Their motives are good—they care about you and your baby and they want to help.

You're Not Alone

One young mother wrote to me and said, "I feel like I'm the only one doing this!" Well, she is certainly not! I have received many letters from parents all over the country, and even from the other side of the world, who feel very strongly about feeding their babies only homemade foods. *Super Baby Food* is now in its third edition and it is more popular now than it was when it was first released! Martha Stewart, Kourtney Kardashian, Cindy Crawford and hundreds of thousand of parents have embraced it. You are most definitely NOT alone! Just as breastfeeding was not accepted a few generations ago, homemade baby food is not fully accepted now. But, in the future, you will be proud to tell your children that you cared enough to make them homemade *Super Baby Food*. And they will be proud of you, too!

2

Starting Solid Foods

The term "solid foods" refers to food (baby cereals, fruits, vegetables, meats, and mixed foods) especially prepared for a baby, usually by cooking and puréeing or straining. "Baby food" includes solid foods and baby juices. Breast milk and commercial infant formula, although the major part of a baby's diet, do not come under either the category baby food or solid foods.

When Should I Start Feeding My Baby Solid Foods?

The answer is: when your pediatrician tells you that it's OK to start solid foods. She will probably agree with the American Academy of Pediatrics, whose guidelines state that the best time to begin feeding your baby solid foods is at 6 months of age, especially if you are breastfeeding. Your baby's body, in its first few months, was designed to digest breast milk, or something similar to it. And, calorie for calorie, no solid food has the nutritional quality of breast milk or formula for your young baby. If you feed your baby solid foods too early, her milk intake may decrease. You'd be replacing milk, the best food for your baby, with foods that are nutritionally inferior and not as digestible. Solid foods should not replace breast milk, they should supplement it.

Why You Should Wait Until At Least 4 Months

Your baby is not physically ready to eat solid foods until he is, at the **very** least, 4 months old. Although your mother or grandmother will strongly disagree, saying that she gave her babies solids when they were only 2 weeks old, there are several reasons to wait at least 4 months before starting your baby on solid foods.

Reason 1: Your baby's digestive system is too immature for solid foods before 4 months. Although he can suck very well, he does not have a lot of saliva to help digest food. Until he is at least 3-4 months old, his system lacks certain digestive enzymes. For example, an enzyme called amylase is needed for digesting cereals (starches or complex carbohydrates). His body has trouble digesting some fats before he is 6 months old. Some foods will pass through him undigested and end up in his diaper. In fact, stool analyses of babies under 3 months of age who have eaten solid foods show undigested food particles. Some high protein foods, like eggs, meat, and even cow's milk, when given too early, may cause problems with your baby's immature kidneys.

Reason 2: Your baby is not developmentally ready to eat solid foods. His throat muscles are not developed enough to swallow solid foods until he is at least 4 months old. And, it is not until about 4 months that he is able to use his tongue to transfer food from the front to the back of his mouth. In fact, when you touch his tongue, he reacts by pushing his tongue outward or forward. This response, called the extrusion reflex or the tongue-thrust reflex, is an inborn mechanism designed to protect your baby from choking on foreign substances that he cannot yet properly swallow. This reflex will not disappear until he is around 16-18 weeks old. The first time you feed him with a spoon, it may seem that he is spitting out the food and closing his mouth at the wrong time. This tongue movement is simply the result of the not-yet-unlearned extrusion reflex and not because he doesn't want the food. It is not until he is about 5 months old that he will see the spoon coming and open his mouth in anticipation.

Reason 3: Your baby must have a way of telling you that he is satiated. He lets you know that he is finished breast or bottle feeding by stopping his sucking or by falling asleep. But until he is able to turn his head to refuse food, which occurs at around 4 or 5 months, he has no way of letting you know he has had enough solid food. Because of this inability, when you feed solid foods to a baby too young, you may be unintentionally force-feeding him. This practice can interfere with his body's self-regulating eating mechanism and lead to problems with being overweight later in life. As with adults, your baby should eat only when he is hungry.

Reason 4: Beginning solid foods too early has been associated with other problems later in life, such as obesity, respiratory problems like bronchial asthma, and food allergies.

Reason 5: Solid foods will not make your baby sleep through the night. Studies show that ¾ of all babies sleep through the night at 3 months of age, whether or not they are eating solid foods. Even if solid foods will help your baby sleep longer, that is still not a good reason to begin solid foods early. I know sleep deprivation is torture—most of us have experienced it. Hang in there. One night he'll sleep right through, and then you can start feeling normal again.

Reason 6: If you are breastfeeding and give your baby solid foods too early, your milk production may decrease.

Don't Wait Longer than 8 Months

After six months, your baby begins to need solid foods for some nutrients, such as iron, vitamin C, protein, carbohydrates, zinc, water, and calories, and delaying food may delay growth. Besides playing a nutritional role, solid foods also help your baby developmentally. It is important that your baby start developing eating and chewing skills between the ages of 7 and 9 months. If you delay the introduction of solid foods past 8 or 9 months, your baby may refuse textured foods when you finally do offer them.

> **NOTE:** Some exclusively breastfed babies have successfully begun solid foods after their first birthday. There are parents who feel very strongly that solid foods should not be started until after their baby's first birthday. If you want to wait to introduce solid foods, discuss it with your pediatrician, and do whatever you and your pediatrician agree is best for your baby. Your pediatrician will probably be concerned about your baby getting enough iron in her diet.

Signs of Readiness for Solid Foods

Your pediatrician looks for certain signs of readiness in your baby before advising you to begin solid foods. Here are some of them:

- She is at least 4 months old, and preferably 6 months.

- She weighs twice as much as her birth weight.

- She weighs at least 13-15 pounds.

- She can sit with support, allowing her to lean forward when she wants another spoonful and backward to refuse.

- She has control over her head and neck muscles and can turn her head to refuse food.

- She has stopped exhibiting the extrusion reflex when you put a spoon in her mouth. If, after several tries, food comes right back out of her mouth when you spoon feed her, she is not yet ready for solid foods.

- She is drinking at least 32-40 ounces of formula per 24 hours and still wants more, or

- She is breastfeeding at least 8-10 times per 24 hours (after the first few weeks), empties both breasts at each feeding, and still wants more.

- The time between feedings becomes shorter and shorter over a period of several days.

- She can bring an object that she's holding in her hand directly to her mouth.

- She shows interest in other people who are eating around her.

- She becomes fussy in the middle of the night, whereas before she slept through with no problem. Or her sleep periods are becoming shorter instead of longer.

Baby Food Mathematics

The signs of readiness for solid foods tend to occur around the same time in your baby's life because of a few simple mathematical facts about calories and your baby's body weight. (Math-phobes may skip the next paragraph.)

The average baby needs about 50 calories per day per pound of body weight. Breast milk and formula provide about 20 calories per ounce. Therefore, for every pound of body weight, your baby requires about 2½ ounces of milk. At 13 pounds, your baby needs about 650 calories or about 32 ounces of milk. These two signs of readiness—a minimum weight of 13 pounds and a daily intake of at least 32 ounces of formula per day—are related. So you see, it's not happenstance that some of the signs of readiness coincide.

Vitamin and Mineral Supplement Considerations

Prescription Vitamins

Your pediatrician has probably prescribed "ACD" vitamin drops, so called because they contain vitamins A, C, and D. When your baby gets a little older, a more complete vitamin supplement may be prescribed.

Your baby should get vitamins from whole foods, which also contain cofactors and other substances needed to work with vitamins. Do not count on vitamin supplements to make up for a bad diet. Vitamin supplements are called "supplements" because they are meant to do just that—supplement a baby's good diet, not replace it. I recommend vitamin supplements, because even a good diet can be lacking in nutrients due to improper storage of foods, too-early harvesting, and the lack of nutrients in our country's depleted soils from poor farming methods.

Exclusively breastfed babies are often prescribed a supplement containing vitamin D. The American Academy of Pediatrics recommends this because breast milk may not have enough of this nutrient, which is produced by sunlight on skin.

> WARNING: Never give your child vitamin or mineral supplements without your pediatrician's OK, especially for those supplements sold without a prescription.

Give vitamin supplements to your baby with her meals, and not on an empty stomach. Vitamins work with food to help with chemical reactions in the body. Fat-soluble vitamins (A, D, E, and K) are best utilized when taken with food containing some fat, such as whole milk or yogurt, eggs, soybeans, peanut butter, tahini, and ground nuts and seeds. They should not be fed with an all-fruit snack, because there is virtually no fat in fruit.

I make sure my baby gets his prescription multi-vitamin drops every day. In fact, I divide the dose and give him half a dropper with breakfast and half a dropper with supper. Some vitamins, such as vitamin C, are better utilized if you administer them in two smaller doses than in one large daily dose. I was concerned that I would not be accurate enough in the dosage by dividing it this way, because there is no mark on the dropper at the halfway point. My pediatrician said that you do not have to be that accurate, and that it was OK to divide up the dose by eye-balling it. If you wish to do the same, please OK it with your pediatrician first.

Iron
Enough Iron in Your Baby's Diet is Extremely Important
A full-term baby is born with enough iron stores from Mom to last him about 4-6 months, or until his birth weight doubles. Premature and underweight babies may have only enough iron stores for 2 months. At these ages, babies must be fed foods high in iron, such as iron-fortified formula or iron fortified cereal. Although breast milk has low levels of iron, its iron is used much more efficiently by the baby's body than iron from formula or food. However, most experts still recommend that a breastfed baby get some form of iron supplementation, whether it is from iron-fortified cereal or iron drops.

If you plan on feeding your baby homemade whole grain cereal instead of commercial iron-fortified cereal, and your baby is not drinking an iron fortified formula, your baby may not get enough iron. Brown rice and millet contain iron, as do eggs and other foods in the *Super Baby Food Diet*. However, most experts consider their iron levels too low for a baby. Iron from plant sources like rice and millet is not as well assimilated as iron from meat and other animal products.

WARNING: Iron deficiency during the first eighteen months of your baby's life may cause serious health and behavior problems and may delay your baby's development.

Ask your pediatrician about giving your baby a daily iron supplement, which you can buy over the counter (no prescription needed). Similar to prescription vitamins, iron drops are in liquid form and dispensed through a dropper into your baby's mouth.

WARNING: Some brands of iron drops have been known to stain the teeth. Your pediatrician will advise you on which brand to buy.

Your pediatrician may advise that iron drops are not needed if you are feeding your baby iron-fortified cereal or iron-fortified formula. Too much iron is not healthy either, and may lead to constipation. Go by your pediatrician's advice, which may depend on the results of the blood test for anemia given routinely to babies. Babies may continue to need iron supplementation until they are at least 18 months old.

Combine Iron with Vitamin C

The body assimilates iron from meat better than iron from grains. To help increase the absorption of iron, feed your baby a vitamin C food or vitamin drops containing vitamin C at the same time your feed your baby eggs or cereals. This combination of foods is built into the *Super Baby Food Diet*.

Iron-fortified Adult Cereals

Don't feed your baby iron-fortified adult cereals and feel safe about your baby getting enough iron. There are different forms of iron, some of which are very poorly absorbed. Adult cereals may contain the poorly absorbed type. Top brand baby cereals are fortified with the correct form of iron, the form that is assimilated well by your baby.

Fluoride

Discuss a fluoride supplement with your pediatrician, especially if you have drinking water that is not fluoridated. The daily dose of fluoride depends on the level of fluoride in your baby's drinking water and her age. If there is no fluoride in her drinking water, supplements are usually started after baby's sixth month.

WARNING: Excessive intake of fluoride by your child from supplements, fluoridated water, concentrated baby formula mixed with fluoridated water, and the swallowing of fluoridated toothpaste and mouthwashes, can also cause problems. Remember to keep toothpaste, mouthwash, and fluoride supplements out of baby's reach. High fluoride levels have been found in some commercial baby foods, specifically chicken, which may put baby at risk for developing fluorosis if he regularly eats more than a few ounces.

NOTE: Boiling fluoridated water does NOT remove the fluoride. As the water evaporates, the fluoride actually becomes more concentrated.

REMINDER: If you are using fluoridated water to mix your baby's formula, remember to discuss this fact with your pediatrician.

3

The Super Baby Food Diet

A Super Healthy Diet for Your Super Baby

The *Super Baby Food Diet* is an extremely healthy diet composed of only whole, natural foods. It is based on these major components: whole grain cereals, vegetables and fruits, yogurt and other dairy products, eggs, nuts, seeds, and legumes. Pediatricians and nutritionists agree that a semi-vegetarian diet (a *lacto-ovo* diet containing milk products and eggs) fulfills all of your growing baby's nutritional requirements.

You may recognize these foods as being those from the "new" food groups, the new "optimal diet" groups. The old food groups were meats, breads and cereals, milk and other dairy foods, and vegetables and fruits. The new optimal diet groups are similar, except that other high protein foods or "meat alternatives" have been added to the protein group: legumes, nuts, and seeds. The meat alternatives usually contain fewer pesticides, hormones, and other toxins than meats, and most of them do not have the sometimes-fatal problem of bacterial contamination (E. coli, salmonella). Nuts and seeds contain the healthy unsaturated fats that your baby needs for development, especially brain development, without the gobs of unhealthy saturated fats found in meats.

How Do I Keep Track of All the Foods My Baby Needs?

The table on the next page lists the major food groups in the diet with a suggested minimum number of daily food servings from each food group. You may be wondering how a busy parent could possibly keep track of all these requirements. Well, the *Super Baby Food Diet* makes it very easy—I promise! Even your babysitter will think so. You will see how as you read through this chapter.

The Super Baby Food Diet	
Food Group and Servings	**Best Super Baby Food Sources and Approximate Portion Sizes for a *One-Year-Old***
Grain Group grains, cereals, breads, pasta 4 servings per day	½-¾ cup cooked whole grains, ie. *Super Baby Porridge* ½ cup dry whole grain cereal (Cheerios®, etc.) ½ slice 100% whole grain bread ½ cup whole grain pasta or noodles 1-2 tablespoons wheat germ
Legume Group beans, legumes, nuts, seeds 2-3 servings per day	⅛ cup (2 tablespoons) dry beans/legumes or ¼ cup cooked beans/legumes, ie. Super Baby Porridge 1-2 tablespoons ground nuts and/or seeds 1-2 tablespoons nut butter or seed butter ½ cup ground seed sprouts 1 ounce tofu
Dairy Group 4 servings per day for a total of 24 ounces or daily amount for child's age	½-¾ cup milk: ie. breast, formula, whole, 2%, or calcium and vitamin D fortified soybean or brown rice milk ½ cup yogurt * ⅔ cup cottage cheese ¾ ounce natural cheese
Vegetable/ Fruit Group 4-6 servings per day	1 or more *Super Green Veggies* ** 1 vitamin C fruit or juice *** ½ vitamin A (orange/yellow) veggie (or 1 every other day) 2 or more other vegetables and fruits
Eggs 3-4 servings per week	½ hard-cooked egg or 1 egg every other day or a scrambled egg, cooked solid
Miscellaneous Nutritional Enhancers as often as once per meal	These nutritional enhancers can be mixed into cereal, yogurt, cottage cheese, and mashed veggies/fruits: nutritional yeast, flaxseed (linseed) oil, powdered kelp, blackstrap molasses, and foods listed as part of other groups above (wheat germ, mashed cooked beans, ground nuts/seeds, tahini, sprouts, tofu, and soybean grits/flour)

*   Yogurt here means plain yogurt, no sugar, organic if possible!

**   Serving size of vegetable is 2-4 tablespoons or 1-2 food cubes.

***   Serving size of fruits is ¼-½ of a fresh fruit, ½-1 cup of raw fruit pieces, or ¼-½ cup juice.

The Super Baby Food Diet Grows with Your Baby

The previous table shows the approximate portion sizes for a 12-month-old baby. A younger baby will eat slightly smaller portions, a toddler will eat slightly larger portions. *The number of portions remains the same for all ages; it's the serving size that varies.* For example, a 6-month-old baby may eat a ¼ cup of *Super Porridge* cereal, a 9-month-old may eat a ½ cup, and a 14-month-old may eat a full cup. But, as the table says, all three babies should have 4 servings of grains each day. The required portions from the different food groups help promote a balanced diet.

My Baby Doesn't Eat That Much!

You may be thinking to yourself, "Let's get real! No real-life baby eats three squares a day!" I hear you, and you're right. Most parents are lucky if their baby (or toddler) eats two good meals a day. In fact, many babies live on one good meal a day, one OK meal a day, breast milk or formula, and maybe a few snacks. If your baby is one of them, the *Super Baby Food Diet* is compatible with his eating habits. As you read the rest of this chapter, you will see that the *Super Porridge Main Meal* works as the one good daily meal, the yogurt meal can be the OK meal, and *Super Snacks* or the third meal can pick up any slack.

Two Well-planned Quick and Easy Meals Per Day

The *Super Baby Food Diet* is based on two main meals a day, a few *Super Snacks*, and a third meal for older babies who eat more food. Even though I call them "main" meals, they are relatively small amounts of food compared to our adult-sized meals. Because baby's stomachs are small, they do well when they eat small amounts of food—mini-meals and snacks—frequently throughout the day. The *Super Baby Food Diet* lends itself to this style of eating.

Each meal is very quick and easy to make. In fact, any given meal takes less than three minutes to prepare! Of course, this assumes that you have done some advance preparation and refrigerating/freezing of foods.

The first main meal is based on *Super Porridge*, the second main meal is based on yogurt, and the other meal and snacks vary from day to day. *Super Porridge* and yogurt, along with being extremely healthy foods alone, are great base mixtures to which dozens of other foods can be added, from puréed veggies to wheat germ and ground nuts/seeds. Keep yogurt and cooked *Super Porridge* ready in the refrigerator, and you can whip up a complete *Super Baby Meal* in minutes.

The next table is an example of a daily feeding schedule for a baby on the *Super Baby Food Diet* who is at least 9 months old.

Sample Daily Feeding Schedule for The Super Baby Food Diet	
Upon Awakening	breast or bottle
Breakfast	a main meal based on *Super Porridge*
Morning Snack	Super Snack
Lunch	a main meal based on yogurt
Afternoon Snack	Super Snack
Supper	a meal that varies from day to day
Bedtime	breast or bottle of water
Plus water after and between meals.	

A Healthy Diet Must Have a Variety of Foods

From the schedule above, it seems that the *Super Baby Food Diet* is the same foods every day. This is not true. *Super Porridge* can be made from dozens of combinations of different cereal grains (brown rice, millet, barley, oatmeal, etc.) and legumes (soybeans, split peas, lentils, kidney beans, etc.). So *Super Porridge* is actually a large variety of foods, even though you cook it the same way no matter what grain and legume you choose. The only exception is *Super Porridge* with soybeans, which will be explained later.

With regard to the yogurt meal, it is true that the yogurt stays the same from day to day. But it is good to eat yogurt every day, and some experts recommend it because of its superb health-giving properties. Even though the yogurt part remains the same, the yogurt meal is still varied due to the other foods and additions to the yogurt that change from day to day. Also, yogurt does not necessarily have to be made from cow's milk. Soy milks (fortified with calcium and vitamin D) and other non-dairy fortified milks can be used as a base for yogurt.

Super Porridge — The Super Baby's Super Cereal

You will frequently see the cereal named *Super Porridge* in the *Super Baby Food Diet*. I call it *Super Porridge* because it is. *Super Porridge* is a cereal made from brown rice or other whole grains. Just as whole grains should be a major part of an adult's diet, *Super Porridge* is the foundation food of the *Super Baby Food Diet*. It is very easy to make—you can make 2-3 days' worth in about 10 minutes. When your baby is 9 months old, you can add beans/legumes to the porridge to make it a complete protein baby cereal.

The Main Meal of the Day — Super Porridge

The main meal of the *Super Baby Food Diet* is outlined in the next box. I fed my baby this meal around 8 or 9 in the morning, after I had gotten the older kids off to school. The baby can wait to eat his breakfast because the milk feeding he drank upon awakening tides him over through the early morning.

The Super Porridge Main Meal

- ½-1 cup of *Super Porridge* cereal
- Either one vitamin A veggie cube or 1 mashed hard-cooked egg (depending on whether it's an egg day) mixed into the *Super Porridge*
- ½-1 teaspoon nutritional yeast mixed into *Super Porridge*
- 1-2 Super Green Veggie food cubes
- Vitamin C source (2-4 ounces of juice or ½ fruit)
- Prescription vitamin drops and iron supplement drops
- Maybe a pinch of kelp and ½-1 teaspoon of desiccated liver (optional)

Preparation Time: 3-4 Minutes

The main meal includes eggs. The *Super Baby Food Diet* includes 3-4 eggs per week. Every second day, a mashed hard-cooked egg is mixed into your baby's *Super Porridge*.

> **TIP:** A good way to keep track of when to include an egg is to go by the day of the week. In our house, Mondays, Wednesdays, and Fridays are "egg days." Most weeks, my baby also gets a fourth egg during the weekend.

On the days that are not egg days, a vitamin A veggie cube is included in the main meal in place of the egg. Sweet potatoes and carrots are so high in beta-carotene that one food cube every two days, plus a daily Super Green Veggie, supplies all of your baby's vitamin A needs.

Preparation Instructions for Super Porridge Main Meal

This entire meal can be mixed in a single bowl, with the exception of the juice, of course. Start by removing a bowl of previously cooked *Super Porridge* from your refrigerator. Remove the Super Green and orange veggie cubes from the freezer and push them into the porridge in the bowl. Thaw the porridge and cubes in a saucepan on the stove for 1½-2½ minutes (or for the amount of time needed). Meanwhile, peel and mash the egg. While mashing, look carefully at the center of the yolk to make sure that it is cooked solid. Prepare fruit or juice. Get the vitamin drops and iron drops ready if recommended by your pediatrician. Get the nutritional yeast ready to be stirred into the porridge.

> **TIME SAVER:** I keep the nutritional yeast bottle (and other nutritional enhancers, such as the desiccated liver bottle and kelp shaker) in an easy-to-reach cabinet, so that it takes me only seconds to open and spoon them into the porridge on the counter directly below the cabinet.

> **TIP:** Keep your baby's vitamins on a surface that you can reach from the feeding area, but out of baby's reach. This way you won't forget them and then have to jump up for them in the middle of the meal.

> **TIME SAVER:** When you are preparing a batch of veggie cubes, mix a few days' worth of Super Green Veggie cubes in with a few days' worth of vitamin A orange veggie cubes in the same small freezer bag. It's easier in the morning to find, open, and close only one freezer bag instead of two.

An Alternate Preparation Method

With above preparation, veggies are mixed in with the *Super Porridge* in the same bowl. If you prefer to feed your baby the veggies in a different bowl than the one with the porridge, so that your baby can enjoy the flavors separately, follow these preparation steps:

Warm *Super Porridge* from the refrigerator on the stove top for a few minutes. Meanwhile, peel egg. Thaw food cubes on the stove top in a separate pot for a few minutes. Place *Super Porridge* in a bowl. While veggies cook, mash egg (look closely to ensure that it's completely cooked) and mix into porridge. Stir nutritional yeast into porridge. Prepare fruit or juice. Get vitamin drops and iron drops ready.

Vitamin and Iron Supplements Should Be Given with the Main Meal

No nutrient works alone. Vitamin supplements work together with the nutrients in food to supply your baby's nutritional needs. Supplements should not be given on an empty stomach. If your pediatrician has advised you to give your baby prescription vitamin drops and/or iron drops, drop them into your baby's mouth in the middle of the *Super Porridge Main Meal* spoonfuls. Don't feed them at the end of the meal, or a coating will be left on the teeth. Alternatively, you can mix the drops into the *Super Porridge* if you are confident he will eat it all.

Vitamin C and Iron Go Together

Vitamin C must be included in this main meal because it helps absorption of the iron from the egg, yeast, and porridge. To remind you of this, the column title in the *Super Baby Food Diet Daily Worksheet* on page 38 reads "Egg + Vitamin C." If your baby's vitamin drops contain vitamin C, you can leave out the fruit or juice from the main meal, especially if your baby is not old enough yet to eat the entire meal.

Nutritional Yeast

Brewer's yeast, torula yeast, and nutritional yeast are nutritional supplement powders or flakes that are high in protein, the B vitamins, trace elements, and other nutrients. Nutritional yeast is consistently one of the top suppliers for the major nutrients, especially the B vitamins and trace elements. Taking a few seconds to add a little nutritional yeast into your baby's morning *Super Porridge* gives it a super nutrition boost. Brewer's yeast does not contain vitamin B12, a nutrient which is sometimes lacking in strict vegetarian diets, so I recommend nutritional yeast instead.

> WARNING: Do not use the yeast for baking breads as a nutritional supplement. If you are not familiar with nutritional yeast, ask your natural foods store employee to help you find it.

Desiccated Liver Powder

If your baby is not a vegetarian, add a little desiccated liver powder (½-1 teaspoon) into the *Super Porridge* along with the nutritional yeast. It contains many trace minerals and iron, and the fact that it is meat will also help iron absorption.

Kelp

Keep a salt shaker with kelp near the nutritional yeast and put just a pinch of it into your baby's *Super Porridge* each morning.

Don't Give Your Baby Milk with the Main Meal

What's obviously missing in the *Super Porridge Main Meal*? Milk. I don't recommend giving milk with this meal for two reasons. First, milk is very filling and your baby may not be able to finish eating the other foods. Second, some studies have shown that calcium binds with iron, and therefore decreases the iron available to your baby. Foods from the dairy group are the easiest to supply to your baby—it's as easy as pouring a glass of formula or breastfeeding—and you can get the required amount in before the end of the day with no trouble.

The Main Meal Gets Your Baby's Day Off to a SUPER START

In my opinion, if you've fed your baby a *Super Porridge Main Meal* this morning, you've already given her more good food and nutrition than that which exists in a whole day's worth of the typical American baby's diet.

Once you get some practice keeping *Super Porridge* in the refrigerator and Super Green veggie food cubes in the freezer, you will realize how little time and money it takes to feed your baby a super healthy homemade diet. With the size of this chapter, you'd swear I was documenting a mission to

Mars. It takes longer to read about how to make the *Super Baby Food Diet's Main Meal* than it does to actually make the meal!

After I give my baby the main meal each morning, I have a real feeling of accomplishment. I get this wonderful sense of security and fulfillment after he finishes eating, because I know that he has had almost all of his required nutrients for the entire day. I hope that you have the same experience with your baby every morning—the feeling that "I done good!"

Once your baby has finished eating the main meal, you can coast for the rest of the day. Feeding your baby will consist of a super easy second main meal based on yogurt, a few Super Snacks, and maybe a third meal.

The Super Baby Food Diet Daily Worksheet

The *Super Baby Food Diet Daily Worksheet* on page 38 is an easy way to keep track of your baby's daily requirements for the food groups. Please look at it carefully, and compare it to the *Super Baby Food Diet Table* on page 20. The worksheet and the table go hand in hand. Note two things:

1. The foods groups in the diet match the columns in the worksheet.

2. The minimum daily servings in the table match the numbers in the bottom row of the worksheet labeled "Suggested Daily Servings."

Ignore the protein combo column for now. The *Super Baby Food Diet* supplies your baby with more than enough protein.

It's simple to use the worksheet. You could probably figure it out by looking at the sample menu and worksheet on pages 38-41. Just fill in the foods your baby eats during the day and place the number of food servings that each food supplies in the column under the proper food group heading. At the end of the day, total up the numbers and compare your totals with the minimum number of servings in the bottom row of the table.

REMINDER: The worksheet is meant to ensure that your baby is getting a proper balance of foods from the main food groups so that there are no nutritional deficiencies in his diet. There's no need to be a slave to it. It is just a tool to help identify a possible weakness in the variety of foods you're feeding your baby.

The Dairy Column of the Worksheet

The bottom total for the minimum daily servings for the dairy column depends on your baby's age. Before your baby is one year old, he should be drinking the amount of breast milk/formula recommended for his age. After your baby is one year old, he should be drinking at least 24 ounces of cow's milk (or fortified soy milk or other equivalent milk product) to meet his calcium and vitamin D requirements.

Milk (Calcium) Equivalents

These milk products have the approximate calcium equivalent of ½ cup or 4 ounces of milk:

- ½ cup yogurt
- ⅔ cup cottage cheese
- 4 ounces tofu (calcium coagulated)
- ¾ ounce of natural cheese
- 1-inch cube of cheddar cheese
- 2 tablespoons of cream cheese
- ⅔ cup ice cream

Vegetables and Fruits Must Supply Vitamins C and A

One of the fruits/vegetables that you feed your baby each day must be high in vitamin C. Kiwi fruit, orange juice, and to a lesser extent, broccoli, kale, and the other foods listed in the vitamin C table in the Appendix. Because vitamin C is a water-soluble vitamin, it must be supplied every single day.

Vitamin A (or more correctly, beta-carotene) must also be regularly included in your baby's diet and is found in sweet potatoes, carrots, broccoli, and kale, among others. Because vitamin A is fat-soluble, and therefore able to be stored in the body, it's OK to skip a vitamin A food cube once in a while. This is why it is OK to have a vitamin A food serving every second day and alternate it with an egg, which contains some vitamin A. The Super Green Veggies that you feed your baby every day contain significant amounts of beta-carotene, as can be seen in the vitamin A table. If you give your baby two veggie food cubes, don't forget to double the numbers in the table, because the 2 tablespoon serving size used in the nutrient tables is equal to only a single food cube.

> **REMINDER:** Make sure that your baby is getting a nice variety of fruits and vegetables. For example, if he eats a lot of bananas and grape juice and no other veggies or fruits, he is probably not getting his nutritional requirements met. A variety of foods are one key to a healthy diet. There are columns specifically for vitamin A and vitamin C fruits/ veggies in the worksheet on page 38 to help you keep track of these two important nutrients.

The Super Baby Food Group Quick Reference Table

The *Super Baby Food Quick Reference Table* on page 39 will help to remind you which foods fit into which food groups. Note that there is a box in the table for each column in the worksheet. Many of the foods fit into more than one food group. For example, flax seeds, tahini, and tofu contain some calcium. Therefore, these foods help to fill the requirements for the dairy group, even though we don't count them there. Milk alone can be counted as a complete protein, but it fits best under dairy. You needn't be concerned with these overlaps because they ensure that nutrient needs are being met. Be concerned only when requirements are not being met, according to the number of suggested daily servings in the bottom row of the table.

You have my permission to make copies for personal use (so you don't have to worry about copyright infringements) of the worksheet on page 38 and the reference table on page 39. The reference and worksheet are purposely juxtaposed so that you can copy both together on one 8½ x 11 sheet of standard paper. Also, the worksheets are available for easy download on the *Super Baby Food* web site. (www.superbabyfood.com)

> **REMINDER:** Keep your completed worksheets for discussion with your pediatrician. Your pediatrician should be aware of and approve of the diet you are feeding your baby.

Writing the Super Porridge Meal into the Worksheet

The main meal is a very important part of the *Super Baby Food Diet*, therefore detailed examples on how to write it into the worksheet are shown on pages 38-41. The *Super Porridge Meal* is shown as the breakfast part of the worksheet on page 38. The identical breakfast part of the worksheet is shown enlarged on page 43 for easy comparison with the box on page 40. Note that the worksheet is an easier method of writing the same information in the box.

If you look at the full sample worksheet on page 41, you will see that the *Super Porridge Main Meal* makes significant contributions to those minimum suggested daily serving totals in the bottom row.

> **TIP:** Ask your babysitter to write into the worksheet any meals s/he gives your baby, and you can easily keep track of his diet.

The Second Main Meal
The Second Meal Is Based on Yogurt
Give your baby yogurt almost every day as part of a second main meal. You can sometimes use cottage cheese instead of yogurt, which is very high in complete protein (½ cup supplies 14 grams of complete protein), but it also has a lot of sodium. Yogurt is preferable because it contains the friendly bacteria so necessary for intestinal health. Yogurt's beneficial bacteria also promote the production of B vitamins in your baby's intestines. This, along with the fiber in the whole grains and legumes in their diets, may be the reason why my babies never got diarrhea or constipation. I realized this one day when my sons and I were watching television and a commercial was shown for the pink stuff used to treat diarrhea. One of my sons turned to me and said, "What's diarrhea?" It's been several years and they still have never experienced it, or constipation either. From what I hear about leaky diarrhea-filled diapers, I consider myself very fortunate.

While I'm bragging about my healthy kids, I'd also like to boast that they are very rarely sick. I was surprised when I read that the average child has 5 to 10 illnesses a year! In fact, my son once complained to me, "How come we never get to stay home sick like everyone else in our class does?" Well, I confess that we now play hooky occasionally to simply enjoy a day off from school—we can afford it! I claim that *Super Baby Food Diet*, with yogurt and *Super Porridge* from whole grains and legumes as its foundation foods, promotes super immune systems in children. Now, I realize that three kids is not a statistically significant number for a scientifically accurate medical study, but I still say it's the *Super Baby Food*. Let some scientist prove me wrong!

Like *Super Porridge*, yogurt is great base for other foods and nutritional enhancers. Yogurt is a good source of complete protein alone, but mixing yogurt with some other foods increases the amount of complete protein. A yogurt-based lunch is also a great way to get the one or two daily servings of ground nuts or seeds into your baby's diet.

> **MONEY SAVER:** Homemade yogurt costs a small fraction of commercial yogurt. And it's so darn easy to make! See instructions beginning on page 298.

If Your Baby is Allergic to Milk

If your baby has a milk allergy, not to worry, your baby can still have the health benefits of yogurt. Buy yogurt made with soy milk or other milk instead of cow's milk. If you can't find this kind of yogurt, buy soy milk, brown rice milk, almond milk, oat milk, or some other non-cow's milk and make your own yogurt—it's just as easy as making yogurt from cow's milk.

Preparation Instructions for a Super Yogurt Meal

First, place frozen veggie food cubes in a pot over low heat to thaw. Second, spoon any whole seeds or nuts into your blender container. Start the blender. Meanwhile, spoon approximately ½-¾ cup of yogurt into a bowl. Stop the blender and mix the ground seeds/nuts into the yogurt. (Note that you grind only the nuts/seeds in the blender—don't put the yogurt in the blender, or some gets wasted and the container is more difficult to clean.) Add any other ingredients that need no preparation, such as tahini, wheat germ, etc. Last, mix the veggie cubes, which have finished thawing on the stove top, into the yogurt. If the veggie cubes get too hot, let them cool first before adding to the yogurt or the heat will kill some of the yogurt's beneficial bacteria. You may want to place the veggies in a separate bowl so that your baby can taste the individual flavors. If you use a second bowl, you can mix some of the ingredients listed on the next page into the yogurt and some into the veggies for more variety.

A Quick and Easy Yogurt Meal

To make a meal out of yogurt for your little one, simply spoon about ½-1 cup of plain yogurt into a bowl. Add one or more of these:

- ½-1 teaspoon of well-ground flax seeds
- Avocado or avocado frozen food cubes (thawed first)
- 1 tablespoon tahini
- 1 teaspoon or more of ground pumpkin seeds or other seeds
- 1 teaspoon or more of ground almonds, walnuts, filberts, cashews, or other nuts
- ½ of one ground Brazil nut
- 1 tablespoon of thinned peanut butter or other nut butter softened for a few seconds on the stove top over lowest heat.
- 1-2 tablespoons wheat germ
- 1-2 vitamin A veggie cubes (sweet potato, carrots, etc.)
- Other veggie cube(s)
- Puréed or fork-mashed ripe banana, peach, kiwi, or other fruit
- Cooked beans, with skins removed and mashed or pureed, or frozen bean food cubes made from the same
- Blackstrap molasses
- A jar or part of a jar of commercial baby fruit or veggie or no-sugar applesauce

Preparation time: 2-3 minutes

Yogurt Is a Great Base for the Healthy Fats Your Baby Needs

Almost every single day, I add a little ground flaxseed or flaxseed oil (which are the absolute best sources of the essential fatty acid omega 3; fish oil is not), and at least ½ food cube of avocado (which is another super source of the unsaturated fatty acids) to my baby's yogurt. Babies need fats for proper brain development, and avocado, seeds, nuts, and nut/seed butters are the best sources of the healthy unsaturated fats.

Super Snacks

Super snacks are an important part of the *Super Baby Food Diet*. They are healthy foods that add nutrients and calories. Follow all instructions to prevent choking beginning on page 337.

Super Snacks Are Real Food

With regard to a baby's or toddler's diet, the word "snack" is a misnomer. We adults tend to think of snacks as sweet little bits of foods that we eat for enjoyment more than to assuage hunger or to provide nutrition. This is not true for your baby or toddler. Snacks should NOT be thought of as "extras" or "treats" for your baby, but as a necessary part of his daily diet that adds calories and nutrition. Snacks may provide your baby/toddler with 20-25% of his daily calories and other nutrients. Because your baby's stomach is quite small, it cannot hold very much at one time, and therefore your baby must eat small amounts of food frequently throughout the day. Snacks fill the need for food in the time stretch between meals and should be as nutritious as baby's main meals. You shouldn't worry that snacks will spoil your baby's appetite for a meal, because snacks are small healthy meals! However, if your baby is hungry and it's near a main mealtime, you may want to skip the snack and move up the time of the main meal.

> WARNING: The foods we consider snacks—potato chips, cookies, cheese twists, candy—should be NO part of your baby's diet. Besides the obvious lack of any nutritional value, most of these snack "foods" are choking hazards for babies and toddlers.

Snacks should be offered at scheduled, predictable times every day and not at random. As hard as it is not to do this, snacks should not be given to a baby/toddler to keep him quiet while you're on the phone or because he is bored. Keep his favorite DVD at the ready or a favorite toy handy instead. Snacks should be eaten in the feeding area, as main meals are, because they ARE meals.

Until your baby becomes proficient at feeding himself, you will be spoon-feeding him his main meals, which will give him most of his daily nutrition. Snacks should consist mostly of finger foods, to allow your baby to practice his self-feeding skills. Ideas for healthy Super Snacks are listed in the recipes in Part VI. Although the Super Snack list may not appeal to you as tasty snacks, remember that they are not meant to be treats or luxuries, but a necessary nutritional part of your baby's daily diet.

> **TIP:** Use an egg slicer to slice pieces of finger food, like hard-cooked eggs and cooked mashed balls of food. A pastry blender will cut soft food into small pieces in no time. A pizza cutter can be used to quickly slice up whole grain bread, French toast, tofu, and fruits and veggies for baby. Be careful that food pieces are not windpipe size, which would be a choking hazard. Cut round foods, such as bananas and hot dogs, lengthwise before slicing.

> **TIP:** Bond with your child while he's snacking. Sit down with him and use a butter knife to spread the fruit slices with the nut butter one at a time, and hand each to your child. They like watching you prepare each piece and it makes you feel very nurturing.

> **TIP:** Toddlers think it's fun to pull string cheese with you.

Batch Preparing and Freezing Super Snacks

Some super snacks, like Cheerios®, need no preparation. But snacks like cooked vegetable pieces do, and they can be prepared in a large batch and frozen to save time and energy. Prepare and cook according to the directions in Part III. To prevent them from freezing together into one big clump, use the *Tray-Freeze Method* and *Nested Plastic Bag Method* of freezing foods. Actually, there's no need to cook snacks separately. Whenever you cook vegetables, save a few finger food-sized pieces and freeze for Super Snacks.

The Super Snack Freezer Bag

In my freezer, I have one large freezer bag known as THE SUPER SNACK BAG, which contains several inner plastic bags (*Nested Plastic Bag Method*) of batch-prepared Super Snacks: cooked veggie pieces, ripe fruit pieces, small tofu chunks, beans with skins removed, and bags of different Toddler Hors d'oeuvres. I remove several of them from the freezer bag the night before I serve them and place them in a covered bowl in the refrigerator. When it comes time for the babysitter or me to give them to the baby, they're thawed and ready.

→ when he can sit up himself

Super Snacks — Finger Foods

- SOFT pieces or wedges of ripe peeled and cored fruit: peaches, mango, papaya, watermelon, cantaloupe, honeydew, banana, pears, cucumber with seeds removed
- SOFT pieces of cooked, diced vegetables: broccoli florets, sweet potato sticks, or cooked white/sweet potatoes rolled into balls
- Raw carrot, grated fine (bigger carrot pieces are choking hazards)
- Small tofu chunks
- Beans cooked until very soft with skins removed
- Peas cooked until soft and smashed slightly with a fork (for older babies only)
- Oatios® or another health food store equivalent of Cheerios®
- Other whole grain and unsugared dry boxed cereal, but with no nut pieces or any hard pieces that can cause choking
- Crumbled egg pieces, cooked solid or scrambled
- Small pieces of soft cheese
- Small lumps of cottage cheese
- Cooked brown rice and other grains
- Whole grain crackers
- Well-cooked small pasta pieces
- Whole grain bread, cut into toast fingers or small pieces
- A whole bagel makes a good teething ring
- Bits of French toast, cooked thoroughly so no raw egg
- Whole grain pancakes
- Toddler Hors d'oeuvres (Chapter 36)
- Ripe, soft apple pieces or crackers topped with grated or sliced cheese and broiled in the toaster oven to melt the cheese.
- Any soft, ripe fruit, such as banana or apple, sliced and spread with thinned peanut butter or other nut butter. Mix freshly ground pumpkin and flax seeds into the nut butter before spreading.
- Make a mash of any combination of ingredients above, form into small balls and other little shapes and serve as finger foods.

TIP: Those infant feeding dishes with the separate compartments are perfect for storing one day's worth of different finger foods—soft cooked carrot pieces for a morning snack in one part, an afternoon snack of diced peaches in another part, and shredded cheese in the third.

> **WARNING:** Make sure that the food pieces are completely thawed, because frozen foods are choking hazards. Transfer them from the freezer to a warm part of the refrigerator THE NIGHT BEFORE, and they'll surely be thawed by snack time the next day.

> **WARNING:** Once these little food pieces are thawed, don't keep them for more than one day in the refrigerator. Throw them out that same day.

All Snacks Can Be Batch Prepared and Frozen

It takes only a few minutes to prepare Super Snacks like tofu chunks (just cut them up) and ripe and soft fruit pieces (wash, peel, and dice), and you can prepare them immediately before feeding to your baby. But it will save time if you batch prepare and freeze them. Freezing them in batches may also help prevent food waste, because once a block of tofu is opened, or a large fruit is cut up, they must be eaten soon if they are stored in the refrigerator. Your baby probably doesn't eat enough to use them before they would spoil.

The Third Meal

All babies are different. A baby can begin eating three meals a day as early as 6 months or as late as 10 months. When your baby is ready for a third meal, you will be able to tell because he acts hungry! Here are some ideas for an additional meal.

Another Super Porridge Meal

For a second *Super Porridge Meal*, instead of mixing in nutritional yeast and a mashed egg/vitamin A cube as you did in the main meal at breakfast, you can add any of the nutritional enhancers listed on page 20 or any food you might add to yogurt. Mix them into the *Super Porridge* bowl or feed from a separate bowl, so that your baby can taste them individually.

Sandwiches and Crackers

As your baby gets older, you can give him meals that require more advanced eating skills than *Super Porridge* that will supply him with as much nutrition. For instance, instead of using *Super Porridge* as a base for nutritional enhancers, spread the enhancers into a sandwich made from 100% whole grain bread or spread them on whole-grain crackers.

Sandwiches are quick and easy to make, especially if you use easy sandwich spreads like tahini, thinned peanut butter, yogurt cheese, other cheeses, prune butter, and hummus. When I make sandwich spreads like hummus, I always make and freeze a batch using the *Food Cube Method*. One cube is the perfect size for a sandwich.

Buy 100% whole grain crackers or make your own. Use the sandwich spreads or a dip like avocado dip for the crackers.

Pasta

Whole grain organic pastas can be found at most supermarkets. Don't use pasta made from white wheat flour from the supermarket. Mix cooked, drained whole grain pastas with just about anything: easy-to-make homemade Super Pasta Sauce (store-bought jars are much too high in sodium), cheese, veggie food cubes, or even sandwich spreads. Sprinkle nutritional enhancers like ground nuts/seeds and a little nutritional yeast in the dish immediately before serving. Pasta is a dish that can be frozen in individual portions and thawed on the stove top for a quick and easy meal. Why pay so much money for the commercial brands of frozen dinners or canned junk made with refined flours and loaded with salt, sugar, and additives? Make a few extra portions and freeze them yourself.

Toddler Recipes

When your baby grows into a toddler, there are hundreds of easy recipes included in this book, some of which the rest of the family will enjoy as well.

A Sample Daily Menu

On page 40 you will find a sample of a full daily menu from the *Super Baby Food Diet*. It's for an older baby or toddler as you can see by the portion sizes. On the page opposite the menu (page 41), there is an example of how you would fill in the worksheet for the sample menu.

The Super Baby Food Diet Daily Worksheet

Date:

	Grains	Legumes	Nuts/Seeds*	Dairy	Super Green Veg	Vitamin C Fruit/Veg	Vitamin A Fruit/Veg	Other Fruit/Veg	Enhancers	Egg + Vitamin C	Vitamin Drops	Iron Drops	Protein Combination
Breakfast													
Morning Snack													
Lunch													
Afternoon Snack													
Supper													
Other Snacks													
Actual Servings Eaten by Baby													
Suggested Daily Servings	4+	1 to 2	1 to 2	24 oz+	1	1	½	2	1+	½	1	1	2+

* Only if no nut allergy

Quick Reference for Super Baby Food Groups

Whole Grains	Legumes	Nuts and Seeds
Super Porridge and other whole grain cereals	*Super Porridge* made with legumes	Ground flax seeds
Whole grain flour	Tofu	Ground seeds
Whole grain bread	Soybeans/soy grits	Ground nuts
Whole grain pasta	Other beans	Tahini
Wheat germ	Lentils	Other seed butters
Oatios/Cheerios®	Split peas	Peanut butter
Whole grain muffins, crackers, bread sticks	Soybean milk (peanuts are actually legumes)	Other nut butters
		Nut/seed milks
		Sunflower seed sprouts and other sprouts

Super Green Veggies	Vitamin C Veg/Fruits	Vitamin A Veg/Fruits
Kale	Orange/orange juice	Sweet potatoes
Broccoli	Other citrus fruit/juice	Carrots
Greens (beet, turnip, dandelion, mustard, collard)	Kiwi fruit	Pumpkin
Brussels sprouts	Papaya	Kale
Asparagus	Tomatoes	Cantaloupe
Swiss chard	Cantaloupe	Peaches, nectarines
Okra	Strawberries	Apricots
Peas (edible pod)	Brussels sprouts	Winter squash
Spinach	Broccoli	Mango
	Sweet green peppers	Spinach

Other Fruits/Veggies	Dairy	Enhancers
Avocado, Bananas	Cow's milk: whole or 2%	Nutritional yeast
Apples, Pears, Plums	Yogurt, whole milk	Flaxseed/linseed oil
Pineapple, Berries	Soy milk, fortified	Wheat germ
Honeydew melon, Watermelon	Cottage cheese	Ground nuts/seeds
Green beans	Natural cheese	Ground sprouts
Cabbage, Cauliflower		Desiccated liver
Beets, Turnips		Blackstrap molasses
White potatoes		Powdered kelp
Tomatoes/sauce		

Sample Daily Menu of Super Baby Food Diet

Upon awakening	Breast feed or bottle of formula
Breakfast Preparation time: 3 minutes	¾ cup *Super Porridge* cereal made from whole grain millet and soy grits mixed with 1 mashed hard-cooked egg and 1 teaspoon nutritional yeast 2 broccoli cubes ½ cup fresh squeezed orange juice Prescription vitamin drops Iron drops
Mid Morning Snack Preparation time: 1 minute	½ cup Oatios (the organic, natural foods store equivalent of Cheerios®) Small, soft pieces of cooked carrot from the Super Snack Freezer Bag (page 34) Breast feed or ½ cup (4 oz) formula
Lunch Preparation time: 2½ minutes	½ cup whole milk yogurt mixed with 1 tablespoon tahini and 1 teaspoon ground flaxseed Avocado cubes Breast feed or ½ cup formula
Mid Afternoon Snack Preparation time: 1 minute	Ripe kiwi fruit, cut into small pieces for finger food or spoon fed directly from peel ½ slice whole wheat bread broken into small pieces for finger food Breast feed or ½ cup formula
Supper Preparation time: 2 minutes	¾ cup *Super Porridge* cereal made from brown rice and lentils mixed with a small mashed banana and Breast feed or ½ cup formula
Bedtime	Breast feed or bottle of formula

Plus a 1-2 tablespoons water after each meal and between meals.

Example of Completed Super Baby Food Diet Daily Worksheet for Menu on Previous Page

	Grains	Legumes	Nut/Seeds	Dairy	Super Green Veg	Vitamin C Fruit/Veg	Vitamin A Fruit/Veg	Other Fruit/Veg	Enhancers	Egg + Vit. C	Vitamin Drops	Iron Drops	Protein Combo
Breakfast													
¾ cup *Super Porridge*	2	1											1
Hard-cooked egg										1			1
Nutritional yeast									1				
Broccoli cubes					1								
Orange Juice						1							
Prescription vitamin drops											1		
Iron supplement drops												1	
Morning Snack													
Oatios or Cheerios®	1												
Carrots							1						
4 oz formula				4									
Lunch													
Yogurt				1									1
Tahini			1										
Flaxseed			1										
Avocado								1					
4 oz formula				4									
Afternoon Snack													
Kiwi fruit						1							
½ slice bread	1												
4 oz formula				4									
Supper													
Super Porridge	2	1											1
Banana								1					
4 oz formula				4									
Other Snacks													
8 oz bottle in morning				8									
8 oz bottle in evening				8									
Actual Servings Eaten	6	2	2	32+1	1	2	1	2	1	1	1	1	4
Suggested Daily Servings	4 +	1 - 2	1 - 2	24 oz+	1	1	½	2	1+	½	1	1	2 +

Compare the numbers in the box below with the numbers in the columns in the worksheet on the previous page and note that they are consistent.

The Super Porridge Main Meal Supplies Foods from Almost All Major Food Groups

The *Main Super Porridge Meal* supplies these food group requirements:

- 2 from **Grains Group** (2¼ cup servings of cooked grains) from the *Super Porridge*. Keep in mind that a ¾ serving of *Super Porridge* contains ½ cup (2¼ cups) of cooked grains and ¼ cup of cooked legumes.

- 1 from **Legumes Group** (a ¼ cup serving of cooked beans) from the *Super Porridge*.

- 2 or 3 from **Vegetable/Fruit Group** from the Super Green Veggie cube, the vitamin C fruit/juice, and the vitamin A veggie cube if it is not an egg day. And technically, you can count the beans in *Super Porridge* as a vegetable—adding one more serving.

- 1 from **Eggs** if it's an egg day.

- 1 or 2 from **Nutritional Enhancers**, such as nutritional yeast and maybe the desiccated liver.

- 1 or 2 **Protein** servings: The grains + legumes in the *Super Porridge* combine to make complete protein, and the egg every other day is a second protein serving.

- **Iron** is supplied mostly by the iron supplement drops, but there is also some iron in the egg, nutritional yeast, desiccated liver, and the whole grains and legumes in the *Super Porridge*.

- Milk or other foods from the **Dairy Group** should **NOT** be given to your baby in this meal, because calcium binds with iron.

Directions on how to cook *Super Porridge* are given in Chapter 4. But briefly, if your baby is 9 months or older and can have beans and other legumes, ¾ cup of cooked *Super Porridge* cereal is made with ½ cup of cooked grains and ¼ cup of cooked legumes, which is two ¼ cup grain servings and one legume serving.

Enlarged Main Meal Part of the Super Baby Food Diet Daily Worksheet												
Breakfast	Grains	Legumes	Nut/Seeds	Dairy	Super Green Veg	Vitamin C Fruit/Veg	Vitamin A Fruit/Veg	Other Fruit/Veg	Enhancers	Egg + Vitamin C	Vitamin Drops	Iron Drops	Protein Combination
¾ cup *Super Porridge*	2	1											1
Hard-cooked egg										1			1
Nutritional yeast									1				
Super Green Veggie					1								
Orange Juice						1							
Prescription vitamin drops											1		
Iron supplement drops												1	

Advantages of the Super Baby Food System
An Advantage for You and the Rest of the Family

The *Super Baby Food Diet* is advantageous for meal planning for the rest of your family, too. You have made one or two very special meals for your baby during the day. By suppertime, after your spouse comes home and the kids are home from school, you can concentrate on a meal centered on the rest of the family, and not your baby. Your baby can join the family table. The main meals and *Super Snacks* that your baby has eaten during the day have supplied the vast majority of your baby's daily nutrient requirements.

The Advantage for the Parent Working Outside the Home

I worked three days a week when my twins were babies. The *Super Baby Food Diet* fit in well with the daily routine, because I could get everything ready the night before. I started with a bowl of *Super Porridge* (already made and refrigerated) added some Green Veggie cubes, nutritional yeast, and a mashed egg or orange veggie cube, and put it back in the refrigerator. I also got a yogurt meal ready with some mixed-in nutritional enhancers, and transferred finger foods/snacks from the *Super Snack Freezer Bag* into a partitioned bowl. All of this took only 5 minutes. The babysitter knew that she was supposed to give him vitamin and iron drops with the *Super Porridge*, as well as some orange juice. The babies were on a regular daily eating schedule of healthy *Super Baby Foods*, and the babysitter found it nice and easy to prepare the foods and feed them.

Shopping for the Super Baby Foods
The Supermarket has Everything You Need

You can buy everything you need for the *Super Baby Food Diet* from your local supermarket: brown rice, oatmeal, lentils, split peas, bags of dried beans, vegetables, fruits, eggs, yogurt, and milk. Grocery stores are now expanding their organic and health food sections. It might also be worth it to take a trip to your local natural foods store.

Get Familiar with Your Local Natural Foods Store

A natural foods store has foods that are much healthier for your baby because they are grown organically. Who knows what long-term effects these supposedly safe pesticides will have on your baby (or you for that matter)? Your baby eats much more food per pound of body weight than we do, so pesticides get more concentrated in her little body. Organic rice and legumes are not much more expensive than those at the supermarket. Compare prices and you will see. New natural food stores are popping up all over the place. Google "health food" with "your town" and you will see all of your options.

Food Shopping Tips

- Shop the inner aisles of the supermarket first and the outer aisles last. I spend a lot of time with coupons comparing prices of toilet paper and spaghetti sauce jars. To prevent broccoli from drooping and frozen juices from melting in my shopping cart while I'm doing math in my head, I don't put them in the cart until I'm done with the room temperature non-perishables in the inner aisles.

- Run other errands first and save grocery shopping for last. That way ice cream won't be melting in the back of the minivan while you are stopping at the dry cleaners, at the car wash, and buying stamps at the post office.

- Discard expired coupons from your coupon holder and clip new coupons immediately before a trip to the grocery store and they will be fresh in your mind when you walk those aisles. Valuable coupons about to expire will be discovered. Place them in a coupon pocket labeled It's now or never! and check this pocket before leaving the store. This prevents the "Oh no! I had a coupon for that and it expired!" phenomenon.

- Use the "bin inventory" method in your home to keep important items in stock. In a special storage bin or closet, place one bar of soap, one roll of toilet paper, one day's worth of diapers, and one of any non-perishable item that must be kept on hand at all times. When you think you've run out, the bin will save you. Note: This method will not work if you do not immediately replace the item in the bin!

- Save grocery receipts with computer-printed prices and item names. Use them to compare for best prices at competing stores.

If this is your first trip to your natural foods store, take a few minutes to check it out. (If you're already a regular customer, skip to the next section.) Walk up and down the aisles looking at the individual items.

By the way, the kind of natural foods store I'm talking about is the local, one room Mom and Pop store, not the "pretend" health food big business store at the mall, which specializes in vitamin jars and cans of protein powders labeled with pictures of gleaming gigantic biceps. From my experience, the people at natural foods stores are knowledgeable in healthy foods and care as much about the quality of their food and your health as their profits. If you let them, they will get to know you and your family as family. One of my local stores let me walk out with $40 worth of unpaid groceries because I forgot my checkbook, trusting me to pay the next time.

Buy Brown Rice and Millet First

If you are going to follow the *Super Baby Food Diet*, here are the first foods that you should buy, and the order that you will need them as your baby grows: brown rice, millet, oatmeal/rolled oats, pearled barley, yogurt, tofu, eggs, juices, tahini, Oatios®, pumpkin seeds, almonds, other nuts/seeds, nutritional yeast, wheat germ, lentils, split peas, beans, natural peanut and other nut butters (or nuts to make homemade nut butters), bulgur, non-degerminated cornmeal, whole wheat pasta, sunflower seeds for sprouting, and by now you're a pro and I don't have to tell you what to buy. Buy only the first two (brown rice and millet) your first time at the store, if you wish. Get the rest, as you need them.

Buying Natural Foods On-Line

If you can't get to a natural foods store, and your supermarket doesn't have the foods you are looking for, the Internet is another option. Some sites may be more expensive, but there is a price you pay for convenience. You can buy everything from natural peanut butter and tahini to organic whole grains and tofu on-line. There are many good web sites that sell natural and organic foods, including Amazon.

Natural Foods Web Sites

The Bread Beckers
www.breadbeckers.com

True Foods Market
www.truefoodsmarket.com

Organic Kingdom
www.organickingdom.com

Organic Direct
www.organicdirect.com

Papa's Organic
www.papasorganic.com

shopOrganic and shopGMOfree
www.shoporganic.com

These sites also carry organic non-GMO herbs, grains, seeds, etc.

Mountain Rose Herbs
www.mountainroseherbs.com

Starwest Botanicals
www.starwest-botanicals.com

Familiarize Yourself with These Items and Their Locations in Your Local Natural Foods Store

- Organic dry whole grains: brown rice, millet, whole oats, oat flakes and oatmeal, quinoa, teff, triticale, barley, etc.
- Whole grain flours and brans: whole wheat flour, soy flour, oat flour, rice flour, millet flour, oat flakes, etc.
- Organic legumes: dried beans, peas, lentils, soy grits, etc.
- Organic nuts and seeds, refrigerated: almonds, walnuts, flaxseed, etc.
- Jarred and canned nut and seed butters, such as organic peanut butter, almond butter, tahini, etc.
- Organic cow's milk, pasteurized and refrigerated
- Yogurt made from organic cow/soy/other milk, refrigerated
- Eggs from free-range, no-hormones-added chickens, refrigerated
- Tofu in sterile packages, refrigerated
- Tofu in aseptic packages that need no refrigeration, which can be kept safely at room temperature for up to 10 months. Once opened, they must be refrigerated.
- Commercial boxed breakfast cereals similar to those in the supermarket, such as Oatios or some other Cheerios®-like cereal, whole grain corn flakes cereal, etc.
- Nutritional enhancements, such as nutritional yeast, wheat germ, nonfat organic dry milk powder, desiccated liver, powdered kelp
- Whole grain pastas, such as lasagna, elbow macaroni, and spaghetti made from whole wheat, brown rice, or other whole grain
- Organic tomato, pasta, and other flavorful sauces, with no added salt, sugar, or hydrogenated oils
- Boxes of non-cow's milk: soy milk, rice milk, Better than Milk®, goat's milk, oat milk, and almond and other nut milks. These boxes can be kept at room temperature until the expiration date, but hey must be kept refrigerated once they are opened.
- Snack-type foods, with no added sugar: whole grain cookies, snack bars, fruit leathers, shredded coconut, and carob chips
- Caffeine-free flavorings and flavored drinks, such as carob powder (a chocolate substitute), grain coffee substitutes, and natural teas
- Books, including those on vegetarianism, nutrition, herbs, natural foods, and cookbooks (including *Super Baby Food*)
- Organically-grown fruits and vegetables
- Organic baby foods, such as organic jarred fruits and vegetables, organic whole grain boxed baby cereals, and organic whole grain teething crackers.
- Environment-friendly laundry detergents and other household cleaning products

Each Meal Takes Only A Few Minutes to Prepare

Batch Cooking Is the Key

Why does it only take a few minutes to prepare an entire home-cooked *Super Baby Food* meal? You have previously cooked batches of baby food and stored them in baby-sized portions in your refrigerator or freezer. They are there, ready and waiting for you to grab them and thaw them on the stove-top, making you capable of whipping up a complete baby meal consisting of vegetables, a fruit, and a cereal or protein food in a few minutes. "Aha," you're thinking, "There's the catch! I have to spend days cooking over a hot stove to prepare these foods in advance!" Not true at all.

Foods You Must Prepare in Advance

There are really only three categories of foods that must be advance prepared in large batches to save time: *Super Porridge*, frozen cooked vegetables, and hard-cooked eggs. That's it. Detailed step-by-step instructions for preparing and storing all of the *Super Baby Foods* are given in Part III of this book, but the box below contains a little information to give you an idea of how you would cook and store them. You just cannot buy these foods. There's no commercial baby food on the market that is as healthy as your homemade. You can prepare these foods in less than 30 minutes per week.

Super Baby Foods To Be Prepared in Advance

- *Super Porridge* is a cooked cereal made from 2 parts whole grain and 1 part beans or other legumes. It takes about 10 minutes to prepare 2-3 days' worth and keeps in the refrigerator for up to 3 days or in the freezer for 2 months. Preparation instructions start on page 54.

- Hard-cooked eggs take about 15 minutes to cook, but almost all of that time is waiting for them to boil. Once cooked, eggs keep in the refrigerator for only one week.

- Frozen food cubes of cooked vegetables and fruits take the most time—about 20 minutes to an hour or more, depending on the amount you're preparing. But you only have to prepare them once every month or two. They keep stored in the freezer in plastic freezer bags for two or more months.

Foods Needing No Preparation in Advance

Other foods in the *Super Baby Food Diet* are fresh and require no cooking or advance preparation, and can be prepared in a minute or two immediately before serving. Some of these foods should not be prepared in advance, because of nutrient loss. For example, fruits are a main source of vitamin C, the most delicate of all nutrients. Preparing them a minute before your baby eats them helps maintain this unstable nutrient, which gets destroyed by air, heat, light, and water. Every minute after you cut open an orange or kiwi fruit means the loss of vitamin C. Other foods, like flax seeds, should not be prepared in advance because they get rancid in just a few hours.

Super Baby Foods That Need No Advance Preparation

- Yogurt, cheese, and other dairy foods: no preparation necessary, although you can make your own yogurt and save a bundle.

- Fresh fruit: takes a minute or two to wash, peel, core, and mash.

- Wheat germ, nutritional yeast powder, flaxseed oil, and other foods used as nutritional enhancers, which get sprinkled into other foods like *Super Porridge* and yogurt: no preparation necessary—just open the jar.

- Raw nuts and seeds: to prevent rancidity, kept them whole in the refrigerator, and then grind to a powder in the blender immediately before eating.

- Tofu: purée or mash and combine with other food, or use small chunks as finger food.

- 100% whole grain bread: no preparation necessary, except for possibly tearing into bite-sized pieces. Toasting destroys nutrients.

Foods that You Can Batch Prepare in Advance, If You Wish

There are other foods you can make yourself in order to save money. But if you don't want to take the time, you can purchase them from the supermarket or natural foods store instead. They will be as healthy as homemade. Foods like yogurt, fruit leather, teething and snack crackers, and whole grain bread cost about one third of store-bought if you make your own. The yogurt and fruit leather are cake to make at home and I would definitely recommend it, but the crackers and bread take time. Someday if you're feeling especially domestic and Martha Stewart-like, you should try them.

Develop Your Own Super Baby Food System

As you become more practiced at making *Super Baby Food*, you will develop your own system. One of my kitchen sessions, which I do every few weeks, is shown on page 53. These kitchen sessions are meant to give you a quick overview of the time necessary to prepare the *Super Baby Foods* and an idea of the steps involved. The details on how to prepare all of the *Super Baby Foods* are in Part III.

Additives in Commercial Baby Food

If you are going to buy commercial baby food, read the labels carefully for added sugar and salt. Some commercial baby food manufacturers still add sugar and salt to their jars of baby food, especially to the "dessert" types of baby food. Also, if you buy baby food, go for the single ingredient jars, which are less likely than the "dinners" to have added salt and the bad type of fat.

Hold the Salt and Sugar

When you are preparing homemade baby food, never add salt or sugar. Sugar causes cavities in the teeth and adds empty calories to your baby's diet. Not only does sugar contain no nutrients, it actually uses up your baby's existing nutrients from other foods for its digestion. If your baby fills up on sugar, there won't be room for the *Super Baby Foods* with their important nutrients.

Although salt or sodium is needed by your baby's body, he gets plenty of it from natural unsalted foods. Salt is an acquired taste, and you should not promote a love of salt in your baby's taste buds. Too much salt is a problem in the typical American diet.

Veggies Take the Most Time, But Are Cooked Infrequently

The veggies are the baby foods that have to be cooked least often because they keep for at least two months in the freezer. Obviously, the larger the batch of veggies, the less often you have to make veggie food cubes. Rarely, when I have a lot of energy, I go all out and do the multi-batch vegetable cooking session. Or, when one particular vegetable goes on sale at the supermarket, I take advantage and stock up on food cubes by cooking using an assembly line-type kitchen session.

Hard-cook Eggs Once a Week

Because hard-cooked eggs keep for only one week in the refrigerator, I do them once a week on the same day of the week—Monday. That way I know when they've expired and should be thrown out.

Cook Super Porridge Once Every Few Days

Super Porridge keeps for only 2-3 days in the refrigerator so, unless you freeze it, it must be cooked two or three times a week. You may have to make it more often if you are blessed with twins, as I was! Although *Super Porridge* takes about 15 minutes to make, you can combine it with other household tasks so that it actually takes only a few minutes of your time.

Simultaneous Preparation of the Three Types of Super Baby Foods to Prepare in Advance: Frozen Veggie Cubes, Super Porridge, Hard-Cooked Eggs			
Time for each step	Steps for vegetables	Steps for Super Porridge	Steps for hard-cooked eggs
10 minutes	Wash, chop veggies, and start cooking on the stove top.		
30 seconds		Place water for *Super Porridge* on stove to boil.	
30 seconds			Place eggs in water on stove to boil.
3 minutes		Measure, mix, grind in blender grains/beans and put by stove, ready to stir into water. Put whisk by stove.	
5-10 minutes wait while veggies cook	Get purée equipment ready.	When water boils, stir in ground grains and beans. Note time when porridge will be done. *Stir Super Porridge* frequently.	Eggs started boiling, set timer, get towel for drying eggs ready. Forget about eggs until timer sounds.
7 minutes	Veggies are done cooking and stand-ing, purée and put in ice cube trays, cover well, freeze.	Keep stirring *Super Porridge* frequently.	
2 minutes		*Super Porridge* done. Pour into individual bowls, cover, and refrigerate.	
2 minutes			Eggs done. Run cold water into pot. Dry well, cover, refrigerate.
Total time: 23-28 minutes.			

Integrating Super Porridge into Your Daily Kitchen Routine

Super Porridge keeps in the refrigerator for 2-3 days, therefore every few days you must make a fresh batch (unless you freeze it). There's no need for it to take more than a few minutes out of your day, if you merge it into the household tasks that you're doing anyway. Plan on making *Super Porridge* when you are going to be hanging around in the kitchen for at least 10 minutes, because you should stir *Super Porridge* every couple of minutes to prevent scorching. I make *Super Porridge* while I simultaneously do my daily 15-minute "quick pick-up" routine. Here's how I fit it in.

Time Super Porridge Right and It Won't Take Any Time

1. Place water on the stove to boil. Remember to always use the back burners and to turn the handles toward the wall so that baby can't reach.

2. Measure and grind grains and beans in blender and place next to stove. Place whisk next to stove. Now everything is ready for when the water begins to boil.

3. While waiting the 5 or so minutes for the water to boil, I do a small "out of kitchen" task, such as: sort or start a load of laundry, pick up some of the toys that are scattered throughout the house, fix a bed, take out the garbage, make a quick phone call, etc. But don't get sidetracked and forget about the pot on the stove as I have done many times!

4. Return to kitchen and sprinkle the ground grain/bean powder into boiling water. If you use the same burner, the same pot, and the same amount of water, you will know exactly how long it will take for the water to boil and you can set a loud timer to signal you to return to the kitchen with perfect timing.

5. Reduce heat and keep stirring until it cools a bit.

6. Now's the time to do 10 minutes of kitchen tasks while stirring the *Super Porridge* every 2 minutes: hand wash the last meal's dishes or empty/load the dishwasher, make a batch of formula bottles, take an inventory of the food staples on page 143 so that you know what to buy on today's trip to the natural foods store, clip coupons, sweep the kitchen floor, wipe off the counter tops, do a quick clean of the refrigerator—throw old food out and wipe off a shelf, call Aunt Erin, put her on speaker and wipe down the top of the refrigerator, check your emails, etc.

7. Pour finished *Super Porridge* into individual bowls, cover well, and refrigerate.

8. Clean the pot.

Voilá! Super Porridge for 2-3 days.

4

Super Porridge Cereals: THE Most Important Part of the Super Baby Food Diet

Super Porridge cereal is THE most important part of the Super Baby Food Diet

Many parents who have used the earlier editions of this book have told me that they used this book to make only vegetables. Vegetables are only part of the *Super Baby Food Diet*. I encourage you to try making *Super Porridge*—it's very easy and, in my opinion, is the unique part of the diet that will make your baby super healthy. I have not done a scientific study, but it seems that babies who have not been fed *Super Porridge* get sick just as often as the "average" American baby—about 5 to 10 times per year. The parents who I know have made *Super Porridge* a major part of their babies' diets claim that their babies never or very rarely get sick. And they all claim that they NEVER have problems with diarrhea or constipation. The fiber in the whole grains and legumes of *Super Porridge* is necessary for colon health and overall health. So please include *Super Porridge* in your baby's diet—you and your baby will be happy you did.

> **TIP:** If you begin your baby on *Super Porridge* at 6 months and feed it to her every single day, she will probably continue to eat it well into the toddler years because she is used to it. Believe it or not, my son is now older than three and he still eats it every day! Here is his daily super healthy meal: Whole grains, legumes, nutritional yeast (yuck!), kale or some other Super Green Veggie cube, and half an avocado cube. It doesn't taste good to me, but he eats it—no problem. He even asks for it! I'm keeping my fingers crossed that he will continue eating it forever. I force myself to eat his leftovers.

Super Porridge is a homemade baby cereal that, when cooked, looks very similar to commercial boxed baby cereal mixed with liquid. But unlike commercial cereal that is processed and refined, *Super Porridge* is a natural cereal made from unrefined whole grains. Whole grains are a very inexpensive source of super nutrition for your baby. These complex carbohydrates are a good source of trace minerals, such as chromium, copper, magnesium, manganese, selenium, silicon, zinc, and others.

Instead of starting baby on commercial rice cereal, you can start your baby on *Super Porridge* made from brown rice. However, your baby should be at least 6 months old before you give her *Super Porridge*, because her digestive system will then be mature enough to digest the whole grains.

You can buy brown rice at your supermarket, but the organic section of your supermarket and/or local natural foods stores have organically grown brown rice.

Storing Uncooked Whole Grains

Don't worry about buying too many whole grains—you'll use them before they spoil. Store dry, uncooked, whole grains in an airtight jar in a dark, cool cabinet and they'll keep for a year or more. Buckwheat groats and oatmeal are exceptions—keep them at room temperature for only one month or refrigerate or freeze them for longer storage—up to 6 months.

Insects love whole grains! Storing grains in sterile mayonnaise jars is a good way to protect them from the little varmints because grain bugs can chew through plastic bags, cardboard boxes, and wax paper coverings.

TIP: Larvae of bugs are sometimes inside the grains—that's how they magically appear, even in tightly covered containers. If you have trouble with little grain bug specks, perhaps because you live in a climate of high heat and humidity. Try one of these preventative measures:

- Store grains in your refrigerator—if you have the room, or

- Place the grains in the freezer for 14 days to kill all insect larvae, or

- Heat the grains in the oven on cookie sheets or in shallow pans at 130°F for at least 30 minutes to kill the larvae, or

- Place a bay leaf or two into the grains, but be sure to remove the leaves and any leaf pieces completely before cooking. (Bay leaves are sharp and can cut your mouth and throat.) Enclose the bay leaves in cheesecloth to prevent pieces from mixing into the grains. Replace bay leaves after about one year.

Making Super Porridge from Brown Rice

Making *Super Porridge* is easy. First measure a cup of water on the stove to boil.

> **WARNING:** Be sure to read the use, safety, cleaning, and maintenance directions for your blender or processor completely before you begin to use it. Be sure that the manufacturer's instructions say that it is OK to grind dry ingredients in your blender or processor, such as brown rice, oatmeal, other grains, and whole nuts and seeds.

While the water is heating to a boil, measure ¼ cup of brown rice into your blender. Grind it very well, for about 2 minutes. Your blender makes a lot of noise, and it's hard to stand there listening to that motor go for so long, but please wait for the full 2 minutes. Even though the motor gets hot, rest assured that your blender is meant to work like this and the motor will not be damaged. I've used (and I mean used!) my blender for 15 years now and it still works as if it's brand new.

> **TIP:** If you are grinding large amounts of grains and the motor sounds like it's laboring too hard, increase the speed. If it still doesn't sound right, grind smaller batches.

This fine grinding is necessary for your beginning eater. If your baby is a little older and eating chunkier food, you may have to grind for only 20 30 seconds to get the proper consistency. You know you're a pro at making *Super Porridge* when you can tell just by the sound of your blender when the grains are finished grinding!

> **WARNING:** Your blender and food processor give off a lot of EMFs (electro-magnetic fields), so don't stand very close to it. Step back a good foot or two while it is grinding.

When the cup of water starts to boil on the stove, turn the heat down to the lowest setting. Sprinkle the ground rice into the water while stirring briskly with a wire whisk. Cover the pot and keep it over low heat for about 10 minutes. Stir frequently with the whisk to prevent scorching on the bottom and to remove lumps. You will have to stir more frequently at first, when the pot is still very hot, than after it's had a few minutes to cool.

> **TIP:** To prevent powdered grain from going all over the kitchen counter when you open the blender, unscrew the blender base from the blender container while holding it over the boiling water in the pot.

> **TIP:** When you open the lid to stir the porridge, hold the lid over the pot so that the condensed steam will drip back into the pot and not on your stove top.

Adjust the Consistency, If Necessary

If your *Super Porridge* is too thick, thin it by simply mixing in a little breast milk, formula, or water. If it is too thin, add a little wheat germ, ground nuts, ground oatmeal, commercial powdered baby cereal, etc. Make sure that the thickener you use is age-appropriate, of course.

> **TIP:** If you are making whole brown rice for the rest of your family, you can make *Super Porridge* from it by puréeing the cooked rice with an equal amount of liquid.

How to Prevent Boiling Over

There's a possibility that the cereal will boil over and make a mess of your stove. One way to prevent this from happening is to use a fairly large pot—the pot should be able to hold three times the volume of cereal. I use glass, see-through cookware. Boil overs seem to be more frequent with this cookware, because the glass gets hotter and stays hotter longer. To prevent boil-overs, I move the pot totally off the burner immediately after I stir in the grains, and stir for about a minute until the electric burner cools down and the porridge stops boiling. Then I place it back on the burner with heat on lowest setting.

> **TIP:** Use the same pot, same stove burner, same heat setting, and the same quantity of water/food and you will know the time and tricks necessary to cook the food quickly and perfectly.

Refrigerate the Two Servings Immediately

After letting the cereal cook over low heat for 10 minutes, it's ready. One cup of water and ¼ cup of rice makes a little more than 1 cup of cereal, or two ½ cup servings. You may want to keep the cereal in the pot and refrigerate until mealtime, or you can divide it into two or three individual microwaveable bowls with lids and refrigerate. Make sure you cover the cereal well so it won't dry up in the dry refrigerator air. Cooked *Super Porridge* will keep in the refrigerator for 2-3 days. If your baby is ready to eat now, make sure the cereal has cooled to a safe temperature before you feed it to her.

Individual Bowls are More Convenient

When my *Super Porridge* has finished cooking, I always pour it into separate bowls with lids before storing it in the refrigerator. When mealtime comes, I grab an individual serving and warm it on the stove top. This is easier than spooning out a portion and returning the pot to the refrigerator. It also saves space in your refrigerator—you can stack three or four bowls with lids in a smaller area than a big pot would take. And emptying the cereal into bowls makes the pot immediately available for other uses.

Corelle® dishes are great for individual servings of *Super Porridge*. I cover the bowls by placing a small Corelle dish over them, which believe it or not, seals tightly enough to keep the porridge fresh. The dish covers also make the bowls stackable. Corelle dishes stack compactly in the cabinet and in the dishwasher—an absolute must in my home. And you don't have to be gentle with them because they are break-resistant. Please know that I have no affiliation with Corelle and, to my knowledge, neither my family nor I own any Corning® stock. I just think their dishes are great for those who prefer practicality to fancy dinnerware.

Freeze Super Porridge for Longer Storage

If you wish, you can freeze *Super Porridge* in individual servings using the *Phantom Container Freezing Method*. It will keep for 2-4 weeks or longer. I usually don't freeze *Super Porridge* because it's so quick to make—I make it every 2 or 3 days and it's always ready in the refrigerator. Freezing changes the texture of the cereal so that it is a little rubbery, though it's fine after you mash it and add a little formula to it. I do occasionally reach into the refrigerator at baby's mealtime and find that I'm out of *Super Porridge*.

Although it takes only 10 minutes waiting time to cook, it does take a while to cool, and my baby is not that patient. For these "emergencies" when I run out, I always keep at least one portion of frozen *Super Porridge* tucked away in the freezer. A few minutes on the stove top, and it's ready to eat.

Making Super Porridge from Millet

Millet is a super healthy whole grain cereal for your baby, and can be used instead of rice as a first cereal. Like rice, it is not likely to cause allergy and is easily digested. A grain of millet is much smaller than a grain of rice, so you must use a different portion when you make *Super Porridge* from millet. Instead of ¼ cup, which is actually 4 tablespoons, use a little less— about 3 tablespoons of millet.

Place a cup of water on the stove to boil and while it's heating, put 3 tablespoons of millet into the blender. Grind for 2 minutes or less. Follow the same directions as for rice: Whisk the millet powder into the boiling water and let it sit over low heat for 10 minutes. Whisk the porridge frequently to prevent burning and lumps.

Making Super Porridge from Barley

Your natural foods store carries organic pearled barley, or you can buy barley at the supermarket if you prefer. Use ¼ cup barley to 1 cup boiling water, as for brown rice, and cook it the same way.

Making Super Porridge from Oatmeal

Your health food store also carries whole grain oats, which look similar to brown rice grains. These, too, should be cooked the same way as *Super Porridge* brown rice. Most of us have probably never seen oat grains. We're more familiar with rolled oats (also called old-fashioned oats). These flakes are made from oat grains that have been steamed and flattened. They take about 15 minutes to cook. Quick-cooking oats are similar to rolled oats, but cook faster—in about 5 minutes—because they have been cut up before being steamed and flattened. Use the old-fashioned rolled oat flakes (not the quick-cooking) to make *Super Porridge*. Whether you are using the oat grains or rolled oats in *Super Porridge*, cook them the same as you would brown rice—grind ¼ cup in the blender and cook the powder for 10 minutes.

The Smaller the Grain, the Less Grain You Use

With millet, it's 3 tablespoons of grains to 1 cup of water; with rice, it's 4 tablespoons or ¼ cup of grains to 1 cup of water. In general, the smaller the size of the grain, the less you use. This is because small grains pack more tightly and have less air space between them, making them denser so that you need a smaller measure of them. So when cooking other grains, compare them to the size of millet and rice and measure accordingly. Brown rice comes in three sizes: large grain, medium grain, and small grain. Use 1 cup of water for ¼ cup medium grain rice. The large grain rice would need 1 to 2 tablespoons less water than the medium grain. The small grain rice packs denser and would need a few tablespoons more water than the medium grain.

> **REMINDER:** As a general rule of thumb for *Super Porridge*, use an amount of water equal to 4-5 times the amount of powdered grains/ legumes.

> **TIP:** When in doubt, use more water. If cereal turns out a little watery, just add a little ground dry oatmeal or wheat germ to thicken.

As Baby Grows, Double the Recipe

In no time at all, you'll find yourself running out of *Super Porridge* before the 2-3 day refrigerator keeping time is up. Then you can double the recipe. Boil 2 cups of water instead of 1, and double the volume of grains: ½ cup of grains for rice and the larger grains and 6 tablespoons of grain for millet and the smaller grains. This will yield a little more than 2 cups of cereal, which can be divided into four ½ cup individual servings or three ¾ cup servings. To save time and cooking, make enough *Super Porridge* to feed your baby for 2-3 days—the refrigerator keeping time of cooked *Super Porridge*.

Mini-Blender Containers

It's worth it to purchase a little blender container for grinding. One mini container holds one cup and has markings on the side for easy measuring, and it's so much easier to use than the big clumsy blender container. Mini-blend containers are also easier to take apart and clean than the big container.

Batch Grinding in Advance

If you don't like grinding grains a quarter cup at a time every 2-3 days, you can grind a big batch of grains and store them in the refrigerator in a tightly closed sterile glass jar. The ground grains will keep in the refrigerator for up to a month. For example, you can grind a cup or two of brown rice all at once and store the powder in a clean mayonnaise jar in the refrigerator. When it comes time to make *Super Porridge*, boil a cup of water on the stove, and sprinkle 3-4 tablespoons of the already ground powdered grain into the pot and cook for 10 minutes. Grinding in batches means you have to take apart the blender and clean it only once.

TIP: Grinding is easier if you grind small amounts (about ¼-½ cup) at a time.

Super Porridge Made from Mixed Grains

When your baby is 7 months old, you can feed her cereals made from mixed grains. Simply mix any two grains together. For example, ¼ cup brown rice and 3 tablespoons of millet can be ground together in the blender and stirred into 2 cups of boiling water and cooked and stored as usual.

Super Porridge with Tofu, Cheese, or Eggs

At 7 months, add hard-cooked egg or a tablespoon or two of mashed tofu into cooked *Super Porridge* to make a high-protein *Super Porridge*.

High Protein Super Porridge

When your baby is 9 months old, he has arrived! At this age, he can eat the ultimate super duper *Super Porridge*—that which is made from a mixture of grains and beans/legumes. *Super Porridge* with beans is no more trouble to cook than *Super Porridge* made from plain brown rice—just mix some beans in with the grains, grind, and cook for 10 minutes. When beans are ground to a powder in the blender, no pre-soaking is necessary, and they cook in 10 minutes just as the grains do. Before grinding, pick through the beans and discard any that are cracked, malformed, or discolored. On rare occasions, you may also find little pebbles mixed in with the beans.

NOTE: The only special treatment needed for *Super Porridge* with beans is when you add one specific bean—the soybean. If soybeans are included in the *Super Porridge* mix, you must cook for 20 minutes instead of 10.

When approximately two parts grains are mixed with one part beans or other legumes, protein is formed that is as high a quality as that from eggs or meats. You don't have to be this exact, but if you want the very best proportions for maximum protein, use ⅓ cup rice or other grain and ⅛ cup lentil or other beans/peas/legumes. This mixture (equivalent to two cups of cooked *Super Porridge*) contains about 7.5 grams of complete protein.

High Protein Super Porridge Made from Mixing Grains with Legumes

To make 2 cups of high protein *Super Porridge*, mix in blender and grind:

- ⅓ cup dry whole grains (brown rice, millet, oatmeal, or any of the grains listed in Chapter 22) and

- 2 tablespoons (⅛ cup) dried legumes (lentils, soy grits, split peas, or any legume listed in Chapter 23)

This makes about ½ cup of powder. Stir powder into 2 cups boiling water, reduce heat to low, and cook for 10 minutes (20 minutes if soybeans are included), stirring frequently with whisk to remove lumps and prevent scorching. Refrigerate for 2-3 days or freeze for up to one month.

Your Natural Foods Store Is "Full of Beans"

That's a compliment. Newcomers probably never knew so many types of beans existed. Of course, you can buy beans and other legumes at the supermarket, but again, your natural foods store may carry a wider selection and you can be sure they are organically grown.

> **TIP:** Finely ground bean flour, such as soybean flour or soy flour, can be substituted for some of the regular flour in baking to boost the nutrition in the baked goods.

Pre-Measure and Pre-Mix Grains and Beans/Legumes in Individual Containers to Save Time

I have about a dozen mini-blend containers that I fill with a variety of grain and bean combinations to make *Super Porridge*. About once a month, when my mini-blend containers have been all used up to make *Super Porridge*, I pull out the grains and legumes. With a ¼ cup measuring cup and a ⅓ cup measuring cup, I get to work mixing grains and beans/legumes into the containers all at one time. One container might have oats and kidney beans, another millet and lentils, etc. Or sometimes I put a tablespoon of rice, millet, and barley in the same container with 1 tablespoon soybeans, a few kidney beans, and a teaspoon of split peas to make ½ cup total—talk about mixed grains and beans!

> **TIP:** To make sure your baby is getting a variety of beans and grains, and that you're not feeding him the same ones over and over again, keep several types in your cabinet. Rotate them (as you would clothes in your closet) so that they are cycled through your baby's diet.

The methods explained in this chapter on how to make *Super Porridge* are summarized on the next page. Use the method that you find most convenient and the one that saves you the most time.

Cook Super Porridge Using the Method that Saves You the Most Time

There are several ways you can make *Super Porridge*:

• You can make 2-3 days' worth from scratch each time, measuring the grains and beans into the blender, grinding them, and stirring them into the boiling water to cook.

• You can proportion your whole grains and beans in several individual containers, and then grind immediately before cooking 2-3 days' worth and refrigerating. (I'm lacking in freezer and refrigerator space, so I use this one. The individual containers of pre-measured unground grains and beans, as in the previous picture, can be kept in the cabinet until grinding time.)

• You can pre-measure and grind a months' worth of beans and grains all at once and store the powder in sterile, airtight glass jars in the refrigerator. Then cook 2-3 days' worth at one time.

• You can cook a whole batch of *Super Porridge* once a month and store it in individual containers in the freezer (this takes a lot of freezer space) and then thaw one portion immediately before mealtime.

• And yet another way to make *Super Porridge* is to cook grains and beans whole as for adults, without grinding them in the blender, according to the directions in the next two chapters and then purée the cooked grains and beans with liquid (water, breast milk, or formula).

How to Make Super Porridge Thicker and Chunkier

I gave my 3-year-old *Super Porridge* almost every single day. You're never too old for smooth, unchunky *Super Porridge*! As your baby gets older, you may want to make whole grain cereals a little chunkier to give your baby practice in chewing. Your baby might be ready for a thicker texture, but not quite ready for whole cooked brown rice and other grains.

The length of time for cooking grains depends on the size of the grain pieces and the hardness of the grain. The bigger the pieces of ground grains, the longer they take to cook. For example, brown rice *Super Porridge* is made from powdered grains and cooks in 10 minutes. Unpulverized whole brown rice cooks in 45 minutes. To make *Super Porridge* chunkier, do NOT chop the grains into bigger pieces and cook for 10 minutes or the cereal will contain gritty, hard pieces of uncooked grain.

The correct way to make a more textured *Super Porridge* is to cook unground whole grains as directed in the next chapter, then purée the cooked whole grains in your processor with water or other liquid. For very smooth *Super Porridge* for a beginning eater, purée the cooked whole grains with an equal amount of liquid until you have a very smooth texture—the same texture as if you had ground the grains to a powder before cooking. For a more textured *Super Porridge*, thoroughly cook the grains whole and unpulverized as directed in the next chapter. Then add a little liquid and purée a bit. The cereal will have some texture and not be quite so smooth, but there will be no hard, uncooked pieces in it.

5

Your Baby's Very
First Meal of Solid Foods

It's Time to Start Solid Foods!

One day you just know it's time to start. Your pediatrician has given you the OK and together you have decided on the food that will be the first, and there's some ready and waiting in your kitchen. The suggestions that follow will help make your baby's very first meal a pleasant experience.

The Best Time of Day for the Very First Meal

The best time to give your baby her very first meal is in the morning or early afternoon. Sometimes babies have allergic reactions to foods. If you feed her in the evening, and she does have a reaction, it will probably occur in the middle of the night. It is better for you, the parent, if you don't have to comfort a gassy baby at 2 A.M., while you're tired and half asleep.

There is another reason why you should feed your baby during the earlier part of the day. It is usually a time when your baby (and you!) is not tired or colicky, as he may be toward evening. We want everybody happy and energetic when your baby has his first special meal. Choose a time when your baby is not tired, fussy, or cranky, such as after his morning nap.

> **REMINDER:** Here is a sleep saving tip. Always introduce any new food to your baby at breakfast or lunch, never supper. If he has an allergic reaction, it is less likely to occur in the middle of the night.

Give Your Baby His Very First Meal When He is Not Too Hungry

Yes, when he is not too hungry. He should be hungry enough to want to eat, but not ravenous. A too-hungry baby urgently wanting to eat may become frustrated during this new unfamiliar eating method, with this strange contraption called a spoon. Feed him his very first meal after he has had a partial breast or bottle-feeding. Give him half a feeding, then introduce his first solid food, and then finish the feeding. Giving him a partial feeding will also help to maintain his milk intake. Or you can give him his first solid food halfway through the time between two breast or bottle feedings, when he's just a little hungry.

The Food's Temperature

Remember that your baby's mouth is much more sensitive to heat than yours, so please do not go by how warm you like your food when heating up your baby's food. The temperature of your baby's food should be moderately warm. Breast-fed babies are accustomed to the temperature of breast milk—body temperature, 98.6°F—and will be comfortable with their first solid food if it is also at body temperature. However, your baby does not mind cool food and heating is not really necessary, although warmed food does have more flavor. If you do wish to warm your baby's food, you can do so on the stove top.

The Amount of Food for Your Baby's Very First Meal

You may be surprised at how little food you should give your baby at her first meal—no more than a teaspoon or two (before it's mixed with liquid). Remember that she will not be very hungry because you will first give her half of a breast or bottle-feeding. Or, if you're giving her first meal halfway between breast or bottle-feedings, it will be at a time that is at least an hour before she expects her next feeding.

The Consistency of the First Solid Food is Not SOLID

"Solid" is a misnomer—to eat foods that are actually solid, your baby would need a good set of teeth, which she won't have for quite some time! Your baby's first food, after breast milk or formula, should be more liquid than solid. In fact, it should be so liquid that it pours off the spoon. Thick food may make him gag or choke. If you're feeding him commercial rice cereal, use only a teaspoon and mix it with about 2 tablespoons of liquid. For liquid, you can use water, but using breast milk or formula is more nutritious and will make the food taste more familiar to him. If you're using cooked sweet potato, ripe banana, or ripe avocado, mash or purée it until it is very smooth and has absolutely no lumps. Then take only a teaspoonful and mix with liquid until it pours off the spoon. To yogurt, add just a little liquid. Or scoop yogurt out from the top, where that yellow-tinged watery liquid (called whey) gathers. Mix the whey into the yogurt to liquefy it so that it pours off the spoon.

TIP: If you tend to hold the bowl of baby food while you feed your baby, you may find it easier to use a coffee cup with a handle.

One More Thing Before You Start Feeding Your Baby

We all know that mealtimes are important to a baby's health and physical growth and development. But before you go wielding that baby spoon, you might want to become more aware of how important mealtimes are to your baby's intellectual, psychological, and emotional development, and to her development of self-confidence and feelings of trust and security. In other words, mealtimes can mess her up in more ways than one!

Get Ready . . .

Now that everything is physically ready for baby's first meal, prepare yourself mentally. Decide that you will not be disappointed or upset if she doesn't do well with the food. Be ready to keep your facial expression pleasant, no matter what happens.

I didn't realize how important my facial expression was as a guide to my babies until one afternoon when I was sitting outside with my twin sons. Unexpectedly, a very loud crack of thunder sounded, and this was a new noise to my sons. They both immediately looked questioningly at my face to see if they should be afraid. When I looked at them and smiled, they were quite relieved and returned the smile. Since then, we love thunderstorms. The point to remember is to keep your face pleasant at baby's meal times. If your face looks anxious, your baby will be anxious, and mealtimes will turn out to be anxiety producing.

Even a baby can see through feigned calmness. I smiled at my sons through an entire commuter flight in a plane the size of a phone booth. My sons didn't fall for it, and they watched me, worried, the whole time. Don't fake it. Be determined beforehand that you will not get frustrated if baby refuses to eat or spits food at you, and then you won't have to pretend.

REMINDER: The more relaxed, confident, and tolerant you are at mealtime, the smoother the feeding will go.

Get Set . . . Go!

Your baby and you are both seated comfortably and you have a relaxed expression on your face. You have just finished giving him half a breast or bottle-feeding and he is still hungry. It's time to go! Put a pea-sized amount of the liquidy food on the spoon, no more than ¼ teaspoon. Place the spoon lightly on your baby's lower lip and slip it gently into his mouth, so that it's on top of his tongue. Let him suck the food off the spoon. If he doesn't, then tip the spoon slightly so that the food pours slowly into his mouth. You may also want to try placing the food a little farther back on his tongue, because of his tendency to thrust his tongue forward. Be careful not to gag him.

Whatever Happens, Smile and Say "Mmmmm!!!!"

Remember that this is a first time for your baby. Don't show disappointment if she thrusts her tongue forward and seems to spit out the food—that's normal. The younger she is, the longer it will take her to learn to swallow. The closer she is to 6 months, the better she will do. If she is spitting out the food, gently scrape it off her chin with the spoon and re-feed it to her. A baby who is truly ready for solid foods will, after a few tries, begin to get the hang of it and retain more of the food in her mouth than she spits out.

If she doesn't handle the spoon well or if she seems at all uncomfortable put the food away and wait a few days before trying to feed her again. Remember that your baby's health will not suffer if she doesn't start eating solid foods today. Take it slowly and never push her to eat. You want your baby to look forward to her meals as relaxing and enjoyable times with you. After a few days, try feeding her again, keeping things relaxed and pleasant. If she still has problems, discuss your concerns with your pediatrician.

> **REMINDER:** Your baby will look adorable when he is eating, but try not to laugh when he spits out his food. It may encourage him to continue to do this after it's no longer cute.

Watch Carefully for Signs that You Should End the Meal

Continue to feed her as long as she wants to cooperate. Keep feeding her until the food is gone, or until she turns her head away or closes her little mouth when she sees the spoon coming. Fussiness is also a sign that your baby is finished eating. Never force your baby to continue eating if she does not want to. When she is finished eating, offer her a little water and the rest of her breast or bottle-feeding.

Water

When your baby begins eating solid foods, it increases the load on the kidneys and necessitates the addition of a small amount of water to your baby's diet as long as the baby is over 6 months old.

What to Do with the Leftovers

Whether you are using commercial jars of baby food or making homemade baby food, it is important for your baby's and family's health and safety that the "food preparer" in the home understands the basics of hygiene and bacterial contamination. Please be sure to read Chapter 31, *Baby, Kitchen and Laundry Hygiene.*

> WARNING: Do not keep baby food—either opened commercial jars or homemade—in the refrigerator for more than 1-2 days. Baby food can be spoiled without necessarily smelling bad. If commercial infant cereal has been mixed with liquid, serve it immediately; discard any leftovers and do not use them for another meal.

> WARNING: If leftover food has come in contact with your baby's saliva, because the spoon from your baby's mouth has been dipped into it, throw the food away. The bacteria and enzymes in your baby's saliva will continue digesting the food in the bowl, breaking down the vital nutrients and causing it to begin to spoil.

If you are using avocado or banana as baby's first food, you will have plenty of leftovers. You can always eat the rest of the banana yourself, but even an adult has trouble finishing a whole avocado minus one teaspoon!

One method that will help prevent leftovers and food waste is the *Frozen Food Cube Method*. The method is explained thoroughly in Part III, but very briefly you would: purée or fork-mash a very ripe avocado, spoon portions into the cubes of a stainless steel ice cube tray, cover with organic, bleach-free wax paper, then aluminum foil to prevent freezer burn and nutrient loss, freeze until solid, and then transfer the frozen food cubes into an organic, bleach-free wax paper-lined plastic freezer bag. When mealtime comes, thaw a food cube or two (following the directions and precautions in Part III) and feed it to your baby. The *Food Cube Method* can be used for cooked puréed sweet potatoes and almost all other *Super Baby Foods*.

> **MONEY SAVER:** Don't cook large amounts of a new food until you know that your baby likes it and will eat it.

Poop Panic!

Beware that your baby's bowel movements (now a major part of your life) will change considerably when he starts eating solid foods. They will have a stronger odor, and they may also take on the color of the food eaten several hours before. My baby's first post-beet poop looked so much like blood I almost went into a panic. Beets and beet greens cause the most severe color change, followed by kale and the other greens. You may also notice orange veggies, like carrots, at the other end, too. Beets may also cause red urine, although this is not as common. Asparagus sometimes lends a strong "fragrance" to a baby's urine.

Your baby's stool may also contain undigested foods. For example, you may see in your baby's diaper the little black seeds from kiwi fruit, which will pass unscathed through your young baby's digestive tract. Sometimes undigested foods are accompanied by small quantities of mucus, especially when your baby starts feeding himself more textured foods. You probably have no cause to be concerned, but it's a good idea to discuss it with your pediatrician.

> **WARNING:** If your baby's stool becomes loose and watery and contains mucus, inform your pediatrician. You may want to retain a stool sample for your doctor to analyze. Your baby's digestive tract might be irritated from a food that he has been eating and you may have to temporarily reduce his solid food intake, especially the suspect food.

> WARNING: Too much fruit juice or even too much fresh fruit can cause your baby's stool to be acidic. This irritates baby's tender skin and may cause a painful, bright red diaper rash that hurts when you wipe. Inform your pediatrician.

REMINDER: Remember to keep your facial expression pleasant when you are changing your baby's diaper. (With some poops, this may be a real challenge!)

Baby's Second Meal and Beyond

Tomorrow, when it's time for your baby's second meal of solid foods, please follow the directions in Chapter 8, *Feeding Your Super Baby During the First Few Weeks* beginning on page 93. Please read the next few chapters before feeding your baby his second meal, as they contain important information on keeping your baby safe. If it is impossible for you to read them in their entirety before your baby's second meal, then please take a few minutes now to skim through them and read just the subheadings.

TIP: If your baby has problems with gas, you may want to consider giving her simethicone drops. These drops act as an antiflatulent to help relieve your baby's gas pains and are claimed to be safe. They are not absorbed by your baby's intestinal system and pass right through it. Sold over the counter under the name Mylicon® Drops, they also come in generic brands which probably work just as well, but are much cheaper. They really helped whenever my third son was screaming with gas pain. As always, get an OK from your pediatrician before you administer any medications to your baby, even those you can buy without a prescription.

TIP: Some experts swear that the carminative oil in fennel is an excellent remedy for colic. Make fennel tea for your baby by pouring 4-5 cups of boiling water over 1 teaspoon fennel seeds. Steep for 10 minutes, strain well, and cool. Administer 1-2 ounces at a time. As always, consult your pediatrician to get his advice first before administering fennel, other medicinal herbs, or any medication to your baby.

Food Allergies and the Four-Day Wait Rule

An allergy is an abnormal reaction by the body's immune system to some substance. An allergic reaction to food occurs when the body perceives an ingested food as a threat and overproduces antibodies to counteract it.

4-7 Days Waiting Period after the Introduction of Each New Food

It is possible that your baby has one or more food allergies, especially if food allergies run in your family. When your baby eats a food that he is allergic to, a reaction (like hives) can occur immediately, or a reaction can be delayed and occur SEVERAL DAYS LATER. Because of this, it is important that you wait several days after the introduction of any new food in order to see if that new food will trigger an allergic reaction. In other words, follow the *Four-Day Wait Rule.*

The Four-Day Wait Rule

Introduce only one new food at a time. After you introduce your baby to a new food, do not introduce another new food for at least four days and watch carefully for signs of allergies.

Note: Some experts recommend a 3-day waiting period, some recommend waiting 5 days, and still others recommend a full week of waiting between new foods. Consult with your pediatrician and follow his recommendation.

It is important that you understand that a 4-day wait does NOT mean that you feed your baby lots of that one new food, or that you feed him only that new food during the waiting period. In fact, only one small feeding of the new food can be enough to cause an allergic reaction. During the waiting period, feed him a variety of foods to which he has been previously introduced as well as some of the new food.

Wait No Longer than One Week

Some authors recommend waiting a full week after each new food. A one-week trial period is fine, but please don't wait any longer than a week before giving your baby other foods. Feeding him one food for too long a time may produce a sensitivity in him to that food. Four to seven days is a long enough time to determine if your baby has an allergy to a food.

Introduce Single Foods Only

Be careful that each new food is a single food. For example, don't feed your baby yogurt that is mixed with peaches for the first time, if peaches haven't been introduced before either. If there is an allergic reaction, you won't know whether it was the peaches or the yogurt. The same goes for commercial "mixed dinners." Do not feed them to your baby until each ingredient in the dinner has been introduced individually using the *Four-Day Wait Rule*. Same goes for multi-ingredient stews and soups.

Watch for Signs of Allergies

After each new food is introduced, watch your baby carefully for the next 4 days, looking for any of the signs of allergies listed in the box below. Most allergic reactions manifest themselves in vague symptoms that you may not notice if you're not watching carefully. Although many of these symptoms are commonly caused by a cold or other illness, there is a possibility that they are indications of an allergy to the most recently introduced new food. Consult your pediatrician to be sure.

Allergy symptoms can occur in almost any part of the body, but most commonly they manifest in the digestive tract (nausea, diarrhea, etc.), the respiratory system (runny nose, wheezing, etc.), and the skin (rashes, hives, etc.). As you can see from the list below, they range from mild to severe, and even death can result. I certainly don't mean to unduly alarm you. Serious food allergies are extremely rare in healthy babies, especially when solid foods are delayed until 6 months of age. And parents are usually aware of food allergies that run in the family. So please don't worry excessively over possible serious allergic reactions.

Signs of Allergies			
Nausea	Cough	Lip swelling	Headache
Vomiting	Wheezing	Face swelling	Irritability
Gas	Breathing difficulties	Rashes	Fatigue
Diarrhea		Diaper rash	Behavior problems
Frequent bowel movements	Asthma	Hives	
Abdominal pain	Runny nose with clear secretions	Itching	Convulsions
Bed-wetting		Eczema	Shock
	Eye swelling	Mouth ulcers	Death

Feeding with Love

Your baby's feeding area should be a happy place to be! You will be spending a lot of time feeding your baby in the next few years. Try not to look at baby's mealtime as a chore. Rather, use it as a quality time for bonding with your beautiful baby. Spoon-feeding your baby will then make you feel very loving and nurturing towards him, and he will become closer to you as he does when you breast or bottle-feed him.

Mealtimes are important to your baby's social development. During your baby's first year, he should develop a sense of trust, and relaxed mealtimes are a large part of the process. If his first experiences with food are within an atmosphere of tension and frustration, eating problems may develop that can last a lifetime. Your baby will actually grow and develop better if he is fed in a loving environment rather than one that is emotionally negative. Feeding your baby involves much more than food.

Entertainment with Dinner

Make silly faces at your baby, smile, and talk to her during mealtime. Do the classic "airplane into the hangar" routine. Sing her songs. My baby's favorite was *How Much Is That Doggie in the Window?* because I said "WOOF! WOOF!" between phrases. (My older boys asked me to refrain from doing this when they had friends over.) However, you should not drag out baby's mealtimes beyond 20-30 minutes. The high chair's main purpose should be eating, not entertainment.

If an older baby gets antsy while you are getting her food ready, give her some finger food to keep her busy. Or place an interesting toy on her high chair, one that she doesn't get to play with at other times and that will endure crashing to the floor after hundreds of throws off the high chair tray. The invention of the suction toy has saved parents many backaches. During the actual meal, remove all toys so that your baby can concentrate on eating. Keep distractions to a minimum.

TIP: Save her absolute favorite small toy for when you are dining out and she is ready to let out a howl. Please remove her from the restaurant if she's noisy. There are a lot of people around you paying for dinner and a babysitter so that they can enjoy a quiet, romantic meal on a rare night out without the baby. By the way, if you are going to take a baby or toddler out to dinner, it's a good idea to take some *Super Baby Food* with you. You can slowly feed her to keep her busy during the wait for the meal (and it's a long wait if you have a toddler with you.)

Eating Is an Important Learning Process

Baby mealtimes are the foundation for a lifetime of the healthy attitudes and the eating habits so necessary for the prevention of adult eating disorders. Allow your baby to participate as much as possible in the feeding process. Eating, like walking or any other skill, must be learned. Self-feeding is important to your baby's physical development, eye-hand coordination, and manual dexterity. It is also important to her intellectual development. Allowing your baby to freely self-feed shows her that you have confidence in her abilities, which increases her self-confidence, independence, and self-esteem. Your tolerance, patience, and acceptance teach her that the world is not a restrictive, formidable place and that she is free to be creative.

REMINDER: It is important to have a positive, cheerful attitude each time you place your baby in his high chair or when you find yourself getting frustrated about the mess.

Pay close attention and you will see that meals are a special education in itself. Learning begins with your baby's very first meal.

Your baby also learns about cause and effect while eating: Raise my hand this way and the cracker reaches my mouth; tip the cup to this angle and liquid will flow out and into my mouth or onto the tray; drop the spoon and it falls to the floor and goes "ting" and Mom/Dad picks it up. The concept of object permanence is reinforced. The spoon still exists, even when it's on the floor and I cannot see it.

WARNING: Restricting a baby from self-feeding during his first year may cause feeding problems later on.

Praise the Good, Ignore the Bad

Most babies spit out food, throw food and dishes on the floor, and perform other seemingly mischievous acts in the high chair. Your reaction will determine whether the behavior will continue or, worse, become a power ploy. Giving "normal baby behavior" attention, even negative attention, may reinforce the behavior. Keep a poker face when your baby does something in the high chair that annoys you—he will notice if you look upset and may begin to practice ~~tormenting~~ entertaining you.

TIP: Try making a game of eating to prevent food on the floor.

TIP: If your baby looks adorable when she experiments and spits food over her chin for the first time, don't smile or laugh. She may enjoy your response and repeat the spitting after it's no longer cute.

DO Play with Your Food

Babies are messy eaters, so make sure that you have the feeding area set up for easy cleanup. It is perfectly normal for a baby to dip his fingers into bowls of food, suck his fingers and fist, squeeze and smear food onto his face and the tray with his palm and fingers, mash it into his hair, spit it out or let it drool down his chin, blow it at you or on the wall, throw it on the floor along with cups and bowls, and spill his drinks.

Be assured that to everything, there is a learning purpose. Your baby is not doing these things to provoke you—he is experimenting and learning about his environment and the texture and feel of his food. She explores her food just as she explores her toys. Restrain your impulse to be neat and encourage self-feeding. Your baby doesn't need Miss Manners' approval.

TIP: Before self-feeding mealtimes, roll up baby's sleeves to keep them clean. Bibs and other "how to keep baby clean" tips are discussed in Chapter 31.

TIP: Although a wet wipe-up towel works fairly well to clean a baby's fingers, a finger bowl (like in fancy restaurants) works even better. Dip your little one's hands into the water and dry them with a wipe-up towel.

TIP: When some babies begin self-feeding, their moms get them used to wearing a hat or shower cap to keep their hair clean. Make it fun and your baby just might go for it.

Self-Feeding Babies Eat Slowly

It seems to take forever for a baby to feed himself, but once again, be patient. Grin and bear it when he endlessly explores his food before putting it in his mouth. As long as some eating is taking place, let him be. When it becomes all play, it's time to end the meal.

Self-Feeding Babies DO Eat Enough

Your baby will feed herself inefficiently, and you may wonder if more food is going into her mouth or onto the floor. She will consume much less food than when you spoon-feed her, but be assured that she will eat enough for her growing needs. Remember—a healthy baby will eat the proper amount of food and will not starve herself. Coincidentally, by the time your baby is skilled enough to self-feed, she will also be growing at a much slower rate and need fewer calories.

6

Food Allergies

In the previous chapter, I introduced the *Four-Day Wait Rule* and watching for allergy signs. In this chapter, you'll learn about the causes of allergies, foods most and least likely to trigger allergies, lactose or milk intolerance, and what to do if your baby has an allergic reaction.

Causes of Food Allergies

Introducing Solid Foods Too Early

A young baby's digestive system is immature. Their intestines are more permeable to large food molecules and they have relatively low quantities of something called sIgA, making them more prone to allergic reactions. This is why it is so important to introduce foods at age-appropriate times, when your baby's system is mature enough to handle them.

Heredity

Allergies run in families. If one parent has an allergy, there is a 50% chance that their child will also have that allergy. If both parents have an allergy, there is a 75% chance that their child will have it. Inform your pediatrician of any food allergies in your family.

Overfeeding of a Particular Food

Feeding your baby too much of a new food over a long period of time may trigger a sensitivity to that food, which may not have occurred during a one week or less waiting period.

An Existing Allergy to a Similar Food

Be aware that if your baby is allergic to a food, he may also be allergic to similar foods. For example, if your baby is allergic to cabbage, then he may also be allergic to other vegetables in the cabbage family, such as broccoli or Brussels sprouts. A baby allergic to oranges may also be allergic to grapefruit, limes, lemons, tangerines, and kumquats.

Always Check the Ingredients

People allergic to milk, or lactose-intolerant, must also avoid canned milk, dried powdered milk, milkshakes, ice cream, yogurt made from cow's milk, butter, margarine, cheese, cream, sour cream, buttermilk, custards made with milk, some hot dogs, and any products containing whey, casein, milk solids, and other foods containing milk products.

People allergic to eggs must also, if they are very sensitive, avoid other products containing eggs: breads and bread products; cookies, cakes, doughnuts, pies and other desserts, pretzels, salad dressings and mayonnaise, some pasta noodles, etc. Always check the ingredients!

Gluten is a part of wheat, barley, and rye. Gluten intolerance is associated with celiac disease, also called gluten-sensitive enteropathy. This disease develops when the immune system responds abnormally to gluten. This abnormal response does not involve IgE antibody and is not a food allergy, but a real disease. Some people, however, are allergic to wheat or other specific grains.

People with a strong sensitivity to gluten should avoid products containing it. Wheat, rye, and other grains containing gluten, breads and bread products; wheat flour, wheat germ, wheat bran; doughnuts, cakes, cookies, pies, and many other desserts made with flour; some gravy and sauces; malt, as in malted milk; soy sauce or tamari; some processed cheeses and meats; some coffee substitutes; and many other products containing wheat. There are, however, many products on the market today that are gluten-free. Look for labels that say "Gluten-Free" or "Wheat-Free."

TIP: Your natural foods store and grocery stores have a variety of wheat-free and dairy-free food items.

The Foods Most and Least Likely to Trigger Allergies

About ninety percent of food allergies are to eight foods: cow's milk, soy, wheat, peanuts, tree nuts, shellfish, eggs, and fish. Please be aware that any child can be allergic to any food, even if there is no family history of food allergy.

Cow's Milk

The food most notorious for causing allergies in young babies is cow's milk. Typically, it's the protein *casein* in cow's milk that is the culprit. It is estimated that more than one in ten babies have sensitivities to milk, which explains the big market for soy-based baby formulas. Fortunately, the majority of these children outgrow milk allergy during their second year of life. Experts used to recommend postponing the introduction of cow's milk for one year, but now suggest that small amounts in yogurt, cheese or baked goods are okay.

Soy, Eggs, Wheat, and Others

The next most common food allergy is to soy, followed by eggs and wheat. Other common allergens are citrus fruits, berries, tomatoes, fish (especially shellfish), corn, nuts, and those listed in the next table. Most of these allergies subside, as children get older, with the exception of wheat, eggs, cow's milk, nuts, and fish, which often remain throughout life.

Artificial Additives

Foods containing artificial additives, chemicals such as MSG (monosodium glutamate), and artificial sweeteners often cause allergies. Never feed your baby (or any living being) artificially sweetened carbonated beverages. They have no nutritional value and are nothing but water, sugar, and chemicals. It is typical for a 12-ounce soft drink to contain 7 or more teaspoons of sugar! Some carbonated beverages also contain caffeine, even the light-colored sodas.

Peanut Allergies

Peanut-allergic children may suffer serious reactions and even death from eating foods containing peanuts. A serious reaction may result if a peanut-allergic child accidentally leans on a counter smeared with peanut butter or peanut oil, even if it has been wiped off!

Some experts recommend waiting until age three before introducing peanut butter, or anything containing peanuts! However, recent studies indicate that introducing peanut products at a younger age may actually prevent allergies from occurring. Ask your pediatrician when you should begin the introduction of peanut foods into your baby's diet. Be sure to make her aware if you have a peanut allergy in your family.

High Risk Allergy Foods	Low Risk Allergy Foods
Beans and other legumes	Apples
Buckwheat	Apricots
Cabbage	Asparagus
Chocolate	Bananas
Cinnamon	Barley
Citrus fruits and juices	Beets
Coconut	Blueberries
Corn	Carrots
Dairy products	Lettuce
Eggs	Millet
Fish	Oats
Mango	Peaches
Melons	Pears
Mustard	Plums
Nuts	Pork
Onions	Rice
Papaya	Squash
Peanuts	Sweet potatoes
Peas	Tapioca
Rye	
Shellfish	
Strawberries	
Soybeans/tofu	
Tomatoes	
Wheat	
Yeast	
Artificial food additives	

NOTE: Recent studies have shown that waiting TOO long to introduce some foods actually boost the chances of an allergic reaction. Ask your pediatrician for advice on the age to begin introducing your baby to the high risk allergy foods listed above.

WARNING: It is possible that your child may have no noticeable reaction when he eats a small quantity of food to which he is allergic, whereas a larger quantity of the food will cause a reaction.

Lactose or Milk Intolerance

Lactose intolerance (or milk intolerance) is different from milk allergy. People with lactose intolerance lack the enzyme lactase in their intestines. Lactase's job is to break down the milk sugar, lactose, which is present in milk and milk products. If a child's intestines lack lactase, lactose is not digested and remains in the intestines, where it absorbs water and becomes food for bacteria. This will cause gas, abdominal cramps, and diarrhea. These symptoms usually occur one to two hours after ingestion, but can start as soon as 30 minutes after eating.

Children with lactose intolerance can sometimes eat yogurt with no problem, because it contains much less lactose than milk. Some children do well with goat's milk. Some natural, aged cheeses, such as Swiss, cheddar, and Colby, may also be well accepted by lactose intolerant children, because some of the lactose is drained off with the whey. Cabot® cheeses, that you can find in the dairy section of many supermarkets, do not contain lactose. Check the labels.

Fresh, unripened cheeses (mozzarella, cream cheese, cottage cheese, ricotta) are not aged and will probably have to be avoided by the lactose intolerant.

LactAID®, a brand of milk containing lactase, is available at most supermarkets. You can also buy lactase pills, chewable tablets or in liquid drop form (LactAID®, Dairy Ease® and some generic brands) in the antacid section of most supermarkets and pharmacies. Be sure to check with your pediatrician before using.

Although yogurt is often recommended as a first food, check with your pediatrician, especially if there is milk intolerance in your family. Children with milk allergy should not eat yogurt or any other milk products.

What to Do If Baby Has an Allergic Reaction

First and foremost, if your baby is having a serious reaction, call 911! Inform your pediatrician. If your baby has a small reaction to a particular food, such as a runny nose, your doctor will probably suggest that you try feeding your baby that food again a month later. If he still shows sensitivity, wait to try again until he is at least one year old. Of course, if your baby has a serious reaction, you should not feed your baby that food culprit again.

Resources for Information about Food Allergies

The American Academy of Allergy, Asthma and Immunology (AAAAI) is a non-profit medical specialty organization representing allergists, clinical immunologists, allied health professionals, and other physicians with a special interest in allergy. To find an allergist/immunologist in your community who specializes in allergies, go to **www.aaaai.org.**

The National Institute of Allergy and Infectious Diseases (NIAID) conducts and supports basic and applied research to better understand, treat, and ultimately prevent infectious, immunologic, and allergic diseases. They are a terrific source of information on allergies.

NIAID
6610 Rockledge Drive
MSC 6612
Bethesda, MD 20892–6612
(866) 284–4107 or (301) 496–5717
www.niaid.nih.gov

Food Allergy and Anaphylaxis Network
11781 Lee Jackson Highway
Suite 160
Fairfax, VA 22033–3309
(800) 929–4040
www.foodallergy.org

Food Allergy Initiative
515 Madison Avenue
Suite 1912
New York, NY 10022–5403
(855) 324–9604
www.faiusa.org

Part II

Feeding Your Baby and Toddler

7

A Month-By-Month Summary Schedule for the Introduction of Foods in Baby's First Year

There seems to be no consensus among the experts on which new foods to introduce at which ages. And the more books you read, the more confused you become. The one fact that experts agree on is: Wait until your baby is at least one-year-old before introducing honey or corn syrup. Most experts say to wait until one year (some say 6-9 months old) before introducing citrus fruits/juices and wheat.

Always Consult with Your Pediatrician

Be sure to discuss your baby's diet with your pediatrician. And remember that if her advice and mine conflict, follow her advice. New knowledge about diet and nutrition is constantly being discovered. Your pediatrician will have the latest information on what is best for your baby.

Take this book with you to your pediatrician's office. Hand it to her opened to the time schedule on the next few pages. Give her a red pen and ask her to modify the schedule as she sees fit. Remember to ask your pediatrician about:

- The amount of water and juice your baby should be drinking and whether she would recommend the local tap water, bottled water, or filtered water. If she recommends a drinking water that is not fluoridated, ask her if she recommends prescription vitamins containing fluoride.

- If you're going to feed your baby homemade cereals and your baby is breast feeding and not drinking an iron fortified formula, remember to ask her if you should give your baby supplemental iron drops.

TIME SAVER: You probably will be constantly referencing the summary schedule on the next two pages. Save time and frustration when looking for it by folding a piece of clear tape over the edge of the page like a tab. You can even place a small piece of paper within the tape with a description of the page. Do this for all pages that you use frequently.

TIP: Keep notes on what you want to ask your pediatrician and remember to take the notes with you when you go for those well-baby visits. I've had the experience of forgetting to ask questions I was SURE I was going to remember to ask. There's something about being in charge of a baby, especially when you are out in public that makes you incapable of thinking clearly. At least I hope that's how it is with everyone—it's certainly that way with me.

Questions I must remember to ask my pediatrician

Summary Schedule for Introduction of Foods During Baby's First Year

Best First Foods for Baby	Best Foods for the Beginning Eater	Foods for Baby 6 Months or Older	Foods for Baby 7 Months or Older
Ripe avocado Ripe banana Iron-fortified infant rice cereal Cooked, puréed sweet potatoes	Single grain iron-fortified commercial infant cereals: Barley Millet Oatmeal Whole-milk yogurt (for babies older than 6 months) Cooked, strained fruits: Apricots Nectarines Peaches Pears Plums Prunes	Homemade whole grain cereals: Brown rice Millet Oat Raw mild fruits: Mango Papaya Pears Winter squash	Homemade mixed cereals Cottage cheese Hard-cooked egg Peaches Cooked, puréed: Asparagus Carrots Green beans Peas Summer squash White potatoes Diluted, strained, mild fruit juices: Apple Apricot Grape Papaya Pear Peach Prune Maybe orange juice
Mix finely puréed food with enough liquid until it pours off the spoon into baby's mouth. Food should be only slightly thicker than breast milk/formula.		Food should still be puréed or mashed until it is a smooth and lump-free consistency. Food can be slightly thicker than for beginners— the consistency of thick cream.	

Please remember to verify this schedule with your pediatrician.

Summary Schedule for Introduction of Foods During Baby's First Year (cont.)			
Foods for Baby 8 Months or Older	**Foods for Baby 9 Months or Older**	**Foods for Baby 10 Months or Older**	**Foods for Baby One Year or Older**
Tahini Ground nuts Ground seeds Nutritional yeast Powdered kelp Tofu Natural cheeses Wheat germ (ask pediatrician permission) Apricot Apple Cantaloupe Honeydew Kiwi fruit Plums Watermelon Peeled and quartered grapes (not whole grapes) Broccoli Okra Cooked parsley	Dried beans, lentils, split peas, ground and cooked Pineapple Brussels sprouts Cauliflower Spinach Beets Kale Eggplant Rhubarb Rutabaga Turnips Finely chopped raw parsley Cooked greens Cooked onion	Peanut butter thinned and creamy (not chunky) Other thinned nut butters Homemade bulgur cereal Cooked whole grain cornmeal with the germ Whole grain pasta Ground sprouts Finely grated, raw: Summer squash Carrots Greens Sweet peppers	Cow's milk Citrus fruits Citrus fruit juices Tomatoes Tomato juice Hard-cooked egg Honey Strawberries, blueberries, and other berries (not whole; cut into small pieces)
Gradually increase thickness, then chunkiness of food. Offer bite-sized pieces of soft finger foods. Watch very carefully for choking or gagging.		Foods should still be fork-mashed or puréed. Never leave your baby alone while eating.	

Please remember to verify this schedule with your pediatrician.

8

Feeding Your Super Baby During the First Few Weeks

Introduce These Foods To Beginning Eaters		
Ripe avocado	Commercial iron-fortified single-grain infant cereals:	Mild fruits, cooked and strained:
Ripe banana		Apricots
Sweet potatoes	Rice	Nectarines
	Barley	Peaches
Yogurt, whole-milk (6 months or older)	Millet	Pears
	Oatmeal	Plums
		Prunes

Feeding Your Baby the Super Baby Food Diet Before 6 Months

Be sure to discuss your baby's diet with your pediatrician. And remember that if her advice and mine conflict, please follow her advice. New knowledge about diet and nutrition is constantly being discovered. Your pediatrician will have the latest information on what is best for your baby.

As of this printing, the American Academy of Pediatrics (AAP) recommends, in most cases, waiting until babies are 6 months old before starting solid foods.

Baby's Second Meal of Solid Foods

Your beginning eater has had his very first meal. It's now day two of solid foods and he's ready for another meal. The amount he is eating depends on his age and weight and his unique appetite. After a few weeks you may want to look at the additional foods that you can give him listed in the next chapter, *Feeding Your Super Baby at 6 Months*.

The First Week of Solid Foods

For the first week (or at least 4 days), give her one meal each day consisting of one single food—the same food you fed to her in her very first meal. As with her first meal, give her some breast milk or formula before the solid food so that she is not too hungry when you spoon-feed her. After she finishes the food, you can give her a little boiled and cooled water and the rest of the breast or formula feeding. For the first few days, each meal should be no more than a tablespoon before mixing with liquid.

The Second Week of Solid Foods

At the beginning of the second week of solid foods, introduce your baby to one new food from the list on the previous page. Wait 4-7 days (the *Four-Day Wait Rule*) and watch for allergy symptoms before introducing another new food.

Continue introducing foods from the previous list, using the *Four-Day Wait Rule*. Your baby will gradually (or quickly if he is older) eat larger food servings and be ready for two meals per day, as discussed later in this chapter.

Soon your baby will become more interested and cooperative in the feeding process. Your beginning eater will develop more mouth and lip control as he gains practice in eating. You may notice him using his lower lip to "hold" the spoon as you feed him. He may draw his lips together as the spoon is exiting his mouth in order to keep the food inside. As his trunk control improves and he sits with more stability, his hands and arms will become active during feeding and he will eventually reach for food or the spoon. At first he may insert a finger or two into his mouth to help him to swallow food. The fingers help him to suck—the only method he employed for swallowing before the advent of solid foods.

Preparation of Foods for Beginners

Avocado, banana, cooked sweet potatoes, and yogurt were discussed in Chapter 5. The single grain cereals listed on the previous page refer to store-bought, brand-name, iron-fortified cereals. Simply mix the cereal with breast milk, formula, or water, or follow the directions on the box. I suggest using an organic brand made of and whole grains. If your baby is already 6 months or older, you may want to skip to the next chapter, *Feeding Your Super Baby at 6 Months*. Six-month-olds have digestive systems mature enough to handle homemade whole grain cereals, which are much healthier for your baby and pocketbook than commercial brands.

Most Fruit Should Be Cooked for Babies Younger than 6 Months

If you must feed your baby before 6 months of age, it is best not to feed raw fruits except for bananas and avocado. Cook fruits to make them soft and more digestible for your baby's immature system. Directions on how to cook fruits are in Part III, Chapter 20. If the fruit contains little bits of peel, it is important to strain them out so that your baby doesn't choke on them. I strongly suggest straining all cooked fruits, even though you think there are no peel pieces, just to be on the safe side.

Food Consistency for Beginners

As in your baby's very first meal, food should be puréed to the smoothest consistency. Mash foods very well with a fork or purée in a blender until all lumps are completely gone. Mix the finely puréed food with enough liquid (breast milk, formula, or water) until the food is very thin and will pour off the spoon into your baby's mouth. Food should be only slightly thicker than breast milk or formula.

Daily Amount of Foods for Beginners

Your baby's first meal consisted of only one teaspoon of solid food. Over the next few weeks, very gradually increase this serving size to 3-4 tablespoons of solid food (before mixing with liquid).

Sample Daily Feeding Schedule for Beginners One Meal Per Day	
Upon Awakening	breast/bottle
Morning	breast/bottle
Noon	give partial feeding from breast/bottle, then solid food, then water, then finish with the breast/bottle
Afternoon	breast/bottle
Evening	breast/bottle
Bedtime	breast/bottle or bottle of cooled boiled water

Daily Amount of Liquids for Beginners

Breast milk or formula is the top priority food. Your baby should be breastfeeding at least 5 times a day or drinking 32 ounces of formula a day. If your baby is not drinking this amount, decrease the amount of solid foods. Your baby should drink a little bit of water after each meal. Limit your baby's water intake to at most 4-6 ounces (maybe more on hot days) per day in order to assure she is drinking enough breast milk or formula.

Two Meals a Day

When you think your baby is hungry enough for two meals a day, offer a second meal in the late afternoon/early evening, as shown in the schedule below. Each meal should consist of only one food serving. For the first few days, make the evening meal the same food as the morning meal. Then the evening meal can be a different food from the morning. Remember that a new food introduced in the evening can cause an allergic reaction in the middle of the night. To prevent loss of sleep, introduce new foods early in the day.

Sample Daily Feeding Schedule for Beginners Two Meals Per Day	
Upon Awakening	breast/bottle
Morning	partial feeding from breast/bottle and a new food
Noon	breast/bottle
Afternoon	partial feeding from breast/bottle and one food serving (same food as in morning or a previously introduced food)
Evening	breast/bottle
Bedtime	breast/bottle or bottle of cooled boiled water
Plus water after and between meals.	

Two Different Foods in the Same Meal

Several days after your baby is eating two different foods a day, you may feed her two different foods in the same meal, such as cereal with bananas. Remember not to introduce two new foods at the same time, because if your baby has an allergic reaction, you won't know which food caused it.

Which One First, the Food or the Breast Milk/Bottle?

After your baby has been eating solid foods for about a month, you can start the meal by feeding her the solid food first and then end with the breast/bottle. The first time you try this, see how she reacts to it. If she'll take the solid food first before any milk from the breast/bottle, fine; otherwise, give her the breast/bottle first and try again a week later.

How Large is a Food Serving?

In the previous table, you see the words "food serving." The amount of food in a serving varies tremendously with the day and the baby. The formal, technical definition of a baby food serving is "however much your baby will eat." The point is that there is no absolute size or standardized amount of food that constitutes a serving for a baby. But just to give you a rough idea, the hypothetical average beginning eater's food serving probably falls somewhere between 1 and 4 tablespoons.

A major part of the *Super Baby Food System* is the preparation of ice cube-sized frozen vegetable cubes. For beginners, a food serving is generally ½ veggie cube to 2 veggie cubes. (Depending on the size of the cubes in your ice cube trays and how full you make them, each cube holds about 2 tablespoons, give or take a few teaspoons. I never said it was an exact system! So 1 food cube is about 2 tablespoons and ½ of a food cube is about a tablespoon.) Start by giving your beginning eater a food cube made by filling the ice cube about half way. If she wants another, don't worry; she'll let you know.

Another major part of the *Super Baby Food System* is the home making of whole grain cereals, where dry uncooked grains are mixed into boiling water to cook. A food serving of homemade cereal for beginning eaters is ¼-½ cup of cooked cereal. This equates to 1-2 tablespoons of dry uncooked cereal, before it's stirred into boiling water. Of course, as your baby gets closer to her first birthday, serving sizes will become a little larger. A one year old may be eating ¾ cup (or larger) of cooked cereal at one sitting.

A beginner's food serving of yogurt is ¼-½ cup. Again, this is just to give you a rough idea. Give your baby as much as he will eat. But watch carefully for signals that he has had enough, and don't try to feed him more food after he loses interest.

Similar-Sized Food Servings

To balance your baby's diet among the food groups, keep food servings about the same size. For example, if your baby's vegetable servings are currently 2 food cubes, keep the fruit servings about the same size: 2 food cubes = 4 tablespoons = ¼ cup. Make cooked cereal servings twice the size of fruit or veggie servings, because cooked cereal is mostly water. For 2 veggie food cubes or ¼ cup fruit, a similar-sized cereal serving would be ½ cup of cooked cereal. (A half-cup of cooked cereal is only a few tablespoons of ground dry cereal before it is mixed with water.) There's no need to become obsessive and use a scientifically accurate scale to weigh servings, just approximate by eyeballing them.

> **REMINDER:** Keeping food servings similar in size will help to promote a nice balance of nutrients from the different food groups in your baby's diet.

Vegetables and Fruits

Feeding your beginner the *Super Baby Food Diet* is a matter of making your own vegetables and fruits, instead of buying the commercial jars of baby vegetables and fruits. Instructions on how to prepare vegetables and fruits are given in Part III. For babies this young, I would suggest purchasing only certified organically grown fruits and vegetables. Until your baby is 6 months old, remember to feed her only those foods listed for beginning eaters and use the *Four-Day Wait Rule*.

Grains and Cereals

Until your baby is 6 months old, she doesn't have the proper enzymes to digest the whole grains in homemade rice and millet cereals. Feeding them to her may cause some digestive problems, like gas. The commercial boxed baby cereals are well digested by a baby younger than 6 months, because they are processed and refined and not whole grain. It's up to your pediatrician and you whether you should feed them to your baby. These cereals are processed and I feel very strongly about feeding only whole, unrefined foods to a baby, which is why I chose not to give them to any of my babies.

Enough Iron is Extremely Important

If you also choose not to feed your baby iron-fortified commercial baby cereals and you are breastfeeding (and not using iron-fortified formula), make sure your baby is getting enough iron. Discuss iron supplement drops with your pediatrician. The iron stores with which babies are born begin to deplete as early as age 4 months, and possibly as early as 2 months for premature infants. If you'd like to go with commercial cereal because of the iron-fortification, check out organic brands of commercial baby food. Be sure your choice is iron-fortified, organic and whole grain.

9

Feeding Your Super Baby
at 6 Months

Introduce These Foods To Your 6-Month-Old	

Homemade single-grain cereals:
  Brown rice
  Millet
  Rolled oats/oatmeal
	Winter squash
	Raw mild fruits:
	  Papaya
	  Mango
	  Pears

Six months is a milestone in the development of your baby's digestive system, which now produces the enzymes necessary for the digestion of your own homemade whole grain cereals. At 6 months, cereals should be made with only one grain—don't start mixing grains together yet. There are instructions on preparing and storing homemade whole grain cereals in Chapter 4. Your 6-month-old is also able to eat the raw mild fruits listed in box above.

At 6 months, your baby is putting everything into her mouth that she can get her little hands on, which helps her to develop self-feeding skills. She may be able to feed herself a cracker and the soft strips of finger food such as teething biscuits or crackers, strips of bread, French toast, soft fruit wedges or veggies cooked until they're soft, whole bagels, pancakes, etc. **Watch your baby carefully for gagging and choking.** Although she holds her bottle and may hold a cup by the handle while trying to manipulate it, her skills are sorely lacking.

Food Consistency for Babies 6 Months Old
Your 6-month-old is learning how to move food around within her mouth. She may now have a few teeth and you may notice within the next few months that she makes chewing motions when you feed her. But because she will not get her first set of molars until she is well into her second year,

it will still be a long time before she will be able to grind her foods. Foods for your baby of 6 months still should be made into a thin, very smooth, liquidy purée.

Daily Amount of Foods for Babies 6 Months Old

Your baby should be eating anywhere from 2 to 6 food servings a day. Each vegetable and fruit serving should be from 1 to 2 tablespoons, or ½ food cube to 1 food cube. Each cooked cereal serving should be ¼ to ½ cup.

Daily Amount of Liquids for 6-Month-Old Babies

Breast milk or formula is the top priority food. Your baby should be breastfeeding at least 5 times a day or drinking 32 ounces of formula a day. If your baby is not drinking this minimum amount, decrease the amount of solid foods you offer him.

Your baby should be drinking water after each meal and between meals. Limit your baby's water intake to at most 4-8 ounces (maybe more on hot days) per day in order to assure she is drinking enough breast milk or formula.

Sample Daily Feeding Schedule for 6-Month-Old Babies	
Upon Awakening	breast/bottle
Morning	one or two food servings and breast/bottle
Noon	breast/bottle
Afternoon	one or two food servings and breast/bottle
Evening	breast/bottle
Bedtime	breast/bottle or bottle of cooled boiled water
Plus water after and between meals. If your baby still seems hungry, offer her a Super Snack in the evening.	

Feeding Your Baby the Super Baby Food Diet At 6 Months

Take a few minutes to reread about the *Super Baby Food Diet* in Chapter 3.

Vegetables and Fruits

Feed your baby certified organically-grown vegetables and fruits instead of the commercial jars of baby food. Instructions on how to prepare vegetables and fruits are given in Part III. Pay attention to the warnings about possible pesticides on some fruits and vegetables.

Super Porridge

You can give away those boxes of commercial baby cereals! Your baby can eat healthy homemade whole grain cereals. Start with brown rice, which is one homemade cereal that is referred to in the *Super Baby Food Diet* as *Super Porridge*. Directions on how to make homemade *Brown Rice Super Porridge* are found on page 57 in Part I. After waiting four days (the *Four-day Wait Rule*), you can introduce *Millet Super Porridge*. Millet is a little round yellow whole grain with a naturally high protein content, which is packed with lots of other good nutrients for your baby.

10

Feeding Your Super Baby at 7 Months

Introduce These Foods To Your 7-Month-Old		
Cottage cheese	Asparagus	Mild fruit juices/nectars, strained and diluted:
Homemade mixed cereals	Carrots	Apple
	Green beans	Apricot
Hard-cooked egg	Peas	Grape
	Summer squash	Papaya
	White potatoes	Pear
	Peaches	Peach
		Prune
		Maybe orange juice

There are over a dozen new foods in the list above that you can introduce to your 7-month-old. There just aren't enough days in the month to introduce them all, as you have to wait at least 4 days between new foods (*The Four-Day Wait Rule*).

The experts don't agree on the ages to introduce foods. Some recommend that you wait until 8 months before introducing eggs and cottage cheese, so you may want to introduce these later in the month and concentrate on introducing the new veggies. Whether you are feeding your baby hard-cooked eggs mixed into *Super Porridge* or scrambled egg bits as a finger food, be careful to cook the yolk thoroughly to kill any possible salmonella. At 7 months, your baby is ready for cereal mixed with fruit or vegetables. Try *Brown Rice Super Porridge* with mashed bananas, or *Millet Super Porridge* with sweet potato food cubes, or just about any combination.

Although your 7-month-old is in the process of developing the pincer grasp, he may still have some time to go before he can handle small bits of finger food. Continue to feed him the finger foods such as teething biscuits or crackers, strips of bread, French toast, soft fruit wedges or veggies cooked until they're soft, whole bagels, pancakes, etc. The rake, palmar, and pincer grasps are discussed in Chapter 16, *Eating and Drinking Skills*.

Food Consistency for Babies 7 Months Old

Your baby's food should still be puréed or mashed to a smooth consistency, although it can be slightly thicker now than it was for a beginning eater. Purée your baby's food until it is the consistency of a thick cream.

Introduce Pasteurized, Diluted, Mild Fruit Juices at 7 Months

Your 7-month-old probably will be awkward when it comes to drinking from a cup, so fill it with small amounts of water or diluted juice to minimize spilling.

Sample Daily Feeding Schedule for 7-Month-Old Babies	
Upon Awakening	breast/bottle
Breakfast	two or three food servings and breast/bottle
Lunch	two or three food servings and breast/bottle
Supper	two or three food servings and breast/bottle
Bedtime	breast/bottle or bottle of cooled boiled water
Plus water after and between meals. Offer 4 ounces of diluted fruit juice once a day.	

Daily Amount of Foods for Babies 7 Months Old

Babies at 7 months of age should be eating two meals a day, maybe three. Each meal should consist of 2-3 food servings. At each meal, your 7-month-old should be eating a total of a ½ cup or 4 ounces or more. Picture the amount in a small commercial baby food jar.

Fruits/Veggies

3-4 servings per day, including 1 vitamin A fruit/veggie and 1 vitamin C veggie/fruit/juice serving. Each serving should be 1-2 tablespoons or a half to a whole food cube. A vitamin A veggie is one of the *Super Green Veggies* or one of the deep yellow/orange vitamin A veggies/fruits listed on page 39. The Super Green Veggies are actually orange too, but their green color hides the orange. Make sure to feed your baby only those veggies/fruits that are age-appropriate.

Grains/Cereals

1-2 cereal or grain servings per day. Each cereal serving should be 1-2 tablespoons dry cereal mixed with formula or breast milk. A serving of grains from cooked homemade *Super Porridge* cereal should be ¼-½ cup, equivalent to 1-2 tablespoons dry, ground grains before cooking.

Egg

Every other day or 3-4 times per week.

Dairy

1 dairy serving every day or every other day. A serving is ⅓-½ cup yogurt and ¼ cup cottage cheese. Plus the breast milk/formula amounts stated in the next paragraph.

Daily Amount of Liquids for Babies 7 Months Old

Breast milk or formula is still the main food for your baby. Your baby should breastfeed 5 times a day or drink 30-32 ounces of formula a day. If your baby is not drinking this amount, decrease the amount of solid foods. Your baby should be drinking water after each meal and between meals. Keep your baby's total water and juice intake to 4-8 ounces maximum per day (maybe more on hot days) to be sure your baby is getting enough breast milk or formula. Also, please read about water on pages 397-400.

Feeding Your Baby the Super Baby Food Diet At 7 Months
Super Porridge

At 7 months, you can make homemade, whole grain *Super Porridge* cereals out of more than one grain. Try rice and millet, or rice and oats, or millet and oats. Directions for making these combined cereals are found in Chapter 4. Remember to use only grains that have been previously introduced individually and checked for allergy using the *Four-Day Wait Rule*.

Meat Alternatives (Protein)

At around 7-8 months, it is recommended that meat be introduced into a non-vegetarian baby's diet. Instead of meat, the *Super Baby Food Diet* uses the healthier meat alternatives to supply protein: tofu, beans and other legumes, nuts, seeds, eggs, and dairy products. This month your baby is old enough to begin eating tofu, a soybean product. At 8 months, you can introduce ground nuts/seeds, tahini, and nutritional yeast and, at 9 months, legumes. Your baby does not need meat to get the protein he needs; the *Super Baby Food Diet* supplies more than enough.

11

Feeding Your Super Baby at 8 Months

Introduce These Foods To Your 8-Month-Old

Apricot	Plums	Tahini
Apple	Watermelon	Finely ground nuts
Cantaloupe	Broccoli	Finely ground seeds
Honeydew melon	Okra	Nutritional yeast
Grapes (peeled and	Cooked parsley	Powdered kelp
quartered, not whole)	Wheat germ	Natural cheeses
Kiwi fruit	(if family allergy, wait	Powdered
Tofu	until after 1 year)	desiccated liver

At eight months, your baby's digestive system is maturing and you can introduce him to more and more foods. Don't slack off and begin giving him too many new foods at one time. Continue to use the *Four-day Wait Rule.*

Tofu (also called "soybean curd" or "bean curd") is a great food for babies 8 months and older. Tofu is a cheese-like product made from soybeans. You may be aware of the nutritional and health benefits of soy products. The "health food" tofu has become so popular that it now can be found in most regular supermarkets. Tofu does not have to be cooked because it is made from cooked soybeans. See page 284 for how to store and freeze tofu. Mashed or puréed tofu can be mixed with your baby's fruit or veggies. Or it can be added to homemade whole grain cereal to create a complete protein meal for your little one.

Your baby is more adept at the pincer grasp and consequently at the self-feeding of finger foods. He also is chewing or, more accurately, "gumming" foods with his molarless gums. Be sure to give him small SOFT bits of finger food with a texture that can be easily and painlessly mashed with baby's sensitive gums. Offer him the teething foods suggested in Chapter 16.

Sometime between now and your baby's first birthday, she will probably grab the spoon and attempt to self-feed. Ignore the mess, realize that your baby needs practice, and encourage your baby's efforts at self-feeding. Show her that you have confidence in her ability.

Wheat and Other Foods Containing Gluten

The gluten contained in wheat, rye, and other foods is a common allergen, as discussed in Chapter 6. Some experts recommend waiting until your baby is one-year-old before introducing it, especially if a wheat/gluten allergy runs in your family. Discuss with your pediatrician whether you should introduce wheat germ, bread, and other products containing gluten this month.

Super Snacks

Somewhere between now and two months from now (age 8-10 months), your baby's food intake will increase substantially. But because your baby's stomach can hold only small amounts of food, she must eat frequently throughout the day to fill her nutritional and caloric needs. Super Snacks fill the void in her tummy between meals, as previously discussed in Chapter 3.

Food Consistency for Babies 8 Months Old

Your baby's food should still be finely puréed. If your baby is easily eating this food, you can gradually decrease the added liquid for a thicker consistency. If your baby gags or chokes or spits out the food, you have made it too thick. At about 8-9 months, babies usually start on the commercial "junior" foods in the 6-8 ounce jars. On your next trip to the supermarket, note their consistency and copy it when you are puréeing homemade *Super Baby Food*.

Tofu is a very convenient finger food that can be served in strips or in small chunks.

Sample Daily Feeding Schedule for 8-Month-Old Babies	
Upon Awakening	breast/bottle
Breakfast	three food servings and breast/bottle or cup
Lunch	three food servings and breast/bottle or cup
Supper	three food servings and breast/bottle or cup
Bedtime	breast or bottle of water
Plus one or two *Super Snacks*, water, and diluted juice.	

Daily Amount of Foods for Babies 8 Months Old
Fruits/Veggies
4-5 servings per day, including 1 vitamin A fruit/veggie and at least 1 vitamin C veggie/fruit/juice serving. Each serving should be 2-3 tablespoons or 1-1½ food cubes. A vitamin A veggie is one of the Super Green Veggies or one of the deep yellow/orange vitamin A veggies/ fruits. Make sure to feed your baby only those veggies/fruits that are age-appropriate. Some of the *Super Snack* finger food ideas listed in Chapter 3 can count as Fruit/Veggies.

Grains/Cereals
2-3 servings or more of cereals or grains per day. Each cereal serving should be 1-2 tablespoons of dry cereal mixed with formula or breast milk. Soon your baby will be eating more food at each meal— he now may be eating 2 cereal servings (2-4 tablespoons of dry cereal) in a single meal. Be sure to feed your baby only those appropriate for his age. Finger foods and *Super Snacks* that can count as grain servings include whole grain baby crackers, whole grain bread pieces, Cheerios® and other cereals for baby, and cooked grains. Any foods containing wheat/gluten should be OK'd by your pediatrician first.

When your baby is 8 months old, she may be able to eat more *Super Porridge* at one meal—perhaps ½-¾ cup of cooked *Super Porridge*, which is equivalent to about 2-3 tablespoons of dry, uncooked ground cereal grains. This counts as 2 grain servings in the *Super Baby Food Diet*.

Protein Foods

1-2 servings of meat alternatives or protein foods: tofu, tahini, ground nuts, ground seeds, and nutritional yeast (added to *Super Porridge* or yogurt). Each serving size of ground nuts/seeds should be about 1 tablespoon before grinding, serving size of tahini should be ½-1 tablespoon, tofu should be 1-2 tablespoons, and nutritional yeast should be ½-1 teaspoon. Mix them in with *Super Porridge* or yogurt, or try some of the more simple *Toddler Hors d'oeuvres Super Snack* recipes with nuts/seeds beginning in Part VI. Make sure your baby has been previously introduced individually to any ingredient in the recipe and watch carefully for choking.

Eggs

Every second day or 3-4 times per week.

Tofu

At least every other day, add 1-2 tablespoons of puréed or well-mashed tofu to *Super Porridge* to make a high protein cereal. Tofu is made from soybeans and forms complete high-quality protein when mixed with the grains in *Super Porridge*.

Dairy

1 dairy serving every day or every other day. A serving is ½ cup of yogurt, ¼-⅓ cup cottage cheese, or ½-1 ounce of grated bits of natural cheeses. Plus the amount of liquids below.

Daily Amount of Liquids for Babies 8 Months Old

Breast milk or formula is still the main food for your baby. Your baby should breastfeed five times a day or drink 29-32 ounces of formula a day. Your baby should be drinking water after meals and between meals. Offer 2-4 ounces of water per day, especially on hot days. Offer a few ounces of diluted fruit juice (½ water, ½ juice) and/or offer a few ounces of nut and seed milks. To be sure that your baby is drinking enough breast milk or formula, do not exceed 6-8 ounces (maybe more on hot days) of total juice, nut milks, and water per day.

Weaning to the Cup

Starting any time now, you may want to start weaning your baby by gradually replacing mealtime bottles with cups of formula. Consider that the first bottle to be eliminated should be the bottle given with the mid-day meal.

Feeding Your Baby the Super Baby Food Diet At 8 Months
Ground Nuts and Seeds

Other super nutritious *Super Baby Foods* that you can start adding to your baby's diet this month are seeds and nuts, especially flaxseed (or flaxseed oil), almonds, filberts, walnuts, and pumpkin seeds. You don't want your baby to miss out on the concentrated nutrition in nuts and seeds. Whole seeds and nuts or even partial pieces of seeds and nuts are choking hazards for babies and toddlers, so you must grind them thoroughly in your blender. Feed ground seeds to your baby immediately after grinding, as they start becoming rancid as soon as their oils are exposed to the air. Another way to get these super foods into your baby's diet is via nut and seed milks, but be sure that they do not decrease your baby's intake of breast milk or formula.

Tahini

I love the convenience of tahini. Tahini is a super healthy spread made from ground sesame seeds (just as peanut butter is a spread made from ground peanuts) and is a very easy food to add into *Super Porridge* and yogurt. It is high in calcium, protein, and the healthy fat that your baby needs for proper development, especially brain development. For nutritional information and tips on tahini, check out Chapter 24.

> WARNING: Be sure to get your pediatrician's OK before you introduce your baby to nuts and seeds, as they are high allergen foods. Please read about peanut allergies on page 82.

Nutritional Yeast

Nutritional yeast, torula yeast, and brewer's yeast are nutritional supplement powders or flakes that are high in protein, the B vitamins, trace elements, and other nutrients. Nutritional yeast is consistently one of the top suppliers for the major nutrients, especially the B vitamins and trace elements. Taking a few seconds to add a little nutritional yeast into your baby's morning *Super Porridge* gives it a super nutrition boost. Nutritional yeast contains vitamin B12, a nutrient that is sometimes lacking in strict vegetarian diets.

> **WARNING:** Do not use the yeast for baking breads as a nutritional supplement. If you are not familiar with nutritional yeast, ask your natural foods store employee to help you find it.

Desiccated Liver and Powdered Kelp

You can begin giving your baby these two nutrition enhancers, which are discussed on page 26.

Begin Using the Super Baby Food Daily Worksheet

Your baby is starting to eat a wide variety of foods. If you have not yet used the *Super Baby Food Diet Worksheet*, you can begin to do so at around this age. Remember that the worksheet is for a one-year-old baby, so your 8-month-old will be eating fewer servings than the numbers recommended in the bottom row labeled "Suggested Daily Servings." And she is not yet eating beans or legumes, except for tofu (from soybeans). However, the worksheet will help you get into the habit of feeding your baby a balanced diet, with foods from each of the major food categories. Remember you can download a blank copy of *The Super Baby Food Worksheet* from the *Super Baby Food* website at www.superbabyfood.com.

12

Feeding Your Super Baby at 9 Months

Introduce These Foods To Your 9-Month-Old

Brussels sprouts	Onion, cooked
Cauliflower	Turnips
Spinach	Pineapple
Beets	Raw parsley, finely chopped
Greens	Beans, split peas, lentils and other
Kale	legumes, ground to a powder
Eggplant	and cooked, or cooked whole
Rhubarb	and mashed with skins removed
Rutabaga	

Your baby's digestive system is almost as mature as an adult's, and you can feed him almost everything an adult eats. Kale is, in my opinion, the most super of the Super Green Veggies. I feed it to my baby at least every second day when it's in season. Buy two bunches at a time, because these and all greens shrink significantly when you cook them.

Your baby's pincer grasp is developing and she is handling her finger foods very well. Your baby can now chew well (ok, gum) and may be able to bite off a piece of food from a larger food. Continue to offer her strips of slices of banana, peeled wedges of ripe pears, peaches, and other fruit, strips of natural cheeses, cooked broccoli spears, peeled cucumber strips, and strips of toast. For other finger food and *Super Snack* ideas, refer back to Chapter 3. Continue to use the *Four-Day Wait Rule*.

Food Consistency for Babies 9 Months Old

As your baby's eating skills develop, gradually make the purée consistency a little thicker by adding less liquid. Also, gradually increase the chunkiness of puréed food by using your blender or food processor on a slower speed and/or for less time. If you manually pulse the food you can stop after each pulse to check for the right consistency.

Besides increasing the chunkiness of your baby's food, another way to slowly accustom him to coarser food is to add a finely minced food to a smooth purée. Try adding finely grated cooked vegetable to yogurt, or add a few teaspoons of grainy cereal to a smooth purée of vegetable. It is important that the chunkier food be very soft, so that your baby can chew them—*gum* them is more accurate—with his sensitive gums.

Sample Daily Feeding Schedule for 9-Month-Old Babies	
Upon Awakening	breast/bottle
Breakfast	three food servings and breast/bottle or cup
Lunch	three food servings cup of formula/breast milk
Afternoon Snack	Super Snack
Supper	three food servings and breast/bottle or cup
Bedtime	breast or bottle of water
Plus one or two *Super Snacks*, water, and diluted juice.	

Daily Amount of Foods for Babies 9 Months Old

You may notice an increase in your baby's appetite and in the quantity of food she eats. Soon, if it isn't already, a one-food-cube serving size will no longer be enough, and your baby will be able to eat 2, or even 3, food cubes.

Fruits/Veggies

4-5 servings per day, including 1 vitamin A fruit/veggie and 1 vitamin C veggie/fruit/juice serving. Each serving should be 2-4 tablespoons or 1-2 food cubes.

Grains/Cereals

3-4 servings of grains per day. Each cereal serving should be 1-2 tablespoons of dry cereal mixed with formula or breast milk. Soon your baby will be eating more food at each meal—he now may be eating 2 cereal servings (2-4 tablespoons of dry cereal) in a single meal. Be sure to feed your baby only those appropriate for his age. Continue giving finger foods and *Super Snacks* that can count as grain servings: whole grain baby crackers, whole grain bread pieces, Cheerios® and other cereals for baby, and cooked grains. Any foods containing wheat/gluten should be OK'd by your pediatrician first.

Your baby is probably now eating ½-¾ cup of *Super Porridge* in one sitting. ½-¾ cup of all-grains *Super Porridge* counts as 2 grain servings on the *Super Baby Food Daily Worksheet*. Previously, *Super Porridge* has been made with all grains, but now your baby is old enough to eat *Super Porridge* made with a combination of grains and legumes.

Protein Foods

2-3 servings per day of protein foods or meat alternatives: tofu; cooked pureed beans, peas, and lentils; ground nuts and seeds; and nutritional yeast. Add these protein foods to *Super Porridge* or yogurt for protein complementarity. A serving of nutritional yeast should be ½-1 teaspoon. A serving is 1-2 tablespoons of ground nuts/seeds or 1-2 tablespoons of ground beans (before cooking), and 2-3 tablespoons of tofu.

The legumes in ¾ of a cup of *High Protein Super Porridge* count as 1 legume serving.

Eggs

Every second day or 3-4 times per week.

Dairy

One dairy serving every day or every other day. A serving is a ½ a cup of yogurt, ⅓ of a cup of cottage cheese, or 1 ounce of grated bits of natural cheeses. Plus the breast milk/formula amounts stated in next paragraph.

Daily Amount of Liquids for Babies 9 Months Old

Your baby should breastfeed at least 3 or 4 times a day or drink 26-32 ounces of formula a day. Offer 2-4 ounces of water daily, especially on hot days. Offer 4 ounces of slightly diluted fruit juice, perhaps 3 ounces juice to 1 ounce water and/or offer a few ounces of nut and seed milks. To be sure that your baby is drinking enough breast milk or formula, do not exceed

6-8 ounces per day (maybe more on hot days) of total water, juice, nut milks, and other beverages.

Feeding Your Baby the Super Baby Food Diet At 9 Months
High Protein Super Porridge

This is the month we've been waiting for—the month that you can add beans and other legumes into *Super Porridge*, making it a complete high protein cereal! Beans and other legumes complement grains to make a complete protein that is as high a quality as meat and dairy products. Chapter 4 has instructions on how to prepare and store *High Protein Super Porridge*. You have already begun adding tofu and ground nuts/seeds into *Super Porridge* made only from grains in order to increase its protein content (and because they are packed with nutrients for your baby). This month, with beans added into the grains before cooking, you are starting with a base of *High Protein Super Porridge* before you add any nuts/seeds or tofu.

Because of the beans, you can now write ¾ cup of *Super Porridge* into the *Super Baby Food Diet Daily Worksheet* as 2 grain servings and 1 legume serving. In fact, your 9-month-old baby is old enough to have the complete *Super Porridge Main Meal*.

13

Feeding Your Super Baby at 10 Months

Introduce These Foods To Your 10-Month-Old		

Peanut butter, thinned (the smooth kind, not the chunky kind)
 	
Other thinned nut butters
 	
Ground sprouts
	Whole grain pasta
	
	Homemade bulgur cereal
	
	Cooked whole grain cornmeal with the germ
		Raw and finely grated:
		  Carrots
		  Greens
		  Summer squash
		  Sweet peppers

At 10 months, you can introduce your baby to nut butters. Peanut butter is not the only kind! You will find walnut butters (high in omega 3), almond butters, cashew butters, and others at the natural foods store. Thick nut butters may cause your baby to gag, so it is important to thin them with milk, water, or even fruit juice. Delicious! Spread them on bread, crackers, and fruit pieces.

> WARNING: Please read about peanut allergies on page 82.

Bulgur, a cracked whole wheat, should not be given if wheat allergy runs in the family. And even if you don't have a wheat allergy in your family, your pediatrician may advise you to wait until your baby is a year old before introducing any wheat products, such as pasta, which usually contains wheat flour. Pasta should be made from 100% whole grain flour, not the white/wheat flour. Continue to use the *Four-Day Wait Rule* with all new foods.

Food Consistency for Babies 10 Months Old

Food should still be fork-mashed or puréed, but continue to gradually increase its thickness and chunkiness. By 10 months, your baby may be eating finger foods very well. Finger foods are becoming a larger part of her diet. Small pieces of plain soft-cooked whole-grain pasta are a good finger food, and they can be frozen in ½ cup portions using the *Nested Plastic Bag Method.*

Sample Daily Feeding Schedule for 10-Month-Old Babies	
Upon Awakening	breast/bottle
Breakfast	three food servings and breast/bottle or cup
Morning Snack	Super Snack
Lunch	three food servings cup of formula/breast milk
Afternoon Snack	Super Snack
Supper	three food servings cup of formula/breast milk
Bedtime	breast or bottle of water
Plus *Super Snacks*, water, and diluted juice.	

Daily Amount of Foods for Babies 10 Months Old

You have probably noticed a big increase in your baby's appetite and in the quantity of food she eats. Servings now consist of 2 or 3 food cubes. In the next two months, your baby should gradually build up to amount of food in the *Super Baby Food Diet* summarized in the table on page 40.

Fruits/Veggies

4-5 servings per day, including 1 vitamin A fruit/veggie and at least 1 vitamin C veggie/fruit/juice serving. Each serving should be 3-4 tablespoons or 1½-2 food cubes.

Grains/Cereals

4 servings of grains per day. Follow the same instructions for Grains/Cereals for 9-month-olds.

Protein foods

2-3 servings per day. New proteins for this month are peanut and other butters, thinned to prevent choking. A serving is 1-2 tablespoons of peanut butter (before thinning) or other nut butter. Other protein foods are the same as for 9-month-olds.

Eggs

Every second day or 3-4 times per week.

Dairy

1 serving per day of dairy or more. A serving is ½ a cup of yogurt, ⅓ cup of cottage cheese, or 1 ounce grated bits of natural cheese. Plus the breast milk/formula amounts stated in next paragraph.

Daily Amount of Liquids for Babies 10 Months Old

Your baby should breastfeed at least 3 times a day or drink 24-32 ounces of formula a day. Offer 2-4 ounces of water daily, especially on hot days. Offer 4 ounces of slightly diluted or undiluted fruit juice and/or offer a few ounces of nut and seed milks. To be sure that your baby is drinking enough breast milk or formula, do not exceed 6-8 ounces per day (maybe more on hot days) of total water, juice, nut milks, and other beverages.

Feeding Your Baby the Super Baby Food Diet At 10 Months

Continue to give your baby *Super Porridge* made from the variety of whole grains, beans, and other legumes from the natural foods store.

The *Super Baby Food System* should now be a part of your daily life. You've developed your own schedule and make *Super Porridge* and frozen food cubes at regular, predictable intervals. Your baby may now be eating the number of servings recommended in the *Super Baby Food Diet Daily Worksheet*.

For the next several months and into toddlerhood, continue with the *Super Baby Food Diet*.

14

Feeding Your Super Baby
at 11 Months

Foods to Introduce at 11 Months
Continue to introduce foods that your baby hasn't had yet using the *Four-day Wait Rule*.

Food Consistency for Babies 11 Months Old
Although you are still feeding your baby her main meals mashed or coarsely puréed, she is probably enjoying quite a few finger foods by now. Sit with your baby while she finger feeds and watch carefully for choking or gagging. Never leave her alone while she is eating.

Daily Amount of Foods for Babies 11 Months Old
Food requirements are similar to those of a 10-month-old baby, but your baby may be eating a little more.

Daily Amount of Liquids for Babies 11 Months Old
Your baby should breastfeed at least 3 times a day or drink 24-32 ounces of formula a day. Offer 4 ounces of water per day (especially on hot days), and offer 2-4 ounces of undiluted or diluted fruit juice and/or a few ounces of nut/seed milk. Remember that you do not have to increase to 100% fruit juice. To be sure that your baby is drinking enough breast milk or formula, do not exceed 6-8 ounces (maybe more on hot days) of total juice, nut milks, and water.

Your Baby's First Birthday
As your baby nears the end of his first year, you cannot remember what it was like in your previous life before kids. You feel that you are the luckiest person in the world to have him. Real joy in living truly comes from loving our children and watching them grow.

Have fun celebrating the end of this first wonderful year at your baby's first birthday party! Check out the recipes in Part VI for *Super Baby* healthy cakes and icings.

15

Feeding Your Super Toddler

Introduce These Foods To Your 12-Month-Old	
Cow's milk	Tomatoes/tomato juice
Citrus fruits/juices	Strawberries, blueberries, and other
Hard-cooked egg white	berries (not whole, cut into small pieces)
Uncooked honey	

Now that your baby is one year old, he is officially a toddler and will remain a toddler until he is three years old. Toddlers are curious little people that get into everything. They have discovered independence and want their own way, and if they don't get it—look out! It is rumored that the word "no" was invented by a toddler.

Toddlers are constantly testing the limit and mealtimes are no exception. Expect plenty of refusals. At mealtimes, you never know when he'll reject a food, even a food that he previously relished. He may adamantly refuse to eat the healthy foods he loved as a baby. When my little guy got to be about 16 months, he wouldn't eat plain *Super Porridge*. I had to add several veggie cubes to it, which was fine with me. Try not to take food rejections personally, and continue to keep mealtimes pleasant and relaxing.

Your toddler can now eat just about anything you do, with the exception of the choking hazards listed on page 338. And, of course, don't feed him foods that are salty, spicy, sugary, or those that contain too much butter. Continue to use the *Four-Day Wait Rule*. You may want to wait to introduce peanuts until your child is three years old—discuss this with your pediatrician.

The Foundation Year for Future Food Preferences
Your baby's second year of life (from 1-2 years old) is THE most important time for establishing food preferences. What she learns to like now will

probably stay with her for the rest of her life. Remember this when you are tempted to treat her with junk foods. Never use food as a reward, even healthy food; instead, substitute a smile, a hug, and a big kiss. And don't make deals to get your child to eat her veggies: "You can have the cookie if you finish your broccoli." In effect, you're saying, "Cookies are better than broccoli and good children get to eat cookies."

How do you get her to eat only good foods? Don't have any junk foods in the house, or hide them and never let your toddler see you or anyone else eating them.

> **TIP:** If your toddler is refusing to eat healthy foods, let the time that lapses between meals be long enough so that your toddler is somewhat hungry for his next snack/meal. He'll be less fussy about what he eats.

After your child's second birthday, he will no longer be willing to try new foods as willingly as during his first and second years. To encourage him, place SMALL amounts of foods nicely arranged on his plate. A too-full plate is overwhelming to a child.

Cut your toddler's food into easy-to-eat pieces. Make healthy foods fun by using the food decorating ideas in Chapter 37.

Distract your child when you offer new or disliked foods. To change the focus away from the food, chat with him about his favorite things, such as the slide at the playground or his favorite book.

Give your toddler as much control over her food choices as possible. But don't ask an open-ended question like "What do you want for lunch?" Give your child less latitude while still allowing her some control by asking a multiple-choice question: "Would you like apples or pears for dessert?"

Along with any new food, also offer a familiar food that your toddler likes.

If you get your toddler involved in food preparation, he will be more likely to eat it. Let him dump the cup of flour into the bowl, tear the lettuce, and wipe up the counter top. It's fun to let your child help, although it will take you three times longer for food preparation!

Keep offering new foods and don't be offended at refusals. Remember to keep mealtimes pleasant and don't start any battles.

While your toddler is eating, let her concentrate. Don't let her get distracted by a television set or other diversion; instead, use mealtimes to spend time with your toddler. You know how easily distracted a toddler can be if you've ever tried to spoon feed your baby a kiwi fruit while she's walking around the family room with her favorite DVD playing—it takes four times as long to finish it.

> WARNING: You should still not leave your child alone while she is eating. Always watch carefully for choking.

Toddlers' Tummies Are Still Small

Your toddler is still eating small amounts of food frequently throughout the day—probably 3 small meals and at least 2 snacks a day. Super Snacks continue to be a big part of your toddler's diet, and will be until your child is 4-5 years old. Although the average two-year-old eats 5 times per day (3 meals, 2 snacks), some children eat as little as 3 times per day and others as often as 14 times per day! (When you feel that all you are doing is feeding and cleaning up after your toddler, think about those children's parents!)

A Decrease in Appetite at One Year

Your toddler's growth rate slows at about the time of her first birthday. Whereas she probably tripled her birth weight during her first year, she will gain only between 3 and 7 pounds during her second. The small weight gain during toddlerhood will produce changes in muscle mass and in the shape of the body, making your toddler look more like a child than a baby. Because she is eating less, it is important to make every bite count nutritionally.

> REMINDER: Never force her to eat or it might be the beginning of a lifetime of eating problems.

24 Ounces of Milk Per Day

Her bones will increase in length and density as calcium and phosphorus are deposited into them. Because of this bone mineralization, it is important to make sure that your toddler is getting enough minerals in her diet. She should continue eating or drinking 24 ounces or 3 cups of milk, yogurt, or other high-calcium and protein foods daily, although some experts hold that 2 cups per day are enough.

Whole or Low-fat Milk?

Now that your baby is a toddler, he can begin drinking cow's milk, unless, of course, he has a milk allergy. Some experts suggest that you continue to feed him whole milk products, and no low-fat or skim milk products, until he is two years old. Other authorities say three years. If you are concerned about your baby's weight or cholesterol levels, you may want to switch to low-fat milk after his first birthday, but consult your pediatrician first. In general, a toddler's fat and cholesterol intake should not be greatly restricted.

> WARNING: Be sure to get your pediatrician's OK before feeding your toddler the commercial milks for toddlers and older children. Some brands contain too much protein and not enough fat.

Iron is Still Important

Too much milk is not good for your toddler if it takes the place of other nutritious foods, especially foods high in iron. Iron continues to be an important nutrient through toddlerhood and milk is not a good source of iron. Milk anemia refers to the iron-deficiency anemia that occurs when a child's diet is lacking in iron because too much milk displaces iron-rich foods. Your toddler's diet should be balanced and consist of foods from all of the food groups, not just the dairy group, to supply the variety of nutrients his body needs.

Iron is a common deficiency among toddlers because they typically stop eating iron-fortified formula and cereals around their first birthday. Iron supplementation should be continued until at least 18 months. Ask your pediatrician how long to continue your child's iron supplements.

Food Serving Sizes for Toddlers

A general rule is to make your toddler's portion sizes equal to 1-2 tablespoons of food for each year of age. A two-year-old should get 2-4 tablespoons, a three-year-old should get 3-6 tablespoons, a 1½-year-old should get 1½-3 tablespoons, etc. If you cannot measure a particular food by tablespoon, give your toddler anywhere from ¼-½ of an adult's portion size. Toddler servings of cooked *Super Porridge* should be ¾-1 cup, which is equivalent to 3-4 tablespoons of dry, uncooked powdered grains and legumes.

Toddlers and Well-Rounded Diets—Fact or Fiction?

There's nothing unusual about a toddler refusing to eat. Some days she will refuse to eat all foods except one, and the next week she will eat a different one to the exclusion of all else. I never had any trouble with my toddlers refusing to eat their *Super Porridge;* in fact, they have always eaten it with gusto. Maybe I was lucky, but I think the trick is to start them on *Super Baby Food* right from the start and keep them on it. A toddler's ignorance of junk food is bliss for us parents! Concerned parents should know that toddlers do not need to eat very much to remain healthy. The *Super Porridge Main Meal* of the *Super Baby Food Diet* plus 2 cups of milk are enough to meet a toddler's daily dietary needs.

> **TIP:** Soup is a quick, easy, and convenient meal for your toddler. But although he is good with solid foods in the spoon, liquidy soup may be a problem. Try this: Use a strainer to collect the solid parts from the soup and place them in his bowl. Let him pierce them with his baby fork or eat them with his spoon. The liquid part of the soup can be poured into his cup for drinking.

Toddler Quirks

Many children don't like their foods to touch each other. If your child doesn't, oblige him by separating and spacing the food on his plate.

Toddlers may hold food in their mouths for hours.

Toddlers may want only one food for several consecutive days or weeks, and then abruptly refuse to eat that food for the next month.

Toddlers may get upset if you do not serve their food the way they are currently thinking that you should. For example, your toddler may be upset if you cut his bread in squares rather than in triangles. Or he may complain vehemently if you gave him juice in his blue sippy cup instead of his purple sippy cup. One day my little guy threw a tantrum when I put his spoon in his bowl instead of in his hand; after that, I never forgot to ask him where he wanted his spoon. Yes, we parents of toddlers learn to walk on eggshells.

Toddlers are extremely active and need to move. After your baby has finished her meal, don't force her to remain at the dinner table listening to adult conversation if she doesn't want to.

House Rules

It is OK to establish and insist upon a few rules for toddlers who should know better. Some rules you may establish may be:

- No food throwing.
- No eating or drinking away from the table/high chair.
- No spitting.

When your toddler begins to act in ways that disturb you with the intent to provoke you rather than to practice skill development, it's time to put your foot down and show that you are the boss. Children need discipline, and they become insecure when you are not in charge. Show that you are serious by taking away the food immediately when established rules are broken. Be firm, but be in control and without anger. You can be kind and loving to your child as you discipline her.

Children Learn by Example

The best way to teach your children manners is to set a good example. Yelling and nagging is just not as effective. Children imitate the actions of adults, so act as you want your child to act. The old "do as I say, not as I do" doesn't work now and it never has. If you wash your hands before a meal, he will too. If you say "please" and "thank you," so will he.

16

Eating and Drinking Skills

Oral Motor and Swallowing Development

As you surely have noticed, your newborn is a veritable sucking machine! A newborn's tongue is large in the mouth and is flat with sides thinned and cupped up to provide a channel for moving liquid backward for swallowing. Sucking pads in the cheeks help provide stability for sucking. Sucking automatically triggers swallowing.

A newborn does not yet recognize the nipple by sight, because cognitive (intellectual) development is too immature. Your newborn will keep crying even though you are directly in front of him obviously getting ready the breast or bottle. But if you touch his lip or cheek, his mouth begins searching for the nipple. His mouth opens wide in order to accept the nipple and his lips move forward in order to surround the nipple. If you place your finger in his mouth, strong sucking is triggered almost immediately. His tongue will wrap around your finger and try to pump liquid from it. If you place your finger in the side of the mouth on top of the gum, his mouth will move up and down in a biting motion. This "phasic bite" is practice for the true chewing he will master in the future.

Between 3 and 6 months, your baby begins to move her mouth more voluntarily, overriding the primitive reflexes with which she was born. She now visually recognizes the nipple and moves forward deliberately. While you feed her, she is learning to handle solid foods within her mouth. Her tongue juts in and out to move the food back into her mouth for swallowing. But her jaw, tongue, and lips move together as one unit and she cannot control them independently. Between 6 and 7½ months, she will begin to chew foods, or because she has no molars at this age, to "gum" foods.

At around 7 to 9 months, your baby learns to move his jaw independently of his tongue and lips. He now opens his jaw to accept the spoon, and his lower lip and upper lip work to remove food from the spoon. He's beginning to coordinate the taking in of food with swallowing and breathing. He can transfer food from the center of his tongue to the sides of his mouth and from the side of his mouth to the center of his tongue, but not yet all the way across the inside his mouth from one side to the other. Although he can get a cracker into his mouth, close his mouth and break off a piece, he will not use precise jaw movements until he is about 9 months old. By then he will be able to make a controlled and more mature bite. By 9½ months, drooling will be significantly reduced because he can better control his lips, tongue, and jaw.

When your baby is 10 to 12 months of age, you will notice that her eating is becoming much more mature. Her bite is more controlled. Her upper lip works better to clean food off the spoon than it did when she was younger. Her cheeks and mouth work to move food around in her mouth, and her mouth is more often closed while she is eating. Her swallowing skills are much improved.

Eating skills continue to mature as your child goes through the toddler years. By the time he is 18 months he will lose very little food from his mouth while eating. His jaw, lips, tongue, and cheek movements will become more finely graded. From 18-24 months, he will begin to practice transferring food from one side of his mouth to the other—a motion that will be perfected by his second birthday.

At two years old, he probably will use his tongue to lick his lips clean and will use his upper teeth to clean his lower lip. He will be able to chew with his mouth closed and has learned to move food around well in his mouth. His jaw openings become better sized for the incoming food.

By his third birthday, he will be able to keep his mouth fully closed while chewing, and even while transferring food across the mouth. He will be able to "feel" food on his lips, and use his tongue to clean it off, and he will use his tongue to clean between his gums and cheeks. The first semblance of adult table manners may appear by your baby's second birthday, but many babies prefer to remain very messy until they are well into their third year. Be patient—civility is bound to come before your child's third birthday.

The Spoon

Baby's gums are sensitive. Feed her with a plastic coated baby spoon. The ZoLi® spoon could be a good choice. The spoon should be small and shallow so that it fits easily into baby's tiny mouth, and should have no sharp edges. For non-self-feeding babies, the longer the spoon handle, the easier on mom's or dad's back muscles and the easier for reaching baby food in the bottom of tall jars. When your baby begins to feed himself, give him a plastic spoon made specifically for this purpose, with a curved handle to decrease the danger of an eye poke.

You can actually use a regular adult spoon if baby can handle it well. If you think it is a problem for baby because she is biting down on it with her sensitive gums, a baby spoon with a soft tip is fine to continue to use. A spoon with a pointed end is not safe for a young child. Plastic coated spoons are often sold with plastic coated forks. Although your baby will not be old enough for a fork until the latter half of her second year, you may save money by buying the set and stashing the fork away until later.

NOTE: The latest fad in baby feeding accessories is flashy-handled spoons and forks, or those with sparkly toys built into the handles, or those with handles shaped like airplanes, etc. These utensils may only serve to distract your baby from what he is supposed to be doing—concentrating on learning how to eat. Your baby doesn't need them.

Do Not Use an Infant Feeder

Although first foods are very liquidy, they should not be fed to your baby through a bottle with an enlarged nipple hole, or with one of those bottle-type infant feeders, which I am surprised are still sold in baby stores. These feeders actually delay learning how to swallow, do not help in desensitizing the gag reflex, and delay the development of other eating skills. They may cause your baby to choke.

Solid foods should be given to your baby at a time when they are needed both nutritionally and developmentally. Nutritionally, they add calories and nutrients to your baby's milk diet. Developmentally, eating solid foods helps in the maturation of a new set of muscles in the tongue that allow swallowing, which were not used in breast or bottle feeding. Proper development of these muscles helps to promote clear speech patterns later in life. If your baby is not developmentally ready to eat from a spoon, then she is not yet ready for solid foods.

When baby eats from a spoon, she starts becoming aware of the process of eating: taking a bite, chewing and swallowing the bite, waiting a moment before taking another bite, and stopping when satiated. Infant feeders do not allow this process and drastically increase the amount of food your baby eats, which may cause problems with overweight and bad eating habits.

The Cup
At First, Hold the Cup While Your Baby Drinks
It may take many months (perhaps until age 16-18 months) for your baby to learn to drink neatly from a cup, but until then keep plenty of wipe-up towels around. Beginning at about 5 or 6 months, let your baby take small sips from a cup while you hold it. There may be a few chokes rather than swallows at first.

Your baby can begin drinking plain water as soon as he begins eating solid foods. You may want to give him this water in a cup after he finishes eating and between meals. Start with about a tablespoon of water and gradually increase the amount. He'll soon become comfortable enough with the cup to grab it and try to drink himself. Let him. He may play with it for a while first, which is a step in learning. It's OK if he spills because there is only a little water in it.

Sippy Cups
You can buy baby cups that have spouts with holes to minimize spilling. If there is an air hole on the opposite side of the spout, it means that liquid will come out faster—you may want to start with a cup without the extra air hole (or cover the hole with tape until baby is older). Some baby cups have different spout attachments that allow for varying liquid flow speeds. The newest invention is the spill-less cup, which doesn't spill even when it tips over. Young babies have an easier time handling a cup with handles on both sides. Those light plastic cups with handles don't do well in the dishwasher—their handles get caught on everything and they are so light that they flip upside down.

Possible Problems with Sippy Cups
Speech Development: For generations, parents have given their babies sippy cups in order to prevent spilling. Recently, experts have become concerned about possible problems from extensive use of the sippy cup. Speech pathologists believe that constant use of the sippy cup can affect your child's speech development, possibly causing slurring and imprecise

articulation. Adult cups help develop muscles in the mouth needed for speech, whereas sippy cups do not contribute to speech development.

Teeth: Extensive sucking on a sippy cup (as with thumb sucking) can place pressure on the palate and push teeth out of place. A second problem with sippy cups and your child's teeth may occur if your child sips any liquid containing sugar from the sippy cup over long periods of time–dental caries. Your child's teeth will be bathed in acids and sugar (natural sugar in juice or the natural lactose in milk) that will cause cavities and erode enamel. Put only pure water in your child's sippy cup or bottle if your child will be sipping on it for more than a short period of time.

Tongue: When a child has her mouth on a sippy cup (or when she is sucking her thumb), her lips are spread apart which causes open-mouthed breathing. The spout is against the top of the mouth and the tongue is misplaced, which prevents her from properly swallowing and suctioning her saliva.

Bacteria: Your baby may leave a sippy cup (or bottle) in the nursery or somewhere else in your home without your knowledge. Bacteria will build up at room temperature after a short time both inside and outside the cup, which you may not smell because of the lid, and your baby may drink it. To prevent this, be diligent about keeping track of all of your child's cups and bottles.

Some experts recommend using straws instead of sippy cups. There are also cups with recessed lids available. Ask your healthcare provider which cups he recommends.

> **TIP:** You can now buy stainless steel cups for babies. They do great in the dishwasher and you don't have to worry about BPA and phthalates.

> **TIP:** To help baby's wet hands get a grip around a handle-less cup, wrap some adhesive tape around it or pieces of self-sticking bathtub appliques, although it will get cruddy after a while. Or cut off the cuff from a small clean sock and stretch it around the cup.

> **MONEY SAVER:** If you don't want to invest in a dishwasher basket, place small items in a partition in the silverware basket and stuff a net scrubber in the top to hold them in.

By 7-8 months, let him feed himself water from the spouted cup. Remember that he may want to just play with it for the first several weeks. Until about 9 months, your baby will drink from it using the same sucking pattern as he would from a bottle.

When he becomes fairly skilled, go all the way and give him an uncovered unbreakable cup, but fill with only small amounts of water or milk to make cleanup easier. Don't make him feel bad when he spills—everyone has to start somewhere. Remember that learning to handle the cup is helping to develop his hand to mouth coordination.

TIP: Drink from a cup while your baby is watching. Babies love to imitate and it's a fun, natural way for them to learn.

From 10-15 months, he will still hold the cup with both hands and may drop it on the floor when finished. Gradually, he will stop using those up and down jaw movements as he is drinking. He will become more skilled at taking several continuous swallows without stopping to take a breath. Observe how his hands, wrist, and elbows consciously work in unison to adjust the angle of the cup in order to successfully move it to his mouth. During these months he will eventually perfect the motion and get the liquid into his mouth without spilling most of the time. By 18 months, he will use the rim of the cup for stability.

TIP: If you can't stand the spills, let your baby practice drinking from a cup in the bathtub, but make sure he doesn't try to drink the bath water when you turn your head!

TIP: Tuck a wipe-up towel between his neck and his bib to prevent drips from going down his shirt. Fold the towel in half to give an extra layer of protection.

TIP: Protect your furniture by teaching baby to place her cup on a coaster. A large plastic lid from a margarine tub makes a large coaster—a bigger target on which baby can place her cup.

By 18-24 months, she will no longer need both hands to hold a cup. Your one-fisted drinker has perfected the tilt of the cup at just the right moment to tip liquid into her mouth. There will continue to be some loss of liquid and spillage until her second birthday, but at least now she is putting the cup back on the table and not throwing it to the floor. Sometime after her second birthday, she will be able to get herself a drink and will even be able to pour from a pitcher and will most likely insist, in the stubborn toddler fashion, on doing it herself.

Gradual Weaning to the Cup

At about 8-10 months, some experts recommend that you begin the process of weaning your baby off the bottle or breast by giving her formula or expressed breast milk in a cup with meals. Many health care providers recommend discontinuing the bottle entirely by the age of 18 months.

> **REMINDER:** The need to suck will continue well into your baby's second year. There's no need to hurry your baby off the breast/bottle. Weaning should be done slowly and gradually and with love. Force should never be used, neither should subtle coaxing or manipulation. In other cultures, moms don't stop breastfeeding until their babies are three or four years old. In the United States, the majority of moms stop breastfeeding before one year.

Wean your baby slowly by eliminating one breastfeeding session or one bottle-feeding at a time. Begin by substituting the feeding with a cup of breast milk or formula at the midday meal. Wait several days or weeks before omitting another feeding. The next feeding to be replaced with the cup should be the feeding with supper, then the morning feeding, and last the bedtime feeding.

It may take more than 6 months before your baby gets all of her liquids from the cup and completely gives up breastfeeding or the bottle. Breast milk or formula should continue to be given in the cup until your baby becomes one year old, when you can start giving cow's milk.

> **TIP:** To help your baby adjust to drinking from a cup, let her drink directly from her open-topped bottle. Or stick a straw into the bottle.

> **TIP:** When your baby begins drinking from a straw, cut it down to baby-size. Cut the straw so that it extends no more than an inch or two above the rim of the cup. And how much fun it is when she discovers how to blow bubbles in her cup! (By the way, bubble blowing is great for your baby's oral muscle development.)

Some Babies Abruptly Stop Breastfeeding

Be aware that some babies wean themselves from the breast at about 10 months, an age where physical progress advances quickly. A friend of mine felt abandoned and rejected when her baby decided one day to quit breastfeeding cold turkey. It is very disconcerting to suddenly have to give up that special intimacy with your baby.

If you need someone to talk to about breastfeeding, there is a compassionate ear available at your local La Leche League, or call the maternity department of your local hospital. I found my La Leche rep very knowledgeable and helpful whenever I had a problem with breastfeeding. Find a local La Leche representative on their web site, www.llli.org. Some terrific online communities for moms are available for your help when you are ready and in need of information.

Finger Foods

Finger foods are food pieces that your baby can pick up and eat by himself. Place them in front of your baby directly on his clean high chair tray, on his feeding table, or on an unbreakable plate. Ideas for finger foods can be found in Chapter 3.

First for Practice, Then for Nutrition

At first, finger foods are mostly tools for practice in self-feeding, which will help your baby to develop manual dexterity and give him more control of his jaw muscles. Practice at finger feeding also promotes the skills necessary for later self feeding with a spoon. It may take up to his 9th or 10th month until he aims accurately enough to get good amounts of finger foods into his mouth. When these skills develop, finger foods will become an important nutritional part of your baby's diet. Until then, your baby will get the majority of his food from your spoon-feeding.

> **NOTE:** Once your baby has begun to self-feed, she may want to eat only food she can feed herself. She may totally refuse to let you feed her with the spoon. Don't be alarmed or try to force her to eat off the spoon. Simply give her ALL finger foods.

The Rake

Before the age of 6 months, your baby scoops up small objects by using the outer palm (pinky finger side) of his hand in a rake-like motion. Because he is not yet skilled at picking up small bits of food, first finger foods should consist of larger food pieces, such as teething biscuits or crackers, strips of bread, French toast, soft fruit wedges or veggies cooked until they're soft, whole bagels, pancakes, etc.

The Palmar Grasp

At around 5 months, the palmar grasp develops. Finger foods are pulled against the palm with the fingers—the thumb is not used and sticks out like a sore thumb. By about 7 months, thumb opposition begins to develop and finger foods will be held against the palm by both the thumb and fingers (radial-palmar grasp).

You can find dozens of different hand grasps in physical therapy (PT) books. If you see the word "radial," think of the thumb side of the hand; "ulnar" is the pinky side. If you see the word "digit" or "digital," think of fingers. In PT, a digit is a finger, and not a number as in math books.

At around 8-9 months, the fingertips, instead of the palm and fingers, begin to hold the food against the tip of the thumb (radial-digital grasp).

It is interesting that your baby will learn to grasp objects months before she will learn to release them voluntarily, which begins at about 11 months.

> **REMINDER:** Along with learning the skill of grasping food comes the repeated practice of opening the hand to release the food—much of the time to the floor! Your baby must practice releasing objects voluntarily, so please be patient with your little one.

The Pincer Grasp

Beginning sometime between 8 and 10 months, your baby will begin to use her index, ring, and pinky fingers against the lower thumb to grasp an object. This crude pincer grasp eventually develops into a neat pincer grasp, where index finger and thumb delicately meet to pick up a small object. This neat pincer grasp (also called the fine pincer grasp), which usually develops around 12 months, allows baby to become skilled at finger feeding small bits of food.

Small and Soft Food Bits

Food bits should be small enough to prevent choking, about the size of a Cheerio®. And they should be soft so that baby can easily chew them or "gum" them with her sensitive gums. In the Recipes chapter, you will find a list of finger food ideas.

Next time you go to the supermarket, look in the baby food section for jarred finger foods. Name brands include pieces of diced apples, peaches, carrots, and green beans. Some of these have added salt and all of them, in my opinion, are overpriced. You can easily make your own finger foods by cooking, dicing, and freezing foods yourself.

> WARNING: Give your baby only 2 or 3 bits of finger foods at a time, otherwise he will probably stuff his cheeks until he looks like a chipmunk. An overfull mouth may lead to choking.

TIP: Sometimes a baby will have trouble picking up pieces of wet fruits or other foods because they are slippery. Help your baby to get a grip by rolling the food pieces in rolled oats/oatmeal ground to a powder in the blender. Or, use whole wheat flour or wheat germ. If the wheat germ is too chunky, grind it to a powder in the blender.

> WARNING: Be careful with slippery pieces of food. They are more likely to slide into the throat or be inhaled into the windpipe. Coat them to make them less slippery as described in the previous tip.

From 12-18 months, you should continue giving your baby plenty of finger foods. At this age, finger feeding will cause more food to reach his mouth than when he spoon feeds. A sandwich is likely to get ripped apart for its filling alone, with the bread discarded. My little guy liked to eat only the peanut butter and leave the crumbled bread in tatters on his tray. When his appetite waned, the food flinging or finger painting began.

Your toddler will become a real pro at finger feeding between 18-24 months.

Teething Foods

Your baby will be getting teeth from 4 months to 24 months, maybe even sooner. You can start giving her teething foods when she is able to bring them to her mouth with her hand—sometime after 5-6 months. Chewing on hard or cool foods will help relieve the teething pain in her gums. Offer her hard toast, hard crackers, cool diluted juices, or a cool baby-safe spoon.

Freeze a fat hard carrot and let her suck on it, but make sure that no pieces will break off and that it is thick enough so that it will not split and cause choking.

> WARNING: With all frozen foods, make sure they are not so cold that they will burn your baby's mouth (example is a child's tongue stuck on a metal pipe at the playground). Rinse frozen food under cool water for a few seconds to prevent ice burns.

TIP: An inexpensive teether is a sterilized sturdy nipple filled with sterile water and frozen. Screw nipple on top of a bottle and baby will hold it easily.

The Baby Safe Feeder® is a popular teething and feeding item for babies that can help prevent choking. It was invented by a father who almost lost his nine-month-old son due to choking on a teething biscuit.

Self-Feeding with a Spoon and Fork

As early as 7 months, your baby will be able to hold a spoon and sometime between 8 and 12 months of age, your baby may grab the spoon and attempt to feed herself. Let her. Encourage her.

Before she attempts to grab the spoon herself, give her a spoon to play with during mealtimes. Accept the banging and clanging—again, it's part of the learning process. When she begins to use the spoon for its real purpose, she will have trouble and will most likely turn the spoon upside down immediately before it gets to her mouth. To help her along, give her foods that will tend to stay stuck to the spoon when it turns over, such as mashed banana, cereal, or organic Greek yogurt (which is thicker than regular yogurt).

TIP: When your baby first starts to use the spoon and has not yet developed enough skills, use two spoons. Let her practice feeding herself with one spoon, while you get a few spoonfuls in with another. Or use two spoons and swap with your baby—an empty spoon for a full spoon.

Proficiency at self-feeding with the spoon takes many months. She will master moving the spoon from bowl to mouth at around 11-12 months of age, before she is able to successfully scoop food from the bowl into the spoon. You can help by filling the spoon with food for her, but let her move it to her mouth and eat. This will help develop her eye-hand coordination.

At 12 months, she may still be turning her spoon upside down right before it reaches her mouth, but within the next few months she will master the spoon and get most of the food into her mouth. Eat with a spoon while your baby is watching. Your baby loves to imitate and it's a fun, natural way for her to learn. She will want to pretend to feed you. Play along and say, "Yummy!"

MONEY SAVER: If she keeps spilling the bowl, you can buy a baby bowl with suction cups on the bottom to anchor it to the tray.

At 15 months, your baby will probably use the spoon to feed himself, although much of the food gets spilled accidentally or deliberately. Between 18 and 21 months, he becomes more skilled with the spoon, but still looks babyish as he uses it because he holds his elbow, arm, and spoon horizontally and raises all three to move spoon to mouth. His other hand comes in handy to help with food on his lips that hasn't quite made it into his mouth. The helping hand may also place dropped food or food from the bowl into the spoon.

From 18-24 months, whole grain cereals (*Super Porridge*) should remain part of his daily diet. The oatmeal-like consistency of *Super Porridge* makes it easy for him to self-feed with a spoon. His other meals should become more coarse in texture and have many soft lumps of food in them. It's time to start letting him use a safe baby fork for learning to spear lumps of food.

By her second birthday, even though her spoon feeding skills are mature, she may still resort to fingers and feeling the food's texture. She may even smell the food. Let her be.

WARNING: Watch your toddler carefully as he eats. Toddlers sometimes get tired of chewing in the middle of a meal and tend to swallow food whole.

Between 24-36 months, your toddler knows whether to use his fingers or a spoon to eat the food before him. He has his black belt in spoon use, although he occasionally spills because his eye-hand coordination is still developing. His skills with the fork are improving and by the end of his third year he will hold it fisted. At three years, he will be able to cut food with his fork. He will be able to spoon his individual portion of food from a serving dish. His mature chewing pattern now mimics that of an adult, with a circular action of the jaw. He may choose moist food over drier foods because he knows from experience that they are easier to chew. Although he may still enjoy playing with his food, don't end the meal as long as there is some eating occurring. Your little one is probably still a messy eater, but he is improving and spilling less and less food from his spoon and his cup.

Table Foods

As early as 7 months, your baby might start eating at the same time as the rest of the family, although she will be eating her own baby foods. Pull her high chair up to the table and let her join the clan. Most table foods are not appropriate for your baby until she is at least one year old.

At 9 or 10 months, she can start eating some unseasoned foods from the family table to which she has been previously introduced, such as mashed potato. Mash the potatoes and take out a baby-sized portion BEFORE you add the salt, pepper, and butter. Or fork-mash some soft unseasoned vegetables, pasta, cheese, etc. By her first birthday, she should be ready to become a full-fledged member at the family table.

> **TIP:** If your family uses placemats, use a paper towel or two for your baby's placemat. Replace when spills occur. At meal's end, wipe up with the paper towel.

Babies imitate the things they see grown-ups do, so try not to let your baby see you using the saltshaker. The salt habit is something our babies (and we adults) can do without.

> **TIP:** Feeding your baby at the table can take your attention away from the other members of your family. You may want to compromise and feed your baby most of his meal before family mealtime, and let baby finger feed himself at the table while you enjoy the rest of your family.

Part III

Purchase, Preparation and Storage of Super Baby Food

17

Food Staples for the Well-Stocked Super Baby Food Kitchen

- Fresh fruit—ripe and ready to eat, especially vitamin C fruits like kiwi fruit and oranges, and vitamin C juices like orange juice
- Frozen fruit—store-bought or home-frozen fruit chunks, or puréed fruit cubes in the freezer for snacks or for use in recipes
- Fresh vegetables, especially the *Super Green Veggies*
- Frozen vegetables—store-bought or home cooked and frozen vegetable chunks or food cubes
- Bread, 100% whole wheat or other whole or sprouted-grain bread from the natural foods store
- Super Flour
- Sandwich spreads such as natural peanut butter, hummus, tahini, cream cheese, and yogurt cheese—batch and freeze
- Whole grain pasta and Super Pasta Sauce (See Recipes)
- Natural cheeses such as Parmesan, Romano, Camembert, Cheddar, Feta, Monterey Jack, Swiss, Provolone, Mozzarella, whole milk Cottage Cheese, Ricotta, Cream Cheese, and many others
- Yogurt—store-bought with active cultures or homemade
- Tofu—aseptically sealed tofu lasts for months at room temperature
- Avocado—whole and ripe and/or frozen in food cubes
- Milk—cow's milk, soybean milk, nut/seed milk, Better Than Milk®
- Nonfat powdered milk
- Butter or natural cold-pressed, un-hydrogenated vegetable oil from the natural foods store

- Raw/hard-boiled eggs from free-running, hormone-free chickens

- A variety of whole grains, especially brown rice, millet, rolled oats, teff, quinoa, and barley

- A variety of dried beans/legumes, especially soy grits or soybeans, lentils, split peas, and garbanzos

- Boxed breakfast cereals, such as bite-sized whole wheat cereal and Oatios® (the health food store equivalent of Cheerios®)

- Healthy canned soups from the natural foods store or your own homemade frozen soups in individual servings

- Your own homemade frozen toddler TV dinners

- Blackstrap molasses

- Maple syrup or honey (honey is for only babies over 12 months old)

- Raw almonds and other nuts and their butters

- Raw seeds and seed butters—pumpkin seeds, flax seeds, tahini

- Nutritional yeast

- Lemon juice ice cubes

- Parsley and other herbs—frozen fresh, frozen in ice cubes, or growing on your windowsill

- Dried fruit—store-bought or home-dried

18

Kitchen Equipment

Most of the equipment needed to make homemade baby food is probably already in your kitchen—bowls, knives, and ice cube trays. Use only stainless steel or glass pots and pans.

Food Processor or Blender

You will need a kitchen appliance that purées food. You must make vegetables and fruits very mushy for your little chewing-impaired sweetie pie. Blenders and mini food processors can be found in local department stores and online for a reasonable cost. In fact, if you are an early bird and expecting a baby, a blender or mini food processor might be a great shower gift idea. If you have either of these, you're set. If you have neither and can only afford one, I'd recommend the blender. It can do almost everything the food processor can do, but it's better at preparing liquidy foods, such as slushies and drinks that have the consistency of milk shakes. You don't really need an expensive, fancy blender. A pulsing feature, which promotes even blending by allowing food to redistribute between pulses, is nice but not necessary. You can alternately press a speed button and the off button to get the same pulsing effect manually.

> WARNING: Be sure to read the use, safety, cleaning, and maintenance directions for your blender or processor completely before you begin to use it. Be sure that the manufacturer's instructions say that it is OK to grind dry ingredients in your blender or processor, such as brown rice, oatmeal, other grains, and whole nuts and seeds.

Mini-Blend Containers

I very strongly recommend that you buy a mini-blend container for your blender. This little container holds about one cup or 8 ounces. It's easy to fill, empty, and clean, and makes grinding grains, beans, and other legumes for homemade *Super Porridge* cereals a dream! I use mine at least once a day and it's the best money I have ever spent. You can order them online or buy in many stores.

Manual Grinders

You could purée with a food mill, but because it's manual, it takes a lot more elbow grease than an electric blender or processor. I don't recommend those small white plastic baby food grinders or mills for making large amounts of baby food. Although a bit cheaper, they are much more work in the end. I have never used mine enough to make it worthwhile.

> **TIP:** If you want a portable baby food grinder for the diaper bag, try a tubular garlic press instead! The press will continue to be useful for pressing garlic and food decorating when you no longer make baby food. A small hand-held grater can also be useful.

Steamers

If you don't have a steamer, buy one—it's worth it. Steaming vegetables retains many more nutrients than boiling them, and it takes less energy to steam vegetables than to boil them. My first steamer was one of the least expensive ones. It was just an insert that I would add to a pot of water. I finally graduated to a top-of-the-line multi-level type with a clear cover, matching steamer insert, and heat-proof handles.

There are many other types of steamers. Invest in a good steamer if you can afford it.

> **MONEY SAVER:** If you don't want to purchase a special steamer, you can always improvise with a metal colander with legs, a flat-bottomed wire basket or strainer, or some similar heat-safe kitchen container with holes, and put it into a pot large enough to wholly contain it.

Strainers

You may need a strainer or sieve for some foods, such as cooked fruits. Small seeds or bits of peel should be strained out for young babies in order to prevent choking or gagging. If you have a strainer, make sure it is in good shape. The metal wires should be unbroken and firm so that they won't break off into baby's food, and there should be no rust. Purchase a strainer or sieve that is bottom-shelf dishwasher-safe even if you don't have a dishwasher. This kind of sieve or strainer tends to be sturdier and you want to be ready just in case you do get a dishwasher some day.

TIP: Always rinse your strainer immediately after using to prevent food from drying on it. If you did let food dry on it, soak in hot soapy water and then scrub gently with a vegetable brush.

How to Strain: Use a rubber spatula (not a metal spoon, which will put undo wear and tear on your strainer) to press the food through the holes in the strainer. For very fine straining, such as for baby juices and nut milks to prevent your baby from choking and so that the holes in the spout of your baby's sippy cup don't get clogged, I find that a yogurt strainer works well. Yogurt strainers can be purchased at kitchen stores, department stores and online for the purpose of making yogurt cheese.

MONEY SAVER: You can improvise a fine strainer for juices and nut milks by lining a colander with layers of cheesecloth, white paper towels, a clean thin kitchen towel, cloth diaper, coffee filter, or even a clean leg part from an old pair of pantyhose.

Larger strainers can be used instead of a colander for rinsing beans and berries and can double as a flour sifter.

Hand Graters

A small hand grater comes in handy when you are feeding a young child. It can be used to quickly grate cheese, raw carrots, apples, and other vegetables and fruits. Buy one that is dishwasher safe.

TIP: When grating several food items, grate the softest food first. Subsequently grating harder foods will clean the softer foods from the grater holes. Use an old sterile toothbrush to clean your grater.

TIP: If you do not have a food processor and want to grate carrots, cabbage, etc. for baby, you can use your blender. Place vegetables in the blender, cover with sterile water, whiz until desired consistency, and pour grated veggies through sieve to strain water out.

Timers

Kitchen timers are lifesavers. The more you have, the better. Never put a pot on the stove without setting a timer. Although timers that make one beep are OK, I prefer the ones that don't stop beeping until I turn them off. (I sometimes miss one beep when I'm in the noisy laundry room or somewhere far off in another part of the house.)

An Organized Kitchen Saves Time, Money, and Energy

Clutter is the worst enemy of an organized kitchen. Get rid of it. If you are short on cabinet space (and who isn't?), place those items that you use once a year up into the attic, down into the basement, or into the back of a closet. I put my ice bucket in the attic two years ago and haven't used it since—but I am using the cabinet space it freed up.

Kitchen items should be stored according to their frequency of use. The more often you use an item, the easier it should be to grab. "Quick-grab" or "easy-access" kitchen spaces are those areas in your kitchen that are very convenient to reach: the front of an eye-level cabinet, the drawer next to the sink, the counter top in your most common work area, etc.

Store infrequently used light items in the upper cabinets and heavy items or fragile items in the lower cabinets. My bunny-shaped cake pan, which I use once a year if I'm lucky, is stored in the very back of the most hard-to-reach top shelf in my kitchen. However, my kitchen wipe-up towels—I seem to need a new clean one every five minutes when I'm in the kitchen—are stored in the big drawer between the sink and the refrigerator, which is the central part of the kitchen where I stand most often.

The quick-grab spots in your refrigerator and freezer are the door shelves and the front of the top main shelves. To prevent food waste, store leftovers with short shelf lives where you'll be sure to notice them every time you open the refrigerator door. Seeing them will remind you to use them up.

Store perishable items in a consistent organization scheme that will rotate food to ensure that older food gets used first. My scheme is named the "book reading" method: left to right, top to bottom, front to back. Let's say you have 12 cans of tomato sauce with different expiration dates. The oldest can goes on the left side in the front row on the top layer. If you make a new batch of formula and still have two bottles left over from the last batch, you should use the two older bottles first, of course. In our home, older bottles are placed on the left side of the refrigerator door shelf and everyone is instructed to "take from the left."

TIP: If bottles keep toppling over in your refrigerator, place them in a cardboard carton six-pack holder or similar container to keep them together and upright.

Traveling Equipment

Unfortunately, homemade frozen baby food cubes don't travel well and neither does homemade *Super Porridge* because it keeps in the refrigerator for only 2-3 days. Traveling is the time to use an organic brand of jarred baby food and boxed organic, whole grain baby cereals.

For baby emergencies, it is a good idea to keep a baby travel bag in the trunk of your car. This is in addition to the usual diaper bag that you carry everywhere. The travel bag is for when you have forgotten to pack something in the diaper bag, for when your baby gets wet or dirty and needs a change of clothes, or for other emergencies. I keep my baby emergency supplies in the trunk in an old duffle bag.

Water	A few diapers
Bottle	Wet wipes
Nipple	Clean burp cloth
Can of formula	Bib
Cheerios®	Blanket
Crackers	Toys
Jars of organic, commercial baby food	Pacifier
Boxed organic cereal	First-aid stuff
Bowl	Jacket (in case it gets cold)
Spoon	Summer shirt (in case it gets hot)
Can opener	Full change of clothes
(all cleaned in paper towel-lined	Sun hat
plastic bag)	Sun screen lotion

TIP: If you're short on clothes, keep a change of clothes in the trunk that is slightly too big or too small. Who cares if they don't fit perfectly in a baby emergency!

MONEY SAVER: Don't buy expensive travel sizes of wipes and lotions. When your regular size wipes or lotions have only a few more uses, open new ones and put the "almost empties" in the trunk. Squeeze every last bit out of a diaper cream (or toothpaste) tube by rolling up a pencil from the end, or use a small rolling pin to push the contents up from the end of the tube, or just step on the tube with your foot. In a pinch, use wax paper as a waterproof changing mat.

TIP: Keep a large paintbrush in the trunk of your car to dust sand and dirt from kids' shoes. Or keep empty freezer bags or plastic grocery bags for kids' muddy shoes to save your car's carpet.

TIP: Let your kids use a homemade lap table (page 586) for doing artwork in the car. Use it to store art materials when not in use.

19

Methods of Freezing and Thawing Super Baby Foods

Throughout this book you will find references to these freezing methods: the *Food Cube Method*, the *Tray-Freeze Method*, the *Phantom Container Freezing Method*, and the *Nested Plastic Bag Method*. This chapter explains how to freeze foods using these methods, and includes other information about freezing and thawing foods.

> **TIP:** Besides veggies and fruits, you can freeze almost all other *Super Baby Foods* including *Super Porridge*, tofu, yogurt, cottage cheese, eggs, pasta, wheat germ, sprouts, cooked beans (frozen whole or puréed, in food cubes), juices, and homemade tomato sauce.

If you're not sure about the "freezability" of a food, refer to specific fruits and vegetables in Chapters 20 and 21. You can also find several good books on freezing and preserving food at your library or online.

> **TIP:** A few hours before you begin making frozen baby food cubes, especially if you're going to make several trays, turn your freezer thermostat down a notch to make the freezer colder than usual. Turn it down to -10°F to get it really cold. The food will freeze faster. A large amount of warm food may affect the foods already frozen in your freezer, so get your freezer nice and cold to prevent this.

Important Rules for All Freezing Methods
Prevent Bacterial Growth

Whether you are using the *Food Cube Method* or one of the other freezing methods, use super clean equipment and utensils because although freezing retards the growth of bacteria, it doesn't kill them.

As soon as each ice cube tray or other container is filled with food, pop it into the freezer immediately. Get it cold as soon as possible to prevent bacterial growth.

Prevent Freezer Burn

Freezer burn occurs when air gets into the package and causes the food to dry up. You probably know how it tastes. Sometimes it looks like pale gray spots, or there are lots of ice crystals in the food. Before freezing, cover all food well with wax paper, then aluminum foil or freezer wrap, or place in a wax paper-lined freezer bag and make it really airtight. Although freezer burn is not dangerous, it causes nutrient loss, dries and toughens the food and has an unpleasant taste.

Always choose plastic and aluminum foil that is made for freezer use by carefully reading the label on the packages. Cheap plastic wrap or sandwich bags alone aren't heavy enough to protect frozen food. Do not reuse aluminum foil in the freezer, because the crinkles allow air to permeate into the food.

> **WARNING:** I believe that the only safe substance to place next to food is **100% all natural unbleached wax paper.** Aluminum foil, plastic wrap, and plastic bags leave residues in the food. That is why I always place a layer of wax paper between the food and an outer layer of aluminum foil, plastic freezer wrap or freezer bags.

NOTE: Whenever you see a reference to wax paper, it always means **100% unbleached all natural wax paper.**

The Food Cube Method

Puréed, cooked vegetables are a large part of the *Super Baby Food Diet*. To save time and energy, cook and purée large batches of veggies all at once and freeze them in ice cube trays using the *Food Cube Method*. Most ice cube trays make food cubes that are about 2 tablespoons in volume, which happens to be the perfect size for a single portion of baby food. You may wish to verify your ice cube capacity by using a tablespoon to measure water into one of the cube compartments. When your baby first starts on solid foods, she will probably eat only a tablespoon at a time, so you may want to fill your ice cube trays only half way. As your baby's food servings grow, you can fill the cubes to capacity. Eventually, your baby will be eating 2-3 food cubes at a time.

REMINDER: I recommend using stainless steel ice cube trays, available online. Although there are BPA-free plastic trays available for sale, why take a risk? Although stainless steel trays are a bit more expensive, you will have them forever!

The Two Steps to the Food Cube Method

1. Placing the food in ice cube trays and freezing until solid, and

2. Transferring the frozen food cubes into plastic freezer bags lined with wax paper.

If you are in the middle of puréeing a big batch of baby food and you run out of ice cube trays, no problem. Use little paper cups. Or scoop the puréed food in little globs onto a tray covered with wax paper and freeze using the *Tray-Freeze Method*, as discussed in the next section. Cover well with more wax paper to prevent freezer burn and nutrient loss.

If ice cube portions are too small for the foods you wish to freeze, you can use slightly larger globs or larger containers, such as empty, cleaned, baby food glass jars, small glass Pyrex containers, and the like.

REMINDER: The puréed food in the ice cube trays should be frozen as quickly as possible. If you have the room in your freezer, do not stack the trays on top of each other. Warm trays will give heat to each other if stacked and will prolong freezing time. Try to place the trays separately in different parts of the freezer. If your freezer has a quick-freezing shelf, use it until trays are frozen, and then move to a regular part of the freezer.

Transferring the Cubes to Freezer Bags

After the food cubes are frozen solid, which may take several hours or overnight (depending on your freezer temperature), transfer them to plastic freezer bags lined with wax paper. The idea here is to keep the food from directly touching the plastic.

REMINDER: Don't accidentally buy "storage bags" instead of "freezer bags." The packages look very similar and I once grabbed the storage type by accident when I was in a hurry and didn't read the box carefully. Freezer bags are heavier and prevent freezer-burn.

Freezer bags usually come in two sizes—quart-size and gallon-size—but I suggest that you use only the smaller size bag. The last food cubes left in the bottom of the larger bags tend not to be very fresh, because it takes some time to use all the cubes in a larger bag. Also, it's easier to find space in a crammed freezer for a little bag.

> **MONEY SAVER:** When your are ready to make the transfer from ice cube trays to wax paper-lined freezer bags, don't waste water by running it over the back of those trays to loosen the cubes. Let the trays sit on the counter for a few minutes. Thawing will occur around the edges just enough to allow the food cubes to easily pop out with a twist of the wrist or a whack on the counter.

> **TIP:** Wax paper has another use! If you are having trouble removing ice cube trays from the freezer because they are stuck to the shelf or other items in the freezer, place a sheet of wax paper under them before freezing.

Place the food cubes in the lined freezer bag, but before zipping shut, remove as much of the air from the inside of the bag as possible

Label and Date Each Freezer Bag

The first vegetable you will probably cook and freeze for your baby is sweet potatoes. At first, there will be only one bag of sweet potatoes in your freezer. After your baby gets older and is eating a variety of veggies, you may gather quite a few bags. Even the keenest eye has trouble telling frozen carrot cubes from sweet potatoes, but you can usually smell or even taste them to differentiate.

Label the bags with the name of the food, the date of freezing, and the expiration date. It depends on the specific food, but it is probably safe to say that veggie cubes will keep for at least two months. You probably will use your cubes well within that time.

> **TIP:** If your freezer bags have "built-in" labels, use them. They are less likely to fall off and get lost in your freezer.

> **TIP:** If you're desperate for a freezer label, use printer label or even a band-aid.

You may have to retrieve baby food bags from the freezer several times per day, so keep them in an easy-to-reach place in the freezer. Being able to grab them quickly will not only save time and aggravation, but will minimize the time the door is open, preventing your freezer from losing its cool.

TIME SAVER: I mix together several days' worth of the orange and green veggie cubes and avocado cubes in the same freezer bag. It's easier every morning to find, pull out, and open one bag instead of three.

WARNING: Keep freezer bags or any type of plastic bag away from your baby/toddler—they are a suffocation hazard!

MONEY SAVER: Use the *Food Cube Method* for all freezable foods when you don't want to discard a small amount of clean leftovers. Often you open an entire can of some recipe ingredient and use only a small amount, such as tomato paste, stock, lemon juice, etc. Measure the leftovers into recipe-sized amounts and freeze in ice cube trays using the *Food Cube Method* or the *Tray-Freeze Method*. Tablespoons of frozen tomato paste can be dropped into sauces without thawing first.

The Tray-Freeze Method

For berries or fruit chunks that you would like to easily retrieve separately, use the *Tray-Freeze Method*. Line a tray or cookie sheet or anything clean, flat, and freezer-safe with wax paper. Arrange the chunks of fruit on the wax paper so that they don't touch each other. Cover with more of the wax paper and then foil or freezer wrap and place in the freezer. When solidly frozen, remove fruit chunks from trays and store in plastic freezer bags lined with wax paper. Later, you can easily remove as many single pieces as you need because they won't clump together.

Puréed sweet or white potatoes can be frozen in ice cube trays using the *Food Cube Method*, or they can be rolled into little balls and tray-frozen. In Part VI, there are many recipes for *Toddler Hors D'oeuvre* that tray-freeze very well.

MONEY SAVER: Check out your local warehouse store or restaurant supply store for very large boxes of wax paper and freezer bags. You must buy a lot, but you will save a lot if you use a lot!

The Phantom Container Freezing Method

Supermarket TV dinners are expensive and contain too many sweeteners, sodium, and preservatives. Make your own—a batch at a time—and freeze them yourself.

You will need a few containers to freeze homemade "TV dinners." There are many shapes and sizes of freezing containers, which can be found in most department stores and supermarkets as well as online. Invest in a few containers that are dishwasher and freezer safe. They'll pay for themselves in no time. Buy those that are shaped for efficient storing, such as the flat ones that can be stacked to make the most of freezer space. I recommend glass containers that are freezer safe and stainless steel containers. Both should come with lids.

You're not limited to the number of containers you have if you use the *Phantom Container Freezing Method*. Here's what to do: Cook several servings of "TV dinners." Good choices are macaroni and cheese, lentil stew, eggplant Parmesan, or almost any casserole. Carefully spoon single servings of food into individual freezer containers. Freeze overnight until very solid.

Freeze soups in individual servings using the *Phantom Container Method* for up to 3 months. Pour soup into individual bowls, freeze, and then pop out of the bowl and into a freezer bag lined with wax paper.

When frozen solid, take the containers out of the freezer and let them sit on the counter for a few minutes until the food thaws around the edges just enough so that you can pop it out of the container. The frozen food will maintain the shape as if there is an invisible or *Phantom* container surrounding it—hence *The Phantom Container Freezing Method*.

Immediately place the block of food in a plastic freezer bag lined with wax paper. (Sounds just like the good old *Food Cube Method*, only for bigger servings.) Or use the *Nested Plastic Bag Method* (discussed next). Label and date the freezer bag and return to the freezer. The empty container is now available for other uses.

When it comes time to serve the "TV dinner," take a food block out of the bag, place it in a small pot, and heat it on the stove. If you are not in a hurry, thaw it in the container overnight in the refrigerator (never thaw food at room temperature). You will save energy reheating it, and while it thaws it helps to keep the refrigerator cold.

TIP: Muffin pans—those with 12 cups—are great for keeping side dishes separate, as are popsicle molds. Both are available in stainless steel versions.

The Nested Plastic Bag Method

The *Nested Plastic Bag Method* is a method of freezing individual toddler-sized servings of finger foods and other foods, which saves you money on freezer bags. Simply nest several sandwich-sized storage bags, which cost much less than freezer bags, inside a large freezer bag. Place individual servings of foods in sandwich bags lined with wax paper. Seal the sandwich bags and then put them inside a larger freezer bag. The sandwich bags keep the individual servings separate, and it doesn't matter that they are not freezer quality because they are inside a larger good-quality freezer bag.

One application for the *Nested Plastic Bag Method* is in the freezing of Super Snacks. (See *Super Snack Freezer Bag*, page 34.) Keep diced carrots in one sandwich bag, chopped peaches in another, pasta pieces in another, etc. Or you can have a Frozen Fresh Herb Bag, where one sandwich bag contains dill frozen in ice cubes, another contains parsley, another oregano, etc.

I also use the *Nested Plastic Bag Method* to freeze cooked veggies for my older boys' lunches. I cook a batch of veggies and divide them into wax paper-lined cheap sandwich bags containing half-cup portions, which I then place into a big good quality freezer bag. In the morning, I take one of the sandwich bags from the freezer bag and pack it in the lunch box. It's thawed and ready to eat by lunchtime.

TIP: When doing a lot of rearranging in your freezer, use oven mitts to protect your hands from the cold.

REMINDER: Foods and liquids expand when they freeze. For those containers that have no flexibility, such as glass jars, remember to leave at least ½-inch of air space for expansion. Leave ½-inch of headroom on top of containers filled with liquid, or the liquid will expand and may seep out of the top during freezing.

TIP: If you are going on vacation and live where power outages are a problem, place two ice cubes in a plastic bag in the freezer. Upon return, check ice cubes and if they are not still in the shape of ice cubes, you'll know there was a power outage. Frozen food may not be safe to eat.

TIP: Some cooked foods, such as pasta, vegetables and grains, become softer after being frozen and reheated. If you find this, try undercooking the recipe a little before freezing it.

NOTE: You may find that my advice on freezing foods conflicts with the advice found in other cookbooks. This is because other authors are concerned about the preservation of food texture during the freezing and thawing processes. For example, I say that you can freeze bananas, but others would disagree because, when thawed, bananas get mushy and darken. Although adults may not like it that way, your baby may! Some experts will tell you to cool the trays first in the refrigerator before putting them in the freezer. Cooling food before freezing reduces moisture condensation. The condensation (water) expands during freezing, breaks food fibers, and causes foods to be limp and soggy. With puréed baby food, we don't have to worry about this, so skip the refrigerator step, and go directly from counter to freezer. You may have heard that before freezing most vegetables and some fruits, blanching is required. Blanching is the process of boiling food briefly and then quickly cooling it to stop the cooking process. Blanching sterilizes and cleans food before freezing. But more importantly, blanching stops enzymes from changing the food's composition (ripening it, decomposing it). Of course, we don't have to worry about blanching because our baby food's enzymes have been deactivated during cooking.

Freezer Space

A well-stocked freezer is more energy-efficient than a half-empty freezer because the empty air space loses cold much faster than solidly frozen material when you open the door. If you don't have enough food to fill up your half-empty freezer, stuff it with newspaper. Even better, fill the empty space with empty, clean milk cartons filled with water. The ice blocks that form will help keep your freezer cold, especially if your electricity goes out for a while. Do leave some space for air circulation to keep your freezer working properly.

As your family grows, you are more likely to have the problem of too little, rather than too much, freezer space. You can make efficient use of your freezer space by using freezer containers that are of uniform size and square-cornered rather than round, because they will fit more tightly together.

The method by which you freeze semi-solid liquids in freezer bags can also save you some freezer space. Don't freeze them initially by placing them directly on the freezer shelf. They'll freeze into a roundish lump and may bulge into the wires of the freezer shelf. Instead, place the bags in the freezer on a flat surface (a cookie sheet, a piece of clean cardboard, etc.) and smooth out their semi-solid contents so that a somewhat flat, square shape is formed. Of if you want to get fancy, you can place the filled freezer bag into a box for a neat box shape.

After the contents are frozen solid, you can then stack them compactly, directly on a freezer shelf. This method is good for pasta with sauce, stews, soups, and casseroles, because they have liquid and can be shaped into squares. Unfortunately, you don't have the flexibility to do this with baby food cubes in freezer bags, which have quite a bit of air space between them, unless you want to spend a lot of time packing the cubes individually so that they fit together like a tight jigsaw puzzle!

> **TIP:** Here's a tip if you find yourself frequently searching for items in your freezer that aren't there, or find outdated frozen food that must be discarded and wasted. Keep an inventory list of freezer items taped to the freezer door. Update it every time you add food or take food out of the freezer. Besides preventing wasted food, this list also saves energy because you don't keep the door open looking for foods that don't exist.

How to Safely Thaw Frozen Baby Foods

"Safely" here has two meanings. First, baby food should be thawed in a way that prevents bacterial growth. Baby food should *never* be thawed at room temperature, and baby food should not be kept at room temperature for more than several minutes.

Second, "safely" means thawing baby food so that it is not too hot or too cold to be a danger to your baby. If it's too hot, it may burn your baby's mouth. If it is too cold, and therefore not thawed thoroughly, it may contain frozen food chunks that are choking hazards to your baby. (Food that is too cold may also "burn" your baby's sensitive mouth.)

Baby's Food Should Be Only Moderately Warm

Note that I have been using the word "thaw" and not "reheat." You want to simply take the chill out of baby's food; you don't want to make it hot. Never feed your baby hot food! Your baby's mouth is much more sensitive to heat than your mouth, and food that does not feel hot to you may burn your baby. Baby's food should be only slightly warm, about the temperature of the body—98.6° F, like breast milk. When you touch the food, it should feel neither hot nor cold.

Stir Baby Food Thoroughly to Evenly Distribute Heat

When using the stove top to thaw baby's food cubes, it is important that you make sure there are no heat pockets or "hot spots" anywhere within the food. It is very possible that one section of your baby's food feels cool or even cold, while other parts are dangerously hot and will burn your baby's mouth.

> **WARNING:** When warming baby food, always thoroughly mix before feeding to baby in order to distribute heat as evenly as possible. Stir completely and then test, test, test.

Always Test the Temperature of Your Baby's Food

One way to test is to insert your clean finger into several areas of the bowl. Although you may be uncomfortable doing this, remember that it is certainly better than burning your baby's mouth.

> **WARNING:** Do not test the temperature of your baby's food by feeling the container. A not-too-hot container does not mean that the food contained within it is a safe temperature for your baby. Each part of the food must be temperature-tested directly.

Another way you can test is to touch each and every spoonful to your upper lip immediately before placing it in your baby's mouth. It is interesting that in some cultures, parents act as natural food processors. They chew food, remove it from their mouths, and feed it to their babies. The parent's saliva partially digests the food, making it easier for the baby to digest.

Baby's Food is Too Hot? How to Cool Food Quickly

If you accidentally make the food too hot and your baby is loudly complaining that she wants to eat NOW, add frozen food cubes and mix thoroughly to cool it fast. Or, try this: Scrape the food into another cool bowl. The flatter the bowl, the more surface area on the food, and the faster it will cool. Place it in the freezer for a minute. Stir the food again thoroughly and it will be much cooler.

Thawing Food Cubes on the Stove

The trick to successful stove-top thawing is to use very low heat or a double boiler. Stir often while thawing.

Thawing Food Cubes in the Refrigerator

Food cubes can be thawed overnight in the refrigerator, where cold temperatures prevent rapid bacterial growth. This method may be the best alternative for parents who do not wish to use the stove. It takes several hours for food cubes to thaw in the refrigerator, which is why thawing overnight might be the best way to thaw in the refrigerator.

> **WARNING:** Always be careful to check that cubes have been thoroughly thawed, and that there are no leftover frozen food chunks inside the cubes on which your baby can choke.

Although you might like your veggies warmed, your baby will probably be perfectly happy with them at refrigerator temperature. If so, you will save time, energy, and nutrients by thawing them overnight in the refrigerator and not warming them at all. However, warmed food does have more flavor. If you wish, you can warm your baby's food from the refrigerator by placing the container in a bowl of hot tap water for a few minutes, or on the stove top over medium-low heat for a minute or so. As always, test for safe temperatures before feeding to your baby.

There is one disadvantage to overnight thawing in the refrigerator. You must discard puréed baby food from the refrigerator within a day or two. If you do not carefully plan the next day's meals, you may have to waste food by throwing it out. Baby food must be discarded after a day or two in the refrigerator because refrigerator temperatures only slow bacterial growth, they do not completely prevent it.

Never Refreeze Thawed Baby Food

Once baby food has been frozen and thawed, do NOT refreeze it, discard it. Do not use frozen vegetables or other frozen foods for making frozen baby food cubes, unless they were fresh and uncooked when they were frozen. **Baby food should not be frozen twice.**

20

Super Baby Food
Vegetables

Vegetable Basics

This chapter explains the general steps for preparing vegetables. Complete information about each vegetable can be found in the at the end of this chapter and are listed alphabetically. For example, turn and look at the details for carrots on page 187. Included is how to choose the best carrots at the supermarket, when carrots are in season, cooking times, how old your baby must be to eat carrots, and other information about carrots.

Buying Vegetables

In the best of circumstances, we would walk out the door of our homes to a beautiful, organic garden growing in the back yard and choose a healthy, ripe vegetable. To obtain the most nutrients, we would cook it or eat it raw immediately. This case is not true for most of us, but let's keep it in mind as the ideal to help us remember how to buy produce.

> **MONEY SAVER:** When buying produce individually instead of by the pound, such as avocados, pints of berries, etc., use the supermarket's produce scale to see which weighs the most.

Be Gentle with Your Produce

Some vegetables and fruits look a lot tougher than they are. For example, pineapples look like they have tough skin, but it is actually very vulnerable to bruising. Damaging the skin of vegetables and fruits leaves them open to decay, which sometimes spreads very rapidly throughout the rest of the flesh. So be gentle with your produce, and treat it with tender, loving care.

How to Choose the Best Vegetables

- Buy produce as free of pesticides as possible; certified organic is best. Pesticides affect small babies more adversely than adults, and become more concentrated in their little bodies.

- Buy local produce. It is more likely to have fewer pesticides and it has not lost nutrients during a long transportation process. Visit your local Farmers' Market or roadside stand for more choices.

- Buy domestic rather than imported produce. Imported produce can contain levels of pesticides several times higher than domestic produce. The FDA inspects fewer than 3% of shipments of imported food. Therefore, imported produce may not have been checked to see if growers have met the pesticide standards of the United States, which are generally stricter than elsewhere.

- If possible, buy vine-ripened vegetables, not those that ripened in a cardboard box. Unfortunately, economics dictate that to maximize profits, produce should be picked before it is fully ripe. Unripe produce is firmer, and therefore won't bruise as easily during the handling and transportation process. Even "vine-ripened" tomatoes are picked when they are still pink, before they turn ripe red.

- Buy produce in season. It will be fresher, tastier and cheaper.

- As a general rule, the smaller the vegetable, the more tender and younger it is.

- I highly recommend fresh, natural food or frozen food over canned food. However, if you choose to feed your baby canned vegetables, buy vegetables without salt or other additives. If you have vegetables with added salt, rinse them under the tap in a strainer to remove as much of the salt as possible.

TIP: Once bought, get vegetables home from the store and into the refrigerator as soon as possible, as some nutrients are destroyed quickly if left sitting at room temperature or in a hot trunk. Run other errands before you shop for food. The supermarket should be your last stop so that you can go directly home. If you can't get veggies home quickly, place them in a cooler in the trunk.

Keep Vegetables Cold

Enzymes are biological catalysts that cause nutrient loss and change the composition of vegetables—and then they rot. Enzymes convert sugar into starch. Over time in storage, this causes vegetables to lose flavor and crispness. Have you ever tasted a pea picked fresh from the garden? It's actually sweet! Older peas are bland, tasteless, and all starch. Enzymes have converted virtually all their sugar. Cold temperatures slow down this enzyme activity.

Store Most Vegetables in High Humidity

The air that circulates in your refrigerator is very dry. Protect vegetables from this dry air by placing them in wax paper-lined plastic bags or in the vegetable crisper drawer of your refrigerator. Vegetables actually contain a lot of water (as do human bodies). If this water dries up, nutrients are destroyed and your vegetables won't taste as good. So keep your carrots from shriveling by leaving them in the lined plastic bag.

> **TIP:** If you have a problem with too much moisture in your refrigerator's vegetable drawer, place a clean, dry sponge in the drawer to absorb it. Or place several layers of white paper towels under produce to absorb moisture. Save paper towels by using brown bag paper as a bottom layer. You can also sprinkle baking soda between the layers to keep the drawer smelling fresh. Replace every week.

Some Vegetables Require a Cool, Dark, Dry Place

Some vegetables, such as pumpkins and potatoes, store well for months in a dry, dark, cool place (45-50°F). If you don't think you have such a place, consider your attic (in winter, but not summer when it gets very hot), or a dark corner of your unheated garage, or even your basement (if it is not damp). A small thermometer can be used to monitor the temperature.

Freezing Is the Best Storage Method for COOKED Vegetables

Super Baby Food vegetables are most nutritious when cooked properly and eaten immediately. If this isn't possible, store vegetables in a way that maintains the most taste and nutrients. Freezing is the best storage method and is, of course, also the most expensive. Canning (or jarring) is popular because it's cheap, but most canned food is not nearly as tasty or nutritious as frozen.

Drying is another method for preserving food. See page 226 for how to make your own fruit leather.

To Peel or Not to Peel

Whether or not you peel off the skin depends on the particular vegetable or fruit. See the specifics in the appendix. For example, you can or cannot peel carrots, depending on their size. Keep in mind that many nutrients are in the skins, and scraping will cause them to be lost. Instead of spending time peeling carrots, I carefully scrub off the dirt with a vegetable brush or a clean nylon scouring pad. You may choose to peel instead, especially if the carrots are not organic and you are concerned about pesticides.

> WARNING: Avoid eating large amounts of orange peels or peels of other citrus fruits, as they may contain carcinogens (cancer-causing substances). Citrus rinds absorb pesticides, so try to buy organic citrus fruits only.

Peel any produce with a wax coating (apples, cucumbers, etc.), not only to remove the wax, but also to remove possible fungicides that are often used in combination with the wax. Peel produce with tough skins (apples, cucumbers, etc.) on which a baby can choke. Remove the outer leaves of leafy vegetables (Brussels sprouts, cabbage, lettuce) for baby. Then carefully wash the inner leaves while thoroughly checking for bad spots and insects.

> MONEY SAVER: Don't discard those organic citrus peels—grate the rinds and freeze using the *Nested Plastic Bag Method* and use as flavorings in muffins, icings, and other recipes.

How to Clean Vegetables and Fruits

Cleaning vegetables and fruits leaves me in a quandary. On one hand, I want to really soak and scrub them to remove as many chemicals as possible (on foods not grown organically) before they get into my little one's mouth. But on the other hand, the more I soak and scrub, the more nutrients get destroyed, especially the water-soluble vitamins. Personally, I'm more afraid of pesticides than vitamin-depletion, so I recommend lots of washing.

Use Water and Soap

Most experts used to recommend cleaning vegetables and fruits with cold water because warm water may soften them. Warm water also may cause a significant loss of nutrients and even the loss of some juice. However, the FDA recommends using warm water to wash produce for better removal of pesticides. I recommend using cold water for certified organic produce, and warm water for non-organic produce.

Vegetable and Fruit Soaps

I recommend the use of one of the soaps specifically made to clean vegetables and fruits. In addition to the pesticides used on non-organic food crops, other chemicals are added to prevent the pesticides from being washed away by rain. Soaps for veggies and fruits may help cut through these chemicals and also remove surface pesticides. Systemic pesticides—those absorbed by the plant during growth—cannot be removed by any amount of washing, which is why it is best to buy certified organic produce for your precious little one.

You will find these special fruit and vegetable soaps at your local natural foods store and in some supermarkets. If not, ask if they can order some for you.

> WARNING: Make sure you use only soap that is food-safe. Other soaps may leave a dangerous residue on food that will end up in your baby's tummy.

If you are going to use vegetable/fruit soap, spray each vegetable piece all over, covering every inch. Then let sit for at least 30 seconds. Or, follow the directions on the label.

Next, take a vegetable brush and hold a piece under the water while gently scrubbing. For hard vegetables, like unpeeled carrots that have little crevices where dirt collects, move the brush up and down and side to side (like you brush your teeth). Rinse well and be sure to rinse off all of the soap. Remember that all this washing is causing nutrient loss. If you have organic produce, go light on the scrubbing—there are no invisible pesticides to worry about.

Wash All Produce

You may not be in the habit of washing fruits with thick peels that will not be eaten, such as oranges and bananas. But these have pesticides all over them and people have been touching them. So please don't forget to wash any fruit or vegetable that you will be giving your baby.

If you're not going to cook the washed vegetables immediately, shake and lightly dry each piece with a towel and return them to the refrigerator as quickly as you can. Too much moisture may cause them to spoil. If you're going to cook them immediately, there's no need to dry them.

> **MONEY SAVER:** Let your soapy water do double duty. Save soap and water by collecting the running tap water in the sink while you are washing produce. Use the second-hand water to wash fruits with peels that won't be eaten, like bananas and oranges.

How to Cook Vegetables

When cooking baby food, your main concern besides safety should be that of nutrition. Negligent cooking techniques can destroy important vitamins needed for your baby's good health. Keep in mind that nutrients are destroyed by heat, air, light, and water. Water-soluble vitamins are lost when they leach into cooking water and the heat, inevitable in cooking, destroys some vitamins. Vitamin C is the most vulnerable vitamin, being both water-soluble and extremely susceptible to heat. Nature knew what she was doing when she put vitamin C into foods we eat raw, like citrus fruits.

Because vegetables for baby are just plain, unseasoned, whole vegetables with no fancy sauces or flavoring, cooking for baby is easy. It involves very little preparation and consists mostly of waiting while the vegetables cook. You just have to keep an eye on them while you do the rest of your kitchen chores.

> **TIP:** Don't discard the water used for cooking vegetables—it contains valuable nutrients. Use it for puréeing baby's food. Or add it to a container in your freezer and use it for soups, stews, and in place of meat broth in recipes. It will keep frozen for up to 6 months. Or pour it over your pet's food or use it to water your plants when cooled.

How to Tell When a Vegetable Is Fully Cooked

Cooking vegetables is a matter of timing. Vegetable cooking times vary due to moisture content, freshness, size, density, and age of the vegetable. The uniqueness of your stove and oven add to cooking time variability. Information on cooking times for specific vegetables can be found at the end of this chapter. Please take a moment and turn to the information on carrots on pages 187-188. Note that times for steaming and baking are stated. Use my recommended times as approximates and depend on your experience with your cooking equipment.

Because heat destroys some vitamins, a minimum amount of cooking time retains maximum nutrients, so test as soon as you think the vegetables might be done. You can always add cooking time if undercooked, but there is nothing you can do if they are overcooked. Test most vegetables for doneness by piercing them with a fork. The fork should slide in fairly easily. Whole vegetables, such as sweet potatoes and beets, should be soft all the way to the center. Leafy vegetables, such as spinach and kale, should look wilted, take on a brighter color, and be crisp tender to bite. (Crisp tender means that the greens are tender, but not so mushy that they don't crunch a little when you bite them.)

> **TIP:** For future reference, make notes in this book on how much time it took to cook a particular vegetable. Every time you open your oven or lift a lid to test for doneness, heat escapes and energy is wasted, so write down the cooking times for your unique appliances. Add any other relevant details. I always write notes in my cookbooks, including specifics about my equipment, mistakes I don't want to repeat, and whether or not my family and I liked the finished product.

Methods of Cooking Vegetables

There are many ways you can cook vegetables: steaming, baking, boiling, pressure-cooking, stir-frying, grilling, deep-frying, and, of course, not cooking them at all—eating them raw. Water and/or heat destroy vitamins; therefore, the best methods of cooking vegetables for your baby are those that have a minimum cooking time and use the least heat and water. Steaming, and baking are best because they use little water. Boiling vegetables in water causes a considerable loss of water-soluble vitamins. If you absolutely must boil, use as little water as possible: no more than a ½-inch in the bottom of the pot. Have the water boiling before you add the vegetables and simmer for as little time as possible. Deep frying vegetables, such as potatoes (French fries), should not even be considered. (See recipe for *French Fries-Not!* on page 457.)

Interestingly, eating vegetables raw is not always the way to get the most nutrients. Some nutrients become more available after cooking, such as the vitamin A in carrots.

Steaming Method

I highly recommend steaming vegetables instead of boiling them, because steaming retains much more of the nutrients. Water-soluble vitamins, such as vitamin C and the B vitamins, leach out into cooking water. Vegetables come into contact with much more cooking water if you boil vegetables rather than steam them, thereby allowing a significant loss of nutrients. Different types of steamers were discussed in Chapter 18.

Steaming Fresh Vegetables

- Place vegetables into the steamer so that they are no more than 2 inches deep, and in even layers. Don't have a big pile next to a small pile.

- If you are steaming whole vegetables, such as Brussels sprouts, place them in a single layer. Don't pile them up like a bucket of balls.

- To steam vegetables, place an inch or so of water into the bottom of a pot. Bring the water to a full boil BEFORE placing the vegetables in the steamer into the pot.

- After the water boils, put the steamer with the vegetables into the pot. Vegetables should be at least one inch above the water so that the water won't touch the vegetables when it is vigorously boiling.

- If the water starts to boil out, add more boiling water. If you are steaming a lot of vegetables, keep a separate pot with water boiling to replenish the water in the steamer when it gets low.

- Make sure the cover fits well on the pot to minimize the escape of steam into the air. Steam takes nutrients with it and the loss of steam impedes cooking.

- Stir or shake vegetables half-way through cooking for even cooking.

Energy-saving Stove Top Cooking Tips

- When boiling a measured amount of water, measure the water BEFORE boiling. Boiling water first and then measuring and discarding the excess wastes both water and energy.

- To save energy with an electric stove, match the stove burner to the size of the pot as closely as possible or heat will be lost to the air.

- Keep burner reflectors clean so they can reflect the heat efficiently. A no-scrub method of cleaning stubborn stains from metal reflectors is this: In a large pot, squirt some dishwashing detergent in water and stir until dissolved. Add burners and make sure they are covered with water. Bring water and dishwashing detergent to a boil and boil the burners for about 5-10 minutes. Crusty black burned-on food will wipe off easily with a scouring pad.

- Keep a lid on the pot when bringing water or other liquid to a boil. The liquid will boil faster and use less energy.

- To save a little energy, turn off an electric burner a few minutes before the end of the cooking time. It will stay hot enough to finish the cooking. Likewise, turn off your oven a few minutes early.

Baking Method

Baking or roasting fresh vegetables preserves nutrients because little or no water is used. Some vegetables, such as sweet potatoes, can be baked whole. Simply pierce their skins and place directly on the oven rack or on a baking sheet. Some vegetables should be sliced and placed in a pan with a little water. For sliced vegetables, pack them tightly into a covered baking dish to retain moisture. Vegetables with high water content, such as zucchini, need no added water.

WARNING: If your oven is within your toddler's reach, never turn it on until you make sure that it's empty and that your little one hasn't placed something in it! You may want to invest in a baby-proof oven lock, which you'll find in baby stores and online.

MONEY SAVER: To save on energy bills, place a batch of vegetables in the same half-empty (conventional) oven you are using to cook dinner.

Minimizing Nutrient Loss from Vegetables During Preparation and Cooking

- Remember that nutrients are destroyed by heat, light, air, and water.

- Most vegetables need to be kept cold to retain their nutrients and stay fresh. Don't let them sit on the counter at room temperature, get them into the refrigerator as quickly as possible.

- Don't peel a vegetable or fruit if you don't have to. The peel contains concentrated nutrients and fiber.

- Cut vegetables into the largest pieces possible. Vegetables lose nutrients due to the cutting, chopping, dicing, and shredding of vegetables. Minimize this nutrient loss by cutting the pieces as uniformly sized as possible, so that each piece will take the same amount of time to cook. If you're cooking whole vegetables, such as potatoes, choose same-sized vegetables at the supermarket.

- Use as little water as possible during cooking. Water-soluble vitamins, such as vitamin C and the B complex, leach into cooking water. Steam cook vegetables instead of boiling them. When steam cooking veggies, make sure that the bottom of the steamer is not submerged in the water, so the water doesn't touch the cooking vegetables. The steamer should be an inch or two above the boiling water. Keep the lid tightly closed to minimize the amount of steam that escapes. When steam goes, it takes nutrients with it and impedes cooking.

- If you do boil vegetables, simmer instead of boil as much as possible. Use no more than a half-inch of water in the bottom of the pot. Have the water boiling before you add the vegetables and simmer for as little time as possible.

- Don't keep food warm—serve it right away. And don't leave leftovers at room temperature—refrigerate immediately.

- Don't use baking soda in cooking water, it destroys water-soluble vitamins.

How to Purée Vegetables

Your young baby cannot yet chew food, so you must purée it to a smooth lump-free consistency. To get the consistency necessary for beginning eaters, water must be added to the food mixture being processed. For most vegetables, use the water in which they were cooked, whether the water is from steaming, baking, or boiling. This water contains valuable nutrients that have leached out of the vegetables during cooking.

Pour the water from the cooking pot into a container with a spout so that it will be easy to pour into the processor. I use a little glass measuring cup with a spout.

> **WARNING:** Never put very hot liquids in your blender. Hot moisture may become trapped and erupt when you open the lid.

I will use the term "processor" to refer to your blender, your food processor, your food mill, or whatever you're using to purée.

Place chunks of cooked vegetables into the bowl of the processor so that it's almost full. Make sure you leave some head room. Add a tablespoon or two of the cooking water.

> **TIP:** If you find that the sweet potatoes and other cooked veggies are too hot to handle while you're puréeing them, use a pair of those rubber kitchen gloves used for washing dishes. Then you can keep the gloves on for clean-up, when you can use really hot water without burning yourself.

> **WARNING:** Always keep your hand on the blender cover to assure that it doesn't come off and spew food all over you and the kitchen. Do this especially when you have hot food in the blender that could burn you. Your baby should be far away from a working blender at all times (even a non-working blender with its sharp blades).

Cover, keep your hand on the lid, and start the processor. Pour more water very slowly through the hole in the top of the processor until food moves freely. If you're using a blender, use a rubber spatula to push the food into the blades, if necessary. Be careful not to let the spatula touch the blades. If food becomes lodged in the blades, stop the blender and wait for the blades to stop moving before using your spatula to remove the pieces.

> **WARNING:** Never use a metal utensil to push food into blender blades. This is dangerous and may ruin your blender's blades if it touches them by accident.

Use the least amount of water necessary to get the consistency you need for your baby's age. For a young baby who has just started on solid food, you must use quite a bit of water to get a very smooth texture.

MONEY SAVER: Do you see how much water you must add to get this fine consistency? Makes you wonder how much of commercial jarred baby food is actually food and how much is water. Next time you're at the supermarket, take a close look at the glass jars of baby food and note their consistencies. Copy their textures when making food for your baby at different ages.

As your baby gets older, she can chew or actually "gum" chunkier food. Then you will, of course, add less water and purée for less time. If you accidentally add too much water, simply add some more cooked vegetables.

TIP: When it comes time that your baby can eat chunky vegetables, fill your food processor only half-way. This will prevent some food from getting over-chopped.

> **WARNING:** You must be especially careful to keep any puréed baby food cold. Never leave it for extended periods at room temperature, because bacteria will thrive in it. The same is true for open jars of commercial baby food. Remember that bacteria grow in temperatures that are not too hot and not too cold—they love room temperature.

How to Store Cooked Vegetables
Refrigerating Small Portions

Store a portion or two of the food you just puréed in the refrigerator to feed to your baby within the next day. Cooked, puréed vegetables will not keep in the refrigerator longer than a day or two. Store them in a small covered glass bowl, and then you can just empty into a pot to reheat. Freeze any cooked puréed food that you will not be using within the next day.

> **WARNING:** Do not store baby food that has been made from frozen vegetables or other frozen foods. For example, if you have bought some commercially frozen broccoli from the supermarket and cooked and puréed it for your baby, do not freeze it for future use. Discard any leftovers. Most foods should not be frozen more than once, especially vegetables.

Freezing—The Food Cube Method

Next to the processor containing the puréed food, place ice cube trays along with a spoon or little measuring cup (⅓ or ¼ cup size). Make sure everything is whistle-clean because although freezing retards the growth of germs in foods, it does not sterilize.

The puréed food can be poured into the ice cube trays if the consistency is very liquefied; just remove the processor bowl and pour into the trays. If the food is too thick to pour, scoop and pat into the cubes with your clean fingers.

TIME SAVER: If you're puréeing a large batch of the same vegetable, you may have to fill your processor more than once. Don't waste time between refills scooping small amounts of vegetable from the bottom of the processor. Keep adding more food in on top and scoop out those last bits only once in the end when you're finishing up.

Freeze using the *Food Cube Method* as detailed in Chapter 19. As soon as each ice cube tray is filled, immediately cover it and place it in the freezer.

While you're at it, you may want to freeze a few portions in little freezer-safe, glass containers with lids to be used when you go out for the day. Take them out frozen, place in a cooler with an ice pack to keep them at refrigerator temperature to prevent bacterial growth and by meal-time they'll be thawed and ready. NEVER thaw foods at room temperature.

TIP: Make your food cubes a consistent size, then you'll know by experience exactly how much stove time is needed to thaw them.

When your baby is very young and needs a very smooth consistency, the cubes will have a lot of water in them and will freeze almost as solid as ice. As your baby grows and you make the cubes lumpier, they will be less icy and thaw and reheat faster.

How to Batch Cook Vegetables

For Your Beginning Eater, Make A Single Batch of Cooked Veggies

When your baby begins to eat solid foods, she will not eat much at all—only about a tablespoon or two a day. The first vegetable you will probably give her is sweet potatoes. Other veggies, like carrots, spinach, broccoli, and others, should not be fed to very young babies because of the nitrates they contain.

As your baby gets older and eats more, you can prepare two batches of veggies simultaneously. While the sweet potatoes are baking in the oven, steam a batch of green beans on the stove top or purée a ripe avocado.

TIP: While you're cooking baby veggies, dice some snack-sized portions of finger food and replenish your Super Snack Freezer Bag (page 34).

For An Older Baby, Four Batches a Month

As your baby gets older, you'll probably have to make about 4 batches of cooked veggies a month. Depending on the vegetable, a "batch" is approximately two ice cube trays. So a month's worth is about 8 trays—an average or 3 or 4 veggie cube servings a day.

Make one batch each week/4 batches a month. I usually keep up with my little one's veggie cube needs by making a single batch once a week. I save time and cleanup by combining baby food cooking with the cooking I do for the rest of my family. For example, when I make steamed broccoli for my family's dinner, I steam an extra bunch of broccoli in the same pot, purée it, fill 2 ice cube trays, and freeze it for the baby. Or if I'm baking a casserole, I simply add another baking dish with vegetables for baby. The puréeing and freezing adds only an extra 10 or 15 minutes preparation time.

You may wish to stock up on *Super Baby Food* and make baby vegetables along with the other two types of baby foods that need advance preparation: cooked eggs and *Super Porridge*. If so, check out the sample session shown on page 53.

Or make all 4 batches once a month. Occasionally, I dedicate the better part of one morning a month to the batch-cooking of large amounts of baby veggies. On the day of the week when fresh produce has been delivered to my supermarket, I buy a month's worth. I run right home and get to work for an hour or two and make several weeks' worth of baby food. The more food I prepare at one time, the more time I save. It's similar to industrial mass production.

While one batch of produce is steaming on the stove and another batch is cooking in the oven, I'm washing and preparing the next batch. If you've got a lot going on at once, there's no time to stand around and wait for something to get cooked. Your time is used very efficiently and you'll be amazed at how much you can get done in one or two hours if you do things in parallel. Also, you clean up only once at the end, another time-saver.

TIP: Before going to the supermarket, make sure your kitchen is clean and the counter tops are cleared off. Go through your refrigerator and freezer and throw out old food to make room for the new.

Advanced Batch Cooking

OK, you've decided to spend the morning making a huge batch of *Super Baby Food*. It helps to decide which foods you're going to make before you go to the supermarket. Super Green Veggies like broccoli and kale, and carrots or sweet potatoes for beta-carotene (vitamin A) should be regulars on your shopping list. The following example assumes you've decided to prepare a bunch of broccoli, 4 sweet potatoes, a bunch of carrots, and an avocado. It pays to think things through for a minute before you start cooking. Roughly estimate how much preparation and cooking time is needed for each food:

Broccoli: Wash, minimally chop, and steam for 15 minutes.
Carrots: Wash, peel, slice, and then steam for 10 minutes.
Sweet Potatoes: Wash and bake 45 minutes.
Avocado: Ripe and ready. Wash. No cooking necessary.

TIP: Always start with the food that takes the most time to prepare.

The box on the next page shows one possibility for the order in which to do the kitchen tasks necessary to prepare and cook the four foods above. Unless you consider yourself a lean, mean, cooking machine, the example will probably make your head spin. It's really not as difficult at it looks. Rest assured, you do not have to do all this cooking in one session! That's why I labeled it ADVANCED. I rarely do 4 batches at once—usually only 1 or 2 batches at a time.

In this example, about 8 trays or over 100 food cubes were made in less than 1½ hours. If your baby eats 2 cubes a day, that's 50 days' worth; if your baby eats 3 cubes a day, that's a month's worth.

A Vegetable Food Cube Assembly Line

It's a little easier to batch-cook the SAME veggie in an assembly line method, as shown with broccoli on page 180. When broccoli goes on sale, I stock up on it and buy enough for 2 months' worth of food cubes. In less than 1 hour, I transform 4 bunches of broccoli into approximately 120 food cubes—that's just pennies per cube!

TIME SAVER: If you have a friend who also makes homemade baby food, consider swapping food cubes for more variety.

When you are able to successfully complete batch-cooking sessions similar to those on the next two pages, consider yourself a black belt in *Super Baby Food*.

Example of Steps Involved in
ADVANCED Multi-batch Vegetable Cooking

Time	Task
5 minutes	Arrange all necessary equipment on counter top.
1 minute	Place an inch or two of water in pot on stove to heat for steaming vegetables.
6 minutes	While waiting for water to boil, wash and chop broccoli and place in steamer. Water is now boiling, place steamer in pot and set timer for 15 minutes.
5 minutes	Wash sweet potatoes, pierce with a fork in several places, place in oven and bake uncovered for 45 minutes.
10 minutes	Wash, peel, and slice carrots in preparation for steamer.
1 minute	Timer goes off to indicate that broccoli is finished steaming. Remove from steamer and put in bowl to wait for puréeing. Wait to purée broccoli until it has cooled somewhat, so that you don't burn yourself.
1 minute	Add water to steaming pot, if necessary. It's easier to take a small glass with water to the pot, rather than bringing the pot to the sink tap.
1 minute	Place sliced carrots in steamer and place in pot after water starts boiling again. Set timer for 10 minutes.
7 minutes	Purée broccoli and fill ice cube trays. Cover well with aluminum foil, and place in freezer.
7 minutes	Sweet potatoes are done cooking. Cut sweet potatoes in half and scoop out flesh from skin. Purée, tray, cover, and freeze. During this step, timer interrupts indicating carrots are done steaming. Do step below and then finish sweet potatoes.
1 minute	Remove steamer with carrots from pot and place on counter to cool.
7 minutes	Purée carrots, tray, cover, and place in freezer.
7 minutes	If you have any energy left, do the avocado. Cut in half, scoop out flesh, purée, tray, cover, and freeze.
15 minutes	Clean up.

Total time: Approximately 1 hour and 15 minutes.

A Broccoli Food Cube Assembly Line

Time	Task
1 minute	Place water in the steamer pot and bring to a boil. Keep a separate pot of boiling water ready to replenish steamer water as you cook batches.
30 seconds	Coarsely chop the first bunch of broccoli.
2 minutes	Place cut broccoli in colander and wash well. A sink hose spray comes in handy for rinsing.
1 minute	Place broccoli in steamer. Set timer to steam for about 8-10 minutes.
2½ minutes	Coarsely chop the second bunch of broccoli and rinse in colander as you did the first bunch. Let it drain while waiting for its turn in the steamer.
5 minutes	While the first bunch of broccoli is cooking, get oven mitts ready as well as a large cooling/holding bowl, food processor or blender, slotted spoon, spouted cup, spoon or scoop, ice cube trays, and aluminum foil to cover the trays.
2 minutes	Timer sounds indicating first bunch of broccoli finished cooking. Spoon cooked broccoli into cooling bowl with slotted spoon.
1 minute	Transfer second bunch of broccoli from colander to steamer, cover and set timer for 8-10 minutes.
2 minutes	Coarsely chop and rinse the third bunch of broccoli in colander. Let it drain while waiting for steamer.
7 minutes	First bunch is in cooling bowl and is cool enough to handle now. Purée, spoon into ice cube trays, cover with organic bleach-free wax paper and the aluminum foil, and place into freezer.
1 minute	Second bunch of broccoli is done cooking—transfer it from steamer to cooling bowl.
1 minutes	Move third bunch from colander to steamer and start timer cooking for 8-10 minutes.
2 minutes	Coarsely chop and rinse fourth bunch of broccoli in colander. Let it drain while waiting for microwave.
7 minutes	Purée second bunch of broccoli, tray, cover, and freeze. And so on . . .

Total time: Less than 1 hour for 4 broccoli bunches.

Specific Vegetables

Acorn Squash, see Squash, Winter

Asparagus

Baby must be at least 7 months old to eat asparagus.

Asparagus is one of the Super Green Veggies.

Equivalents: 12-16 stalks = 1 pound = 3½ cups of pieces.

In season: Available February through July; peak April through June.

Choosing: Buy asparagus loose so that you can take a close look at each piece. Select asparagus whose tips are closed and compact. The stalks should be brittle, straight, firm, not limp, and almost totally bright green. The stalks also should be perfectly round, not angular, and with no vertical ridges. Fatter is better. The thicker the stalk, the more tender.

Storing: Get them into the refrigerator quickly, as room temperature rapidly deteriorates asparagus. Remove any rubber bands. The bottom should be kept damp: wrap the ends in wet white paper towels and place in a glass container with lid in the refrigerator. Or, if you have the refrigerator room, store them upright in a container with their ends in water, as you would a bunch of flowers. They will keep for up to 3 days.

Preparation for cooking: Don't throw away half your asparagus. Cut off only the very tough bottom inch or so and peel the stalk as you would a carrot. It's difficult to find asparagus without sand or grit. To clean, soak in cold water for 30 minutes and then rinse thoroughly.

Steam: Steam whole asparagus for 10 minutes, cut asparagus pieces for 5 minutes.

Freezing: Use the *Cube Method* or *Tray-Freeze Method*, and keep for up to 2 months.

Beans, Edible Pod: Snap, Green, Yellow, or Waxed

Baby must be at least 7 months old to eat beans.

Equivalents: 1 pound of green beans = 3 cups fresh = 2½ cups cooked.

In season: Available year round; peak May through October.

Choosing: Select beans that are brightly colored green or yellow with as few brown spots as possible. Brown spots can be cut away because they are bruises and not decay. Pods should be smooth, thin, and well-filled, but with no ridge and no bulges, which indicate that the beans are too mature. They should be stiff, so that they would snap easily, and not wilted or flabby. Pick beans of uniform size for even cooking.

Storing: Wrap in organic bleach-free wax paper and then a plastic bag and store in the refrigerator for up to 4 days.

Preparation for cooking: Snap or trim ends (it's really only necessary to trim the stem end), but leave small beans whole. Cut very large beans in half.

Steam: Steam for 9 to 12 minutes.

Freezing: Use the *Cube Method* or *Tray-Freeze Method*, and keep for up to 2 months.

Beets

Baby must be at least 9 months old to eat cooked beats; raw and grated, 10-11 months. See warning about nitrates.

Grated beets can be fed to your baby raw. Cooked beets are tasty and very colorful. They can be used as a decorative touch or even a food coloring in baby's food. Beets stain, so use a good bib when feeding your baby beets. Be aware that several hours after your baby eats beets, her stool will be quite red in color. I panicked the first time I saw the red during a diaper change—my first thought was blood! Beets are a good indicator of the time it takes food to pass through your baby. **NOTE: Beet stains are impossible to get out of cloth, plastic surfaces and wood.**

Equivalents: 6 medium beets = 1 pound = 2 cups sliced.

In season: Available year round; peak June through October.

Choosing: Beets are sold with or without their green tops. The tops, called "beet greens," should be fresh-looking, thin-ribbed, and deep green, with no brown or red edges, and with no trace of slime. If they are a little wilted, the flavor of the red root should not be affected because the greens rapidly deteriorate while the root remains good. Beet greens are edible.

Beets without their greens should have at least ½ inch of stem left on top and their bottom roots should be at least two inches long. The bulbous root should have a lush, deep red color and smooth, firm skin with no cuts or soft spots. Roots should have no scaly areas or circles on the top and they should be a nice round shape, not elongated. Buy small to medium-sized beets, as large beets tend to be tough with inedible, woody cores.

Storing: As with other root vegetables, immediately remove the greens so that they do not pull moisture from the root. Leave an inch or two of stem on the root, or it will bleed during cooking. Store beets in the refrigerator wrapped in organic, bleach-free wax paper and then in a plastic bag for up to 10 days.

Preparation for cooking: Scrub well under cold-running water.

Steam: I don't recommend steaming. It takes about 60 minutes!

Boil: Simmer whole beets for two hours. Peels will easily come off and juices will be better retained in whole beets.

Bake: Wash thoroughly, place on a baking sheet and bake at 400°F for 90 minutes to two hours—the larger the beets, the longer the baking time.

Peel and purée: After cooking beets, remove stems. If you wish, slip off peels under cold running water before puréeing.

Freezing: Use the *Cube Method* or *Tray-Freeze Method*, and keep for up to 2 months.

Beet Greens, *see* Greens
Butternut Squash, *see* Squash, Winter

Broccoli

Baby must be at least 8 months old to eat cooked broccoli.

We all know how good broccoli is for us. This Super Green Veggie, a good source of vitamins A and C, calcium, and many other nutrients, should be a regular food in your Super Baby's diet. Your baby should have a Super Green Veggie serving every single day, and broccoli is one that is available year round.

Equivalents: A 1-pound head of broccoli = 2 cups florets.

In season: Available year round; peak October through May. The plants do well in cool weather.

Choosing: Select medium-sized bunches with small, tightly closed green buds that crowd together tightly. Stalks should be slender and feel firm, but not too tough and woody. Stalks should also be tender, especially in the upper portion toward the florets. Any leaves on the stalk should be fresh and not wilted and brightly colored green. Avoid bruised or wilted broccoli and broccoli whose buds are spread instead of tight. Do not buy broccoli with yellow flowers in the buds, as they indicate age. The more yellow, the less desirable the bunch is. Avoid those with any soft slippery spots. Also, use your nose. If the broccoli has a strong odor, pass on it.

Storing: Refrigerate unwashed wrapped in organic, bleach-free wax paper and then in a plastic bag for up to 3 days. Dolores Riccio, author of *Superfoods*, says that a better way to store broccoli "is to treat it like a bunch of flowers. Slice off the ends of the stalks and stand them in a pitcher with about two inches of water, loosely cover the head with a plastic bag, and refrigerate." (*Editor's note:* We suggest wrapping in organic, bleach-free wax paper.) She recommends that we eat broccoli 4 to 5 times a week. I almost agree. We, and our babies, should have at least one of the Super Greens every day—it doesn't have to be broccoli.

Preparation for cooking: While rinsing, use your fingers to open florets so that water flows between them and gets them really clean. Broccoli sometimes causes gas in babies (and adults). To prevent gas, slightly undercook broccoli. Undercooking maintains the green chlorophyll, which counteracts gas-causing sulfur compounds.

Trim off any tough part on the bottom of the stalk—leave about 3 or 4 inches under the florets. You can cut the broccoli lengthwise into spears or crosswise leaving the florets whole. If the florets are too large, cut them into pieces so they'll fit in the steamer. If you will be cooking only the florets for baby, cut the stems very close to the florets and they will separate automatically into individual florets. Broccoli florets cook faster than the thick stalks, so slash the entire length of the stalks 5 or 6 times to cause them to cook as fast as the florets. You can eat the stalk and the leaves. The leaves cook very quickly, as other greens do. Pull them off and save them. Then throw them into the pot for the last minute or two of cooking.

Steaming: Place broccoli in steamer, stalks on bottom, florets on top. Steam for about 15 to 20 minutes for large pieces and about 8 to 10 minutes for smaller pieces.

Freezing: Use the *Cube Method* or *Tray-Freeze Method*, and keep for up to 2 months.

Buying frozen broccoli: Short spears are best; they are mostly florets. Whole spears are next best. Broccoli cuts contain too many stalks, and chopped broccoli is almost all stalks. I always put frozen veggies into a strainer or colander and run them under water for a few seconds to remove that frosty covering which sometimes gives them an off flavor. Try not use frozen broccoli for making baby food cubes.

Brussels Sprouts

Baby must be at least 8 months old to eat cooked Brussels sprouts. Never feed your baby raw Brussels sprouts.

Brussels sprouts are a Super Green Veggie.

In season: Available year round; peak September through March.

Choosing: Select small Brussels sprouts whose leaves are tight, firm, and bright green. They should feel heavy for their size. Avoid those with bruises, worm holes, or yellow leaves that are soft, wilted, or puffy. If they are packaged, you'll have to look very carefully for insect damage (tiny holes in the leaves). Large Brussels sprouts are coarse with a strong flavor and odor. Buy the smallest ones you can find. Check that the stem is not cut too close, otherwise the outer leaves will fall off during cooking.

Storing: Pull off any yellow or yellowish-green leaves. Place in organic, unbleached wax paper and then in plastic bag in refrigerator for up to 3 days. Use as soon as possible or their flavor will be too strong.

Preparation for cooking: Don't overcook Brussels sprouts or they will get mushy and have a strong flavor. Trim the stems off the bottom. Cut two slashes into the bottom perpendicularly (like a cross) and this will help them cook evenly.

Steam: Steam whole for 15 to 20 minutes or until stem end is done.

Freezing: Use the *Cube Method* or *Tray-Freeze Method*, and keep for up to 2 months.

Cabbage

Baby must be at least 12 months old to eat cabbage because it tends to cause digestive problems.

Equivalents: ½ head = 1 pound cabbage = 4½ cups raw, shredded = 2½ cups cooked.

In season: Available year round; peak October through May.

Choosing: Cabbages are sold with or without outer leaves, called wrapper leaves. Inside the wrapper leaves the head is very firm, spherical, tightly packed, and a very pale green—almost colorless. Wrapper leaves should be crisp and fresh, with no signs of wilting or decay. If wrapper leaves have been removed, make sure the inner head is fresh, moist, and hard, not puffy, and feels heavy for its size. Inspect the base of the cabbage to ensure that leaves are firmly attached to the stem and there is no separation from the stem. There should be no splits. Avoid cabbage with discolored veins. Use your nose; fresh cabbage does not have a strong cabbage odor.

Storing: Remember that the more you cut vegetables, the most nutrient loss from air exposure, so don't shred the cabbage until you're ready to use it. If shredded cabbage is exposed to air, especially warm air, it loses lots of its vitamin C. Store whole cabbage in organic, unbleached wax paper and then in a plastic bag in the refrigerator for up to two weeks. If you use only part of the cabbage head, keep the unused section in one piece and store tightly wrapped in the refrigerator for up to two days.

Preparation for cooking: Cabbage is rich is vitamin C, which is destroyed by heat, so cook for as short a time as possible. Pull off any wilted outer leaves, but only if badly wilted because the outer leaves are richest in nutrients. Cut in half lengthwise and remove the inner core. Cut into wedges or shred. Shredding cabbage allows for a shorter cooking time. Cabbage contains sulfur compounds which causes cooking odors—keep a tight lid on to minimize the smell.

Steam: Steam wedges for about 15 minutes.

Stuffed Cabbage: To prepare cabbage for stuffed cabbage, first cut out core of whole cabbage with a sharp knife. Then submerge head in boiling water and let cook for 5 minutes. Then move it to a bowl of cold water. Or, wash and dry a head of cabbage and freeze, uncooked, in organic, unbleached wax paper and then in a plastic bag. When thawed, the leaves are easy to pull off and use for stuffed cabbage. Who really has time for stuffing cabbage, anyway? Get the same taste results by baking shredded cabbage and the stuffing in layers in a baking dish.

Freezing: Use the *Cube Method* or *Tray-Freeze Method*, and keep for up to 2 months.

Carrots

Baby must be at least 7 months old to eat cooked carrots; 10 months old to eat finely grated raw carrots. See warning about nitrates.

Carrots are loaded with beta-carotene, a form of vitamin A that is not toxic, even in large doses. Don't believe anyone who tells you not to feed your baby too many carrots (within reason, of course) for fear of vitamin A toxicity. In fact, you should give your baby a vitamin A veggie every day. It's the vitamin A from animal products and vitamin pills that causes toxicity. The beta-carotene in carrots is made more available to the body by cooking. Also, grating raw carrots makes the beta-carotene more available. Raw carrots are said to lower cholesterol levels. You can't go wrong—eat them raw or cooked!

Equivalents: 6 or 7 medium carrots = 1 pound = 3 cups shredded.

In season: Carrots are available year round. They are at their peak in the summer.

Choosing: Carrots are sold "topped" (green top stems removed) in plastic bags. You may also find carrots complete with their bushy green tops. If you buy them this way, cut off their tops immediately to prevent them from pulling moisture out of the orange root. Select carrots that are clean and bright orange, indicating large amounts of beta-carotene. Buyer beware: Sometimes carrots are packaged in orange-tinted plastic bags that may hide pale carrots. In this case, check for freshness by bending them. They should be firm, not flabby or shriveled, and have no decaying spots or splits. Smaller carrots are sweeter and more tender. Large, thick carrots may have tough, woody cores. But instead of the overpriced carrots labeled "baby carrots" in the supermarket, go for the small to medium-sized regular carrots—they're tastier. Avoid carrots with green spots because they will taste bitter. Green discoloration or "sunburn" in the orange stem is a sign that the carrots have been left in sunlight (sunlight helps plants produce green chlorophyll).

Storing: Carrots need cold temperature and high humidity. Store in the refrigerator in a glass container with a lid that allows for air, which helps to retain moisture and protect from the refrigerator's dry air. Keep carrots away from fruit, if you can. Make sure to remove their green tops immediately to prevent sap from flowing into them, taking nutrition and flavor with it. Fresh carrots will keep in the refrigerator for up to two weeks. And good news—they keep their nutrients when properly stored.

Preparation for cooking: Nutrients are most concentrated in the peels of carrots and just below. You don't have to peel or scrape young or small carrots if you give them a good scrubbing with a vegetable brush. Older, bigger carrots are probably better peeled.

Steaming: Steam whole carrots 15 minutes; carrot slices about 10 minutes.

Baking: Large carrots can be baked in the oven. Scrub them and leave whole and unpeeled. Bake at 350°F for 30-40 minutes.

Freezing: Freeze puréed carrots using the *Food Cube* method, and keep for up to 2 months.

Cauliflower

Baby must be at least 9 months old to eat cooked cauliflower.

The off-white florets (called the "curd" because it looks like curd) are usually sold surrounded by some green outer leaves. Cauliflower contains vitamin C, potassium, fiber, and the B vitamins. Watch your baby for signs of gas after you feed her cauliflower.

Equivalents: 1½ pounds = 2 cups cooked.

In season: Available year round; peak September through November.

Choosing: The curd should be clean, creamy white, heavy, firm, dense, and tightly crowded together. If it has a yellow tinge or has begun to spread and is loose, don't buy it because it's old. The florets can be either smooth or bristly, but not too granular or rice-looking, and they should not easily crumble if you scratch them. Avoid cauliflower with a lot of brown or black spots on the florets; if there is just a little bit, you can trim it off and the rest is OK to eat. The outer leaves should be fresh and crisp. If the leaves drop off, don't buy that head. It's OK if there are a few green leaves growing out of the curd if they haven't begun to flower.

Storing: Store the head wrapped in organic, bleach-free wax paper and then a plastic bag in the refrigerator for about a week. Use as soon as possible, as old cauliflower develops a strong taste and odor. Raw florets cut from the head will keep for only one day. Cooked cauliflower keeps in the refrigerator for up to 3 days.

Preparation for cooking: Turn the head upside down, remove all leaves, and use a knife to cut out most of the center stalk. Cut florets in large pieces. Although most people throw away the leaves, you can actually eat them cooked or raw. Cook them with the cauliflower or separately. Instead of cutting up the head, you can leave it whole. To get rid of any insects, soak head down for at least a half-hour in cold water, to which has been added about a teaspoonful of salt. Then rinse thoroughly. However, I suggest you simply cut it into florets and check carefully for bugs. The soaking leaches out nutrients and the longer cooking time required for the whole head destroys more nutrients. Cauliflower contains sulfur compounds that cause cooking odors—keep a tight lid on to minimize the smell.

> **Note:** It is best to undercook cauliflower; overcooking makes it mushy and the flavor too strong.

Steam: Steam florets for 10 minutes, whole head for 20-30 minutes.

Boil: Boil florets for 12 minutes.

> **Tip:** To prevent cauliflower from yellowing while boiling, add one or two tablespoons of milk to the water first.

Freezing: Use the *Cube Method* or *Tray-Freeze Method*, and keep for up to 2 months.

Celery

Baby must be at least 7 months old to eat cooked celery; 10 months old to eat very finely grated raw celery. Make sure there are no hard celery pieces, because they are choking hazards. Remove all strings from celery. **Never give a baby celery with strings—strings are also a choking hazard.**

Equivalents: 1 stalk = ½ cup diced.

In season: Available year round.

Choosing: Select a bundle of medium length and thickness with green, fresh top leaves or only slightly wilted top leaves, which have no sign of yellow. The ribs should be very crisp, brittle, and rigid, ones that will snap easily. The ribs should have a good glossy green color: light, medium, or dark green is OK depending on the variety. Remember that more green means more vitamin A. Don't buy limp, rubbery, lifeless celery with any brown or gray discoloration on the stalk or rust-colored marks near the base. Gently open the bundle to check that the insides of the stalks are fresh-looking and smooth with no holes or off-color patches. Feel the insides with your fingers and don't buy if there is roughness or puffiness.

Storing: Do not remove leaves for storing. Store in paper bags in the refrigerator. Or wrap in white paper towels, then store in glass container with a tight lid in refrigerator for up to two weeks. If you have the refrigerator room, place the stalk end in a shallow bowl of water (like flowers in a vase) and cover with organic, bleach-free wax paper and then plastic wrap.

Preparing: Pull the stalks from the bundle. Trim off the leaves, wash very well, and use fresh to flavor soups, salad, or stew. Or dry the leaves and make into a powder by rubbing through a sieve; use powder as a flavoring. Trim the bottom of the stalks.

Clean each stalk thoroughly with a vegetable brush, rinsing well. Whole outer stalks are best for cooking; tender, inner stalks are good for salads or eating raw. Celery can be finely diced for use as a *Healthy Addition* for older children.

Remove all strings from celery for baby. Remove the stalk's tough part and strings with a vegetable peeler. Or remove strings from outer stalks by using a knife to pull strings from the top to the bottom and throw them away. Or remove strings by snapping the stalk about an inch from the top and while it's still partially attached, pull down the length of the stalk pulling the strings out. Celery strings, as well as hard slices of celery or hard celery pieces, are choking hazards for babies and toddlers.

Steam: Whole ribs for 20 minutes, 1-inch pieces for 10 minutes.

Freezing: Use the *Cube Method* or *Tray-Freeze Method*, and keep for up to 2 months.

> **Tip:** If your recipe calls for fresh parsley and you're out of it, use celery leaves.

Collard Greens, see Greens

Corn
(Sweet Corn, Maize, Zea)

Baby must be at least 12 months old to eat corn. Corn tends to cause digestive problems and whole corn kernels are choking hazards.

Corn gives us so many things: cornmeal, cornstarch, corn oil, and livestock feed (made from the cobs). Its tall corn stalks give us paper and much more. The instant an ear of corn is picked, it quickly converts its sugar to starch. Every minute counts. At room temperature, half of corn's sugar gets converted to starch in one day. Heat or cold stop the conversion, so rush home from the store and either eat, boil, or refrigerate the corn immediately. (Scientists supposedly have come up with a new variety of corn that doesn't convert its starch to sugar so quickly, but we've yet to see it.)

Equivalents: 1 medium ear = ½ cup kernels.

In season: Peak May through September. Fresh corn is definitely one vegetable that you should buy only when in season.

Choosing: The husks of corn should be green, moist, snug, and flexible, not yellow, wilted, or rigid. The bottom stem end should also be green and moist, not dry and brown. Don't buy husked corn (corn with green husks removed), unless it is refrigerated, and really not even then. The silk should be moist, golden yellow, not brown, and free from decay and worm damage. Peel back the husk and make sure the kernels are tightly packed together and neither oversized or undersized. Kernels should be plump and juicy, not shrunken or shriveled. If you dare, stick one with your thumbnail—it should break easily and squirt a thin, milky juice. The rows of kernels should be even and close together with no space between them. Yellow or white, don't rely on color for freshness, but yellow corn has more beta-carotene (vitamin A) than white. Very dark yellow, though, indicates old corn.

Storing: Don't! Use it the same day you buy it. If you can't use it the same day and must store, keep husks on and wrap ears in damp paper towels and refrigerate in organic, bleach-free wax paper and then in plastic bag for no more than a day or two. Or cook the corn as soon as you bring it home, cool it quickly in cold water, and store it in a covered glass container in the refrigerator for up to 3 days.

Preparation for cooking: Remove husks and all of the silk.

Tips to remove silk: To remove silk, rub from top to bottom with a damp paper towel. Another method is to use a vegetable brush or a sterilized toothbrush in a downward motion. If it is still difficult to remove the silk, brush it under running water.

Cooking tips: Your baby doesn't need sugar or salt added to cooking water, and besides, salt hardens the kernels. A teaspoon or two of lemon juice in the cooking water will keep corn a nice yellow color.

Cooking fresh corn off the cob for your toddler: Remove corn from the cob by standing the cob on end and using a sharp knife to cut off a few rows at a time from top to bottom. Do not cut deeply—too near the cob. Then use the back of the knife to scrape the germ off the cob and into the pot. See the nutritional importance of the germ on page 258. Cook the kernels, covered, with a little milk or formula over medium-high heat for only about 3 minutes. Then purée and freeze using the *Food Cube Method* for up to 2 months.

Tip to remove corn kernels from the cob: Use a clean shoehorn.

Oven roasted unhusked corn: Preheat oven to 450°F. With husk still on corn cobs, thoroughly wet under running water. Bake in oven for 45 minutes, turning occasionally. Protect hand with oven mitt and turn with corn tongs. Remove husk and enjoy! No pans to wash.

Steam: Steam husked corn on the cob in one layer for 10 minutes.

Boil: Boil one inch of water (or half water and half milk) in a large pot. Drop corn on the cob, husks and silk removed, into boiling water one ear at a time so as not to disturb the boiling. Cook for 4-6 minutes.

> **Tip:** If you have pot with a colander insert, use it so you won't have to remove each cob individually with tongs. The corn can then be drained easily over the sink.

Tip for buttering corn on the cob: Don't rub a butter stick directly on the cob, it wastes too much and is messy. Use a pastry brush and melted butter for a thin coat. In a pinch, the leaves on top of a celery stick will work, but not as well as a brush. For your large barbecue party, fill a tall thin bottle with hot water and a stick of butter. When butter melts and floats to the top, slowly dip an ear of corn into the bottle so that it gets coated with a nice layer of butter.

Dandelion Greens, see Greens

Eggplant

Baby must be at least 9 months old to eat cooked puréed eggplant. Do not eat raw eggplant.

Equivalents: 1½ pounds = 2½ cups diced.

In season: Available year round; peak June through September.

Choosing: Select small, firm, shiny, tight, smooth, rich purple eggplant with only a small scar on the blossom end. An eggplant should feel heavy for its size. Press gently on the skin—it should cause a dent that immediately springs back when you release. If you can't dent it, it's too young; if it doesn't spring back, it's too old. Avoid those with dark brown or rust-colored spots or those with shriveled tips or cracks.

Storing: Keep in cool place (about 50°F) up to one week. If your house is too warm, keep it wrapped in organic, bleach-free wax paper and then in a plastic bag in the refrigerator for only a few days. If stored longer than that, it will probably look good, but it will taste bitter. Cut eggplant can be stored, well covered, in the refrigerator for up to 2 days.

Preparation for cooking: Do not eat raw eggplant. It's up to you whether you want to eat the peel or not. You should buy only small eggplant, but if you have a large one, you probably should peel it. If eggplant is to be cooked for a long time, don't peel it; for a short time, peel it. It's easier to remove the skin of an eggplant after it has been cooked. Do not undercook eggplant as you would other vegetables. Many cookbooks will tell you to soak or salt the eggplant to remove bitter juices. Avoid doing this, because it leaches out the water-soluble vitamins. Instead, buy small eggplant, which are more likely to be sweet and tender. If you already have a large eggplant, it may not cook well because it contains too much water. To draw out the bitter juices, slice and sprinkle both sides with salt. Let sit for 30 minutes, rinse very well to remove the salt, and dry with paper towels

> **Note:** Eggplant absorbs oil like a sponge, so never fry it, unless you want to eat a lot of fat.

Steam: Cut into uniform pieces. Steam for 15-20 minutes.

Bake: Slice in half lengthwise. Place on buttered cookie sheet with cut side down. Bake in pre-heated 350°F oven for 30 minutes.

Freeze: If you like, add a little lemon juice (if your baby is old enough for citrus) to puréed eggplant to keep it from discoloring. Freeze cooked eggplant using the *Food Cube Method* and keep for up to 2 months.

Green Beans, see Beans

Greens

Baby must be at least 9 months old to eat cooked greens, 10 months old for finely chopped raw greens. See warning about nitrates in collard greens and spinach.

Super Green Veggies include beet greens, collard greens, dandelion greens, kale, mustard greens, sorrel, spinach, Swiss chard, and turnip greens. Light green iceberg lettuce is a nutritional waste of time—go for the dark, leafy greens. Buy at least 2 bunches at a time when making baby food cubes because they shrink a lot during cooking. You can use the dandelion greens from your backyard, but make sure that they are totally organic and have never been sprayed with chemical fertilizers or weed killers. The dandelion greens I've cooked up from my backyard tasted very, very bitter.

In season: Beet greens, June through October; collard greens, dandelion greens, kale, and mustard greens, January through April; sorrel, July through October; spinach, all year, peak in April and May; Swiss chard, July through October; turnip greens, October through March.

Choosing: Buy greens that are loose and not in plastic bags. Greens are very short-lived, so you should be able to have a good, close look at each leaf. Leaves should be young and tender with no thick veins, bright green, crisp and not wilted, insect-free, and have no bruises, decaying spots, or slime. Don't buy greens with yellow, red, or brown spots. Beet greens should contain red color. Swiss chard stems should be thick and white or red. Dandelion greens should have part of the root still attached. If the supermarket regularly squirts a wet mist on the greens, check them carefully for dark or decaying spots, as wet greens rot quickly.

Storing: Rush home from the supermarket and cook and freeze greens the second you walk in the door. If you must store them, wrap them in white paper towels and place in organic, bleach-free wax paper-lined plastic bags in a cold part of the refrigerator or the vegetable crisper. Use them fast—within a day or two. Greens are tough to get into a plastic bag: turn the plastic bag inside out and with your hand inside the bag, grab the greens and turn bag right side out while enclosing the greens.

Preparation for cooking: Discard leaves with a lot of yellow or decay. Trim off any thick stems and small blemishes before cooking—stems are much more difficult to remove after cooking. If you wish, coarsely chop into uniform pieces. Wash each leaf under cold running tap water. For leaves with a lot of sand, such as spinach, wash them this way: first swish them in a sink full of lukewarm water to send sand to the bottom of sink. Drain the sink, making sure all sand is cleaned out. Refill sink, this time with cold water, swish, and drain again. Repeat with cold water until no sand is left in the sink. The more curly the leaves, the more places dirt could hide, and the more thoroughly you should wash them.

Preparing kale: Kale is a *Super Duper Green*. Get your baby used to the flavor and stir a kale cube into your baby's *Super Porridge* as often as possible! To prepare kale, swish in a sink full of cold water. Remove stems before cooking.

Here is the best method I've found from my experience de-stemming countless numbers of kale leaves. (If I had a nickel for every kale leaf I've prepared for my babies, I wouldn't have had to write this book!) First fold the leaf in half along the stem line. While holding leaves in your right hand, use left hand to hold the stem on the bottom and rip upwards using your right hand in a "hinged palm-up" motion from bottom to side. On large and long leaves you will have to move your right hand up and rip several times to get the whole stem off. Discard the stem in your left hand. Then use both left and right hands to rip leaves into smaller uniform pieces. (If you are left-handed, change left hand to right hand and vice versa in these instructions.)

I feed my baby a LOT of organic kale and I usually batch cook three kale bunches at a time, so I had to find a quick and efficient way of ripping kale apart from its stem. It is important that you remove the stem BEFORE cooking, because it's more trouble to remove after cooking—even if the kale is not hot.

To reduce flavor: Greens have a strong flavor, which some babies dislike. If your baby refuses to eat greens, try steaming them uncovered, which will reduce the strong flavor. Cooking uncovered does cause nutrient loss, though. Instead, to hide the strong flavor of greens, try mixing them with a more pleasant tasting food, such as mashed banana. I reduce their strong flavor by mixing only one food cube with a full cup of *Super Porridge*.

Steam: Steam whole leaves 5 minutes; pieces 3 minutes.

> **Tip:** Greens like spinach are sometimes too soggy for adults after cooking. Remove excess liquid by squeezing between two dinner plates.

Raw greens: Greens can be used in salads and in place of lettuce on sandwiches. However, for these purposes, use only very young, small, tender leaves.

Purée: As you purée cooked kale, it will have the consistency of tiny hard flakes in dark green water. Push the purée against a spoon to squeeze off as much water as possible and then spoon into ice cube tray. The "drier" the kale, the less ice cube trays you'll need. If it's too dry in your baby's *Super Porridge*, add a little milk to the *Super Porridge*. When you are done puréeing, scrape and pour what's left in the processor into a strainer and you may get enough for a whole new cube. I actually FORCE myself to drink the leftover green water! My life insurance company gives me a discount because of this! I call it "self-flagellation for good health."

Freezing: Freeze puréed greens using the *Food Cube Method* and keep for up to 2 months.

Kale, see Greens

Lettuce

Baby must be at least 10-11 months old to eat finely diced lettuce.

Besides fiber and a little vitamin A, tasteless anemic-green iceberg lettuce is a nutritional waste of time for your baby (and you). Go for the greens, dark greens, instead. I include it here only for completeness. Romaine lettuce is more nutritious than iceberg.

In season: Available year round; peak May through July.

Choosing: Iceberg leaves should be crisp, bright, and light green, but not pale. The head should give slightly when squeezed; it should be firm, but not hard. Don't buy iceberg lettuce if it is irregularly shaped or if the leaves are brown at the tips. Romaine lettuce is more oval than iceberg and darker green. Its leaves are looser and not so crisp. Buy lettuce that is being refrigerated in the store and not stacked up on a middle display box at room temperature. The latter may last only a day once you bring it home. **Storing:** Do not remove leaves for storing. Store lettuce in paper bags in the refrigerator. Or wrap in white paper towels, then store tightly-wrapped in plastic bag with air holes or lettuce crisper in refrigerator for up to one week. Lettuce is tough to get into a plastic bag: turn the plastic bag inside out and with your hand inside the bag, grab the head of lettuce and turn bag right side out while enclosing the lettuce. Be sure to tear lettuce for salads immediately before serving—not before storing—to retain maximum vitamin C and to prevent wilting.

Preparation: Don't discard the outer (wrapper) leaves if they are undamaged, as they have most of the nutrients. Remove core of lettuce by cutting it out. Or, better than cutting, which causes brown spots: Hold the head with its core end down and smack it sharply on the counter to loosen the core, and then twist the core and pull it out. Wash leaves by rinsing under cold running tap water, letting water flow between leaves. Shake off water, drain well or dry with clean towels. Tip: Line a colander with nylon net for rinsing lettuce. Then just lift the lettuce out of the netting and squeeze gently to drain.

Freezing: Don't.

> **Tip:** Never put salt on lettuce—it will toughen it and wilt it. To keep salad really fresh, nest your empty salad bowl inside a slightly larger bowl containing water and freeze. Both bowls should be freezer-safe, of course. Weight down the inner bowl so it will not float on the water in the larger bowl. The ice layer that forms between the two bowls will keep the salad in the inner bowl cool and crisp .

> **Tip:** To prevent greens from becoming limp, place a small inverted bowl/saucer at the bottom of your salad bowl so that excess water will collect under it. For picnics, first put salad dressing on bottom under the bowl (after the salad has drained well and you have poured off the water) and toss immediately before serving. You won't need to pack the salad bottle and bring it home. Tip: When using oil and vinegar as a salad dressing, first pour on the vinegar and second the oil, otherwise the oil will just slide off the lettuce.

> **Tip:** Use old spice jars or baby food jars to hold salad dressing for travel.

Mushrooms

Baby must be at least 9 months old to eat cooked mushrooms. Raw mushrooms and raw mushroom pieces are choking hazards and should not be given to a baby under 4 years old as they are a choking hazard.

Unless you're a mushroom expert, don't eat mushrooms from your backyard. Some very pretty harmless-looking white mushrooms grow wild, but contain poisons. Mushrooms are widely thought to have no nutritive value, but they do contain potassium, fiber, and the B vitamins.

Equivalents: ½ pound of fresh mushroom = 2 cups sliced.

In season: Available year round; least in August; peak October through June.

Choosing: It's better to buy loose mushrooms than packaged mushrooms, so that you can get a good look at them. Select clean, firm, young, small or medium-sized fresh mushrooms that have a uniform color of white, off-white, or light tan. The caps should be bright, smooth, and tight around the stem, revealing little or none of the gills (paper thin tissue under the cap). Gills should be light tan. Avoid mushrooms that are slimy, shriveled, spongy in texture, discolored, bruised, or pitted. Don't buy mushrooms that are bleached (label must inform you of this) or those with preservatives. As mushrooms mature, their caps open and expose more of the gills, and they get darker in color. Mature mushrooms have a stronger flavor, which some people prefer. You can buy mature mushrooms, but they will have a shorter storage life, of course.

Storing: Mushrooms are mostly water. Don't wash them before storing; clean immediately before using. Place in refrigerator in an open container, such as the cardboard container they came in or a folded back open paper bag, and cover loosely with a wet paper towel wrung half dry to keep them from shriveling. They should keep for up to 3 days. Or, cook and cover mushrooms and store in refrigerator up to 4 days.

Raw mushrooms: Don't feed raw mushrooms to your baby as a finger food. They are slippery and hard to chew. Your baby may swallow one whole before she gets a chance to chew it; therefore, they are a choking hazard.

Preparation for cooking: Do not peel mushrooms. Remove any tough stems. Never soak mushrooms, for they absorb water and become waterlogged. To clean, wipe gently with a wet paper towel or a sterile soft toothbrush (no need to buy a fancy mushroom brush). Or, rinse quickly under running cold tap water and drain between paper towels. If some mushrooms are much larger than others, cut in half lengthwise for a more uniform size for cooking.

Steam: Don't steam mushrooms, as the mushrooms' moisture will drip out the holes into the boiling water.

Sauté: Clean and slice or chop mushrooms. Place 2 or 3 tablespoons of butter for each pound of mushrooms in a heavy frying pan over medium-high heat. Add mushrooms and sauté, uncovered, for 3 or 4 minutes, stirring so that the butter coats the mushrooms. If mushrooms get too hard, next time try sautéing over a higher heat.

Bake: Bake, covered, for 15 minutes in a pre-heated 350°F oven.

Freezing: You can freeze whole raw mushrooms without blanching. They'll lose their texture and won't be good to eat raw after thawing, but they will be good for cooking. Cooked mushrooms with their pan juices (puréed or not) keep in the freezer for up to 2 months. To use up leftover mushrooms before they go bad, purée and freeze them using the *Food Cube Method*. Use in soups, stews, sauces, etc.

Tip: An egg slicer is great for quickly slicing mushrooms into uniform pieces.

Mustard greens, see Greens

Okra

Baby must be at least 8 months old to eat cooked okra.

Okra is a *Super Green Veggie* used more for thickening than flavoring. Its gluey, syrupy juice typically is used to thicken soups and stews, such as the Southern gumbo and Creole stews. Okra combines well with tomatoes and corn. It has good amounts of vitamins A and C, along with other nutrients. Okra can be eaten raw in salads.

Equivalents: 22-28 pods = 1 pound = 5 cups.

In season: Available year round in the South; peak June through October.

Choosing: Select small, crisp, bright-green okra pods that are less than 4½ inches long—ideally from 2 to 3½ inches. Their tips should bend with very slight pressure. Avoid those that are flabby, wilted, pale, tough, woody, stiff, or those with hard bodies. Don't buy those that are pitted or those with black spots.

Storing: Store okra in the vegetable crisper in the refrigerator for up to 3 days. Make sure there is no moisture on the okra and that it is very dry before you put it in the container. Any water on the skin will turn it slimy. Cooked okra can be stored, covered, in the refrigerator for up to 4 days.

Preparation for cooking: Too much contact with water makes okra sticky, so rinse lightly and quickly, using a vegetable brush to remove the fuzz. Don't peel okra. Cut off the stems carefully, so as not to pierce the pods. Leave small pods whole. Slice larger pods in half. Don't overcook okra; it will become slippery and gummy.

Steam: Steam whole okra for 15 minutes.

Bake: Bake on cookie sheet for 30 minutes at 350°F.

Freeze: Purée and freeze using the *Food Cube Method* and keep for up to 2 months.

Onions

Baby must be at least 9 months old to eat cooked onion, and 18 months old to eat raw onion. Raw onion might cause digestive problems.

Equivalents: 1 medium onion = ¾ cup chopped or sliced.

In season: Available all year.

Choosing: Select onions that are firm, hard, bright, and shiny. The outer skin should be dry, papery, and crackly. Check under the skin for dark, moldy areas. Examine the neck closely—it should be small, tightly closed, firm, completely dry, and free from decay. Avoid spongy, soft onions or onions with hollow woody centers. Don't buy onions that are sprouting, those with green sunburn spots, and those with any wet spots. Buy onions loose, so that you can examine each one. Or buy them bagged in netting, but make sure you check each one for decay, because one bad onion spreads its decay to the others.

Storing: Store in a cool, dry, place with good air circulation for up to 2 weeks. Spread onions out in a single layer and store in one of those wire mesh hanging baskets, which allows air circulation. Or use an old clean pair of pantyhose. Onions will store loose, in the refrigerator for up to 2 months, but they pass their odor to other refrigerator inhabitants. Onions that have been cut, if wrapped tightly in covered glass container, will keep in the refrigerator for up to 3 days. To prevent odor from getting into other foods, store cut onions in a glass jar with an airtight screw lid; they will keep a few days longer stored this way. Cooked onions in a tightly covered container will keep in the refrigerator for up to 5 days. Do not store onions near potatoes, because each releases gasses that shorten the others' storage life.

Tip: Rub butter over the cut part of an onion before storing in the refrigerator to keep it fresh longer.

Preparation for cooking: Wash, peel off outer skin, and cut out any damage. Leave small uniform-sized onions whole, or cut large onions into halves, quarters, or slices. To prevent the center of the onion from "telescoping" (poking out during cooking), cut a small X into each stem end.

Steam: Steam whole onions for 30 minutes.

Bake: Remove outer skin from whole onion. Bake for 30 minutes until outside is crisp and inside is tender.

Freezing: Onions don't need blanching before freezing. Peel and chop onions—use your processor to chop to save tears. Freeze them for up to 1 year by wrapping chopped onion in organic, bleach-free wax paper and then in a plastic bag. Many recipes call for only a little chopped raw onion. Chop and freeze leftover onion to use for these recipes. You may want to pre-measure by tablespoon, half-cup, or whatever measure your favorite recipes require. Freeze pre-measured amounts.

Eating raw onions: If you find that raw onions are too strong, slice and separate into onion rings and soak in cold water for about one hour.

Dried onions: Slice onions paper thin and separate into rings. Spread on baking sheet and let dry in a 275°F oven for about 45 minutes until they are dry and lightly browned. Chop and refrigerate in an airtight screw-top glass jar and they will keep for up to one month. Use in recipes as you would dried onions.

Tips for less tears: When you cut into an onion it releases an enzyme, called allinase, that converts into sulfenic acid molecules, which spontaneously rearrange to form syn-propanethial-S-oxide, the chemical that triggers your tears. To prevent your eyes from tearing, wear your swim or ski goggles or wrap-around sun glasses. Start slicing at the top of the onion and cut off the root end last. Or, peel them under cold running water to dilute the gas before it gets released into the air—you will lose some nutrients this way and raise your water bill. Or, keep rinsing only your hands under running water. Refrigerate onions to make them cool before peeling to slow down the gas. Keep your mouth closed tightly while peeling. Work under your kitchen's exhaust fan. Or try holding an unlit match between your teeth; the match's sulfur reacts with the gas and helps reduce tears. Or use your food processor instead of cutting onions manually.

Parsley

Baby must be at least 8 months old to eat cooked parsley; 9 months old to eat finely chopped raw parsley.

Parsley, too often used as a decorative garnish to be dismissed with the dirty plate, should be eaten, and eaten often! This herb is a powerhouse of nutrition, rich in vitamins A, C, and iron. Herbs are easy to grow in your kitchen. See *How to Grow Herbs on Your Windowsill*, page 601. You can just snip some fresh leaves off the living plant with clean scissors (can't get any fresher than that!) for use in omelets, cereals, etc. Always add parsley to cooked dishes immediately before the end of the cooking time; cooked parsley tastes bitter. In your favorite recipes, substitute 1 tablespoon chopped fresh herbs for 1 teaspoon dried herbs. In other words, 3 parts fresh herbs equal 1 part dried herbs.

In season: Available year round; slight peak October through December.

Choosing: Fresh parsley comes in flat leaf and curly leaf varieties. Either way, buy only crisp, fresh, bright green leaves and never those that are yellow or brown. Avoid parsley that has watery areas or is wilted.

Preparation for storing or freezing: Discard tough stems. Cut off any damaged, yellow, or wilted leaves. Rinse well under running tap water. Gently shake to remove most of the water.

Storing: Wrap prepared parsley in white paper towels and refrigerate in plastic bags for up to 4 days.

Freezing parsley (and other herbs): Prepare as above and pat dry with white paper towels. (You don't have to blanch herbs before freezing. You can blanch for 10 seconds, if you wish, but why destroy nutrients when you don't have to?) Make sure the leaves are very dry so they won't stick together when frozen. You can freeze fresh herbs whole, cut into large pieces, or chopped into small pieces. Place them into the freezer in a freezer proof container, or wrap in organic, bleach-free wax paper and then in a plastic freezer bag. When needed, cut off the amount you want and immediately put the rest back into the freezer. Freeze for up to a year. (To prevent basil leaves from losing color, dip in boiling water for 2-3 seconds before freezing.)

Another way to freeze fresh herbs: Chop or purée herbs and place in ice cube trays, cover with water and freeze. Store cubes in a freezer-safe container. Freeze for up to 4 months. Frozen cubes can be dropped, unthawed, into stews or soups to flavor and add nutrients. Or, let frozen herb cubes sit in a strainer over a bowl or glass until the ice melts. For quicker thawing, melt the ice cube in a saucepan on the stove top and pour through a strainer.

Herb vinegars: Make your own herb-flavored vinegars by placing fresh, clean herbs (not basil) in apple cider vinegar in a tightly covered airtight screw-top jar in the refrigerator. Make sure the jar and top is sterile before filling. It's ready for use after 2 weeks. Strain. Keep refrigerated.

Drying parsley and other herbs: Dried herbs are concentrated fresh herbs. Drying causes the same flavor concentration in herbs as it does in fruits. 1 teaspoon of dried herbs is equal to 3 teaspoons of fresh herbs, so be careful about adding dried herbs to your recipes. Adding too little is no problem, you can always add more; but if you add too much, you've blown it.

To dry herbs, such as parsley, oregano, sage, basil, mint, and others, rinse them and gently shake off excess water. Herbs can be dried in bunches by hanging them leaves down with the stems tied together like an upside-down bouquet. This will allow the essential oils in the stems to flow into the leaves, making them more flavorful. To prevent the herbs from getting dusty while drying or getting broiled in the sun, and preventing leaves from falling all over the floor, place the bouquet upside down in a paper bag. Cut several holes or slits in the bag for air circulation. Tie the paper bag closed at the stem end of the bouquet. Let it hang in a warm, dry place for up to 3 weeks, until the leaves are so dry that they will crumble.

Herbs dry much faster in your conventional oven, of course, than they do hanging upside down in a paper bag. Pre-heat your oven to 175°F.

Spread herbs loosely on a dry cookie sheet and place in oven. Wait two minutes and turn the oven off. Let the herbs sit in the oven with the door closed for about 8 hours or overnight. (If you have a gas oven, you can use only the heat from the pilot light to dry your herbs. Place the cookie sheet in the oven and let them dry for several days.)

When dry, remove the leaves from the stems and store them tightly covered in a small glass jar away from air, light, and heat. You can crush the leaves before storing, but their oils keep better if you leave them whole; crush them just before using for maximum flavor. Store them in a dry, cool, dark place in glass jars. Don't use paper or cardboard containers, because they will absorb the essential oils and the herbs will be tasteless. I like to keep my dried herbs out in the kitchen, keep covered with jar lid to prevent light from penetrating. Keep dried herbs away from any heat source: stoves, refrigerators, etc. The glass jars should be as small as possible, no bigger than the 4 ounce glass jars of baby food or mustard jar. The larger the jar, the more flavor loss from frequent opening to the air. Use a small piece of masking tape on the bottom of jar to label with date.

Herb butter: See recipe on page 482.

Growing: Grow parsley and other herbs in your kitchen—pages 601-604.

> **Tip:** Chew parsley after a meal—it is a delicious and natural breath freshener.

> **Tip:** If your recipe calls for fresh parsley and you're out of it, use celery leaves.

Peas
(Green Peas or Shell Peas)

Baby must be at least 7 months old to eat cooked puréed peas. Whole peas are a choking hazard until at least 3 years, but whole peas smashed lightly with a fork make a nutritious finger food for older babies.

The peas in this section are those where the pod is not edible. See Beans section for green beans and other edible-pod peas. Also, see dried split peas in the legume section.

Peas are very perishable and quickly turn from sugar to starch, so eat them as soon as possible. Don't remove them from their pods until the last possible minute. Peas right from your backyard garden, when shelled and eaten immediately after the picking, are sweet and delicious. I find shelling them tedious. My family eats fresh peas very rarely—only when they come straight from a relative's or our home garden. However, my baby eats dried split peas as part of his *Super Porridge* very frequently.

Equivalents: 1 pound of pods = 1 cup shelled peas.

In season: Available March through November; peak March through June.

Choosing: Select crisp, bright green pods that are filled with peas, but not bulging. Avoid those that are flat, dull, bloated, light green or yellowed, gray-spotted, mildewed, or wilted, even just a little wilted. Buying frozen peas (the "petite" ones are best) is an option, but do not use these for frozen food cubes. Remember: **Never refreeze thawed baby food.** Canned peas, which are completely tasteless, should be outlawed.

Storing: Eat them the same day you buy or pick them. If you must store, refrigerate in pods wrapped in organic, bleach-free wax paper and then in a plastic bag for up to 4 days. Store cooked peas in refrigerator for up to 4 days.

Preparation for cooking: Remove peas from pods. Place in colander or large strainer and rinse under tap water.

Steam: Steam peas (removed from pods) for 8 minutes.

Freezing: Freeze puréed peas using the *Food Cube Method* or *Tray-Freeze Method* and keep for up to 2 months.

> **Tip:** Boiling causes a great loss in nutrients, but if you choose to boil, cook the peas IN the pods. The peas will come out of the pods during boiling and you won't have to manually remove the pods.

Peppers
(Bell Peppers, Sweet Green Peppers, Sweet Red Peppers)

Baby must be at least 10 months old to eat finely grated sweet peppers.

The peppers you feed to baby are the sweet green or sweet red ones, not the hot peppers! By the way, all peppers start out green and turn to another color (or stay green) when ripe. Peppers are a good source of that unstable nutrient, vitamin C. It is better to serve them to baby puréed or diced raw because cooking destroys this vitamin.

Equivalents: 1 large bell pepper = 1 cup chopped.

In season: Available year round; slight peak May through October. This vegetable is OK to buy out of season—the vitamin C content is great for preventing winter colds.

Choosing: Select firm peppers with bright color that feel heavy for their size. Look for glossy, thick, smooth skins. Buy only peppers with their stems still on. Try to find peppers without that darned wax coating, which causes accelerated bacterial growth inside peppers. Also, wax used on produce is supposedly safe, but it may contain pesticide residues. Avoid soft, flabby, wrinkled, wilted, cracked, or spotted peppers or those with thin, flimsy walls. Look carefully for soft watery spots, which reveal decay underneath.

Storing: Don't keep peppers at room temperature. Place immediately in refrigerator wrapped in organic, bleach-free wax paper and then in a plastic bag or put them in a paper bag in the vegetable crisper. Keep for not more than 5 days. Place cut pepper in a sealed container and refrigerate for up to 2 days.

Preparation: Wash and remove stem. Slice lengthwise and remove seeds, membranes, and pith. (The pith is the soft, spongy core in the center.) If you cut carefully, the seeds and pith will come out in one piece. Purée pepper for young baby, or dice it well for an older baby. Slices of green or red peppers are great for decorative touches on toddler food. Or stuff pepper halves with ground nut/seed and cheese mixtures for older children.

Freezing: No need for blanching diced or sliced peppers before freezing. Purée and freeze raw peppers using the *Food Cube Method*, or slice or dice peppers and freeze using the *Nested Plastic Bag Method*. Freeze for up to 6 months.

> **Tip:** When you are chopping up one green pepper, chop up an extra one or two and freeze using the *Nested Plastic Bag Method* for future use in soups, stews, and other recipes.

> **Tip:** Before baking stuffed peppers, rub skins with olive oil to prevent them from splitting.

> **Tip:** When freezing green peppers whole, as for stuffed peppers, slice off tops, remove seeds and membrane, blanch, and freeze peppers nested one inside the other to save freezer space.

Potatoes, White

Baby must be at least 7 months old to eat cooked white potatoes.

The potato is a tuber, not a root vegetable. To preserve as much as possible of the high vitamin C content, cook potatoes in their skins. As usual, nutrients are found in large amounts in the skins and just underneath. By the way, potatoes can be eaten raw, and their vitamin C is intact since no cooking has destroyed it, but eat raw potatoes immediately after you cut them, because they oxidize very rapidly. Serve cooked potatoes puréed (for adults, they are called mashed) with a little yogurt or cottage cheese (made smooth in the blender) instead of high-fat sour cream. Potatoes aren't fattening; it's the butter, sour cream, and other fatty flavorings that we add to potatoes that are fattening. Avoid dehydrated instant potatoes, which are almost vitamin C-less and have chemical preservatives added.

Equivalents: 1 medium potato = ½ pound.

In season: Available year round.

Choosing: Buy uniform medium-sized (½-pound) baking or general purpose potatoes that are firm, unshriveled, relatively smooth, and fairly well-shaped. Give the potato a gentle squeeze—its skin should fit tight. There should be very little peeling, eyes, and sprouts, and no deep cracks or sticky or decaying spots. One bad potato spoils the others, so fish around and do a careful check of all potatoes in the bag.

Don't buy potatoes with green discoloration. Green patches caused by sunlight have a chemical called solanine, which is similar to nicotine and toxic in large doses. Green patches caused by artificial light, rather than sunlight, are not poisonous, but how do you know which light caused the green? Don't take a chance and avoid potatoes with any green spots.

Don't buy a potato with black eyes, which indicates that the potato was accidentally frozen. Look for dirty potatoes—potatoes grow underground and naturally come out dirty. If they have been commercially washed, they are sometimes more expensive and may have absorbed water and lost nutrients. (Some disagree: They say to buy clean potatoes, because dirt harbors microorganisms. Use your own judgment.)

Storing: Don't wash potatoes until just before use because moisture will cause decay. Store potatoes in a paper bag or something that will allow air circulation and moisture release. Or use a leg from an old clean pair of pantyhose. Store unwashed potatoes in a cool (about 50°F), dry, dark place for up to 2 months. Make sure you keep them completely out of natural sunlight to prevent greening. If you store them at room temperature, do so for no more than 2 weeks.

Don't store potatoes near onions, because each releases gasses that shorten the other's storage life.

If you refrigerate potatoes, let them sit for a day or two at room temperature before using. Refrigeration changes the starch in potatoes to sugar; room temperature will change the sugar back to starch.

Leftover cooked potatoes will keep in a tightly closed container in the refrigerator for up to 5 days.

Some say to place peeled potatoes in cold water to prevent darkening, but I disagree because this causes nutrients to leach out. Instead, store cut or peeled potatoes in an airtight glass container.

Preparation for cooking: Scrub with vegetable brush under cold water. Remove any damaged areas, and eyes and sprouts, which are toxic. Cut away the green areas; don't worry, the solanine in the green area doesn't "spread" into the surrounding white area.

Steam: Steam 30 minutes for whole, unpeeled potatoes; 8 minutes for ½-inch slices.

Boil: Boil enough water to cover potatoes. Place washed, whole, unpeeled potatoes in boiling water, cover pot, and cook for 20-30 minutes until tender.

Bake: Scrub and wash the skin and dry with a white paper towel. You may wish to rub a little butter on the skin to keep it soft and prevent cracking during baking. Pierce potatoes in several places with a fork. Place on baking sheet or directly on oven rack. For a medium sized potato, bake at 325°F for 1½ hours; at 400°F for about 50 minutes to an hour; at 450°F for about 45 minutes. Potatoes are done if they feel soft when pressed or when a fork goes into the center easily. A metal kebab skewer inserted through a whole potato lengthwise will cut its baking time in half. Or use the metal prongs sold at kitchen stores for baking potatoes. A potato boiled for 5 minutes will bake in half the time. It is not true that a potato wrapped in aluminum foil will bake faster. Foil slows down the heat transfer from the oven and does not allow the peel to get crisp.

Tip: If you have many potatoes to bake, place them on their ends in a 12-cup muffin tin.

Tip: Use leftover baked potatoes, diced, for some breakfast hash browns.

Tip: For a nice presentation, slit the baked potato in half and, with your hands, squeeze the skins causing the flesh to pop up out of the half.

Leftover baked potatoes: See recipes for leftover baked potatoes in Part VI: *Potato Skins, Baked Potato Cubes,* and *At-the-Ready Frozen Baked Potatoes.*

Mash: You don't have to make mashed potatoes with boiled potatoes, use baked potatoes for more nutrition. Mash cooked potatoes with a fork or potato masher or an electric mixer. You can try using your blender, but it may cause the potatoes to take on a plastic consistency. Add a quarter cup of warm liquid (milk) and 1 or 2 teaspoons of softened butter for each medium potato, if you wish. Do not add flavorings (herbs, grated cheese, etc.) into mashed potatoes until immediately before serving.

Tip: At the last minute, stir in ½-1 cup of shredded cheddar cheese into mashed potatoes and they will contain streaks of gold.

Leftover mashed potatoes: Coat leftover mashed potatoes with flour, wheat germ, or ground oatmeal and fry in a little butter or vegetable oil. See recipe for *Potato Burgers* on page 477. Or place them in a casserole dish, brush top with butter, cover, and bake 30 minutes at 250°F.

Freezing: Mashed potatoes will keep well-wrapped in the freezer for up to 10 months. Freeze whole baked potatoes for up to 3 months; thaw in the refrigerator overnight and bake at 350°F for 30 minutes. Bake frozen, unthawed whole baked potatoes at 350°F for 45 minutes.

Reheating: Dip whole cooked baked potatoes in hot water for a few minutes and re-bake for 20 minutes at 350°F.

Tip: Before boiling potatoes whole, peel a small band of skin around the "waistline" of the potato to prevent the skin from bursting.

Tip: If you have too many potatoes, store a few apples in with them to help prevent them from sprouting.

Pumpkins, see Squash, Winter

Rhubarb

Baby must be at least 9 months old to eat cooked rhubarb. Never feed baby (or yourself) raw rhubarb.

Rhubarb is technically a vegetable, but frequently referred to as a fruit due to its flavor.

Equivalents: 1 pound rhubarb = 3 cups slices = 2 cups cooked.

In season: Available January through August; peak May.

Choosing: Select bright, shiny, firm, crisp rhubarb that is a good red or pink color. Stalks should be neither too thick or too thin. Avoid wilted, flabby, stringy, or rough-textured rhubarb.

Storing: Store covered in organic, bleach-free wax paper and then in a plastic bag in refrigerator for up to one week.

Preparation for cooking: Do not eat rhubarb leaves; they are toxic and can be fatal. Eat only the stalks. Discard leaves, and wash and slice the stalks into 1½ inch slices.

Steam: Steam 20 minutes.

Bake: Bake in covered dish in a 350°F pre-heated oven for about 30 minutes.

Serve: Purée cooked rhubarb stalks and add about 3 tablespoons maple syrup for each pound. Add thickener (ground oatmeal, wheat germ, whole grain bread crumbs) if too watery. Store leftover cooked purée in refrigerator tightly covered for up to 5 days.

Freezing: Freeze using the *Food Cube Method* and keep for up to 6 months.

Rutabagas and Turnips

Baby must be at least 9 months old to eat cooked rutabagas or turnips. See warning about nitrates.

These two root vegetables are very similar to each other, with rutabagas having the stronger flavor.

Equivalents: 2-3 medium sized rutabagas/turnips = 1 pound.

In season: Available all year; peak October through March.

Choosing: Choose those that are smooth, firm, solid, well-shaped, and heavy for their size. They should be no more than 3 or 4 inches in diameter.

If turnips come with their green tops, make sure that they are fresh-looking and green. For turnip greens, see *Greens*.

Storing: Store turnips wrapped in organic, bleach-free wax paper and then plastic bag in refrigerator for up to 1 week. As with other root vegetables, immediately remove the greens so that they do not pull moisture from the root. Store rutabagas for up to two weeks in the refrigerator and up to 1 week at room temperature.

Preparation for cooking: Wash, peel with a vegetable peeler, and cut into uniform, large pieces. Don't eat the peel because it tastes bitter. Do not overcook.

Steam: Steam for 10 minutes.

Bake: Place pieces in shallow baking dish. Dot with butter and/or sprinkle with a little water. Bake at 400°F for 30-45 minutes.

Freezing: Purée and freeze using the *Food Cube Method* and keep for up to 10 months.

Snap Beans, see Green Beans

Sorrel, see Greens

Spinach, see Greens

Squash, Summer

Baby must be at least 7 months old to eat cooked summer squash, 10 months old to eat raw grated summer squash.

The many summer squashes include: chayote, English yellow, sunburst, yellow crookneck, and the zucchinis (also called Italian marrows or Italian squash). These squash grow quickly and are harvested while their seeds are still small and immature and their rinds are still thin and tender. Cook and purée squash for your baby. Or serve grated raw summer squash as a *Healthy Addition* to tofu, cottage cheese, yogurt, etc. Shredded zucchini is great in bread.

Equivalents: 1 pound summer squash = 3½ cups sliced.

In season: Available year round; peak July through September.

Choosing: Select young, small or medium summer squash—they are soft and moist. Skin should be tender enough to be easily punctured with your fingernail. Skin also should be bright, smooth, glossy, and have good color.

Zucchini skin should be bright green. Summer squash should feel firm and heavy for their size. They should have an inch of stem still attached. The best size is about six inches long and one inch in diameter or smaller. Don't buy summer squash that is dull, flabby, soggy, dry, hard, tough, or with soft spots.

Storing: Refrigerate uncut covered in organic, unbleached wax paper and then in plastic bags for up to 5 days.

Preparation for cooking: Cut off ends and discard. Do not peel. Cook small, whole zucchini that are uniform in size, or cut larger zucchini into uniform slices.

Steam: Steam small, whole squash for 12 minutes. Steam slices for 5 minutes.

Bake: Bake in covered baking dish in 350°F oven for 25 minutes. No need to add water for baking.

Freezing: Purée cooked squash and freeze using the Food Cube Method. Grate raw zucchini and freeze using the Nested Plastic Bag method. Pre-measure 1 cup per bag or the amount needed for zucchini bread or your favorite recipe.

> **Note:** Chayote squash should be peeled. It will keep longer than other summer squash in the refrigerator—up to 2 weeks.

Squash, Winter

Baby must be at least 6 months old to eat cooked winter squash.

Winter squash have thick, hard shells and fully-grown seeds, unlike summer squash, with their thin rinds and immature seeds. Winter squash have those wonderful fall colors (indicating a high vitamin A content), such as deep-orange pumpkins and dark-green acorn squash. Other winter squash are banana, buttercup, butternut, and Hubbard. Less commonly-known are Chinese, delicata, golden acorn, and sweet dumpling.

Equivalents: 1 pound of raw winter squash = 1 cup cooked and puréed.

In season: September through March.

Choosing: Select those with bright, hard, tough, thick shells that feel heavy for their size. Variations in skin color are OK, but don't buy squash with tender or soft rinds or those with soft, decaying spots, mold, or cuts. If squash is cut, make sure that it has a bright orange or yellow color and that it is not stringy. Small pumpkins are best for eating; large pumpkins are best for jack-o-lanterns.

Storing: Whole winter squash will keep for up to 2 months if you keep them in a cool, dark, dry, and well ventilated spot. Store cut pieces wrapped in organic, unbleached wax paper and then in plastic bags in the refrigerator for up to 5 days.

Preparation for cooking one medium squash (1 pound): Cut squash in half lengthwise. Remove seeds and fibers, but leave skin intact. Or, peel squash and remove seeds and fiber. Cut into 1 inch cubes. If you're really having trouble cutting a very hard squash, try microwaving the whole squash very briefly (30 seconds or so), just enough to soften it up a little. Pierce several places with a fork first to prevent an explosion.

Steam: Steam large squash pieces for 25 minutes.

Bake: Place prepared squash halves in a baking pan. Spread cut surfaces with butter or lemon juice (if your baby is old enough for citrus) if you wish. (Some suggest to place them cut side down, but I find baking them cut side up gives them a better flavor.) Bake in pre-heated 350°F oven for 30 to 45 minutes, depending on size. Peel or scoop out flesh and purée for baby. Or, place cubes into uncovered baking dish. Sprinkle with butter, lemon juice (if your baby is old enough for citrus) and/or water. Bake in pre-heated 350°F oven for 45 minutes.

Baking a whole squash: Place on a dry baking pan. Bake in a pre-heated 350°F oven for about one hour until done. After cool, slice off top and scoop out seeds and membranes.

Testing a whole squash for doneness: Test by wrapping your finger in a towel and pressing to see if it feels soft. Don't burn yourself! Or, test for doneness by piercing with fork—squash should be tender.

> **Tip:** To remove the flesh from squash halves, especially acorn squash, try using a serrated scoop or grapefruit spoon. It will cut out the flesh easily and cleanly.

Purée: From squash halves, peel or scoop out flesh and purée. Do not feed peel from winter squash to baby. After baking, cooled squash peel very easily. Make sure to remove all strings from the purée— they are choking hazards. Use an electric mixer to purée and those pesky strings will adhere to the beaters and then strain to remove any remaining strings.

Freezing: Freeze purée using the *Food Cube Method* and keep for up to 2 months.

Baking a large pumpkin: Cut the top off the pumpkin just under the stem. Scoop out seeds and membranes. (Save those wonderful, nutritious pumpkin seeds.) Replace the top and place on a dry baking pan. Bake in a pre-heated 350°F oven for 1-1½ hours. Test for doneness by following directions for a whole squash above.

Baking pumpkin seeds: Remove pulp and string and rinse seeds. Place in a single layer on ungreased baking sheet. Bake in pre-heated 325°F oven for 15-20 minutes until dry and lightly brown, or for 30-40 minutes if you like them crispy. Use as a snack or garnish for adults.

Note: Using fresh pumpkin for pies is a lot of work. I did it once and that was enough. If you are going to try it, make sure the pumpkin purée is not too watery. To make it thicker, cook the purée in a saucepan over low heat until enough water has evaporated to make it the proper consistency. What's the proper consistency? That of canned pumpkin, of course.

Tips for carving a Jack-O-Lantern: Cut stemmed top lid out of pumpkin with knife angled inward, not vertically, to prevent lid from falling inside. Make a mark or leave a notch on lid to indicate how to turn and place the lid so that it will fit perfectly every time. Cut a small hole in lid to act as a chimney for candle smoke.

Use an ice cream scoop to make hollowing out pumpkin easier, and leave a thinner wall in front so that the face will be easier to cut. (Save seeds and bake as directed above.)

Tape a paper pattern to front of pumpkin; use tip of knife to punch pinholes through paper into pumpkin rind, "tracing" the design into the rind with pinholes. (Use a copy of a picture from your child's favorite story book or a copy of a photograph of your child, carve your child's name, or have your child draw a picture.)

Buy a saw-like knife made especially to cut jack-o-lanterns—they are cheap and it makes cutting so much easier.

If your jack-o-lantern dries up, rehydrate by soaking in water until it's as good as new.

To preserve your jack-o-lantern, spray inside and out with an antiseptic spray to kill bacteria.

Place a candle on a small flat fire-proof dish or layers of aluminum foil. To stabilize, adhere candle to dish by "gluing" with melted wax. Light candle with fireplace match or dry stick of spaghetti or tape a few matches to a butter knife. Lighting the candle is easier if you cut the large initial hole in the bottom of the pumpkin instead of the top. To light the candle, lift the pumpkin by the stem, leaving the bottom hole and candle exposed for lighting.

Or don't use a candle at all—line the jack-o-lantern with aluminum foil and place a small string of Christmas lights inside. The cord and plug can be pulled through a hole in the back of the pumpkin. Or use a small flashlight.

Toddlers: Toddlers can safely decorate their own jack-o-lantern by drawing on a pumpkin with washable, non-toxic, felt-tip markers.

String Beans

Beans with strings no longer exist. Green bean growers have worked hard to make beans without strings. You probably want green beans—see **Beans**.

Sweet Potatoes (Yams)

Baby must be at least 4 months old to eat cooked, puréed sweet potatoes.

Puréed sweet potato is an excellent first food for baby. The sweet potato is one of the most complete foods. Like carrots, it is a super source of beta-carotene (vitamin A). Sweet potatoes are also a good source of magnesium, potassium, and other vitamins and minerals. The dry-fleshed variety (see next paragraph) can replace white potatoes in most recipes, and they take less time to cook and reheat better. Try them instead of white potatoes in potato salad and potato pancakes. Sweet potatoes are also one of the easiest vegetables to prepare. Just pierce them with a fork, bake them, cut them in half, scoop out the flesh, and fork-mash for baby.

There are two varieties of sweet potato sold in the United States: moist-fleshed, which has bright orange flesh that is sweet and moist when cooked, and dry-fleshed, which has ivory-colored flesh that is dry and mealy (like white potatoes) when cooked. The moister and sweeter variety is usually labeled "yam," even though it's really a sweet potato. Real yams are foreign-grown and cannot usually be found on our supermarket shelves. This is good because yams have virtually no vitamin A, but sweet potatoes are loaded with it. Be gentle with sweet potatoes, as they damage easily.

Equivalents: 3 medium sweet potatoes = 1 pound = 3 cups sliced = 2½ cups puréed.

In season: Available year round; peak October through December.

Choosing: Buy them loose so you can get a good look at each one. Select small- to medium-sized, thick, chunky, well-shaped sweet potatoes that taper toward the ends. Skin should be dry, firm, bright, smooth, and uniformly colored. Try to get them unwaxed. Wax used on produce is supposedly safe, but it may contain pesticide residues. Avoid potatoes with cuts, worm holes, or other damage. Decay, found often in sweet potatoes, can be in the form of shriveled ends or wet, soft, discolored, or sunken areas in the skin. Cutting out a damaged area does no good. One bad spot ruins the whole potato and the rest of the potato that still looks good will probably be affected and taste bad. So, discard the entire potato if there is any serious injury.

Storing: Store in a dark, cool (50°F) place in a perforated (so moisture doesn't build) plastic bag after loosely wrapping in organic, bleach-free wax paper for several weeks. Or, keep them at room temperature for up to one week. You may hear that you shouldn't store raw sweet potatoes in the refrigerator. Actually, you can store them as described above in the refrigerator for up to 10 days if you make sure they don't freeze. If even a little part of a potato freezes, the whole potato will taste bitter. After cooking, store them in the refrigerator for up to 5 days.

Preparation for cooking: Wash by scrubbing gently and do not peel.

Steaming: Steam whole sweet potatoes for 30 or more minutes.

Baking: Pierce several holes in the potatoes with a fork. If you wish, rub skin with butter. Bake, uncovered, in a 400°F oven for about 45 minutes, or in a 375°F oven for 55 minutes.

Boiling: Boil enough water to cover potatoes. Place washed, whole unpeeled, potatoes in boiling water, cover pot, and cook for 20-30 minutes until tender. Drain boiling water and drop potatoes into cold water and peels will slip right off.

Puréeing: Cut cooked potato in half. Scoop out flesh and mash with fork, potato masher, or mixer to purée. (If peeled, as in previous boiling paragraph, you can just put the whole potatoes in a bowl and mash.) For young babies who need a very smooth consistency, use your food processor or blender. For large sweet potatoes, which tend to be fibrous, a mixer is better to purée because the stringy fibers will collect on the beaters and leave the mash smooth. Make sure to remove all strings from the purée—they are choking hazards. Use an electric mixer to purée the strings will adhere to the beaters and then strain to remove any remaining strings.

Freezing: Freeze puréed sweet potatoes using the *Food Cube Method* and keep for up to 2 months. Add a little lemon juice to prevent discoloration, if your baby is old enough for citrus. I never do, and my sweet potato cubes stay a nice orange color anyway.

Swiss Chard, see Greens

Turnips, see Rutabagas

Waxed Beans, see Beans

Yellow Beans, see Beans

Yams, see Sweet Potatoes

Zucchini, see Squash, Summer

21

Super Baby Food
Fruits

We may consider fruit to be produce that tastes sweet, but fruits are actually the parts of plants that contain the seeds. Avocado, tomatoes, pumpkins, eggplants, rhubarb, and cucumbers are technically classified by botanists as fruits, not vegetables. All fruits grow above the ground on trees, vines, or shrubs. Fruits grown closest to the equator (bananas, figs, and dates) get more exposure to the sun than those grown in more temperate zones. This causes them to have a higher percentage of natural sugar and taste much sweeter. For the same reason, different parts of the same fruit are sweeter than others. The blossom end of an orange is sweeter than the bottom because it gets more sun.

The best way to feed fruit to your baby is to take a whole, fresh, ripe uncut piece of fruit from the refrigerator—wash, peel, and purée it—and feed it to her immediately. For older babies, peel and dice it into small pieces and serve immediately as finger food. (Watch out for those slippery foods!) Make sure the fruit is very soft and ripe to prevent choking. Minimize the amount of time fruit is exposed to warm room air and light to maximize the amount of nutrients retained, especially the very unstable vitamin C. Get the fruit from inside its peel to inside your baby as soon as possible!

Complete information about each fruit can be found in the at the end of this chapter and are listed alphabetically.

Choosing Fresh Fruit

Buy fruit individually and not packaged in plastic so you can take a close look at each piece. In general, there should be no bruises, mold, cuts in the skin, or bad odor. You can't necessarily judge a fruit by its color. Sometimes color is important, and sometimes color means nothing. Did you know that green oranges are probably better than orange oranges?

Buy fruit that has begun to ripen a little in the store, in order to be sure that the fruit will, in fact, ripen. Fruit should feel firm, but not rock hard. Smell the fruit—if it smells slightly sweet, it's a sign that it has started ripening. Don't buy overripe fruit, even if it's on sale; many parts won't be edible.

The ripeness tests in the Specific Fruits and Vegetables appendix are not very objective. If you don't have much experience with fruit and think you'll have trouble determining subjective characteristics like "firm, but not hard" and "slightly sweet," don't worry. Take this book to the supermarket with you and test many fruits. With a little experience, you'll become a real expert.

It's All in the Ripening

Fruits should be ripe before we eat them. We don't let broccoli (a vegetable) get ripe, but we do let all fruits (including tomatoes) get ripe. Most mass-grown fruit arrives at the supermarket unripened and hard. If it hasn't fully ripened on the grocer's shelf, you must let it ripen at home. Some fruits, like bananas, will ripen no matter how green. But, some fruits will never ripen. I bought a few avocados that never ripened and remained hard for weeks, and I had to toss them. At the time, I didn't know to ripen them at room temperature and not in the refrigerator! Ripen most fruits by keeping them at room temperature out of direct sunlight, turning occasionally. For each commonly used fruit, ripening instructions are given at the end of this chapter.

Fruit Ripeners

There is such a thing as a fruit ripener, which is nothing more than a glass bowl with holes. If you use one, clean it often to remove invisible bacteria or mold, which can be passed from one batch of fruit to the next. An inexpensive, but equally effective emulation of a fruit ripener is a simple paper bag punched with small holes or left slightly open. The holes will allow carbon dioxide and excess moisture to leave and oxygen to enter. It is interesting that ethylene gas, which is naturally produced by the fruit itself, helps the fruit to ripen. The fruit ripener or paper bag concentrates the gas around the fruit, which acts as a catalyst.

TIP: Try this if you want to speed a fruit's ripening: Place a very ripe piece of fruit, such as a black banana, in the same bag with hard fruit. It will emit lots of ethylene gas and cause quick ripening of the hard fruit.

Storing Fruit

Fruit should be kept uncut until needed. If fruit is cut, keep it tightly wrapped to prevent exposure to air. Most ripe fruit should be kept cold and in high humidity—so wrap it in unbleached, organic wax paper and then plastic wrap and/or put in the vegetable crisper to keep it from being exposed to the very dry air circulating in your refrigerator and freezer. Don't keep ripe fruit in light, especially direct sunlight. Light destroys vitamin C, therefore ripe fruit should be kept in the dark. This is why the light automatically turns off when you close your refrigerator door. I wonder how much vitamin C really exists in fruit juice that is packaged in clear plastic or glass bottles that do nothing to stop light penetration.

TIP: Light and warmth destroy vitamin C very quickly. Keep orange juice in a cold and dark place. Buy orange juice in opaque cartons in the refrigerator section of the supermarket. Or better yet, give your baby vitamin C by feeding him a fresh kiwi fruit or by squeezing him juice from a fresh orange.

Cleaning Fruit

To wash most fruits, follow the same instructions for cleaning vegetables in the previous chapter.

Berries must be cleaned differently. Blueberries, strawberries, and other berries bruise very easily and must be treated gently. Immediately remove decayed, moldy, or bruised berries before the damage spreads to the others. Ideally, berries should not be washed until you are ready to use them. But, I wash them before they go into the refrigerator so they are ready to grab for quick snacks. (It's against my kids' religion to wash fruit!)

Berries are best cleaned by placing them in a colander or large strainer and dipping them in water or gently spraying them with the sink hose or slow-running tap water. Don't soak berries because their juice will be replaced with the water through osmosis. Let the berries drip dry for a short while and then place them back into the container they came in— usually a plastic basket or perforated cardboard container. Or place them in a colander. Don't layer them too deep or the berries on the bottom will be crushed. Cover them well with a paper towel.

Refrigerating Fruit

See the end of this chapter for the number of days each specific fruit will keep in the refrigerator. Remember that those times are for whole, uncut fruit. Most cut up fruit and cooked fruit will keep for only a day or two. Any fruit that has been cooked and/or puréed should be kept in the refrigerator for only one day and then discarded. To prevent food waste, purée only one day's worth of fruit for baby, or freeze larger amounts using the *Food Cube Method*.

Freezing Fruit

It is best to feed your baby fresh, ripe fruit. However, you may wish to freeze fruits with short peak seasons, such as strawberries, so that they may be enjoyed throughout the year. Frozen fruit tends to be soft, and maybe even mushy when thawed, because the moisture expansion within the fruit during freezing causes the cell walls to break. Your baby probably won't mind.

Fruit can be frozen raw—it doesn't need to be blanched or cooked first. Clean the fruit, cut into chunks, and let dry on paper towels. Follow the instructions for specific fruits.

There are several methods of freezing fruit. The *Tray-Freeze Method* is best if you want to retrieve a few small fruit pieces from the freezer at one time. If not, and you do not mind if the fruit chunks clump together in one big blob, it is OK to freeze plain fruit chunks in an air-tight container with no liquid (this is called the "dry pack" method).

For light-colored fruits that lose their color and flavor when frozen, some experts recommend freezing fruit chunks in liquid (the "wet pack" method). The liquid, whose purpose is to keep the fruit from coming in contact with air and discoloring, is usually a syrup solution (actually nothing but sugar water) mixed with some ascorbic acid (vitamin C).

In my opinion, baby food should not have added processed sugar, and you don't want to overload your baby with too much vitamin C. If you wish to use the liquid, I recommend that fruits be submerged and frozen in orange juice instead of the syrup solution. Orange juice, with its natural sugar and vitamin C, is a healthy alternative to sugar water. Of course, do not use orange juice if your baby is not yet old enough for citrus, use the *Tray-Freeze Method*.

If your baby is at least 9 months old, she is old enough for pineapple. Freeze fruit chunks under pineapple juice instead of orange juice. Simply place the washed fruit chunks in a freezer-safe glass container and cover them with juice. The fruit pieces may float on top of the juice. To keep them submerged, place crumpled wax paper on top of the fruit chunks to keep them submerged under the juice so that they are not exposed to any air. Leave a little head room for expansion, cover tightly, and freeze.

Freezing Puréed Fruit in Food Cubes

To prevent discoloration of puréed fruit that will be frozen, mix a little lemon or pineapple juice into the purée before freezing. (If your baby has not yet been introduced to citrus fruits/pineapple, leave out the juice.) For freezing instructions on specific fruits, refer to the Specific Fruits and Vegetables appendix.

How to Thaw Fruit

It is best to thaw fruit in the refrigerator for several hours or overnight. If you need to thaw fruit fast, thaw on the stove top over very low heat or in a double boiler. Remember that heat and air destroy nutrients, so thawing fruit well covered in the refrigerator is best.

> WARNING: Fruit that has been frozen and thawed keeps for a shorter time than fresh fruit, so discard within 24 hours.

How to Cook Fruit

Before 6-7 months of age, it is best not to feed raw fruits to your baby (except for bananas and avocado). Cook fruits to make them soft and more digestible for your baby's immature digestive system. Cook fruits as you would vegetables, until they are tender and soft. Then strain them thoroughly to remove the fruit peels, which are choking hazards.

Canned Fruit

I always recommend fresh, natural food or frozen food over canned food. However, if you choose to feed your baby canned fruit, buy those in their natural juices. If you have fruit that is canned in sugary syrups, rinse it under running tap water in a strainer to remove as much of the syrup as possible.

Too Much Fruit May Cause Diaper Rash

Too much fruit juice or even too much fresh fruit can cause your baby's stool to be acidic. This irritates baby's tender skin and may cause a painful, bright red diaper rash that hurts when you wipe. Inform your pediatrician.

Dried Fruit

Drying food actually can preserve it because bacteria, molds, and yeasts cannot grow without sufficient moisture. The presence of mold on dried foods is an indicator that the food is not dry enough. Food drying is the process of dehydrating or removing most of the water from foods. Most fruits are more than 70% water, but it varies. Strawberries are 90% water, apples are 84% and bananas are 65%. After drying, their moisture content drops to about 15-20%, causing them to significantly shrink in weight and size. In fact, it takes at least six pounds of most fresh fruit to make one pound of dried fruit.

Drying concentrates the natural sugars (and some nutrients) of fruit, which explains why dried fruit taste so sweet. Dried fruit contains a lot of sugar, natural sugar, but sugar just the same. Therefore, you should prevent your child from eating limitless quantities.

Drying foods causes significant nutrient loss, especially vitamins A and C, but some minerals are fairly well retained. Still, dried fruits are healthy snacks for our children, especially when compared to the sugar-laden empty-calorie junk that kids ask you to buy in the supermarket.

Dried fruits, such as banana chips and fruit leather, are good finger foods and snack foods for your baby or toddler. You must first chop them into small pieces and make them very soft by re-hydrating them (described later), so they are not a choking hazard.

TIP: Dried fruit is easier to chop if it is cold. Place it in the freezer for about an hour to chill. Use kitchen scissors to cut into small pieces. To prevent sticking, rub butter or oil on the scissors (or a knife), or dip them into hot water. Chop dried fruits in your food processor a little at a time. If sticking occurs, try soaking them in cold water before putting them in your processor.

Dried apple rings (not re-hydrated) are good for teething rings, but they must be very dry and hard so that your baby cannot bite off a piece and choke. They also must be large enough to not be a choking hazard.

You can buy dried fruits at the supermarket and natural foods store, or you can dry them at home yourself. The advantages of drying food at home are similar to those of making baby food at home: it saves you money, it gives you control over the quality of the ingredients, and it eliminates the need for preservatives. Your own home-dried fruits and fruit leathers are much healthier than most commercially dried fruits and rolled-up fruit snacks that may contain added sugar, partially hydrogenated oils, and chemicals.

> **WARNING:** Watch out for top-name brands that add partially hydrogenated oils to their raisins and other dried fruits. Read the label carefully.

Food dryers are now available at department and kitchen stores and online. Perhaps you've seen the infomercial! If you have a food dryer, you know how well they work for making dried fruits, dried herbs, beef jerky, and even dried flowers. If you don't have one, you can use your oven (conventional, not microwave) for making small amounts of dried foods. Your oven is not as reliable as a food dryer, or as energy efficient, but it gets the job done. My favorite book on food drying is by Deanna DeLong, *How To Dry Foods*. Another excellent book that discusses food drying as well as food canning and much more is *The Big Book of Preserving the Harvest* by Carol W. Costenbader.

Storing Dried Fruit

The best way I've found to store dried fruit is the *Nested Plastic Bag Method*. Store individual servings in the organic, bleach-free wax paper lined inside bags with the air removed and place them in a stronger, thicker big freezer bag. This way, you can open the outer freezer bag without exposing the dried fruit to air. It is important to keep dried fruit from air, because it begins to absorb moisture from the air immediately, and moisture in dried fruit means mold. Store the bag in a cool (around 50°F), dry, dark place, and the dried fruit should keep for up to 2-4 weeks. At room temperature, it will keep for only about half that time. For longer storage, refrigerate for up to 2 months or freeze for 6 months to 1 year.

TIP: If raisins and other died fruit clump together; place them in colander and rinse under hot running water.

Rehydrating (Plumping) Dried Fruit

You can eat dried fruit or use it in recipes as is, but you may find that it is more tasty and easier to chew if you "plump" or rehydrate it. You must rehydrate dried fruit for your baby to help prevent choking. Raisins, often "plumped" raisins, are a very commonly used dried fruit in recipes.

There are several ways to rehydrate dried fruit. Soak dried fruit overnight in water in the refrigerator to rehydrate. Or pour boiling water over dried fruit (1½ cups of boiling water per cup of dried fruit) and let sit until rehydrated. This may take as little as 10 minutes for small fruit pieces (raisins) to one or two hours for large fruit pieces (apricot halves). Plump raisins or other small dried fruit pieces by steaming them for 3-5 minutes over boiling water.

> **WARNING: Once dried food has been rehydrated, it spoils quickly. Eat immediately or throw it away.**

TIP: During baking, roll wet raisins and other dried fruit and nuts in flour before mixing into batter while using your fingers to separate the pieces. This helps prevent fruit pieces from sinking to the bottom of the batter.

MONEY SAVER: You're paying top dollar for the convenience of those little boxes of raisins. Buy in bulk and keep refilling the boxes. One pound of raisins = approximately 3 cups.

Fruit Leather

Take a stroll down the boxed snacks aisle at the supermarket and read the ingredients list on a fruit roll type snack box. These dried fruit snacks, made with "real fruit" (as it so boldly states on the package), are nothing more than fruit leather with added sugar, hydrogenated oils, artificial colors and flavors, and other chemicals. Without coupons, the 6-ounce boxes cost so much more than making the fruit leather yourself. We sure do pay a lot for packaging and convenience. Is the super hero on the package really worth it? If your kids think so, make them Fruit Leather Pinwheels and I bet they'll change their minds.

One day I was puréeing fruit for fruit leather, and a friend of my sons asked me what I was doing. When I told him, he replied, surprised, "What? You can make those?"

Fruit leather can be made from fresh fruit, thawed frozen fruit, or even drained canned fruits. If you're using fresh fruit, choose good quality, ripe fruits. Actually, slightly overripe fruit is also good for fruit leather, due to its full flavor and sweetness. Almost-black bananas and overripe juicy peaches are great for fruit leather.

Leathers can be made from fruits that are either raw or cooked. Cooking fruits causes nutrient loss, but the leathers made from cooked fruits are bright and glossy. Raw fruit leathers tend to look dull, but have more of a fresh fruit flavor. Try making some of each and decide for yourself.

How to Make Fruit Leather in Your Oven

Prepare a large cookie sheet or 10 x 15 flat baking sheet by lining it with unbleached parchment/wax paper or greasing the cookie sheet with oil or a spray. If using wax paper, make sure to wrap over the edges and underneath the cookie sheet so there is enough slack for the sheet to hold it down in place.

Wash the fruit well. You can peel the fruits, but it's OK to leave the skins on for fruit leather. Slice or chop the fruit and place in a food processor or blender to purée. To prevent discoloration, add a tablespoon of lemon juice if you wish. Purée the fruit and add a minimum amount of water or juice, if necessary. Keep in mind that the more liquid you add, the longer it will take to dry. The consistency should be like that of molasses or thick applesauce. Two cups of fruit purée, give or take ¼ cup, is a good amount for a batch of fruit leather.

If you wish to cook the fruit, pour the purée into a saucepan and bring it to a boil over medium-high heat, stirring continuously. When it boils, keep stirring, turn off the heat, and let the purée simmer for 3-5 minutes. Let cool to room temperature.

Spread the fruit purée on the prepared cookie sheet until it is ⅛-¼ inch thick. Tilt and turn the tray or use a spatula to spread. Spread as evenly as possible so it will dry uniformly. Leave a border of at least 1-2 inches between the purée and the edges of the cookie sheet. Use two cookie sheets if you find you have too much purée. Or freeze the extra purée for drying another time; when ready to use, simply thaw, spread on sheets, and dry.

> **TIP:** You can make fun shapes while spreading the leather: circles or pancakes, teddy bear faces, clovers, hearts, etc. Use different colored fruit purées and garnishes (discussed later) and bring out the artist in you. Or wait until after it's dry, when you may find it easier to make designs out of already dried leather—see Cutting Fruit Leather on the next page.

Fruit Leather Drying Method One: Place the tray in the oven with door slightly open. If you have an electric oven, leave the door open 1-3 inches. If you have a gas oven, leave the door open 6 8 inches. Keep the oven at 115 120°F. Dry for 6-8 hours. Then flip the leather over, and dry for another 6- 8 hours.

Fruit Leather Drying Method Two: Place the tray in a preheated 175°F oven with the door slightly open for about 3 hours. If the bottom is not dry, flip and continue drying.

Fruit Leather Drying Method Three: Place the tray in a preheated 275°F oven with the door closed for 30-35 minutes. Then turn off the oven, leave the oven door closed, and let dry overnight or for at least 8-10 hours.

Fruit Leather Drying Method Four: You can also dry fruit leather in the sun, but it may take from 1-3 days, depending on the temperature and humidity. Protect it from insects by covering it with cheesecloth or netting.

After it's dry, place it in a preheated oven set at 200°F for 45 minutes before cooling and storing. Fruit leather is finished drying when it feels tacky, but is pliable and will pull away from the baking sheet or parchment paper. It is better to over dry than under dry. By the way, the dryer the leather, the longer it will keep So, if you want your leather to last many months, dry it until it is no longer tacky and completely dry.

> **TIP:** If you've accidentally let the leather dry too long and it has become brittle and crackly—not to worry! Break it up into little leather chips by hand or in the processor and use them as *Super Baby Food Healthy Extras*. They are good as is, or rehydrate them. Use them as a flavor enhancer for cereal, yogurt, tofu, beverages, etc. And what possibilities leather chips are for decorative touches!

Rolling Fruit Leather

You can roll fruit leather to make it look like the boxed supermarket fruit roll snacks. Simply roll it up as you would a sleeping bag or jelly roll. The leather will be easier to roll if it is still slightly warm. You can place it on a piece of wax paper and roll it. Then cut the roll into single snack-sized pieces that are about one inch wide. Cutting is easier if the leather is chilled first.

Cutting Fruit Leather

Instead of rolling, you can cut the slightly warm fruit leather into rectangular pieces and stack between strips of wax paper. Or you can cut designs out of the leather and use them as decorative touches.

> **TIP:** There's nothing like fruit leather for cutting detailed shapes for decorative touches. You can easily spell out a child's name, or cut numbers for the age of the birthday child to put on the cake. Stencils can be used to make your letters and numbers professional. Use a clean utility knife or pizza cutter to make cutting easy, but first place the fruit leather on some wax paper over old magazines or several layers of newspaper to protect your table top. Use a copy machine to copy your child's favorite picture from a book, then use the copy as a pattern to place over the fruit leather and cut the design. Before drying, you can add food coloring to light colored fruit purée, such as apple or banana, for custom colors—like the purple of imaginary dinosaurs, or the green of Christmas trees.

Storing Fruit Leather

Place single servings of fruit leather in small organic wax paper-lined plastic sandwich bags, remove as much air as possible, and tie a tight knot. Place the individual sandwich bags in a large plastic freezer bag. (This is the *Nested Plastic Bag Method*). Now you can open and reopen the large freezer bag without exposing the leather in the individual bags to air and moisture. Stored this way in a cool (around 50°F), dry, dark place, the leather should keep for 2-4 weeks. At room temperature, it will keep for only about half that time. For longer storage, refrigerate for up to 2 months or freeze for 3-4 months. Leather with garnishes or fillings should not be stored at room temperature; refrigerate or freeze them.

Fruit Leather Recipes

It seems that there are infinitely many combinations of fruits, flavorings, garnishes, and fillings for fruit leather. Apples are a favorite fruit for making leather, because their pectin content helps to thicken the purée. Some fruits, such as citrus fruits and blueberries, are too bland or juicy to be used alone. They should be combined with apples or other fruits to improve flavor and texture. Pears are best if they are not dried alone; combine them with apples or pineapple.

Fruit Combinations for Fruit Leather

These combinations of puréed fruit work well and taste good together in fruit leather:

apple-banana	apple-strawberry
apple-any berry	apple-apricot
apple-peach	apple-orange
apple-any fruit	apricot-plum
banana-cherry	cherry-pineapple
nectarine-pineapple	nectarine-plum
peach-blueberry	peach-plum
pear-apple	pear-pineapple
strawberry-peach	strawberry-pineapple

Tip: Add a crushed vitamin C tablet to a light fruit purée (peach, pear, banana, etc.) to keep it from browning.

The Easiest Ever Apple Fruit Leather

Open a jar of applesauce, spread on the cookie sheet, and dry.

Variation: Add ¼ teaspoon of cinnamon into applesauce before drying. Or mix into applesauce a 4-ounce jar of baby fruit, such as peaches, apricots, prunes, etc.

Quick Strawberry Leather

Thaw a package of frozen strawberries according to package directions. Purée in processor adding water or fruit juice until good consistency. Dry.

Mango Leather

Purée 2 cups of mango and dry.

Pumpkin Leather Jack-O-Lanterns

Open a 16-ounce can of pumpkin, stir in ½ cup of honey or maple syrup, and add ½ teaspoon of pumpkin pie spice. Dry. Cut into Jack-O-Lantern shapes and use garnishes and decorative touches for eyes, mouth, stem, etc.

Fruit Leather from Canned Fruit

Open a can or jar of fruit. Drain fruit and reserve liquid. Purée fruit in processor, adding only enough reserved liquid until good consistency. Dry.

Flavoring Fruit Leather

During blending, a teaspoon or more of honey or other sweetener can be added, if you wish, but it is not really necessary if your fruit is naturally sweet and ripe. Flavorings like lemon juice, almond extract, vanilla, and cinnamon, nutmeg, and other spices can also be added.

Garnishing Fruit Leather

Chopped nuts, raisins, shredded coconut, and other garnishes can be sprinkled onto fruit leather near the end of the drying period while it is still slightly sticky. The garnishes add a nice touch to leather cut into flat pieces. You can cut fancy shapes out of the leather and use garnishes to decorate. Or the garnishes can be rolled up into the leather, like jelly in a jelly roll.

Fruit Leather Pinwheels

These are the ultimate fruit leather snack! After the leather has dried, but is still slightly warm, spread a thin layer of filling over it, leaving an inch of margin around the edges. Then roll up jelly-roll style. Cut the roll into ½ to 1-inch pieces. Cutting is easier if the leather is chilled and stiff. For filling, use plain or sweetened tofu, softened cream cheese, softened peanut butter or other nut butters, tahini, yogurt cheese, a contrasting color jam or jelly. You can sprinkle garnishes over the filling and roll them in. Store the pinwheels in the refrigerator or freezer, not at room temperature. Children (and older folks) love the look of these pinwheels or spirals, and they are delicious!

Specific Fruits

Apples

Baby must be at least 8 months old to eat peeled raw grated apple. At least 4 years old for unpeeled, because apple peels are choking hazards.

Apples can be served as a sweet dessert that does not cause a quick rise in blood sugar levels as other sweet desserts do. Although apples are not found much in the vitamin and mineral bar chart tables in the nutrition section of this book, they do contain modest amounts of many vitamins and minerals. They are abundant in pectin, a fiber found on the apple peel and just below, which is known for its cholesterol-lowering effects. Whenever possible, eat apples unpeeled. And remember, "An unpeeled apple a day keeps the doctor away." Unfortunately, apple peels are choking hazards for babies and toddlers.

Note that apple juice does not lower cholesterol. How does juice differ from cider? Apple cider is fresh-crushed apple in season. Apple juice is pasteurized and bottled for a long shelf life. "Clarified" apple juice is filtered to remove all pulp. Vinegar is made from the fermentation of a sugar. Wine vinegar is made from grapes. Apple cider vinegar is made from fermented apple cider. Use plain white vinegar for cleaning, and apple cider vinegar for eating—it's much healthier than plain vinegar. Store cider vinegar in a cool dry place for up to 6 months, or according to the expiration date. See how to make apple cider vinegar below. Apples are known as "Nature's Toothbrush." Pack an apple in your child's lunch box and instruct her to eat it last. It doesn't replace brushing, but it helps clean the teeth and massages the gums.

Equivalents: 3 medium apples = 1 pound = 2½ cups peeled and sliced.

In season: Available year round; peak for Cortland, October to January; for Empire, October to April; for Granny Smith's, April to July; for McIntosh, Newton Pippin, and Red Delicious, September to June; for Golden Delicious and Spartan, September to May; for Ida Red, Rome Beauty, and Winesap, October to June.

Choosing: Choose apples that are smooth and not shriveled. Bruises seriously affect apples, so check carefully for small depressions in the skin. Apples should be very firm and not yield when pressed. Be especially careful to check for firmness in large apples, which age more quickly than small apples. Small brownish or tan freckles on the skin are OK. Try to buy unwaxed apples. Wax used on produce is supposedly safe, but it may contain pesticide residues.

Ripening and storing: As apples ripen, they become sweeter. Some varieties, such as Granny Smiths, stay more sour or tart than others. If apples are too firm or sour, ripen at room temperature for a day or two and they will ripen quickly. Place ripened apples in an organic, bleach-free wax paper-lined plastic bag in the refrigerator. Apples keep in the refrigerator very well, up to four weeks before they begin to soften. Apples will keep longer if they don't touch each other—but who has the room! Soft apples can be eaten raw, but they are better for baking or applesauce.

Freezing applesauce: Freeze unsweetened applesauce using the *Food Cube Method* and keep for up to 2 months.

Apricots

Baby must be at least 8 months old to eat apricots.

Equivalents: 8-10 medium apricots = 1 pound fresh = 2 cups sliced; 1 pound dried apricots = 3 cups.

In season: Available May to August; peak June and July.

Choosing: Buy juicy-looking, plump apricots with a uniform golden-orange color. Skin should have a little give when pressed and should not be hard or shriveled. Blemishes will not affect the flavor if the skin is not broken. Avoid firm fruit and those that are pale yellow or have a greenish tint.

Ripening and storing: Keep at room temperature for no more than two days in a loosely closed paper bag until ripe (soft but not mushy). Store in refrigerator in a glass container for up to 3 days after ripe.

Serving: Peel with vegetable peeler. Purée for young babies. For older babies, peel and dice soft apricot pieces and use as finger food.

Freezing: Peel and purée and freeze using the *Food Cube Method*. Or freeze in chunks using the *Tray-Freeze Method*. Apricots will keep in the freezer for 10 to 12 months.

Dried apricots: It takes 6 pounds of fresh apricots to make 1 pound of dried apricots, which really concentrates the sweetness and nutrients. Dried apricots are nutritional snacks eaten as is, or they can be ingredients in other dishes to add a natural sweetness. Dried fruits should be eaten in moderation because of their concentrated sugar.

Avocados

Baby must be at least 4 months old to eat avocados.

Avocados are a great first food for your baby. They are an excellent source of unsaturated fatty acids and have a higher proportion of this "good" fat than any other fruit except the olive. Yes, they are actually fruits, even though they are commonly thought of as vegetables. Try using mashed avocado as a "vegetable butter," a replacement for butter that can be spread on crackers or sandwiches.

Equivalents: 1 medium avocado = 1 cup.

In season: Available year round; peak December through May.

Choosing: When selecting avocados, look carefully for damage, which shows up as soft dark spots in the skin. Tan-colored patches are OK. When picked up, an avocado should feel heavy for its size. If you're not going to eat the avocado for a few days, select an avocado that is firm, but not rock hard, and ripen it at home. If you plan on eating it immediately, select a ripe avocado as described next.

Ripening: Firm avocados will never ripen in the refrigerator—let them sit at room temperature for up to 6 days. Place them in a brown paper bag to speed ripening. Avocados are ripe when they yield to gentle pressure and feel soft all over. Another way to test for ripeness is to gently squeeze the whole avocado with all five fingers. (Using all five fingers prevents bruises.) If the flesh feels like it is separating from the seed, the avocado is ripe. As avocados ripen, the skin becomes a darker green. Still another way to test for ripeness is to insert a toothpick in the stem end. If it moves easily, the avocado is ripe. Avocados are easy to peel when they are ripe; the peel is hard to remove when avocados are underripe.

Storing: After ripened, store the whole avocado in the refrigerator in the vegetable crisper for up to two weeks. Your very young baby will certainly leave you with avocado leftovers. Store cut avocados by leaving the skins on and keeping the pit in the uneaten portion. You can brush the fruit part with lemon juice (if baby is old enough for citrus) to keep it from turning brown. It's OK to eat the brown part, but you can easily scrape it off with a knife. Wrap in organic bleach-free wax paper and then a plastic bag and store in the refrigerator.

Bananas

Baby must be at least 4 months old to eat bananas.

Bananas are God's gift to parents (second to the baby, of course). They are one of the easiest, handiest baby foods—simply peel, fork-mash, and feed. I'll never understand why parents pay a fortune for jarred baby bananas when fresh are so easy. Because they are prepackaged in their own peels and require no cooking, they can be thrown in the diaper bag at the last minute for an instant traveling baby snack.

Mashed bananas are one of the most versatile ingredients in homemade baby food. You can add almost anything to mashed bananas—yogurt, cream cheese, cooked cereal, ground sprouts, (and) nutritional yeast. Your baby will love these combinations because the bananas give them a naturally sweet taste.

Nutrition-wise, bananas are known for their high level of potassium and fiber, and contain fair amounts of many other nutrients.

Equivalents: 3-4 medium bananas = 2 cups sliced = 1½ cups mashed.

In season: Available year round.

Choosing: Select bananas with no bruises. The entire peel should be intact with part of the stem still attached. Bananas are a rare fruit in that they actually ripen better off the tree. It's OK to buy bananas in any stage of ripeness, from totally green and unripe to totally yellow with black flecks. However, the more ripe, the more easily the banana will bruise, so be gentle.

Red bananas are generally larger than yellow bananas and take a little longer to ripen, but they taste the same. The skins of red bananas take on a deeper color as they ripen. Avoid bananas with a dull, grayish color, which means they have been stored in cold temperatures and will never ripen.

We eat dozens of bananas in our house each week. I buy some that are all yellow with brown specks (ripe), some with green tips (slightly underripe), and some totally green (very underripe). As they yellow and ripen, they get eaten. In rare cases where some are around long enough to turn black, they get baked into healthy, delicious breads or muffins.

Ripening: Ripen bananas by leaving them uncovered at room temperature. People like bananas at different ripeness stages. Some like them slightly underripe (yellow with a little green at the stem), and some like them very ripe (all yellow with black flecks). Feed your baby very ripe bananas, because that's when they are at their nutritional height and mash very easily. Their starch has turned to sugar and is easily digested.

Storing: When bananas are at just the right stage of ripeness, place them in the refrigerator to keep them at that ripeness stage. Their peels turn black in several hours, but their flesh remains unchanged and they will keep in the refrigerator for up to 6 days. Unpeeled bananas stored in an airtight plastic bag or jar in the refrigerator will last even longer. If you do not have room in your refrigerator, but want to slow the ripening of bananas at room temperature, place them in a plastic bag with as much air removed as possible.

Storing a partially peeled banana: Your baby will probably be able to eat only part of a banana at first. Eat the rest yourself. Or, partially peel the banana, uncovering only the amount your baby will eat. Remove part of the banana and replace the peels by wrapping them around the cut part of the leftover banana. Store in the refrigerator with a piece of wax paper on the open end. The cut will darken, but it is OK to eat.

Freezing banana purée: Yes, you can freeze bananas! That's fortunate for those of us who bought too many at a sale or who let their bananas get black. Just fork-mash or purée and freeze in ice cube trays. You can add 1 tablespoon lemon juice (if baby is old enough for citrus) for each cup of banana to prevent darkening. Bananas will keep frozen for up to 3 months. When thawed, they'll be mushy—perfect for your little one or as an ingredient in baked goods.

Freezing whole bananas: Bananas can be frozen whole for up to 6 months. Place them whole and within their peels inside a large airtight freezer bag lined with organic, bleach-free wax paper. To use, thaw completely in the refrigerator. Then slice off the stem and squeeze the mushy banana flesh out through the hole.

Blueberries

Baby must be at least 9 months old to eat mashed raw blueberries. Wait until three years or older for whole blueberries because they are a choking hazard.

Purée or mash blueberries for babies from 9 months to a year of age and make sure there are no large peels. Blueberries might be helpful if your baby (or you) has diarrhea. Fresh blueberries are a nice finger food for toddlers over 3 years old.

Equivalents: 1 pint berries = 2 cups.

In season: Available May through September; peak June through August.

Choosing blueberries: Select those that are firm and plump, dry but not shriveled, and with no decay (caused by too much moisture). Avoid light-colored blueberries or those that are green or have a reddish tinge. A dark blue color with a silvery sheen (a natural protective coating) indicates good flavor. Don't buy watery, soft, or moldy blueberries because they are overripe.

Cleaning and storing berries: Blueberries, strawberries, and other berries bruise very easily and you must treat them gently. Immediately remove decayed, moldy, or bruised berries before the damage spreads to other berries. Ideally, berries should not be washed until you are ready to use them. But, I wash them before they go into the refrigerator so they are ready to grab for quick snacks. (It's against my kids' religion to wash fruit.) Berries are best cleaned by placing them in a colander or large strainer and dipping them in water or gently spraying them with the sink hose or slow-running tap water. Don't soak berries because their juice will be replaced with the water through osmosis. Let the berries drip dry for a short while and then place them back into the container they came in—usually a green plastic basket or a perforated cardboard container. Or place them in a colander. Don't layer them too deep or the bottom berries will be crushed. Cover them well with a piece of organic, unbleached wax paper and then plastic wrap. Blueberries will keep for a week or maybe even two.

Tip: To prevent berry juice from dripping in your refrigerator, place the container on a flat bowl or dish. To remove berry stains from your hands, rub with lemon juice.

Freezing berries: Pick berries over, wash them, and freeze in an organic, bleach-free wax paper-lined plastic freezer bag or in a glass container, or use the *Tray-Freeze Method*. Leave a little head room (½ inch) in any rigid container for expansion. Label and date them. Blueberries are great for freezing and will keep frozen for up to a year.

Thawing berries: Frozen berries in a waxed paper-lined plastic bag can be thawed by placing the bag in a big bowl of cold water for 10-20 minutes— move them around a bit during thawing. (This bowl method can't be used to thaw big pieces of fruit because it would take too long at room temperature for them to thaw. Foods should never be thawed for more than several minutes at room temperature)

Tip: To use frozen berries in pancakes (blueberry pancakes) or muffin recipes, there's no need to thaw them first. Simply add the frozen berries to the batter.

Cantaloupe

Baby must be at least 8 months old to eat cantaloupe.

The orange color of the cantaloupe means a high beta-carotene (vitamin A) content. Cantaloupes are also a good source of vitamin C, potassium, magnesium, B vitamins, and more.

In season: May through October, peak June through August.

Choosing: When a good, ripe cantaloupe is harvested, the stem comes off in a nice clean break. Look at the stem end. There should be a smooth, shallow, circular depression with no jagged edges. There should be no stem remaining. The opposite (blossom) end should give slightly when pressed. A cantaloupe will feel springy if you squeeze it gently between your palms. Be careful, though, cantaloupes are not strong, even though their peels are thick. The webbing should be course, thick, dry, raised, and look "three-dimensional," not flat. The background under the webbing should be yellow, not green.

Gently shake the melon, if you hear sloshing inside, pass on it. Buy cantaloupes that are oval (or, less desirable, round), with no flat or dented sides. Avoid those with bruises or off-color spots, because the damage probably goes into the flesh. The stronger the cantaloupe scent, the riper the cantaloupe. But don't buy an overripe cantaloupe, which smells too sweet, feels soft and flabby all over, and has a bright yellow color, because it will be tasteless and watery.

Storing: If necessary, ripen at room temperature for 2 or 3 days. It will get no sweeter, but it will get softer and juicier. Store ripe, whole cantaloupe in a plastic bag lined with organic, bleach free wax paper (to keep the smell from other produce) in the refrigerator for about a week. Cut cantaloupe, when tightly wrapped and refrigerated, will keep for only a day or two. Leave the seeds in halved melons for longer freshness.

Freezing: Cut into slices or use a melon baller. Place in a rigid (glass) freezer-safe container and cover with orange juice—its vitamin C content will prevent darkening and flavor changes. To keep melons submerged under juice so that it is not in contact with the air, try placing crumpled organic, bleach-free wax paper in the container. Leave a little head room.

When completely thawed, melon is mushy, so serve to adults when still a little bit frozen for better texture. Different melons (cantaloupe, honeydew, watermelon) can be mixed in the same freezer container and will keep in the freezer for 10 months to a year.

Cherries

Baby must be at least 9 months old to eat finely chopped raw cherries, or 1 year if an allergy runs in the family. Do not feed whole cherries to children under 4 years old.

Equivalents: 1 pound fresh cherries = 2 cups pitted.

In season: May through August; peak June and July.

Choosing: Select firm, plump, and glossy cherries that are not shriveled or soft. Color is very important in determining freshness and sweetness. In sweet cherries, look for a brightly-colored mahogany (like cherry wood), deep-reddish brown, purple, or even black surface; dullness is a sign of age. Sour cherries are lighter red; they should have a bright, uniform color.

Avoid cherries without stems, as the empty hole opens the cherry to decay. The stems should be fresh-looking, not dark or dry. Look very carefully for decay, which can be camouflaged by the dark color of the cherries. To help detect decay, look for leaking spots and mold.

Storing: Clean and store cherries as you would berries. Don't wash until ready to use. Place in the refrigerator in an organic, bleach-free wax paper-lined plastic bag for up to 4 days.

Freezing: Wash first. Then de-stem and remove pits (use a specially-made cherry pitter, the top of a vegetable peeler, or other makeshift utensil) and freeze for up to 10 months. Label and date them.

Citrus Fruits and Juices
(Oranges, Lemons, Limes, Grapefruits, and Tangerines)

Baby must be at least 12 months old for citrus fruits/juices or younger with your pediatrician's OK. Oranges are acidic and babies sometimes have a sensitivity or intolerance to citrus, so watch your baby carefully.

Citrus fruits are a super source of vitamin C. A good way to get the vitamin into your baby is fresh squeezed orange juice. Vitamin C is very unstable and is lost quickly with exposure to heat, light, or air, so you must squeeze and feed immediately. The body uses vitamin C within a few hours, so it's best to give a little portion of vitamin C foods to your baby several times a day, instead of one big dose.

In season: Available year round; peak depends on variety.

Choosing: Citrus fruits are not picked until they are mature, so you don't have to worry about unripeness. The most important factor in selecting good citrus fruit is feel. Oranges, grapefruits, lemons, limes, and tangerines should all feel firm and heavy for their size. Their peels should be smooth and fine-grained; large pores are not good. Rough, shriveled, or wrinkled peels mean the fruit probably will have thick skin and be pulpy and not juicy. Avoid fruit with soft spots or mold. Non-organic citrus fruits are often waxed and sprayed with fungicide, so wash very well with warm water even if you are not going to eat the peel.

Storing: Store citrus fruits in a plastic bag lined with organic, bleach-free wax paper or the vegetable crisper. They will keep for at least two weeks.

Freezing: For later squeezing, citrus fruits can be frozen whole in plastic freezer bags lined with organic, bleach-free wax paper. Wash well first.

Oranges: Some variety of oranges are available all year. Valencia oranges are available all year; peak April through October. Navel oranges are available October through April. When choosing oranges, don't be concerned with color. Green or orange doesn't determine freshness or ripeness. Brown spots on the peel are fine and usually indicate a good orange.

Grapefruit: Available year round; peak January through June. 1 medium grapefruit = ½ pound = 1 cup sections. You'll find grapefruits that are either white or pink—they taste the same. The pink color comes from beta-carotene (vitamin A), so pink grapefruit is better than white from a nutritional standpoint. Judge a grapefruit by its skin—thin skins probably mean a nice juicy fruit. Pass on those with thick skins, rough or wrinkled skins, or deep pores. Choose grapefruits that are firm, but not hard, and with thin skins that are springy to the touch. Grapefruits should be well-rounded and flat, not pointed, at both ends. The color and look of the skin is not important.

Lemons: Available year round; peak March through September. The peel of the lemon should be oily or glossy, thin, and yellow. If it has a green tinge, all the better; it's very fresh, has a good flavor, and will store longer than a yellow lemon. Choose small to medium-sized lemons, as larger lemons tend to be thick skinned and less juicy. Buy those that are least pointed on the ends. Check the stem end for soft spots, mold, decay, or discoloration. Lemons store in the refrigerator for a month or more, so keep some handy to flavor everything from iced tea to yogurt. See below for how to freeze lemon juice cubes.

Limes: Available year round; peak June through August. Persian limes should have shiny green peels; Key limes should have light yellow peels. Limes should be glossy, firm, and have no dark patches. When limes begin turning brownish yellow, use them fast. Freeze lime juice as lemon juice below.

Tangerines: Available October through April; peak November through January. Tangerines are easy to peel. Select lustrous, glossy tangerines that are deep-yellow or orange, almost red, not pale yellow or greenish. They don't have to feel very firm, but don't buy those that are too soft.

Commercial baby orange juice: If you've read about vitamin C, you know that warmth and light destroy this very unstable nutrient. I wonder how much vitamin C remains in the clear glass jars in which commercial baby orange juice is sold. The glass lets in light and these jars are stored at room temperature, not in the supermarket's refrigerator section. And look what you're paying! It is much more economical, natural, and nutritious to buy fresh and squeeze it yourself. Or, if you don't want the inconvenience of squeezing your own, buy the half-gallon cartons of pasteurized orange juice in the refrigerator section of the supermarket. The containers keep out light and they are also kept cold.

Squeezing your own citrus juice: To get the most juice from citrus fruits, roll them on a hard surface before squeezing to break the inner tissues. Some recommend warming them in hot water or in the oven for a minute or two or keeping them at room temperature for a while before squeezing to increase the amount of juice, but warmth destroys vitamin C. So keep citrus fruits cold until immediately before serving. A medium-sized orange will yield about ⅓-½ cup of juice; a lemon, about 3 tablespoons; a grapefruit, about 1 cup; and a lime, 1½-2 tablespoons of juice. Refrigerate fresh-squeezed juice for up to 2 days. Remember to protect from air and heat to minimize vitamin C loss.

Tip: If you need only a few drops of juice, use a fork to prick a small hole in the peel and squeeze a little out.

Freezing juice: You can freeze fresh-squeezed (or non-frozen commercial) juices. Do not refreeze concentrated fruit juices. Juice can be frozen in cubes and then transferred to organic, bleach-free wax paper-lined plastic bags, as in the *Food Cube Method*. Cubes will keep for up to 3 months.

Tip: Buy fresh lemons (or limes) when they are on sale and squeeze and measure tablespoons of their juice in ice cube trays. Transfer the pre-measured recipe-sized lemon juice cubes into wax paper-lined plastic freezer bags, where they will be ready to thaw for your favorite recipes.

Tip: Concentrated frozen fruit juice is often used as a healthy sweetener in recipes. Buy in bulk, proportion frozen juice into recipe-sized amounts without letting the juice thaw, and freeze in small containers or use the *Nested Plastic Bag Method*.

Citrus zest (dried citrus peel): Zest is the colored part of the peel and doesn't include the white pith, which has a bitter flavor. Don't pay for the expensive supermarket varieties when it's so easy to make your own! Choose citrus fruit with thick peels, such as Navel oranges. Use only organic fruit for citrus peels in recipes. Wash and scrub the fruit well, peel off the zest diagonally, which is easier than straight up and down. Remove any white part and chop finely. Dry by spreading out in a single layer on an ungreased baking sheet for 20 minutes in a 200°F oven or overnight at room temperature. Store in a small airtight jar in the refrigerator (baby food jars are a nice size) or freeze. A medium orange will yield 2-3 tablespoons grated zest; a medium lemon will yield 2 teaspoons; a medium lime will yield 1 teaspoon grated zest. These are great for flavoring your herbal tea. Or stir into plain hot water for a beverage or kids' tea. If you wish you can grind into a powder in the blender.

> **Tip:** Use a vegetable peeler to remove peels without white rinds. Grating is easier while the fruit is still whole and uncut. Freeze citrus peels for easier grating.

Granulated zest: Combine the lemon zest from one lemon (about 2-3 teaspoons) with 1-2 tablespoons of granulated sugar and grind to a fine powder in the blender. Store as you would zest (see above). Great in herbal tea!

Cucumbers

Baby must be at least 8-10 months old to eat raw puréed cucumber, because cucumber tends to cause digestive problems.

Equivalents: 1 medium cucumber = 1½ cups sliced.

In season: Available year round; peak May through August.

Choosing: Select small or medium cucumbers that are dark green, solid and firm all over, slender, even-shaped, and have many small lumps on their skin. Whitish tips are OK. Avoid mushy cucumbers with shriveled ends and overgrown cucumbers, which are puffy, large, dull-looking, and possibly yellowed—these will taste bitter. It is almost impossible to find non-organically-grown cucumbers that are not waxed. Wax used on produce is supposedly safe, but it may contain pesticide residues. If you remove the wax by peeling, you also remove a lot of the vitamin A. Don't peel if the cucumber is young and has very tender skin. Use finely diced cucumber as a *Healthy Extra*. Or slice them lengthwise or crosswise for older children to dip into yogurt.

Storing: Store wrapped in an organic, wax paper-lined plastic bag or unwrapped in the vegetable crisper for up to a week. Wrap cut cucumbers well before placing in the refrigerator or other foods will pick up their odor. Sliced, wrapped cucumbers or cucumbers in dressing keep in the refrigerator up to 3 days.

Freezing: Don't.

Purée: Peel, scoop out seeds with a spoon or knife tip, and purée in a blender. Serve immediately and don't freeze.

> **Tip:** To remove seeds from a large cucumber, peel and cut in half lengthwise. Then remove seeds with a melon baller, or run the tip of a teaspoon down the center of each half. Use cucumber sticks as "stirrers" in beverages.

Grapefruit, see Citrus Fruit

Grapes

Baby must be at least 8 months old to eat cut up grapes. Never feed a baby whole grapes; she can choke. Peel them and chop them into small pieces.

Equivalents: 1 pound of grapes = 2½ cups.

In season: Available July through March; peak July and August.

Choosing: Select grapes that are bright, dry, and plump. Avoid shriveled, leaky, wrinkled, or damaged grapes. They should have a good, bright color for their variety. Red grapes should be good and red, but the seedless, common green grapes, to be sweetest, should have a yellowish cast. The grapes should be of good color around each stem and stems should be pliable. Grapes do not ripen off the vine, they must be ripe when picked. They don't get sweeter or juicier either. To test for freshness, pick up a bunch of grapes by the top stem and jiggle it very gently. The grapes should stay firmly attached. The more grapes that fall off, the older the bunch.

Storing: Remove any damaged grapes and store in a plastic bag lined with organic, bleach free wax paper in the refrigerator for up to 5 days.

Freezing: Freeze only the seedless grapes, unless you want to take the time to remove the seeds. Wash grapes and remove stems. Freeze in a freezer bag lined with organic, bleach free wax paper.

For my older children, I keep frozen grapes in an open container on the freezer door, for easy grabbing. They don't have time to get freezer burn because they disappear so fast. Kids love these nice little refreshing snacks throughout the hot summer days. Whole frozen grapes are for older children only, they are choking hazards for babies and toddlers.

Honeydew Melons

Baby must be at least 8 months old to eat Honeydew melons.

In season: Available year round; peak June through October.

Choosing: Ripe melons should have a creamy white, ivory, or pale yellow color, even on the underside, and a faint and pleasant scent. Mature honeydews have a light velvety feel to their rind. Don't buy a slick, bald feeling melon—it's too mature. A ripe melon has a slightly soft blossom and stem end. The stem will not necessarily be smooth. Avoid those with punctures in the rind or water-soaked areas, and those with a greenish white or white color. Gently shake the melon, if you hear sloshing inside, pass on it. Buy large honeydews that are at least six inches in diameter and weigh at least five pounds. A cut melon's flesh should look soft and juicy and have a pleasant scent.

Storing: If necessary, ripen at room temperature away from sunlight for up to 4 days. It will get no sweeter, but it will get softer and juicier. Store ripe, whole melon in a plastic bag lined with organic, bleach free wax paper in the refrigerator for about a week; store cut melon for up to 5 days. Leave the seeds in halved melons for longer freshness.

Freezing: Follow directions for freezing cantaloupe.

Tip: Use an ice cream scoop to remove seeds from halved melons.

Kiwi Fruit

Baby must be at least 8 months old to eat peeled kiwi fruit; peels are choking hazards.

Kiwi fruit is a funny-looking brown, fuzzy, egg-shaped fruit with beautiful insides. The bright green flesh, little black seeds, and cheesecake-like center can be used as *Super Baby Food Decorative Touches* in many toddler meals. Kiwi fruit is a good source of vitamin C and babies love its natural sweet taste. For a quick and easy snack, I grab a cool, ripe kiwi out of the fridge, wash it, cut it in half, and use a spoon to feed my baby right out of the peel. Don't be surprised if you see the little black seeds in your baby's diaper!

In season: Available year round; peak June through March.

Choosing: Select fruit that is plump with no bruises. A ripe kiwi yields to gentle pressure and feels soft (as a ripe peach does), but not mushy or spongy. In the store, it will probably still be firm, so you must ripen at home. Make sure it is evenly firm with no soft or shriveling spots.

Storing: Ripen at room temperature out of sunlight, turning fruit occasionally. Refrigerate ripened kiwis in plastic bag lined with organic, bleach free wax paper or vegetable crisper for up to one week.

Serving: Cut in half and scoop out flesh and edible seeds. Mash with fork and serve immediately before the vitamin C is destroyed by air, light, and warm temperature. Kiwis are quite watery—you may want to mix with a thickener, such as or ground dry oatmeal or wheat germ. For older babies, you can slice or dice the fruit and serve as finger food. Peel first to prevent choking.

Freezing: Peel kiwis with vegetable peeler. Purée and freeze using the *Food Cube Method* and keep for up to 2 months. You may want to add a little lemon juice (if your baby is old enough for citrus) to prevent darkening. You can also freeze kiwis sliced, diced, or left whole. Follow directions for freezing cantaloupe.

Kiwi and gelatin: Gelatin will not set if has kiwi in it because kiwis contain a protease enzyme called actinidin that will keep the gelatin from setting.

*Lemons, see **Citrus Fruits***

Limes, see Citrus Fruits

Mangoes

Baby must be at least 6 months old to eat mangoes.

Besides being delicious (and expensive), mangoes are nutritious with their vitamins A (orange color indicates beta carotene), C, and D. Mangoes are antiviral; mango juice poured into a test tube with live viruses actually deactivates them.

In season: Available May through August; peak June and July.

Choosing: Select fresh-looking, plump mangoes with a pleasant fragrance and smooth, undamaged skin. They should be at least 5 inches in diameter. Choose those with the fewest possible black spots, where the damage will move into the flesh when the fruit is very ripe. When ripe, mangoes are orange-yellow or red and feel soft. You can buy them firm and partially green and ripen them at home, but don't buy them completely green, as they may not ripen.

Storing: Ripen, uncovered, at room temperature out of direct sunlight before storing. Store ripened fruit in an organic, bleach-free wax paper-lined plastic bag for up to 3 days.

Peeling: With a sharp knife, slash the peel. Over a bowl, slowly tear back the peel and scoop out the flesh. Or slice completely into the fruit to the pit and divide into two half bowls. Scoop out flesh. Purée for young baby. Give diced pieces to older baby. Serve immediately to prevent air and warmth from destroying the vitamin C.

Freezing: Peel, pit, purée, add a little lemon juice (if your baby is old enough for citrus) to prevent discoloring if you like, and freeze using the *Food Cube Method* and keep for up to 10 months.

Nectarines

Baby must be at least 6 months old to eat cooked nectarines, 7 months for raw puréed.

Nectarines can be used in any recipe in place of peaches. Their hue indicates a good beta-carotene (vitamin A) content and they also contain some vitamin C.

Equivalents: 3 or 4 medium nectarines = 1 pound = 2 cups peeled and sliced.

In season: Available June through August; peak in July.

Choosing: Select plump, smooth nectarines with a bright color. Color hues (red, yellow, tan flecks, or even green spots) are not good indicators of ripeness. Look for a bright color and avoid dull fruit. Unfortunately, the brightness may come from a wax coating. Wax used on produce is supposedly safe, but it may contain pesticide residues. They should feel slightly soft along the seam. Don't buy dull, hard, wrinkled, or shriveled fruit or fruit with soft spots, mold, or broken skin. Use your nose and buy only fruit that has a sweet fragrance.

Storing: Ripen, if necessary, at room temperature for up to 3 days. Store ripened fruit in an organic, bleach-free wax paper-lined plastic bag in the refrigerator for up to 5 days. If cut, store tightly wrapped nectarine pieces in refrigerator for at most 2 days. If you want to prevent exposed cut flesh from darkening, rub it with lemon juice (if baby is old enough for citrus).

Freezing: Wash and peel nectarines with vegetable peeler. Remove pit, purée, and freeze using the *Food Cube Method* and keep for up to 2 months. You may want to add a little lemon juice (if your baby is old enough for citrus) to prevent darkening. Or, you can freeze nectarine halves. Wash, peel, remove pit, place in rigid (freezer-safe, glass) container and cover with orange juice (if your baby is old enough for citrus) to prevent darkening. Leave a little head room for expansion. Nectarine chunks or halves will keep in the freezer for up to a year.

Oranges, see Citrus Fruits

Papaya

Baby must be at least 6 months old to eat cooked papaya, 7 months for puréed raw papaya.

The orange-colored flesh of the papaya indicates its high beta carotene (vitamin A) content. Papayas are loaded with vitamin C.

In season: Available year round; peak April through July.

Choosing: Select fruit that is smooth, well-shaped, unbruised, unbroken, and at least half yellow with as little green as possible. Avoid fruit that has any soft spots or is mushy or shriveled. You will probably find papaya in the market unripened and firm. Let it ripen at room temperature for up to 5 days. Ripe papaya turns all yellow, has a pleasant fragrance, and becomes soft like a ripe peach, so that it yields to gentle pressure.

Storing: Store ripe papaya in a plastic bag lined with organic, bleach free wax paper in refrigerator for up to 2 weeks.

Serving: Cut in half lengthwise and remove seeds for baby. (The seeds are edible. You can grind them in the blender until they are the size of coarsely ground pepper and add them to drinks or salad dressings.) Mash some papaya and serve immediately to your baby, before the warmth and light in the room destroy the vitamin C.

Freezing: Remove black seeds and follow directions for freezing cantaloupe.

Papaya and gelatin: Gelatin will not set if has papaya in it because papayas contain a protease called papain, which will keep the gelatin from setting.

Peaches

Baby must be at least 6 months old to eat cooked peaches, 7 months for puréed raw peaches.

Equivalents: 4 medium peaches = 1 pound = 2 cups peeled and sliced.

In season: Available May through September; peak July and August.

Choosing: Select firm or slightly soft peaches with a nice fragrance. Pick peaches that have a good shape with a seam that is easily distinguishable. Avoid peaches that are very hard or very soft or those with flattened bruises, which mean inner decay. Color is important. Peaches should have a yellow or cream-colored background, and most varieties also have a red blush. Don't buy peaches that have any green color.

Storing: Ripen at room temperature for a day or two, until the peaches feel soft and yield to gentle pressure. Ripe peaches will have a strong and sweet scent. Store ripe peaches in organic, bleach-free wax paper-lined plastic bags in the refrigerator for up to 5 days. Store cut peaches tightly wrapped in the refrigerator for one or two days. A little lemon juice (if your baby is old enough for citrus) rubbed on the cut flesh will prevent darkening.

Freezing: Peel ripe peaches using a vegetable peeler. Remove pit, purée, and freeze using the *Food Cube Method*. Or freeze peach halves following directions for nectarines.

Pears

Baby must be at least 6 months old to eat cooked pears, 7 months for raw, very ripe pears.

Pears are a good source of fiber and a fair source of vitamins C, B, A, and iron.

Equivalents: 3 medium pears = 1 pound = 2 cups peeled and sliced.

In season: Available year round; peak August through November, depending on variety.

Choosing: In general, pears are usually sold green and turn yellow as they ripen. Select pears that are plump and firm, but not hard. Make sure that the areas around the stem and blossom ends are not weak. Avoid pears that are wilted or shriveled, for they are immature and will never ripen. To be sure that pears will ripen, buy those that are a little soft, indicating that they have already begun the ripening process. Don't buy pears with soft spots or those that look dull. Try to get pears that haven't been waxed. Wax used on produce is supposedly safe, but it may contain pesticide residues.

Color is important: Bartlett (this summer pear is probably the most common) should be pale to rich yellow or dark red, peak availability is July through November; Bosc pears should be greenish yellow to brownish yellow background with differing intensities of reddish blush; Comice pears should be light green to yellow green or dark red; Winter Nellis should be medium to light green. In the one case of the d'Anjou variety, color does not indicate ripeness.

Storing: Ripen at room temperature for up to 5 days, until they become soft and yield to gentle pressure. Store ripe pears in an organic, bleach-free wax paper-lined plastic bag in the refrigerator for up to 5 days. Store cut pears wrapped tightly in the refrigerator for a day or two. If you wish, rub cut flesh with lemon juice (if your baby is old enough for citrus) to prevent darkening.

Freezing: Freeze and purée pears that are still a little firm, before they turn completely soft. Peel, remove core and seeds, and purée flesh. Add a little lemon juice (if your baby is old enough for citrus) to prevent darkening. Pears will keep in the freezer for up to one year.

Pineapples

Baby must be at least 9 months old to eat pineapple. Pineapples can be acidic, so watch for reactions.

Pineapples are fun! They also contain a good amount of vitamin C and manganese.

Equivalents: 1 medium pineapple = about 3½ pounds = 3 cups peeled and diced.

In season: Available year round; peak March through July.

Choosing: Select the largest pineapple possible; it will give you more fruit. Buy only those pineapples that are plump, firm, glossy, and bright. Don't buy pineapples that are a dull yellowish-green, as they may never ripen. Spikes (leaves on top) should be fresh-looking and green. It is important that the fruit have a strong, sweet fragrance—a sour or fermented smell means it's overripe. Soft or dark spots or bruises are a sign of decay, which will spread rapidly underneath. The pips, or eyes, should be flat, glossy, and slightly separated. Avoid pineapples whose eyes are either pointy or sunken.

Ripening: Leave the pineapple at room temperature for up to 2 days to get it softer and juicier. When the pineapple is ready to be eaten, the spikes will pull out easily. The mature unripe pineapples are green and turn yellow and orange and become softer and juicier as they ripen. A ripe pineapple will sound solid, not hollow, if you thump your finger against it.

Storing: Store whole pineapple in an organic, bleach-free wax paper-lined plastic bag in the refrigerator for up to 5 days. Cut pineapple keeps longer than whole pineapple. Place pieces in an airtight bag or container for up to one week. (Yes, cut pineapple lasts longer than whole pineapple.)

Preparation: Here's an easy way to cut up a pineapple. Slice lengthwise into quarters. Use a knife, preferably curved, to slice core off top of each quarter. Slice the edible flesh from the peel. Discard the core and peel. Purée or dice the flesh. A medium-sized pineapple yields about 3 cups of diced fruit. If you wish to use only part of a pineapple, slice it whole starting from the bottom, and peel and core each disc individually. Cover the cut end of the pineapple very well before refrigerating.

Tip: Wear an oven mitt while slicing pineapple for a good "unpicky" grip.

Canned: Although I usually don't recommend canned food, unsweetened canned pineapple is a nice treat for baby, and it's a fair source of vitamin C. Crushed canned pineapple, if finely chopped is a good finger food. It can be added as a natural sweetener to yogurt, cottage cheese, tofu, etc. Transfer opened canned pineapple to a glass dish, cover tightly, and it will keep in the refrigerator for up to one week.

Freezing: Freeze the purée from fresh (not canned) pineapple using the *Food Cube Method* or freeze diced pineapple pieces covered in their own natural juice. For a better texture, serve thawed pineapple to adults while it is still a little bit frozen.

Pineapple and gelatin: Don't add fresh pineapple to a recipe with gelatin. It contains a protease enzyme called bromelain that prevents the gelatin from setting because it breaks down proteins (this is why it makes meat tender). There is no problem with canned pineapple, because the canning/ heating process destroys the bromelian. Use agar instead of gelatin and there will be no problem with any pineapple, fresh or frozen.

Plums and Fresh Prunes

Baby must be at least 8 months old to eat fresh plums.

Fresh prunes and plums are almost the same fruit. One difference is that fresh prunes are "freestone"—the pit pulls out easily from fresh prunes, as peach pits do. It's no easy job to remove the flesh from a plum pit. It really hangs on! Another difference is that fresh prunes don't ferment during the drying process, which is why dried prunes are so common. Also, fresh prunes are firmer, sweeter, and more acid than plums.

Equivalents: 8 medium fresh plums = 1 pound = 2½ cups pitted.

In season: Peak July through August.

Choosing: Choose fruit that is brightly colored for their variety. They should be firm, not too soft and leaky and not too hard and wrinkled. Feel the skin—it should be slightly soft and yield to gentle pressure. Don't buy dull or bruised fruit.

Storing: Ripen firm fruit at room temperature for a day or two. Store ripe fruit in a vegetable crisper or in an organic, bleach-free wax paper-lined plastic bag in the refrigerator for up to 5 days.

Preparation: Wash, peel, remove pit, and purée.

Freezing: Freeze purée using the *Food Cube Method* and keep for up to 3 months. Add a little lemon juice (if your baby is old enough for citrus) to prevent darkening, if you wish. You can freeze plums or fresh prunes whole in their peels in an organic, bleach-free wax paper-lined plastic freezer bag for up to 3 months. Before thawing whole frozen fruit, dip in cold water for 15 seconds and rub off the peels—they'll come off easily. Thaw and serve.

> **Tip:** Replace butter/oil with prune butter. Prune butter—a thickened prune purée—can be substituted in equal amounts for butter or oil in baked goods. Substitute up to ¾ of the butter/oil called for in the recipe with prune butter and you will still have a nice texture in the final product. Prune butter goes especially well in brownies and other recipes with cocoa powder, dark muffins, quick breads, cakes, and cookies. You can buy prune butter, also called "lekvar," in your supermarket or natural foods store. Or you can use jarred baby prunes instead of prune butter, but they are usually more expensive. Or you can make your own.

*Prunes, see **Plums***

Rhubarb

Baby must be at least 9 months old to eat cooked rhubarb. NEVER feed baby (or yourself) raw rhubarb.

Rhubarb, or "pieplant," is technically a vegetable, but frequently referred to as a fruit due to its flavor.

Equivalents: 1 pound rhubarb = 3 cups slices = 2 cups cooked.

In season: Available January through August; peak May.

Choosing: Select bright, shiny, firm, crisp rhubarb that is a good red or pink color. Stalks should be neither too thick or too thin. Avoid wilted, flabby, stringy, or rough-textured rhubarb.

Storing: Store in plastic bag lined with organic, bleach free wax paper in the refrigerator for up to one week.

Preparation for cooking: DO NOT eat rhubarb leaves; they are toxic and can be fatal. Eat only the stalks. Discard leaves, and wash and slice the stalks into 1½ inch slices.

Steam: Steam 20 minutes.

Bake: Bake in covered dish in a pre-heated 350°F oven for about 30 minutes.

Serve: Purée cooked rhubarb stalks and add about 3 tablespoons of maple syrup for each pound. Add thickener (ground oatmeal, wheat germ, whole grain bread crumbs) if too watery. Store leftover cooked purée, tightly covered, in the refrigerator for up to 5 days.

Freezing: Freeze using the *Food Cube Method* and keep for up to 6 months.

Strawberries

Baby must be at least 9 months old to eat mashed raw strawberries. Strawberries are a common allergen and your pediatrician may want you to wait until your baby is one year old (some say 2 years old) before you introduce them to your baby. Check first, especially if there is an allergy to strawberries in your family.

Purée or mash them for babies from 9 months to a year of age and make sure there are no large peels.

Equivalents: 1 pint berries = 2 cups.

In season: Available March through September; peak April through June

Choosing strawberries: Select strawberries that are firm, plump, lustrous, moist-looking, those that smell sweet, and those that are completely deep red. Leaf caps should be attached and fresh. Avoid strawberries that are greenish or with large uncolored areas, dull, shrunken, shriveled, bruised, soft, or those with dry, brown leaf caps. Don't go by the nice berries on top—make sure you check all berries in the bottom of the container. The container should not be stained or sticky—check the bottom. Don't buy those in large containers because the bottom ones definitely will be crushed.

Cleaning and storing strawberries: Strawberries, and other berries bruise very easily and you must treat them gently. Immediately remove decayed, moldy, or bruised berries before the damage spreads to other berries. Ideally, berries should not be washed until you are ready to use them. But, I wash them before they go into the refrigerator so they are ready to grab for quick snacks. (It's against my kids' religion to wash fruit.) Berries are best cleaned by placing them in a colander or large strainer and dipping them in water or gently spraying them with the sink hose or slow-running tap water. Don't soak berries because their juice will be replaced with the water through osmosis. Let the berries drip dry for a short while and then place them back into the container they came in—usually a green plastic basket or a perforated cardboard container. Or place them in a colander. Don't layer them too deep or the bottom berries will be crushed. Cover them well with a piece of organic, unbleached wax paper and then plastic wrap. Strawberries may get moldy within a day or two. One way you can prolong strawberries' keeping time is to wash them and let them dry completely. Then place them in a glass jar with an airtight screw top lid, place a paper towel over them in the jar to absorb moisture, tightly close the jar, and refrigerate. Leave strawberries' green caps on when you store them—open areas in strawberry flesh left from ripping out the caps will decay rapidly. Clean strawberries by rinsing them well before removing their stems or they will become soggy.

Freezing berries: Pick berries over, wash them, and then remove the leaf caps. Freeze in an organic, bleach-free wax paper-lined plastic freezer bag or in a glass container, or use the *Tray-Freeze Method*. Leave a little head room (½ inch) in any rigid container for expansion. Label and date them. Strawberries will keep frozen for up to 6 months.

Thawing berries: Frozen berries in a wax paper-lined plastic bag can be thawed by placing the bag in a big bowl of cold water for 10-20 minutes— move them around a bit during thawing. (This bowl method can't be used to thaw big pieces of fruit because it would take too long at room temperature for them to thaw. Foods should never be thawed for more than several minutes at room temperature)

Tangerines, see Citrus Fruits

Tomatoes

Baby must be at least 1 year old to eat raw tomatoes or tomato juice.

If you've ever tasted a fresh ripe red tomato right off the vine, you know that there's no comparison in taste to the supermarket variety. It would be too expensive to let mass-grown tomatoes ripen on the vine, so commercially grown tomatoes are picked and then ripen after. Even "vine-ripened" tomatoes are picked when they are still pink. Some agribusiness tomatoes are even ripened in the truck while in transit. If you can't get your hands on yours (or a friend's) home-grown tomatoes, the next best thing is your local Farmers' Market or roadside stand. Vine-ripened tomatoes will have much more vitamin C and other nutrients than those gassed-to-ripeness or those ripened off the vine. Tomatoes are really a fruit, not a vegetable. Small chunks of the soft inner part of raw tomatoes, without seeds or peels, are a nutritious finger food for toddlers.

Equivalents: 3 medium tomatoes = 1 pound = 1½ cups peeled, seeded, and chopped.

In season: Available year round; peak June through August.

Choosing: Select firm, plump, smooth, well-formed tomatoes with good uniform color. They should feel heavy for their size. It's OK if there are a few small scars near the stem, but don't buy those with large cracks. Those that were vine-ripened have a fresh tomato-y smell, whereas those gas-ripened are odorless. Don't buy overripe tomatoes—soft or watery tomatoes and those with wet spots, depressions, mold, or bruises. Cherry tomatoes are usually flavorful.

Ripen: Ripen at room temperature away from sunlight for up to 5 days, but only if they have not been previously refrigerated. Ripe tomatoes will be a good red color and yield to gentle pressure. If you need a ripe tomato fast, put a tomato in a paper bag with an apple. The apple will release ethylene gas and speed the tomato's ripening. Sunlight will not speed tomatoes' ripening, it only softens them.

Storing: Once ripened, tomatoes will store for up to another week at room temperature. Keep them away from sunlight. Try to use tomatoes before you must refrigerate them, because cool temperatures take away their sweetness. If a tomato is becoming overripe, then go ahead and put it in the refrigerator. When it comes time to eat, place it at room temperature for an hour or so, until the chill goes. Tomatoes taste much better at room temperature than when chilled. Store cut tomatoes in a tightly sealed container or in an organic, bleach-free wax paper-lined plastic bag in the refrigerator for up to 2 days. Remember to keep cut tomatoes out of air, warmth, and light to preserve the vitamin C.

Preparation: Cut in half and remove seeds. Scoop out the flesh and purée.

Tip: For tomatoes in salads, slice vertically and the slices will stay firmer.

Freezing: Freeze purée using the *Food Cube Method* and keep for up to 1 year. Whole tomatoes or pieces don't need blanching before you freeze them in a organic, bleach-free wax paper-lined freezer bags—but core them first. Frozen tomatoes are very easy to peel. When thawed, tomato pieces will be mushy; use in sauces, soups, and stews.

Canned tomatoes: Sometimes canned tomatoes are better than the poor quality raw tomatoes discussed above. Read the label carefully and don't buy cans with salt, sugar, or preservatives added. Tomato paste or tomato purée in the can should not be fed to your baby—both are concentrated, but they are OK to use in baby's pasta sauce. Try to buy cans with an expiration date, as canned tomato products don't keep as long as other canned vegetables. Store opened canned tomato product leftovers in tightly covered glass jars for up to 1 week in the refrigerator. If you leave them in the can, they sometimes pick up a tinny or metallic flavor.

Sauce: Don't go through the trouble of peeling and seeding tomatoes for sauce. Throw the whole tomato in the processor and blend away.

Watermelon

Baby must be at least 8 months old to eat watermelon.

In season: Available April through September; peak June through August.

Choosing: Select whole melons that feel smooth and look slightly dull, not shiny. They should be symmetrically shaped with full rounded, not flat, ends. The rind should be light green with dark green veins. The underside should have a cream or light yellowish color, not white or pale green. All of these indicators still do not insure a good watermelon. You just can't judge a watermelon by its cover. It's best to buy melon already cut. Look for red, crisp, firm, and juicy flesh, which is not dry, mushy, fibrous, or stringy and has no white streaks running lengthwise through it. Seeds should be dark and black or dark brown, not white, which is a sign of immaturity.

Storing: Keep whole melon in the refrigerator for up to one week. If you don't have the refrigerator room, whole melons can be kept at room temperature for a few days. If melon is cut, wrap pieces tightly in an organic, bleach-free wax paper and then plastic and store in refrigerator for up to 4 days.

Freezing: Follow directions for freezing cantaloupe.

22

Whole Grain Super Baby Foods

Whole Grains vs Processed Grains

There is an enormous nutritional difference between whole grains and the enriched, processed grains used in most of America's food products. The word "enriched" means that more than a dozen natural nutrients have been destroyed during processing and a few synthetic ones (thiamin, riboflavin, niacin, iron, and maybe calcium) have been replaced in unnatural proportions. See the comparison table on the next page. (Enriched is not the same as "fortified," which indicates that nutrients have been added that were never present in the first place.)

endosperm
bran
germ
Whole wheat kernel

Let's take whole wheat as an example. In the natural foods store on the grains shelf, you will see whole wheat kernels that look very similar to brown rice. If you were to dissect a kernel of whole wheat, you would find that it has the three parts pictured on the left.

- **The bran** (as in wheat bran) is about 14% of the wheat kernel. It contains almost all of the fiber, some minerals, B vitamins, and a little incomplete protein. This layered outer covering of the grain is stiffer and harder than the inside of the kernel and offers it some protection against the outside world, as an apple peel protects the innards of an apple. It makes sense that the bran contains most of the fiber of the wheat kernel.

- **The germ** (as in wheat germ) is less than 3% of the wheat kernel, but it contains almost all of its nutrients, including vitamin E and unsaturated fatty acids or oils. The germ is the seed of the wheat plant and contains the stuff to grow new life.

- **The endosperm** is 83% of the wheat kernel. It is almost all starch with minute amounts of nutrients. White flour is made from the nutrition-less endosperm.

The whole wheat kernel, with its germ and surrounding support system, is actually the seed of the wheat plant. Plant it and it will grow; place it in water and it will sprout.

When whole wheat is ground into flour, it contains the germ and the bran. But when whole wheat flour is refined into white flour, the germ and bran, along with all their nutrients and fiber, are removed. White flour is the stuff from which most commercial breads, rolls, biscuits, pretzels, muffins, cookies, cakes, and hundreds of other food products are made. In addition, 40% of the chromium, 89% of the cobalt, and 48% of the molybdenum is removed during refinement.

Comparison of Whole Wheat Flour, White Flour, and Enriched White Flour - Nutrients in a half-cup			
	Whole Wheat Flour	White Flour	Enriched Flour	% Removed In Refinement
calories	203	226	226	
protein	8.22	6.40	6.40	22%
fat	1.12	0.61	0.61	
carbohydrate	43.54	47.31	47.31	
fiber	1.26	0.15	0.15	88%
calcium	20.00	9.00	156.24	
iron	2.33	0.73	2.88	
magnesium	83.00	13.00	13.00	84%
phosphorus	208.00	67.00	67.00	68%
potassium	243.00	66.00	66.00	73%
sodium	3.00	1.00	1.00	67%
zinc	1.76	0.44	0.44	75%
copper	0.23	0.09	0.09	61%
manganese	2.28	0.42	0.42	81%
thiamine	0.27	0.27	0.49	
riboflavin	0.13	0.02	0.31	
niacin	3.82	0.78	3.66	4%
pantothenic acid	0.61	0.27	0.27	55%
vitamin B6	0.21	0.03	0.03	87%
folic acid	26.00	16.00	16.00	38%

Note: Folic acid has been added to enriched flour since 1998.

In 1998, food manufacturers began to add folic acid to enriched processed flour. Folic acid helps to prevent some birth defects, such as spina bifida and others. Folic acid is the B vitamin that the fetus needs in the first few weeks of pregnancy—usually before the woman knows that she is pregnant.

Why do manufacturers go through the trouble to remove the germ and the bran? After all, the process must cost them money. The reason is simple. White flour has an indefinite shelf life. The oils contained in the germ make whole wheat flour go rancid, get bitter and spoil quickly. Refined white flour lasts forever because it's virtually lifeless. And then, as if removing the germ and bran were not enough, food manufacturers go even further to strip white flour of any minute food value left in it by bleaching. Bleaching makes it very white and pretty.

Incidentally, the reason why wheat flour is so often used for bread products, rather than rye flour or some other flour, is because of its high gluten content. Gluten is the ingredient in flour that makes breads and bread products become soft and elastic and rise high.

Keep Whole Wheat Flour Refrigerated

Whole wheat flour keeps only for about a week at room temperature, so refrigerate it if you don't plan on using it soon. And always refrigerate it on hot days. You can tell if whole wheat flour is fresh by tasting it. If it has the least amount of bitterness, it is spoiled. Breads made from whole wheat flour at your natural foods store are usually frozen.

BUYER BEWARE:
Misleading Advertising:
"Wheat" does not mean "Whole Wheat"

If a package says "wheat flour," it does NOT mean whole wheat flour. White flour IS wheat flour—the nutrition-less endosperm part of the wheat kernel. I believe that the manufacturer is hoping that the uninformed consumer will take "wheat flour" to mean "whole wheat flour." Manufacturers may also put in big letters on the package that a product is "Made from whole wheat." Well, there may be only a small amount of whole wheat flour in the product, while most of it is actually wheat flour (white flour). Read the ingredients list. Another trick of the food manufacturing trade is the use of the word *wholesome*. "Made from wholesome wheat flour" means that it's made from plain old wheat/white flour, which, in my opinion, is not wholesome at all!

"Wheat bread" does not mean "Whole Wheat bread"

BUYER BEWARE: Nutritionists used to recommend that you eat dark bread, because it was made from whole grains. Then the food manufacturers caught on and added caramel coloring to their bread to make it a dark color, so that consumers would think it was healthier. Protect yourself by reading the ingredients list.

Bread Is Not the Only White Flour Product

Beware that typical American supermarket bagels, breakfast cereals, rolls, crackers, pretzels, spaghetti and other pasta products, buns, pizza crusts, pastries, cakes, cupcakes, and cookies are made from white flour.

> **WARNING: Read the ingredients list thoroughly and do not buy any bread or bread products containing hydrogenated oils.**

Other Whole Grains

White rice is to brown rice as white flour is to whole wheat flour. De-germinated cornmeal is to whole grain cornmeal as white flour is to whole wheat flour. The word de-germinated sounds like something good, doesn't it? Take the germs out. Well, now we know that the germ is the staff of life, and foods that are de-germinated might as well be labeled denatured and de-nutrified. "Enriched" is another word that makes white flour sound healthy, as discussed earlier in this chapter. Even at the natural foods store, these food manufacturers' tricks are used. Make sure a product is labeled "whole millet flour," "whole cornmeal," "whole corn flour," "whole rye flour," etc.

NOTE: Cream of Wheat® is not a whole-grain cereal.

How to Cook Whole Grains

Of course, grinding grains and making *Super Porridge* is one way to cook whole grains. But for older folks and for your baby, when he gets old enough to eat food that is not puréed, grains are usually cooked without grinding them first.

Rinsing Grains Before Cooking

Some people recommend washing grains before cooking by rinsing them under cold running tap water. Rinsing causes a loss of B vitamins. I don't rinse mine, unless I can actually see surface grit. I buy organic so I don't have to worry about pesticides, and I feel that the boiling water will sterilize the grains. However, if you prefer, you can rinse your grains.

Cooking Grains on the Stove Top

Cooking whole grains is as easy as boiling water. Bring the recommended amount of water to a boil (see table on next page). Use a pot large enough to hold the grains and the water, with a little (or a lot of) headroom leftover. Note that the heavier the pot, the less the chance of scorching. Sprinkle whole grains into boiling water. Stir once and only once. Cover the pot and turn heat down to the lowest setting. Let simmer for the recommended time. Do not stir again because you can damage the grains and cause them to cook unevenly and be gummy. Keep a close eye on the pot for the first several minutes in case it starts to boil over. Then you can quickly move it off the burner and turn down the heat.

Another way you can cook whole grains on the stove top is to put them in cold water and then bring it to a boil. Cover the pot and turn heat down to lowest setting. Let simmer for the recommended time. The grains will be creamier, as you would want for puddings. However, the grains are not as fluffy with this method.

Although you may have to wait up to 45 minutes or more for grains to cook, it is all wait time. That's why cooking grains is so easy—they require no attention.

Grain Cooking Quick Reference

For each cup of dry grain	Use this many cups of water	And simmer for this many minutes
amaranth	2	25
barley, pearled	2¾	40-45
brown rice	2	45
buckwheat groats	2	15-20
bulgur	2	15-20
couscous	1¾	4
kamut	2	50
millet	3	45
oatmeal/rolled oats	2	15
oats, whole	3	45-60
quinoa	2	15-20
rye berries	4	60
sorghum	3	45
teff	3	15
triticale	4	60
wheat, cracked	2	25
wheat berries	3	120

For cornmeal, see recipe for polenta, page 470.

TIP: Replacing some or all of the water with stock makes the grains much more flavorful. Or use milk, which will add to the nutrition and protein content. Or try undiluted tomato juice. You can also use apple juice or other sweet fruit juice, but replace no more than ⅓ of the water or the grains will be too sweet.

TIP: For a distinct flavor, toast grains for a few minutes in a heavy skillet on the stove top in a little butter. Then cook as discussed above.

Cooking Grains in the Oven

Grains can be baked in the oven. In a casserole dish, combine boiling water and dry grains using proportions in the table above. Bake, covered, at 375°F for 30-45 minutes or until water is absorbed. Or you can use your oven as a slow grain cooker. Mix grains with water (cold or boiling) in a covered casserole and bake at 200°F for 4 hours or more, until water is absorbed. Slow cooking at this low heat saves nutrients that would be destroyed at higher temperatures.

Grain Steamers

You certainly do not need to buy one, but if you already have a rice steamer, a vegetable steamer, or any food steamer, you can use it to cook whole grains. The metal units that look like a crock pot work well. Follow the instruction manual for how to cook rice in order to use the steamer to cook any other grain.

Storing Cooked Whole Grains

Grains cooked whole can be kept refrigerated, covered well, for up to 5 days. Reheat on the stove top.

Cooked grains freeze well and will keep frozen for up to 3 months. Divide into individual portions and freeze using the *Nested Plastic Bag Method*. To reheat frozen grains, transfer them out of the bag and into a small pot on the stove top. Defrosting is not necessary. Add a tablespoon of water for each cup of grains, or as needed to achieve the desired consistency.

> **TIP:** Use leftover grains as an addition to soups to make them more hearty and to add a nutritional boost. Mix them with a little salad dressing. Make fried brown rice or other grain by sautéing in a little oil with chopped onions/scallions, mushrooms, cooked peas, etc.

Making Super Porridge from Cooked Grains

Super Porridge can also be made from grains that have been cooked whole with no grinding. First, cook grains as described previously, using the proper amount of liquid. Then mix the COOKED grains with ADDITIONAL liquid and grind in the processor until you have a smooth consistency. For the smooth texture needed for a beginning eater, use an amount of liquid equal to the amount of cooked grains and purée to a smooth consistency.

For example, let's say you have cooked some brown rice for the adults in your family and you'd like to use some to make into *Super Porridge* for the baby. For a ½ cup of the cooked brown rice, add a ½ cup of liquid (water, breast milk/formula) and grind in the blender or processor until smooth. For a ¼ cup of cooked brown rice, use a ¼ cup of liquid, etc. Use the same amount of liquid as cooked grains. If necessary, add more liquid during processing to get a smooth consistency.

As your baby gets older, she will be ready for a more textured and chunkier *Super Porridge*, but not quite ready to eat whole cooked unground grains (like the rice we eat as adults). When she's in this "in-between" stage, here's how to make a more textured cereal: Make *Super Porridge* as instructed in the previous paragraph, but with less grinding. In other words, don't grind until the cereal is very smooth—leave a little chunkiness in it. As your baby becomes ready for even more texture and chunkiness, try adding less liquid and grind for even less time. Gradually decrease the liquid and increase the chunkiness until she can handle adult-style whole grains.

TIP: The INCORRECT method for increasing chunkiness in *Super Porridge* is to follow the directions in the last chapter with less grinding. For grains to cook in 10 minutes, they must be ground into a powder. If you incompletely grind dry grains and leave big chunks of dry grain in the powder and cook for only 10 minutes, there will be hard, undercooked grain pieces in the *Super Porridge*. Therefore, the way to increase texture in *Super Porridge* for an older baby is to cook the grains completely as described in this chapter and then grind less and use less additional liquid.

Wheat Germ

Wheat germ is actually the seed of the wheat kernel and, like all seeds, is a super nutritious food. It is one of the parts of the wheat kernel that is removed when whole wheat is refined into white flour or wheat flour. You can buy wheat germ raw or toasted. Because of its oils, it is quite perishable and must be refrigerated or frozen in a tightly closed container. Toasting, although it reduces its nutrient content, will extend its shelf life for up to 6 months in the refrigerator. Toast your own raw wheat germ by spreading it thinly and evenly on an ungreased baking sheet and baking in a pre-heated 325°F oven for 15-20 minutes until lightly browned.

NOTE: Don't feed your baby wheat bran, oat bran, or other bran.

Say Goodbye to White Bread

Every time I see an advertisement containing a sandwich made of glowing white bread I want to scream. It looks very pretty, but as discussed previously, it is a nutritional nightmare. Even worse are the breads that would be lily-white but for the addition of caramel color to darken the bread, which tricks some consumers into thinking it's healthy.

While I'm on the subject of food advertisements, let me blow off some more steam here. How about those advertisements for "big kid nutrition," where they show a hot dog on a white flour roll with French fries and a cola beverage! Aarrggghh!

To prepare an actual nutritious meal, try to buy your bread at your natural foods store or the natural, organic section of your grocery store and read the label carefully. The first ingredient should be "whole wheat flour" or "whole some-other-grain flour" or "whole sprouted grains of wheat," etc. You might find it in the freezer case. When you bring it home, keep it in the freezer until the night before you're going to use it. Then switch it into the refrigerator where it will thaw in several hours. (If you forget the switch and need a quick sandwich, thaw a few slices in the toaster.) The loaf will keep for a couple of weeks in the refrigerator, whereas it would only keep for a day at room temperature. Be prepared to pay more for a loaf of real bread, and remember that, in this case, you get what you pay for.

> **NOTE:** Everything I have read about storing bread says that refrigerating bread hastens the staling process. But this certainly has not been my experience with the whole grain bread I buy from the natural foods store. If not kept in the refrigerator, it gets stale and hard within a day or two. The 100% whole grain bread I have occasionally bought at the supermarket does well at room temperature or in the refrigerator. I suspect that it is white bread that goes stale in the refrigerator.

> **MONEY SAVER:** Don't discard the ends of bread if your family won't eat them. Use them as veggie burger buns. Or grind them into healthy whole grain bread crumbs.

Whole Grain Pasta

Whole grain pasta is an easy and convenient food for babies older than 10-12 months. Buy pasta at your natural foods store, where you'll find it made from whole grains such as whole wheat and brown rice. For babies with wheat allergy, use brown rice or other whole grain pasta. The typical supermarket pasta is made from white flour. Remember, if the ingredients list says "wheat flour," it's only white flour. Spinach pasta actually has very little spinach in it, and is also usually made with wheat flour (white flour), so check the ingredients list. Whole grain pasta is an easy third meal for your baby, and it freezes well.

Freezing and Thawing Pasta

Freeze pasta in individual portions using the *Nested Plastic Bag Method* or the *Phantom Container Method*. Although you can freeze plain pasta (for finger foods), pasta freezes better if it is in sauce. Thaw pasta on the stove top. Reheat dishes you can stir, such as macaroni and cheese, on stove top until warmed throughout, stirring half-way through cooking time. Use a bit of milk to regain a creamy consistency. You can also thaw and reheat pasta by placing it in a strainer and dipping it into boiling water.

Other Whole Grain Products

You will find many other products made from 100% whole grains at the natural foods store: muffins, English muffins, rolls, biscuits, bagels, pizza crusts, pie crusts, cakes, pita, hot cereals, and boxed breakfast cereals.

Home-Baking Whole Grain Bread

"Bread is the staff of life" is a saying that refers to whole grain breads, and not the nutritional disaster made from refined white flour found on the shelves of every supermarket in America. You can buy good quality breads, but they can be found primarily in natural foods stores and in the ever-expanding organic whole foods aisles—thank goodness in increasing numbers. They are expensive, but again, you get what you pay for. My family lived on sprouted 7-grain bread that cost a pretty penny at my local natural foods store. Now, the comparable bread that I bake at home is about a third the price.

As when you make your own baby food, you can be assured that you are using only high quality, wholesome ingredients when you make your own homemade bread. No artificial preservatives are needed in the bread coming fresh out of your own oven. Most people consider it beyond the realm of their abilities to bake their own bread. For most of my life, I had a fear of baking bread—not those quick breads that have baking powder or baking soda as leavening (rising) agents, but the breads that involve yeast and kneading and rising. Every time I saw the words "active yeast" in a cookbook, my mind would automatically say, "Turn to next recipe." But I've recently gotten into baking whole grain yeast breads, and it's not difficult at all. Of course, you can always buy a bread machine that bakes 100% whole grain breads!

If you'd like to learn how to bake whole grain breads by hand, I highly recommend that you buy, or borrow from your local library, some books on bread baking. My favorite is *The Laurel's Kitchen Bread Book: A Guide to Whole-Grain Breadmaking* by Laurel Robertson. Maybe you do bake bread, but only with white flour, because your experience with whole wheat flour has been negative. (No one could eat my first whole-grain loaves without breaking their teeth, so heavy and dense were they.) Perhaps you bake bread with SOME whole wheat flour (less than ½ or ⅓ of the flour) because that's what you thought was necessary to get light loaves. Good news! It IS possible to get light, delicious bread from 100% whole wheat flour if you follow the methods and tips that follow.

Tips for Making Whole Wheat Bread

- When you knead whole wheat dough and want to reduce stickiness, add as little flour as possible to the kneading surface or your fingers—just a light dusting. Or use a little water instead of flour to reduce stickiness. Or don't use any flour or water and use a plastic kitchen scraper or spatula to scrape the dough off the kneading surface and your fingers. Too much flour is one of the most common causes of brick-hard whole wheat bread. It is better for whole wheat dough to be too wet than too dry. If you're used to baking with white flour, know that whole wheat flour will still feel tacky even after it has been thoroughly kneaded.

- To get a good rise, the yeast must be fresh and of good quality. Also, make sure the liquid is at the right temperature for the yeast (110°F or the temperature stated on the packet instructions). The temperature of the warm rising place should be between 80°F and 90°F for a nice, slow, good rise. Also, a longer rising time, or a little extra sweetener, will increase the rise.

- Use whole wheat flour that is as fresh as possible; it should be less than 2 months old. You can tell if whole wheat flour is fresh by tasting it—it should have no trace of bitterness. Whole wheat and other whole grain flours keep at room temperature for only about one week. If you won't use them in that time, refrigerate for up to 2 months, or freeze for up to 6 months. If you really get into baking with whole grains, invest in a home mill to grind flour at home. There's nothing like a loaf of bread made with freshly ground flour. You can get freshly ground coffee beans at the supermarket. Maybe freshly ground flour will be available some day.

- Use whole wheat flour of good quality, which you will find at your local natural foods store. The best flour for bread comes from HARD red spring wheat, because it forms stronger gluten when kneaded. Buy flour with a high gluten content. Look for flour with at least 14% protein content. Buy only "bread flour" and not "all purpose" or "pastry flour."

- To get a light loaf, you must knead whole wheat dough longer than white flour dough. When recipes call for 10 minutes of kneading white flour, you may have to knead whole wheat dough for 15-20 minutes, or even longer. Good things take time.

- If your bread is dry or hard, reduce the oven temperature or shorten the baking time. Also, try using a little less yeast.

- If the top or edge of your bread has split or cracked, your oven temperature may be too high.

- Replace a little of the whole wheat flour with gluten flour to increase the dough's elasticity and produce a lighter loaf. Gluten flour, made from wheat flour, is more than half pure gluten. Use this as a last resort, because gluten flour is processed.

- When mixing the dough ingredients, add one teaspoon of baking powder or soda to the dry flour before mixing it with the yeast liquid. It will help the rising.

- After all ingredients have been mixed and before the first kneading, sprinkle ¾ teaspoon of lemon juice or vinegar for each cup of flour in the recipe into the dough mixture to help increase its elasticity. Use no more than ¾ teaspoon per cup of flour, or the acid will inhibit yeast fermentation.

- These tips also hold for other bread products, such as buns, rolls, pizza crusts, pretzels, and breadsticks. Substitute all of that unhealthy white flour for 100% whole wheat flour in your favorite recipes.

About Yeast

Bread yeast is alive. It is a tiny plant, a fungus, which has been used for thousands of years to raise bread. When mixed with warm water, it becomes active, starts eating the sugar and flour, and produces gas (carbon dioxide) as a by-product. Look closely at a slice of bread from your kitchen. Do you see those tiny air holes throughout the bread? That's what makes bread light and airy. The air holes are caused when tiny gas bubbles produced by yeast get caught and held within the bread. The bubbles are retained down in the dough when the dough's consistency is elastic enough to stretch and expand and encase the bubbles. Just as a balloon will stretch and expand and hold air, so will elastic dough. If a balloon is old and dry and not elastic enough, it won't hold air and will burst. If dough is not elastic enough, it will not be able to hold the bubbles within its structure. It is the retention of gas within the dough's structure that causes the dough to expand and "rise." As discussed later, kneading and gluten are necessary to make the dough elastic.

Non-yeast breads (quick breads), pancakes, muffins, cakes, cookies, etc., also have air holes. These bread products are too liquidy and thin or have a non-elastic consistency, which makes slow-working yeast ineffective at raising them. Instead, gas is produced by a chemical reaction among their ingredients. Baking soda (an alkali), when mixed with an acid (buttermilk, yogurt, orange juice, apple cider, molasses, etc.), will produce carbon dioxide gas. Baking powder is a mixture of baking soda (alkali) and an acid (cream of tartar, etc.) and will produce carbon dioxide when mixed with water and other liquids that produce a good acid/alkali balance.

TIP: To test baking soda for freshness, mix a little with a few drops of vinegar or lemon juice. It should bubble. To test baking powder, mix a teaspoon with $1/3$ cup of hot water. It should bubble.

MONEY SAVER: See recipe for Self-Rising Super Flour, page 330.

Bread yeast comes in two varieties: active dry yeasts and quick-rising yeasts. Quick-rising yeast multiplies twice as fast and cuts rising time in half. Active dry yeast retains more nutrients and gives bread a better flavor, so I use active dry yeast in bread recipes. Bread yeast can be purchased in packets or in cakes—one packet is equal to one cake. It used to be that one packet contained a full tablespoon of yeast, but in these days of constantly rising prices, a packet now contains only about 2 teaspoons. I guess manufacturers discovered that the new lesser amount has almost the same leavening power as a tablespoon.

MONEY SAVER: It is much cheaper to buy yeast in bulk from the natural foods store (or Sam's Club, BJ's, or Costco). Keep it in the refrigerator or in the freezer and it will be good for at least 6 months. You'll know if it is no longer good if it doesn't bubble when added to warm water.

> **WARNING:** Don't use brewer's, nutritional, or torula yeast for baking. These yeasts, although I recommend them as nutritional enhancers, will not raise bread because they are inactive.

The Major Steps in Making Yeast Bread Are:

- Mix the dough ingredients
- Knead the dough
- Let the dough rise
- Punch the dough down
- Shape the dough into loaves
- Let the dough rise again
- Bake at 350°F
- Let cool
- Eat!

Basic Whole Wheat Bread Dough Recipe

(makes two loaves)

1 tablespoon active dry yeast or 1 packet active dry yeast

¾ cup warm water (110°F or temperature indicated on yeast packet)

2 cups warm water

3 tablespoons honey

6 cups whole wheat bread flour

2 tablespoons oil

2 teaspoons salt

Making 100% Whole Wheat Bread
Mix the Dough Ingredients

Warm a measuring cup under hot tap water and then measure ¾ cup warm water into it. When the temperature is right, thoroughly stir in the yeast. Put in a warm place for 5-10 minutes or until bubbly. (If it does not get bubbly, the yeast is dead. Buy new yeast and try again.)

Mix 3 tablespoons of honey into 2 cups of warm water. Put 6 cups of flour into a large bowl and stir the salt into it. Make a well in the middle of the flour and slowly pour the honey/water mixture into it. Then add the yeast/water mixture.

Stir dough with a wooden spoon, beginning at center and moving outward. Wet your fingers and hand-mash the dough until it is evenly mixed. The dough should be wet and sticky, but able to hold its shape. If it is too wet and runny, add another few tablespoons of flour. The dough should still be sticky, but not stiff. If it is stiff, making it difficult to squeeze, add one or two tablespoons more water.

Knead the Dough

Dump the dough ball onto the kneading surface and knead for at least 20 minutes. Be careful about adding flour to the kneading surface to reduce stickiness. It is best to use a plastic kitchen scraper or spatula to scrape off dough that sticks to the kneading surface and your fingers. Your kneading will eventually reduce stickiness. If the dough becomes too stiff during kneading, add a little water to your hands.

Kneading is the process of rubbing dough particles against each other either by hand or by machine. (Now you know what that loud clacking sound is from your bread machine in the middle of the night.) Kneading by hand is what people are referring to when they say that making bread is a lot of work. The purpose kneading is to make the dough elastic. The component of the dough that becomes elastic during kneading is called gluten. Wheat flour (either white flour or whole wheat flour) is the flour that contains the most gluten, which is why wheat breads are so common. Other flours, such as rye flour, contain only small amounts of gluten that are not enough to make dough rise. Read the ingredients on a package of commercial rye bread and you will see that white or wheat flour is the main ingredient. Rye flour will be found lower on the list of ingredients, indicating that there is less rye flour than wheat flour in a loaf of rye bread.

Every baker has their own method of kneading. Some pound and throw the dough on the table; some push, pull, and fold; and some use their knuckles. Any method you like is good, as long as you're mushing up that dough. Here's my method: Push on the dough ball with the palms of your hands using the weight of your torso, grasp the dough furthest from you with your fingers and fold it almost in half toward you, push down again, and then give the dough a quarter turn. Fold and repeat the sequence over and over again. When you first start kneading, be gentle during the first few minutes, and then get more vigorous.

When you knead, use a non-sticky surface, such as a wooden board, a marble tabletop, a Formica® kitchen counter top, granite or even a glass surface. Make sure that the surface is at a comfortable height, not so low that you have to bend over to knead and hurt your back, or so high that your elbows aren't at the right angle to give you leaning power.

Most recipes tell you to knead for about 10 minutes. That 10 minutes actually means 15 minutes if you're taking it easy and barely pushing on the dough, or it means 5 minutes if you're angry about something and taking it out on the poor dough. If you need stress relief (and what new parent doesn't), kneading is a good and wholesome outlet. Speaking of wholesome, the first time I kneaded bread dough, I was surprised at how good and natural it felt, even though I had no idea what I was doing. It gets less fun after several minutes though, and I suggest you have something to think about or listen to, like music or the news on the television, to make the time go faster. Or chat with your children—it's good quality time and they'll look back and remember you as the perfect mother. There are two times when I can't keep my eyes off the clock—when I'm on my exercise bike and when I'm kneading—but in both cases, I feel so good when I'm done!

Whole wheat dough will start out being sticky, but will gradually become less sticky and more elastic during kneading. Some recipes instruct you to generously flour the kneading surface and your fingers to reduce the stickiness, perhaps with as much as one tablespoon for each cup of flour in the recipe. This is OK for white flour, but not for whole wheat. Too much flour is one of the most common causes of brick-hard whole wheat bread, so use as little flour as possible—only a light dusting. Or try using a little water instead of flour to reduce stickiness during kneading. I don't use any water or flour. Instead, I scrape the dough off the kneading surface and my fingers with a scraper, butter knife, or whatever flat, straight (but not sharp) edge is available. The stickiness significantly subsides about half-way through kneading, but even after whole wheat dough is thoroughly kneaded, it will still feel tacky.

After you've been kneading for a while, you can check how far along you are by gently pulling the dough apart. Eventually craters will form over the surface and it will tear apart easily. Keep kneading until the dough becomes silky smooth and, when gently pulled apart, forms a very thin sheet or strand that doesn't tear. The dough will still feel tacky, but despite its stickiness, it will feel springy. When this happens, you're done kneading.

Another indicator that dough is sufficiently kneaded is the appearance of little wrinkles on the dough's surface. With whole wheat, you must knead a lot longer than a white flour recipe instructs—perhaps twice as long. All good, healthy things take time. This 100% whole wheat recipe requires at least 15-20 minutes of kneading, so get ready for a good workout.

For my first several loaves, I was never sure whether I kneaded enough. So I just assumed I was kneading strenuously enough, kneaded for the time suggested in the recipe, and added about 3 minutes. Since the loaves turned out well (after my first brick disaster, that is), I guess I did OK. Kneading is like anything else—with practice comes confidence, skill, and success.

TIP: If you're not sure that you've kneaded enough, continue kneading for a couple more minutes. Although it is possible to over knead by hand, it takes a LOT of extra time. If you under knead by even a few minutes, your bread won't rise well. So err on the over kneading side. This is true only for hand kneading—if you're using a machine, over kneading is very possible.

Let the Dough Rise

Place a teaspoon of oil in the bowl and turn dough to coat all surfaces. Cover with a warm, damp towel. Let rise in a warm place (80°F to 90°F is best for the yeast to do its work) for about 1½-2 hours, until doubled in size.

Punch the Dough Down

Take your fist and punch it right into the center of the dough. Whomp! You can leave the dough in the bowl if you like. The purpose of punching down is to remove air from the dough. You may hear a hissing sound as the gas escapes. After punching, fold the edges in toward the center and into the imprint of your fist. Knead the dough for a short time to squeeze out more air. You don't want big pockets of air in your bread; you want lots of little tiny holes for even rising. (We've all had slices of bread with huge holes.) Punching down also redistributes the yeast and gives it access to fresh dough to eat during the second rise.

It is during this short second kneading after punching down the dough that you would add any larger or chunky optional ingredients, such as raisins or other dried fruits, seeds or chopped nuts, cheeses, herbs, or sprouted grains. Or, you can flatten the dough, sprinkle bulky ingredients onto the dough, and roll up the dough jelly-roll style.

Shape the Dough into Loaves

After you've punched down and kneaded a little, divide the dough into halves and shape it into two loaves (or many pretzels or bread sticks or buns or pizza crust). Place the loaves into greased loaf pans or place the loaves on a greased flat baking sheet. Grease the pans with butter, not oil. Butter will form a non-stick layer between the dough and the pan, whereas some of the oil may be absorbed into the dough and cause some sticking to occur. If you're using loaf pans, gently flatten the dough so that it covers the bottom of the pan. There should be room for upward expansion in the loaf pans. Or, use a slightly smaller loaf pan and fill it ⅔ full. The dough will rise up over the top of the loaf pan, making a nice mushroom shape. You may want to sprinkle sesame or poppy seeds, chopped nuts, rolled oats, slivered sautéed onions, or dry flour onto the top of the loaf after shaping, which will enhance the look and taste of your bread.

Let the Dough Rise Again

Now that the bread is shaped and placed in pans or on a baking sheet, cover it and place in a warm place as before. Let it rise until doubled in size—it should take a little less time than the first rise. After this second rise, the loaves are ready for baking.

Bake

Place the loaves in a cold oven. Turn the oven on and set the temperature to 350°F. The smaller the loaves, the shorter the baking time, of course. And if you have very small pieces of dough, such as bread sticks or pretzels, the recipe will probably tell you to bake at a high temperature for a short period of time. A higher heat will cause a crisp outer crust, such as is common for bread sticks and pretzels. If the bread is far from being done and the crust is starting to burn or get too brown, cover the crust with aluminum foil (shiny side up) to slow its baking. You may want to cover all small dough pieces, like pretzels and bread sticks, with aluminum foil to keep them from burning.

Testing for Doneness

There are several ways you can tell when the bread has finished baking. The bread will begin to pull away from the sides of the pan. A cake tester or other thin wire pushed into the thickest part of the loaf will come out clean. A toothpick can be used in small pieces of dough, such as buns. A tap on the bottom or top crust will produce a hollow thump rather than a solid-sounding thud, indicating the presence of light airy dough and the absence of thick raw dough.

I like this very reliable method: Dump the loaf out of the pan upside down into your toweled hand. Insert a thin knife through the loaf from the bottom until it almost touches the top crust. It will pull out clean if the loaf is done. If you cannot tell whether the knife has raw dough on it or just moisture from steam, gently wipe it across the towel. The steam will wipe away and the dough will stay.

Let Cool

It is important to cool each loaf thoroughly so that steam does not cause sogginess on the bottoms or sides. Take each loaf out of its pan and cool on a wire rack, or anything that allows air to circulate underneath. Use an oven rack or the rack from a broiling pan, or just prop the loaf over two or three butter knives.

Store the Baked Bread Properly

Unlike white bread, whole wheat bread will keep at room temperature for only a few days if placed in a ventilated bread box, or wrapped loosely in a paper bag, that allows air flow to prevent mold. Let the bread cool completely before storing so that it doesn't become soggy. Store it in the refrigerator, tightly wrapped, for 2-3 weeks.

It will keep much better if you freeze it, even if you will be eating it within a few days. If you wrap it very well in organic, bleach-free wax paper and then aluminum foil, baked bread may keep for up to a year.

Before freezing bread, it's a good idea to slice it so that you can easily remove a piece at a time and toast it—you practically need an electric saw to cut off part of a frozen loaf!

Thaw frozen bread for about 4 hours at room temperature. Leave it in the aluminum foil, so that any ice crystals can be reabsorbed back into the bread. If you plan on eating it for breakfast, leave it out overnight. Or, thaw frozen bread by baking it wrapped in aluminum foil for 15-20 minutes at 375°F, until the center is warm. Frozen bread keeps very well and tastes almost like freshly baked bread when thawed or toasted.

Good luck in your baking!

23

Legumes:
Dried Beans, Peas, and Lentils

Dried beans, peas, and lentils are called "legumes" or "pulses." Legumes come from plants that have pods. Legumes are second only to whole grains as our most important food source. Like whole grains, legumes are storehouses of vitamins, minerals, and fiber. Mixed with grains, they form complete protein. Learn more about protein complementarity on page 412.

How to Buy and Store Legumes

Choose legumes that are bright in color; dullness indicates age and long storage. They should also be uniform in size, so they will take the same amount of time to cook. Otherwise some will be overcooked and some will be undercooked and tough. Look for beans with no tiny holes, which signify a bug infestation. Whole dried beans will keep for up to a year in a tightly covered container in a cool, dry place. Uncooked whole dried beans will keep indefinitely in the freezer.

Preparing Legumes for Cooking
Rinsing Beans

Before cooking, pick through the beans and remove any cracked, malformed, discolored beans, and any pebbles or other debris. Place in a colander or strainer and clean by rinsing under cold-running tap water or the sink hose.

Slowly Rehydrating Dried Beans: The Overnight Soak

Before most dried beans are cooked, soaking must rehydrate them. (Lentils, split peas, and soy grits are exceptions.) The easiest and most energy-efficient way to soak beans is to place them in cold water that is at least 3 times their volume for 6-8 hours or overnight.

Soak them in the refrigerator. (Some authors recommend refrigeration for soybeans only, but I recommend soaking all beans in the refrigerator, where cooler temperatures prevent fermentation and spoilage, especially during hot summer nights.) Cover the water and beans to protect them from the refrigerator air.

After the soak, remove any beans that are floating on top of the water. Floating beans were harvested prematurely, causing the beans to shrink within their seed coats. They may have gotten moldy and there might be dirt in the space under the seed coat.

> **TIP:** To save washing a bowl, soak the beans in the same stainless steel or glass pot that you will cook them in.

The Fast Way: The Quick Soak Method

If you can't wait all night for your beans to soak, there is a quicker way. Boil water that is 3-4 times the volume of the beans. Drop the beans into the boiling water gradually, so as not to stop the water from boiling. Continue boiling all the beans for 2 more minutes, and then remove the pot from the stove. Cover and let it sit for at least one hour. The boiling process breaks the shells of the beans so they absorb water faster.

Because heat destroys nutrients, the *Overnight Soak Method* is preferred over the *Quick Soak Method*. It also saves energy.

> **MONEY SAVER:** Some beans are sold as "quick-cooking" beans, meaning that they have been presoaked, re-dried, and packaged. These beans are usually more expensive, however. If you do buy them to save some time, cook them by following the directions on the label.

Cooking Beans

Now that the beans have been either soaked overnight or quick-soaked, place them on the stove top. For all beans except the soybean, use the same water for cooking that you used for soaking. This helps preserve nutrients. To prevent bitterness in soybeans, drain the soak water and replace it with fresh water. Make sure that the beans are covered well with water. If the water is at a low level in the pot because the beans soaked it in, add more water.

Place the beans over low heat (no need to boil first) and let them come to a simmer and cook for the recommended time. Beans do take a long time to cook, but, as with grains, it's all waiting time and your attention is not necessary until they are done.

Always cook beans by simmering, not boiling, because boiling will break the skins and cause the beans to separate. Boiling may also cause boil-overs. Do not stir the beans while cooking or you may break the skins. Beans will have a firmer texture if you cook them uncovered. Cook beans in a covered pot for your baby, however, because they will be softer.

Bean Cooking Quick Reference			
For each cup of dried beans:	Use this many cups of water:	Soaking required?	Cooking Time
Adzuki	4	yes	50 minutes
Black or turtle	4	yes	1 hour
Black-eyes pea	4	yes	1 hour
Fava	4	yes	1 hour
Garbanzo (chick peas)	4	yes	2 hours
Kidney	3	yes	1½ hours
Lentil	4	no	30 minutes
Lima	4	yes	1 hour
Lima, baby	4	yes	50 minutes
Mung	4	yes	1½ hours
Pinto	3	yes	1½ hours
Soybean	4	yes	3 hours
Soy grits	2	no	30-45 minutes
Yellow or green split peas	3	no	40 minutes
White or Great Northern or navy bean (pea bean)	4	yes	1 hour

REMINDER: Tofu is made from super nutritious soybeans. Tofu is a convenient no-cooking-necessary way to get beans into your family's diet.

For Quick Cooking, Freeze Uncooked, Soaked Beans

Beans soaked overnight can be frozen before they are cooked. Freeze them in small portions using the *Nested Plastic Bag Method*. Frozen beans will take only about 20 minutes to cook. This is because the freezing process breaks the strands that hold the beans together (similar to what happens in the *Quick Soak Method*), which greatly shortens the cooking time.

How to Tell If Beans Are Finished Cooking

Test beans for doneness by tasting them. They should be firm, but tender, and smooth, not gritty. Another way is to blow on them. If they split, they're cooked. Squeeze one between your thumb and index finger. If the inside is hard, the bean is not finished cooking.

TIP: Gas is sometimes a problem with beans and babies (and adults). Introduce beans to your baby in small amounts, and then feed him more when his body gets accustomed to them. If gas is still a problem, try this: Don't cook beans in the soaking water—discard it and use fresh water. Or change the water once or twice during soaking. Or replace the cooking water once or twice during cooking. Although this will decrease the nutrient content of the beans, it will also decrease the complex sugar, raffinose in beans, which are the cause of flatulence.

WARNING: Some flavorings should not be added to beans before they are thoroughly cooked. Acidic foods (tomatoes, tomato sauce, lemon juice, wine, etc.) react with the seed coats' starch and toughens them. Calcium interferes with the cooking process, so do not add molasses or any other food containing calcium until beans have finished cooking. Salt reacts with the seed coat and prevents liquid from being absorbed and toughens beans. Add any of these ingredients only when beans have finished cooking.

TIP: Flavor beans when cooking them for adults by adding chopped onion, minced fresh garlic, ginger, or other fresh herbs and spices to the beans' cooking water.

No Need to Pre-soak Soy Grits, Lentils, and Split Peas

These are the legumes to use if you forgot the overnight soak because you can cook them with no prior soaking. Soy grits are nothing more than coarsely chopped soybeans. I use them frequently instead of whole soybeans, which have to be soaked overnight and then cooked for 3 hours. You can cook these three legumes in the same pot with grains for complete protein because they take approximately the same amount of time to cook. Of course, you can always mix any previously cooked beans with any previously cooked grains in a 1-part-beans-to-2-parts-grains ratio, but it's more trouble to cook them in separate pots for different lengths of time.

Let's say you wanted to mix brown rice and soy grits: put ½ cup brown rice (which will expand to 1 cup) and ¼ cup soy grits (which will expand to ½ cup) in a pot with 1½ cups boiling water (1 cup of water for the ½ cup of rice and ½ cup of water for the ¼ cup of soy grits). Turn the heat down and let simmer for 45 minutes and you've got a complete protein dish. Feed some to the family, purée a little portion with an equal amount of liquid for the baby, and freeze any leftovers.

NOTE: Even though these three legumes do not have to be soaked, you can place them in a clear bowl and cover them with water for the purpose of finding the defective ones, which will float to the top.

Refrigerating and Freezing Cooked Whole Beans

Cooked whole beans, covered 'well, will keep only 3-5 days in the refrigerator. Beans spoil quickly, so freeze them using the *Nested Plastic Bag Method* in individual 1 cup or ½ cup portions for up to 4 months.

Puréed Bean Frozen Food Cubes

Purée cooked beans in the processor and refrigerate for up to 3 days. Or use the *Food Cube Method* to freeze bean purée for up to 6 weeks. Add puréed bean food cubes to your baby's yogurt or mix with vegetables as a *Healthy Extra*.

Bean Flour

Bean flour, such as soy flour or soybean flour, can be used in recipes to increase the nutrient content. Just as wheat flour is nothing more than ground up wheat kernels, bean flour is ground up dried beans. You can buy bean flours at the natural foods store. It takes a while to use up a bag of soy flour, so I suggest that you freeze it. When baking bread, muffins, or quick breads, grab a bag of ground bean flour and replace some of the flour in the recipe.

You can grind your own bean flours. A blender can be used to grind beans, but the powder is a little too coarse for flour. There are manual grinders for grains and beans that look like meat grinders. These make better flour than the blender, but it's still a little coarse. I grind many different grains and beans into flour all at once, and then freeze them. That way I only have to take it apart and clean it once.

TIP: A food grinder or pasta maker that won't stay firmly in place is a nuisance. Place a small piece of folded sandpaper, rough side out, between the clamp and table.

There are also electric grinders available at retail stores and online, but they are, of course, more expensive than manual grinders. Some coffee grinders may work, but first check with the manufacturer to make sure that beans will not damage the unit.

Bean Equivalents

One pound of dried beans equals about 2½ cups of uncooked dried beans and about 6 cups, give or take ½ cup, of cooked beans.

One 15-ounce or 16-ounce can of beans is approximately equal to 1¾ cups of drained cooked beans or about ¾ cup uncooked dried beans. Home-cooked legumes are easy, healthier and more economical than canned beans, but canned beans are better than no beans at all! Always thoroughly rinse canned beans containing sodium to remove as much salt as possible. Rinse beans in a colander/sieve/strainer under running tap water.

Tofu: A Most Convenient Bean Food

Tofu, also called "soybean curd" or "bean curd," is a product made from soybeans, which contains almost all of the nutritional benefits of the soybean. Like the soybean, it is one of the few plant products high in complete protein. Tofu contains some calcium and the numerous other nutrients found in soybeans. Tofu comes in three textures—soft, firm, and extra-firm. Firm tofu has excess water extracted, making it denser and easier to slice or cube.

You can buy tofu at most supermarkets and at any natural foods store. Some tofu is packaged so that it has to be refrigerated—make sure that it is refrigerated in the store. Some tofu is packed in aseptic boxes that will keep unrefrigerated for up to 10 months.

Once a tofu package has been opened, it must be refrigerated. I remember the good old days when blocks of tofu were sold in an open refrigerated barrel at my local natural foods store and customers would bag their own. But tofu is no longer sold that way, due to the liability of unfriendly bacteria. For your baby, be sure to buy tofu in sealed packages only.

Tofu (also known to small children as "toe food") is a great food for a babies 8 months and older. It does not have to be cooked because it is made from cooked soybeans. Purée or mash it and add it to *Super Porridge*, fruits, veggies, yogurt, anything. Small tofu chunks or strips of tofu make great finger foods. There are several tofu recipes in the Recipes chapter.

Refrigerating Tofu

You must store tofu under water in the refrigerator. You might get away with an airtight container, but under water is always good. The water must be changed daily. You may have seen this bumper sticker: *Have you changed your tofu's water today?* Treat it well and it will keep in the refrigerator for up to a week.

Freezing Tofu

Freeze tofu in its original carton. Or, freeze opened tofu in water. Freeze the whole block submerged in water, or place little chunks of tofu in ice cube trays, cover them with water, and freeze using the *Food Cube Method* and keep for up to 2 months. Thaw overnight in the refrigerator.

> **WARNING:** There are many brands of tofu, and some are firm, some are soft. Freezing changes the texture of some tofu so that it becomes rubbery. Before giving thawed tofu to your baby, make sure that it is not difficult to chew so that your baby will not choke.

TIP: Steaming tofu causes it to develop a consistency similar to egg white. For people who would rather not eat eggs or for those with an allergy to eggs, try substituting steamed tofu for cooked egg whites in potato salad and other recipes. Steam tofu for 7-12 minutes, depending on its firmness.

Sneak Beans into Recipes

For older children who simply won't eat beans, you can still manage to sneak them into their diets. Substitute some bean flour for regular flour in baked goods. Mix a little bean flour into pancakes, muffins, and other baked goods. Mix mashed cooked bean purée or tofu into just about anything: sandwich spreads, sauces, gravies, veggie burgers, mayonnaise, salad dressings, omelets, casseroles, milkshakes, soups, pasta sauces, and believe it or not, even puddings and ice cream.

24

Nuts and Seeds

WARNING: Be sure to get your pediatrician's OK before you introduce your baby to nuts and seeds, as they are high allergen foods, particularly peanuts. Make sure your pediatrician knows of any peanut allergy in your family! Peanut-allergic children may suffer serious reactions and even death from eating foods containing peanuts. A serious reaction may even result if a peanut-allergic child accidentally leans on a counter smeared with peanut butter or peanut oil, even if it has been wiped off!

Nuts and Seeds Are Nature's Nutrient Powerhouses

Seeds are loaded with nutrients. If a seed is placed in the ground, it grows. If a seed is placed in water, it sprouts. Nature must have put a concentrated store of nutrients in the seed, which can grow a new plant with no soil and nothing more than plain water. The seed is the nucleus of a plant, the part that maintains survival of the species, and the part that is most important to nature. If there is a variation and lack of nutrients in the soil, the other plant parts suffer at the expense of the seed. In infertile soil, the roots forage for every trace nutrient they can find in order to first form the seed. The seed is life itself.

I read once where if you are going to be shipwrecked on the proverbial desert island and you could choose only one food to take with you, you should choose sunflower seeds. They supposedly have every nutrient needed for human survival except vitamin C, but when sprouted they produce vitamin C. I am certainly not suggesting that your baby live on sunflower seeds alone, but I do recommend that ground sunflower and other seeds be a regular part of your baby's diet.

WARNING: Sunflower seeds are packed with nutrients, but they have a problem with rancidity. If they are yellowish in color and don't smell right, don't use them.

Seeds Are More than Just Seeds

Whole grains are the seeds of grassy plants, such as wheat, millet, rice, etc. Nuts are the seeds of nut trees. Dried beans are seeds. Legumes are seeds. Plant them and care for them and they will grow into a whole new plant. The healthiest foods for you and your baby are seeds, because they are living stores of nutrition.

It Just Doesn't Get Nutritionally Better than Seeds

Whole grains, beans/legumes, nuts, and seeds are the best natural sources of essential fatty acids, the healthy fats needed for your baby's brain development. They contain large amounts of protein, vitamin E, the B complex vitamins, tons of other vitamins, minerals, and trace elements.

So there you have it, the absolute optimum diet for human beings: whole grains, beans/legumes, nuts, seeds, fruits, and vegetables. I memorized that list, and whenever I stand in my kitchen thinking about dinner, I say to myself "whole grains, beans, nuts, seeds, fruits, and vegetables." For babies, add breast milk/formula, yogurt (even yogurt is alive with friendly bacteria), and eggs.

TIP: To get nuts and seeds into your family's diet, grind them and add them to pancakes, oatmeal, omelets, casseroles, pasta sauces, and sprinkle them into cold breakfast cereal and milk.

How to Buy Seeds
Fresh, Raw, Whole Seeds and Nuts

Try the natural foods store or the organic section of your supermarket. If you think of nuts as canned, salted and oiled, and seeds as bottled, salted sunflower seed snacks, please change your thinking. You can buy a variety of fresh, raw, organically grown seeds and nuts. It's easiest when you buy them already hulled (shell removed).

Look them over to see if they are shriveled—a shriveled nut is a spoiled nut. If you are going to buy them in the shells, test for freshness by shaking. If they are loose in the shell and make a noise, don't buy them—they are shrunken and spoiled. Remember that this was also true of a spoiled bean, which floats to the top of the soak water because it had shrunk inside its outer coating and contains air space. A shelled nut should break in two when you snap it. If it bends instead of breaks, the nut is old.

TIP: Removing the shells from Brazil nuts is easy if they are first frozen. Freezing makes the shells brittle and the nuts come out whole instead of broken into pieces.

Nut and Seed Butters

Your natural foods store carries a variety of nut and seed butters. Peanut butter is nothing more than ground peanuts and maybe some added non-hydrogenated oil to help make a smooth consistency. Walnut butter is made from ground walnuts. Almond butter is made from almonds. Tahini, or sesame seed butter, is made from ground sesame seeds. I highly recommend that these nut/seed butters from the natural foods store be included in your baby's diet.

MONEY SAVER: Use a small spatula to scrape every last bit of nut/ seed butter out of the jar. You will be surprised at how much you would have wasted by throwing it away.

Homemade Nut Butters

It's easy to make your own nut butters. To make homemade nut butter, grind nuts in a blender or food processor with a little cold-pressed safflower oil (about 1 tablespoon of oil for each cup of raw nuts). Start by measuring ¼ cup of nuts and 1 teaspoon of oil and gradually add the rest of the nuts and oil.

> WARNING: Commercially made nut butters are closely scrutinized for mold that may contain aflatoxin, a carcinogenic fungal toxin commonly found in mold. If you are going to make your own nut butters, use only the freshest nuts. Ask a store employee about the age of the nuts you plan to use.

Choosy Moms Choose Natural Peanut Butter

Most of the peanut butter in the "peanut butter aisle" at the supermarket contains added salt, sugar, and poisonous partially hydrogenated oils. You can find organic peanut butter. Read the ingredients list and make sure that the jar you select contains only ground organically-grown peanuts.

Natural Peanut Butters Separate

Because healthy, natural peanut butters (and other nut and seed butters) do not contain stabilizers, they separate and the oil gathers on top of the jar. If this doesn't happen, you should question that brand of nut butter. Use a butter knife to stir the butter. When you find it difficult and frustrating to stir the oil into the nuts, remind yourself that you are doing it for your baby's health. Know that, after it gets cold during refrigerator storage, you won't have to stir it again. The cold keeps it from separating.

> **TIP:** A few days before opening a new jar of nut/seed butter, place it on its side so that the oil will move. Turn the jar frequently. Keep the jar on the kitchen counter, where seeing it will remind you to turn it often. This turning will help pre-mix the butter before you open it, and make stirring easier for you.

Storing Nuts, Seeds, and Their Butters

Nuts and seeds must be kept refrigerated in a closed container to protect them from warmth and dry refrigerator air. Refrigerated shelled nuts will keep for 3-4 months; frozen they will keep for 8 months.

Seeds contain oils that go rancid quickly when exposed to air after grinding. To prevent rancidity, seeds should be kept whole and refrigerated, and should not be ground in the blender until immediately before serving.

Both nuts and seeds should be ground to a fine powder in the blender, not only to prevent your baby from choking on them, but also to promote the digestion of their many nutrients.

> **REMINDER:** Once natural peanut butter jars and other nut and seed butter jars are opened, they must be refrigerated.

> **TIP:** Use peanut butter on your breakfast toast instead of butter or margarine. It's much more nutritious. Drizzle a little honey (for babies older than one year) or maple syrup over the peanut butter for an extra delicious treat.

Feeding Your Baby Nuts and Seeds

Introduce your baby first to tahini. Mix a little in his *Super Porridge* or yogurt. Then you can try raw almonds and pumpkin seeds—grind them and all nuts and seeds in the blender immediately before feeding them to your baby. Also good are peanuts or peanut butter, hazelnuts (filberts), flax seeds, and chia seeds. Flaxseed or its oil (also called linseed oil—the food grade oil, not the stuff found in turpentine) should be a part of your baby's diet every single day for EFAs.

> WARNING: You know this, but I still want to say it: Never feed a baby or toddler whole (or even partially whole) seeds or nuts. They are choking hazards. Grind your baby's nuts and seeds in the blender or processor until they are a fine powder. Make sure there are no chunky pieces. Serve immediately before they become rancid.

Grind them for yourself and the older members of your family, also. Seeds and nuts must be chewed very, very well in order to get their nutrients, or they'll pass right through the body. This is especially true of the smaller seeds, like chia seeds, flax seeds, and sesame seeds. Eat them well-ground to get maximum nutrients. This is one reason why I recommend tahini—thoroughly ground sesame seed butter—for your baby rather than sesame seeds, along with the fact that it is so very convenient to add a spoonful into baby's yogurt or *Super Porridge*.

TIP: If seeds and nuts clump in your blender while grinding, try adding a little flour to keep them moving.

TIP: Again, I want to point out the convenience of the mini-blend container. I must use mine at least twice a day, and I know if I had to use the big container it would be a real inconvenience.

I find it a real inconvenience to have to eat seeds immediately after they have been ground to prevent rancidity. I do one grinding in the morning and serve them at breakfast to get them into my family's diet every day. Breakfast is convenient for me because everyone is together at one meal and the foods are very flexible. Ground seeds and nuts can be easily added immediately after grinding into cold cereals, omelets, hot oatmeal, pancakes, waffles, or fruited yogurt. Then, after everyone has left for the day, I put the leftovers into my baby's *Super Porridge*.

TIP: Rinse nut/seed powder from bowls immediately after you're finished eating. Don't let them dry up or they become welded to the bowl. And don't ever let any flax or chia seed pieces get into your dishwasher or you'll be rewashing everything, especially the glasses. If you accidentally let seed parts dry on a bowl, let the bowl soak for a while in plain or soapy water and they'll rinse right off. If seed parts are stuck on the lip of the bowl, nest it inside a bigger bowl, fill the bigger bowl so that the water covers the lip of the smaller bowl, and let it soak.

Nut/Seed Milks

Another way to get nuts and seeds into your children's diets is with nut/seed milks. See recipes for *Super Milks* in Part VI.

TIP: Whole nuts and seeds are DELICIOUS when rehydrated! Soak them in water in the refrigerator overnight and enjoy them in your cereal in the morning or as a snack. Don't feed these whole nuts/seeds to your baby, though, because are choking hazards.

25

Dairy Foods

Cheese

Cheese is an easy and convenient baby food that, like milk and yogurt, is high in protein and calcium. Grated soft natural cheese and small lumps of cottage cheese are nice finger foods for your baby. Remember that babies needs fat, so buy whole milk cheeses for your baby.

Buy Only Natural Cheese

United States government standards require processed cheeses to be only 51% real cheese, so do not buy products labeled "processed cheese," "cheese spread," or "cheese food." Processed cheese has been altered for long storage life and many contain artificial colorings and preservatives. Buy only natural cheeses for your baby: Parmesan, Romano, Camembert, Cheddar, Feta, Monterey Jack, Swiss, Provolone, Mozzarella, whole milk Cottage Cheese, Ricotta, Cream Cheese, and many others.

When buying cheese, inspect the wrapper carefully for damage or stickiness and remember to check the expiration date. Avoid buying old cheese that looks dry or has cracks in it. The color should be uniform from center to edge. White cheeses, such as ricotta, become yellow as they age. Look carefully for mold, which looks like white, blue, pink, or green flecks or furry patches. Avoid cheese with a greasy surface, which indicates that the cheese has been warmed.

Storing Cheese

Store natural cheese in an airtight container in the refrigerator. Cheese that comes in a rind should be kept in the rind until you are ready to use it.

> WARNING: Discard any cheese with even the tiniest bit of mold on it. Experts say it's OK to cut off the moldy part and eat the rest, but I say never take chances with children.

Cheese can also be frozen in an airtight container. Freeze cheese pieces separately in chunks no larger than a ½ pound. Be ready for a change in texture: firm cheeses may turn crumbly and soft cheeses may separate. Your baby will probably not mind the texture. Freeze cottage and ricotta cheese using the *Food Cube Method* and keep for 4-6 months. Thaw overnight in the refrigerator and be sure to use thawed cheese within a few days.

Cheese Tips

- Cheese is easier to slice with a dull knife. Warm the knife under hot tap water for easier slicing.

- It's cheaper to buy cheese in bulk, grate it, and freeze it in small quantities in individual bags using the Nested Plastic Bag Method. If you hate shredding your own, you can buy already-shredded cheese in bulk and freeze. Soft cheeses (cottage, ricotta, etc.) can be bought in bulk and frozen using the *Food Cube Method*.

- Rub oil or butter on your grater or oil-spray it and grating cheese will be easier. The grater will be easy to clean, too.

- Soft cheese will be easier to grate if first placed in the freezer for 15-30 minutes.

- Small chunks of cheese can be grated with a garlic press.

- Use a potato peeler to make strips of cheese for "hair" or other Decorative Touches.

- To prevent mold from forming, wrap a cheese block in white paper towels dampened with apple cider vinegar before placing it in a plastic bag to refrigerate. Periodically re wet the paper towels with the vinegar.

- A sugar cube stored with hard cheese in the same container helps to prevent mold.

- Store cottage cheese, ricotta cheese, sour cream, and yogurt with the carton upside down in the refrigerator. The cheese pressing against the lid helps to seal it and keep the container airtight, extending storage life.

- Block cheese dries out quickly if not properly stored. To rehydrate dried-out cheese, soak in buttermilk. Prevent cheese from drying out by rubbing cut edges with butter or oil or by oil-spraying the surface.

Nonfat Dry Milk

Nonfat dry milk is dried and concentrated pasteurized skim milk in a powder form. Fresh nonfat dry milk is odorless.

> WARNING: Use only NONFAT powdered milk and not dry whole milk, because the cholesterol in whole or low-fat powdered milks has been damaged during the drying process, making it harmful.

Add the instant kind into baby's foods and beverages as a nutrition booster to add calcium and protein. Or use it to thicken homemade yogurt.

TIP: For older family members who don't need the fat in milk, mix a tablespoon of nonfat powdered milk into a cup of skim milk to thicken it and make it creamier.

Store an unopened box of nonfat dry milk in a cool dry place and discard it after the expiration date. Once you open a packet, store it in an airtight glass container in the refrigerator and it will keep for weeks.

Nonfat dry milk also can be mixed with water in the proportions given in the directions (usually about 3 tablespoons of powder to one cup of water) to make liquid milk that you can drink or cook with, but the flavor isn't the same as regular milk. Store the mixed liquid milk in an airtight container in the refrigerator and use within three days.

Yogurt

In this chapter, I saved the best for last—yogurt! Yogurt has been around for thousands of years and is a *Super Baby Food* and a *Super Adult Food*. Yogurt is a good source of calcium, protein, phosphorus, potassium, riboflavin, vitamin B12, and pantothenic acid. It is said that yogurt has many health benefits, from preventing cancer and high blood pressure to curing vaginal yeast infections. Yogurt has been shown to enhance the body's immune system by increasing the production of gamma interferons, which play a key roll in fighting certain allergies and viral infections.

TIP: If you have a problem with vaginal yeast infections, try eating a daily cup of yogurt containing the Lactobacillus acidophilus culture for several months. There's a good chance that it will help.

Yogurt is a tangy, fermented (curdled) milk that contains living bacteria. But unlike "bad" bacteria, yogurt bacteria cultures are friendly and very beneficial to health. Yogurt bacteria cultures, which multiply at body temperature, produce B vitamins in the intestines and attack harmful bacteria in the colon. Yogurt soothes stomach ailments and its cultures help digest casein, a milk protein. Yogurt helps restore the health-giving flora that naturally occurs in the human intestines and helps to prevent gastrointestinal infections. Yogurt is easily digested and well-tolerated by babies and its protein is better assimilated.

Antibiotics, for example, kill friendly intestinal flora. People on antibiotics should eat two servings of yogurt a day, starting with the first dose and continuing until 10 days after antibiotic use has ceased. Antibiotics promote diaper rash, which is caused by the unfriendly bacteria that grow in the absence of these flora. Antibiotics also make your baby susceptible to thrush (a yeast which looks like a "whiteness" on the tongue) and other fungal infections, because they kill the good bacteria in the mouth, too. If you are breastfeeding, your baby's infection may spread to your nipples causing redness, burning, and itching. Acidophilus powder (available at the natural foods store) mixed into your baby's formula once a day may help. Acidophilus is a healthy, intestinal bacteria also found in yogurt that is killed by antibiotics. If you are breastfeeding, the powder can be mixed into a little water and administered a few times per day. Get your pediatrician's OK before giving the powder to your baby. She may want to prescribe some anti-fungal medication for your baby.

Some people who cannot drink milk because of lactose intolerance can eat yogurt without any problem because yogurt contains much less lactose than milk. The bacteria predigests the lactose. Lactose is a milk sugar that causes diarrhea and bloating in lactose-intolerant people. The active yogurt cultures create lactase, the enzyme in which lactose-intolerant people are deficient. People with milk ALLERGY should not eat yogurt made from cow's milk. However, they can have yogurt made from soy.

Plain low-fat yogurt can help reduce dietary fat by acting as a replacement in many recipes for sour cream, heavy cream, whipped cream, and buttermilk. It can replace all or part of the mayonnaise called for in a recipe. Yogurt can be used as an ingredient in dozens of recipes, from buttermilk pancakes to cheesecake.

How to Buy Commercial Yogurt

Commercial yogurt is exorbitantly priced. Before I started making my own yogurt, I cringed whenever I bought two 32-ounce containers of store-bought yogurt to make one mock cheesecake. Now, I make my own yogurt and instead of paying for commercial yogurt. I buy ½ gallon (64 ounces) of milk to make homemade and save loads of money. The last section of this chapter contains directions for making homemade yogurt.

Buy Only Yogurt with Live Bacteria

Carefully read the package and look for words like "live and active cultures." Commercial manufacturers sometimes pasteurize yogurt after culturing to increase its shelf life. Unfortunately, this heat treatment kills the beneficial bacteria. If you see words like "pasteurized," "stabilized," or "heat-treated after culturing," beware that they are euphemisms for "all the good bacteria are dead."

Don't Buy Old Yogurt

Fresh yogurt has "stronger" bacteria, which become less vigorous as the yogurt ages. Check the expiration date. Although UNOPENED yogurt can keep in the refrigerator up to 10 days past the expiration date, the cultures will be fairly weak by that time. If you're going to use commercial yogurt to start your own homemade yogurt, buy the freshest yogurt possible.

Buy Whole Milk or Low-fat Milk Yogurt for Baby

Your baby needs fats and you should not restrict his fat intake until he is at least one year old. Also, the fat in yogurt helps make the friendly bacteria more hardy and healthy.

Buy Plain Yogurt with No Additives

Avoid the yogurt with sugar, flavorings, gelatins, and artificial sweeteners. Besides the obvious reasons, these additives interfere with bacterial activity. Some commercial yogurts have fruit on the bottom, which you mix in, and some have pre-blended fruit already distributed throughout the yogurt. Some "farm-style" commercial yogurts come with a layer of yogurt cream on the top, which has a high fat content. Don't buy any of these. Buy only PLAIN yogurt and add your own flavorings.

Add Your Own Flavoring

Commercially flavored yogurt usually contains excessive sugars and additives that your baby doesn't need. Your baby will be happy with plain, unflavored yogurt, but use yogurt as a base for *Healthy Extras*, pages 328-331. Flavor plain yogurt with any of the suggestions in the box on the next page. Gently stir or fold flavorings into yogurt. If you stir too roughly, you will thin the yogurt. If convenient, the best time to add flavorings is immediately before eating. There is one exception—add dried fruit several hours before eating so that it softens, or soak the dried fruit to soften it and then add it to the yogurt. If you're making homemade yogurt, add flavorings AFTER it's done incubating.

Home-Added Yogurt Flavoring Suggestions

Stir these flavorings into yogurt gently or yogurt will become thin and runny:

Fresh fruit: apples, berries, peaches, pears, etc., chopped or puréed
Frozen no-sugar-added fruits, chopped or puréed
Natural jam or jelly
Canned fruits, drained and chopped or puréed
Jarred commercial baby fruit
Applesauce
Rehydrated dried fruit, chopped or puréed
Crushed, well-drained, canned pineapple
Blackstrap molasses
Maple syrup
Honey (for babies over 1 year)
Molasses
Vanilla
Wheat germ
Lemon or lime juice
Frozen orange juice concentrate, or any other frozen fruit juice concentrate

Apple butter, prune butter, any fruit butter
Well-ground nuts or seeds
Thinned creamy peanut butter
Thinned almond or other nut butter
Thinned tahini or other seed butter
Puréed cooked carrots or sweet potato (thaw a food cube or 2)
Finely diced cucumber pieces
Finely chopped parsley
Cinnamon
Nutmeg
Healthy Extras (page 328)

For mommies and daddies only, not baby:
Butterscotch syrup
Chocolate (or carob) syrup
Chocolate chips
Chocolate syrup/chips and peanut butter
Instant coffee and sweetener
Jamocha (chocolate syrup and instant coffee)
Chili or curry powder, chili sauce

Freezing Yogurt

You can freeze yogurt in its original container for up to 6 weeks. If you can't use yogurt within 5-7 days, freeze it, well covered, in an airtight container or by using the *Food Cube Method*. Yogurt bacteria grows just like other bacteria and survives freezing temperatures.

Flavored frozen yogurt is as popular as ever, but the commercial varieties are loaded with sugar and additives. Make your own frozen yogurt ice cream—see recipe, page 519.

Yogurt Cheese

Yogurt cheese is nothing more than yogurt with the whey (yellow-tinged liquid) drained from it. Yogurt cheese can be used as a healthy substitute for cream cheese and sour cream. To make yogurt cheese, use only plain, unflavored commercial or homemade yogurt with no gelatin added, which prevents the whey from draining out.

Place the yogurt into a container that will allow the liquid whey to drip through it. Yogurt cheese "funnels" can be purchased at kitchen and some department stores, but you don't have to buy one. Use a colander, strainer, or steamer and line it with a coffee filter, several layers of white paper towels or heavy white paper napkins, a double thickness of damp cheesecloth or a damp, clean, white cloth napkin. Place the colander over a bowl to catch the whey (the yellow-tinged liquid that drains out).

Cover the colander with plastic wrap and place in the refrigerator. Let it drain for several hours in the refrigerator. Stir occasionally with a rubber spatula. The longer you let it drain, the thicker it will become. In a few hours the yogurt will have the consistency of sour cream; overnight it will resemble cream cheese. A pint of yogurt makes about one cup of yogurt cheese. Keep yogurt cheese refrigerated and it will keep for about one week.

> **TIP:** Yogurt cheese will become liquidy if you mix or beat it too hard, so be gentle when stirring it into recipes.

> **TIP:** Don't throw away that whey—it contains calcium and other nutrients. Drink it straight; use it in flavored beverages, as the liquid in muffins and other baked goods, and in soups and gravies.

Making Homemade Yogurt
Homemade Yogurt is Delicious!

You can tailor-make yogurt according to your individual taste. If you're missing out on the health benefits of yogurt and don't eat it because you don't like the tart flavor of store-bought, you absolutely must try making your own. Fresh—and I mean really fresh, as fresh as one-day-old—homemade yogurt is delicious, in that it has no tart flavor if made with new starter. You can add fresh puréed fruit, maple syrup, or any of the flavorings mentioned previously, and it tastes like a sweet pudding, not like yogurt at all. If you like the tart flavor of yogurt, you can make that as well. Homemade does develop the tart taste after a few days in the refrigerator.

Homemade Yogurt is Cheap!

Commercial yogurt manufacturers do not want you to know how easy and cheap it is to make your own yogurt. An even greater discrepancy in price exists when you compare smaller quantities of yogurt; an 8-ounce single serving container of plain name-brand yogurt currently costs much more per quart. Store-bought yogurt costs about 3 times that of homemade, even when you consider the heat (gas or electric) necessary for making homemade.

Homemade Yogurt is Easy!

When you make yogurt, you actually breed friendly bacteria. You may not want to mention this to your older children who may refuse to eat "germs." Making yogurt entails heating (to sterilize) and cooling some milk, adding yogurt bacteria as a "starter," and letting it incubate (grow and multiply) in a warm place for several hours until it becomes thick and custardy.

Use Whole or Low-fat Milk for Your Baby

Yogurt can be made with almost any kind of milk. You can use whole milk, 2%, 1%, skim, pasteurized, homogenized, organic, raw, diluted evaporated, dry milk powder, cow's, goat's, water buffalo's (no kidding), and soybean milk. (A friend asked me about breast milk. I wouldn't do it, but who knows!) The thinner the milk, the thinner the yogurt. For example, skim milk yogurt is much thinner than yogurt made from whole milk. Powdered milk can also be used to thicken yogurt. For your baby, whole or low-fat milk is best, because a babies need fat and the yogurt cultures remain more viable than in skim milk. Also, the fat content increases the assimilation of fat-soluble vitamins. Whole or low-fat milk yogurt is also more digestible than skim milk yogurt. If you're concerned that your baby has a weight problem, you can feed low-fat or skim milk yogurt to your baby after his first birthday if your pediatrician says that it is OK.

> **TIP:** Try to buy only organic milk for making yogurt. They now sell organic cow's milk at natural foods stores and in the organic isle of your supermarket. Soy milk is usually made from organic soybeans, but check the label before you buy.

Milk made from reconstituted dried nonfat, non-instant milk powder or evaporated milk can be used to make yogurt. Use boiled water cooled to 110-120°F and mix it with the powder or canned milk. Read the package directions for reconstitution and use a little more powder or canned milk than the directions call for. Use only fresh powdered nonfat milk—it should be odorless if it's fresh—and use only the non-instant kind. Check the expiration date on canned milk.

> **WARNING:** Some authors say to use warm tap water to dilute dried or evaporated milk, because it's just the right temperature. **NEVER** use warm or hot tap water for drinking purposes. The warmth helps lead and other heavy metals from your pipes leach into the water.

Steps in Making Homemade Yogurt

Briefly, the steps in making yogurt are:

1. Sterilize the milk to kill all bacteria.
2. Cool the milk to the incubation temperature for growing yogurt.
3. Optionally, add nonfat dry milk.
4. Introduce friendly yogurt bacteria (the starter) into the milk.
5. Let the yogurt bacteria incubate.
6. Refrigerate the finished yogurt.
7. Optionally add flavoring to the yogurt.

Sterilize the Milk

When you buy milk, it is not sterile even though it has been pasteurized. After heating, a few bacteria are still left, and another few have been introduced during handling. That's why milk spoils if it is old, even if the carton is not opened. Milk straight from the cow must be boiled for at least 10-15 minutes to kill all bacteria.

If you're using powdered or evaporated milk and cooled boiled water, there's no need to scald the milk after it's mixed as is called for in the next section. The powder and canned milk should be sterile, and you boiled the water so it's free of bacteria, too.

Stove top scalding. Pour a quart of milk (or any amount) into a pot for heating on the stove. Use a metal spoon. You can use any pot, but glass, stainless steel, or enameled are best because they won't affect taste.

Scald the milk, which means to heat the milk until it's almost boiling, when small bubbles form around the edges and steam begins to rise. This occurs around 180-185°F. I recommend the use of a yogurt (or candy) thermometer to check the temperature. They can be purchased from kitchen stores, natural foods stores, and many department stores. Clip the thermometer on the pot and keep it submerged in the milk at least 2 inches deep while heating. Watch the red mark rise to 185°F.

> **TIP:** To verify the accuracy of your thermometer, place it in boiling water to see if it reads 212°F.

> **TIP:** To prevent the milk from scorching the bottom of the pot, heat the milk slowly and stir often. Scorching not only makes the pot difficult to wash, it also spoils the flavor of the yogurt. Use a double-boiler, if you have one.

Jar-in-pot scalding. Here's another way to save washing a pot. Nest a thick, sturdy, heat-proof glass jar (I use a quart-size mayonnaise jar) with the milk into a pot of water on the stove top and bring it to a boil. Keep the thermometer submerged in the milk to watch for 185°F. The milk will not scorch and the pot won't get dirty because it contains only water. When the water boils, the jar will rattle loudly. You may want to place a small piece of cloth under the jar in the pot to stop the clacking.

MONEY SAVER: After you remove the jar from the pot to let it cool, use the boiling hot water in the pot to sterilize utensils.

> **WARNING:** Make sure your hands are super clean, along with any pots and utensils that will touch the milk. You don't want to introduce and incubate "bad" bacteria in the milk. Wash your hands with soap. Use containers and utensils straight out of the dishwasher or wash them in very hot water and dish detergent.

TIP: If you have a dishwasher, wash the thermometer in it. When the cycle is finished, store the thermometer and a sterile spoon directly out of the dishwasher to keep it clean and ready for making yogurt.

After scalding the milk, you can remove any skin that forms on top, if you wish.

Cool the Milk to the Incubation Temperature

Now that all the bacteria are dead and gone, cool the milk to a temperature that will allow yogurt bacteria to grow and thrive. Let it cool at room temperature, or place it in the refrigerator to speed the cooling.

Keep a spoon in the milk for frequent stirring to evenly distribute the heat, or use the thermometer to stir. Place the thermometer at an angle where it can be quickly seen with a peek into the refrigerator.

The perfect temperature for growing bacteria is about 112°F. Keep the thermometer in the milk and watch it. It may take a good hour at room temperature to cool, so plan on sticking around the kitchen for a while.

If you don't have a thermometer, place a drop of milk on your wrist; remember that your body temperature is around 98.6°F, so it should feel lukewarm.

Another way you can test for 112°F is to put your clean little finger into the milk and slowly count to ten (one thousand and one, one thousand and two, . . .). If you have to pull out your finger because the milk is too hot, the milk must cool some more. You really don't need to be very accurate—actually any temperature from 90-120°F is fine for incubating bacteria, but the closer you stay within 105-110°F, the better.

Optionally, Add Nonfat Dry Milk Powder

You may wish to add some nonfat dry milk powder to increase the nutritional content of the yogurt. The powder will also thicken the consistency of the yogurt. Nonfat dry milk powder is sterile, so you don't have to worry about it containing bacteria. Add about ¼ cup powder per quart of cooled liquid milk and mix very well. See nonfat warning, page 293.

Add the Starter

Now that the milk is at the right temperature, add the friendly bacteria culture—the "starter." One way to introduce yogurt bacteria cultures into the milk is to simply add some yogurt.

The first time you make yogurt, you can use store-bought yogurt for your starter. Buy a small container of plain yogurt, but make sure that the label indicates that the yogurt contains live bacteria. Look for words like "live and active cultures." Also make sure that the yogurt is not too old. For each quart of cooled milk, gently fold in about 2 tablespoons of yogurt. The next time you make yogurt, you can use a few tablespoons from this first batch to start the next batch.

Let the starter yogurt sit at room temperature while the milk is cooling, so it will not be too cold when you add it to the milk. If you wish, take a little milk from the jar and mix it with the starter, and then add it back to the rest of the milk.

Another starter, which can be purchased at any natural foods store, is freeze-dried bacteria culture sold in packets. Although more expensive, this starter is more reliable than yogurt from a previous homemade or commercial batch.

Incubate the Yogurt and Let the Cultures Grow

Pour the milk from the pot into smaller clean individual containers (Pyrex® bowls or custard cups are good). Or use a wide-mouthed jar or bowl. I like to use empty glass mayonnaise jars to hold my yogurt—they can be washed in the hot cycle of the dishwasher. Pre-warm the mayonnaise jars or containers immediately before you pour the yogurt mixture into them.

Warm them in whatever way works best for you: by filling them with hot water, placing them on a wood stove, warming them in a 100°F oven, taking them from a warm dishwasher, etc. If you used the *jar-in-pot* method to scald the milk, you won't have a pot to pour from because you already have the milk in a jar of perfect temperature.

Cover the yogurt during incubation so it's not open to the air, which always contains bacteria. Use the cover of the jar or place plastic wrap over the bowl, making sure the plastic never touches the mixture.

Keep the yogurt warm during incubation. Place the yogurt mixture in a warm place to allow the bacteria to grow and the yogurt to thicken. Remember that bacteria grow when the temperature is neither too hot nor too cold. Keep the temperature at 105-112°F, although yogurt bacteria will survive between 90°F and 120°F. The consistency and taste of homemade yogurt varies with the milk used and also with the temperature at which it was incubated.

REMINDER: The lower the temperature, the sweeter the yogurt; the higher the temperature, the tarter the yogurt. But remember to keep the temperature in the range of 90°-120°F, or the bacteria will die from being too hot or become inactive from being too cold.

TIP: The first few times you make yogurt, baby-sit it. In other words, don't go out for the day or let it sit overnight. Be there so that you can check the temperature every hour or so.

Don't give up if you mess up your first batch of homemade yogurt. My first batch failed. When I told my older children with a feigned sad expression, "I killed my yogurt," they laughed hilariously. This I did by not realizing how darned long it took my oven thermometer to adjust its temperature reading. I turned up my oven temperature, the thermometer read 110°F, and I walked away thinking that the thermometer was finished adjusting. Half an hour later, I came back and was surprised that it read 150°F. Needless to say, that yogurt batch was ruined, but not all was lost—we used the hot milk to make cocoa.

TIP: If you're using your oven to incubate yogurt, pre-warm it before putting the yogurt into it and give the thermometer at least 15-30 minutes to adjust. That way you can be sure it's not hotter than it looks.

Warm Places to Grow Yogurt

Before you actually use a "warm place" to incubate yogurt, test its temperature by doing this: Fill a mayonnaise jar or a bowl with about a quart of warm water. Place the jar in the warm place for several hours. Keep your yogurt/candy thermometer dipped into the jar and check it about every hour or so to make sure the temperature stays within the range of 90-120°F—the closer to 112°F, the better. Once the warm place has been tested, you can confidently try it for incubating the real stuff.

Conventional Oven. Wrap the jar of yogurt in a thick towel or yogurt towel bag and place it in your oven on the lowest temperature (about 110°F). To monitor the temperature, I use a regular outside/inside air thermometer. The oven should never get hot enough to go above the thermometer's maximum temperature mark and break it.

You can use an oven thermometer, but the markings usually start at about 200°F—a temperature that will kill your yogurt. With an oven thermometer, you usually must estimate where the 110°F mark is. If you have only a yogurt or candy thermometer, place it in a bowl of water in the oven. Remember that your oven will be unavailable for cooking other food for several hours.

Conventional Oven II. Instead of leaving your oven on throughout the incubation period, heat it periodically. First turn on your oven, heat it to 120°F, and turn it off. Keep an eye on the thermometer (hopefully you have a window so you don't have to open the oven door). When it drops to near 100°F, turn on the oven for only a minute, wait, and watch the thermometer to see if it reads 120°F again. This is the method I must use with my electric oven, because if I leave it on continuously, even if it's set to the lowest temperature, it gets too hot and kills the yogurt cultures.

It usually takes around 2 hours for my oven to drop to 100°F and need reheating. If I'm going to let the yogurt incubate overnight, I certainly don't get up in the middle of the night to reheat it. (Those of us with babies know what a luxury uninterrupted sleep is.) Instead, I set the "Timed Bake" to turn on automatically, let it heat for one minute, and turn off automatically. Keep the jar of yogurt wrapped in a thick towel or yogurt towel bag to protect it from the variations in temperature inside the oven.

Conventional Oven III. Keep the oven off completely. Use only the pilot light in a gas stove or the light bulb in an electric oven. The low heat generated will probably be warm enough. Don't use this method if it costs a fortune to replace your electric oven's light bulb.

Picnic Cooler (the typical plastic insulated cooler that you take to the beach, or even a cheap Styrofoam one). Place the yogurt in a warm water bath (not your Jacuzzi, although it might work). Pour warm water (around 115°F) into the cooler so that it comes at least halfway up the jar containing the yogurt. Close the cooler tightly and don't peak too often—every time you open the cooler, heat gets lost.

Picnic cooler II. I make yogurt successfully by boiling a pot of water and placing it into a picnic cooler with the yogurt. The hot pot of water keeps it warm long enough for incubation. Use this method instead of the warm water bath and you don't have to pick up a heavy cooler to dump the water out. And if you are using *jar-in-pot* scalding, you can use the same water and pot.

The kitchen sink. If you don't have a picnic cooler, there's always the kitchen sink, the bathroom sink, or even the bathtub. Run a few inches of warm tap water (around 115°F) in the bottom of your sink so that it comes at least halfway up the yogurt container. You may want to cover the sink with towels, a carpet, a blanket, a newspaper, or whatever's handy to retain the heat. You may have to check every few hours to make sure the water doesn't get too cold.

If it's unheard of in your house to make the kitchen sink unavailable for several hours, and this may be going too far, use baby's little bathtub to hold warm water. You get the idea—use just about any large container that will hold water.

The stove top. Put a pot of water on the stove over the lowest heat setting. Place the jar of yogurt into the water. Make sure it doesn't get too hot. After an hour or two, my old electric stove brings the water temperature to 130°F, so I either have to watch it carefully and turn it on and off every so often, or use a double boiler.

An electric fry pan. Fill it with warm water and set it to 100-110°F. Place yogurt containers in the pan and, if possible, place the pan's cover on them.

A crockpot. If your crockpot has only a low and high heat setting, it's probably too hot to incubate yogurt. Usually, a crockpot's low heat setting is 200°F and the high setting is 300°F. But if your have a rare crockpot where you can set the temperature, fill it partially with warm water, place the jar in it, and set it to 110-115°F. Verify with a thermometer that your crockpot stays at the proper temperature.

A warming tray. Use the kind that keeps foods warm at a party or the ones that keep baby food warm. Place a bowl with water on it and the yogurt jar in the bowl. If too hot, try putting layers of cloth towels between the tray and the bowl, but this wastes energy.

A heating pad. Wrap the yogurt in some thick towels or put it in a yogurt towel bag (see page 308) and place on a heating pad on low setting.

A hot water bottle. A hot water bottle is another heat source that can be placed in a picnic cooler or in a stock pot with the jar of yogurt. Wrap the pot in a large thick beach towel, blanket, carpet, newspaper, or put it in a yogurt towel bag to help retain warmth.

A home-heating source. Try a radiator, wood stove, or heating duct. Wrap the yogurt in some thick towels or put it in a yogurt towel bag and place it on or near a home-heating source.

A major appliance. Try the top of your refrigerator or the top of the water heater.

Electronic equipment. Your TV, stereo, or other electronic equipment may be releasing enough heat to incubate yogurt. I think this worked several decades ago when vacuum tubes and transistors were state-of-the-art. Today's integrated circuits are just too energy efficient!

A wide-mouthed thermos. Wash it out with hot water and soap and rinse very well. Pre-warm it by rinsing with hot water. Pour the yogurt mixture into the thermos, cover it, and leave it undisturbed for several hours. (You may have a problem with the formation of a vacuum within the thermos during incubation. The only way to know is to try it.)

Solar energy. Use the green energy effect to your advantage—place the yogurt in a hot car or in a sunny window.

Down. A sleeping bag, vest, or jacket may work to keep your yogurt warm and cozy.

Microwaveable neck warmers. Don't go out and buy one, but if you happen to already have one of those neck warmers that you heat for a few minutes in the microwave that stays warm for hours, try using it to incubate yogurt. Wrap the yogurt container in a thick towel or put it in a yogurt towel bag and then surround with the neck warmer.

An electric commercial yogurt maker. As a last resort, you can always buy the appliance especially designed to incubate yogurt. This is too easy for those of us who like a challenge. Effortless and worry-free, you may find that it's worth it to buy one if you plan on eating yogurt every day, as you should.

The human body. While climbing a mountain, the heat from your body will keep a flask of yogurt at the right temperature.

Anywhere warm. You probably have the idea by now. Anything you can use to keep the yogurt at a comfortable temperature will do. You'll be surprised at what you'll find around the house.

Keep the yogurt still during incubation. Place the yogurt mixture in a place where it won't be disturbed or have to be moved for several hours. Movement will cause the whey to settle out from the curd. Jiggling the yogurt will cause it to take more time to thicken, it won't ruin it.

Wait several hours until the yogurt is finished. The yogurt will take anywhere from 4 to 12 hours to become thick and pudding-like. Test for doneness by touching the top with your clean finger. The longer you let it incubate, the more tart the flavor.

If you make yogurt in your oven during the day, remember that your oven will be unavailable for cooking other foods for a significant stretch of time.

> **TIP:** Although it takes a lot of time to make yogurt, don't let that deter you. Yogurt making does not require constant attention; only occasional temperature-taking that requires you to hang around the house for a while. This probably isn't difficult for those of us with new babies—most of us have happily dropped out of the jet set.

Yogurt Towel Bag

Make a thick towel bag to fit around your yogurt jar. Take an old towel, fold it into several layers, and sew it into a pocket shape to fit the jar fairly snugly, similar to a sleeping bag. All parts of the jar are then covered neatly with several layers of thick toweling, so that the yogurt is kept at a fairly even temperature throughout many hours of incubation. The insulation of the towel bag prevents the yogurt from being too susceptible to outside hot or cold temperature fluctuations.

Refrigerate the Finished Yogurt

Cover and refrigerate the finished yogurt for several hours before serving. The yogurt will keep in the refrigerator for 1 to 2 weeks. If you're going to use some of this current batch as a starter for your next batch, make sure that it is no more than 5-7 days old so that the bacteria is still strong.

As with store-bought yogurt, the longer you store yogurt, the tarter it becomes. A yellow-tinged watery liquid, called "whey," forms on top of the yogurt. Pour it off to thicken the yogurt, stir it in if you want a thinner yogurt.

Optionally, Add Flavoring or Nutritional Enhancers

Follow the same instructions for flavoring commercial yogurt on page 296. Experiment until you get the taste and texture you want. The taste and texture of homemade yogurt depends on many factors: the milk used, the scalding method, the starter, the temperature during incubation, the stability of the temperature during incubation, the length of incubation time. Experiment until you find a yogurt that tastes best to you.

To Thicken Yogurt

Yogurt will thicken once it's refrigerated. Frequently pour off the whey. If, after refrigerating, it's still too thin for your taste, next time try using a yogurt with more fat. Skim milk makes thinner yogurt than low-fat milk, which makes thinner yogurt than whole milk. Or, try adding powdered milk when you add the starter.

Or, "gel it." Add one packet (or one tablespoon) of agar flakes or unflavored gelatin to the yogurt after it is finished and just before you place it into the refrigerator. First, dilute the agar or gelatin in a few tablespoons of hot water, then mix it into the finished yogurt.

Increase/Decrease the Tart Flavor

I personally do not like the tartness of yogurt. I like my yogurt thick and creamy with no taste at all. Know that the longer the incubation time, the tarter the yogurt. Also, the longer the yogurt is stored in the refrigerator, the tarter it becomes. If your starter is tart, the yogurt will be, too. When my starter gets tart, I throw it out and use a new starter.

Keep in mind that the lower the temperature of the yogurt during incubation (but still within the range 90-120°F), the less sour the flavor of the yogurt. I let mine incubate for at most 5 hours at around 100°F to minimize its tartness. To decrease the tart flavor of refrigerated yogurt, add some lemon juice.

If Your Yogurt Didn't Turn out Right

If your yogurt is much too runny, don't throw it out. Dissolve a tablespoon of agar or unflavored gelatin in 4 tablespoons of warm. Stir into the yogurt and refrigerate. Here is a list of problems that may have ruined your yogurt:

- You let it get too hot. Temperatures above 120°F will kill yogurt bacteria.

- You let it get too cold. Yogurt cultures become inactive at temperatures below 90-95°F.

- There were antibiotics in the milk. Buy organic milk for making yogurt.

- Your starter may have been too old. Some advise you to begin with a new starter every month or so, although there is rumored to be yogurt alive today that's been passed down from generation to generation for hundreds of years.

- If your yogurt tastes sour and/or separates, your heat source may be a little too warm. Or too much starter was introduced into the milk—use a little less next time or incubate for a shorter time period.

- If you place yogurt into the freezer to cool it first, before placing it in the refrigerator, the consistency will be more even.

- If your yogurt tastes or smells strange, other bacteria may have taken up housekeeping in your yogurt. Toss it and start with a new starter. Make sure everything is scrupulously clean.

- Don't bake bread the same day or the day before you make yogurt. The yogurt may taste like bread yeast because it may pick up airborne yeast particles.

Summary: My Easiest Yogurt Making Method

I wanted to give you complete detailed instructions on how to make yogurt because you will use a lot of it if you're feeding your baby the *Super Baby Food Diet*. Making homemade yogurt will save you a ton of money.

After years of trying to find the easiest, most effective, and "least dishes to wash" method of making yogurt, here's what I've come up with. It works every time with my refrigerator, my microwave oven, and my conventional oven. With trial and error, you will find the exact times for your equipment and find the easiest method for you.

1. Pour a quart of milk into a clean mayonnaise jar. I usually use organic soy milk enriched with calcium and vitamin D.

2. Nest the jar into a saucepan on the stove top with water that comes halfway up the side of the jar. Put a yogurt thermometer into the milk (not the water) and bring milk to 185°F. (If it clacks too much while heating, try putting a small towel under the jar.) From the refrigerator, remove the little jar containing the starter (see tip below) and let it warm to room temperature while milk is scalding and cooling.

3. When milk is 185°F, cover jar with lid and place in refrigerator to cool. Set my timer for 45 minutes, which is how long it will take in my refrigerator to cool to 115°F.

4. Place the spoon and other utensils in the scalding water in the sauce pan on the stove top in order to sterilize them.

5. When milk in refrigerator is 115°F, stir dry milk powder and starter into jar and replace lid.

6. Place jar in pre-warmed homemade yogurt towel bag (see below) and into pre-warmed oven. (I stick the towel bag in the oven while the oven preheats so that it will get pre-warmed with the oven.)

7. Five hours later, yogurt is firm. Move it to the refrigerator.

TIP: Before you begin to eat a freshly-opened container of yogurt, set aside a little of it to be used as a starter for your next batch of homemade yogurt. Save some of the yogurt by scooping 2 or 3 tablespoons into a small sterile glass baby food jar. Cover and keep in a cold spot in the refrigerator. Storing these tablespoons in a separate jar will keep it cleaner and ensure that you won't eat all the yogurt and forget to save some to start your next batch.

Get to Know Your Oven Intimately

Your oven is a good place to incubate homemade yogurt, let bread rise, and dry foods like fruit leather. But an oven that is too hot will kill the bacteria in the yogurt, the yeast in the bread, and will fry your foods instead of dry them.

On days when you are not using your oven, learn about it by using trial and error to test how fast it heats. Figure out the exact number of seconds it takes to heat your oven to about 110°F.

First, put a thermometer into your oven—one that has markings as low as 100°F. Use a timer that is accurate to the second—the digital timer on your microwave or a separate digital timer works well. Close your oven door and set the timer for 60 seconds. Turn your oven off exactly when the timer beeps.

Now watch the temperature inside the oven for the next few hours. See how hot it gets and how long it remains at 110°F. If 60 seconds wasn't long enough, try 90 seconds on another day. When you actually put the yogurt or bread in the oven, it will decrease the temperature, of course, which is OK. A slightly cooler oven will only prolong the process, and you can always adjust the temperature by turning the oven on for a few extra seconds.

26

Eggs

Eggs Are Not as Bad as They Are Cracked Up to Be

Perhaps the first thing you think of when you think of eggs is cholesterol. Well, it's true that eggs do have a lot of cholesterol, but remember that we are not restricting fats from your baby's diet. Your baby needs fats. Eggs are a very nutritious food for your baby; they contain vitamin A, five grams of complete high quality protein, vitamin B12 (a problem nutrient for strict vegetarians), and many other nutrients. They contain about six grams of fat, of which four are unsaturated and two are saturated.

> WARNING: Never eat raw eggs and NEVER, EVER feed them to your baby.

While it used to be a recommendation to wait to feed egg whites to babies under one year, that has changed! Authorities believe that egg whites no longer pose a problem and may be introduced alongside egg yolks at 6 months of age. If your family has a history of allergic reaction to eggs, however, check with your pediatrician before introducing to your baby.

Wash Eggs Immediately Before Cracking

Dangerous bacteria may lurk on the shells of eggs, which may contaminate the inside raw egg as it pours out of the shell. Therefore, wash the outside of the egg with warm water and dish detergent (not dishwasher detergent). Rinse well. Do not wash eggs before storing, because you will remove the natural protective coating (called the "bloom") that helps protect against bacterial penetration through the pores in the shell. Therefore, leave the bloom on the egg as long as possible and wait to wash the shell until immediately before you're ready to use the egg.

Separating Egg Yolks from the Whites

Crumbled bits of hard-cooked egg yolk and pieces of scrambled egg yolk are nice finger foods for your baby. To separate the yolk from the white of a raw egg for scrambling, place the raw egg in a small funnel nested in a cup. The yolk will remain in funnel and white will run into the cup. Or place the raw egg in the palm of your clean hand and let the white run off through your fingers. Most of us probably separate eggs by pouring the yolk back and forth between the two half-shells, but this method may cause bacteria from the surface of the shell to contaminate the raw egg.

> **WARNING:** As with meat, be scrupulously clean when working with raw eggs. Wash well with hot water and soap anything that touched the eggs: your hands, pots, dishes, utensils, the counter, etc. Follow all safety precautions for handling meat when you work with eggs.

Buying Eggs

It is best to buy eggs that are organic wherever you can find them: the organic isle of your supermarket, the natural food stores, your local farmer's market, etc. These eggs are from free-running, synthetic hormone-free, healthy, happy chickens that have not been forced to sit in a cage their whole lives, never to see the light of day. These eggs are more expensive, but they are worth it.

You might find it most convenient to buy large eggs, rather than medium or extra-large, because large eggs are the default size used in most recipes.

Look for the expiration date on the package. To make things unnecessarily complicated, some packages have a Julian date instead of an expiration date. It is a number from 1 to 365 where 1 indicates January 1 and 365 indicates December 31. The Julian date is either the day that the eggs were packed or 30 days after the eggs were packed. Use eggs within one week after you bring them home. Although they may be OK for a month past the Julian date, their freshness diminishes.

The Egg Wiggle Test: Open the egg carton and gently turn each egg to make sure it moves freely. If it's stuck, the egg is cracked and the inside has leaked and dried. Don't buy them.

How to Test for Freshness of an Egg

The words "fresh eggs" on the container mean only that they have been kept refrigerated since they came out of the chicken. Fresh eggs may not be fresh.

To test for freshness, place an egg in a pan of water. If it sinks immediately, it's fresh. If it floats, it's too old to use. If it tilts, it's 3-4 days old; if it stands upright, it's about 10 days old.

The movement of an egg under water is determined by the amount of air contained within the shell, which enters slowly over a period of time. The more air, the more the egg rises in the water.

Old eggs have runny whites that flatten out in the pan, instead of thick whites that stand high. The runniness is caused by the thinning and breaking down of the white because of the release of carbon dioxide through the eggshell. Fresh egg shells are rough and chalky while old egg shells are smooth and shiny.

Never Eat Raw Eggs

Because of the risk of salmonella, you should never eat raw eggs, and you should certainly never risk giving them to your baby. As stated previously, even eggs with no cracks that are bacteria-free outside the shell can contain salmonella inside from the chicken's intestines. So washing an egg does not make it safe. Whether you are feeding your baby hard-cooked egg or scrambled egg, make sure that it is cooked through and solid, with no raw parts.

> WARNING: Before feeding your little one a hard-cooked egg, break it open with a fork and make sure that the yolk is solid all the way to the center. No part of the yolk should be undercooked because it may contain live salmonella.

How to Refrigerate a Raw Egg

Store eggs large end up, which is the way they come in the egg packs from the store. Keeping them large end up maximizes the distance between the air bubble inside the egg and the egg yolk, which is heavier than the white and sinks to the bottom. (Once cooked, it doesn't matter which side is up.) The large end of the egg is less likely to break if bumped.

> WARNING: Keep eggs refrigerated every minute! Do not let them sit out while you're making breakfast—return them to the refrigerator immediately.

Don't transfer eggs from the store container to the egg molds on the doors of old refrigerators. The door is usually the warmest part of the refrigerator, and eggs should be kept cold. The movement of the door may cause the eggs to form small invisible cracks.

Eggs must be kept covered when refrigerated to prevent a loss of moisture from the dry refrigerator air. Covering them also helps to prevent eggs from picking up odors from other foods.

Raw egg whites can be stored in the refrigerator, tightly covered, for about one week. (Raw eggs can also be frozen, as discussed later.) Egg yolks can be refrigerated covered with water for up to 3 days. Place some cold water in an air-tight container and slide unbroken yolks into the water. Cover the container well and refrigerate.

How to Hard-Cook an Egg

I have found that this method of hard-cooking eggs is less likely to cause cracks in the shell. Place the eggs in a saucepan and cover completely with cold water. Heat the water slowly over medium high heat until it boils. Continue to cook the eggs in slowly boiling water for 15 minutes. The water should be boiling, but not so rapidly that the eggs clack wildly and crack. After 15 minutes, plunge them into cold water to stop the cooking. I just stick the stainless steel pot into the sink and run cold tap water into it. Incidentally, quickly stopping the egg from cooking will make peeling easier.

There are other ways to hard-cook an egg. One is to slowly lower a raw egg into boiling water and continue to boil for 15 minutes. I always get a lot of cracks with this method. If cooking does cause a crack in one of your eggs, use it immediately.

Egg Tips

- Many recipes call for room temperature eggs, but leaving eggs at room temperature for extended periods allows bacteria to grow. Instead, place eggs from the refrigerator into warm (not hot) water for 5-10 minutes immediately before using.

- 5 large eggs = 1 cup, 7 whites = 1 cup, 13-14 yolks = 1 cup, ½ large egg is equal to about 1½ tablespoons

- Many recipes call for whipped raw egg whites, which may contain salmonella. This is OK, as long as they will be baked or cooked at a high temperature that will kill all bacteria. For recipes that do not involve heating (such as Egg Nog, Caesar salad, etc.), raw egg whites can be replaced with a pasteurized egg white product. Many egg white products are available at your natural foods store and supermarket organic food isle.

- While whipping egg whites, make sure you use a clean bowl because any oil or grease will prevent whites from rising. Make sure that all yolk has been completely removed. Remember that you should never eat raw eggs because of the danger of salmonella. Used whipped raw egg whites only in recipes where they will be cooked thoroughly to kill all bacteria.

- To get the smoothest scrambled eggs, don't rush it. Start with a cold buttered frying pan and stir frequently while cooking slowly over medium-low heat. Add one tablespoon per egg of cream, evaporated milk, or regular milk. For really creamy eggs, add ½ tablespoon of sour cream for each egg.

- To prevent raw egg yolks from hardening on a plastic spatula making it difficult to clean, spray oil or butter the spatula first.

- Drop a raw egg on the floor? Use a baster to suck it up. Clean baster very well afterwards. Or, instead of the baster, sprinkle salt on the raw egg on the floor and wait 20 minutes. A paper towel will pick it up easily.

- Add about one teaspoon of wheat germ for each egg before scrambling to increase nutritional content.

- There's no major nutritional difference between white and brown eggs. The color of the shell has to do with camouflaging the egg from its natural predators.

- It is common to add milk to eggs when scrambling them. Try orange juice instead, and see how you like the flavor.

- Wet your fingers before handling whole raw eggs. It will give you a good grip and you will be less likely to drop them and make a mess!

- To lessen the chances of breaking a yolk during cracking, hold the egg at an angle instead of straight while hitting it on the top edge of the pan or bowl.

- Crack each egg into a cup first before adding it to a recipe. If the egg is spoiled, it won't ruin the entire recipe.

- For easy peeling, tap a hard-cooked egg on all sides on the counter top. Roll gently between your palms to crackle. Pull the shell off beginning with the large end. Optionally, pull off shell while holding under cold running tap water. Another method is to crack the shell all over, insert a small WET spoon (baby has one) under the membrane and turn egg while prying the shell off.

- For easy peeling of many eggs at one time, follow directions for *How to Hard-Cook an Egg*. After boiling, pour off the hot water, and crack each egg with the back of a spoon. Cover eggs with cold water and keep running cold tap water into the pot until the water remains cool. Store pot in refrigerator for an hour or more to allow the water to get between the egg and shell. Peel and shells will come off easily.

- Separate an egg and use the nonfat whites for your breakfast omelets. Cook the whole yolk for baby by simmering in water for 10-12 minutes. As always, break the cooked egg yolk open to look and make sure it is cooked through thoroughly with no raw parts.

- Sliced eggs are great for *Decorative Touches* (page 559). If you have trouble with yolks crumbling while trying to get a pretty slice, try dipping knife in cold water first before slicing.

- Add two tablespoons of vinegar per quart of cooking water to help prevent cracks in eggs. Or rub eggs with a cut lemon or lemon juice to help prevent cracking during cooking.

- Use a pastry bag to stuff deviled eggs. Fill bag with stuffing and squeeze.

- Deviled eggs look best when yolks are centered within the white. To help yolks stay centered, gently stir water and eggs for the first few minutes of boiling to set the whites. Also, the white will be stronger and will be less likely to break when stuffed.

- Use the (cooled) cooking water from boiled eggs to water plants. The minerals that leached into the water from the eggshells make a very nutritious fertilizer. Place discarded eggshells into your watering can. Dry egg shells in the oven, pulverize them in the blender, and use the powder to fertilize houseplants.

- Read about egg substitutes at the end of this chapter.

Storing Cooked Eggs

Eggs must be refrigerated both before and AFTER COOKING. Thoroughly dry each cooked egg with a clean wipe-up towel and do so very gently so as not to cause cracks. Refrigerate immediately after cooking to minimize the time the eggs are in the danger zone temperature range for bacterial growth. Bacteria in the air can enter the shell through minute invisible cracks, so get eggs cooled as quickly as possible after cooking to prevent bacterial growth.

Plunging them into cold water after cooking helps to cool them quickly. Store cooked eggs in the refrigerator, well covered, and, as with raw eggs, do not store in egg molds on the doors of old refrigerators. Eggs must be kept covered and cold, and the door is the warmest part of the refrigerator.

Keep cooked eggs no longer than one week. Use or discard hard-cooked eggs within one week after they have been cooked.

> **TIP:** I always hard-cook 4 eggs for my little guy on the same day of the week, Monday. If I crack an egg during cooking, he eats that one the same morning. He gets an egg in his *Super Porridge* on Monday, Wednesday, and Friday (which my family and I call "egg days") and maybe once during the weekend. Cooking eggs on the same day each week helps you to remember to discard them when they become a week old.

> **WARNING:** Don't eat eggs from Easter egg hunts. You never know how old they are or how well they've been kept cold.

Freezing Eggs

So eggs have gone on sale, and you took advantage and bought a gross. Good thing for you eggs can be frozen.

Hard-cooked egg whites become rubbery when frozen. Hard-cooked egg yolks can be frozen in a organic, bleach-free waxed paper-lined, plastic freezer bag for up to two months. Thaw frozen cooked yolks overnight in the refrigerator and use within one day. Do not refreeze.

Freeze only eggs that are fresh and don't have a cracked shell. First, do not freeze whole raw eggs in the shell, or they will expand and break the shell. Whites freeze well, but egg yolks gel and get sticky and thick unless you add salt or sugar.

Break four whole raw eggs into a sturdy freezer container. Very gently mix the eggs so that the yolks break, or pierce the yolks to break them. Don't stir up foam or you'll have dry, freezer-burned eggs. Stir in a ¼ teaspoon salt OR 2 teaspoons of sugar or corn syrup for each of the four raw eggs. Choose salt or sugar depending on how you will use the eggs when thawed. Leave no more than ½ inch of headroom, cover well, label, and freeze for up to 6 months.

You can also freeze the whole egg mixture using the *Food Cube Method*. Approximately 3 tablespoons is equal to one egg. Thaw (see below) and use scrambled, in omelets, or in baking.

Freezing Raw Egg Yolks

To freeze raw egg yolks, place the yolks in a sturdy freezer container and pierce them so that they break. Gently stir in ⅛ teaspoon salt or ½ teaspoon sugar or corn syrup for every four yolks to prevent coagulation. Freeze for up to 3 months. Approximately one tablespoon of thawed egg yolk liquid is equal to one egg yolk.

Freezing Raw Egg Whites

Raw egg whites freeze well. No need to add anything to them. Freeze them using the *Food Cube Method*—one egg white per cube—and keep for up to 6 months. Instead of cubes, you can freeze a whole bunch of egg whites in a sturdy freezer container with no more than ½ inch headroom. Approximately two tablespoons of liquid egg white is equal to one egg white.

Thawing Raw or Cooked Eggs

Thaw frozen eggs overnight in the refrigerator and use within one day. Do not refreeze.

What's That Green Stuff?

The green discoloration you sometimes see on the outer surface of a hard cooked egg yolk may be unattractive, but it is harmless and you can safely eat it. It is caused by a chemical reaction between the iron in the egg yolk and the sulfur in the white. There are two things you can do to minimize it. Cook eggs in simmering water rather than water at full boil, and don't overcook them. Plunging eggs into cold water after 15 minutes of boiling will quickly stop the cooking.

Blood Spots

The blood spots you see occasionally when you break a raw egg were caused by the rupture of a blood vessel on the yolk's surface when it was being formed. The egg is perfectly safe to eat. If you wish, remove the blood spot with the tip of a knife.

How to Tell a Raw Egg from a Cooked Egg

Spin it. A cooked egg will spin; a raw egg will wobble. Find out for yourself by comparing the movements of a spinning cooked egg and a raw egg.

> **TIP:** To keep track of which eggs are raw and which are cooked, keep them in separate containers in your refrigerator. If you're short on refrigerator space as I am, keep them in the same egg carton and mark the cooked eggs with a "C" using a non-toxic marker or crayon. Or, store raw eggs large end up and cooked eggs small end up, but you'll need good eyes with this method to tell which end is up. Or, store raw eggs on the right side of the container and cooked eggs on the left; remember that raw and right both start with "R." Some people can smell the difference between a raw and cooked egg. The most fun way to distinguish raw from cooked eggs is to put a few drops of food coloring and a little vinegar into the water while boiling to "color code" cooked eggs.

Egg Safety Information

For more information on the safe handling and storage of eggs, check out the USDA website: **www.USDA.gov.**

Egg Substitutes

Most commercial egg replacement products are nothing more than egg whites with no yolks and a small amount of other ingredients such as vegetable oils, nonfat milk, emulsifiers, stabilizers, artificial colors, and others. For vegans, those who are allergic to eggs, or those who wish to cook without eggs for another reason, here are some homemade egg substitutes you can use instead of the commercial variety:

- For each egg to be replaced in a baked product, use one heaping tablespoon of soy flour or cornstarch plus 1½ tablespoons water. The soy flour is the more nutritious of the two.

- Use half of a mashed banana instead of an egg in muffins and cookies.

- In place of an egg, use one ounce of mashed tofu.

- Replace hard-cooked egg white in recipes like potato salad with steamed tofu.

- Instead of using eggs to bind ingredients in meatless loaves and burgers, use mashed potato, moistened whole grain bread crumbs, rolled oats, or tomato paste.

27

Super-Duper Baby Foods

Kelp

Powdered kelp (which is actually a seaweed) can be purchased at your natural foods store. My family uses it instead of iodized salt as a source of iodine. You may want to put just a pinch of powdered kelp in your baby's *Super Porridge* each morning. I keep kelp in a saltshaker—it's very convenient for sprinkling small amounts onto foods. If you have the approval of your pediatrician, introduce kelp to your baby at 8 months.

> WARNING: Some kelp may have a high arsenic content. Be careful about where you buy the kelp you feed to your baby.

Vegetable Oils

Typical supermarket brands of cooking oil are processed at high temperatures and have added chemicals. They are not at all natural, and have been processed, refined, deodorized, and bleached. Avoid them. And avoid margarines, which have partially hydrogenated oils. Be sure to read the label and avoid any oils containing BHT or BHA.

Flaxseed or flaxseed oil from the natural food store is a must for inclusion your baby's diet, as discussed at length in the nutrition section beginning on page 406. As for other oils, buy only cold-pressed, unrefined vegetable oil. Olive oil is one of the least likely to be rancid. Natural, unprocessed oils should be kept under constant refrigeration to help prevent rancidity; they will get cloudy because of the lecithin they contain, but that doesn't affect the quality.

There are two camps when it comes to using fat for cooking and frying. Some experts claim that vegetable oils should NEVER be used for cooking or frying because heat causes them to become carcinogenic. They suggest using butter instead. Other experts don't agree with the use of butter because of its saturated fat.

WARNING: Never heat oil to the smoking point. It may ignite.

Homemade Oil Spray

Pam® and other commercial spray cooking oils are expensive, and they are nothing more than lecithin and alcohol. Save money by making homemade oil-spray with similar ingredients to those in commercial products (see the ingredients list on the can).

Pour a ½ cup of vodka or other flavorless alcohol from the liquor store (do NOT use rubbing alcohol) into a sterile spray or pump bottle. Add 2 teaspoons of liquid lecithin (from the natural foods store). Shake very well and use like Pam. The vodka acts as an emulsifier to make the thick lecithin disperse easily. The vodka will evaporate during cooking, leaving only a thin coat of lecithin, which will prevent sticking and wash off easily. Keep refrigerated.

Instead of the previous recipe, you can smear liquid lecithin directly on the pan, but you tend to use a lot of lecithin this way and it is thick and messy.

If you are having trouble finding liquid lecithin, use 4 tablespoons granular lecithin (very easy to find) mixed into a ½ cup of corn oil. Mix thoroughly in your blender and keep the spray bottle refrigerated.

TIP: I have found that plain cooking oil (without alcohol) works just fine in a spray bottle as a Pam® substitute. Or use a squeeze bottle and smear with a small piece of paper towel. As with all oils, keep refrigerated.

The bottle containing homemade oil-spray does tend to get messy. Clean it by emptying it and then filling it with very hot soapy water. Replace the spritzer and spray many times. Then fill with clear water and replace the spritzer again and spray many times to rinse out the soap. Repeat this rinsing with a fresh batch of clear water for a second rinse and again for a third rinse until you are sure that all traces of soap have been rinsed away.

Coconut Oil

Coconut oil is extracted from the fruit of mature coconuts. Since coconuts are grown on palm trees in soil that is loaded with nutrients, coconuts have lots of nutrition. And it's delicious! Coconut oil has a sweet, nutty taste, and is often used as a substitute for shortening or butter in a vegan diet.

For baby, coconut oil is also an excellent source of healthy fats, which babies need for their growing brains! It is an ingredient in infant formula, which makes perfect sense because it is one of the few natural sources of lauric acid, which is also found in breast milk. To include this yummy, healthy oil in your child's diet simply add a teaspoon or two to his prepared baby food meal.

Coconut oil can also be used in cooking the family meal as well. Since it has a high smoke point, it is good to cook with instead of other vegetable oils. You can find coconut oil in your natural foods store and some supermarkets.

You can also find coconut milk, dried coconut flakes—the kind used on cupcakes, and coconut flour. Recommended reading: Bruce Fife's two excellent books: *The Coconut Oil Miracle* and *Cooking with Coconut Flour: A Delicious Low-Carb, Gluten-Free Alternative to Wheat.*

TIP: Use coconut oil on your and your baby's skin. It is a wonderful moisturizer, with no chemicals.

Agar

Did you ever notice the gelatinous goop that pools around chicken parts? That jelly contains the same ingredient in animal gelatin, which is made from the connective tissue in bones, hoofs, ligaments, cartilage, and tendons of animals. Gelatin is a substance that dissolves in hot water and solidifies in cold. We all have eaten or have at least seen Jell-O® gelatin—a dessert made from animal gelatin, artificial colors, and other ingredients.

Agar, also called "agar agar," is a gelatinous substance made from seaweed (red algae). Unlike gelatin, it is not made from animal products and therefore is favored by vegetarians. Agar can be found at your natural foods store and comes granulated or flaked. Substitute 1-2 tablespoons (depending on the brand) of agar flakes for each tablespoon of gelatin or packet of gelatin called for in your favorite recipes, or follow the directions on the package. Granulated agar is more "dense" and you need less of it: substitute ½-1 tablespoon of granulated agar for each tablespoon of gelatin. One tablespoon of flakes or ½ tablespoon of granules will gel one cup liquid.

> **TIP:** Don't add fresh pineapple, kiwi fruit, papaya, guava, ginger, or figs to a recipe with gelatin. They contain an enzyme called bromelain, which breaks down proteins and prevents the gelatin from setting. (This is why it makes a good meat tenderizer.) There is no problem with canned pineapple, because the canning/heating process destroys the bromelain. Use agar instead of gelatin and there will be no problem with any pineapple, fresh or frozen.

Arrowroot

Arrowroot is a thickener derived from the tropical maranta plant root. It's more nutritious than cornstarch and does not have the raw flavor of whole wheat flour. Arrowroot is easily digested by infants and young children. One tablespoon of arrowroot will thicken one cup of liquid. Do not overstir, or the mixture will become thin again.

Use a little less arrowroot when substituting for flour in your favorite recipes, because arrowroot's thickening power is stronger than flour. Substitute two teaspoons of arrowroot for each tablespoon of flour. Like cornstarch, arrowroot should be mixed with enough cold liquid to make a paste before stirring into a hot mixture. Substitute the same amount of arrowroot for cornstarch in a recipe.

Blackstrap Molasses

You can buy blackstrap molasses at the natural foods store and many supermarkets. Use it as a licorice-like sweetener in yogurt, baking, and beverages. I should warn you that many people do not like the strong taste of it.

Blackstrap molasses is actually a waste product from the refinement of table sugar, and it is the only sweetener that contains any significant amount of nutrients. Besides other nutrients, most brands of blackstrap molasses are very high in iron, depending on the manufacturing process.

After opening the jar, store blackstrap molasses in the refrigerator.

TIP: Blackstrap molasses is as "slow as molasses" in January. Try to buy a jar with a wide mouth, so that you can spoon it out instead of pouring.

Honey

> **WARNING: Do not feed your baby honey or corn syrup until he is at least one year old, because of the possibility of botulism poisoning.**

Honey is just another sugar. It does have minute traces of nutrients, but not enough to mention. One advantage of honey over table sugar is that you can use less of it to get the same sweetness in recipes. Substitute approximately ⅔ cup honey for each cup of sugar called for in the recipe. If the original recipe does not contain any honey, reduce the baking temperature by 25°F to prevent over-browning. For each cup of honey substituted, add an extra ¼ teaspoon of baking soda to neutralize the acidity. Also, reduce the liquid in the recipe by about ¼ cup for each cup of honey. Honey substitutions in baked products are risky and, unless you are daring, substitute no more than half the sugar called for in the recipe with honey.

Honey doesn't spoil. Store honey at room temperature away from direct sunlight. Prevent water from getting into the honey, because moisture will cause mold to grow. You can keep it in the refrigerator, but colder temperatures will speed crystallization.

Natural honey will eventually crystallize at room temperature. To re-liquefy crystallized honey, place the open jar in hot water or in the oven at 250°F for several minutes and stir every few minutes. The time it will take to liquefy depends on the amount of honey in the jar, of course.

Maple Syrup

Real maple syrup is also just another sugar, but it is more natural and healthier than the supermarket brands of "pretend" maple syrup, which are actually made from cheap corn syrup, preservatives, and artificial colorings. Real maple syrup must be kept refrigerated after the bottle is opened.

TIP: Wipe the lid and jar of blackstrap molasses, maple syrup, or honey with a damp towel before recapping to prevent sticking. Optionally, spritz the cap with oil-spray before recapping.

TIP: When measuring blackstrap molasses and honey, warm the measuring cup by rinsing with hot water. The warmth will cause the sweetener to flow better. Or, if a recipe also calls for oil, use a measuring cup to measure the oil first. Use the same oil-lined cup to measure the sweetener—it will slide out freely.

WARNING: Blackstrap molasses, honey, and syrup are infamous for causing dental cavities.

28

Healthy Extras

Throughout this book you will frequently see the words "add *Healthy Extras.*" *Healthy Extras* are exceptionally nutritious "health foods," which you should feed to your baby as often as possible. (They look a lot like the food staples on the previous page.) Some of them, such as nutritional yeast, don't taste very good, but several of the recipes give you a chance to sneak them into your baby's foods without her noticing. Some of the *Healthy Extras*, such as wheat germ and ground oats, absorb liquid and cause the food to be a little dry. Add a little more liquid than is called for in the recipe to correct for them.

Healthy Extras to Add as Super Nutrition Enhancers

Nutritional yeast
Wheat germ
Ground dry oatmeal or rolled oats
Tofu
Yogurt
Cooked crumbled egg
Shredded or diced raw vegetables (carrots, broccoli, celery, cabbage)
Chopped fresh or frozen parsley
Mashed (or whole for babies over 3 years) cooked dried beans or frozen puréed cooked bean food cubes
Cooked soy grits
Bean flour
Ground nuts (almonds, walnuts, filberts, etc.)
Nut and seed butters (peanut butter, almond butter, tahini, etc.
Ground seeds (pumpkin, flax, chia, etc.) Eat immediately
Cooked brown rice or millet grains or any cooked whole grains
Milks: breast, formula, super milks, instant nonfat dry milk
These healthy extras can double as sweeteners:
Shredded or diced fresh fruits (apples, pears, kiwi, etc.)
Chopped dried fruits, rehydrated (apricots, papaya, etc.)
Blackstrap molasses
Mashed fresh or mashed frozen strawberries and other berries
Concentrated frozen all-fruit juices
Natural no-added-sugar all-fruit jams or jellies

Super Flour

Please make sure to read the chapter on whole grains, which discusses the nutritional difference between refined and whole grain flours. You can use plain whole wheat flour as Super Flour in any of the recipes, or you can add to the protein and nutritional value of Super Flour by mixing it with soybean flour and other nutritional extras. To make one cup of Super Flour, place the following ingredients into a one-cup dry measuring cup:

1 tablespoon soy flour
1 tablespoon wheat germ
1 teaspoon nutritional yeast

Top off the cup with whole wheat flour to fill the balance of the cup.

Or use the mixture below as Super Flour, which is a well-known formula devised by Dr. Clive McKay of Cornell University. The Cornell Formula is mostly white flour, but there's no law that says you cannot replace the white flour with whole wheat flour!

The Cornell Formula

To make one cup of Cornell Formula, place the following ingredients into a one-cup dry measuring cup:

1 tablespoon nonfat dry milk solids
1 tablespoon soy flour
1 teaspoon wheat germ

Top off the cup with unbleached, unbrominated white flour to fill out the balance of the cup. Or use my formula on the next page for a home-enriched white flour. I add back the wheat germ and the bran that were removed during the refinement of white flour.

Home Enrichment Formula for White Flour

Place the following ingredients into a one-cup dry measuring cup:

1 tablespoon wheat germ
1 tablespoon wheat bran or oat bran
1 teaspoon soy flour (optional)
1 teaspoon nonfat powdered milk (optional)
1 teaspoon nutritional yeast (optional)

Top off with unbleached, unbrominated white flour to fill out the balance of the cup. Make a cup for each cup of flour called for in the recipe. Or use part whole wheat flour and replace the other part of the flour in the recipe with the mixture above.

Self-Rising Super Flour

No need to buy self-rising flour. Make your own by putting 1½ teaspoons baking powder and ½ teaspoon salt into a one-cup dry measuring cup. Fill it to the top with Super Flour and level with a knife to make one cup total.

TIP: Although soy flour is a great nutrition booster, which complements the wheat flour to form complete protein, it has a bitter taste. Don't add more than one tablespoon of soy flour per cup of recipe flour or its taste may affect your bread's flavor.

TIP: Whole wheat, germ, and bran absorb more liquid than white flour absorbs, so you may have to decrease the flour or increase the liquid in standard bread recipes by a few tablespoons. If you are replacing the white flour in a recipe with whole wheat flour, use a little less than is called for in the recipe, because it also will absorb more liquid.

TIP: You can replace white flour with whole wheat flour in your favorite recipes, but whole grain flour tends to leave bread products flat and dense. I have been teased by my family and friends many times about being able to use my cakes and quick breads as doorstops. For these recipes, I have reluctantly resolved myself to replace ONLY PART of the white flour called for in the recipe with whole grain flour—no more than ¼ to ½ —depending on the recipe. So before you go replacing all the white flour with whole wheat flour in a cake recipe for the school bake sale or your child's birthday party, make sure you've tested it beforehand.

Healthy Recipes for Commercial Food Products

Next time you are at the supermarket, take a look at the list of ingredients on any boxed food product: salt, sugars, partially hydrogenated oils, artificial flavors, pesticides, coloring, wheat flour (same as nutritionless white flour), and other nutritional horrors. Then check the amount or weight in the box and the cost—an exorbitant price for a minute amount of junk food! Someone has to pay for all of that expensive advertising and attention-getting, environment-unfriendly packaging. Natural food stores have commercially boxed food products with healthier ingredients, but you are still paying high prices for their convenience. See if you recognize the familiar recipes with slightly modified brand names in the recipes in Part VI.

Part IV

Safety First

29

Important Safety Information

The importance of safety in the kitchen and in the home cannot be overemphasized. Thousands of accidents and deaths occur in homes each year because people are either careless or just not aware of the hazards. I certainly don't intend to make you a basket case about your baby's safety. My intention is to make you aware of some precautions that you can take to minimize the chance of food problems, and kitchen and other household accidents.

Other rooms in your home besides the kitchen can be dangerous, of course, but this book's focus is on baby food and the kitchen. For a more thorough coverage of household safety, read one of the many good books available on the subject, such as Vicky Lansky's *Baby Proofing Basics 2 Ed: How To Keep Your Child Safe*. Although Debra Lynn Dadd's book, *Home Safe Home*, is not specifically a baby safety book, I highly recommend it as an overall home safety book. Your local library and, of course, the internet are good sources of free information.

Emergency Phone Numbers

Create several copies of an emergency sheet based on the information on the next two pages and hang them in strategic places and near every phone in your home. Update the emergency information sheet every few months or whenever the information changes. Keep a copy in your purse, the diaper bag, the glove compartment, your office, at the babysitter's or day care, etc.

Review the emergency sheet with babysitters, grandparents, neighbors, and anyone else who will be staying with your baby. Tell them to take a copy to the hospital with them. Tape a copy next to the door so it can be seen and grabbed quickly on the rush to the hospital.

It has been my experience that people hesitate to make emergency calls because they are nervous or afraid, and the younger the person is, the more s/he hesitates.

Stress to them that they should not hesitate to call the **Poison Control Center or 911 IMMEDIATELY.** Make it clear that it is much better to have an ambulance when it is not needed than to need an ambulance to save your child's life and not have one.

> **TIP:** For the babysitter, leave a Post-it-Note® by each phone with the phone number and name of the place you can be reached. (Save the notes for re-use.) You could have the babysitter program your name and cell phone number in his or her phone before s/he babysits for the first time for easy access, every young person has a cell phone in their pocket at all times!

> **REMINDER:** Be extra careful there is nothing in your way when you pull out of your driveway. Know exactly where your children are before you begin driving your car.

Emergency Information and Phone Number Sheet

Write up a sheet of paper with important facts and phone numbers. Make several copies and hang them all over the house and near every phone. Include this information:

- Poison Control Center's phone number.
- Fire department, ambulance, and police department phone numbers.
- Electric company's and gas company's emergency phone numbers.
- The precise address and phone number of your home.
- Directions to your home from the main street or well-known landmark in your town and the time it will take to get there.
- The full name of the baby, the hospital where she was born, blood group, immunizations, and medical problems. State any unusual fears your child may have.
- Pencil in your baby's current age and weight—keep it updated.
- Information on allergies to foods or medications. If your baby has no allergies, state that she has "no known allergies."
- Mom's and Dad's work numbers, full names, and work addresses. (I highlight these phone numbers with a yellow highlighter pen.)
- Any other phone numbers where Mom and Dad might be, such as cellular phone numbers, work numbers, the YMCA, frequently visited restaurants, etc.

- Phone numbers of other people to call in case Mom and Dad cannot be reached, such as Grandpa, Aunt Casey, Uncle Sean, the neighbor you trust, another babysitter. These should be listed in the order of the ones to call first.

- Names, addresses, and emergency phone numbers of your baby's pediatrician, pediatric dentist, ophthalmologist, and the nearest all-night pharmacy that delivers. Leave an emergency cash envelope with your babysitter. If you have a preferred hospital in your community, list its name.

- A copy of your medical insurance cards. (Copy them and cut and paste them directly onto this emergency sheet.)

- A notarized note signed by you saying that any hospital or emergency facility can administer emergency treatment to your baby. Hospitals will not give emergency treatment to your baby unless her life is in danger or unless they have permission from a parent. Call the emergency room of every hospital in your community and ask for the necessary procedures to have your written permission on file.

- The location of keys to doors in the house, in case your child locks himself in the bathroom or some other room in the house. Or drape a thick towel over the tops of doors to prevent them from fully closing.

- The date that this sheet was last updated.

Choking Hazards

There is a risk that young babies will choke on any foods, but hard, whole foods are especially dangerous. The foods in the table below are all considered choking hazards and should not be fed to a baby before he is at least three years old. Choking is not uncommon in children, even children older than three- to five-years-old.

WARNING: A child who has had a chocking episode should be examined by a doctor in order to determine if any food pieces remain lodged in his upper respiratory tract. Food pieces may cause swelling and strangulation to occur within a few days.

Foods That Are Choking Hazards to Avoid Before Age Three

popcorn	sliced hot dog "coins" and any other windpipe sized foods
marshmallows	
grapes	hard, underripe fruit pieces
ice cubes	peels of vegetables and fruits
celery sticks	strings from vegetables, such as celery, sweet potatoes, and winter squash
all berries	
olives	watermelon seeds and other seeds from vegetables and fruits
peas	leafy vegetables
raisins	whole corn kernels (cooked or uncooked)
any dried fruit	raw carrot, celery, mushroom, and other hard vegetable pieces
pretzel pieces	
pieces of bacon	apple pieces and other hard fruit pieces
gristle from meat	too thin carrot sticks (pieces can break off)
candy of all kinds	any nut butter (unthinned or chunky style)
gum	caramel candy and other thick, sticky foods
	whole or partially chopped nuts and seeds nuts hidden in candy bars
	potato chips, corn chips, and other chips

NOTE: Some of the foods listed as choking hazards above are very nutritious and it would be a shame to miss their nutrients. When baby is older and chewing and swallowing very well, you may want to feed her some of the foods above if you watch her very carefully. Ask your pediatrician for advice.

Prevent Your Baby from Choking

- Always watch your baby carefully while he is eating, and never turn your back or leave the room. Forget about your housework until after he is finished eating. Use his mealtimes as quality times to bond with your beautiful baby.

- Food pieces should be small enough so that, even if baby doesn't chew them at all and swallows them whole, they won't become lodged in the throat or food pipe.

- Before feeding your baby tofu dogs, do NOT slice them crosswise into round coin-shaped pieces. These pieces are dangerous choking hazards and the perfect size and shape to block a child's windpipe. First slice the whole tofu dogs lengthwise and then into small pieces less than an inch long.

- Never let baby eat unless he is seated and in an upright position. For example, don't let him lie on the floor and eat a cracker. Eating while he is walking or running may also cause choking.

- Be especially careful to watch a baby who has had teething medicine rubbed in his mouth. His ability to swallow may be impaired.

- Give your baby only a few bits of finger food at a time so that he doesn't cram too much in his mouth at once and possibly choke.

- Foods like cookies, crackers, muffins, breads, and biscuits should be either too hard for baby to bite off a piece or so soft that they dissolve almost immediately when put into baby's mouth.

- Be careful with slippery foods, such as wet fruits, which your baby can easily inhale into his windpipe.

- Do not prop your baby's bottle, as your baby may choke.

- Baby's mealtimes should be pleasant and fun. However, a baby laughing too much may choke on his food, and that's not fun. Use your own judgment as to how much is too much.

- Stress to your children to take small bites and chew carefully and thoroughly before swallowing.

- Balloons and broken balloon pieces are not food, of course, but they are known choking hazards for young children, especially when deflated.

- Choking hazard measures are available at major toy stores for a few dollars. Any toy, toy part, or item that is smaller than 1¾ inch should be considered a choking hazard to children, especially children under three years old. Use an official measuring device like the OneStepAhead® "Choke Tube Tester" to measure small toys for safety.

Warn Older Children about Choking

Older children should be made aware of the dangers of choking and your baby. Tell them never to leave food where baby can reach it and never to feed your baby anything that has not been OK'd by you. Warn even the babysitter about feeding unapproved snacks/foods to your baby. I heard of a case where the babysitter fed a candy bar to a baby who choked on a nut inside the candy bar. Nuts are especially dangerous because nut oils may cause lung infections if inhaled.

Know What to Do If Your Baby Is Choking

Reading about the Heimlich maneuver and CPR (cardio-pulmonary resuscitation) in a book or online cannot prepare you like real-life practice under an expert's instruction. Call your local chapter of the American Red Cross or ask your pediatrician for information on classes given in your area. Local YMCA's are a terrific source of First Aid classes.

I can't say enough good things about the American Red Cross. Their volunteers are extremely understanding and helpful. My twins had premature apnea and were on monitors for six months after they came home from the hospital. A trained Red Cross volunteer actually came to my house to give instruction on infant CPR and the Heimlich maneuver to a group of my twins' significant others, including grandmas, grandpas, aunts, uncles, neighbors, and babysitters. Any donation you give to the American Red Cross goes to a very worthy cause.

I warn you that this paragraph is upsetting and scary: I once took an American Red Cross First Aid course where the instructor related a very sad true story. It was about a panicking mother who, in an effort to help her choking baby, hurriedly pushed her hand into the baby's mouth without looking, and accidentally drove the food further down the baby's throat, causing him to suffocate. Never reach into baby's mouth unless you can see the food piece. Swipe it sideways and out, do not push it back. It's a good idea to keep a working flashlight handy to look into baby's mouth for food pieces.

You are less likely to panic in an emergency situation if you know what to do. Emergency training will take only a few hours of your time. Your baby is well worth it.

For older children and adults, it is probably best not to interfere with choking if the person can breath, cough, or speak. If he cannot breathe, call for help immediately.

Be Ready to Call the Poison Control Center at Any Time

Please put this book down and do this right now: Write the phone number for the Poison Control Center near every handset in your home and program it in your cell phone! In the United States, the phone number is **800-222-1222** and their website is **www.aapcc.org**.

Many poisonings can be managed over the phone if you call the Poison Control Center right away. If you even think there is a possibility of a poisoning, do not hesitate and call the center immediately.

When you call, the Poison Control Center will want to know:

- The age and weight of the child.
- The substance that the child swallowed—take the open pill bottle or other container to the phone. Or take the container of the substance that was splashed on the child's skin or in the child's eyes.
- An estimate of the amount of the substance swallowed by the child.
- An estimate of how long ago the child swallowed the substance.
- Symptoms: vomiting, irregular breathing, rapid sweating, weak pulse, a change in skin color or unusual skin color, drowsiness, sluggishness, diarrhea, burns around the mouth, odor on breath, poison still in mouth or on child's teeth, etc. If the child is old enough, ask her how she feels and if it hurts: head, stomach, can she see clearly, etc.
- Keep anything you find for analysis by medical personnel. The pill bottle, the cleaning container, parts of the houseplant or outdoor plant. Keep some of the vomit; this is not time to be squeamish—a life could be at stake.
- Follow the Poison Control Center's instructions. The center will call you back with a follow-up call later to make sure the child is OK.
- If the child is unconscious, call 911 first, and then administer CPR.

Syrup of Ipecac

Buy some Syrup of Ipecac, which is a liquid used to induce vomiting (an "emetic"). Buy the bottle with the latest expiration date. Place the Syrup of Ipecac bottle in an easily seen, easy to reach, centrally located place in your home, but out of baby's reach. Point out to everyone that it is there and what its purpose is. You may want to stick it right onto the wall in a center hallway. Store another bottle of syrup of ipecac with the first aid/ medical supplies, a bottle in the glove compartment of each car, and one in the diaper bag.

> **WARNING: Do not use Syrup of Ipecac to induce vomiting unless the Poison Control Center specifically instructs you to. Bringing some poisons back up through the esophagus and throat through vomiting can cause more damage than if it remained in the stomach.**

Vitamin/Mineral Supplements

The most common cause of poisoning deaths for children under age six in the United States is the swallowing of iron-containing products. So be as careful about keeping vitamin bottles out of baby's reach as you are with your other medicines. Children can die by consuming as few as five iron-containing pills.

Don't Let Children Mimic You

Do not let your children see you using cough syrups, pills, throat sprays, or any other medications. Babies love to imitate you. Even something as seemingly innocuous as eye drops can cause a child to go into a coma if he drinks enough of them. ALL prescription and over-the-counter medications should be locked up and out of sight.

Child-Resistant Caps Are Not To Be Trusted

Don't be mislead into thinking that a poisonous substance in a child-resistant bottle is child-proof. Manufacturers claim that the purpose of child-resistant caps is to give you some extra time to remove your baby from the danger. They are meant only to give you a few extra seconds to prevent your baby from eating or drinking the toxic product inside.

Possibly Poisonous Foods

Probably the best way to allay your fears about food poisoning is to learn about bacteria, how it grows, and how you can prevent its growth.

> **WARNING: Do not eat rhubarb leaves.**
> **They are toxic and can be fatal.**

Honey, Corn Syrup, and Infant Botulism

Do not feed uncooked honey or corn syrup to your baby before she is one year old. Honey and corn syrup may contain spores of bacteria that cause clostridium botulism, a disease that can be fatal. Because infants have not yet developed intestinal flora (their bowel is alkaline, not acidic) or defense mechanisms that fight this bacteria, it can multiply in the intestines. By one year, a baby's stomach acidity is close to that of an adult's. Symptoms of botulism include constipation, poor appetite, and weakness.

What about cooked honey/corn syrup? If baked into food, such as breads, it is probably safe for a baby to eat, but not definitely. Although bacteria is killed during baking, the bacterial spores are very hardy and need to be in high temperatures for extended periods of time in order to die. The spores can survive through baking and possibly cause botulism, especially if your baby is younger than 6 months. Why take the chance?

Don't feed your baby honey or corn syrup, even if it has been cooked or baked into foods. I suggest that you be safe and wait to give your baby those delicious whole grain honey graham crackers from the natural foods store until after her first birthday!

NOTE: The corn syrup used in infant baby formulas is safe.

Raw Eggs and Salmonella

Eggs are a regular part of the *Super Baby Food Diet*, but eggs must be cooked thoroughly to be safe for baby and adults. Raw eggs, especially if they contain cracks in the shell, are a hospitable breeding ground for salmonella bacteria. Even perfect and un-cracked fresh eggs can contain bacteria inside their shells, because chickens (and other animals) actually have harmful bacteria in their intestines, which get deposited into the egg before it comes out of the chicken!

Washing it on the outside does not make a raw egg safe. Eggs must be hard cooked or scrambled and cooked solid to be safe for your baby.

REMINDER: Never eat raw eggs or any foods that contain raw eggs, such as eggnog, Caesar salad, whipped raw egg whites, easy-over eggs with partially raw parts. And this one's a killer for me because I love raw cake batter, especially chocolate: Don't let your children "lick the bowl" or beaters or eat from the mixing bowl from cake batter/cookies if you've used raw eggs as an ingredient.

WARNING: While we're on the subject of salmonella, you may be surprised at the fact that 90% of reptile-like pets, such as iguanas and turtles, have been found to contain salmonella. Some babies have died from salmonella poisoning after touching or being near these animals. (As if we parents didn't have enough to worry about.)

General Safety Precautions and Tips

- Metal seat belt buckles get burning hot when the sun shines on them or when the inside of your car gets hot. Cover the metal parts with terrycloth wrist bands or with the cuffs cut from old socks.

- Tape old shoulder pads to the sharp corners of tables and other furniture to prevent baby from getting bruised. Or use stuffing from an old pillow, a rolled up sock, or half or a quarter of a tennis ball.

- The corners and edges of cardboard boxes can be taped over the edges of table corners or on a brick fireplace raised hearth. Add some padding under the cardboard to prevent bruises. Or sew your baby's old crib bumpers together and use as a padding.

- Instead of buying plastic covers for your electrical outlets, improvise a baby-proof cover with plain electrical tape. Unscrew and remove the cover of the outlet, place electrical tape over the slits, and then replace the cover. The cover should hold the tape securely in place. The disadvantage of this method, of course, is that you cannot plug an appliance into the outlet.

- Keep kids riding bicycles out of the street by stretching an extension ladder across the end of the driveway.

- For a clean play area, place a child who is not mobile on a large flat sheet. Toys can be picked up in a moment by gathering the corners, and the sheet is easily machine washed.

- Drape a towel over the top of the bedroom/bathroom door to prevent children from locking themselves in.

- Prevent your toddler from opening a door at Grandma's or a friend's house by using a strong rubber band to hold a sock over the doorknob.

- Place large sponges under crib wheels to prevent it from the crib from "walking" when baby shakes it.

- Keep unopened fast food packets of ketchup in your freezer for use as an ice pack for little boo-boos. Or small balloons filled with water and frozen. A package of frozen peas or other frozen vegetables wrapped in a thin cloth is good for bigger boo-boos.

- Decorate a band-aid with stickers or non-toxic markers. If it hurts to remove a band-aid, try rubbing it with vegetable oil or heating the adhesive with a hair dryer.

- Before removing a splinter, numb the area with an ice cube or some teething pain reliever.

- In a public place, "label" your child with a suitcase address tag or a pet tag engraved with your child's name, address, and phone number. Use a safe diaper pin to attach it to your child's coat. A pet tag is small enough to fit on your child's shoe.

- Be ready for anything while away from home. Keep emergency supplies in the trunk of your car along with the supplies listed on page 149.

- When in public, your family should always have a pre-determined place to meet if you lose each other. Choose a unique, familiar, and easily-seen landmark: the center fountain in a mall, the ferris wheel at the amusement park, etc. A default rule to have in case you forgot to set a meeting place is this: young folks remain clearly visible in a safe place and wait for the adults to find them. Otherwise, if you both walk around looking for each other, you can pass each other like two ships in the night for hours. Teach your little one what to do if she gets lost. For example, go to the nearest cash register and tell the person in the dark blue coat that you are lost. Or put a sheet of paper with information in her pocket and tell her to give it to a "safe" adult. Go over the plan several times until she can repeat it back to you.

> **WARNING:** A baby or toddler can drown in a pail or bucket of water within minutes. Watch both the pail and your baby every second until you've poured the water down the drain and put the pail away. Keep the lids locked down on your toilets, too. A little baby boy in my own hometown tragically drowned in a toilet. It can happen to anyone.

30

Kitchen and Baby Food Safety

The Feeding Area

Set up a feeding area in your home where you will feed your baby most of the time. Babies like stability and predictability. She'll know just what's coming if you feed her in the same high chair in the same corner of the kitchen each day.

Make the feeding area as comfortable for you as it is for your baby. Place your chair in front of your baby's feeding chair so that you can be face-to-face with him, to chat and smile at him as he eats. Feeding time will become another pleasant bonding time for the two of you. It's very nurturing to give food to your baby, as it is to breast or bottle-feed him.

Have a tabletop or counter surface within your reach and out of your baby's reach. Place on it wipe-up towels, vitamin supplements, bibs, and anything else you use during baby's mealtime.

If the floor in the feeding area is carpeted or covered with some other material that will be ruined when baby starts dropping food to the floor, protect it by covering it with something waterproof. Baby departments and online stores carry "drop-cloths" specifically for baby feeding areas. A piece of plastic tarp, an old waterproof tablecloth, or an old shower curtain (by the way, shower curtains are machine washable) will work; but use one only if it's not slippery. Or you can get a piece of non-slip linoleum remnant from the nearest floor-covering store (ask them if it will ruin carpeting if placed over it).

If you're at Grandma's or a friend's house, rip a big plastic garbage bag at the seam so that it lays flat in one layer. Be very careful not to slip on it, because plastic garbage bags are as slick as ice. Layers of newspaper, brown paper bags from the grocery store, or even a flattened large cardboard box also can be used to temporarily protect floors.

The walls near the feeding chair should not be covered with fine velvet wallpaper; if so, protect them also. The nicest babies have been known to throw food. Walls are also threatened by the ominous full-mouthed sneeze, which has been known to project wet food as far as several feet in all directions. Practice a quick draw with a wipe-up towel to cover baby's mouth when you suspect one is about to occur.

> WARNING: Make sure that wall mountings, electrical outlets, and objects on counter tops are out of baby's reach from the feeding chair. Also, your baby should not be able to grab something and use it for leverage to tip the chair over.

The High Chair
Safety First
Thousands of children are injured each year because of careless practices with high chairs, so please read the warnings in this section carefully.

> WARNING: Never leave your baby alone in a high chair. High chairs are safe only when an adult is present to make sure that our energetic babies don't try any acrobatics while seated in them.

Stability
There now exists a vast array of high chairs on the market. Safety should be your first criterion in choosing a high chair. Pick one with a wide base for stability. Before buying a chair, shake it and push it sideways to see just how much it takes to tip it over.

Always place the chair on a level floor surface to prevent instability. And if your chair has wheels, always make sure the wheel locks are in good working condition and fully engaged before seating your baby. A wiggly baby can maneuver a mobile chair to the nearest staircase in the twinkling of an eye.

> WARNING: Never allow your older children to play in baby's high chair or hang onto it. Their weight may tip the chair over, causing injury. Keep older children and pets away from your baby when he's in his high chair.

JPMA Certification

Make sure that the chair you buy is certified safe by the Juvenile Products Manufacturers Association (JPMA). The JPMA is a national trade organization representing most companies that manufacture or import infant products. There is a wealth of information on their web site including recall information. Look for it at **www.jpma.org**.

> WARNING: Do not assume that because one chair model from a specific manufacturer is certified by the JPMA, that all models from that manufacturer are. Some manufacturers have only a few of their chair models certified. Make sure that the specific model that you have chosen is certified by looking for the JPMA seal on the box or on the high chair itself.

The Consumer Product Safety Commission (CPSC)

The CPSC (www.cpsc.gov) is an independent Federal regulatory agency that helps keep American families safe by reducing the risk of injury or death from consumer products. If you have any question about the safety of a high chair or another type of feeding chair or just about any product—from mini-blinds to portable cribs—call their hotline at 800-638-2772, or write CPSC, 4330 East West Highway, Bethesda, MD 20814. You can also call or write the CPSC to report an unsafe product.

Safety Strap

The high chair should have a waist strap to prevent your baby from standing up in the chair and/or climbing out the top, possibly causing it to teeter over. A crotch strap also should be part of the restraint system to prevent your baby from sliding out the bottom. Some babies love to slither down slowly until they are under the tray, while others prefer a rapid chute.

> WARNING: All kidding aside—always use the full restraint system including the waist and crotch straps when seating your baby in the high chair—never use the tray alone. The tray is not intended to be a restraint. Numerous deaths have occurred from babies slipping down in the seat and catching their heads on the tray (called "submarining entrapment"). Submarining entrapment can also occur in strollers and other baby seats—always use the full restraint system as described in the manufacturer's instructions.

REMINDER: For your child's safety, remember to clean the chair and its restraint system on a regular basis. Clumps of food and dried liquids can prevent the restraint system and tray from working properly.

> WARNING: A high chair safety strap is wonderful for preventing babies from sliding out, but it can be life-threatening if your baby is choking and you can't quickly release her from the chair. Practice opening that buckle until you're as quick as lightning and you can do it blindfolded. There is a chance that she could be moving so much that you can't get to the buckle. Study the chair and see where you can cut the strap with a knife or scissors to release her, in the rare case where this would be necessary. Find a place on the back or side of the chair where you can safely and easily cut the strap and not your baby.

The Tray

Choose a high chair with a large removable tray so you can take it to the kitchen sink and give it a good washing and so that you can use the sink hose to rinse off every last trace of soap. Your baby will be eating finger foods directly off the tray, so you want to keep it as clean as possible.

If you can remove the tray with only one hand that is even better. Plan on spending some time in the store when you shop for a high chair. Remove each high chair's tray and figure out which one feels easiest and best to you. You shouldn't have to peer under the tray to find the catch to remove it—it should be easily found by touch.

The tray should have a raised lip around the edge to stop inevitable spills from getting to the floor or baby's lap. The lip may also help prevent baby from pushing food pieces and dishes off the tray and onto the floor, although I wouldn't count on it. The tray should be angled so that liquids spill to the front.

Another reason for a removable tray is the ability to move the chair to the family table when your baby gets older. Make sure the instructions say that the chair is safe at a full-sized adult table without its tray.

> WARNING: After your baby is seated, always make sure that the full restraint system is in place and that the tray is securely locked into position. An unlocked tray is a danger to your baby. Give the tray a good forward yank to verify that it's locked in place.

REMINDER: Get into the habit of knowing where tiny fingers are before you slide the tray onto the high chair so that you don't accidentally pinch them. Always give a quick look before you close or collapse anything: high chair trays, folding strollers, car doors, house doors, cabinets, reclining living room chairs, lawn chairs, etc. To do a quick check of several children at one glance before slamming a car door, play "Simon says 'Hands on Your Head.'" Odds are that this quick check habit, which takes only a second, will eventually save your child pain and injury.

TIP: If the high chair tray is no longer sliding on and off smoothly, try rubbing the metal runners with a sheet of waxed paper, or rub them with a bar of mild soap, or put a little petroleum jelly on the runners, or use a vegetable oil spray to lubricate them. Use the same to make metal crib runners move smoothly and noiselessly, for sticking dresser drawers, squeaky doors, etc.

Adjustable Height

The ability to raise and lower the height of the high chair is a nice feature. This will allow you to adjust the seat height when you are feeding your baby so that you and your baby can be face-to-face. The adjustable height feature is also nice for when your baby moves to the family table.

Comfort

Padded seats are usually more comfortable for babies than wooden seats. The covering should be thick so it will not puncture easily. Feel the seams to make sure they are smooth and won't scratch your baby's legs. Check over the entire chair for any protrusions or sharp edges that can injure your baby. If you have your baby with you, and she is willing, test her in your favorite chair before you buy it. She'll let you know if she doesn't like it!

MONEY SAVER: Some high chairs recline to an infant seat-type angle, an expensive option that is useful for a very short time. If he's uncomfortable in a high chair and your lap, why not just use your infant seat until he's older? Remember to always strap him in securely and never place the seat on a chair or table because it can fall off and cause your baby serious injury. Place the infant seat on the floor and sit on the floor next to him to feed him. He can't fall off the floor!

WARNING: Your baby should be seated in an upright position, whether it is in the high chair, an infant seat, or your lap, in order to prevent choking during eating. Also, don't let your baby crawl around with a cracker or other food, as he may lie facing upward and choke.

TIP: If your baby sits up well, but tends to wobble sideways in the high chair, use a few rolled-up terry cloth towels to support her on each side.

"Previously Owned" or Older High Chairs

If you have inherited an older-model high chair or purchased a used chair, make sure that it is safe. It should be sturdy with a complete working restraint system and tray. Older chairs with only a crotch bar do not prevent a child from climbing out the top. If parts are missing, check online, or call or write the manufacturer to see if you can get replacements.

Call the JPMA to verify that a used or older chair has been certified, that there have been no recalls or safety problems, and to obtain any other warnings or information on that particular model chair from that manufacturer.

NOTE: No matter which feeding chair you are using, take the time to read and follow all instructions carefully. Periodically check all assembly screws to make sure that they are fully tightened. Check that all clamps and locking mechanisms are working properly. The instructions will include details on how to clean and maintain the chair.

REMINDER: Remember to stop using the seat when your child has reached the recommended maximum height OR weight; it may help you to remember this if you write yourself a note with the height and weight where you will see it often. Busy parents of young children have a tendency to forget things!

Cleanability

Your baby's high chair will eventually become a modern art piece of crusty layers of dried food. To clean a high chair, take it in the bathtub (place rags under the legs to prevent scratches in the tub) and give it a shower massage with an old vegetable brush or toothbrush. Or use the hose outside on a nice warm sunny day, or take it to the car wash and blast it with the pressure hose (make sure to rinse very well to get all the harsh detergent off).

> **TIP:** For those really dried on food splatters, lay a wet towel or sponge on them for an hour or so, and they'll wipe right off. If food is dried around the arms of the chair or in corner crevices, take a dripping wet rag and drape it or tie it around the hard-to-reach dried food. Let it sit for a few hours and then use an old toothbrush or vegetable brush to scrub out the softened food. If you're in a hurry, try using a baker's bench knife to get stuck-on food off a high chair or counter top. They are available in kitchen stores.

Preventing Burns in the Kitchen

I'm sure you've heard a lot of warnings lately to be careful with hot food in the kitchen. We sometimes don't think that accidents will happen to us and that they happen only to other people. It's only those who have been through pain and misfortune who understand how important it is to be cautious. I still remember, when I was a 12-year-old candy striper, the sight of a 2-year-old child who was hospitalized for months. She had been burned over most of her body from scalding liquid that her mother accidentally spilled on her. She cried out in pain whenever touched, making it impossible for her mother to pick her up and hold her. The baby couldn't even be covered with a bed sheet because it hurt too much. I'm telling you this horror story, which I know is making you cringe or cry (I get bleary-eyed every time I think about it), so that you will have a healthy fear of burns from kitchen accidents. Perhaps it will prompt you to be extra cautious in the kitchen. These memories have made me so phobic of burn accidents that I note the whereabouts of all of my children and even my dog to make sure that they are completely out of the kitchen before I move a hot pot.

Use these Safety Precautions to Prevent Burns in the Kitchen

- Use the back burners on your stove, so if your baby reaches up and touches the front burners, she won't burn her fingers. Buy a stove shield and switch covers for your stove—ask for them at your local toy/department store or look for them in baby catalogs. (One Step Ahead also carries these)

- Turn the handles of the pots toward the back of the stove, so they are not extending out in front of the stove. Your baby can reach up and pull an extended handle and cause a pot of boiling food to pour on her. ALWAYS turn pot handles backward, even when you are home alone, so that it becomes a habit. Get other family members into the habit too.

- Pack your tablecloths away until baby is older. He can pull the tablecloth down on himself along with heavy items and hot food.

- When you are moving pots of hot food, verify that baby is not in your path, and that you cannot possibly spill hot food on him. Never hold your baby by a hot stove. If possible, keep your baby out of the kitchen while you are cooking. If no one is around to watch your little one while you cook, place him in the high chair in the kitchen. He'll love to sit and watch you, especially if you talk and sing to him or even dance around to entertain him (as a drastic measure). Strap him in so that he won't surprise you underfoot and get burned. Also, don't set him in your path or in the path of any hot pot you're moving from stove to counter. Make it impossible to fall on him with hot food or to spill hot food on him.

- Don't drink hot coffee, hot liquids, or eat hot soup or other food while holding your baby. You may accidentally spill some on him.

- Keep a fire extinguisher and a fire blanket in your kitchen. Put them in a convenient and visible place, where they will be away from possible fires. For example, don't place them on back of the stove where you won't be able to reach them when the stove is on fire!

- Don't smoke around your baby or allow anyone else to. Besides the danger of cigarette burns, second-hand smoke is very unhealthy. Don't worry about hurting their feelings; simply tell them kindly to put it out.

- Do not lean with your back on the range top or reach over or across the stove top, especially if you have long hair or are wearing loose-fitting clothing or an untucked shirt. Of course, never allow your child to climb on the stove top.

- While dining out, keep baby out of the paths of waiters/ waitresses. Be especially careful to keep servers carrying hot coffee pots to refill customers' cups away from your baby. Some have no experience around babies and they just don't think.

- Always put dangerous objects, such as hot pots, sharp knives, etc. on the back of the counter towards the wall out of baby's reach and not near the edge of the counter. Divide kitchen counters with an imaginary line or with red strips of tape to remind the family to keep dangerous objects behind the line where baby's hands cannot reach.

- Don't forget to keep wax paper and other wraps with a sharp cutting edge built into the box away from baby so she doesn't get cut. And keep plastic wrap, garbage bags, freezer bags—all suffocation hazards—away from baby as well.

- Mark the hot water faucets in the kitchen and the bathroom with red tape, stickers, or nail polish, and warn your toddler not to touch them. Set your hot water heater's thermostat to a safe temperature to prevent scalding. The American Academy of Pediatrics recommends a setting of 120°F. There now exist anti-scald devices for spigots—inquire at your local hardware store or ask a plumber.

- Be careful not to burn your baby's mouth. Your baby's mouth is more sensitive to heat than yours and baby's food should be only moderately warm.

- Before turning on your oven, always first check inside for teddy bears, plastic toys, used diapers, and the cat.

How Does Your Bacteria Grow
Small Amounts Are OK

Bacteria are everywhere! They are on your hands and skin, inside your mouth and nose, in meat and eggs, on the surface of fruits and vegetables, on insects, and worst of all, bacteria are in the air attached to dust particles. Food is constantly being contaminated with bacteria, which is why you must take such care in handling your baby's food. But these bacteria usually exist in small amounts, and because they are small amounts, they don't give us much trouble. It's when they grow and multiply into large amounts that they poison our foods and make us sick.

Bacteria Need a Proper Environment to Reach Dangerous Levels

The environment must meet these four criteria to allow bacteria to multiply to dangerous numbers:

- **Moisture.** Food must be composed of enough water (more than approximately 15%) for bacteria to be able to grow. Most foods do contain enough moisture, although some foods, such as dried fruits and flour, contain less than bacteria need.

- **Warmth.** Food must be at the proper temperature for bacterial growth to occur, which is between 40° and 140°F. High heat kills bacteria, but cold only temporarily disables them, as discussed later in this chapter.

- **Proper pH.** Most fruits are too acidic and most vegetables are too alkaline to support bacterial growth. This is why you can leave fruits at room temperature to ripen. Meats, eggs, and other foods are in the proper pH range.

- **Time.** It takes time (2 or more hours) for bacteria to multiply and grow to dangerous levels. It may take as little as one hour or less in warm temperatures conducive to bacterial growth.

Food Preservation Methods Must Prevent Bacterial Growth

Methods of preserving food and protecting it from bacterial growth take advantage of one or more of the above bacterial needs. For example, dried foods, such as dried apricots and beef jerky, have most of their moisture removed, enough so that bacteria cannot multiply. Freezing keeps food too cold for bacteria to multiply. Canning involves heating food to kill bacteria and packing it in bacteria-proof containers.

Shallow Containers are Best

To get food cooled as quickly as possible, store them in small and/or shallow containers. Deep or large containers may allow the food in the middle to remain at a bacteria-friendly temperature. Bacteria will have time to multiply before the middle food cools and will become alive again when the food is warmed. That's why ice cube trays are ideal for the quick-freezing of baby food—they are not only shallow, but the dividers between the cubes also help the food to freeze quickly.

Storage Temperature is an Important Bacterial Deterrent

It is very important not to leave food sitting out at room temperature for extended periods, because bacteria will grow rapidly in it. However, it does take time, possibly as long as 2 hours or more, for bacteria to multiply to dangerous levels and cause illness. That is why no one got sick at the last summer picnic from eating foods that sat outside on the tables. To be safe, do not leave food, especially baby food, at room temperature for more than a few minutes. Keep hot food hot and cold food cold.

Freezing Does NOT Kill Bacteria

Temperatures higher than 165°F will kill most bacteria. It is important to note that cold temperatures—40° or lower—as in your refrigerator and freezer, only inactivate bacteria and temporarily prevent them from multiplying. Cold does not kill bacteria. When the temperature warms up, bacteria kick in and multiply at warp speed.

Bacteria Thrive at Room and Body Temperature	
165-212°F	Most bacteria killed at these temperatures.
140-165°F	Bacteria do not multiply at these temperatures, but some do survive.
120-140°F	Many bacteria survive these temperatures.
60-120°F	DANGER ZONE! Rapid bacterial growth with toxins produced by some bacteria.
40-60°F	Food poisoning bacteria can grow in this range.
32-40°F	Bacteria that spoils food grows slowly at these refrigerator temperatures.
0-32°F	Freezing temperatures inactivate bacteria, but they survive and will begin to multiply as soon as warm temperatures recur.

Never Thaw Foods at Room Temperature

It is important not to let foods, especially meat, thaw at room temperature or in warm water. The outer layers can become warm enough for bacteria to multiply, even though the inside is still frozen. Thaw all foods in the refrigerator, where the outside layers will remain at a temperature too cool to allow bacterial growth. (Never marinate at room temperature—always marinate in the refrigerator.)

WARNING: Due to the possibility of bacterial growth, never refreeze food that has been cooked then frozen and then thawed.

Thaw Baby Food So That Bacteria Cannot Multiply

Puréed baby food must be handled very carefully to protect it from an influx of bacteria. Keep it cold right up to the minute before feeding your baby. Do not let it sit at room temperature for more than several minutes. Some baby food cookbook authors suggest thawing food cubes by taking them out of the freezer and letting them sit at room temperature for an hour before mealtime. I do not recommend this method, because it may give bacteria a chance to grow.

REMINDER: Keep hot foods hot and cold foods cold.

Safely Handling Baby's Food
Introduce as Little Bacteria as Possible

Minimize the introduction of bacteria into baby food by having all cooking equipment that touches the food whistle-clean, including utensils, ice cube trays, blenders, counter tops, and your hands.

TIP: Once you've cleaned utensils that will be used for baby's food, hide them from the rest of the family. If you put them in the silverware drawer, other family members (who may have forgotten to wash their hands) will touch them. Store them in a clean drinking glass in the back of a cabinet, or roll them up in a clean paper towel or wipe up towel and hide them in the back of a drawer. While emptying clean dishes out of the dishwasher, I always store a few spoons and other utensils that I plan to use for making baby food away from the rest of the family dishes.

Move food from cooking pan to refrigerator/freezer as quickly as possible to minimize the time that food is in the temperature range for fast bacterial growth. Cooking will destroy most bacteria, but it is inevitable that some bacteria will sneak into the food from utensils and other equipment or even from the dust in the air. To stop those bacteria before they begin to multiply, cool the food immediately after cooking. If you are concerned that the hot container will warm the inside of your refrigerator, set it in ice or cold water until it cools down a bit. Be careful with any hot glass container because it may crack if you put it on ice or cool it too quickly.

TIP: It's worth it to spend a few dollars on a refrigerator/freezer thermometer, available at the local kitchen store department or specialty kitchen store. Use it verify that your freezer's temperature is 0°F or colder. Do this by placing the thermometer in the front of your freezer near the top and leaving the door closed overnight, or for at least 6-8 hours. If it reads higher than 0°F, lower the freezer's thermostat and check the reading again after keeping the door closed for 6-8 hours.

Use the same method as for the freezer to verify that your refrigerator temperature registers somewhere between 32-40°F. As a general rule, try to keep your refrigerator as cold as possible without freezing the milk. The coldest part of most refrigerators is at the bottom (cold air sinks). A thermometer can find the coldest and warmest parts of your refrigerator— leave it overnight in each part and compare to find out which part is coldest.

> **WARNING:** The length of time for foods to be kept safely frozen stated in this book assume a freezer temperature of 0°F. If your freezer is warmer, the times should be significantly shortened.

Dip with a Clean Spoon

Always use a clean spoon when removing food for baby from a large container. For example, when dipping yogurt or spooning cooked cereal out of a refrigerator container, use a clean spoon that has not come in contact with saliva or counter top bacteria. You don't want to introduce bacteria into the food.

If you take too much, you must discard any leftovers. It's OK if your baby doesn't eat all of the food—the days of the "clean plate club" are over.

If you've taken too little and your baby wants more, do not worry; she will let you know. Or you can ask her if she wants more (it's OK if she doesn't). You can then use a new clean spoon and take more out of the container.

With commercial baby foods, it's OK to feed your baby by spooning directly from the jar if he is going to eat the whole jar. Throw out leftover food in the jar if baby's saliva has been introduced into it. If your baby is going to eat only part of the food, use a clean spoon to dip out his portion and immediately replace the top and refrigerate the rest.

MONEY SAVER: To prevent food waste, use a clean spoon to take from the large container a small amount of food that you are sure your baby will finish, because you will have to discard any leftovers.

Baby Food Precautions

- **Baby food can be spoiled without necessarily smelling bad.** If you have any questions about the safety of a food that looks or smells strange, don't take a chance, discard it. Don't taste it to see if it's OK. **When in doubt, throw it out!**

- Do not keep baby food or juices, either opened commercial jars or homemade, in the refrigerator for more than two days.

- Any leftover homemade or commercial baby food or juice that has come in contact with your baby's saliva, because the spoon from your baby's mouth has been dipped into it or because your baby drank from the cup or container, must be discarded. The saliva's enzymes and bacteria will continue digesting the food or juice, breaking down the vital nutrients and causing it to begin to spoil.

- If commercial infant/baby/toddler cereal has been mixed with liquid, serve it immediately. Discard any leftovers and do not use them for another meal.

- Once frozen or refrigerated baby food/juice has been sitting at room temperature for more than a few minutes, do not refreeze it or return it to the refrigerator. Bacteria from the air and other sources have been introduced into the food, even if your baby's saliva has not touched it. Its quality has deteriorated and bacteria may have started to grow to dangerous levels, making it unsafe for your baby to eat.

- Do not make baby food from frozen vegetables or other frozen foods and refreeze it using the *Food Cube Method.* Baby food should not be frozen more than once.

- Never eat food that has mold on it. The mold you see is only the tip of the iceberg—poisons from molds form far under the surface and may not be visible. Don't cut off the moldy part of food and eat the rest. Throw away all of the food, even though only part of it is moldy.

- To prevent bacterial growth, never thaw baby food at room temperature and do not keep baby food in the danger zone for bacterial growth (see chart on page 356) for more than a few minutes.

Canned Foods

In general, canned foods are nutritionally inferior to fresh or frozen foods, and canned vegetables and other foods are frequently high in sodium.

> WARNING: When you buy a can of food, check it out carefully. Don't buy cans or jars that are sticky or those with stains. Make sure there are no bulges, dents, broken seams, rust, or small holes in the can. These indicate spoiled or contaminated food.

> WARNING: Carefully examine the color and clarity of any liquids, syrups, or juices from cans. If the liquid is supposed to be clear but looks cloudy, do not use it—throw it out.

After opening cans of food, do not store leftovers in the original can. Transfer them to a sterile, air-tight glass jar and place them in the refrigerator. Metal elements from the can may cause the food to acquire a "tinny" taste, and some may even leach into the food.

Wash Cans and Jars Before Opening

You never know what's on the outside of cans/jars of food from the supermarket—dust, dirt, germs, and who knows what else. Some supermarkets even spray insecticides directly on the shelves. So make sure to wash the outside of food containers thoroughly and rinse, rinse, rinse before you open them to prevent contamination of the food inside when you're opening them.

And remember to keep your can opener clean—use detergent and a sterile toothbrush after every opening to scrub off dried food and rinse well with hot water.

"Pop!" Goes the Jar or Throw it Out

Some baby foods are packaged in vacuum-sealed jars. Listen carefully while you twist open a jar of baby food. If the button on the jar's lid doesn't pop up when you open it, discard the entire jar because it may be contaminated. Or, better yet, return it to the store and get your money back.

> **WARNING:** Never bang on a glass jar to loosen a top that won't open, which can cause little pieces of glass to get into the food. Use one of those rubber grasper gadgets sold explicitly for the purpose of opening tight-lidded vacuum-packed jars, or use rubber gloves, a large rubber band like those that comes with broccoli bunches, a damp wipe-up towel, or sandpaper. Or let hot tap water run over the top to loosen it. A gritty or grating sound when opening a glass jar may be caused by small pieces of broken glass—so listen carefully and discard the whole jar if you hear anything suspicious.

TIP: It is best to avoid breakable dishes when there's a baby in the house. I recommend Corelle® bowls and dishes because they don't break. They also stack compactly in the cabinet and in the dishwasher. (Please know that I have no affiliation with the Corning® company, financial or otherwise.) I called the company and they said that their dishes do not contain any lead.

TIP: If glass gets broken, pick up every sliver before your baby does. Pick up the largest pieces by hand. Vacuum thoroughly or sweep with a broom, using a damp newspaper as a dustpan. Use damp paper towels to wipe up the entire area. Glass can fly far from the break site so do the entire floor area, table tops, and any other surfaces that may have caught some glass. Turn the lights off and use a flashlight to search carefully from every angle for small. Hopefully, any glass you missed will twinkle. I do one final step (being the self-sacrificing parent that I am): I walk around in my bare feet over the entire area—better for me to get glass in my foot than my baby.

Food and Drug Administration (FDA)

The FDA is a Federal agency that ensures that all the food (except meat and eggs) we eat is safe and wholesome, that the cosmetics we use won't harm us, and that medicines, medical devices, and radiation emitting consumer products, such as microwave ovens, are safe and effective.

For general questions on food safety, you can call the FDA's Consumer Hotline at 888-463-6332 or visit their web site, www.fda.gov.

If the situation is critical, call their emergency number, 301-796-8240, which is staffed 24 hours a day.

The FDA's Center for Food Safety and Applied Nutrition and Seafood Hotline toll-free number is 888-463-6332.

For questions about prescription or non-prescription medicines or to report a problem with an adverse reaction to medicines, call the FDA MedWatch Hotline, 800-332-1088; but first, of course, you should call your doctor immediately.

31

Baby, Kitchen and Laundry Hygiene

Good Hygiene is Necessary to Prevent Food borne Illness

Food borne illness (commonly referred to as food poisoning) can be prevented if you follow the rules of kitchen and personal hygiene discussed in this chapter. Mishandling and improper storage of food in the home is the most prevalent cause of food poisoning. Babies and children are more susceptible than adults, so we must be very careful whether we are handling either our own homemade *Super Baby Food* or commercial baby foods.

Hand Washing—Yours and Your Baby's

Washing your hands is probably the most important thing you can do to keep baby food clean. Keep a pump bottle of soap by the kitchen sink and use it frequently. When you wash your hands, rub the soap over every inch of your hands for at least 30 seconds, getting between your fingers, under your rings, and under your fingernails. With fingertips downward, rinse hands thoroughly under very warm water—the hottest you can stand. Dry with a clean paper towel or a freshly laundered wipe-up towel.

> **REMEMBER:** When washing your hands, remember to thoroughly rinse off all soap so no trace of it ends up in baby's food.

> **MONEY SAVER:** Keep a spray bottle filled with water mixed with a few tablespoons of a dishwashing liquid near the sink. A few squirts on your hand or a dish/pot that you are washing individually is more economical than a squirt of liquid at full concentration.

> **NOTE:** Some believe that over-using antibacterial soaps may cause super strains of bacteria (similar to the super strains of germs that have become immune to antibiotics).

Remember to repeat hand washing if you've touched yours or your baby's eyes, nose or mouth, sneezed into your hands, touched a pet or pet's dish, touched meat, eggs, or other raw animal products, and, of course, if you've gone to the bathroom or changed a diaper.

> **WARNING: Cover any open cuts, especially those on your hands, with sterile adhesive strips or band-aids before feeding your baby.**

When baby starts self feeding, wash his hands thoroughly before each meal because you never know what he's been touching! Unlike adults who usually eat with utensils, baby's hands go directly into the food and into his mouth.

> **WARNING: Puppies are wonderful! But be especially careful to wash your baby's hands thoroughly if she touches one. If she puts her hands in her mouth or eats with them before you wash them, she can get worms internally. Scary, I know.**

Preventing Dental Problems

Take good care of your baby's teeth, even though they will eventually fall out and be replaced by permanent teeth. Baby teeth are important for holding permanent teeth in their proper positions.

Fluoride

Your baby (over 6 months old) may also need a fluoride supplement if her drinking water is not fluoridated or be at risk of fluorosis (discolored teeth) from getting too much fluoride.

Nutrition and Sweets

Good nutritious food and a minimum of sweet junk foods help promote dental health. Acids produced by sugars in foods actually remove calcium from the enamel of teeth.

> WARNING: After your child eats a sweet food, make sure that you clean his teeth, or at least make him rinse with water, immediately afterward to prevent tooth decay. Blackstrap molasses and dried fruits, such as raisins and apricots, are especially bad to leave on the teeth because of their concentrated sugars and stickiness, which prolongs contact with tooth enamel. Chewy candy, hard candy, and lollipops are definite no-no's. Besides being choking hazards, they bathe the teeth in sugars for extended periods—tooth decay's heaven. Good snack foods that have a cavity fighting effect include cheese, yogurt, milk, peanut butter, and apples.

Drink Water or Rinse after Meals

Get your child into the habit of drinking a little water after every meal, which he should be doing anyway as soon as he starts on solid foods. Teach an older child to brush or at least rinse with water after every meal.

> WARNING: Do not allow your child to suck or chew on ice cubes. Besides being a choking hazard, biting and chewing on ice cubes may cause the teeth to crack or may cause parts of the teeth to break off.

Clean Your Baby's Teeth Often

When your baby's teeth start coming in, "brush" them at least once a day with a piece of gauze, a handkerchief, or a washcloth. Some experts recommend cleaning the gums before the first tooth appears. After there are a few more teeth, you can switch to a soft toothbrush. The brush should be very soft to prevent wearing down of baby's enamel and irritation to baby's sensitive gums.

NOTE: There are all kinds of baby toothbrushes now on the market. Toothbrushes that fit on your fingertip, brushes with cartoon characters on them, glow-in-the-dark toothbrushes, eco-friendly silicone baby-specific toothbrushes, and who knows what else they'll think of. Use a toothbrush that has been approved by the American Dental Association.

Clean your baby's teeth within 5-10 minutes after each meal. Ideally, you should clean your baby's teeth after every meal, but do so especially at bedtime after the last feeding. Don't forget to floss between his teeth, as soon as he has two next to each other.

Do not use toothpaste until your baby is at least two years old, and then use only a pea-sized bit or a drop the size of a match head. Be careful about letting your baby swallow fluoridated toothpaste, because too much fluoride can actually cause dental and other problems.

TIP: If you can't prevent your child from eating toothpaste, use a toothpaste without fluoride or a toothpaste with low fluoride levels. Many natural toothpastes without fluoride and artificial sweeteners are available at your natural foods store and organic section of your supermarket.

Your child will not be able to proficiently brush his own teeth until he is at least 7 years old. Teach him how by standing behind him in front of a mirror and holding his hand over the toothbrush while you show him how to move it. Use a gentle up and down motion and be careful not to gag him. Place an hourglass minute egg timer on the bathroom sink and instruct your child to use it for timing his tooth brushing.

TIP: Bacteria accumulate in toothbrushes. Experts recommend discarding toothbrushes after six weeks of use. Regularly soak toothbrushes in Listerine® or similar mouthwash and rinse very well before placing in baby's mouth. Or run toothbrushes through the dishwasher in the silverware basket, which will also remove those annoying accumulations of gel toothpaste.

No Sleeping with Bedtime Bottles or While Breastfeeding

Don't let your baby fall asleep with a bottle of milk or juice—make sure that he finished his bedtime bottle before he falls asleep. First, the liquid can pool in his mouth and cause tooth decay, even if his teeth have not yet come through the gums. Second, when your baby falls asleep, his saliva flow significantly diminishes. Saliva helps bathe the teeth and washes away food particles, helping to prevent cavities. So teeth get a double whammy when the baby falls asleep with milk or juice, and dental cavities may form. Referred to as nursing bottle caries or bottle-mouth caries, this tooth decay is most common in children between eighteen months and three years old. It is more likely to occur in the top teeth, because the tongue tends to cover and protect the bottom teeth.

Nursing bottle caries are not limited to bottle-fed babies. Breast-feeding baby for long periods during the night while Mom falls asleep also can cause this decay. Perhaps Dad can let Mom sleep and take baby away. Incidentally, sleeping with bedtime bottles or while breastfeeding may also cause ear infections, because liquids may flow through the Eustachian tube and into the inner ear.

Beware of giving your baby a bottle of plain water at bedtime, if he insists on keeping and sleeping with a bottle. Although this will not cause dental problems, there is still a chance that the baby can choke on it. In addition, the AAP recommends no water for baby until after 6 months due to danger of water intoxication. Check with your pediatrician to discuss feeding any water to your baby.

Another cause of dental caries is the feeding of sweet food before bedtime, because the sugar may remain in his mouth. Always brush your child's teeth after sugary, sticky treats.

No Honey-Coated Pacifiers

It used to be a common practice to place honey on a baby's pacifier. Raw honey will not only promote cavities, but also may cause botulism poisoning in babies younger than one year old.

> **TIP:** For an approximation of the number of teeth your baby should have at a given age, subtract 6 from your baby's age in months. For example, a baby 10 months old should have about 4 teeth. Use this rule for babies under 2 years old.

Keeping Your Kitchen Clean
Use Antibacterial Dish Detergent

Antibacterial dish detergent is great because when hand-washing dishes, we sometimes don't use water hot enough to kill bacteria. Use hot water to wash and rinse dishes and dry with a freshly laundered wipe-up towel.

> **TIP:** I hate washing dishes—who doesn't? I find that I hate it much less if I have a pair of rubber gloves on. Then I don't mind putting my hands in mush and I can use very hot water without burning myself. Sprinkle a little cornstarch or baking soda into your gloves to make them slide on and off easily. Use a warm hair dryer to dry the inside of rubber gloves, but watch carefully to prevent them from burning or catching fire.

Keep Your Sink and Faucets Clean

Use antibacterial soap, hot water, and an old toothbrush or vegetable brush to wash your kitchen sink faucets and sink interior daily. You don't want your clean hands to pick up germs from your sink faucets.

> **TIP:** Old toothbrushes are great for cleaning little nooks and crannies in blenders, hand graters, in the edge around the stove, electric can openers, strainers, garlic presses, etc. Run the toothbrushes through the dishwasher in the silverware basket to sanitize.

Cleaning Your Blender and Food Processor

Bacteria can hide in the cracks and crevices of your blender and/or food processor. It is important that you take them apart after every use and clean them. Use very hot water. If you have rubber gloves on, don't accidentally put a hole in them with the sharp blades. Thoroughly clean and dry each individual piece before re assembling. As you know from reading the manufacturer's instructions, those large holes in the cutting blades are for the purpose of picking up the discs safely without touching the sharp edges that cut and grate.

> **TIP:** Clean your blender soon after each use and never let it wait so long that food dries on the blades. If you simply cannot clean the blender right away, pour some hot tap water into it and let it soak until you can get to it. If you accidentally did let something dry in your blender so that it is impossible to clean off (orange pulp is the worst!), rinse out as much as possible and then blend some water and ice. The cracked ice will blast it off.

> **TIP:** To help get your blender clean before disassembling, place a little dish detergent in the blender with about a cup of hot water and, optionally, a ½ teaspoon of baking soda and run on low speed for 30 seconds. Use only a small drop of dish detergent, only one molecule, unless you want a kitchen full of suds!

> **TIP:** Blenders and food processors are loud. Buy a thick pad of rubbery plastic in a stationery shop for keeping office machines quiet, and place it under the blender to make it run more quietly. Or use an old computer mouse pad.

Cutting Boards

They used to say that the surfaces of wooden spoons and cutting boards were breeding grounds for millions of bacteria, and to use only plastic or metal. Now they say that bacteria do not grow on wood. Who knows! I still do not recommend wood cutting boards. Plastic cutting boards are supposedly safe when cleaned well. They should be discarded when deeply scarred because bacteria can grow within the cuts.

I use a small plastic cutting board with a claim on the label that will not dull knives. I wash it after every use in the dishwasher. It is small and takes up little room.

Disinfect Kitchen Surfaces Often

You can buy disinfectant for kitchen counter tops and other kitchen surfaces, but it's cheaper and just as effective to use plain old chlorine bleach. A strong solution that will kill any germ in its path is 1 part chlorine bleach to 4 parts water. Let sit for 5 minutes and rinse. When it not longer smells, the bleach is dissipated and gone. Chlorine does give off toxic fumes in amounts well below recognized safety levels for adults. But I recommend that you disinfect only when the baby is not around and when you are in a well-ventilated kitchen.

> WARNING: Never let chlorine bleach touch a metal sink or other surface or metal utensil. For metal surfaces, buy a special purpose disinfectant.

NOTE: Some experts insist that frequent household germ-killing is futile because it has such a short-term effect, and that the disinfectant treatment is actually more dangerous than the germs. Others claim that the only important preventative measure is frequent and diligent hand washing. Others believe that babies need to be exposed to germs to develop their immune systems. Still others recommend major household disinfection only if there is a contagious disease in the home. Ask your pediatrician for the latest advice, which I can't keep up with because it seems to change every month!

Meat Safety Deserves Special Attention

If you prepare meat in your kitchen, make sure to wash thoroughly, in very hot water and soap, anything that touched meat or its juice, including your hands, utensils, cutting boards, etc. Or mix one tablespoon of chlorine bleach into one gallon of hot water to wipe surfaces clean. Allow surfaces to air dry. Utensils can also be sanitized by soaking in plain hot water (at least 170°F) for at least 30 seconds. Dishwashers working properly should reach this temperature.

Keep a separate cutting board for meat—not the one you use for produce and other foods—or cut meat on waxed or parchment paper and discard immediately. Wear rubber gloves when handling meat to protect cuts and abrasions on your hands from infection, and wash the gloves well with soap when done.

Safe handling of meat begins at the grocery store. In your shopping cart, keep meat, poultry, and fish away from produce, cans of food, boxes, and all other groceries. Bag meat separately from all other food items in its own plastic bag and tie the bag shut so that any leaking liquids will remain contained. Do not let the meat get above refrigerator temperatures for more than a few minutes. Shop for meat last, so that it will remain cold as long as possible. Get meat home and into the refrigerator as soon as possible. If you cannot get home quickly, keep a cooler with ice in your car to store the meat in to keep it cold. Keep meat and its liquids away from other food items in your refrigerator and freezer, as you did in your grocery cart. Put meat on a lower shelf where its liquids will not drip on and contaminate other foods.

The Garbage

Regularly clean your kitchen garbage pail by taking it into the bathtub and washing it with disinfectant and hot water from the shower massage.

Hide your kitchen garbage pail in a locked cabinet for the next few years. If your baby is like mine, he loves to throw things like remote controls and other expensive items into the kitchen garbage can. He also enjoys chewing on discarded banana peels and other food from the garbage.

> WARNING: Plastic garbage bags are a suffocation hazard for toddlers; keep them safely locked away from them.

Dishwasher Tips

If you are fortunate enough to have a dishwasher, that's great! Use it to the max and follow these tips:

- If you know you will soon be preparing a batch of baby food or formula bottles, load your dishwasher with everything you will need. Use the heat boost during the main wash cycle to kill every last germ. When the dishwasher finishes, it is the perfect time to prepare baby food or formula, when dishes, pots, bottles, nipples, ice cube trays, and utensils are freshly sterilized and still untouched by human hands inside the dishwasher. It also saves put-away time—take the bottles and bowls from the dishwasher and use them right away. There's no need to put them away. They may never see the inside of a kitchen cabinet!

- **Pre-rinsing Is Not Necessary.** It's not necessary to rinse off your dirty dishes before you put them in the dishwasher—it's just a waste of water. If you don't believe it, try just one dishwasher load with no pre-rinsing. You'll be surprised that the dishes get perfectly clean anyway. One time I remember being so exhausted that I threw half-full bowls of cereal into the dishwasher without any scraping at all. I dreaded opening the door after that wash cycle, but to my surprise and relief everything was perfectly clean! The only non-meat foods that you must pre-rinse, to my knowledge, are flax and chia seeds. Because they are mucigelatinous (you'll know what I mean if you eat them), they stick to everything, especially glassware. Rinse them off well and do so immediately after a meal, before they become hardened to the plate.

- **Don't Use the Delay Option.** If you have a delay option on your dishwasher, so that it starts in the middle of the night and not during peak electricity daytimes, you may not want to use it. Here's why: Water sitting in your pipes loses heat, which means that the water that fills your dishwasher at night is much cooler than water coming fresh from the hot water heater (unless you have midnight bathers in your home). This problem gets magnified the farther your hot water heater is from your dishwasher and the colder your basement is. The heat boost option during the main wash cycle helps to reheat the water, but it is best to have hot water for all wash and rinse cycles.

- **Run Hot Tap Water Before Starting.** Immediately before you start your dishwasher, run tap water into your kitchen sink until it gets its hottest. This way the water cooled from sitting in the pipes won't fill your dishwasher. Turning up the thermostat on your hot water heater

371

will make tap water hotter, but I don't recommend it. There's a danger of people, especially children, getting scalded in the shower or bath when your tap water is very hot. A temperature setting of 140°F is the maximum for hot water in the kitchen and safety in the bathroom. However, please note that the American Academy of Pediatrics, whose main concern with water temperature is the prevention of scalding, suggests a setting of 120° or lower.

- While letting the tap water run until it gets hot, don't let it run down the drain, save it in jugs for watering plants or other purposes.

- Dishwasher detergent becomes ineffective with exposure to air, so don't fill your dishwasher cups far in advance of starting the cycle. This is another reason that the delay option may not be a good idea. Fill the detergent cup that will be closed first and the open cup second. This way if you spill detergent on the door while filling the closed cup, it won't be wasted because you can count it towards the amount you need in the open cup. Decrease the amount you pour in the open cup by the amount you spilled.

> **WARNING: Dishwasher detergent is poison to babies/toddlers. Keep it out of baby's reach—both the bottle and the liquid in the cups on the open door of your dishwasher.**

- **Use only detergent meant for dishwashers.** Hand dish liquids will cause too many bubbles that may clog the drain and prevent the jets of water from doing their job.

- **Load Carefully and Don't Overload.** Your dishwasher will get your dishes clean only if the water jets can do their job. Make sure you don't place a big bowl or broiling pan in the way of baby bottles or any other dishes, or they will prevent the water from shooting at them and getting them clean. And don't overload your dishwasher, save the extra dishes for the next load.

- **Load ice cube trays** by placing them back to back and upright between the bars of the top rack of your dishwasher.

- **Dishwasher Baskets.** I use two baskets on the top rack of my dishwasher to stop small items from flying around inside. I put everything from bottle caps to small plastic measuring cups in them. In my opinion, they are well worth the price.

- **Empty clean dishes from the bottom rack of your dishwasher first.** Then if some trapped water spills from a dish/cup as you're emptying the top rack, no dishes on the bottom rack will get wet and have to be towel dried. Grab the silverware basket by the big handle and move it to the counter over the silverware drawer to save steps in emptying.

Wipe-up Towels Help Keep Your Baby and Kitchen Clean

The handiest thing you can have in your kitchen to keep it clean, whether or not there is a baby in the family—but especially if there is—is a dozen or two of those cheap white terry cloth finger towels or wash cloths. You can buy them at the local store. Or you can find similar cloths in large packages labeled "carwash cloths" in the automotive section of department stores. Make sure you buy only 100% cotton terry cloths.

I use them to wipe up everything from my baby's face and hands, to the kitchen counter tops and floor (not the same one, of course). There are always several clean wipe-up towels in a special kitchen drawer used only for the purpose of holding these towels, and everyone in the family uses them. Buy two or three dozen and you'll always have a fresh clean towel to dry your hands and for wiping up.

> **TIP:** Wipe the cleanest thing first and the dirtiest thing last, and then you will need only one wipe-up towel. For example, at the end of the meal, wipe your baby's face first, her hands next, then the high chair tray and seat, and last the floor. If you've used the towel to wipe the floor first, then you'll need another clean towel to wipe her face.

> **TIP:** If your baby acts insulted when you try to wipe his face with a towel, use your wet fingers to clean him up, and wipe your fingers instead of his face with the towel.

> **WARNING:** Sponges are breeding grounds for bacteria. Wipe-up towels are better—they have many more purposes than sponges and are always clean because you wash them after every use. If you insist on using sponges, run them through the dishwasher on the top shelf. Or disinfect by soaking in ¾ cup of household bleach in a gallon of water for 10-15 minutes; then rinse them out very well.

You probably already use white cotton diapers as general-purpose wipes and spit-up rags for your baby. These are fine, but I find them too thin and large for kitchen use. Terry cloth wipe-up towels or washcloths are so much more absorbent. They are also small enough for single-use purposes, as you would use disposable paper towels.

TIP: Buy different colors of wipe-up towels for different uses: yellow can be for wiping up kitchen counters and hand and dish drying, green can be for appliances, white can be for baby's hands and face, etc.

REMINDER: You will want to wash them first before you use them, of course. Wash and machine-dry them separately the first time, because they will shed an incredible amount of lint the first time they are washed.

There are three reasons why these little terry cloth towels are so practical. One, you can use them to wipe up anything. They are so cheap that you don't care if they get stained or ripped. You can even use them on baby's bottom if you sterilize them afterward by washing them in hot water and bleach. Two, they'll save you money on paper towels. Three, their laundering cost is negligible, because you can add them into the washing machine with ANY other clothes or laundry. You can even wash them with a new red shirt, because you don't really care if they turn pink—they're rags.

TIP: Even though they are rags, you can still extend their lives. If snags form in them, don't pull them, cut the threads instead. Do this also, of course, for your good terry cloth towels.

I do laundry at least every other day. In every load, there are several of these wipe-up towels. I usually wash my towels in hot water with bleach to sterilize them. Sometimes I don't have any other whites to wash them with, and it would be energy-inefficient to wash a few wipe-up towels in bleach and hot water in a large washing machine alone. So here's what I do to save water and energy.

Place the wipe-up towels in the empty washing machine. Set the machine for hot water wash and the water level to low. Pour in detergent and bleach and begin the wash cycle. Let the machine go through the wash cycle and the first rinse and spin cycle, and then open the lid. The rags are now clean from a hot water and bleach wash (but not thoroughly rinsed) and are in the bottom of the washing machine.

Now begin all over again from scratch for the rest of the laundry. Place the regular load of laundry into the machine with the wet, clean wipe-up towels. Set the water temperature and level and add detergent according to the rest of the load. The towels will be washed again and finish the rinse and spin cycles with the rest of the load.

From my experience, it seems that there is not enough chlorine bleach left on the towels after the first rinse and spin cycle to do any color damage to the other clothes, but you may not want to do this with clothing that is susceptible to color fading.

The only time you have to go through this procedure is when you feel that your wipe-up towels need to be sterilized in hot water and bleach, such as when you used them on baby's bottom or on the kitchen floor. Wipe-up towels used only on baby's face and kitchen counter tops probably don't need hot water and bleach, especially when you're going to dry them in a hot clothes dryer.

TIP: An adaptation of this washing method can be done when you have clothes that should be washed in different cycles and different temperatures. Let's say you have two small bunches of clothes: one is more durable than the other and should be washed in hot water with normal agitation and lots of detergent in a long cycle, and the other bunch consists of more delicate clothing that should be washed in cooler water. Throw the durable bunch in the machine first with the full amount of detergent, set the water level to low and the water temperature to hot, and start the machine on a long-timed wash. When the machine is almost done with the wash cycle, set the water level to high and allow cold water to fill the wash basin to the top, making the water now warm or cool instead of hot. Then add the delicate clothes into the water and let them agitate for the short time left on the wash cycle. Both bunches get rinsed (in cold water) and spun dry together. In effect, you've done two different load types in one!

Children Are More Important than the Carpet

Brace yourself before reading this paragraph. This is a heartbreaking true story about someone I've known since childhood. Back a few generations ago, when most moms were stay-at-home and cabinet locks were not yet invented, a neighbor and dear friend of mine got under his mother's sink during his toddler years. The crystal drain opener, which looked like candy, was easy to reach. He tasted it. It burned his mouth instantly and so badly that he was deformed for life. He's embarrassed about his looks and his dribbling. Kids constantly made fun of him. He has had over a dozen painful plastic surgeries, but as an adult, his injuries are still obvious. He has suffered as much emotionally as physically. His mother never forgave herself.

I'm sorry. I know this is terribly upsetting. But I would rather have you be upset than to have anything like this happen to your child. Children are more important than a sparkling clean house. For your children's sake, choose to use only baby-safe products. Before your baby becomes mobile, go through your entire house, including the basement and garage, and get rid of any poisonous substances: insecticides, weed killers, drain cleaners, etc. You don't need them if you use the recipes in this chapter. Make sure that any other home or building your baby may visit—grandma's, the babysitter's, a friend's, etc.—is as safe for your baby as your home is.

> WARNING: BLEACH + AMMONIA = DANGER!! Never mix bleach (or any product containing bleach) with ammonia (or any product containing ammonia). Mixing bleach and ammonia will cause a dangerous gas to form, which is a health hazard if inhaled and may even be lethal. The same is true for BLEACH + VINEGAR and BLEACH + TOILET BOWL CLEANER.

Baby-Safe Cleaning Products

Do NOT keep poisonous household cleaning products in your home, grandma's home, the babysitter's house, or any other place your child may be. You just do NOT need them.

Ingredients for Safe Household Cleaning Solutions

Here are some staples to have on hand for the recipes in this section:

- Baking soda (sodium bicarbonate)—the same stuff you use in cakes and other baked goods. Buy it in bulk at the supermarket, department store, or your natural foods store.

- Washing soda is similar to baking soda in that it is mined from the same mineral (trona) and is refined to sodium bicarbonate. But not as refined as baking soda. It is therefore more caustic, non-edible, and less expensive. Look for it near the laundry detergents in the supermarket.

- Plain white vinegar is mentioned a lot in this section. It is much cheaper to buy the generic brand by the gallon than it is to buy the top named brands in the small glass bottles.

- Vanilla smells delicious and is used in some of the recipes here. Why buy vanilla scented cologne when you can dab real vanilla extract behind your ears to smell pretty?

- Cornstarch. The same white powder you use for thickening sauces.

- Liquid soap, not detergent, from the natural foods store.

- Borax is found near the laundry detergents at the supermarket. It is a mineral that occurs naturally and is safe for the environment, but it is not baby-safe so keep it out of baby's reach. It is also an eye and skin irritant and is harmful if swallowed. But sometimes you do need something strong to get parts of your home clean, and borax is one of the acceptable ingredients for these purposes. It is a disinfectant and a deodorant. Just be very careful when the baby is around.

- Next time you're at the local X-mart department store, pick up some empty transparent plastic trigger spray bottles for your homemade cleaning solutions. Do not use poisonous aerosol spray cans in your home; they only serve to deposit toxins in the air and into your family's lungs.

- Check out the cleaning products that are environmentally friendly and baby safe at your local natural foods store. Many supermarkets now carry Seventh Generation products, "products in harmony with the earth." Online at www.seventhgeneration.com.

- Products containing ammonia should not be used in a home with a baby (or any living beings). Ammonia is dangerous if swallowed and its fumes should not be inhaled. It is an eye and skin irritant and may cause burns. Never use any product containing ammonia in an aerosol can.

Pesticides

Pesticides kill living things. Let me repeat that. Pesticides kill living things. Who knows what long-term effects these supposedly safe levels of pesticides used on our nation's crops will have on your baby (or you for that matter), especially since "safe" pesticide levels on our nation's crops are set according to tolerances by adults and not babies! Another problem with pesticides and your baby is this: Your baby eats much more food per pound of body weight than adults do, so pesticides get more concentrated in her little body. Babies are especially vulnerable to pesticides because their immune system, their organs, and their developing brains are so immature.

> WARNING: The American Academy of Pediatrics recommends that you wait until your baby is between 7 and 9 months old before you introduce homemade carrots, beets, turnips, spinach, or collard greens. In some parts of the country, these crops contain nitrates, and may cause a type of anemia (methemoglobinemia) in young infants. Nitrates also form cancer-causing nitrosamines. Commercial baby food manufacturers can test for nitrates, but we parents can't. Some health professionals believe that any health risk from high-nitrate vegetables in babies under 7 months is so small that restriction is not really necessary. No matter how small the risk, do not take the chance. Wait until your baby is at least 7 months old before feeding her these homemade foods.

Certified Organic Foods are Best for Baby

Only certified organic foods should be used to make food for your precious baby. "Certified" organic means that the food has been grown and handled according to strict uniform guidelines and that the farm fields and processing facilities have been inspected to assure that organic standards are being met, according the Organic Foods Production Act of 1990.

For more information about organic food, contact the Organic Trade Association, PO Box 28, Brattleboro, VT 05301 (www.ota.com).

NOTE: If your child is eating a lot of one single food, she may be getting much more of a particular pesticide than a child who is eating a variety of foods.

The Environmental Protection Agency (EPA)

The EPA is responsible for protecting human health, safeguarding the environment, and establishing safe levels of pesticides for humans.

If you have questions about pesticides, contact the National Pesticide Information Center: 800-858-7378 or online at npic.orst.edu

For questions about drinking water, call the EPA's Safe Drinking Water Hotline at 800-426-4791, or find them online at water.epa.gov.

Baby-Safe Household Pesticides

Ants

Instant grits is a safe solution to your ant problems. Sprinkle where they enter and the workers will take the grits back to the queen ant. She'll eat them, expand, and blow up. Ants will not cross a line. Find where they are entering your home and draw a line with any of these: blackboard chalk, liquid dish soap, bath powder, white flour, paprika, red chili powder, dried peppermint, or cream of tartar. (Be careful with liquid dish soap. It may stain walls and is slippery and it's more trouble to wipe up.) Try dusting the area with ground cinnamon. Fill cracks with flour or white glue. Try washing counter tops, floors, cabinets, etc. with equal parts white vinegar and water. Repel ants on vertical surfaces like windowsills, doors, and cracks in your home's foundation by spraying liberally with equal parts white vinegar and water. For places where children never go, mix two parts borax and one part sugar or white flour and sprinkle around the foundation of your home. Keep borax away from children.

Ants and Snails and Slugs

Place beer (yes, regular six-pack type beer) into a aluminum pie tin and place in the ground level with the soil. Keep snails from a young plant by pushing a soup can with both ends removed into the soil around the plant. The can encircles the plant and protects it from snails.

Cockroaches

Kill cockroaches by petrifying them. Mix equal parts cornstarch and Plaster of Paris and sprinkle in cracks and crevices. Keep Plaster of Paris away from children and follow warnings on the label. Or mix two parts flour, four parts borax, and one part cocoa and place in a saucer where they crawl. For cockroaches or silverfish, mix one part boric acid (keep away from children) with two parts sugar in a small amount of water. Leave bowl where insects crawl, but safely out of children's reach. Or try sprinkling equal parts baking soda and powdered sugar where they crawl.

Fleas

Remove vacuum cleaner bags immediately after vacuuming. Seal the bag and dispose of it outside your home. Add a bit of vinegar to your pet's drinking water—about one teaspoon to a quart of water and it will help repel fleas and ticks. Including nutritional yeast in your dog's diet may also help. Use Murphy's® Oil Soap to wash your dog. It kills fleas on contact (no 10-minute wait for flea soap to work), makes fur shine, and is natural so your dog can safely lick herself.

Flypaper

Make your own flypaper by mixing together and bringing to a boil corn syrup, sugar, and a little water. Coat strips cut from brown grocery bags and hang.

Mice

Mice hate peppermint. Repel them by placing fresh peppermint sprigs where they run. Or use a piece of cardboard saturated with oil of peppermint (available at some pharmacies). Nontoxic but cruel: Leave mashed potato buds or powder in their paths, along with a saucer of water nearby. They will eat it and die from bloating. Humane mouse traps are available at hardware stores.

Plant Pests

Place a raw white potato slice on the surface of soil in your potted plants. It will draw out plant-damaging worms.

Put hot sauce on a ball of cotton and place in your houseplant pot to repel plant pests.

In your blender, mix water and some garlic and pepper sauce or hot peppers or red pepper powder and optionally some raw onion. Strain and spray to coat plant leaves. Make sure to spray under leaves too. Or spray plants with one part Dawn® dishwashing detergent or other biodegradable dish soap to four parts water. Wait one hour before rinsing clean with water. Or soak raw onions and garlic in some water for a week. Place in spray bottle and use as a natural insecticide for plants.

Bugs don't like dead bugs, especially dead bugs that are in their family! Gather together some dead bugs and mix them in your blender with water. Strain until you can spray the mixture. Truly a bug spray!

Ring a houseplant with your dog's flea collar. Cover plant and collar together in a plastic bag and let sit for two days. The tiny pests will be gone. Be sure to keep the collar and the plastic bag out of reach of children. Do not do this with houseplants that you plan to eat, such as herbs.

Kill grass growing in cracks by pouring boiling water on it. Or sprinkle with salt. Or wet with undiluted white vinegar.

For More Information on Pesticides

Contact Beyond Pesticides, 701 East Street SE, Washington, DC 20003 202-543-5450 (www.beyondpesticides.org).

Part V

Nutrition for
Your Super Baby

32

How Much Should My Baby Eat?

A Healthy Baby Will Eat The Proper Amount of Food

The question "How much should my baby be eating?" is so often asked of pediatricians, that it is clear that food amount is a great concern to new parents. They are worried that their babies are either eating too much or too little. Don't worry. Your baby will tell you how much he should eat. Your concern should be to include as much nutrition as possible into every calorie that goes into your baby's mouth. As your baby gets older, feed him a balanced variety of healthy foods and you can be confident that he's eating right.

The Amount Your Baby Eats Will Vary from Day to Day

The quantity of food your baby will eat will vary from day to day, sometimes by great amounts. Don't be surprised if she acts like you starve her one day and eats like a little bird the next. An extended period in which she eats very little is usually followed by a period where she eats a lot. Remember that it is atypical for a baby to be consistent in the amount of food she eats and with her food likes and dislikes from one day to the next.

You know your baby. You can tell if she's not eating because she is sick. If you have any doubt, it's always best to call and ask your pediatrician. Don't be afraid to "bother" your doctor when you have a concern. If he or she makes you feel like you are a nuisance, find another doctor.

Growth Spurts

The "average" baby doubles her birth weight by five months and triples it by one year. That means if your baby weighed 7 pounds at birth, she should weigh about 14 pounds at 5 months and about 21 pounds at 1 year. Imagine tripling your weight in one year!

Your baby's entire first year is a growth spurt, with temporarily bigger growth spurts occurring at certain times. The first several growth spurts are signaled by increased milk consumption. The first growth spurt occurs about a week after birth, the next at 3 weeks, then 6 weeks, and then at about 3 months. After about 5 or 6 months, you may notice that your baby is eating less, which may be because he is growing at a slower rate at this time or because of teething pain.

Another growth spurt begins between 8 and 10 months of age, when you will see a significant increase in the food your baby eats. You may notice an increase in your baby's appetite when he begins crawling and walking, an effect of his using more energy.

When he begins his second year of life, his growth rate again decreases and he will consequently eat less. This is the time, shortly after the first birthday, that many parents become concerned by the drop in their baby's appetite. Your pediatrician will be watching your baby's growth and development. Discuss with her any changes in appetite you notice in your baby, not only to make sure that your baby is OK, but also to reassure you.

NOTE: Steady weight gain is not necessarily an indicator of a healthy baby. Rely on your pediatrician's expertise to monitor your baby's growth and development.

I'm Worried That My Baby is Eating Too Much
A Healthy Baby Will Stop Eating When Full

Your baby's appetite is self-regulating. If your baby is eating a lot, he needs to. As long as he's not eating junk foods and stays with *Super Baby Food*, there's probably no need to worry.

REMINDER: When your baby cries, first try to comfort him by holding and talking to him. Use food to stop him from crying as a last resort, when you are sure that he is crying because he is hungry.

My Baby is Too Fat

Many babies, even breast-fed babies, are fat before they start crawling and walking. But when they start to move, they quickly slim down. Never put your baby on a reducing diet. And never feed an under one-year-old baby skim (nonfat) milk, because it contains too much protein and salt and because babies need fat in their diet. The estimates on the percentage of fat from calories that should be in a baby's diet range from 30% to 55%, which is higher than the percentage recommended for us adults. If you are concerned about your baby's weight, consult your pediatrician before making any changes in your baby's diet.

I'm Worried That My Baby Is Not Eating Enough
A Healthy Baby Will Not Starve Himself

You know your baby. You can tell when he is sick or if something is wrong. If your baby is not losing weight, seems healthy and happy, and your pediatrician says that he is developing well, you probably have no cause to worry.

I've heard on more than one occasion a mother say, "My baby won't eat for me." That statement indicates that a power struggle has developed between Mom and baby. For example, Baby does Mom a favor by eating, and punishes her by not eating. How to prevent this? Do not over-react when your baby refuses to eat. And always keep mealtimes relaxed and pleasant.

You Can Put a Baby in a High Chair, but You Can't Make Him Eat

Never force your baby to eat. When that little head turns or those little lips close tight, it is time to put the food away. Never, never, never force a baby to eat. Never make him finish the last spoonful in the bowl—throw it away. Never make him finish the last half-ounce in the bottom of the bottle— throw it away. Finishing that last bite will start your baby in the bad habit of eating when he is not hungry and throws off his body's self-regulating mechanism, which may lead to being overweight later in life.

Some parents are so concerned about their baby's lack of appetite that they may resort to shoving a spoonful of food into baby's open mouth when he is not paying attention, or forcing or manipulating food into their baby by some other means. This kind of feeding is doing more harm than good. If you find that you are resorting to such methods, give yourself an "A" for effort and for the fact that you care so much about your baby. But please stop, and instead, ask your pediatrician for advice on what to do about your baby "not eating enough."

WARNING: If your baby begins to hold food in her mouth for extended periods, or spit, gag, or vomit food, this may be an indicator that your baby views mealtimes as stressful. Re-evaluate your feeding methods and make sure that you are not force feeding your baby—either purposely or unintentionally.

What to Do When Your Baby Won't Eat a Certain Food

Don't push it. Put it away and try again in a few weeks. There are certain things in the *Super Baby Food Diet* that even I won't eat alone, such as nutritional yeast. It tastes awful. It must be mixed in with small amounts of other food to hide its bitterness.

Sometimes your baby will not eat something that is sweet and tastes good to you. With my baby, it was applesauce. I was surprised (but not upset!) that he simply would not eat it. A few months later, he began eating it with gusto and has loved it ever since. It must have been something about the acidic flavor.

If you are afraid a toddler will not like a particularly healthy new food, such as kale, use a little reverse psychology to get her interested. Don't give her any and eat it in front of her; have the whole family eat it in front of her. She will want some. Be hesitant, but agree to give her some. If you're lucky, she will love to eat it because it makes her feel like a big girl who fits in with the rest of the family.

> **REMINDER:** Babies will almost always make a face when offered a new food, especially if it has a strong flavor. Do not go by her facial expression. Offer her another spoonful and if her little mouth opens to accept a refill, continue feeding.

> **TIP:** You may wish to have this rule in your home: You have to try one bite of a new food. If you don't like it, you don't have to eat it, but you have to try it. Remind your child of Dr. Suess's *Green Eggs and Ham*. You may like them, Sam I am.

Small Amounts of Food Frequently Throughout the Day

It's not unusual for a baby to eat only one major meal a day, with the rest of his food coming from snacking. Snacks are necessary in a baby's diet and should consist of smaller portions of the same healthy foods that are part of larger meals. A baby may not begin eating three baby-sized meals until he is 10 months old, although he may start as early as 4 months.

Snacks should be offered at scheduled, predictable times every day and not at random. Snacks should be eaten in the feeding area, as main meals are, because they ARE meals.

The "Average" Food Amounts Given in this Book

In the chapters for each month of your baby's first year, I included a section about the daily amounts of foods that you can expect your baby to eat at that age. These amounts are based on the hypothetical "average" baby. Babies differ enormously in height, weight, activity level, and appetite.

However, sometimes a great deviation from the average may be a sign that something is wrong. If your baby eats a VASTLY different amount of food than the one stated for her age, you may have a reason to be concerned. If you're worried, call your pediatrician.

Baby Food Diary

If you are concerned that your baby is eating too much or too little, begin keeping a baby food diary. Include a description and amount of each food and drink your baby has consumed with the day and time of each meal or snack. After you have gathered several days of "data," consult with your pediatrician.

> **REMINDER:** Your pediatrician should be a person you feel comfortable with. You should not hesitate to ask him or her a question. Many Moms have come to me with questions and when I asked them what their pediatricians advised, they tell me that it never even crossed their minds to ask their doctors!! Do not hesitate to pick up the phone and call your pediatrician's office with a question. There are no "dumb" questions. If your doctor makes you feel like there are, or in any other way makes you feel uncomfortable about the concerns you have for your baby, find another doctor.

Table of Baby Food Portions

The table on the next page is a brief summary of the complete information given in Chapters 9-15. The table is meant to give you only a rough sketch of the number of meals and the size of food servings that your baby might eat at those ages. Please be very flexible when you feed your baby and go by her cues that she is still hungry or satisfied.

Super Baby Food Daily Servings and Portion Sizes				
Food	**7 Months**	**8 Months**	**9 Months**	**10-11 Months**
Veggies and Fruits	3-4 servings 1-2 tbsp per serving	4-5 servings 2-3 tbsp per serving	4-5 servings 2-4 tbsp per serving	4-5 servings 3-4 tbsp per serving
Super Porridge Cereals	1-2 servings 1-2 tbsp dry cereal or ¼-½ cup cooked cereal per	2-3 servings 1-2 tbsp dry cereal or ¼-½ cup cooked cereal per	3-4 servings 1-2 tbsp dry cereal or ¼-½ cup cooked cereal per	4 servings 1-2 tbsp dry cereal or ¼-½ cup cooked cereal per
Legumes, Nuts and Seeds	1-2 tbsp of tofu purée every day or every 2nd day	1-2 servings For serving sizes, see protein foods on p. 409-414	2-3 servings For serving sizes, see protein foods on p. 409-414	2-3 servings For serving sizes, see protein foods on p. 409-414
Dairy	1 serving per day or every other day ⅓-½ cup yogurt, or ¼ cup cottage cheese	1 serving per day or every other day ½ cup yogurt, or ¼-⅓ cup cottage cheese, or ½-1 oz natural grated cheese	1 serving per day or every other day ½ cup yogurt, or ⅓ cup cottage cheese, or 1 oz natural grated cheese	1 serving per day ½ cup yogurt, or ⅓ cup cottage cheese, or 1 oz natural grated cheese
Eggs	**One egg every second day** or 3-4 eggs per week			
Nutritional Enhancers	none	Add ½-1 tsp. of nutritional yeast and a pinch of kelp into *Super Porridge* at least once a day, and maybe ½-1 teaspoon of desiccated liver, too.		
Solid Food Meals per Day	2-3 meals per day of 2-3 servings each	3 meals per day of 3 servings each + snack or 2	3 meals per day of 3 servings each + snack or 2	3 meals per day of 3 servings + 2 or more snacks
Breast feedings or Formula per Day	30-32 oz. formula or 5 breast feedings/day	29-32 oz. formula or 5 breast feedings/day	26-32 oz. formula or 3-4 breast feedings/day	24-32 oz. formula or 3-4 breast feedings per day
Juice and Water	4 oz. max.per day	6-8 oz. max. per day	6-8 oz. max. per day	6-8 oz. max. per day

Be very flexible with meals and food serving sizes. This table is meant to give you only a rough idea of what your baby might eat at these ages.

Length and Weight Charts

Weight and length charts for children up to three years old, developed by the National Center for Health Statistics in collaboration with the National Center for Chronic Disease Prevention and Health Promotion are included here for your convenience. If you are concerned about your baby's size, have a talk with your pediatrician.

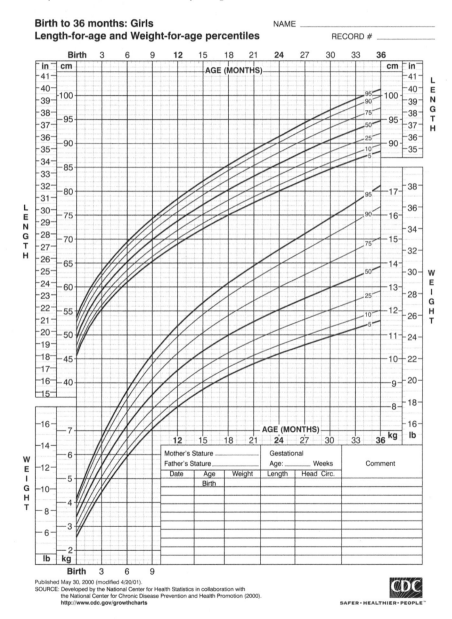

Birth to 36 months: Girls
Length-for-age and Weight-for-age percentiles

NAME _____
RECORD # _____

Published May 30, 2000 (modified 4/20/01).
SOURCE: Developed by the National Center for Health Statistics in collaboration with
the National Center for Chronic Disease Prevention and Health Promotion (2000).
http://www.cdc.gov/growthcharts

CDC
SAFER·HEALTHIER·PEOPLE™

391

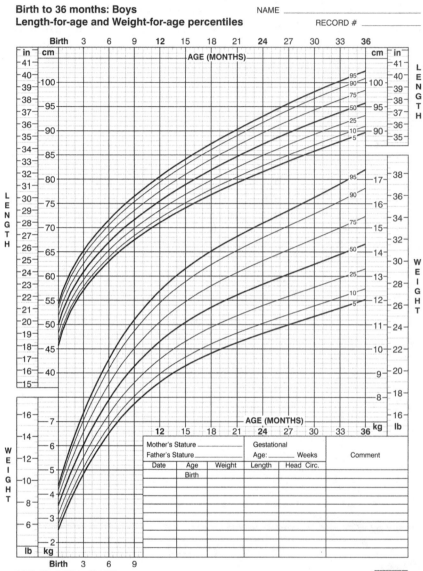

Birth to 36 months: Boys
Length-for-age and Weight-for-age percentiles

NAME _____

RECORD # _____

Published May 30, 2000 (modified 4/20/01).
SOURCE: Developed by the National Center for Health Statistics in collaboration with
the National Center for Chronic Disease Prevention and Health Promotion (2000).
http://www.cdc.gov/growthcharts

SAFER·HEALTHIER·PEOPLE™

33

How Much Should My Baby Drink?

Breast Milk/Formula Before Introducing Solid Foods

As a general rule, a baby drinking breast milk or formula exclusively—that is, one who has not yet been started on solid foods—should be drinking about 2½ ounces of milk per day for each pound of body weight. Age plays an important factor. For example, a baby younger than 6 weeks may drink more than 3 ounces of formula per pound of body weight because of a fast growth rate, whereas a baby 15 weeks old may drink only 2 ounces per pound. Of course, a 20-week-old baby who has begun eating solid foods may be drinking only 2 ounces per pound of body weight, due to the increased calories from the solid food. Examples of the number of average daily ounces according to pounds of body weight are given below.

Average Amounts of Daily Breast Milk/Formula by Body Weight for Babies Not Yet Eating Solid Foods	
6 pounds	15 ounces per 24 hours
7 pounds	17½ ounces per 24 hours
8 pounds	20 ounces per 24 hours
9 pounds	22½ ounces per 24 hours
10 pounds	25 ounces per 24 hours
11 pounds	27½ ounces per 24 hours
12 pounds	30 ounces per 24 hours
13 pounds	32 ounces per 24 hours

Is Your Baby is Drinking Enough Breast Milk or Formula?

Breast milk or formula is the most important food for your baby during her first year, and especially in her first 8 months. It is very important that the introduction of solid foods not decrease her breast milk or formula intake during the first eight months. Calorie for calorie, there is no solid food that is as nutritious for your baby as breast milk or formula. Initially, solid foods should supplement milk, not replace it. If your baby is not drinking the recommended amount of breast milk/formula for her age, (see the chart in the previous chapter) cut back on her solid food intake so that she will be hungrier for breast milk or formula. For smaller babies, this may not work; please consult your pediatrician.

> WARNING: When mixing formula, always use the recommended ratio of water to formula. Parents who are concerned that their babies are not drinking enough formula may think that less water is the answer. Do NOT make formula more concentrated than it should be by adding less water than instructed. Sodium, protein, and other ingredients in the formula must be mixed with the proper amount of water so as not to strain your baby's kidneys and for other health reasons.

Formula-fed Babies and the 32-Ounce Rule

If your baby is older than 6 months, most experts agree that your baby should not be drinking more than 32-40 ounces of formula per day. If your baby wants more than this limit, offer her a bottle of water instead. If she won't drink water, offer her pasteurized and diluted juice as described in the Juice section further in this chapter.

Please note that the "no more than 32 ounces per day" rule holds only for babies older than 6 months. Before the age of 4-6 months, experts say that too much formula is not a problem and that a hungry baby should be given a bottle instead of solid food. Your pediatrician may not agree; follow her advice on this issue.

No Cow's Milk Until One Year

Breast milk or formula is the only milk you should give to your baby throughout her first year. Cow's milk is different in composition than human milk—it's "designed" for baby cows, not baby humans. Cow's milk contains more salt than breast milk/formula and its protein content is different from human milk, which may strain your baby's kidneys. Introducing your baby to cow's milk too early can cause milk allergy to those who are susceptible.

Cow's milk leaves an infant at risk for anemia because it is low in iron, a very important nutrient for your baby in her first years of life. Cow's milk is also low in vitamin C, another important nutrient. Vitamin C also helps in the absorption of iron, so the lack of it in cow's milk increases the risk of anemia. And to even further risk iron deficiency anemia, cow's milk can irritate the digestive tracts of very young infants (younger than 6 months) and cause tiny amounts of bleeding, with a consequent loss of blood and its iron.

> **NOTE:** Although cow's milk should not be used as a replacement for breast milk or formula during the first year, it is OK to introduce it as an ingredient of solid foods in the rest of the diet, such as yogurt.

Parents may wish to begin cow's milk as early as possible because it is less expensive than formula. Some experts are more lenient about this one-year rule and advise that once your baby is getting half of his calories from solid foods, it's OK to start him on cow's milk. Others say it's OK when your baby is eating at least six ounces of solid foods a day. Go by your pediatrician's advice.

> **TIP:** When it comes time to make the transition from formula to cow's milk, it may be easier for your baby if you start by mixing a small amount of cow's milk into your baby's cup of formula or breast milk. Gradually decrease the amount of formula and increase the amount of cow's milk until the mixture is all cow's milk with no formula.

Once your baby starts on cow's milk, it should be whole milk and not skim or low-fat, which is too high in salt and protein. Your baby needs the fat from whole milk for calories and nutrition. You can find organic milk at the natural foods store and many supermarkets. Organic milk is milk from cows that haven't been administered drugs or fed hormones. It is usually pasteurized, but don't buy it unless it states that it is pasteurized on the label. Don't confuse organic milk with raw milk, which may contain dangerous bacteria.

It's probably safest to purchase commercially pasteurized milk for your baby, rather than home pasteurizing. Be sure to properly refrigerate the milk. Do not keep it at room temperature for more than a few minutes, and discard at expiration date. Bacteria in milk do grow in the fridge, but they grow slowly, which is why you must get rid of it after a while.

I strongly recommend that you buy only certified organic pasteurized milk for your baby. It is from cows that have not been given antibiotics and growth hormones and which have been fed grass with no pesticides. All cow's milk will have natural hormones in it, since the cow is giving milk because it is supposed to be nursing its calf. Organic milk doesn't have added growth hormones.

Organic pasteurized milk should be safe in the refrigerator until its expiration date if not left at room temperature for more than a few minutes. It is still not safe for children with milk allergies. It still contains lactose and should not be given to children who are lactose intolerant. Organic pasteurized milk might be more expensive, but it is one of the foods that is worth the money to buy organic.

The Dangers of Raw Milk

Milk is a liquid in which bacteria grows quickly, so milk sold to the public is pasteurized. Pasteurization is a heating process done to milk to destroy harmful microorganisms. Many people have begun drinking raw milk because they believe the high-heat pasteurization process destroys nutrients in milk and makes it unhealthy. Raw milk is often sold in health food stores. People also buy raw milk from neighbors that have cows. Raw milk has to be handled using extremely sanitary methods in order to prevent bacteria from taking root.

The FDA claims that raw milk poses serious health risks. Their web site, www.fda.gov/Food/ResourcesForYou/Consumers/ucm079516.htm, has more information about this.

Despite the FDA's recommendations, some people still choose to drink raw milk. The microorganisms, which may grow in raw milk, are especially dangerous for people who have weak immune systems, such as babies, small children, the elderly, pregnant women, and people with chronic illnesses.

Raw milk is much healthier than pasteurized milk, if it is free from dangerous germs. The problem is the possibility of dangerous bacteria, which are killed during pasteurization. Adults with strong immune systems are taking a chance when drinking raw milk. Giving raw milk to babies with immature immune systems may be fatal. Experts recommend not feeding your children raw milk. It's a shame that it's not considered safe to give babies and children raw milk, just as it's a shame that raw sprouts, honey, raw eggs, and other healthy foods should not be fed to children. It's just too risky. The risk might be low, but why take the chance when these foods can be lethal!

One option for people who wish to drink raw milk is home pasteurization. It can be done at lower temperatures than commercial pasteurization, thereby minimizing the destruction of nutrients. In general, the lower the heat, the longer you must heat the milk in order to kill all bacteria; the higher the heat, the less time you must heat the milk. Search the web for "home pasteurizing milk" for complete information. Here's a good source: www.motherearthnews.com/ask-our-experts/pasteurize-raw-milk-at-home.aspx.

Baby's Bottle Should Contain Only Formula or Breast Milk

Some experts recommend that your baby's bottle contain only formula or breast milk. In other words, although it is fine to let your baby drink milk or water or juice from the cup, some authorities advise that it is best to offer only milk, and never water or juice, in the bottle.

Water
Water Is Important to Kidney Functioning

When you introduce solid foods, begin giving your baby a little water after and between meals. It will help her kidneys dilute the more concentrated waste products of solid foods.

The amount of water needed varies with the baby. You may start by giving your baby a tablespoon of water after his meal and before the rest of the breast or bottle-feeding. Gradually increase the amount of water until he is drinking a maximum of 4-6 ounces of water per day. Maintain this maximum until your baby is about one year old, so as to ensure that his drinking other liquids does not decrease his milk intake.

> WARNING: Water intoxication is a risk for a baby under 6 months. Consult your pediatrician.

Besides helping the kidneys, water is needed by your baby's body to replace that which is lost through the urine, feces, sweating, evaporation, and breathing (as can be seen in cold weather). This he gets from milk, water, juice, and food, which is part water. You must make sure your baby gets enough liquids to prevent dehydration, especially on hot days. Ask your pediatrician how much water your baby should drink.

Getting enough liquid is as important for a baby as for an adult, maybe even more so, because a baby's body is made up of a higher proportion of water than an adult's. While adults require a daily an amount of water equal to 2-3% of their body weight, a baby requires about 15%! If you're not interested in the math, skip the next paragraph.

For example, a 20-pound baby requires approximately .15*20=3 pounds (48 ounces) of water every day. Let's say he drinks 32 ounces of formula, 2 ounces of juice, and 2 ounces of water, for a total of about 36 ounces. That leaves about 12 ounces to be obtained from food. If he eats 2 half-cup servings of cereal, 4 quarter-cup servings of vegetables, and 2 quarter-cup servings of fruits, that's 2½ cups or 20 ounces of food. It is safe to say that more than half of these foods is water, and so there you have it—12 ounces of water.

Babies do not dehydrate easily because the main part of their diet is fluid. But your baby may dehydrate if she is vomiting or has diarrhea, so be sure to consult with your pediatrician.

Tap Water

Tap water may be safe for your baby to drink. Ask your pediatrician, who should be familiar with the local water supplies. If your pediatrician isn't sure and you are concerned about lead and other tap water dangers, call the EPA's Safe Drinking Water Hotline at 800-426-4791 or go their web site, water.epa.gov/drink/hotline/index.cfm, for a list of certified water testers in your area. National Testing Laboratories, Ltd. in Cleveland, Ohio at 800-458-3330 www.ntllabs.com/residential.html also tests drinking water.

Beware of free water testing offers. If you are going to use a home lead test kit, first call the EPA to make sure that they approve of the manufacturer. If a test determines that a problem exists with your water, get it retested by another certified water tester.

WARNING: Never use tap water that has been sitting in your pipes for an extended period of time, because it may contain heavy metals (cadmium, mercury, lead) that leached in from the plumbing. For example, you wouldn't want to drink the first glass of water out of the kitchen tap in the morning, because that water has been sitting in the pipes all night. Flush out stagnant water from the pipes by letting the water run for a few minutes, until it gets as cold as it will get. Don't waste this water: rinse dirty dishes with it or save it to water plants.

WARNING: Never use hot tap water for drinking or cooking purposes. The warmth helps lead and other heavy metals from your pipes leach into the water. If you need warm/hot water, draw cold water and heat it on the stove.

No Standards for Bottled Waters

When you buy bottled water, you may be wasting money. Most bottled waters are not natural mineral water at all, and are actually nothing more than processed local tap or well water. This is true if the label says "spring fresh," "spring type" or "spring pure." Some bottled waters have added sodium and may have more bacteria than your tap water, and even more lead! There are no federal standards on any bottled waters if they are bottled and sold in the same state!

One type of bottled water, distilled water, has nothing in it but H_2O. Distilled water has no minerals and may even absorb minerals from your body. Drinking water should be a dietary source of many healthful minerals, so distilled water is not good to drink. (Some people disagree with this, and claim that drinking distilled water is healthful.)

Hard Water vs Soft Water

Hard water refers to water that has high levels of minerals, specifically calcium and magnesium. Hard water is known for making white clothes gray after washing, leaving a bathtub ring, and depositing crystals in your tea kettle and hot water heater. Water softeners were invented to undo the hardness of water. But soft water contains high levels of sodium. It makes more bubbles in the bathtub and causes soap to lather more readily, so that you can use less soap. Soft water more easily dissolves metals from your plumbing. Hard water is the more healthy drinking water, so if you plan on buying a water softener, hook it up to your hot water pipes only and drink only from the cold. Call your local water company to determine your water hardness.

Hard Water is Healthier than Soft Water		
Water hardness (ppm)	Minerals-grains per gallon	Parts per million
soft	0-3.5	0-60
moderately hard	3.6-7	61-120
hard	7.1-10.5	121-180
very hard	10.6 and above	181 and above

MONEY SAVER: If you have soft water, although it's not good for drinking, it sure is good for saving money on detergents. We have very soft water in our community and I get away with using less than half the recommended amount of laundry detergent and dishwasher liquid! I use the money I save on detergent to have healthy drinking water delivered to our doorstep.

The Best Drinking Water The best water you can drink is probably water bottled directly from a local spring. The spring should be in an area with little or no industry, so pollutants can't get into the water. The bottle will say something like, "Natural spring water bottled directly from the source." Call the company and ask about their water's hardness and if/how often they test their water for pollutants, lead and other heavy metals, and other toxic substances.

Baby's Water Must Be Boiled and Cooled
The water you give to your very young baby must be boiled to kill all bacteria. Boil it for 5-10 minutes and store it in a sterile container in the refrigerator. Make sure it is thoroughly cooled before giving it to baby. Do not keep it at room temperature for more than a few minutes. Store in the refrigerator for no more than 2 days and then discard it. It will not be long before you can feed your baby water without boiling it first. Ask your pediatrician when it is no longer necessary to boil your baby's water.

Juice

At about 7 months, you can begin giving your baby diluted, mild fruit juice. Your pediatrician may advise the introduction of juice several months earlier.

It's Important that Juice Not Replace Baby Milk

To keep your baby's breast milk/formula intake up, limit your baby's juice intake to 3-4 ounces of juice per day. Babies who drink too much juice may not be drinking enough breast milk or formula to obtain the fat, calories, and protein they need for proper development. Too much juice and not enough breast milk/formula may adversely affect your baby's growth and may lead to decreased weight and height.

Start with Mild Fruit Juices

Start with mild juices, such as apple, apricot, white grape, papaya, pear, peach, and prune, remembering to use the *Four-day Wait Rule*. Although some experts recommend orange juice and other citrus juices at 6 months, others recommend waiting until 12 months, especially if allergy to citrus runs in the family. Citrus is one of the foods that are a common allergen and the acidity may be a problem. Ask your pediatrician when you should start giving your baby orange juice.

Apple juice seems to be very popular because it has a low chance of allergy, although a friend of mine uses it because it doesn't stain the carpet. It certainly is no more nutritious than other non-citrus juices, unless it is vitamin C fortified.

Juices for Baby Must Be Pasteurized

You may be aware of the recent problem with E. coli bacteria in commercial unpasteurized apple juice and apple cider. Make sure that any juice fed to your baby is pasteurized—it should be indicated on the label. Beverages in bottles, cans, and juice boxes stored on the supermarket shelf at room temperature are supposedly pasteurized. I recommend that you not trust them, though, unless it specifically says that they are pasteurized on the label.

WARNING: Do not feed your baby apple cider, juices, or any beverages bought from roadside stands. And do not feed your baby "fresh" juices, as they are not pasteurized.

Refrigerate and Discard Open Bottles of Juice Within Two Days

If you are feeding your baby commercial baby juices, make sure to refrigerate any opened bottles with unused portions immediately. Do not leave opened jars of baby juice at room temperature for more than a few minutes. Store opened jars of baby juice tightly covered in the refrigerator. Keep for no more than two days before discarding.

How to Pasteurize Juice

If you are not sure that juice for baby has been pasteurized, bring it to a full boil and boil it for it for 3-5 minutes to kill any bacteria. Store in a sterile container in the refrigerator immediately. Never leave it for more than a few minutes at room temperature and keep refrigerated. Discard after 2 days.

Juice Should Be Diluted When First Introduced

Juice contains large amounts of sugar, and natural or not, too much sugar is not good for your baby. For example, it takes an entire apple to make one ounce of apple juice. Therefore, four ounces of juice contain the natural sugar found in four apples—that's a lot of sugar!

Excessive sugar from fruit juices may cause susceptibility to yeast overgrowth (specifically candida albicans), which manifests in throat and ear infections, eczema, and chronic nasal congestion. Too much sugar causes a temporary decrease in your baby's white blood cell count, and consequently a decrease in the strength of her immune system—yet another reason why too much sugar causes illness.

Sorbitol (a sugar alcohol found in pear and apple juices) has been shown to cause gastrointestinal disorders, such as gas and bloating, abdominal pain, and diarrhea.

Bottled baby juice is 100% juice with no water added and therefore should be diluted. If your pediatrician OKs it, you can save money and use regular adult juices and dilute them yourself. Buy those juices that are only 100% juice and make sure they are pasteurized. Do not feed your baby "pretend" juices—those juice drinks, which have added sugar. These nutritionally void drinks are nothing but sugar, water, and food coloring. Read the label and watch out for ingredients ending with "ose". Although natural juice does contain a lot of sugar, it does contain some other nutrients. It is best to buy baby juice fortified with vitamin C, a necessary nutrient that will also help with iron absorption.

At first, dilute 1 ounce of juice with 3 ounces of water, giving a 4-ounce serving. Over a month's time, gradually increase to half juice and half water. In subsequent months as your baby grows older, you can, if you wish, gradually increase to 100% juice with no added water.

> **REMEMBER:** There is really no need to build up to 100% juice, which contains so much concentrated sugar. If you wish, you can continue feeding your baby diluted juice throughout his childhood and even into adulthood. It's a good idea to start diluting your families and your juice, too. We're better off without all that concentrated sugar!

Some Juices Must Be Strained to Prevent Choking

Most natural foods stores have a nice selection of organic fruit juices, but they sometimes have solid particles that should be strained out to prevent baby from choking. Home-squeezed juices also need straining. As discussed above, remember to check that all juice has been pasteurized.

Home-squeezed Juice

If you squeeze juices at home manually or with a juice extractor, feed them to your baby immediately after squeezing so that bacteria do not have a chance to multiply. Drinking home-squeezed juices is similar to eating fresh fruit. However, do not store home-squeezed juices (even in the refrigerator or freezer) for baby unless you first pasteurize them as directed on the previous page. After pasteurizing, strain the juice. Refrigerate in a sterile container. As with all juice, discard after two days.

Before juicing, remember to wash the fruit/vegetable well to remove as much of the pesticides as possible. Although pasteurization kills bacteria, it does not remove the pesticides. I recommend using only certified organically grown produce for making home-squeezed juices.

Protect Your Baby's Teeth from Sugar in Juice and Other Beverages

Use a baby cup instead of the bottle to feed your baby juice in order to minimize the time the juice remains in his mouth. Don't let your baby sip from a bottle or cup of juice, milk, formula, or any other carbohydrate-containing liquid throughout the day. The natural sugars and acids in the liquid will remain for extended periods on his teeth and may cause cavities. If your baby insists on sipping from a bottle, make it water.

> WARNING: Too much fruit juice or even too much fresh fruit can cause your baby's stool to be acidic. This irritates baby's tender skin and may cause a painful, bright red diaper rash that hurts when you wipe. Inform your pediatrician.

Cola and Other Carbonated Beverages

NEVER give your baby cola drinks or other sweet carbonated beverages, even when she's 21 years old. Besides gobs of unhealthy sugar, some of these drinks also contain caffeine, which has a much greater affect on a 20-pound baby than it does on a 150-pound adult.

Nut/Seed Milks

Other Super Baby (and Super Adult) beverages are nut milks and seed milks. As discussed previously, nuts and seeds are one of nature's most nutritious foods. Nut/seed milk is not actually what we tend to think of as "milk." It is actually water with added liquefied nuts or seeds, which makes the water look like a thin and watery milk. Nut/seed milks are very easy to make if you have a blender.

Beginning at about 8 months, you can introduce your baby to these Super Milks. But just as with juice and water, nut/seed milks should supplement and not replace breast milk or formula.

Some experts advise using nut/seed milks for non-breastfeeding babies who cannot tolerate any brand of formula. If your baby has this intolerance, discuss with your pediatrician the use of nut/seed milks.

REMINDER: For your baby to develop properly, he needs a recommended amount of breast milk/formula every day. Water and juice should not replace breast milk/formula. Limit your baby's juice intake to 3-4 ounces of undiluted juice per day until he is one year old. Limit your baby's total daily intake of juice, water, and other beverages to 6-8 ounces per day so that he will drink his recommended amount of breast milk/formula. On hot days, your baby may need a little more water to replace perspiration.

34

Nutrition 101

Proper nutrition is about eating the proper foods in the correct amounts and combinations so that our bodies can carry on their biological processes and use energy. The more you study the minute details of nutrition, the more complicated it gets, and the more you realize that you should just leave it to nature. In other words, eating a variety of whole, natural foods— whole grains, legumes, nuts, seeds, vegetables, fruits, and yogurt—is the best diet we can eat to insure optimum health.

This chapter gives the basics of nutrition, an understanding of which will help you to give your baby and yourself a good diet. Also included in this chapter are many warnings about the food industry and their advertising practices, which, I believe, are meant to mislead the uninformed consumer and increase their profits.

Baby-Sized Portions

Note that the food portions are baby-sized for your convenience. Keep this in mind if you compare these numbers to numbers in other books, which will usually be much larger because of adult-sized portions. Most of the vegetable servings are one ounce (1 oz) servings. One ounce is approximately equal to 28 grams, 2 tablespoons, ⅛ cup, or approximately 1 food cube. Of course, your food cubes may be slightly larger or smaller and they contain varying amounts of water from puréeing, so allow for inaccuracies. If your baby is eating two food cubes instead of one, remember to double the number in the table. Many fruit portions for babies are given in fractions: ⅛ cantaloupe, ¼ orange, ½ kiwi fruit, etc. When trying to figure the size of these portions, picture in your mind a medium-sized fruit. The fruit portions are quite small. If your baby loves fruit and eats more than these small portions, (like mine does), adjust the numbers accordingly. The portions for grains, legumes, nuts, and seeds are also 1 ounce. The nutrient numbers are for dry, uncooked grains and legumes as you buy them from the store before grinding in the blender.

REMINDER: 1-ounce portions are approximately ⅛ cup or 2 tablespoons. To get a feel for a 1-oz portion, picture the amount of veggies, grains, beans, nuts, or seeds that would fit in a small scoop.

Food Groups

In 1943, the United States Department of Agriculture (USDA), in order to form a more perfect union of the foods in Americans' diets, came out with the "basic four:" meats, vegetables and fruits, starchy foods/potatoes, and milk. The USDA recommended having one food from each of the four groups at each

meal, thereby making them "square meals." For optimal health, one was to eat three square meals a day. Many baby boomers like myself grew up on these "meat and potatoes" meals.

People are beginning to become aware of the importance of a high-fiber, low-fat diet for good health. The USDA's *MyPlate*, which has replaced the old *Food Pyramid*, reflects this awakening.

Fruits

Any fruit or 100% fruit juice is part of the fruit group, including fresh, canned, frozen, or dried. Fruits may be whole, cut-up, or pureed.

There are some foods in the fruit group that are healthier than others, and particularly whole fresh fruit. As the old adage goes, "An apple a day keeps the doctor away." Lots of fruits and vegetables, high in vitamins and antioxidants, in your child's diet helps strengthen his immune system. Fruits, like vegetables, have no fat or cholesterol and are high in water content; filling up on them helps to prevent obesity.

Vegetables

There are some foods in the vegetable group that are healthier than others. It wouldn't do to eat the same few veggies all the time, because there are so many thousands of nutrients that vegetables supply and you need a variety to make sure you are getting all of them.

Vegetables can be divided into five sub-groups: dark green vegetables such as broccoli, spinach and kale; beans and peas; starchy vegetables such as corn and potatoes; red and orange vegetables such as acorn squash, carrots and sweet potatoes; and "other" vegetables such as mushrooms, celery and zucchini.

High-quality veggies are loaded with vitamins and minerals. Fresh picked organically grown vegetables grown in nutrient-rich soils are best. Eat only the most nutritious vegetables, particularly steamed carrots and broccoli and legumes. Eat dark green veggies like kale and swiss chard instead of iceberg lettuce, which is light green in color with a lot less nutrients than the darker green leafy vegetables. And iceberg lettuce is commonly sprayed heavily with pesticides.

Grains

There are some foods in the grain group that are healthier than others. **Eat More** of these grains: 100% whole wheat bread, 100% whole wheat pasta, oatmeal, ready-to-eat breakfast cereals made from 100% whole grains, *Super Porridge*, cooked brown rice and other cooked whole grains, such as quinoa, millet, and buckwheat.

Eat less of these grains: white rice and products made from refined grains, such as white bread, pasta, bagels, pretzels, breakfast cereals made from enriched white flour and corn flake breakfast cereal made from degerminated corn flour, and lots of sugar like cookies, cupcakes, sweetened breakfast cereals, danish, croissants.

I recommend that you and your family eat ONLY organic 100% whole grains or foods made from organic 100% whole grain flours. In Chapter 22 I discussed the nutritional difference between whole grains and processed grains, explained how to cook whole grains such as brown rice and *Super Porridge*, and showed you how to read misleading food labels that want you to believe you are buying a whole grain product that really isn't.

WARNING: If you or your child is used to eating mostly processed grains, ask your healthcare provider how to change to 100% whole grains. Too much fiber too fast, when the body is not used to a high fiber diet, can cause gastrointestinal distress. You may want to do a gradual change by increasing the number of servings of whole grains per day by only one serving every several days.

Breakfast Cereals

Commercial ready-to-eat breakfast cereals, such a Cheerios®, are part of the whole grain group. But Cheerios are not organic and they do have a little added sugar, so you may want to choose a similar O-shaped cereal made from organic oatmeal with no sugar added, such as Oatios®. These used to be available only in natural foods stores, but now many supermarkets are carrying them. One cup of Oatios is considered one serving of whole grains. Natural foods and many grocery stores have a variety of organic 100% whole grain ready-to-eat breakfast cereals similar to the major brands.

Dairy

All fluid milk products and many foods made from milk are considered part of this food group. Foods made from milk that retain their calcium content are part of the group. Foods made from milk that have little to no calcium, such as cream cheese, cream, and butter, are not. Calcium-fortified soy milk is also considered by the USDA to be part of the Dairy Group.

Foods in the Dairy Group provide nutrients that are vital for health, including calcium. Calcium is used for building bones and teeth. Dairy products are especially important to bone health during childhood and adolescence, when bone mass is being built.

Protein—The Body-Building Nutrient
There is NO Fiber in Meat

Instead of a Meat Group, MyPlate exhibits, well, not even a Food Group but a nutrient group—Protein! "Protein" was an easier way, the USDA learned from their research, to describe the variety of sources from which a person could get their protein including meat, eggs, dairy, nuts, seeds, beans, soy, etc.) Of course, meat is NOT part of the *Super Baby Food Diet!*

The human body is constantly in need of protein to continuously replace its parts. Perhaps you have heard that your body completely replaces its skin every seven years. All of our fat cells get replaced within a year's time, and no blood cell in our bodies is more than 4 months old. Your baby needs even more protein than an adult proportionate to his size, because along with all of this replacing of body cells, he also is growing at a rapid rate and adding new body cells each day. While the adult body needs about one-third gram of protein for each pound of body weight, your baby needs approximately a full gram of protein for each pound of body weight, or proportionately 3 times the adult amount.

The Super Baby Food Diet Supplies Lots of Protein

It is the norm for Americans to over consume protein. In our meat-centered culture, many people believe that meat is required in the diet to supply protein requirements and other nutrients. They may be concerned that the *Super Baby Food Diet,* a lacto-ovo vegetarian diet (a vegetarian diet that includes dairy products and eggs), will cause stunted growth or other health problems in their baby. If you have this concern, perhaps the table on the next page will reassure you that your baby will get more than enough of her protein requirements from the *Super Baby Food Diet.* Pediatricians agree that a lacto-ovo vegetarian diet is a healthy and safe diet for a growing baby. It is a strict vegan diet that causes concern for most health professionals.

Amino Acids are the Building Blocks of Proteins

Our bodies are constantly building proteins to be used for maintenance, growth, and repair. The substances it uses for all this protein synthesis are called amino acids. Surely you remember eighth grade health science class—"Amino acids are the building blocks of proteins." You routinely answered the test question on this memorized fact correctly, but had no idea why you had to know it. Here's why: It will help you to understand *protein complementarity* so you can give your baby a super healthy diet.

Essential Amino Acids

There are 22 amino acids. Of them, only 9 cannot be manufactured by the body and must be provided by foods in the diet, 10 if you include arginine, required for the young, but not for adults. The 9 amino acids are called **essential amino acids**. (Remember what *essential* means in nutrition—a nutrient that cannot be made by the body, and therefore must be supplied by the diet.)

It used to be thought that you needed to eat all 9 essential amino acids together in the same meal. Recent studies have shown that as long as you eat a variety of foods containing all the EEAs on daily basis you will be getting your required amount.

Your Baby's Protein Needs

The Super Baby Food Diet supplies your baby with more than enough protein. Please look at the next table. It shows the number of protein grams in the foods if they are eaten separately, in other words, if you discount any protein complementarity that may be taking place. Many of the foods in the *Super Baby Food Diet* naturally complement each other for additional protein.

Your Child's Average Daily Protein Requirements

Newborn to 3 years	13 grams
4 to 8 years	19 grams
9 to 13 years	34 grams

Protein Grams from Super Baby Foods Eaten Separately

Super Baby Food	Grams	Super Baby Food	Grams
2 T broccoli	1.0	⅛ C mung beans	7.0
2 T Brussels sprouts	1.0	½ oz soy flour	5.0
2 T asparagus	1.0	⅛ C split peas	7.0
2 T beet greens	1.0	⅛ C navy beans	6.0
1 oz Calif. avocado	1.0	⅛ C kidney beans	7.0
2 T sweet potatoes	0.5	⅛ C Great Nor. beans	6.0
2 T cauliflower	1.0	⅛ C pinto beans	6.0
2 T canned pumpkin	0.2	⅛ C adzuki beans	6.0
1 oz mashed banana	0.3	⅛ C black turtle beans	6.0
2 T beets	0.4	⅛ C lima beans	6.0
2 T carrots	0.2	⅛ C chickpeas	5.0
½ C fresh orange juice	1.0	⅛ C soybeans	10.0
⅛ C amaranth	4.0	1 oz tofu	4.0
⅛ C triticale	4.0	1 T nutritional yeast	4.5
⅛ C rye berries	4.0	1 T textured veg. protein	3.0
⅛ C couscous	4.0	1 oz peanuts	7.0
⅛ C quinoa	4.0	1 T peanut butter	4.0
⅛ C millet	3.0	1 oz almonds	6.0
⅛ C teff	4.0	1 T almond butter	2.0

Super Baby Food	Grams	Super Baby Food	Grams
⅛ C pearled barley	3.0	1 oz filberts	4.0
⅛ C buckwheat groats	3.0	1 oz cashews	5.0
1 T toasted wheat germ	4.0	1 oz English walnuts	4.0
1 T raw wheat germ	3.0	1 oz Brazil nuts	4.0
⅛ C brown rice	2.0	1 oz flaxseed	5.0
⅛ C whole wheat flour	4.0	2 T chia seeds	4.0
⅛ C rolled oats/ oatmeal	4.0	1 oz sunflower seeds	6.0
⅛ C cornmeal, whole grain	2.0	1 oz pumpkin/squash seeds	7.0
⅛ C lentils	7.0	½ C breast milk	1.5
⅛ C bulgur	3.0	½ C most formula	4.0
½ C milk	4.0	1 oz ricotta, part skim	3.0
¼ C cottage cheese	6.0	1 T grated Parmesan	2.0
½ C whole milk yogurt	4.5	1 oz cheddar cheese	7.0
1 oz natural Swiss cheese	8.0	1 oz mozzarella, part skim	7.0
1 large egg, whole	6.3	1 large egg yolk	3.0

Protein Complementarity

With few exceptions, only foods from animals, such as meat, milk, and eggs, contain all the essential amino acids in the proper proportions to make significant amounts of complete proteins. Grains, beans, vegetables, and other plant foods, when eaten alone, do not supply enough complete proteins for the body because they are lacking in one or more EAA. However, if we combine a plant food lacking in one EAA with another plant food strong in that EAA, complete protein is formed. The protein is equal to or better than the protein from meat and other animal products, and you don't have to kill any animals or eat all of the fat and toxins that go along with meat. This process of combining non-meat foods to make complete protein, so that one food's weakness in EAAs is compensated by another food's strength in those EAAs, is referred to as protein complementarity.

High Protein Plant Food Combinations	
Super Baby Food Combinations That Form Complete Protein	**Example Food Combinations (T=tablespoon, t=teaspoon)**
2 GRAINS+1 LEGUMES Combine approximately 2 parts grains with 1 part beans, peas, or other legumes.	2 cup rice + 1 cup beans ½ cup rice + ¼ cup lentils ½ cup millet + ¼ cup soy grits 1 cup whole wheat flour + ¼ cup soy flour or powder 1 cup bulgur + ⅓ cup split peas ½ cup rice + 3 oz tofu 1 slice whole wheat bread + 1 oz tofu 1 slice whole wheat bread + 1 T peanut butter ½ cup pasta + 8 oz tofu
PEANUTS + MILK	½ cup milk + 5 T peanut butter ¼ cup yogurt + 2½ T peanut butter
SEEDS + MILK	½ cup yogurt + 5 T tahini
GRAINS + MILK	¼ cup rice + ⅓ cup milk or yogurt 1 cup whole wheat flour + ⅔ cup milk or yogurt 1 slice whole wheat bread + 1 t cheese 1 cup macaroni + ½ oz cheese
MISCELLANEOUS	¼ cup rice + 1 T nutritional yeast 1 slice whole wheat bread + 1 T peanut butter ½ pound white potatoes + ¼ cup grated cheese 1 cup milk or yogurt + ½ cup beans ½ pound white potatoes + ¾ cup yogurt ½ cup cornmeal + ⅛ cup dry beans scalloped potatoes broccoli with cheese sauce eggplant Parmesan

The table on the previous page shows some plant food combinations that form complete protein. You can learn more about protein complementarity by reading the single best book on the subject: Frances Moore Lappé's classic book *Diet for a Small Planet*.

The measures in the table are for dry, uncooked grains and legumes. For example, when you see *2 cups rice* that means 2 cups of dry brown rice before cooking in water. *1 cup beans* means 1 cup of dry beans or legumes before soaking and cooking in water. Rice can be replaced with oats, barley, millet, and other grains with a similar effect in protein complementarity. Peanuts are technically legumes (because of the pod), but they should be treated like nuts when combining foods for complete proteins.

Nutrients

The food we eat provides our body with the substances necessary for energy and with the structural components necessary for bodily growth and repair. These substances are called nutrients. The amount of nutrients we need depend on body weight, age, activity level, and many other factors.

In general, the younger a person is, the more nutrients he needs per pound of body weight. For example, a 150-pound, 30-year old woman requires more or less 13 calories per pound of body weight per day or about 2000 (13x150) calories. But a 25 pound, 18 month old toddler requires about 50 calories per pound of body weight per day or 1250 calories. A toddler needs more than 3 times more calories per pound than an adult! This disparity exists with almost all other nutrients. Nutrients are needed in much greater proportions by your baby because of her fast growth rate and her activity level—as we parents know so well. It is therefore very important that you feed your baby the healthiest foods possible, to insure that she grows up to be big and strong!

The Major Nutrient Classes

The nutrients needed by the human body are classified into 6 types:

1. Carbohydrates
2. Fats
3. Proteins
4. Vitamins
5. Minerals
6. Water

Carbohydrates, fats, and proteins are called macronutrients because you body needs lots of them. Vitamins and minerals are called micronutrients because your body needs very little of them, relative to the macros. However, the fact that we only need a little bit of the micros doesn't mean that they aren't just as important as the macros.

No nutrient works alone. Nutrients are needed in proper proportions, as they are found in whole, natural food.

Macronutrients

Carbohydrates and fats from foods are the main sources of energy for the body. Each gram of carbohydrate supplies 4.1 calories, and each gram of fat supplies 9.3 calories. Fat is a more concentrated source of fuel for the body, and is more "fattening" than carbohydrate. Although proteins are mainly for maintenance and repair, they can also be used for energy when carbohydrates and fats are not available. Proteins, like carbohydrates, supply 4.1 calories per gram. The breakfast cereal commercial that reminds you to lose the fat, not the muscle, is referring to the loss of protein when muscle tissue is broken down and used for energy because of a lack of carbohydrates and fat in the diet, due to crash dieting. (Incidentally, that cereal is not whole grain.)

Carbohydrates Supply Energy

Carbohydrates are the most important source of energy for the body. There are three classifications of carbohydrates: sugars (simple carbohydrates), starches (complex carbohydrates), and fibers (also complex carbohydrates). Carbohydrates are found almost exclusively in plant foods, with the exception of milk, which contains lactose or milk sugar, a simple carbohydrate.

Simple Carbohydrates or Sugars

Sugars are called simple carbohydrates because their simple molecular makeup allows them to be digested very easily and quickly—in fact, too easily and too quickly. These sugars include common white sugar or table sugar, brown sugar, powdered sugar, honey, molasses, and the crystallized white fructose that looks like white sugar.

Empty Calories and Nutrient Debt

We know that too much of these sugars are not good for us, but why? After all, they are natural: sucrose (table sugar) is found in sugar beets and sugar cane, fructose (fruit sugar) is found in fruits, which are very good for us, and honey is very healthy for bees. Well, first of all and probably least important is the fact that these concentrated sugars are a major cause of tooth decay. A bigger problem with these sugars is that they supply empty calories—calories with only energy and without any significant amounts of other vitamins and minerals. Eating large amounts of them makes you feel full for a short while, but you burn them up very quickly and soon find yourself hungry again. It's like building a campfire out of leaves instead of logs: You get a big, big fire for a few minutes, but then it quickly fizzles out. Complex carbohydrates (covered next) are like logs—they burn slowly and steadily for a long time.

And here's a surprising fact about sugars: Not only do simple carbohydrates supply no other nutrients, but they actually rob vitamins and minerals already existing in your body to digest them! Eating refined sugars is like going into nutrient debt. This occurs with all simple carbohydrates, even honey, which is not much better than table sugar, with only a minute amount of nutrients.

Refined Sugars Wreak Havoc with Blood Sugar Levels

The main problem with simple carbohydrates exists in their concentration. In nature, sugars are found diluted in large amounts of water in fruit and sugar beets, coexisting with fiber and many other nutrients. When removed from their original plant sources, table sugar and other simple carbohydrates are refined, processed, and concentrated. They cause a reaction in the human body more akin to that of a drug or chemical than that which would occur from the natural, whole foods from which they were derived. When eaten in large amounts, these concentrated sugars cause a rapid and dramatic rise in blood sugar levels, which causes the pancreas (a digestive organ that produces insulin to counteract blood sugar) and other digestive organs to go wild trying to handle this instantaneous influx of excessive sugar. This over-reaction eats up too much sugar, causing a precipitous drop in your blood sugar level. This plummet affects your brain before any other organ: You feel tired, irritable, nervous, and lightheaded, and may have other low blood sugar (or hypoglycemic) symptoms. In order to alleviate these symptoms, you grab a jelly doughnut and a cup of sugared coffee, and the roller coaster ride starts all over again.

Macronutrient Food Sources		
Macronutrient	Super Baby Food Sources	Other Sources
Carbohydrates	whole grains beans and legumes nuts and seeds starchy and other vegetables and their juices fruits and their juices dairy products blackstrap molasses	wheat flour (not whole), same as white flour white sugar white rice cakes, pies ice cream colas and other soft drinks
Fats	nuts and seeds flaxseed (linseed) oil avocado eggs dairy products whole grains	meat butter margarine processed vegetable oils lard shortening
Proteins	eggs dairy products combinations of grains, beans, legumes, nuts, seeds, and nutritional yeast	red meat pork poultry fish

BUYER BEWARE: Avoid the OSEs on the Label

The food industry takes full advantage of the fact that these sugars can technically be labeled "natural." To increase sales, they make their food products taste good by loading them with lots of sweet-tasting sugary additives, and mislead the uninformed public that their product is healthy because it's "all natural." Think about it, a five pound bag of white sugar (sucrose) is, in fact, all natural. Don't fall for the advertising. Ignore all healthy and natural claims written in big, brightly colored letters on the front of the package and go for the jugular—the ingredients list. In general, look for ingredients that end in *ose*; they're the sugars.

Names That Mean Sugar in Lists of Ingredients

sucrose	glucose	mannitol	sorghum syrup
dextrose	lactose	sorbitol	high fructose corn syrup
maltose	molasses	honey	fruit juice concentrate
fructose	corn sweetener	syrup	and, of course, sugar

BUYER BEWARE: The Hidden Sugar Amount Trick

Here's a trick that food manufacturers use to make you think you're getting less sugar than is actually in their products. Let's say that a jar of peaches actually has more sugar than peaches, but the manufacturer doesn't want you to realize this. The list of ingredients on the side of the jar may read: peaches, dextrose, sucrose, and fructose. (This is a simplified version of the trick. A real package intersperses several other ingredients between the ose's, so they're not as obvious.) Because peaches are first on the ingredient list, the unwary consumer may think that they are actually getting more peaches than anything else. Well, there may be more peaches than dextrose, and more dextrose than sucrose, and more sucrose than fructose, but when you add up the quantities of dextrose, sucrose, and fructose, the total sugar content is greater than the amount of peaches.

5 grams = 1 teaspoon

The new mandatory nutrition labels make it difficult for a food manufacturer to hide the actual total sugar amount in their products. Look at the second line from the bottom in the label; it has the word *Sugars* followed by a number of grams. Consider every 5 grams of sugar one teaspoon. (Actually, 1 teaspoon of sugar is equivalent to 4.76 grams or about 4¾ grams.) For instance, if a cereal has 15 grams of sugar per serving, that's the equivalent of more than 3 teaspoons of sugar. Some children's breakfast cereals are more than 50% sugar! Soft drinks are other high-sugar offenders, with colas containing about 9 teaspoons of sugar per 12 ounces, and orange soda with almost 12 teaspoons per 12 ounces. Picture taking a 12 ounce glass of water and stirring 12 teaspoons of sugar into it and feeding it to your children! This is what you are giving your children when you feed them soft drinks, except soft drinks have more junk added: chemicals, food colorings, etc.

Our Taste Buds Previously Insured a Balanced Diet

It is a shame that the stuff that tastes so good to us is so bad for us. Every wonder why? I once heard a good explanation. In the environments of our ancestors, complex carbohydrates were plentiful and easily acquired from the abundance of plant life. Foods containing fats and sugars were scarcer, so nature (knowing that a variety of foods helps to insure a balanced diet) supposedly built into our taste buds a love for the rare fats and sweets. Hence, our ancestors had a great desire for them, and would go through more difficult maneuvers to obtain them.

A friend of mine has a cute cartoon on his office door. Under a picture of a little boy saying a prayer at his bedside reads this caption: Dear Lord, Please put my vitamins in candy instead of broccoli.

Sugar Substitutes

Sugar substitutes have no place in a baby's diet. Nutrasweet®, saccharin and Equal® are not natural, in my opinion, no matter what the ads say. Artificial additives and chemicals should not be put into your baby's body. At the time this book was printed, some scientists believe that the risk of brain cancer may be increased by the use of some artificial sweeteners, which have been sold for years as being "safe." How true this is, we don't know, but why take the chance!

Sugar in Baby Foods

Baby food manufacturers have stopped adding sugars to most baby foods, thanks to pressure from the public, but they still add it to the dessert-type baby foods. Read the label and don't buy them.

Complex Carbohydrates or Starches

Whereas simple carbohydrates (sugars) have simple molecular structures that are digested too quickly and easily by the body, complex carbohydrates have complex molecular structures that take hours to be digested. A complex carbohydrate molecule is actually a very long chain of thousands of simple sugar molecules, which gets broken down and released into the bloodstream slowly and steadily. Blood sugar levels stay at an even keel, along with organ activity and your emotions. After eating complex carbohydrates, you don't feel hungry again for several hours and your desire for food again comes back slowly. It is much healthier to eat whole foods with complex carbohydrates that your body breaks down into sugars, than to let food manufacturers refine whole foods into simple sugars before they even reach your plate.

Complex carbohydrates, also called starches, are found in grains, beans, legumes, nuts, seeds, and the products made from them, such as breads and pastas, and in starchy foods such as potatoes and other vegetables.

Fiber

Although some refer to fiber as a nutrient class by itself, it is actually a type of complex carbohydrate. Fibers, like starches, are long chains of sugar units, but the bonds between them cannot be broken by our systems, and they pass through the body undigested. Fiber, sometimes imprecisely referred to as "roughage," comes only from plant foods. There is no fiber in meat, milk, eggs, and cheese. It is found in whole grains, legumes, nuts, seeds, and in parts of fruits and vegetables, such as in the peels of fruits, the membranes between orange segments, and in the strings of celery. Fiber is listed in the ingredients on commercial food products as pectin, cellulose, and guar gum. Fibrous additives change the texture of the food. Another fiber ingredient is lignin, which is actually a woody material from the stems and bark of plants.

There are two types of fiber found in food: insoluble and soluble. Insoluble fiber (lignin, cellulose, hemicellulose) does not dissolve in water and adds bulk to the diet. It speeds up passage of food through the intestine, which helps prevent constipation and speeds carcinogens out of the body before they can do much harm, thereby reducing cancer risk. Soluble fiber (pectin, gums, psyllium), which does dissolve in water, also increases bulk in the diet. It slows down the absorption of carbohydrates and sugars, which helps manage diabetes. Soluble fiber has also been found to lower blood cholesterol levels.

Babies Eating Super Baby Food Do Not Need Bran

We all know that bran is a good source of fiber, but I don't recommend adding it to your baby's foods. If he is eating the *Super Baby Food Diet*, he is getting plenty of fiber and he doesn't need bran. In fact, too much bran is not good because it binds with certain nutrients and carries them out of the body before they can be assimilated.

Food Sources of Water Soluble Fiber	Food Sources of Water Insoluble Fiber
whole grains (in cereal, bread, pasta, crackers, muffins, rolls, etc.) vegetables and fruits with peels nuts and seeds	legumes (dried beans, peas, lentils) oats and oat bran, barley apples, pears, plums oranges and other citrus fruits

Fats: The Good, the Bad, and the Ugly

The family of lipids (the scientific name for what we commonly call fats) includes fats, oils, cholesterol, triglycerides, and other lipids. Fats, along with carbohydrates, are the two major sources of energy for the body. Fats are also needed to provide insulation to keep the body warm. In general, women have a higher percentage of fat stored in their bodies than men, which is why they can supposedly stand colder temperatures than men. Fats are also needed in the body to hold essential fatty acids and the fat-soluble vitamins (A, D, E, and K).

Fatty acids (so named because their molecular structure contains an acid group) are classified as either saturated or unsaturated, depending on whether their structures are holding a maximum amount of hydrogen. If they contain a maximum amount of hydrogen, they are referred to as saturated fatty acids, because they are "saturated" with hydrogen. If it is possible for a fat to hold more hydrogen, and hence not saturated with hydrogen, they are called unsaturated fatty acids.

The Bad—Saturated Fats

Saturated fats are found mostly in animal products, such as meats, poultry, lard, shortening, butter, and eggs. They are also found in a few vegetable products: cocoa butter, coconut oil, palm oil, and palm kernel oil. Saturated fats are solid at room temperature. (Virgin coconut oil, although technically a saturated fat, is high in lauric acid, a medium-chain fatty acid that raises both good and bad cholesterol. Opinions of health professionals are swaying toward coconut oil being a healthy alternatives. Stay tuned.)

BUYER BEWARE: Saturated Fat in Plant Oils

Some vegetable products (cocoa butter, palm oil, and palm kernel oil) do contain large proportions of saturated fats. If a product is labeled "Non-dairy" or "No animal products," that doesn't necessarily mean that it contains no saturated fats.

Our bodies are able to internally manufacture all the saturated fat it needs from other fat sources in our diets, and therefore we can be perfectly healthy if we never ate a gram of saturated fat. Studies have shown that saturated fats from animal products clog arteries and increase the chance of heart disease. They also interfere with the body's production of the good fats, such as EFAs (discussed next). But there is good news for us chocoholics. Recent studies have brought into question the heart-damaging effects of saturated fats from plant products, such as cocoa butter. They might not be so bad after all.

BUYER BEWARE: Pork—The Other White Meat

White meat generally contains less fat than red meat. In my opinion, the slogan "*Pork. The other white meat,*" misleads the uninformed public into thinking that pork has a low fat content similar to poultry. Not true. Most pork is much more fatty than white meat, and some pork is actually more fatty than some red meat. Compare:

Grams of Fat in 3½ Ounces		
Pork	**Beef**	**Roasted Chicken**
ground pork 31	hamburger 20	with skin 15
pork chop 32	rib roast 40	without skin 3
bacon 52		fried drumstick 10

The Good—Unsaturated Fats

Unsaturated fats are usually supplied by plants, and include oils from vegetables, such as corn oil. Unsaturated fats are liquid at room temperature. The two types of unsaturated fats are monounsaturated fats, found primarily in vegetable oils such as avocado, olive, and canola or rapeseed, and polyunsaturated fats (PUFAs), found mostly in seed and nut oils, such as sunflower, safflower, walnut, corn, and soy. PUFAs are also found in fish oils, because of the sea plants eaten by the fish. It is important to note that although we need some unsaturated fats in our diet, an overabundance may lead to serious health problems. PUFAs, when consumed in excess, may lower HDL (the "good" cholesterol) levels in the bloodstream. Monounsaturated fats are the only fats that have managed to keep a clean bill of health through all the scientific studies.

The Refrigerator Test

Most oils are part saturated fat and part unsaturated fat. The more saturated the fat, the more it tends to solidify at room temperature or at temperatures slightly cooler. To determine the amount of saturated fat contained in a bottle of oil, place it in the refrigerator and wait for it to get cold. The parts that become solid are the saturated fat, and the parts that become thick or cloudy, but remain liquid, are the polyunsaturated fat, and the liquid parts are the monounsaturated fat.

Essential Fatty Acids or EFAs

The word "essential" in the world of nutrition refers to a nutrient that cannot be made by the body, and therefore must be supplied by the diet. In other words, it is essential that an "essential nutrient" be part of your diet.

Essential fatty acids (EFAs) are the fats we must get from our diet, because our bodies cannot manufacture them. Of all the fatty acids, only two are essential: linoleic acid (LA) and linolenic acid (LNA or ALENA). The two EFAs are both polyunsaturated fats. They are part of every single solitary cell in our bodies, and make up a large percent of brain tissues. EFAs also have a lot to do with the way cholesterol works in our systems.

Omega 3 and Omega 6

Lately, the EFAs omega 3, a linolenic acid, and omega 6, a linoleic acid, have been mentioned frequently in the popular press. Omega 6 is found in corn oils and other oils from warm weather plants, such as sunflower and safflower oils. Omega 3 is found in cold water fatty fish (tuna, cod, mackerel, salmon), green leafy vegetables, some nuts, and cold weather plants like flaxseed. You may have heard that Eskimos, who eat lots of cold-water fish, have a low incidence of heart disease.

The typical American diet contains more than enough omega 6, but is sorely lacking in omega 3. Researchers believe that there should be a one-to-one ratio of omega 3's to omega-6's in the human diet. It is estimated that the current ratio is about ten-to-one (10 omega 6's to one omega 3)! Omega 3 deficiencies are believed to cause heart disease, arthritis, skin problems, problems in the immune system, and mental illness.

Forget Fish Oils and Go for the Flax

The popular press has been giving much attention to the fact that eating more fish can decrease the incidence of heart disease because of its omega 3 content. This is true, but fish may have high amounts of heavy metals from water pollution, such as lead and mercury. I don't understand why the press, along with some authors of "good fat" and omega 3 books, seem to concentrate only on fish. They completely ignore the absolute best source of omega 3: the small brown flaxseed.

We "health faddists" have known for years about the fabulous flaxseed. Flaxseed is THE food highest in the omega 3 fatty acid linolenic acid, and one of the best food sources of the other essential fatty acid, linoleic acid. Flax does not have the problem of heavy metals, and no fish have to be slaughtered in order to get flax. To get the amount of omega 3 found in flaxseed, you would have to eat quite a few fish meals, probably more than most people would want to eat. For example, three grams of flax seeds (about ½ tablespoon) have 2372 mg of omega 3 fatty acids, whereas a half a can of white tuna fish has only 700 mg and 3½ ounces of rainbow trout has less than 600 mg.

Somehow I feel I must be fair to the fish, though, and say that the best fish source, sardines, does have quite a bit of omega 3—5000 mg per 3½ ounce serving. And two other fish—sockeye salmon and Atlantic mackerel, have 2500-3000 per 3½ ounce serving. All other fish are under the 2000 mg mark. Other non fish sources of omega 3 are: walnuts and walnut butter, canola oil, olive oil, alfalfa sprouts, soybeans, and spinach.

Flax for Your Baby

I suggest that you feed your baby about a ½ teaspoon of whole raw flax seeds every day. First, you must grind them well in your blender or they may pass through your baby's system undigested. Feed them to your baby immediately after grinding, because they become rancid in just a few hours after grinding. Mix them into his *Super Porridge*, yogurt, or other food.

You can buy flaxseed oil at the natural foods store. (Flaxseed or linseed oil from the hardware store is not for human consumption. Do not eat!) Dr. Leo Galland, author of *SuperImmunity for Kids*, recommends a teaspoon of flaxseed oil per day added to baby's formula bottle. Or you can rub a teaspoon on his skin and let it get absorbed. If it smells "fishy," don't worry, that's normal.

You must keep flaxseed oil refrigerated or frozen. Keep only until the date on the label, or ask the natural foods store cashier how long it will keep. The oil usually keeps for up to 2 months in the refrigerator, or up to 4 months in the freezer. Be careful that the oil has not become rancid. Shake it before using, and taste it every time. If it is even slightly bitter, throw the whole bottle out.

> **WARNING:** Flaxseed oil should never be used for frying, as the high temperatures destroy all of the beneficial EFAs and may create TFAs (discussed on the next page).

I prefer flaxseed over flaxseed oil because it is a whole food and contains the fiber, whereas the oil does not. Also, whole flaxseed (before it is ground in the blender) does not become rancid quickly as the oil does.

> **WARNING:** Omega 3 greatly increases the effectiveness of B vitamins. If you eat flaxseed regularly, do not take megadoses of the B vitamins.

Essential Fatty Acids and Rancidity

Essential fatty acids and other unsaturated fatty acids are unstable and become rancid quickly if not stored carefully. When the oils containing EFAs are exposed to air, they attract oxygen. This ability to easily attract oxygen is one property that is very beneficial to the body, because EFAs help carry oxygen through the body. Unfortunately, it is also the property that causes a problem with rancidity.

This problem with air exposure causing rancidity is the reason why it is so important to eat seeds immediately after grinding. Ground seeds are broken open and their oils are exposed to oxygen, causing oxidation to occur and the seeds' oils to become rancid.

One way to prevent rancidity in vegetable oils is to keep them under refrigeration, a storage method that is expensive for the food industry. A much cheaper method of preventing rancidity is hydrogenation.

The Ugly and Very Bad—Partially Hydrogenated Oils and TFAs

Hydrogenation is a chemical process that adds hydrogen to unsaturated fatty acids. Remember that unsaturated fatty acids are not holding the maximum amount of hydrogen—they are not saturated with hydrogen. Hydrogenation makes oils more saturated: monounsaturated oils become more polyunsaturated, and polyunsaturated oils become more saturated. Hydrogenation adds to the saturation, and therefore also to the solidity, of previously liquid vegetable oils, making their texture more palatable to some people.

Adding hydrogen is a cheap way to make fats less prone to rancidity. It greatly extends the shelf life of fats. Unfortunately, it may also greatly reduce the life of people that eat them. If an oil is completely hydrogenated, it is similar to a saturated fat and as stable. Partially hydrogenated oils are worse than fully hydrogenated or totally saturated oils. If an oil is only partially hydrogenated, the part that has not taken on hydrogen—the unsaturated part—is open to the formation of trans fatty acids. Trans-fatty acids (TFAs) are carcinogens (cancer-causing agents), and also have been found to raise LDL (the bad cholesterol) levels in the bloodstream and decrease HDL (the good cholesterol) levels. They are not found naturally in foods, and are brought about by heating oils to high temperatures or by chemical processes such as hydrogenation.

BUYER BEWARE: Partially Hydrogenated Oils
Avoid any food products containing partially hydrogenated oils as you would avoid plutonium.

BUYER BEWARE: Margarine and TFAs
Margarine is more solid than liquid because their healthy liquid oils have been partially hydrogenated to make them solid. Even though margarine may not contain TFAs (and the manufacturers advertise that they do not contain trans fatty acids, trans fats, or TFAs), their partially hydrogenated oils most likely will turn to TFAs.

Cholesterol
Cholesterol is a not really a fat—it's actually a sterol, another member of the lipid family. Cholesterol, unlike fats, is not an energy source of the body. It is an essential structural component in every cell in our bodies, and is also needed to build hormones like testosterone and estrogen. The cholesterol contained in human skin is converted into vitamin D by exposure to sunlight.

The brain contains a higher concentration of cholesterol than any other organ in the body. Cholesterol is not essential in the diet because the liver can manufacture it.

Dietary cholesterol (the cholesterol in the foods we eat) is present only in animal products like meat, poultry, eggs, and dairy products. Serum cholesterol (or blood cholesterol) is the cholesterol in the bloodstream resulting from cholesterol in the diet or from being manufactured by the liver.

High levels of dietary or serum cholesterol have been associated with greater risk of heart attack. But authorities believe that it's not just the cholesterol in our diets that promotes heart disease; it is more the total amount of fat and lipids that we consume. We Americans just eat too much fat! Although we adults should restrict all dietary fats, including cholesterol and saturated fats, we should not restrict fats in our babies' diets.

HDL and LDL

Because fats and cholesterol cannot dissolve in blood, they must hitch a ride on a certain kind of protein in order to get around the body through the bloodstream. These proteins, called transport proteins or lipoproteins (lipo for fats, proteins for proteins), act as little taxis to move fats and cholesterol around in the body.

There are two types of lipoproteins: high-density lipoproteins or HDLs (the "good" cholesterol) and low-density lipoproteins or LDLs (the "bad" cholesterol). HDLs carry cholesterol out of the arteries back to the liver for reprocessing or out of the body. Therefore we consider them good lipoproteins because their act of removing fats helps prevent heart disease.

A way to remember that HDL's are the good cholesterol is to remember that we want a high level of high-density lipoproteins in our bloodstream. LDLs carry cholesterol out of the liver and into the bloodstream. An excess of LDLs causes cholesterol to get deposited in the artery walls, a process known as "hardening of the arteries." We want a low level of LDLs in our blood. So, you see, all cholesterol is the same. When people say that cholesterol is "good" or "bad," they are actually referring to the type of lipoprotein that is carrying it in the blood.

BUYER BEWARE: "No Cholesterol!" May Raise Your Cholesterol

An excess of saturated fat in the diet has been proven to contribute to elevated blood cholesterol levels. On some food products with high saturated fat, I believe that the food manufacturer purposely puts the words **No Cholesterol!** on the labels to mislead the consumer that their product is heart-healthy. Although it may be true that their product contains no cholesterol, the high level of saturated fat contributes to high blood cholesterol and makes it very heart-UNhealthy.

Triglycerides

Triglycerides are "bundles" of individual saturated and unsaturated fats and are a major form of storage for fatty acids in the body. Triglycerides are also found in the bloodstream, and a common question heard in the doctor's office is, "How are my triglycerides?" High triglycerides levels are correlated with heart disease.

Free Radicals

Fats in the body sometimes change into reactive compounds called "free radicals," which do serious damage to body cells. Free radicals are believed to cause cancer and heart disease. The more fats you eat, the higher the chance that free radicals will occur in your body. Antioxidants (vitamins A, C, E, and selenium) have been found to help rid the body of free radicals. And, as nature would design it, the low-fat foods—fruits, vegetables, and whole grains—are the foods that contain lots of antioxidants. Fill up on them and you won't have room for fatty foods.

Fats and Your Baby

Babies need fats. One of the main problems with a STRICT vegetarian diet for babies is a lack of fat and calories, because fat is a concentrated source of calories. The *Super Baby Food Diet* includes these foods that contain fats: eggs, dairy products, nuts, and seeds. Breast milk and formula contain fat. Some fats also exist in whole grains and beans, especially soybeans and tofu.

Food Sources of Fats and Oils

The next table summarizes the main food sources of saturated and unsaturated fatty acids.

Food Sources of Saturated Fatty Acids	Food Sources of Unsaturated Fatty Acids	
	Monounsaturated*	Polyunsaturated*
hydrogenated oil	avocado	pumpkin seeds
margarine with partially	avocado oil	flaxseeds
hydrogenated oil	canola (rapeseed) oil	sesame seeds
meat	safflower oil	sesame oil
bacon	sunflower oil	sunflower seeds
beef tallow	olives	sunflower oil
chicken fat	olive oil	safflower oil
lamb tallow	peanuts	Brazil nuts
salt pork	peanut oil	walnuts
poultry	almonds	pine nuts
shortening	almond oil	butternuts
lard	filberts or hazelnuts	soybeans
dairy products, such as	cashews	soybean oil
butter, milk (not skim),	macadamia nuts	mayonnaise made from
cheese, yogurt	pecans	non-hydrogenated oils
coconut oil	pistachios	
palm oil	acorns	
palm kernel oil	beechnuts	
	hickory nuts	

* Nuts contain both monounsaturated and polyunsaturated fatty acids. Nuts are classified here in the category of the predominant fatty acid.

BUYER BEWARE
Misleading Advertising: "90% Fat Free" Can Mean 75% Fat

Products often claim to contain some percentage of fat that is very misleading, because the percentage is calculated by weight instead of by calories. Here is a simple example to see how this trick is done. Let us say that you have in one glass 10 grams of oil, which is all fat and contains 90 calories because each fat gram is 9 calories. In another glass you have 90 grams of sugared water that has no fat and 30 calories. Mix the two glasses and you have 100 grams altogether, 10 grams of which are fat and 90 grams of which are nonfat. By weight, the fat content is 10 grams out of 100, which is 10% fat by weight, or 90% nonfat. The mixture can be legally advertised as 90% fat free! But by calories, the more appropriate way to measure fat content, the fat percentage is much higher. The mixture is 90 calories from the all-fat oil and 30 calories from the no-fat sugar water, for a total of 120 calories. Since 90 calories out of the 120 calories come from fat, 75% (90 divided by 120) of the calories come from fat. By calories, the mixture is 75% fat, even though by weight it was only 10% fat. So go by the nutrition label and not the advertising on the front of the package. To get the percentage of fat by calories, take the number of fat grams from the nutrition label, multiply by 9, and divide by the total number of calories.

Vitamins and Minerals—The Micronutrients

Vitamins act as catalysts in the biochemical reactions of the human body. Our bodies need very small amounts of vitamins and minerals, which is why they are called "micronutrients," but if we don't get the proper amounts, severe illness or even death may result. Whereas the macronutrients are measured in grams, vitamins and minerals are measured in milligrams (mg) or micrograms (mcg). There are 28 grams in one ounce. A milligram (mg) is one thousandth of a gram; a microgram (mcg) is one millionth of a gram, and that's pretty small!

Fat-soluble vs Water-soluble Vitamins

Vitamins come in two varieties: those that are fat-soluble (vitamins A, D, E, and K) and those that are water-soluble (all other vitamins). The water-soluble vitamins are found in the watery parts of foods and do their work in the water-filled parts of the body. Excesses of water-soluble vitamins get flushed out of the body in the urine and therefore are rarely toxic. In contrast, excesses of the fat-soluble vitamins are stored in the body, making toxicity possible. Because excesses of the water-soluble vitamins are excreted and not stored by the body, it is important that they be part of your diet every day. You can be a little more lax about getting fat-soluble vitamins daily, because of the body's ability to store them.

Nutrient Supplements

Many experts now agree that vitamin and mineral supplements are helpful, but only in small doses and in the same proportions in which they are found in nature, as in a good multivitamin/multimineral supplement. Our food supply does not always supply us with the vital nutrients we need because of nutrient-depleted chemicalized soils, too-early harvesting, long transportation times, and less-than-optimal storage conditions. Nutrient supplements can help assure that we are getting the vitamins and minerals missing in our foods. Some people eat too much processed, denatured, sugared, salted, canned and boxed pretend foods. They think they can make up for it by pumping vitamin pills into their systems. But supplements are meant to be just that—supplements. They should supplement a good diet, not make up for a bad one.

Today, there's much talk about taking megavitamins and megaminerals. Taking large amounts of pills may not only be unhelpful, it may actually be harmful. No nutrient works alone, it must be in proper proportion with other nutrients as they are found in nature. Taking megadoses of one nutrient can leave us deficient in another, or worse yet, can cause toxicity. This is especially true of the fat-soluble nutrients. Fat-soluble nutrients are stored in body fat, unlike the water soluble nutrients, which are not stored by the body. Too much of the fat-soluble vitamins can build to toxic amounts in the body. In contrast, too much of the water-soluble vitamins will most likely be excreted in the urine. It is said that Americans have the healthiest urine in the world.

> **REMINDER:** Take fat-soluble vitamin supplements with foods that contain fat (as little as 3-4 grams of fat is all you need) so that they will be better assimilated.

How Many Calories Does My Baby Need?

You may know that to approximate your daily caloric requirements, you multiply your body weight in pounds by about 13 calories. A 150 pound woman needs about 13x150 or about 2000 calories per day to maintain her weight. You can do the same to get the approximate number of calories needed daily by your baby. But instead of using 13, use the number 50, because your baby needs about 50 calories per pound of body weight. Wouldn't it be nice if we could use that number? That same 150 pound woman would be able to eat 7500 calories a day without gaining weight!

A baby needs a lot more energy per pound than we do, because of his fast growth rate and activity level.

Your Baby's Caloric Needs

Your baby knows how many calories she needs and will eat accordingly. If you are concerned that she is eating too little or too much, the next table may help in determining if your concerns are legitimate. Of course, calorie requirements vary with each baby, but the averages in the table will give you a rough idea of the number of calories your baby should be eating. If your baby is eating significantly less or more than the amount recommended for her age, consult your pediatrician. These numbers that follow are average caloric recommendations for babies at the age and weight.

A More Accurate Daily Caloric Requirement for Your Baby

A more accurate number for your individual baby's recommended daily calories can be computed by multiplying her weight in pounds by the number associated with her age below. Depending on the individual baby and the particular day, calorie requirements will still vary from this number by up to 10% above or below.

0-3 months	55 calories per pound of body weight
3-6 months	52 calories per pound of body weight
6-9 months	50 calories per pound of body weight
9-12 months	47 calories per pound of body weight
1-3 years	45 calories per pound of body weight

Example: If your baby is 10 months old and weighs 19 pounds, multiply 19 by 47 to get 893. Caloric needs can vary by 10% above or below. 10% of 893 is about 89, so the lower limit is 893 89 = 804, and the upper limit is 893 + 89 = 982. Therefore, your baby should be getting between 804 and 982 calories per day.

Your Baby's Fat Needs

It is important for proper growth and development that your baby get enough fat. The table below lists the amounts of fat in the *Super Baby Foods*. The second numeric column gives the fat grams in the food, and the third column gives the number of calories in the food that come from fat. The fourth column gives the percentage of fat in the foods. Nuts, seeds, and avocado are mostly fat—the good fat that your baby needs for growth and proper brain development. Eggs, milk, yogurt, and cheese also supply good amounts of fats, but these fats are saturated and less healthy than the unsaturated fats in nuts and seeds.

To use the table to determine if your baby is getting enough (or too much) fat in his diet, total up the number of fat grams from the food that your baby has eaten in one day and confirm that the number fits in the recommended range at the top of the table for your baby's age group.

Your Baby's Average Daily Recommended Calories and Fat

0 to 6 months (13 lbs)	715 calories and 25-40 fat grams
6 to 12 months (20 lbs)	1,000 calories and 33-52 fat grams
1 to 3 years (29 lbs)	1,300 calories and 50-79 fat grams

Calories and Fat in the Super Baby Foods

Calories and Fat in Super Baby Foods	Calories	Fat Grams	Calories from Fat
2 T Brussels sprouts	12	0	0
2 T beets	12	0	0
2 T carrots	10	0	0
2 T broccoli	10	0	0
2 T asparagus	6	0	0
2 T beet greens	6	0	0
2 T cauliflower	7	0	0
2 T sweet potatoes	21	0	0
2 T canned pumpkin	10	0	0
1 oz Calif. avocado	47	4	36
1 oz mashed banana	25	0	0
½ C orange juice	56	0	0
⅛ C rolled oats/oatmeal	109	2	16
1 oz toasted wheat germ	108	3	27
1 oz raw wheat germ	101	3	27
⅛ C millet	94	2	10
⅛ C amaranth	31	1	5
1 oz teff	103	1	6
1 oz couscous	32	0	0
⅛ C brown rice	27	0	0
⅛ C triticale	94	1	5

Calories and Fat in Super Baby Foods	Calories	Fat Grams	Calories from Fat
⅛ C quinoa	103	2	15
⅛ C buckwheat groats	97	1	6
⅛ C rye berries	94	1	6
⅛ C cornmeal, whole grain	101	1	8
⅛ C whole wheat flour	95	1	4
⅛ C bulgur	96	0	0
⅛ C pearled barley	24	0	0
1 oz tofu	21	1	11
⅛ C soybeans	32	2	15
⅛ C chickpeas	34	1	7
⅛ C mung beans	90	0	0
⅛ C navy beans	32	0	0
⅛ C split peas	40	0	0
⅛ C pinto beans	97	0	0
⅛ C lentils	99	0	0
⅛ C adzuki beans	92	0	0
⅛ C black turtle beans	95	0	0
⅛ C Great Northern beans	95	0	0
⅛ C kidney beans	94	0	0
⅛ C lima beans	95	0	0
1 oz Brazil nuts	186	17	166
1 oz walnuts	183	18	164
1 oz filberts	176	17	154
1 oz almonds	163	14	126
1 oz cashews	160	12	108
1 T pumpkin seeds	56	5	45
1 oz sunflower seeds	149	11	98
1 oz peanuts	161	14	125
1 T flaxseed	33	2	19
1 T chia seeds	69	5	54

Calories and Fat in Super Baby Foods	Calories	Fat Grams	Calories from Fat
1 T almond butter	102	9	81
1 T tahini	89	8	67
½ C breast milk	80	4	46
½ C formula	72	4	36
½ C milk, 3.25%	73	4	36
½ C milk, 2%	69	3	21
½ C whole milk yogurt	75	4	35
1 oz cheddar cheese	113	9	84
1 oz natural Swiss cheese	108	8	68
1 oz mozzarella, part skim	71	4	39
½ C cottage cheese	116	5	46
1 oz ricotta, part skim	39	2	19
1 T grated Parmesan	22	1	13
1 T butter	100	11	100
1 large egg, whole	72	5	45
1 large egg, yolk	54	5	41
1 T blackstrap molasses	58	0	0
¾ cup Super Porridge*	100	2	18

* The amount of calories and fat in *Super Porridge* depends, of course, on the grain and legume ingredients.

Nutritional Analysis of a Sample Menu for Calories, Fat Grams, Protein Grams, and % of Calories from Fat

Meal	Calories	Fat	Protein
morning 8 oz formula/breast milk	160	8	8
Breakfast			
¾ cup Super Porridge	100	2	4
1 whole egg	72	5	6.3
2 T broccoli	10	0	1
1½ tsp nutritional yeast	20	0	3
½ cup orange juice	56	0	1
Morning Snack			
⅓ cup Oatio's	49	.7	.9
2 T carrot	10	0	0
½ cup (4 oz) formula/breast milk	80	4	4
Lunch			
½ cup yogurt	75	4	4.5
1 T tahini	89	8	3
1 tsp flax seeds	25	2	1
2 oz avocado	94	8	2
Afternoon Snack			
3 oz kiwi fruit	51	0	0
½ slice whole wheat bread	33	.5	1.5
½ cup formula/breast milk	80	4	4
Supper			
¾ cup Super Porridge	100	2	4
banana	90	0	1
½ cup formula/breast milk	80	4	4
Bedtime			
8 oz formula/breast milk	160	8	8
TOTAL	1,431	60.2	61.2

For complete nutritional information and nutrient tables for all *Super Baby Foods*, visit my web site, **www.superbabyfood.com** for a free download.

Part VI

Recipes

35

Baby Recipes

Remember to check with your pediatrician before starting solid foods!

All of these recipes are designed around the following commandment:

**Thou shalt spend the least possible amount of time
in the kitchen and the most possible amount of time
enjoying your beautiful baby.**

Most of these recipes are super healthy for your baby or toddler and take only a few minutes of your time to prepare. There is not a fancy, two-dozen-steps, gourmet recipe in the bunch. The recipes are quick because they contain few ingredients—foods that are natural, whole, and minimally processed. It is ironic that the healthiest baby foods are also the foods that require little or no preparation: fresh fruits, yogurt, cheeses and other milk products, cereals, raw nuts and seeds, and plain vegetables. Lucky thing for us busy parents that these plain, simple foods are the absolute best and most nutritious foods for our babies.

> **TIP:** To make your kids feel special, name recipes after them. For example, the "Johnny Casserole" or the "Mary Broccoli Recipe." I once named a yogurt dip after one of my sons, and literally a year later (after I had long forgotten it), he remembered it was named after him. This is also a great way to get your kids to eat a healthy food that they don't particularly like!

Food Staples

Almost all of the ingredients in the recipes are staple foods that you should always have on hand in your kitchen. Many of them keep well at room temperature for extended time periods. Some, such as grains and legumes, store for up to a year. Because you don't have to worry about limited refrigerator or freezer space, or a short shelf life and wasted food due to spoilage, you can stock up when they go on sale.

You may want to further increase your food savings by joining a food co-op (short for cooperative). A co-op is a group of people that join together to buy foods in bulk at reduced prices.

Keep on hand as many as possible of the food staples listed in Chapter 17. If you haven't read the rest of the book, know that each of these food staples is discussed somewhere in this book, with details and instructions on how to prepare and store each one.

> **TIP:** Running out of milk is a catastrophe in a house with a toddler. For just this emergency, always keep a can of evaporated milk (not sweetened condensed milk, which is 40% sugar!) or some nonfat dry milk on hand in the cabinet and follow the directions to reconstitute it. Or, better yet, pick up a can of Better Than Milk. Use it when you run out of fresh milk, or in place of fresh milk. Soy milk enriched with calcium and vitamin D is another type of staple milk. It will keep unopened in the aseptic box for months until its expiration date—so always keep some in the cabinet. Give your baby enriched soy milk to get him used to the taste, so that he will continue to drink it into adulthood.

Baby Recipes – Purées!

Purée Vegetable Basics

Puréeing is all the rage and thank goodness. With just a few tips under your belt, you can prepare your baby food using organic, delicious vegetables and here is the best part—you will know exactly what is in the food you give your baby! I will use the term "processor" to refer to your blender, your processor, your food mill, or whatever you are using to purée. To get the correct liquidy consistency necessary for beginner eaters, water must be added to the food mixture being processed.

For most vegetables, use the water in which they were cooked, whether the water is from steaming, baking, or boiling. This water contains valuable nutrients that have leached out of the vegetables during cooking.

Place chunks of cooked vegetables into the bowl of the processor so that it is almost full. Make sure you leave some head room. Add a tablespoon or two of the cooking water. Cover, keep your hand on the lid, and start the processor. Pour water very slowly through the hole in the top of the processer until the food moves freely. Use the least amount of water necessary to get the consistency you need for your baby's age.

Purée Fruit Basics

Place whole fruit, complete with skin (think nectarine, peach, apple, pear) in boiling water for approximately 45 seconds. Remove the whole fruit with a slotted spoon and into a bowl filled with a few ice cubes and some cold water (an ice water bath.) The skins should be easy to remove with fingers or a paring knife. Once skinned, remove the pit or seeds and cube the reminder of the fruit.

Save the water in which the fruit was cooked for later use.

Place the cubed fruit into your blender with a bit of the reserved liquid. Since fruit has a lot of liquid anyway, you might not need to add much reserved water. Purée away!

Once blended put the pureed fruit through the holes of a strainer to remove small seeds and any bits of remaining peel.

The recipes that follow will give you ideas for beginner baby foods. The variations are endless. Once you get the hang of it you can easily create your own. I encourage you to share your creations with everyone on our website at www.superbabyfood.com.

Recipes for Babies 6 to 7 Months Old

Consistency at this age should pour off the spoon into the baby's mouth!

The Avocado Smash

Avocado is a terrific first food for baby!

- Take a sharp knife and cut avocado in half crosswise.
- Remove the huge seed.
- Use a spoon to scoop out flesh from peel and place on a flat dish.
- Use a fork to mash flesh on dish.
- Adjust the consistency with some breast milk or formula.

The Banana Smash

Talk about handy, bananas are nutritious and versatile—when the time is right you can add many goodies to it.

- Peel an organically-grown banana.
- Fork mash or purée in your blender.
- Adjust the consistency with some breast milk or formula.

Puréed Cooked Pears

- Select firm, plump pears. Rinse well.
- Place pears in a pot of boiling water for 45 seconds.
- Remove from pot with a slotted spoon and put into an ice bath.
- Remove peels with fingers or a paring knife.
- Remove seeds and cube the remaining fruit.
- Place fruit cubes in blender and purée away!
- Add a bit of liquid to achieve desired consistency.
- Push purée through strainer to remove any seeds and/or peels.

Puréed Cooked Peas

- Select crisp, bright green pea pods.
- Remove peas from pods. Place in a colander and rinse well.
- Steam peas for 8 minutes or until tender, reserving the liquid.
- Place peas in blender with some reserved liquid and purée away!
- Place purée through a strainer to remove remaining skins.

Puréed Cooked Sweet Potato

- Wash sweet potato by scrubbing gently.
- Steam whole sweet potato for 30 or more minutes or
- Place potatoes in a pot of boiling water on the stove and cover for 20-30 minutes until tender.
- Drain boiling water (save a bit of the liquid) and drop potatoes into cold water, the peels will slip right off.
- Cut cooked potato in half and then half again.
- Place pieces into blender or processor with a bit of the reserved liquid.
- Make sure there are no fibers left in the puree as they are choking hazards (a mixer is sometimes better with a larger potato because the fibers stick to the beaters).
- Add liquid (breast milk or formula) for desired consistency.

Puréed Cooked Peaches

- Select firm, or slightly soft peaches. Rinse well.
- Place peaches in a pot of boiling water for 45 seconds.
- Remove from pot with a slotted spoon and put into an ice bath.
- Remove peels with fingers or a paring knife.
- Remove pit and cube the remaining fruit.
- Place fruit cubes in blender and purée away!
- Add a bit of liquid to achieve desired consistency.
- Place purée through strainer to remove remaining peels.

Puréed Cooked Nectarines

- Select plump, smooth nectarines. Rinse well.
- Place nectarines in a pot of boiling water for 45 seconds.
- Remove from pot with a slotted spoon and put into an ice bath.
- Remove peels with fingers or a paring knife.
- Remove pit and cube the remaining fruit.
- Place fruit cubes in blender and purée away!
- Add a bit of liquid to achieve desired consistency.
- Place purée through strainer to remove remaining peels.

Single Grain Super Porridge

¼ cup brown rice (organic, whole kernel)

1 cup water

- Measure 1 cup of water and place into a pot on the stove to boil.
- Measure ¼ cup brown rice into your blender. Grind well, for about 2 minutes. (it's going to be very loud, but it's important to let the blender grind the brown rice down) If you have a coffee grinder, you may find it works better than a blender. Do not use a food processor, as it does not grind grains well.
- When the water starts to boil on the stove, turn the heat down to the lowest setting.
- Sprinkle the ground rice into the water while stirring briskly with a wire whisk.
- Cover the pot and keep it on low heat for about 10 minutes.
- Whisk frequently to prevent scorching and to remove lumps.
- Let cool.
- Adjust the consistency with some breast milk or formula.

Recipes for Babies 8 to 9 Months Old

Consistency at this age should be as thick as cream: smooth and lump-free!

Puréed Cooked Summer Squash

- Select young, small or medium summer squash. They are soft and moist.
- Wash thoroughly.
- Cut off ends and discard the ends.
- Cut into uniform pieces.
- Steam pieces for 5-7 minutes or until tender, reserving the liquid.
- Place pieces in blender with some reserved liquid. Purée away!
- Place purée through a strainer to remove remaining skins.

Puréed Cooked Carrots

- Select small to medium sized carrots that are firm.
- Wash thoroughly and peel.
- Cut off ends and discard the ends.
- Cut into uniform pieces.
- Steam pieces for 20 minutes or until tender, reserving the liquid.
- Place pieces in blender with some reserved liquid. Purée away!

Brown Rice and Millet Super Baby Porridge

¼ cup brown rice, organic whole kernel
3 tablespoons millet
2 cups water

- Ground brown rice and millet together into fine powder in blender.
- Bring water to a boil and then reduce heat to lowest setting.
- Sprinkle the powder into the water and stir with a wire whisk.
- Adjust the consistency with some breast milk or formula.

High Protein Super Porridge

¼ cup brown rice, organic, whole kernel
hard cooked egg yolk
1½ tablespoons tofu – mashed
1 cup water

- In a blender, ground brown rice to a fine powder.
- Bring water to boil, then reduce heat to lowest setting.
- Sprinkle the fine brown rice powder into the water while stirring with a wire whisk.
- Add mashed egg yolk and mashed tofu.
- Adjust the consistency with some breast milk or formula.

Recipes for Babies 10 to 11 Months Old

Consistency at this age should be gradually thickening!

Puréed Cooked Broccoli

- Select medium bunches with small, tightly closed green buds.
- Wash thoroughly.
- Cut off 1 inch at the end. Peel the stalks as you would a carrot.
- Cut so that only the florets remain.
- Steam broccoli florets, 8-10 minutes or until tender, reserving the liquid.
- Place pieces in blender with some reserved liquid. Purée away!

Puréed Cooked Asparagus

- Select firm, bright green, fat stalks.
- Wash thoroughly.
- Cut off 1 inch at the end. Peel the stalks as you would a carrot
- Cut into uniform pieces.
- Steam pieces for 5 minutes or until tender, reserving the liquid.
- Place pieces in blender with some reserved liquid. Purée away!

Recipes for Babies 11 to 12 Months Old

Consistency at this age should be thickening more!

Puréed Cooked Cauliflower

- Select clean, creamy white cauliflower.
- Wash thoroughly.
- Cut so that only the florets remain.
- Steam florets, 10 minutes or until tender, reserving the liquid.
- Place pieces in blender with some reserved liquid. Purée away!

Puréed Cooked Kale

- Select kale that is loose and not in plastic bags.
- Wash each leaf under cold water.
- Discard unwanted leaves.
- Remove stems.
- Steam leaves, 5 minutes, reserving the liquid.
- Place pieces in blender with some reserved liquid. Purée away!

Note: Kale has a very strong flavor; try mixing with mashed banana!

Legume Super Porridge

Makes 2 cups of high protein *Super Porridge*

⅓ cup brown rice, organic, whole kernel (or millet or oatmeal)

⅛ cup dried lentils

2 cups water

- Ground brown rice and lentils in blender to a fine powder.
- Bring two cups of water to a boil.
- Sprinkle the fine powder into the water while stirring with a wire whisk.
- Reduce heat to low and cook for 10 minutes, stirring frequently.
- Adjust the consistency with some breast milk or formula.

Baby Applesauce

This recipe makes about 1 cup.

2 medium-sized apples

1½ tablespoons water or juice

- Wash apples and peel, if you wish.
- Remove seeds and core, and chop.
- Purée in blender or food processor, adding just enough apple juice or water so that food moves freely.

- Add a little lemon juice, if you wish, to prevent darkening.
- Serve with *Healthy Extras.*

Store, tightly covered, in refrigerator for up to one week, or freeze for up to 2 months.

Variation: Cook the apples after chopping. Place the apple pieces in covered pot with 1½ tablespoons of water or juice. Cook over low-medium heat for 2 minutes per apple. Pour apple pieces and water/juice into blender to purée—extra liquid will not be necessary.

36

Toddler Recipes

Use The Batch and Freeze Method

There are a few recipes that have too many ingredients, take too many steps, and require too many mixing bowls and pans to be called simple. For these more involved recipes, I suggest that you make and freeze several batches. You've been making *Super Baby Food* for the last several months (I hope), so batch cooking and freezing is nothing new to you.

Toddler TV Dinners

Supermarket TV dinners are expensive and again, in my opinion, not worth the convenience. They're also high in sodium and loaded with junk—just look at the long list of unpronounceable ingredients. Why not make your own? When you're cooking, double or triple the recipe and freeze the extras to create your own homemade TV dinners. Do this for your family's meals as well as your toddler's meals, if you have enough freezer space. Luckily, toddler-sized meals don't take up much room in the freezer.

Toddler Take-Along Lunches

Don't buy those over-priced lunch packs that are nothing more than a few pieces of salty luncheon meat, crackers made from white flour, and candy pieces. The convenience of the packaging will ruin your pocketbook and our planet. (What will the food industry think of next!). Put whole grain crackers, natural cheese slices, halved-grapes, and other Super Snacks into a BPA-free lunch container. Cut the cheese slices and other foods into fun shapes using cookie cutters. You don't need to have a different food in each compartment—alternate the foods to make it look like there is a nice selection. Cover with wax paper to keep the foods in their bins. Add a napkin over the wax paper. Tape a picture inside the top of the container so your child will see it when she opens the carton. A heart to remind your child that you love her will help make your child happy while she's away from home.

Super Healthy Two-Minute Meal

Mash an avocado and or banana and, optionally, add a little lemon juice. Add *Healthy Extras*, like wheat germ, ground nuts/seeds, and mashed beans for a complete meal. I put this simple recipe here to remind you that as long as you have some *Healthy Extras* as food staples in your kitchen and bananas on the counter, you've got a very healthy meal that your child will love. Keep "whole grains, beans, nuts, seeds, fruits, and veggies" in your kitchen as a constant reminder to add whole grains, cooked beans, and raw nuts and seeds to your child's food as often as possible.

Fruit Recipes

Cold Fresh Fruit Purée Soup

In a blender or food processor, purée fresh juicy fruits, such as cantaloupes, peaches, watermelon, kiwis, or honeydew. Put them in the freezer for ½ hour to make them really cold. Add a touch of lemon or lime juice. This soup can be served in natural melon rind bowls.

Variation: Add one tablespoon of plain yogurt for each ½ cup of "soup." Add *Healthy Extras*.

Broiled Fruit Wedges

Broil fruit wedges (apples, bananas, pears, pineapple chunks, peaches, orange wedges) under broiler about 5 minutes or until tender. Optionally sprinkle with lemon juice first. Serve plain or with yogurt/fruit topping.

Applesauce Custard

Preheat oven to 350°F. In blender, mix until smooth:

    1 cup applesauce
    ½ cup pears or other puréed fruit or more applesauce
    1 cup low-fat milk
    4 beaten eggs
    ½ teaspoon cinnamon

Place in individual custard cups and top with a pinch of cinnamon. Set cups into shallow baking pan filled with hot water so it comes up 1 inch on sides of cups. Bake 50 minutes or until cake tester or toothpick comes out clean. Refrigerate, covered well, and eat within 2-3 days. Serve cool.

Apple Smiley Face

Grate an apple in the processor. Mix with 1 tablespoon of peanut butter or other nut butter. Optionally add 1 teaspoon honey or maple syrup or blackstrap molasses and a pinch of cinnamon and/or nutmeg. Add

Healthy Extras—grated carrots are good. Place on small plate and form into pancake-shaped face. *Decorative Touches* form eyes, nose, hair, etc.

Apple Crisp
Preheat oven to 350°F. Blend using pastry blender or fork until flaky:
- ¾ cup Super Flour
- ½ cup brown sugar
- ½ teaspoon cinnamon
- 4-6 tablespoons butter

Arrange 4 cups of peeled, cored, sliced apples in an 8-inch square baking dish. Sprinkle mixture over apples. Bake for 60-90 minutes until apples are tender.

Baked Apples
Wash a few uniformly-sized apples. Remove the cores without cutting through the bottom of the apple. Leaving a little of the core in the bottom will prevent the stuffing from leaking out.

Slit the peel in a few spots to prevent wrinkles. Stuff them with plumped raisins or dates, re-hydrated dried apricot pieces, and/or ground nuts or seeds. Optionally add a dash of cinnamon and/or nutmeg. It's not necessary, but add a teaspoon or two of maple syrup or honey if you wish.

Press the stuffing firmly into the cored hole with your fingers or the back of a teaspoon. Dot a bit of butter on top of the stuffing, if you like.

Place apples in a covered baking pan or dish with a little water or apple juice in the bottom to prevent scorching. If they are wobbly, slice a little off the bottoms to make them flatter and more stable, or place them in a muffin tin for support.

Bake at 350°F for about 45 minutes or until tender. Toaster ovens are a nice appliance for baking a few apples. After baking, you might want to add a bit of yogurt, whipped cream, or *Mock Whipped Cream*, and a dash of cinnamon, or vanilla ice cream on top of the apples.

Or while baked apples are still hot, top with a little honey to be absorbed by the apples—it will not get burned as it would when spread on top before baking.

Tip: Bake apples in muffin tins. Fill tins with a little apple juice or water first.

Baked Stuffed Apples
These are very similar to baked apples, except instead of just removing the core of the apple, you also remove most of the fruit inside. In other words, hollow out the apple as much as possible with a spoon or a melon baller.

Leave enough inside the apple so that it won't collapse—about ½-inch walls. Preheat oven to 350°F.

Cut a ½-inch slice horizontally off the top, so that you have access to the innards. Purée the apple pulp in your processor with ¼ cup of tofu for each apple.

Place mixture in bowl and add for each apple:

> 1 tablespoon of shredded mozzarella cheese
> 6-7 raisins
> 2 tablespoons of cooked millet or other grain
> pinch of cinnamon and nutmeg

Spoon mixture into apples and cover with apple tops. Bake for about 45 minutes or until tender.

Avocado Cube Salad

Cut small cubes of avocado and/or banana and/or tofu. Drizzle with a little lemon juice and honey (about 1 tablespoon per cup of cubes). My kids loved this as an outdoors summer afternoon snack.

Banana Pancakes

Mash or purée banana. Shape into small pancakes and dredge in ground nuts/seeds. Serve raw immediately.

Banana Sandwiches

Slice banana in half lengthwise. Spread peanut butter inside and put banana slices (which act as bread slices) together to make a sandwich. These are a little messy, but fun to eat!

Variation: Apple sandwiches can be made with 2 apple slices or 1 cracker spread with peanut butter and topped with an apple slice. Or, instead of peanut butter, use another sandwich spread.

Broiled Bananas

Peel banana and cut lengthwise and then horizontally into small pieces. Place on oil-sprayed baking sheet cut side up and sprinkle with cinnamon, nutmeg, and a little honey/brown sugar. Broil until warmed.

Healthy "Hot Dog"

Spread one slice of whole grain bread with peanut butter. Place a small whole banana dog on the bread and fold bread up around sides of banana, so that it resembles a hot dog. Paint a face on the banana with extra peanut butter.

Variation: Use tahini or jelly/jam instead of peanut butter.

Canoes for Riding the Rapids

A slightly curved, shorter banana is good for this recipe. Wash the outside of a banana. Make a vertical slit down one side of the unpeeled banana leaving about ½ inch uncut at each end. If the banana is curved, make the slit on the "upside" so that it's shaped like a canoe. Open slit and carefully scoop out the flesh.

Fork-mash half of the banana and mix with ½ cup of mashed tofu, 2 tablespoons of ground seeds, 1 tablespoon of wheat germ, and honey to taste. Spread banana peel open gently and make bottom of canoe flat by pressing with fingers so that it will be stable, being careful not to rip ends.

Return mixture to inside of banana. You can trim around the slit with a sharp knife to make the opening wider.

Use the other half of the banana flesh to shape fish and rocks, roll in wheat germ, and place them around the canoe. These dangerous rocks must be avoided to prevent the canoe from breaking apart.

Make oars out of carrot or celery sticks or anything else handy. Place small plastic toy figures (large enough not to be swallowed or choked on) in canoe or make your own out of *Decorative Touches*.

Submarines Exploring the Deep

Make the canoes in the previous recipe, but close the slit after stuffing. You'll have to use a little less filling. Place a piece of banana on the top middle of the submarine as its periscope, and add a banana piece shaped like a propeller to the back. Leftover banana pieces can be fish, sharks, turtles, and octopuses. No need for missiles, because this is a peaceful voyage.

Dolphins in the Ocean Blue (Blueberry Bake)

Preheat oven to 400°F. Grease a 2 quart casserole. In a large bowl, mix:
    4 cups of blueberries
    2½ tablespoons arrowroot
    1 tablespoon lemon juice
Pour fruit mixture into casserole. In a large bowl, mix:
    1 cup Super Flour
    1 teaspoon baking powder
    1 tablespoon butter or oil
    1 cup milk
Pour over fruit mixture. Bake for 50 minutes until nicely browned.

Serve with yogurt topping: 1 cup yogurt mixed in blender with 2 tablespoons honey or maple syrup and enough blueberries to make the yogurt an ocean blue color. Place a small toy ship and/or dolphin on top or use blueberries or other *Decorative Touches* to draw them.

Variation: Instead of dolphins, let there be sharks. Stick triangular-shaped *Decorative Touches* into the topping to simulate shark fins. Or for a more tame depiction of fish in water, use deep yellow or orange veggie pieces to make goldfish in a pretty blue aquarium. Green veggies can be ocean turtles or seaweed. Or buy those commercial fish cracker snacks.

Variations for topping: Instead of blueberries, use strawberries and make a pinkish-red topping for a Valentine Cake. On top, make a heart-shape with strawberry halves for your special Valentine. Or you can make this any day as an "I Love You" cake. Blueberries and strawberries mashed together make purple, like the color of imaginary dinosaurs.

Kiwi Health Cereal

Dice or mash a kiwi with fork. Add cottage cheese, wheat germ, and a little honey or maple syrup. Add a pinch or two of brewer's yeast (whose bitter flavor will be hidden by the sweetness of the kiwi and honey) for an extra nutritional punch. The vitamin C in the kiwi works well with the calcium in the cottage cheese and the iron in the wheat germ.

Variation: Instead of kiwi, you can use banana; instead of cottage cheese, you can use yogurt or yogurt cheese.

Melon Baskets

Carve a watermelon, cantaloupe, or other melon into a basket with a handle. Fill with melon balls, grapes, and other fresh fruit pieces.

Variation: Instead of a basket, design a whale out of a watermelon.

Melon Yogurt Bowls

Wash uncut whole cantaloupe (or honeydew or papaya). Cut cantaloupe in half (lengthwise or width-wise) and reserve the rind shells for later use as bowls. Scoop out seeds. Use melon baller to scoop out balls. Place melon balls into shell bowls with ¼ to ½ cup plain yogurt for each bowl. Sprinkle ground nuts on top. Serve immediately for maximum nutrients.

Kids will love the natural bowls. If the bowls are rolling around and unstable, slice a little piece off the bottom to make it flatter. On picnics, bowls are also disposable.

Stuffed Peach Halves

Slice ripe peach in half and remove pit. Stuff with mixture of:
  1 tablespoon peanut butter
  1 tablespoon tahini

1 teaspoon maple syrup

2 drops vanilla

Variation: Use an apricot or a nectarine instead of peach.

Dried Peach Millet Pudding

Preheat oven to 325°F. In processor, grind 1 cup dried peaches (or other dried fruit) into a powder.

In a baking dish, mix peaches with:

4 cups milk

½ cup uncooked millet

¼ cup honey

Bake, uncovered for 2½ hours, stirring occasionally.

Refrigerate and pudding will thicken as it cools.

Pineapple Tubbie or Sailing Ship

Like melon rinds, the pineapple shell makes a great natural bowl. We pretend it's a bathtub and the fruit purée is the bubble bath water. Put little plastic toy people or other cartoon characters in the tub and pretend they're bathing.

To make the tubbie, wash and slice the pineapple in half lengthwise. You can leave its stem sticking out at one end or cut off the stem and stick it into the tubbie. (Your child will come up with some explanation for what the stem is.)

Remove the flesh with sharp knife, leaving ¼ inch wall and floor. Be careful not to cut through the bottom of the shell. Discard the hard core part and use the tender flesh to make the fruit purée or diced fruit.

Add other fruits to the tubbie if you wish.

Strawberry Pizza

Preheat oven to 350°F. For crust, mix:

½ cup wheat germ

½ cup ground oatmeal

1 beaten egg

1 tablespoon melted butter or oil

Press into bottom of a 9-inch pie plate; don't go up the sides. Bake for 10 minutes.

For filling, mix:

½ cup of yogurt cheese (or cottage cheese)

1 tablespoon of orange juice or other fruit concentrate

Spread filling on crust.

For topping: Arrange fresh strawberries over filling into a design or shape or letter. Cut with pizza cutter. Keep refrigerated or freeze.

Variation: Replace strawberries with other fruit or use a mixture of fresh fruit.

Easy Fruit Pastries

Preheat oven to 325°F. Cream together:

3 tablespoons melted butter

¼ cup tofu

½ cup Super Flour

Chill dough in refrigerator until firm. Roll between waxed paper , making a 12 x 12-inch square. Cut dough into 16 squares.

Place 1 teaspoon of fruit purée or jam in center of each square. Pull up the 4 corners of each square over the center and crimp edges together, encasing the fruit and forming an X. Bake for 18-20 minutes until edges become slightly browned.

Vegetable Recipes

Acorn Squash Bowls

Bake squash. Scoop out flesh, being careful to keep rind intact. Add a tablespoon or two of orange juice, maple syrup, or honey into mashed flesh. Return mashed squash to acorn bowls. Add *Healthy Extras*.

Cream of Broccoli Soup

2 cups milk

1 cup chopped raw broccoli

1 tablespoon butter

1 cup vegetable stock or water

Blend in blender until smooth. In saucepan, bring to boil. Cover and cook over medium heat for 20 minutes, stirring frequently.

Cabbage Coleslaw

Shred some raw cabbage. For each cup of shredded cabbage, add:

⅓ cup of mayonnaise

1 teaspoon lemon juice

½ 1 teaspoon honey or maple syrup

½ teaspoon apple cider vinegar

"Creamed" Cabbage

Finely shred 2 cups of raw cabbage (about ¼ of a small head). Cook, covered, in a pan over medium heat with 1 teaspoon of water and 1 tablespoon butter for 4-5 minutes until tender. Remove from heat, stir in 3 tablespoons yogurt or yogurt cheese, cottage cheese, or sour cream and serve. Sprinkle with fresh parsley.

Pineapple Flavored Cabbage

Over low heat in covered pan, cook sliced cabbage in pineapple juice (about ½ cup juice per half head of cabbage) until tender. Optionally add a tablespoon of butter or olive oil for more flavor.

Carrot Salad

Shred a cup of raw carrot in the processor. Mix in 2 teaspoons lemon juice or orange juice and 2 tablespoons yogurt cheese or cream cheese. Add *Healthy Extras*. Optionally, substitute raw zucchini for carrot.

Pennies for Your Thoughts (Parsleyed Carrots)

Toss 1 pound sliced, cooked carrots with:
- 1-2 tablespoons butter
- 1 tablespoon lemon juice
- 2 tablespoons finely chopped fresh parsley

Play the game "A Penny for Your Thoughts" with your child. Every time your child eats a carrot slice—a penny, you have to tell him one of your thoughts: I think you're great! I'll always love you! What a lucky Mom/Dad I am to have a daughter/son like you! And every time you eat a penny, your child has to tell you her thought.

Cucumbers and Yogurt

Mix 1 tablespoon lemon juice into plain yogurt. Add sliced or diced cucumbers. Add *Healthy Extras*. Or use sliced cucumbers for dipping into yogurt mixture.

Eggplant Pizza

Preheat oven to 350°F. Slice a small eggplant into thin (¼-inch) slices. Place slices on cookie sheet and cover with tomato sauce or pizza sauce and top with shredded cheese. Add other toppings if you wish. Bake 15-20 minutes until cheese is melted and lightly browned. Use spatula to place on serving dish.

Tasty Eggplant Slices

Preheat oven to 450°F. Slice eggplant into ½-inch thick slices. Spread with tofu mayonnaise from the natural foods store. Sprinkle with wheat germ or whole grain bread crumbs, grated Parmesan cheese, and oregano. Bake on cookie sheet for 15 minutes.

Stuffed Froggies

Stuff half of a green pepper with *Super Porridge* or any *Super Sandwich Spreads*. Place upside down on a plate. Add eyes using a green olive sliced in half, legs shaped from the other half of the green pepper, and warts! Warts can be flax seeds or brown rice grains or any other small food pieces. If eyes and warts won't stick to the green pepper, wet the pepper with water or honey before sticking.

A-C-E-G: All Children Eat Grass

Cook greens according to one of the methods below. Place on a plate and pretend they are a green field of grass on a farm. Add little toy farm animals. Your toddler will love to pretend he's a cow eating the grass. But make sure you make it clear to him that he's not to eat the grass in the back yard!

Cooking Method 1: Thaw two or three green veggie cubes. Sauté over medium heat 2 3 tablespoons chopped onion and 2 3 tablespoons walnuts in 1 teaspoon olive oil or butter until soft. Toss sautéed onions and walnuts with cooked greens. Sprinkle with 1 tablespoon lemon juice and serve immediately.

Cooking Method 2: Thaw two or three green veggie cubes. Sauté ⅓ cup chopped onion in 1 teaspoon olive oil over medium heat until soft. Add ⅓ cup of sliced fresh mushrooms and sauté 2 minutes more. Decrease to low heat and add greens. Cook, covered for 2-3 minutes. Stir frequently and watch for burning. Add 1 tablespoon of Dijon mustard and cook and stir for 2 minutes more. Serve immediately.

Variation: An adult golf enthusiast can pretend with your toddler that they're enjoying a round of golf.

Frosty the Potato Man/Woman

Place two or three circular globs of mashed potatoes on a plate. Use a spoon or ice cream scoop to shape like a snowman. Use Decorative Touches to add a hat or hair, eyes, nose, mouth, buttons, scarf, and arms.

Super Potato Porridge

1 raw potato, shredded in processor
1 cup boiling water
2 tablespoons fresh parsley (optional)
1 tablespoon melted butter (optional)

Sprinkle shredded potato into boiling water, cover, and let sit 5-10 minutes. Add parsley and melted butter.

French Fries-Not!

Don't deep fry potatoes in all that oil. Bake them instead.

Pre-heat oven to 425°F. Cut up well-washed potatoes (white or sweet) into uniform-sized quarters, eighths, French-fry shapes or ¼-inch slices. You can peel them if you wish, but it's better to leave the peels intact because they contain many nutrients.

Place the cut-up potatoes in a bowl and toss them with melted butter or olive oil. Use only one teaspoon of melted butter per potato.

Spread buttered cut-up potatoes on a cookie sheet sprayed with non-stick cooking spray. (For slices, it's easier to spread melted butter onto baking sheet and coat each side with butter.)

Bake for 20 minutes or more or until browned on all sides, turning and flipping for uniform cooking. If you wish, during last few minutes of cooking, turn on broiler and let potatoes broil for about 3 minutes, until light golden brown. Flip the chips and broil the other side. Optionally, sprinkle lightly with powdered kelp. Serve while still hot.

Baked Potato Cubes

Cube leftover baked potatoes into ½-inch cubes (leave skins on), toss in plastic bag with olive oil and herbs. Bake uncovered, flipping once or twice, at 425°F for about 45 minutes until crisp and golden brown.

At-the-Ready Frozen Baked Potatoes

Cut leftover baked potatoes in half. Scoop out flesh and mix with cheese, yogurt, chives, parsley, etc. Freeze using the *Tray Freeze Method*. Check out the prices for these commercial flavored baked potatoes in the freezer section of the supermarket!

Potato Skins

Remove the flesh from leftover baked potatoes. Brush olive oil on skins, cut into ½-inch strips, and sprinkle with a little salt, pepper, and optionally chili powder. Bake for 10 minutes at 400°F until crisp. Eat as snacks or crumpled over salads.

Healthy Potato Chips

Preheat oven to 450°F. Slice well-washed, unpeeled potatoes (about 1 pound) very thin using your processor or by hand. Spread one layer thin on a large buttered or oil-sprayed cookie sheet. Brush tops with oil. Bake for 8-10 minutes until lightly browned. Turn cookie sheet halfway through cooking for more even browning. Shake potato chips, while still warm, in paper lunch bag with 2 tablespoons of seasoning. Store in cool, dry place in plastic zipper bag.

Potato Pancakes

Chop 2 raw medium potatoes and 1 small onion in your food processor. In bowl, beat 2 eggs. Place a lightly buttered or oil-sprayed frying pan over medium heat. Mix potatoes and onions into eggs and add 1 tablespoon of Super Flour into which ¼ teaspoon of baking powder was mixed. Use a quarter cup measuring cup or a tablespoon to spoon onto lightly greased pan over medium heat. Flatten with spatula. Cook 3 minutes on each side until lightly browned. Drain on paper towels. Serve with sour cream or yogurt cheese.

Drain tip: Rip up brown paper bags and place under paper towels as bottom layers for draining grease. Saves money on paper towels.

Whole Grain "Shake and Cook" Potato Coating

Preheat oven to 350°F. Mix in bowl:
  3 tablespoons Super Flour
  1 tablespoon wheat germ
  ½ cup whole wheat bread crumbs
  2 teaspoons sugar
  1 teaspoon salt
  1 teaspoon Italian seasoning
  1 tablespoon olive oil
In plastic freezer bag, shake mixture with potatoes cut into ½-inch chunks. Place coated potato chunks on oiled baking sheet and bake for 30 minutes until brown. Store leftover mix in airtight container in refrigerator.

Mr./Ms. Sweet Potato Heads

Slice 2 cooked sweet potatoes in half. Scoop out flesh, being careful to keep skin intact to be used as a bowl later. Mash flesh and mix with:
  2 tablespoons yogurt
  1 tablespoon maple syrup or honey
  2 tablespoons orange juice

Replace mashed potato mixture into reserved skin bowls. Use Decorative Touches to make eyes, nose, mouth, hair, etc. Serve to children. For adults, you may have to reheat in oven or microwave.

Variation: Make mashed potato mixture by mixing flesh from the sweet potatoes with ¼-½ cup of puréed pineapple chunks.

Sweet Potato Pancakes

Make potato pancakes as in previous recipe, but use sweet potatoes instead. Serve with yogurt and/or applesauce.

Sunny Sweet Potato Cups

Bake a sweet potato. Meanwhile, wash one whole orange. Slice in half and remove flesh, being careful to keep rinds intact to be used as bowls later. Purée cooked sweet potato and mix with 3 tablespoons orange juice squeezed from orange flesh. Spoon into reserved orange rind bowls. Use *Decorative Touches* to draw smiley face or other design on top.

Sweet Potato Salad

4 large sweet potatoes, cooked and diced
1 onion, finely chopped
½ cup finely chopped celery
2 hard boiled eggs, sliced
½ cup mayonnaise (tofu mayo is good)

Mix together and refrigerate. Serve cold.

Spinach Loaf

Preheat oven to 350°F. Combine:
2 cups cooked frozen chopped spinach
white sauce
2 beaten eggs
1 sauteed onion, optional
½ to ¾ cup shredded cheese, optional

Pour into buttered casserole and bake 35-40 minutes until inserted knife comes out clean.

Zucchini Cheese Slices

Place Swiss (or other natural) cheese on top of zucchini slices and slip under the broiler until cheese has melted.

Zucchini Lasagna

Preheat oven to 350°F. Cut a zucchini lengthwise into lasagna-size strips about ½-inch thick. Layer in baking dish with spaghetti sauce and cheeses. Bake uncovered for about 25 minutes.

Veggie Custard

Preheat oven to 350°F. Mix until very smooth by hand or in blender:
  4 egg yolks or 2 whole eggs
  ½ cup soy or cow's milk
  4 veggie cubes—thawed or ½ cup puréed vegetables
Place in four individual custard cups. Set cups into shallow baking pan filled with hot water so it comes up 1 inch on sides of cups. Bake 50 minutes or until cake tester or toothpick comes out clean. Refrigerate, covered well, and eat within 2-3 days. Serve cool.

Veggie Marinade

In a small saucepan over low heat, mix in this order:
  ¼ cup apple cider vinegar
  2 cloves crushed garlic
  1 teaspoon dried herbs or 1 tablespoon fresh (parsley, basil, dill, etc.)
  ½ cup olive oil
Let simmer very gently for 5 minutes. Remove from heat and set aside to steep.

Meanwhile, lightly steam one pound veggies: broccoli, cauliflower, carrots, etc. Place in bowl or large freezer bag and mix with marinade.

Marinate in refrigerator for at least an hour (overnight is good). Mix occasionally. Will keep for up to one week in the refrigerator.

Variation: Add some bite-sized tofu chunks or cooked chick peas and other large beans and let marinate with the veggies.

Tip: Always marinate in the refrigerator, and never at room temperature to prevent bacterial growth.

Yogurt Recipes

Yummy Yogurt

Don't buy the flavored commercial yogurts—they are too expensive and contain too much sugar. Flavor yogurt yourself by adding fruit, vanilla, or any of the other suggestions on page 296. For extra nutrition, add *Healthy Extras*, especially freshly ground nuts/seeds and eat immediately.

Apple Cinnamon Yogurt

Add to 1 cup yogurt:
  ½ cup applesauce
  ¼ teaspoon cinnamon
  ½ teaspoon vanilla

Peanut Butter and Jelly Yogurt

Soften 2 tablespoons of creamy peanut butter for a few seconds in the microwave. Mix softened peanut butter and 2 tablespoons jelly into 1 tablespoon of milk to make it liquidy. Gently fold into plain yogurt.

Variation: Try substituting tofu for yogurt.

Tofu Recipes

Tofu can be used in addition to or instead of cheese/eggs on pizza, in sandwiches, in omelettes, and in pasta dishes.

Tofu Fingers

Preheat oven to 350°F. Slice tofu into strips. Dip into melted butter, milk, or water. Dip into and cover with a mixture of whole grain bread crumbs, wheat germ, Parmesan cheese, oregano, onion powder, and/or garlic powder. Bake on ungreased cookie sheet for 15-20 minutes, turning once. Or cook in microwave until heated through.

Tofu McNuggets

Make previous Tofu Fingers recipe, except cut tofu into chunks or cubes instead of strips.

Veggie Tofu

Mash together:
  2 tablespoons tofu
  1 thawed frozen veggie cube
  or 2 tablespoons mashed cooked veggie

Sprinkle on top:

  1 tablespoon shredded cheese (cheddar is good)

Microwave for 30-60 seconds until cheese melts or place under broiler to melt cheese.

Cherry Tofu Cream

Mix 2 parts silken tofu with 1 part frozen cherries. Mix in blender with a little lemon juice.

Maple Tofu Cream

Mix 4 parts silken tofu with 1 part maple syrup or honey. Mix in blender with a little lemon juice.

Yummy Tofu

Most of the flavor suggestions for yogurt can also be used to flavor tofu. Use silken tofu for a creamy smooth mixture. With tofu you do not have to be gentle when stirring. For extra nutrition, add *Healthy Extras*, especially freshly ground nuts/seeds and eat immediately.

No-Cook Tofu Pudding

In blender or processor, mix until smooth:
    ¼ cup soy or cow's milk
    1 cup tofu
    2 tablespoons lemon juice
    1 teaspoon honey or other sweetener or to taste
    ⅛ teaspoon vanilla
Pour into bowl or individual containers, cover well, and refrigerate. Use within a day or two.

No-Bake Tahini Tofu Custard

    1 10-ounce box tofu
    ¼ cup ground almonds
    ¼ cup tahini
    ¼ cup honey or maple syrup
    1 teaspoon almond extract
Mix all in blender. Serve chilled.

No-Bake Sweet Potato Tofu Pudding

    ½ cup cooked puréed sweet potatoes or thawed food cubes
    2 cups silken tofu
    1 teaspoon vanilla
    ½ teaspoon cinnamon
    ½ cup honey or maple syrup
Mix all in blender. Sprinkle with ½ cup ground almonds. Serve chilled.

Scrambled Tofu

Mix about two tablespoons of mashed tofu with a ¼ tsp. tamari/soy sauce. Optionally add an egg yolk or whole egg (the white part of the egg will help bind together). Mix together and fry in 1½-2 teaspoons of butter or oil.

Oven-Barbecued Tofu

Slice a pound of tofu into about 8 slices. Butter a 9 x 13 pan. Bake slices for 10-15 minutes. Flip and bake other side for 10 more minutes. Brush tops of tofu with barbecue sauce and bake 7-10 more minutes. Serve on whole wheat hamburger buns. You can also barbecue them on your outdoor grill instead of in the oven.

Tofu Salad

Grate a medium carrot. Add ½ cup or more mashed tofu and a tablespoon of lemon juice.

Tofu Cheesecake

Preheat oven to 350°F. Mix ⅔ cup wheat germ with ⅓ cup ground nuts and press into a greased 9-inch pie plate to form the crust. In a small saucepan over medium-high heat, mix 3 ounces of agar or unflavored gelatin with a 6-ounce container of fruit juice concentrate, such as orange juice or lemonade. Pour juice mixture into blender or food processor. Add:

1 pound tofu
1 tablespoon vanilla
¼ cup Super Flour

Blend until smooth. Pour into prepared pie shell and bake 25 minutes.

Variation: Make personal sized cakes by lining individual muffin tins with cupcake liners. Press crust into each liner ²/₃ up the sides. Pour tofu mixture into crusts and bake for 20-25 minutes. These freeze well.

Apple Tofu Custard

1¾ cups applesauce
1 10-ounce box silken tofu
4 eggs
1 teaspoon cinnamon

Preheat oven to 350°F.

Mix all ingredients in blender. Pour into 4 or 5 custard cups. Sprinkle a little cinnamon on top of each cup. Place the cups into a baking pan filled with water 1 inch deep. Bake 45-50 minutes, until inserted toothpick comes out clean. Refrigerate, covered well, and eat within 2-3 days. Serve cool.

Variation: Replace ½ cup of the applesauce with a 4 ounce jar of baby peaches or apricots.

Hawaiian Tofu Stir Fry

Cut a block of tofu into ½ inch cubes. Sprinkle with ¼ cup tamari/soy sauce. Drain and reserve juice from 1 can pineapple chunks. Cut 1 green and 1 sweet red pepper into triangle, square, and other shapes. Cut 1 onion into small wedges. Drain a small can of sliced water chestnuts.

In a small saucepan, whisk together ¼ cup apple cider vinegar and 2 tablespoons arrowroot or cornstarch, then mix in ¼ cup honey, ½ cup vegetable stock, and the reserved pineapple juice. Cook over medium heat until clear and bubbly while whisking continuously.

In large fry pan or wok, melt 4 tablespoons butter/oil on medium high heat. Cook onion wedges for 2 minutes, then add tofu and cook for 1-2 minutes more. Add rest of ingredients, sauce last, and stir until heated through. Serve over cooked whole grains.

Egg Recipes

Monster or Cat Eyes Stuffed Eggs

Slice 2 hard cooked eggs in half. Remove yolks and use a fork to mix yolks with:

  ½ teaspoon fresh minced parsley
  ¼ teaspoon apple cider vinegar
  ½ teaspoon prepared mustard
  2 tablespoons tofu mayonnaise

Stuff egg whites. Place olives in the middle of yolk mixture for irises of eyes. To stop eggs from rolling around, slice a bit of egg white off the bottom to flatten and make more stable. These "eyes" now look up at you!

Tip: Use a cake decorator to stuff eggs using pretty designs. Or mix stuffing for eggs directly in a freezer bag, remove air and zip bag shut, clip a corner, and squeeze stuffing into egg whites.

Sailboats

Use recipe for stuffed eggs above and place small triangular cuts of cheese slices for sails.

Variation: Use a wedge of pie instead of a stuffed egg for the boat.

Green Eggs and No Ham

Scramble an egg with broccoli, kale, or other green veggie purée. Or use a well-drained thawed food cube. To thicken, add *Healthy Extras* with the consistency of powder, such as ground oats, wheat germ, or a pinch of nutritional yeast.

Tip: A drop or two of blue food coloring added to the yellow of an egg yolk will make green eggs.

Eggs Florentine or Another Green Eggs and No Ham

Make a nest with a food cube or two of Super Green Veggies. Warm in oven for a few minutes. Scramble an egg (solid through with no raw liquid) put it in the nest. Top with a sprinkle of fresh parsley and some cheese.

Egg McHealthy Muffin

Preheat oven to 450°F. For each muffin, split a whole grain English muffin and place cut side up on an oil-sprayed baking sheet. For each muffin, beat together in a bowl:

1 egg
2 tablespoons of shredded cheese (cheddar is good)
a little parsley, oregano, basil, or other fresh herbs or
¼ teaspoon dried herbs for each muffin
a pinch of powdered kelp or salt
a pinch pepper

Place mixed ingredients on muffin and bake for 5-10 minutes.

Baked Egg Custard

4 eggs, well beaten
¼ cup maple syrup
1 teaspoon vanilla
2 cups milk

Preheat oven to 325°F. Mix first 3 ingredients. Heat the milk until it just boils and remove from heat. Pour hot milk slowly into other 3 ingredients, beating with whisk. Transfer to 6 well-buttered custard cups. Set the cups into a shallow a pan of hot water approximately 1-inch deep. Bake for 45 minutes until inserted toothpick comes out clean and custard is set. Refrigerate, well covered, and serve cool. Eat within 2-3 days. Top with *Mock Whipped Cream*.

Vanilla Custard

Preheat oven to 325°F. Combine:
⅔ cup nonfat dry milk powder
2 cup water
Then add:
⅓ cup honey
2 beaten eggs or 4 egg yolks
1¼ teaspoon vanilla

Pour into four custard cups set in a shallow pan of hot water 1 inch deep. Bake 50 minutes or until toothpick or knife comes out clean. Refrigerate, covered well, and eat within 2-3 days. Serve cool.

Pumpkin Custard

Preheat oven to 350°F. Combine:

1½ cups pumpkin purée or canned pumpkin or sweet potato purée
½ cup honey
3 beaten eggs
1⅓ cups milk
1 tablespoon arrowroot or cornstarch
1 teaspoon cinnamon
½ teaspoon ginger
¼ teaspoon ground cloves
¼ teaspoon ground nutmeg

Pour into greased baking dish and bake for 45-50 minutes or until set. Refrigerate, covered well, and eat within 2-3 days. Serve cool.

Jack-O-Lantern: Use a circular baking dish and draw triangular eyes, nose, mouth, and stem with green-colored cream cheese or yogurt cheese.

French Toast Sticks

Beat together:

2 eggs
½ cup apple juice OR milk
½ teaspoon vanilla

Pour mixture on small cookie sheet. Tear 2-3 slices of whole grain bread into pieces or sticks. Place the pieces in the mixture and wait until they completely soak up the liquid. Cook thoroughly on stove top in a greased or oil-sprayed pan so that none of the egg remains raw. Serve immediately with one of the Pancake Syrup Ideas toppings.

Banana French Toast

Mix one over-ripe banana with 2 eggs and ¾ teaspoon cinnamon. Add some milk if too thick. Use for French toast.

Baked French Toast

Instead of cooking French toast on the stove top, bake in a preheated 450°F oven on a baking sheet. Place dipped bread on sheet and bake for about 8 minutes. Flip and bake for another 8-10 minutes until all egg has been thoroughly cooked through and no raw egg remains.

Artistic Eggs

Plain scrambled eggs are unexciting. Use a baster or a clean squirt bottle to make designs for your toddler. The trick to prevent running is to let the liquidy egg mixture very slowly out of the baster and then wait until it starts to solidify. For your toddler, one egg mixed with a tablespoon of milk or apple juice is enough.

Eggie in the Middle

Take a piece of whole wheat toast and cut a circle out of the middle with the rim of a can. Place it in a greased or spray-oiled non-stick fry pan. Take a spatula and flatten the bread down, especially at the rim edge of the circle. Pour a scrambled egg into its middle. The egg won't run into the bread if you firmed up the rim of the circle with the spatula. Flip the bread and egg with the spatula to cook the other side. I sometimes have trouble doing that, so I remove the bread and just flip the egg. You can use *Decorative Touches* to make a smiley face or other design on the egg.

Grains and Cereals

Banana Super Porridge

Add a mashed banana into Super Porridge.

Oatmeal Pudding

Cook oatmeal in milk instead of water. Add a little vanilla and sweetener to taste. Tastes like pudding!

Oatmeal and Apples

Add 1 shredded apple to cooked oatmeal. Optionally add a teaspoon of maple syrup or other sweetener and a ¼ teaspoon of cinnamon.

Hodgepodge Skillet Meal

Into a large skillet, stir in one food from each of the following four groups:

Group 1: One cup of raw whole grain (rice, millet, etc) or pasta.

Group 2: A can of soup (cream of potato, cream of mushroom, tomato soup, etc.) mixed with 1½ cans of milk or water.

Group 3: ½ cup cooked beans or eggs

Group 4: 2 cups cooked or raw veggies

Bring to a boil, reduce heat to low, cover pan, and simmer 30-45 minutes until grains are done. Stir occasionally. Optionally add ½-1 cup of cheese or tofu.

Overnight Oatmeal

For the creamiest, most delicious oatmeal for breakfast, mix in a saucepan:

1 cup oatmeal
1½ cups milk
½ cup apple juice

Let sit overnight in the refrigerator. In the morning, it takes only a few minutes to warm and it is luscious! Optionally add fresh apple pieces for extra flavor and texture. And always consider adding *Healthy Extras*.

Whole Grain Crockpot Breakfast

Before going to bed, mix together in crockpot:

2 cups whole grain (1 cup brown rice and 1 cup barley go well together)
2 peeled and chopped apples
½ cup chopped dried fruit or raisins
5 cups water
¼ teaspoon cinnamon

Cook overnight on low and serve in the morning with a little honey or other sweetener and some cow's or soy milk.

Cinnamon Oatmeal

1 cup water
⅓ cup raisins
½ cup rolled oats
¼ teaspoon vanilla
½ teaspoon cinnamon
2 tablespoons tahini

In saucepan, bring water and raisins to a boil. Slowly stir in oats. Lower heat. Add vanilla and cinnamon and let cook for 10 minutes. Mix in tahini.

Cinnamon Toast

Toast lightly a slice of 100% whole grain bread. Butter one side and sprinkle with cinnamon sugar. In oven or toaster oven, broil until sugar bubbles.

Homemade Granola

Preheat oven to 350°F. Spread 5 cups oats in a 9 x 13 pan and heat in oven for 10 minutes. Meanwhile, combine in a bowl:

⅓ cup vegetable oil or butter
½ cup honey
1 teaspoon vanilla
1 cup coconut, sweetened or unsweetened
½ cup well-chopped nuts (almonds are good)

½ cup toasted wheat germ

1 teaspoon cinnamon

Mix into pan with oatmeal and bake for an additional 30 minutes, stirring frequently for even browning. After mixture cools, add:

1½ cups dried fruit (raisins, etc.)

½ cup sunflower seeds

Keep refrigerated in a tightly covered container.

Dried Fruit Cereal

Into boiling water, add ¼ cup dried apple or other dried fruit for each ½ cup of dry grains. Cook as you would *Super Porridge* or whole grains.

Pineapple Brown Rice

Cook 1 cup brown rice in 1½ cups water + ½-cup pineapple juice (instead of two cups water). When rice if finished cooking, stir in:

1 cup yogurt

1 can drained pineapple chunks or crushed pineapple

½ cup ground nuts (and/or seeds if you're going to eat it immediately)

Variation: Use another whole grain instead of brown rice and, of course, adjust water and pineapple juice amounts proportionately.

Grain & Cottage Cheese Squares

Preheat oven to 400°F.

1 cup cooked whole grains

1 cup cottage cheese, puréed smooth in blender

1 tablespoon fresh chopped parsley

1 teaspoon finely minced onion

3 eggs, separated

Mix all ingredients except egg whites. Beat egg whites until stiff and fold into mixture. Spread ½ inch thick in a rectangular buttered pan. Bake about 30 minutes.

Millet Loaf

Preheat oven to 350°F. You will need:

½ cup chopped onion

1½ cups cooked millet

2 cups cooked lentils

2 cups coarsely chopped greens (spinach is good)

In 4 tablespoons melted butter/oil, cook onion for one minute. Add chopped greens and cook for another 2 minutes. Add millet and lentils.

Add:

    2 beaten eggs
    2 medium apples, grated
    1 tablespoon lemon juice
    1 tablespoon parsley, fresh

Turn into oiled loaf pan and bake 35-40 minutes.

Polenta

Boil 2 cups water on stove. Slowly sprinkle 1 cup whole grain cornmeal into water while continuously whisking to prevent lumps. Turn heat to low and simmer for 10-15 minutes, stirring frequently. Serve with Honey Butter.

Variation: Before the last 5 minutes of simmering, add ½ cup of cheddar cheese and ½ cup of Parmesan cheese.

Wheat-Nut Loaf

Preheat oven to 350°F.

    1 cup ground nuts
    1 cup wheat germ
    1 cup shredded cheddar cheese
    1 cup tomato juice, no salt
    1 teaspoon brewer's yeast
    2 beaten eggs
    1 onion, finely chopped

Mix all ingredients and turn into greased loaf pan and bake 45 minutes.

Whole Grain Stir-Fry

Sauté in butter/oil ½-cup sliced carrots (or broccoli or other veggie) for 5 minutes. Mix in:

    1 cup cooked grains
    1 tablespoon tamari
    2 teaspoons tahini
    2 teaspoons fresh parsley

Sauté 5 minutes more.

Fried Rice

Saute ¼ cup of finely chopped onions in 1 tablespoon of butter/oil. Remove from pan. Add more butter/oil to pan and saute 1 cup cooked brown rice. Add ⅓ cup cooked green peas and 1 beaten egg and continue to saute until egg is cooked through. You can double or triple this recipe.

Variation: Replace some onion with minced green peppers and/or celery.

Bird's Nest

Make a "bird's nest" by placing cooked brown rice or other grain or mashed potatoes or other puréed vegetable into a bowl. Using the back of a spoon, form a hole in the center. Place balls of Toddler Hors d'oeuvres (page 553) in the nest as "bird's eggs." Or spoon a different vegetable, a stew, a thick soup, or other food into the nest.

Gilligan's Island (*Substitute your child's name for Gilligan*)

On a dinner plate, place a mound of cooked dark grains, such as brown rice. Some mashed banana or a little butter (softened butter, peanut or other nut butter, or tahini or other seed butter) can be used to cement them together.

Encircle the dark grains with lighter colored cooked grains/beans, such as barley, millet, or soy grits. Then surround the lighter colored grains with a light green or light blue colored purée of mashed potatoes, mashed bananas, mashed white beans, yogurt, or other white food.

The dark grain mound is the soil of the island, the light grain is sand on the beach of the island, and the green/blue food is the ocean.

The grains could be puréed for young toddlers, or use Super Porridge. Use small broccoli stalks, celery sticks, and other raw or cooked green veggies for the island's trees and shrubs. Use *Decorative Touches* to make huts, boats, fish in the ocean, sharks, etc.

Variation: Instead of going through the trouble of three circles of dark and light grains and a colored ocean, use just one mound of grains/beans with a few green veggies poked in. It's Mom's or Dad's enthusiasm that makes it fun, not a detailed work of art.

Beans, Peas, Legumes

Bananas about Beans

Mash together two tablespoons (or one food cube) cooked puréed beans, lentils, or other legumes with ⅓ to ½ banana.

Easy Bean Soup

Purée 1½-2 cups of cooked beans (or a 15- or 16- ounce can of beans) with about a cup or so of broth for a thick and creamy soup base. Add another cup or two (or another can) of whole cooked beans, not puréed. Optionally add seasonings. Heat and serve.

Easy Bean Chili

Combine in large pot:

    16-ounce jar of tomato sauce

    16-ounces of stewed tomatoes

    16-ounce can of red kidney beans or 1½-2 cups of cooked beans

    1 teaspoon blackstrap molasses

    1 teaspoon sugar or honey (optional)

Let simmer for one hour, adding up to one cup of water as chili cooks down, if needed. Before serving, stir in until melted:

    2 cups of shredded cheese (sharp cheddar is good) and/or crumbled tofu

Variation: Replace some or all of beans with reconstituted TVP.

Leftover Legume Loaf

Preheat oven to 350°F. Mix thoroughly:

    1 cup cooked legumes

    1 cup wheat germ, ground nuts, or whole grain bread crumbs or combination

    1 cup liquid (milk, soy milk, or tomato juice)

    parsley, powdered or minced garlic, onions, and other seasonings

Place mixture into loaf pan and bake about 30 minutes until firm.

Garbanzo Loaf

Preheat oven to 375°F.

    3 cups cooked garbanzos (chick peas), mashed

    ¾ cup chopped celery

    ½ cup chopped onion

    1 cup whole wheat bread crumbs

    ⅓ cup tomato sauce

    2 tablespoons Super Flour or wheat germ

    1 cup ground nuts

    3 tablespoons vegetable oil or melted butter

    3 tablespoons chopped fresh parsley or 1 tablespoon dry

    2 beaten eggs

Mix all ingredients and turn into greased loaf pan. Bake for 30 minutes or until set.

Easy Soy Loaf

Preheat oven to 350°F.

2½ cups cooked soybeans, mashed
¾ cup cottage cheese
¼ cup tomato paste
2 eggs
2 tablespoons vegetable oil
1 teaspoon salt
½ cup wheat germ

Mix above and turn into greased loaf pan. Bake for one hour or until set.

Easy Baked Beans

Preheat oven to 350°F. Place 4 cups drained, cooked beans into a large casserole dish. Mix in 2 cups barbeque sauce and 1 finely diced onion. Cover and bake for one hour, stirring occasionally, until beans are bubbly. Add a little water if beans start to dry out during baking.

Layered Soy Cheese Casserole

Preheat oven to 375°F. In heavy saucepan, sauté one chopped onion in 3-4 tablespoons of butter/oil. Add to soft onion:

2 cups cooked soybeans
1 cup evaporated milk
1 teaspoon ketchup

Stir and cook until heated through. Stir in:

3 beaten eggs

Transfer half mixture to greased casserole dish. Layer ½ cup shredded cheese over mixture or cover with cheese slices.

Layer other half of mixture over cheese. Place another layer of shredded cheese on top. Then sprinkle on top a combination of whole wheat bread crumbs and wheat germ. Bake for 40-45 minutes.

TIP: To re-heat casseroles without heating up the oven, place the covered casserole dish in a larger pan partly filled with water on the stove top.

Garbanzo Snack

Preheat oven to 400°F. In bowl, toss COOKED garbanzo beans or canned garbanzos with olive oil and herbs. Use about 1 tablespoon olive oil and 1-2 tablespoons of herbs per cup of beans. Bake on cookie sheet until nicely browned and crispy. Serve hot. Refrigerate leftovers in airtight container. Re-heat leftovers before serving again—they are much better when eaten warm.

Falafel (Garbanzo Croquettes)

1¾ cups cooked garbanzos, puréed or mashed well
1 tablespoon wheat germ
1 tablespoon bread crumbs
1 egg, well beaten
2 tablespoons fresh parsley
½ teaspoon cumin

Mix all and form into about 16 balls and flatten. Fry in a little oil three minutes on each side over medium heat. Serve with Lemon Tahini dressing.

Meatless Patties and Meatless Meals

Any of these patty mixtures can be formed into little meatless balls instead and served as *Toddler Hors d'oeuvres.*

Tip: Use the bottom of a very clean small can of tomato paste to make child-size patties. Trim whole grain bread end slices into circles the same size to make a child-size sandwich.

Tip: Use a melon baller or small scoop to make child-size patties and an ice cream scoop to make adult sized patties.

Tip: When freezing several patties, place between layers of waxed paper.

Protein Burgers

Preheat oven to 350°F. Mix 1 cup cooked grains to ⅓ cup mashed beans/legumes. Add a few tablespoons of any of these until you have the consistency of a hamburger patty:

nut butter
tahini
beaten egg
softened butter/oil
whole wheat bread crumbs
ground nuts/seeds

To flavor, add:

minced onion/garlic or powder
tamari/soy sauce or barbecue sauce
parsley/oregano

Bake in the oven at 350°F for 15-20 minutes.

Lentil Burgers

2 cups cooked lentils, mashed
1 beaten egg
2 cups cooked millet
1 chopped onion

Mix above and form into patties, adding whole wheat bread crumbs if necessary. Dip into milk and then roll in whole wheat bread crumbs or wheat germ. Fry in butter.

Apricot Burgers

In blender or processor, finely chop separately:

3 dried apricots

½ medium carrot, grated

2 tablespoons ground nuts

Mix above thoroughly with:

1½ cups cooked brown rice, bulgur or other whole grain

¼ cup raisins

In blender, process together until smooth:

1½ tablespoons tahini

2 tablespoons maple syrup

¼ cup firm tofu

Stir into apricot mixture. Shape into 4-5 adult-sized or 6-8 child-sized patties, optionally dredge in whole grain bread crumbs, and broil on each side on oiled sheet in oven or on outdoor grill until heated through and browned.

Tofu Burgers

8 ounces firm mashed tofu

1 medium minced onion

2 tablespoons wheat germ

2 tablespoons Super Flour

2 teaspoons garlic powder

2 tablespoons tamari sauce

Mix all ingredients above and shape into 4-5 adult-sized or 6-8 child-sized patties, optionally dredge in whole grain bread crumbs, and broil on each side on oiled sheet in oven or on outdoor grill until heated through and browned.

Avocado Soy Patties

1 medium avocado, mashed

1 cup cooked soybeans, mashed

¼ cup cooked brown rice

½ cup minced raw onion

1 tablespoon prepared mustard

1 tablespoon tomato paste

2 tablespoons wheat germ

Mix all ingredients and add enough whole wheat bread crumbs until your can form into patties. Fry patties in butter/oil until browned.

Rice Burgers

1 cup brown rice
3 tablespoons minced onion
2 tablespoons chopped green peppers
3 tablespoons chopped celery
1 beaten egg
¼ rolled oats
¼ cup wheat germ
1-2 tablespoons Super Flour

Mix all ingredients except Super Flour. Add enough Super Flour until good consistency for patties. Makes 8 adult-sized or twice as many or more toddler-sized patties. Dust with more wheat germ, then fry on both sides in a little butter/oil. Optionally, melt a slice of cheese on top of each patty.

Tofu and Grain Patties

Preheat oven to 400°F. Mix in a bowl:

1 cup mashed tofu
1 cup cooked whole grains (cooked brown rice is good)
½ cup minced celery
2 cloves garlic, minced
1 tablespoon nutritional yeast
1 tablespoon peanut butter
2 tablespoons tamari
½ teaspoon olive oil
½ teaspoon sage

Shape into about 10 child-sized patties or 6 adult-sized patties. Coat both sides of patties by dredging in whole grain flour or wheat germ and bake on well-greased baking sheet 25-30 minutes until golden brown, flipping patties half-way through baking.

Soybean Steak

In blender/processor, mix:

1½ cup cooked soybeans
¾ cup cooked whole grain (rice, etc.)
½ medium onion

Add:

½ cup wheat germ
¼ cup oat or wheat bran

¼ cup whole grain cornmeal

1 beaten egg

2 teaspoons tamari sauce

½ teaspoon powdered kelp

1 teaspoon nutritional yeast

Mix all and shape into balls or 4-5 adult-sized patties or 6-8 toddler sized patties. Freeze between wax paper.

Potato Burgers

Here's a use for those leftover mashed potatoes. Form into patties. Dip into beaten egg and then whole grain breadcrumbs. Let sit in refrigerator for one hour. Fry until brown on both sides and serve immediately.

Vegetarian Hot Dogs

Grind in blender:

1 cup cooked garbanzo beans

1-2 slices of bread

egg replacer equal to 1 egg

¼ teaspoon garlic, minced

¼ teaspoon red peppers, diced

½ teaspoon salt

pinch of pepper

Shape into about 10 hot dogs and chill for at least hour. Deep fry until browned and serve with mustard and relish as you would meat hot dogs.

Sandwiches and Pizzas

Easy, No-Cook Vegetable Pizza

Lift handset of telephone and call local pizza place that delivers. Order a pizza with mushrooms or other vegetable topping. Wait 30 minutes or until doorbell rings. Pay delivery person. Eat and enjoy.

Pizza Crust, Quick No-Rise

Mix in this order:

1½ cups Super Flour

2 teaspoons baking powder

½ teaspoon salt

½ cup soy or cow's milk

3-4 tablespoons oil

Use fork to mix. Knead gently to finish mixing for only 10-12 strokes. Shape and roll to fit greased pizza pan. Add toppings and bake in preheated 425°F oven 15-20 minutes. Make several pizza pies and freeze.

Super Quick Pizza Bread

On a slice of untoasted or slightly toasted whole grain bread, spread tomato, spaghetti, or pizza sauce. Sprinkle with shredded mozzarella cheese. Toast in toaster oven or under broiler for a few minutes until cheese melts. This happens fast, so watch carefully.

Variations: Add a few canned or fresh mushrooms before broiling or sprinkle with Parmesan cheese. Add a dash of fresh or dry oregano into the sauce before spreading.

Super Quick Garlic Bread

Follow the *Super Quick Pizza Bread* recipe above, but brush bread with olive oil or melted butter instead of sauce. Sprinkle with shredded cheese and minced fresh garlic or garlic powder.

Super Quick Mini Jelly Roll

Take a slice of untoasted whole grain bread. Remove crusts (save crusts for Whole Wheat Bread Crumbs). Flatten with a rolling pin or with the palm of your hand. Spread with all fruit no-sugar-added jelly or jam. Roll bread up as you would a sleeping bag. (If it is too difficult to roll up the bread because it too thick, try using a rolling pin to make it thinner.) Stab with a skinny carrot or celery stick to keep from unrolling. Instead of, or in addition to, the jelly, use peanut butter, cream cheese, tahini, hummus, or any sandwich spread. One of the sandwich spreads should be a colorful jelly so your child can see the swirl.

Bagel Ferris Wheel

Slice a whole grain bagel in half. Slice a small piece off the outer edge of the bagel, making a flat edge on which the ferris wheel can stand. Fill the bagel with a Super Sandwich Spread. Use *Decorative Touches* for passenger cars, which stick half way out of the spread.

Never a Plain Old Sandwich

Don't just cut a sandwich in half, be imaginative! Cut a heart-shaped sandwich to tell your little one you love her. Or let her decide on a shape. Does she want a star, a circle, a triangle, an oval, a parallelogram? She's never to young to start learning geometry!

Cookie cutters will work well on fairly flat sandwiches. If your whole grain bread is too thick, cut each slice into two thinner slices to make a flatter sandwich. It's easier to slice bread like this if it's slightly frozen. Or use only one slice of bread and place a cheese slice on it. Cut it into shapes and then broil to melt cheese.

Cut a bread slice into a heart shape, spread with red jelly and give your heart to your toddler.

Cut a sandwich into 9 square blocks and use raisins or re-hydrated dried apricot pieces to play *tic-tac-toe*, or any small food pieces can be used. These blocks can also be stacked into a brick wall. Or, leave the sandwich uncut and open-faced and use sticky peanut butter as a canvas for a picture created with *Decorative Touches*.

Sandwiches are more fun if made with two different slices of bread, such as one slice whole wheat and one slice of rye. Or don't use bread at all and make a sandwich with a whole grain tortilla, bagel half, or pita bread or even a rolled up lettuce leaf.

Freezing Sandwiches

I have to get up at 6 am to get my kids off to school on time. It's so nice when I don't have to make their lunch sandwiches, because I previously made and froze them—batch and freeze to the rescue again! Most frozen sandwiches placed in lunch boxes in the morning thaw and are ready to eat by lunch time. If a sandwich is quite thick, move it from freezer to refrigerator the night before to insure thawing by lunch. At home, the babysitter can remove the chill by placing it in the toaster oven or under the broiler.

Sandwiches made with these fillings can be frozen for up to 2 months: peanut butter, jelly, cream cheese, hummus, prune butter, tuna salad, mashed banana, yogurt cheese. Use day-old bread and spread the butter/peanut butter on the insides of both slices to prevent a wetter filling, like jelly, from making the bread soggy. In other words, don't place jelly directly on the bread, separate with a layer of peanut butter. Or place a slice of cheese between wet filling and bread.

Do not freeze egg salad (it gets rubbery), tomatoes (they get mushy), or salad veggies (they go limp). Ketchup freezes well, as does mustard and pickle relish. Mayonnaise separates and curdles unless you mix it with cream cheese or a similar spread; it should be no more than one third of the mixture.

Freeze sandwiches using the *Nested Plastic Bag Method*, and the sandwich will be in its bag, ready to go into the lunch box. When mass-producing and wrapping sandwiches, use a spatula to slide sandwiches into sandwich bags.

Tip: When making several sandwiches with butter, mix a little milk into softened butter with a small whisk to decrease saturated fat content and save money.

Tip: Prevent soggy lunch box sandwiches. When packing a sandwich for lunch, keep tomatoes, pickles, and other soggy ingredients in separate wax-paper lined plastic bags and have the diner place them on the sandwich immediately before eating.

Super Sandwich Spreads

All sandwich spreads must be kept refrigerated. Or freeze them using the *Food Cube Method* for up to 2 months. Thaw one or two cubes in the microwave and your sandwich spread is ready for spreading. (The assembled sandwich can also be frozen, as discussed in the previous section).

Tip: Keep little packets of ketchup, mustard, etc. from fast food restaurants for lunch box sandwiches. Store salt and pepper in portable shakers by filling drinking straws and twisting ends up.

Tip: Yogurt cheese and cream cheese in sandwiches are great places to hide *Healthy Extras*.

Tofu Cream Cheese

Mix together:
   ½ cup tofu, pressed between towels to drain very well
   3 ounces cream cheese, mashed
   1 tablespoon yogurt cheese
Add *Healthy Extras*.

Egg Salad Spread

Mix a crumbled hard-cooked egg with 1 tablespoon of mayonnaise and a tablespoon of any or all of the following: diced celery or onion, fresh parsley, tofu, and mashed beans.

Egg-less Salad Spread

Mix together:
   1 pound tofu, crumbled
   ¼ cup tofu mayonnaise
   2 teaspoons prepared mustard
   ¼ teaspoon garlic powder
   1 green pepper, minced
   1 celery stalk, finely chopped
   ½ medium onion, minced
   ½ teaspoon tamari

Super Sandwich Spread Combinations

Combine one or more of these ingredients:	with one or more of these sweet ingredients:
Yogurt cheese	Mashed banana
Tofu	Shredded apple or other fresh fruit
Cream cheese	No-sugar added fruit jelly or jam
Shredded natural cheese	Honey
Cottage cheese	Apple butter
Ricotta cheese	Prune butter
Peanut or any nut butter	Rehydrated dried fruit, such as
Tahini or any seed butter	raisins, dates, figs, apricots, and
Mashed avocado	pineapple
Puréed cooked beans	Powdered dried fruit
Mashed cooked egg yolk or	Mashed sweet potato
whole egg	Shredded or mashed carrots
And add one or more of these: Ground nuts Ground seeds (eat immediately) Chopped fresh parsley or other herb	**If too thick to spread, add a little milk or fruit juice.**

Super Butter (Mock Margarine)
Mix equal parts softened butter with a good quality cold-pressed non-hydrogenated oil from the natural foods store.

Honey Butter
You can buy commercial honey butter, but the price is ridiculous. All you have to do is mix one part honey into two parts softened butter. Your kids will love it. Refrigerate or freeze using the *Food Cube Method*.

Honey Peanut Butter
Make honey butter with peanut butter instead of butter.

Parsley Lemon Butter
Mix:
    ½ cup softened butter
    2 tablespoons lemon juice
    1-2 teaspoons finely minced fresh parsley

Herb Butter

Beat fresh herbs from your kitchen window garden into butter. Use 3-4 tablespoons of finely minced fresh herbs (or 1 tablespoon dried herbs) for each ½ cup (4 ounces) softened butter. Try one of these: basil, dill, chive, marjoram, tarragon, and, of course, parsley. Make a big batch and freeze for up to 6 months.

Churn Your Own Butter

Into a 32-ounce mayonnaise or similar jar, pour one pint of heavy whipping cream. The jar must have a lot of head room for shaking. You can add a little salt too, but it is not necessary. Shake for 15 minutes or more until you hear the solid pieces hitting the sides of the jar. Strain through sieve to get solid butter parts. Place pieces into ice cube trays or molds. Refrigerate.
Variation: Add fresh herbs before molding.

Prune Butter

Your kids will love this sweet high-fiber spread on whole grain bread or crackers.

   1 cup pitted prunes
   ½ cup apple juice
   1 tablespoon orange juice
   ¼ teaspoon vanilla

Combine all ingredients in saucepan. Simmer over low heat for about a ½ hour, stirring frequently. Cool and purée in processor until smooth. If too thick add a little more apple or orange juice. Keep refrigerated in an airtight jar.
Variation: Mix cooked prune butter with a little butter.

No-Cook Prune Butter

In blender, mix until smooth:

   8 ounces (1⅓ cup) soft pitted prunes
   ⅔ cup frozen apple juice concentrate, thawed in refrigerator
   ¼ teaspoon vanilla (optional)

Keep refrigerated in air-tight jar.

Easy Apple Butter

Make apple butter by simply reducing applesauce. Place about 1 cup applesauce (optionally add a dash of cinnamon) in a saucepan and bring to a boil. Turn heat to low and simmer, stirring occasionally, until desired consistency is reached. Yields about ½ cup.

Variation: Instead of applesauce, use puréed fresh fruit to make pear, pineapple, blueberry, mango, papaya, peach, pear, or plum butter.

Avocado Spread

Mix equal parts mashed avocado and mashed banana. Add 1 tablespoon lemon juice for each cup to prevent darkening.

Garbanzo Cream Cheese Spread

1 cup cooked garbanzos, well mashed

3 ounces cream cheese

$\frac{1}{3}$ cup tofu

½ cup celery, minced very fine for toddlers

Mix all ingredients. Makes about 2 cups.

Mr/Ms Sunshine

Place a scoop of sandwich spread in the middle of a canned pineapple ring. Use *Decorative Touches* to make facial features on the spread.

Fruit Flowers

Instead of the pineapple ring in the previous recipe, arrange apple, orange, pear, or other fruit wedges around the scoop of spread, making a flower like picture.

Stuffed Buns

Stuff an uncut bun jelly doughnut-style by cutting a hole in the top and piping sandwich filling inside. This method also can be used for Sloppy Joes to make them less sloppy.

Tofu-Nut Butter Spread

Mix in blender:

1 cup tofu

½ cup peanut butter or other nut butter

2 tablespoons maple syrup

Healthy Extras

Banana-Lemon Spread

Add a little lemon juice to mashed banana. Use about 1 teaspoon per ½ cup mashed banana. Simple and good with crackers.

Dried Fruit Spread

Mix dried fruit and a little water in the blender until spreadable consistency. Dates and figs are good.

Hummus

This spread is super healthy and combines tahini, chick peas, and whole grain bread to make complete protein. It's also super delicious and one of my favorites. Purée until smooth these ingredients in the blender/processor:

1 cup cooked chick peas
2 tablespoons tahini
2 tablespoons lemon juice
1 tablespoon olive oil
2 teaspoons minced fresh parsley

Optionally, add ½ clove pressed garlic or a pinch of garlic powder (not garlic salt).

Hummus from Canned Chick Peas

1 16-ounce can of chick peas/garbanzo beans (equivalent to a little less than 2 cups home-cooked)
6 tablespoons lemon juice
½ cup tahini
1 tablespoon olive oil
2 cloves pressed garlic (optional)

Process all until smooth in food processor.

Orange Hummus

3-4 cups cooked garbanzo beans
½ cup orange juice
¼ cup tahini
3 garlic cloves, crushed
1 teaspoon kelp or salt
1½ tablespoons apple cider vinegar
½ teaspoon paprika
½ teaspoon ginger
½ teaspoon coriander
½ teaspoon cumin
½ teaspoon dry mustard
¼ teaspoon turmeric

Process all above until smooth in food processor. Add more orange juice if necessary. Stir in 3 finely minced scallions.

Flying Saucers

Make your child's favorite sandwich on whole-grain English muffins or rolls. Name different sandwiches after planets; for example, peanut butter and jelly is from Venus, yogurt cheese and prune butter is from Mars, etc. Ask which planet your child would like his sandwich from today. You soon develop a repertoire of personalized recipes especially for your child.

Pocket Sandwiches

Don't buy the commercial frozen pocket sandwiches—make your own! For each pocket sandwich, take about two tablespoons of whole grain bread dough (homemade or commercially bought) and roll it out flat. Top with shredded Monterey or other cheese, cooked broccoli or other veggie, etc., or make a pizza- flavored pocket sandwich with mozzarella and tomato sauce/paste. All fillings should be thoroughly cooked before stuffing and drain the fillings well so that the sandwich will not be soggy. Roll dough up and pinch the sides down to contain the filling. Bake according to dough directions. Refrigerate or freeze. Thaw and reheat in the toaster oven.

Quick Breads

Apple Surprise Bread

Preheat oven to 350°F. Grease a 9 x 13 x 1 pan and arrange on the bottom:
　　1 apple or pear, sliced
In a large bowl, mix dry ingredients:
　　2 cups Super Flour
　　¼ cup wheat germ
　　¼ cup bran
　　1 teaspoon baking soda
　　1 teaspoon baking powder
Then add to dry ingredients:
　　½ cup ground nuts
　　1 apple or pear, grated
In a small bowl, mix wet ingredients:
　　2 beaten eggs
　　1 cup milk
　　1 tablespoon melted butter/oil
　　1 teaspoon vanilla
Make a well in dry ingredients and pour in wet ingredients. Mix until combined, but do not over-mix. Bake for 30-35 minutes. Let cool before icing. For icing, mix 1 cup yogurt with 3 tablespoons maple syrup or 2 tablespoons honey and drizzle over cool cake.

Zippity Zucchini Bread

Preheat oven to 350°F. Mix in this order:

    2 cups Super Flour
    1 teaspoon baking soda
    ½ cup melted butter/oil
    1 beaten egg
    1 8.75 oz. can of crushed pineapple, not drained
    ½ cup plumped raisins
    ½ cup grated zucchini

Pour into greased loaf pan and bake 60 minutes, until toothpick or cake tester comes out clean. Cool loaf on wire rack to prevent sogginess.

Banana Nut Bread

Preheat oven to 350°F. Mix wet ingredients in one bowl:

    1 beaten egg
    3 medium ripe bananas, mashed
    3 tablespoons melted butter/oil
    3 tablespoons honey
    2 tablespoons frozen orange juice concentrate
    1 teaspoon vanilla

Mix dry ingredients in another bowl:

    1½ cups Super flour
    1 teaspoon baking soda
    a pinch of salt

Mix wet ingredients into dry ingredients and add ¾ cup chopped nuts (walnuts, filberts, and almonds are good). Bake 50-60 minutes.

Variation: Replace all or some of the nuts with sunflower seeds.

Awesome Orange Bread

Preheat oven to 325°F. Mix in this order:

    3 beaten eggs
    ½ cup melted butter/oil
    1 cup orange juice
    2¼ cups Super Flour
    1 teaspoon baking soda
    1 teaspoon baking powder
    2 teaspoons cinnamon
    1 cup chopped nuts

Bake in greased and floured 9 x 5 loaf pan for 50-60 minutes until cake tester or toothpick comes out clean. Cool on wire rack. Serve with topping of ½ yogurt cheese and ½ orange juice concentrate or with Orange Topping.

Corny Corn Bread

Preheat oven to 350°F.

    1 cup whole grain cornmeal
    ⅔ cup Super Flour
    ½ cup nonfat dry milk
    2 teaspoons baking powder
    2 beaten eggs
    1 cup yogurt
    3 tablespoons melted butter/oil

Mix all ingredients and place in an 8-inch square baking pan. Bake 30 minutes until lightly browned. Cut into 16 or 20 squares.

Honey Corn Bread

Preheat oven to 400°F. Grease a 9-inch loaf pan. Mix these dry ingredients:

    1¾ whole grain cornmeal from the natural foods store
    ½ cup Super Flour
    2 tablespoons wheat germ
    1 teaspoon salt
    3 teaspoons baking powder

Mix these wet ingredients in another bowl:

    2 beaten eggs
    2 tablespoons vegetable oil or melted butter
    2 tablespoons honey
    1 cup milk

Combine wet and dry ingredients. Bake 25 minutes or until done.

Peanut Butter in the Bread

Preheat oven to 350°F. Grease a 9-inch loaf pan. Thoroughly mix wet ingredients:

    ¾ cup peanut butter
    1 cup milk
    ½ cup honey

Mix dry ingredients in separate bowl:

    2 cups Super Flour
    1 tablespoon plus 1 teaspoon (4 teaspoons) baking powder
    ½ teaspoon baking soda
    ¾ teaspoon salt

Combine wet and dry ingredients and bake for 45 minutes.

Banana Bread

Preheat oven to 350°F. Mix wet ingredients:

    1½ cups mashed ripe banana

    ¼ cup oil

    ½ cup honey

    1 teaspoon vanilla

    1-2 beaten eggs (optional)

Mix dry ingredients:

    2 cups whole wheat flour or Super Flour

    ½ cup wheat germ

    1 teaspoon baking soda

    1-2 teaspoons baking powder (optional)

Add dry ingredients into wet, then fold in:

    ½ cup chopped walnuts

Bake in oiled loaf pan for about an hour.

Bread Products

Whole Grain Bread Crumbs

Don't throw away bread crusts and the end slices from whole grain bread. Save them in a paper bag in the cabinet until they get stale and hard. Then break them into small pieces and whiz them in your blender or food processor to make whole wheat bread crumbs.

Or put them in a plastic bag and crush them with a rolling pin and you'll have more control over the coarseness. Store in a tightly-covered jar in your kitchen cabinets. Three slices will make about one cup of crumbs. I think they taste fine, but if you find that the bread crumbs taste like stale bread, try drying fresh bread on an un-oiled baking sheet in a single layer at 300°F until completely dry and lightly browned. Let cool completely before pulverizing.

Whole Grain Italian Bread Crumbs

To each cup of whole grain bread crumbs in previous recipe, add:

    2 tablespoons grated Parmesan cheese

    ½ teaspoon dry oregano

    ½ teaspoon dry basil

    1 tablespoon dry parsley

    ½ teaspoon garlic powder

    ½ teaspoon sugar (optional)

Store in an airtight container in refrigerator for up to two months or until expiration date on cheese label, or freeze.

Bread Crumb Substitutes

Crackers, uncooked rolled oats/oatmeal, whole grain corn flakes, or any dry cereal whirled in the blender make cracker crumbs, which can substitute for bread crumbs in recipes. Or use plastic bag/rolling pin method.

Whole Wheat Breadsticks/Croutons

Cut up slightly dry whole grain bread into narrow rectangular strips for breadsticks or into cubes for croutons. Lightly coat with melted butter/oil and herbs, or if you find it easier, coat with butter and herbs before cutting bread into strips or cubes. I find that the easiest way to coat cut bread is to shake everything together in a plastic bag. Use about 1 tablespoon of butter/oil and 1 teaspoon of dry herbs per ½ cup of bread.

Optionally add ½ teaspoon of seasoning per ½ cup of bread, such as garlic powder or onion salt, grated Parmesan cheese, etc.

On large baking sheet in a single layer, bake 300°F for about 10-15 minutes. Stir during cooking for even drying. Let cook completely.

Store in airtight container in the refrigerator for up to two months or freeze using the *Nested Plastic Bag Method* for up to 6 months.

Shake before using.

Tip: Don't throw out leftover bread or the bread ends that no one will eat. Freeze them in a freezer bag until you have enough for a batch of croutons or breadsticks.

Whole Grain Top-of-Stove Stuffing Mix

Save bread ends, crusts, and leftover bread to make this economical and healthy stuffing mix.

2 cups of cubed dry/stale bread
1 teaspoon dry parsley flakes
1 tablespoon bouillon powder or 1 bouillon cube
1 tablespoon dried minced onion
2 tablespoons dried minced celery
½ teaspoon thyme
½ teaspoon pepper
pinch of powdered kelp
¼ teaspoon sage

Mix all ingredients in a bowl. Double or triple recipe if you wish.

For each cup of stuffing mix, stir in ¼ cup water and 1 tablespoon olive oil or melted butter. Toss well and warm on top of the stove, or bake at 350°F in oven until warmed through.

Store in refrigerator for up to 3 months or in freezer for up to one year.

Variations: Per cup of stuffing mix, add 2 tablespoons plumped raisins, 2 tablespoons canned mushrooms, 2 tablespoons chopped or ground walnuts or other nuts, and/or a tablespoon of Worcestershire sauce.

Homemade Whole Grain Breakfast Cereal Flakes

Boxed breakfast cereals are overpriced and sometimes contain unhealthy ingredients and preservatives. It's easy and much cheaper to make your own using the whole grain flours found at your local natural foods store. If your family is used to a high-sugar cereal, begin by making homemade cereal with high sugar content and gradually decrease to the recipe below. Or completely leave out the sweetener altogether for toddlers and those lucky folks who have not developed a sweet tooth.

    2 cups of whole grain flour (wheat, millet, oat, corn) or Super Flour
    ½-1 teaspoon powdered kelp or salt
    ½ cup sweetener (honey, maple syrup, blackstrap molasses (optional)
    2 cups water

Grease a cookie sheet. Mix ingredients together, adding water slowly as the last ingredient until you have the mixture of a thin paste.

Pour mixture onto sheet while shaking to distribute over entire surface of sheet. As soon as you have enough to cover the cookie sheet as thinly as possible, stop pouring. If you've poured too much, simply return the excess back into the mixing bowl.

Bake in pre-heated 350°F for about 15 minutes until dry and lightly browned. Peel off cookie sheet, let cool, then break into pieces that look like commercial corn flakes. Or you can break into designs and shapes.

Homemade Breakfast Nutty Grape Cereal

Mix in a bowl until smooth:

    3½ cups Super Flour or whole wheat flour
    1 cup brown sugar
    2 cups yogurt, buttermilk, or sour milk
    1 teaspoon baking soda
    ¼ teaspoon kelp or salt

Spread on two greased cookie sheets. Bake for 25-30 minutes until golden brown. While still warm, grind a bit in processor or grate by hand using the large holes.

Whole Grain Popper Tarts

Mix ingredients below for dough.

    2 beaten eggs
    ¼ cup olive oil

2 tablespoons melted butter

¼ cup + 2 tablespoons honey

2 cups Super Flour

2 teaspoons baking powder

Chill for one hour.

Roll dough into six 8 x 12 inch rectangles. These rectangle will be folded in half to make 8 x 6 inch pastries.

Spread about a tablespoon of filling (jam, jelly, strawberry preserves, etc.) on one half of the rectangle, leaving room for sealing edge. Fold in half, enclosing filling by crimping edges with a fork or pastry wheel.

Bake in preheated 350°F oven for about 20 minutes.

Let cool.

Make a frosting by mixing:

2 tablespoons honey or confectioners' sugar

¼ teaspoon vanilla

1 tablespoon milk

Dribble a design on each tart with frosting.

Store using the *Nested Plastic Bag Method*. Refrigerate for up to one week or freeze for up to three months. You can also double or triple this recipe to make 12 or 18 pastries instead of six. Reheat in toaster for 2 minutes (or 4-5 minutes if frozen).

Variation: If your family likes a particular commercial toaster tart, read the ingredients list and experiment to create a healthier, cheaper homemade version.

Quick Breadsticks

Makes about 16 sticks. Mix dry ingredients:

1 cup Super Flour

½ cup oat or wheat bran

½ teaspoon baking powder

In another bowl, mix wet ingredients:

1 beaten egg

4 tablespoons melted butter/oil

¼ cup of water

Make well in dry ingredients and mix in wet ingredients. If dough is too dry, add water; if too wet, add flour or bran. Keep dividing dough in halves until you have 16 balls.

Roll into sticks about ½ inch in diameter. After shaping, you can optionally wet them with a mixture of one beaten egg mixed with 2 tablespoons of water and roll them in sesame seeds or wheat germ.

Place on greased baking sheet and bake in pre-heated 350°F oven for 20 minutes, until crisp and golden-browned.

Store in an air-tight container.

Whole Grain Soft Pretzels

In a large mixing bowl, mix:

1 cup Super Flour
1 tablespoon canola oil
1 cup apple juice (not concentrated)
1 tablespoon active dry yeast or 1 packet active dry yeast

Beat with electric mixer for 3 minutes. Add:

1 cup Super Flour

Knead 10-15 minutes, adding a little water or flour for good consistency. Roll about 16 pieces of dough into long snakes and form into pretzel shapes.

Preheat oven to 450°F. Place pretzels on oiled baking sheet and let rise for 30 minutes.

Beat one egg in a small bowl and brush beaten egg over pretzels. If desired, sprinkle with coarse salt or kelp granules.

Bake 14-16 minutes or until pretzels become a nice golden brown. Let cool a little before eating to prevent mouth burns.

Whole Wheat Buttermilk Biscuits

Preheat oven to 425°F. Sift together:

1¼ cups whole wheat flour
¾ cup unbleached, unbrominated white flour
2 teaspoons baking powder
½ teaspoon baking soda
1 teaspoon salt

While mixing, slowly add:

¾ cup buttermilk or milk
¼ cup oil (safflower or corn)

Knead about 2 minutes. Roll out to ½-inch thick. Use 2-inch biscuit cutter to cut out a dozen or more biscuits. Bake on greased cookie sheet for 12-15 minutes, watching carefully for burning at end of cooking time.

Whole Grain Biscuit Mix

4 cups Super Flour
1 teaspoon salt
½ cup oil
⅔ cup instant nonfat dry milk
3 tablespoons baking powder

Whole Grain Master Baking Mix

Use for pancakes, waffles, etc.

    2 cups whole wheat flour
    2 cup unbleached white flour
    1 cup wheat germ
    3 tablespoons baking soda
    ¾ tablespoon salt
    ¾ tablespoon cream of tartar
    2 tablespoons honey

Cut in until consistency of cornmeal:

    1 cup vegetable shortening

Add:

    1 cup dried milk

Store in tightly-covered container at room temperature or in refrigerator.

To use: In bowl, beat together:

    1 cup milk
    1 beaten egg
    1½ cups master baking mix

Whole Wheat Popovers

Popovers rise because of trapped steam and not leavening agents such as baking powder. Preheat oven to 450°F.

    1 cup whole wheat flour
    1 cup unbleached, unbrominated white flour
    2 tablespoons honey
    4 egg whites
    2 cups milk

Generously grease 12 muffin tins (do not use paper, popovers will stick).

Beat the eggs and gradually stir in milk. Mix in remaining ingredients.

Fill tins ⅓-½ full. Bake for 10 minutes.

Reduce heat to 350°F and continue baking for 15 minutes.

To prevent falling do not open the oven until end of cooking time, or the hot air inside the popovers that is raising them will escape and cause the popovers will collapse. Popovers should be nicely browned before you take them out of the oven, under-baking will cause them to collapse.

When done baking, immediately prick popovers with fork in several places to let the steam escape to prevent sogginess. If popovers stick, run a knife around the edge and use more grease on the tins next time.

Serve with jam, honey, or cheese. Or split and stuff with scrambled eggs.

Freeze popovers in an airtight container for up to 3 months; heat by placing frozen popovers on an ungreased baking sheet in a preheated 450°F oven for 10-15 minutes.

Super Muffins

Tip for filling muffin tins: Use a small measuring cup tins for uniform sized muffins. If you have an ice cream scoop with a lever, all the better, the batter comes out of scoop easily. Or put batter into a clean milk carton for easy pouring, especially if you are using mini-muffin tins. Do not fill tins more than ¾ full or you'll have flat tops. For beautiful rounded muffin tops, grease tins only halfway up the sides.

Tip for oiling muffin tins: Use a pastry brush and oil or melted butter to stick-proof each muffin tin. Or a crumpled piece of paper towel to grease the tins. Or oil-spray. Run a knife around the edges of muffins before removing.

Surprise Muffins: Place a surprise in the middle of each muffin, which your child will discover while eating it. Ideas: a soft cooked and pitted prune or piece of plumped dried papaya or apricot or other plumped soft dried fruit, a peeled piece of apple or pear, glop of peanut butter, carob chips, banana chunk, or anything that would not be a choking hazard.

Don't Warp Your Muffin Tins: The recipes here require the use of muffin tins for baking. If you find that you don't have enough batter to fill all of the tins in the pan, and some must be left empty, fill them halfway with water. This will prevent the muffin pan from burning or warping.

Mini-muffins: These recipes will make 12 regular sized muffins. You can make 2-3 dozen mini muffins instead—kids love things their own size. Bake mini muffins a few minutes less and watch carefully for burning.

Batch and Freeze

Save time by doubling the recipe to make two batches of muffins and freeze one. Freeze muffins in a single layer in a large freezer bag for up to 3 months. Thaw overnight in refrigerator and heat in a 325°F oven loosely wrapped in foil for about 10 minutes.

Heart Shaped Muffins

Make "I love you" muffins for your child by placing aluminum foil between the paper muffin cup and the metal muffin tin to form the muffin into the shape of a heart. Crunch the foil into a ball the size of a marble so that it will cause an indentation on top. Crunch foil into rectangular shapes to push in sides on bottom to form point. Exaggerate the heart shape by decorating with frosting in a heart shape.

Bunny Muffins

Make muffins into bunnies by adding eyes, ears, nose, and whiskers using *Decorative Touches*.

Muffin Frisbees

Slice leftover muffins horizontally into thin circles and bake like cookies in the oven or toaster oven until lightly brown or toast both sides by broiling. Spread with butter or jam.

Orange Juice Muffins

Preheat oven to 425°F. In large bowl, combine the dry ingredients:

 1½ cups Super Flour
 3 tablespoons wheat germ
 1 teaspoon baking soda
 ¼ teaspoon cinnamon
 ½ cup raisins

In a small bowl, combine the wet ingredients:

 2 eggs, beaten
 1 cup orange juice
 2 tablespoons melted butter/oil

Blend the wet ingredients into the dry ingredients and do not over mix. Pour into greased or lined muffin cups. Bake 15 minutes or until a toothpick or cake tester comes out clean. Serve with Orange Topping for an Overly Orangy Taste.

Eggless Apple Muffins

Preheat oven to 350°F. Mix dry ingredients in large bowl:

 2 cups Super Flour
 ½ cup rolled oats
 2 teaspoons baking powder
 1 teaspoon baking soda
 ½ teaspoon cinnamon

Mix wet ingredients in a small bowl:

 1 23-ounce jar applesauce
 ½ cup yogurt
 2 tablespoons molasses
 ½ cup plumped raisins

Mix wet ingredients into dry. Pour into greased or lined muffin cups. Decorate with ground nuts. Bake 25-30 minutes.

Polenta Mini-Muffins

Preheat oven to 350°F.

    1½ cups water or stock
    ½ cup whole grain cornmeal
    2 beaten eggs
    ½ cup shredded cheddar cheese
    ½ cup yogurt
    ¼ cup shredded cheddar cheese

Bring water or stock to a boil on the stove. Slowly add cornmeal into boiling water or stock, stirring continuously with whisk to remove lumps. Thicken by cooking over medium heat for 5 minutes, stirring constantly. Remove from heat. Stir in the beaten eggs, ½ cup cheese, and yogurt. Spoon into 24 greased or lined mini-muffin cups. Sprinkle ¼ cup cheese on top of muffins. Bake 18-22 minutes until firm. Let cool slightly before removing from pan. Serve with tomato sauce.

Variation: Add a little mashed beans to the mixture before baking.

Pizzazzy Pizza Muffins

Preheat oven to 400°F. Combine dry ingredients in a large bowl:

    1¾ cups Super Flour
    2 teaspoons baking powder
    1 teaspoon baking soda
    1 tablespoon fresh oregano or 1 teaspoon dry oregano

Combine these wet ingredients:

    1 beaten egg
    ½ cup homemade tomato sauce
    1 cup yogurt
    ½ cup shredded mozzarella cheese

Mix wet ingredients into dry. Pour into greased or lined muffin tins. Place a slice of tomato on top of each muffin. Sprinkle more shredded cheese on top of tomato slice. Bake 20-25 minutes.

Banana Nut Muffins

Preheat oven to 375°F. Mix dry ingredients in large bowl:

    1¾ Super Flour
    ½ teaspoon baking powder
    ½ teaspoon baking soda
    1 teaspoon cinnamon
    ½ cup ground walnuts

Mix wet ingredients in small bowl:
- 2 beaten eggs
- ¼ cup yogurt
- 2 tablespoons melted butter/oil
- ¼ cup maple syrup
- 1 tablespoon lemon juice
- 3 small mashed ripe bananas (about 1 cup)
- ½ cup plumped raisins

Mix wet ingredients into dry ingredients. Pour into greased or lined muffin tins. Decorate each muffin with a walnut on top (not for babies/toddlers, whole nuts are choking hazards). Bake 20 minutes or until golden.

Peanut Butter Muffins

Preheat oven to 350°F. Mix in this order:
- 2 beaten eggs
- ¼ cup creamy natural peanut butter
- ¼ cup mashed banana
- ½ cup thawed apple juice concentrate
- 1 cup milk
- ½ cup melted butter/oil
- 2½ cups Super Flour
- 1½ teaspoons baking powder
- 1 teaspoon baking soda
- 1 cup finely chopped peanuts

Pour into greased or lined muffins tins and bake 15 minutes.

Cholesterol Killing Bran Muffins

Preheat oven to 425°F. Combine these dry ingredients in a large bowl:
- 2 cups oat bran
- ¼ cup wheat germ
- 1 teaspoon cinnamon
- 1 tablespoon baking soda

Combine these wet ingredients:
- ½ cup evaporated skim milk
- ¾ cup frozen apple juice concentrate
- 1 beaten egg
- 2 tablespoons maple syrup

Mix wet ingredients into dry. Add:
- 1 unpeeled apple, cored and finely grated
- ⅓ cup ground/chopped nuts

Pour into greased or lined muffin tins and bake 18 minutes. These muffins will not rise much because of all the bran, so don't worry that they will seep out of the muffin tins.

Easy Bran Muffins

Preheat oven to 400°F. Mix these dry ingredients in a large bowl:

    2 cups Super Flour
    1 cup wheat or oat bran
    2 tablespoons baking powder
    ¾ teaspoon salt

In a separate bowl, beat together:

    2 eggs
    2 cups milk
    ½ cup applesauce
    ½ cup molasses or honey
    ⅓ cup blackstrap molasses

Combine wet and dry ingredients. Pour into 8 greased or lined muffin tins until ¾ full and bake 15 minutes, until nicely browned.

Variations: Add raisins or other dried fruits.

Wonderful Waffles

I used to buy the commercial, expensive, frozen waffles with imitation blueberries from the supermarket. Yes, I let myself get roped in by those darn coupons. When my son started asking me to buy more, I realized that sometimes he was eating 3 or 4 a day! I decided to invest in a waffle iron, which paid for itself in no time. Every few weeks I pull it out and make and freeze dozens of Super Flour waffles with real blueberries. I no longer cringe when I see him reaching into the freezer. Use of the batch and freeze method and waffles will keep in the freezer for up to 6 months. For waffles that you know will be frozen, you may wish to slightly undercook them.

Tip: Before freezing, cool completely on wire racks. Heat directly from freezer (without thawing) in toaster, or toaster oven at 350°F for 5 minutes.

Wonderful Waffles

Separate 2 eggs. Mix in this order:

    2 beaten egg yolks
    1¾ cups milk
    2 cups Super Flour
    1 tablespoon plus 1 teaspoon baking powder
    ½ cup melted butter/oil

Beat egg whites until soft peaks form. Fold into other ingredients. Bake in preheated waffle iron until steam stops and waffles are golden brown.

Tip: I use oil-spray or a butter spray and spray the waffle iron between waffles.

Variations: Add 1 shredded apple or a 1 cup frozen blueberries (no need to thaw) or other berries.

Tip: Use an old sanitized toothbrush to clean batter from crevices in your waffle iron.

Tip: To keep your waffle iron clean, make waffles that are slightly small and then they won't "overflow" and make a mess. Use the same scoop or measuring cup until you know the exact amount to make a perfect waffle with your particular waffle iron.

Waffle Pizza

Onto cooked waffles, smear peanut butter and jam or jelly for the pizza sauce. Add *Decorative Touches*, such as slices of banana for pretend pepperoni, etc. Make a smiley face pizza.

Crêpes

Whole Wheat Crêpes
(makes one dozen)

Crêpes: Beat 2 eggs in a bowl. Add:
  1½ cups skim milk
  1 cup Super Flour

Mix with whisk or in the blender to remove lumps. Heat a small non-stick skillet or crêpe pan over medium heat. Lightly butter or spray pan with vegetable oil. Remove pan from stove top, quickly pour ¼ cup of batter to thinly coat bottom of pan. Turn and tilt pan to even out batter and made the crêpe as circular as possible. Pour any excess off and back into bowl. After about a minute, when dry on the top and brown on the bottom (check by peeking under edge), flip. Cook the second side for about 30 seconds until blotchy brown. Place finished crêpe on wire rack to cool while you make the next crêpe. Stack cooled crêpes on a plate. Cooled crêpes will not stick together as readily as warm crêpes. Re-grease pan before cooking next crêpe, if necessary.

Variation: Add ½ teaspoon of cinnamon to crêpe mixture. And/or replace a tablespoon of Super Flour with wheat germ.

Filling: There seems no end to the possibilities for crêpe filling.

yogurt cheese

cottage cheese

shredded cheese

Prune Butter

applesauce

any puréed fruit

jelly, jam, or marmalade

re-hydrated dried fruit

any fruit mixed with any cheese

soft-cooked vegetables

Healthy Extras

Topping:

Mock Whipped Cream (page 527)

plain yogurt

yogurt mixed with jam, sweetener, or puréed fruit.

Batch and Freeze: Double the recipe and freeze using the Tray-Freeze Method.

Pancakes

How to Cook Pancakes

Don't over-beat the batter, stop stirring once the ingredients are moist (a few lumps are OK) or your pancakes will be tough. Adjust batter by diluting with milk or other liquid if too thick and adding flour if too thin. Heat griddle or skillet until hot. Its temperature is just right when a few drops of cold water dropped on the griddle will jump and sizzle. If the griddle is not hot enough, the water will just lie there and boil; if it is too hot, it will instantaneously evaporate. To prevent pancakes from sticking, add butter/oil after frying pan is hot. Pour a small amount (about 2-3 tablespoons) of batter onto the griddle until the pancake is the size you want. Make even smaller pancakes for your little ones. Cook about 2 to 3 minutes or until the surface is filled with bubbles and the underside is slightly brown. Raise the edge of the pancake with the spatula to test if it is firm and brown. If so, flip and cook the other side 1 to 2 minutes more. Do not flip again or the pancake will be tough. Do NOT use the spatula to press down the pancake (it feels so right to do this, doesn't it?) or it will be heavy.

Tip: Your child will love watching you make pancakes. If you have an electric frying pan, cook them at the table. If not, let your child have a high seat a safe distance away from the stove.

Tips: Mix pancake batter in a large measuring cup or a wide-mouthed pitcher instead of a bowl for easier pouring. Or put the batter into a clean milk carton—it's spout makes for easy pouring. Or use a squeeze bottle for more control when pouring batter for pancake art. Sometimes it's easier to use scissors to cut fun shapes out of plain circular pancakes. Mom and Dad can eat the scraps.

Tips: Substitute room temperature club soda for liquid in these recipes for a fluffier pancake or waffle, but use immediately and do not store. Or separate eggs and mix yolks into rest of batter. Last, whip egg whites until stiff and fold gently into batter.

Variation: For fruity tasting pancakes, try substituting orange juice for the milk in pancake batter. Optionally add a tablespoon of citrus zest. Or use peach nectar instead of orange juice and add ½ cup chopped soft and ripe fresh peaches.

Pancake Additions Ideas

Add any of the following to the Basic Pancake recipe:

½ cup of frozen or fresh blueberries or strawberries (no need to thaw frozen berries first)

thinly sliced pieces of an apple or other fresh fruit

seedless grapes sliced in half

raisins

carob chips

dates

dried apricots or other dried fruit

chopped walnuts or other nuts

Or replace some of the milk with another flavorful liquid: crushed pineapple, or apple, orange, or other fruit juice.

Batch and Freeze Pancakes

I think pancakes are a lot of trouble to make, maybe because I make a mess that takes time to clean up, so I make a big batch and freeze the leftovers. Pancakes freeze well if you cool them completely on wire racks before freezing. Freeze them in freezer bags between sheets of waxed paper for up to 3 months. To reheat, place frozen pancakes single layer on a baking sheet in a 325°F oven or toaster oven for 7-10 minutes.

Pancake Syrup Ideas

For Heaven's sake, don't give your precious children the pretend maple syrup sold in supermarkets. It's nothing more than corn syrup and caramel coloring. Serve real maple syrup, even though it's expensive. If you use the shot glass idea (see below), you don't use much syrup at all. Another nice topping for pancakes is fruit jelly—use a brand that contains no added sugar and is all fruit. Liquify it by adding a bit of water and maybe maple syrup or honey or melted butter/oil. For large breakfasts, create a selection of flavored pancake syrups by adding a few tablespoons of different jellies or jams to separate containers of maple syrup. This is a good way to use the last bit of jelly left in the jar—heat the jar a little and the jelly will come right out. Try plain applesauce, or a purée of banana with applesauce, using some added apple juice or water to thin it. Or, make your own syrup with fresh fruit: Blend fresh fruit and a little water or juice in the blender. You can buy fruit syrups at the natural foods store, but you can make your own for ⅓ the cost. Yogurt makes a nice base for a pancake syrup. Add a couple of tablespoons of frozen concentrated orange juice, honey, or other sweetener and/or jam and/or a few drops of vanilla or almond extract. Cooked prunes and yogurt (2 tablespoons yogurt per prune) makes a delicious pancake spread. Add some blackstrap molasses to any syrup as a nutritional enhancer, but go light with it because it has a strong taste. Sprinkle some fresh strawberry or banana pieces over the pancakes for an extra special touch. Serve syrup warmed on the stove for extra flavor and to prevent cooling the pancakes.

Have a Shot of Syrup

If I let them, my kids would pour an entire quart of maple syrup over one pancake. I confess, even I would love to use lots of maple syrup. But REAL maple syrup is expensive, and too much sweetener is not good for anyone. Here's a way to use maple syrup so that you get maximum taste from a minimum amount. Fill a shot glass halfway with maple syrup—this takes only about 1 tablespoon! Dip pancake fork-fulls (cut thin so that they will fit) into the shot glass so that only the tip of each fork-full gets covered with maple syrup. Place on tongue, syrup first, to get a full syrup flavor from only a small drop. When you're finished eating your pancakes, you'll be surprised at how little syrup you actually used. If you don't have a shot glass, use any small, shallow container with a thin circumference. The tiny dipping cups for sauces or butter in restaurants are great. Take home the plastic ones, but don't take the metal ones!

Dried Fruit Syrup

Combine ½ cup dried fruit and ½ cup water in a saucepan. (If you have a real sweet tooth, use fruit juice or concentrated frozen fruit juice instead of water.) Bring to a boil and simmer for 20 minutes. Cool. Then whip in a blender, adding water very slowly until mixture reaches syrup consistency. (This will take anywhere from ½ cup to 1½ cups of water, depending on the dried fruit.) Store in refrigerator or freeze using the Food Cube Method. Warm on the stove before serving over pancakes.

Blackstrap Syrup

Combine ½ cup blackstrap molasses, ½ cup honey, and 1 teaspoon vanilla in blender. Keep refrigerated.

Pancake Flour Alternatives

In the Basic Whole Grain Flour Pancake recipe below, try substituting oatmeal for some of the flour. Or, try using some cooked whole brown rice grains, or millet grains, or other whole grains. Cooked mashed beans or bean flour mixes well into pancakes, too. Pancakes are a good way to use leftover cooked grains and beans that are getting old in the refrigerator.

Basic Whole Grain Pancakes

Mix in this order:
   2 cups Super Flour
   2 teaspoons baking soda
    OR 2 teaspoons baking powder
   2 lightly beaten eggs
   2 cups milk
   2 tablespoons oil or melted butter
   Healthy Extras
Follow directions for How to Cook Pancakes.

Tip: Pancakes are a great way to get ground flax and pumpkin seeds and nuts into your child's diet. Grind into powder, sprinkle in to batter, and eat immediately.

Peanut Butter and Jelly Pancakes

Spread a pancake with peanut butter and jelly. Roll up like a sleeping bag. Your toddler can eat these with her hands.

Gingerbread People Pancakes

Pour pancake batter into gingerbread people shapes.

Banana Pancakes

1 cup Super Flour

¼ cup wheat germ

¼ cup oat or wheat bran

½ cup cooked millet or brown rice

½ cup milk

½ cup mashed bananas

2 beaten eggs

1 tablespoon melted butter/oil

Mix ingredients and cook.

Variation: Slice bananas lengthwise and then crosswise into small pieces. Pour pancake batter into pan, quickly add sliced bananas in a design. Flip pancake and finish cooking. Add ground nuts/seeds.

Personalized Picture Pancakes

Pour Basic Whole Grain Pancake batter onto griddle. Place *Decorative Touches*, such as blueberries, walnuts, etc., into the cooking batter to make a smiley face, a heart or other shape, or your toddler's initials. Finish cooking the pancake. Place on your child's plate with the best-looking side facing up. If your decorative touches are hidden inside the pancake and can't be seen, next time remember to either gently push then down into batter or let them float above the batter.

Teddy Bear Pancakes

Pour batter to make a regular pancake. Then pour two small circles on top of the pancake for the bear's ears. Finish cooking. You can add Decorative Touches to make eyes, nose, and mouth.

Tip: Use clean empty food cans with both ends opened and removed as molds for perfect circular pancakes.

"What's in a Name" Pancakes

Spell your child's name in pancake batter. Simply pour the batter so that it forms the letters of your child's name, using a baster or cake icing applier with large-holed tip for more control. Finish cooking. Place it on the plate so that it is right side up, not backwards, of course.

ABC Pancakes

Shape pancakes into letters and numbers. Do free-hand or use cookie cutters.

Smiley Face Pancakes

On skillet ready for cooking pancakes, drop two eyes, a nose, and a smile. Let cook for just a few seconds. Then pour a circular pancake over them. Flip and your pancake will smile at you.

Variation: If your child will enjoy it, do a sad face, a mad face (sloped eyebrows and straight line mouth), a surprised face (open mouth), etc.

Great Pumpkin Pancakes

1 beaten egg
1 cup canned pumpkin
2 tablespoons blackstrap molasses
½ cup Super Flour
½ teaspoon baking powder
½ teaspoon pumpkin pie spice

Mix in bowl and cook. Top with a mixture of yogurt and orange juice concentrate.

Bunny Pancakes

Use the Great Pumpkin recipe above and substitute puréed cooked carrots for the canned pumpkin.

Nutty Millet Pancakes

1 beaten egg
1 cup milk
3 tablespoons melted butter/oil
2 cups millet flour
1 tablespoon baking powder
1 cup chopped nuts

Add more milk if too thick.

Variation: Add 1 cup reconstituted dried fruit or fruit purée.

Oat-Yogurt Pancakes

2 beaten eggs
2 tablespoons melted butter/oil
1 tablespoon maple syrup
1 cup yogurt
1 cup rolled oats
¼ cup wheat germ

Add more wheat germ if necessary. Mix in bowl and cook.

Brown Rice Pancakes

2 cups cooked brown rice
1 cup yogurt
1 tablespoon lemon juice
¼ cup Super Flour or wheat germ
milk

Mix all ingredients, adding enough milk to pour for pancakes. Makes 6.

Crackers

The How To's of Cracker Rolling

Cracker dough should not be kneaded, as is bread dough. It is best to have all ingredients, except eggs, at room temperature before mixing the dough. The cracker recipes below require that you roll the dough very thin—from ¹⁄₁₆ to ⅛ inch thick. It is important that you roll the dough to a uniform thickness, to promote even baking. The thinner you roll the crackers, the crisper they'll turn out after baking. Use a good rolling pin, and roll the dough on a cold, smooth, flat surface, such as a Formica® counter top.

Flour the surface with a couple of tablespoons of flour. Roll the dough gently from the center of the dough out, flipping occasionally. Use a little more flour if the dough is sticking.

Place the entire flat dough sheet on a baking sheet. Use a pizza cutter, a sharp knife, or an unused hair comb to cut almost all the way through the dough. The baked crackers will break easily at these score lines. You can also cut the dough into separate crackers before placing on the baking sheet. Or, cut the dough into squares, rectangles, circles, etc.

To make a nice edge around each cracker, press lines into the edges of each cracker using a fork. Before baking, prick several holes in each cracker all the way through the dough with a fork. These air holes are not really for decoration, their purpose is to help the crackers to stay flat during baking. Of course, you can always poke holes so that they make a design.

Dough Tip: Rolling out dough is easier if you roll it on wax paper. To keep the wax paper from sliding around, place a few drops of water between the paper and the countertop.

Preventing Sogginess in Crackers

After baking, it's a good idea to cool the crackers on a wire rack before storing to prevent sogginess. After they are completely cooled, store in an airtight container in a dry, cool, dark place. Include in the container a few grains of dry rice—these will absorb moisture and help keep the crackers crisp. (A few grains of dry rice in your salt shaker will help keep it flowing freely.) If the crackers are stale or smell bad, throw them out. If they become soggy, but have no odor and taste OK, you can save them.

Dry them by cooking for 3-5 minutes in a preheated 300°F oven and they will keep for another week. Fresh crackers stored in airtight canisters or plastic bags will keep for up to 3-4 weeks at room temperature, up to 3 months in the refrigerator, and up to 6 months in the freezer.

You can add seeds (sesame is good) as a garnish to your crackers before baking. To insure that the seeds stick to both sides of the crackers, sprinkle some seeds on the rolling surface. Place the flat, pre-rolled dough over them, sprinkle some on the top of the cracker dough, and gently roll to press them into both sides of the dough.

A Dozen Quick Crackers

Preheat oven to 350°F. Mix in a bowl:

1 cup Super Flour
¼ teaspoon salt
4 tablespoons cold-pressed canola oil

Gradually stir in 3-4 tablespoons very cold water until the dough is the consistency of pie crust. Refrigerate dough for an hour to chill. Roll very thin to ⅛-¼ inch thickness. Use pizza cutter to cut dough into rectangles, triangles, and other shapes. Prick air holes with fork all the way through the dough. Bake on oiled baking sheet for 10-15 minutes until lightly browned and crisp.

Whole Wheat Teething Crackers

For babies older than one year

Preheat oven to 325°F.

2½ cups Super Flour
½ teaspoon salt
1 tablespoon honey
1 beaten egg
½ cup milk

Mix all ingredients together. Add more milk, a tablespoon at a time, until the dough forms a cohesive ball. Roll thicker than other crackers (about ⅜ inch thick). Use pizza cutter to almost cut through dough to from rectangular shapes crackers, approximately 3 x 1½ inches. Prick air holes in each cracker with a fork completely through the dough. Bake until very dry—about an hour. Cool on wire rack. If crackers are not hard, return to oven for 5-15 minutes.

Applesauce Crackers

Preheat oven to 350°F. Combine:

    1 cup Super Flour

    ½ cup plus 1 tablespoon applesauce

    4 tablespoons melted butter/oil

Roll and bake for 10 minutes. Flip each cracker over and bake for another 5-10 minutes.

Variation: You can make these crackers into twist shapes. Cut rolled dough into rectangular strips, about 3 x ½-inch. Hold the strip with two hands by the ends, twist in opposite directions, place on baking sheet and gently press the ends down onto the sheet to prevent unwinding. Bake.

Oatmeal Wheat Germ Crackers

Preheat oven to 325°F.

    ¾ cup oatmeal

    ¾ cup wheat germ

    ½ teaspoon salt

    1 tablespoon honey

    ¼ cup softened butter/oil

    3 tablespoons milk

Mix all ingredients together. Add more milk, a teaspoon at a time, until the dough forms a cohesive ball. Bake 15 minutes. Flip and bake for an additional 5-10 minutes.

Peanut Butter IN the Crackers

Preheat oven to 325°F.

    1 cup Super Flour

    2 tablespoons melted butter/oil

    2 tablespoons softened peanut butter

    ¼ cup milk

Combine ingredients. Add extra milk, a teaspoon at a time until a soft dough is formed. Knead 5 minutes and roll until ⅛ inch thick. Use pizza cutter to cut almost through dough to form rectangular shaped crackers. Prick air holes in each cracker with a fork completely through the dough. Bake about 12 minutes or until lightly browned. Cool on wire rack.

Tahini Crackers

Preheat oven to 325°F.

    1 cup Super Flour

    2 tablespoons tahini

    2 tablespoons melted butter/oil

2 tablespoons water

Combine ingredients. Add extra water, a teaspoon at a time until a soft dough is formed. Roll until ⅛ inch thick. Use pizza cutter to almost cut through dough to from rectangular shaped crackers. Prick air holes in each cracker with a fork completely through the dough. Bake about 10 minutes or until lightly browned. Cool on wire rack.

Millet Crackers

Preheat oven to 350°F. Mix in this order:

2½ tablespoons melted butter/oil

1½ teaspoons honey

4 tablespoons water

½ cup raw millet, ground to a powder in blender

¾ cup Super Flour

Add more flour, a tablespoon at a time until good dough consistency. Knead for a few minutes and roll until ⅛ inch thick on buttered baking sheet. Score with a knife in diamond shapes. Bake about 20 minutes or until lightly browned. Cool on wire rack.

Whole Grain Cheese Thins

Mix in this order:

1 cup Super Flour

½ teaspoon salt

¼ teaspoon paprika

2 cups grated Cheddar cheese

2 tablespoons oil

Shape into roll and refrigerate overnight in wax paper. Slice very thin, shape into fish or crescent designs as with commercial cheese thins, and bake on greased cookie sheet in pre-heated 350°F oven for about 10 minutes, watching carefully at end for burning. Store in airtight container for up to two weeks in a cool, dark cabinet. Use in soups or for dipping.

Cheesy Thins

Combine with your fingers or a pastry blender until dough consistency:

¾ cup Super Flour

½ cup extra sharp Cheddar or Swiss cheese or combination, grated

2 tablespoons butter, grated

Use only high quality cheeses. Knead about 30 seconds only and chill in refrigerator until firm. Roll very thin. Cut into strips 2½ inches long and ¾ inch wide. Bake in pre-heated 400°F oven for 5 minutes, watching carefully for burning. Makes about 30 thins.

Pasta Recipes

Cooking Pasta: Save some energy by experimenting with pasta cooking. Bring water to a rapid boil. Add pasta and turn off heat. Let stand for a 15 minutes or until done.

Leftover Pasta: Refrigerate leftover pasta, covered well. If pasta sticks together, boil for just one minute or two. Use leftover pasta the next day—sauté in a little butter/oil and garlic. Delicious! Or use leftover pasta for breakfast. For breakfast, mix with scrambled eggs, veggies, cheese, and/or tofu to make Macaroni and Scrambled Eggs.

Tip: Make whole grain pasta often. It's healthy and inexpensive. And pouring boiling water down drains helps to keep them clear.

Tip: Let cold tap water run in the sink while you are pouring off boiling water from pasta. It may help prevent steam and splashes from scalding you.

Super Pasta Sauce

Most commercial spaghetti sauces have too much sodium. Make your own by mixing plain tomato paste (read label and make sure that there is no added salt) with the amount of water specified on the label. Add your own fresh herbs, such as oregano and parsley, and even shredded cheese and other *Healthy Extras*. Freeze using the *Food Cube Method* or the *Phantom Container Method*.

Tip: Cut off both ends of a tomato paste can and freeze. Store in a small freezer bag. Cut off a slice when needed. Remember never to refreeze any food that has previously been frozen, due to possible bacteria contamination. If using a thawed frozen tomato paste to make sauce, do not refreeze the sauce. Keep refrigerated and use within 24 hours.

Quick Super Pasta

Cook some whole grain pasta. As a sauce, thaw a few Super Pasta Sauce food cubes (previous recipe) or vegetable food cubes or both. Add some cooked beans (whole or mashed) or cooked soy grits to the sauce. Heat sauce on the stove or in the microwave. Or don't heat at all, the heat from the pasta will warm it. Pour sauce over cooked, drained pasta. While pasta and sauce are still hot, sprinkle with shredded mozzarella or other natural cheese and let cheese melt. Or melt cheese by placing dish in the microwave for several seconds. Serve immediately. There's no end to the *Healthy Extras* you can add to a pasta dish. This is another meal you can freeze using the *Phantom Container Freezing Method*.

Easy Macaroni and Cheese

1 cup cooked whole grain pasta
¼ cup grated natural cheese
¼ cup cottage or ricotta cheese
1 teaspoon butter
2-3 tablespoons of milk

Mix all ingredients. Heat on stove top until cheese and butter melt. Add a sprinkle of wheat germ on top.

White Sauce

Mix together with whisk or fork in saucepan:
2 tablespoons melted butter/oil
2 tablespoons arrowroot
1 cup milk
⅛ teaspoon pepper (optional)
1 teaspoon salt (optional)

Stir constantly over low heat until thickened. After sauce has thickened, cook for an additional minute.

Macaroni and Cheese Bake

Cook 8 ounces whole wheat elbow macaroni. Preheat oven to 375°F. Beat together:
2 beaten eggs
1 cup milk

Make alternate layers in a greased, 2 quart casserole:
cooked macaroni and
2 cups of grated natural cheese (Mozzarella, Swiss, Cheddar, etc.)

Pour egg/milk mixture over layers. Bake for 40-45 minutes.

Blender/Stove-top Macaroni and Cheese

Cook 8 ounces whole wheat elbow macaroni. Mix in blender:
1½ cups milk
1½ cups shredded cheese or an 8 ounce package
2 tablespoons arrowroot or unbleached white flour
½ teaspoon powdered kelp or salt
1 tablespoon oil or melted butter

Put cooked macaroni in large frying pan and pour blender mixture over macaroni. Cook over low heat, stirring frequently, until thick (about 5-10 minutes). Sprinkle top with whole grain bread crumbs or wheat germ and place under broiler until browned and crunchy.

Homemade Egg Pasta Noodles

3 beaten eggs
1 tablespoon oil
1½ 1¾ cups whole wheat flour

Add beaten eggs to oil. Mix with flour until you have a stiff dough. Knead for 3-5 minutes. Roll out with rolling pin until very thin.

Let dry for 1 hour. Cut into strips. Cook immediately in boiling water for 4-5 minutes or freeze.

Spinach Noodles

Make same as homemade egg noodles, but replace one egg with a small food cube of finely puréed spinach or other Super Green Veggie Cube.

Tofu Lasagna Roll Ups

Cook 1 package of whole wheat lasagna noodles (about 8 noodles) and rinse under cold water. Meanwhile, get ready:

2½ cups tomato sauce
2 cups shredded mozzarella cheese

Mix:

1 cup mashed tofu
¼ cup grated Parmesan cheese

On each cooked noodle, spread a thin layer of the tofu mixture and about 2 tablespoons of tomato sauce, then sprinkle with some shredded cheese. Roll up the noodle jelly-roll style and place it on its side in the baking pan so that you can see the spiral from the top view. When finished with all the noodles, pour the rest of the sauce over them and sprinkle with the rest of the mozzarella cheese. Bake, covered, in a preheated 350°F oven for 30 45 minutes. Freeze leftovers.

Tip: You may wish to cut the noodles in half to make them shorter, so that the spirals will be toddler size.

Alfredo Pasta

In blender, mix until smooth:

one part milk
four parts cottage cheese
two parts grated Parmesan
fresh dill and/or parsley (approximately 1 tablespoon per two cups of cheese or to taste)
nutmeg to taste
black pepper

Toss with hot whole wheat pasta.

Mushroom-Tofu Sauce

Over medium heat, sauté ½ cup onion and ½ cup mushrooms in 1 tablespoon butter or olive oil. Optionally add 1 clove garlic and sauté for an additional minute. Turn heat down to low. Meanwhile, blend tofu (about 1 cup) in processor. Add 1 teaspoon Worcestershire sauce and ⅓ cup vegetable stock or water to processor. Mix tofu mixture into pan and stir until warmed through. Serve over cooked pasta or grains.

Casseroles

Tip: Save time in the kitchen by making two casseroles and freeze one using the Phantom Container Freezing Method. Thaw overnight in refrigerator. As a general rule, an unthawed frozen casserole should be cooked about twice as long as a thawed one. To test a casserole for doneness, insert a butter knife in the middle of the casserole, leave for 10 seconds, remove and feel for heat. If knife is cold, continue cooking.

Easy Bread Casserole

Mix in this order:

    1 cup whole wheat bread crumbs
    1¼ cups milk
    1 large beaten egg
    ½ cup cheese
    1 tablespoon or more wheat germ and/or ground nuts

Bake in pre-heated 375°F oven for 30 minutes.

Cheery Cheese Casserole

Preheat oven to 375°F. In large bowl, mix in this order:

    3 beaten eggs
    ½ cup oil or melted butter
    ½ cup soy or cow's milk
    1 cup cottage cheese
    2 cups grated jack or cheddar cheese
    ¼ cup Super Flour
    ¼ cup wheat germ

Pour mixture into buttered casserole dish and bake for 40 minutes until set.

Lentil Stew

    2 tablespoons olive oil
    2 cups chopped onion
    1 sliced raw carrot
    ½ cup diced celery with leaves
    2 tablespoons minced garlic

3½ cups broth
1 pound dry lentils
½ cup uncooked medium pearl parley
16-ounce can crushed tomatoes
1 teaspoon salt
½ teaspoon pepper
¼ teaspoon oregano
1 package frozen chopped spinach

Sauté onions, celery, and garlic in oil for 8 minutes. Add 8 cups water, the broth, lentils and barley. Cover, bring to a boil, reduce heat and simmer 1 hour or until very tender. Add crushed tomatoes, carrot, and seasonings. Bring to boil, reduce heat, and simmer uncovered for 5 minutes. Add spinach and stir to separate. Simmer another 5-7 minutes. Sprinkle this stew with lots of Parmesan cheese and it's even more delicious!

Easy One-Dish Casserole

Preheat oven to 300°F. Mix in a covered casserole dish:
½ cup uncooked lentils
¼ cup soy grits
½ cup whole grains (millet, brown rice, etc.)
1 small chopped onion
3 cups vegetable broth
1 tablespoon parsley
½ teaspoon sweet basil
¼ teaspoon oregano
¼ teaspoon thyme
1 teaspoon garlic powder

Cover and bake for 90 minutes. Add shredded or grated cheese on top for last 15 minutes of baking.

Tofu, Rice, and Parsley Casserole

Preheat oven to 350°F. Mix in blender:
1 cup milk
1 cup tofu
½ cup sharp cheese
1 egg
1 large onion
one bunch fresh or frozen parsley
1 green pepper, in large pieces

Grease a casserole dish and add 2 cups cooked brown rice or other grain. Pour mixture from blender over rice and bake covered for 45 minutes.

Quick Broccoli-Rice Casserole

Preheat oven to 350°F. In bowl, mix in this order:

    1 beaten egg

    ½ cup milk

    ½ cup grated cheese

    2 cups leftover brown rice

    1 cup broccoli, finely chopped

    1 chopped onion (sauté first if you wish)

Mix all and turn in buttered casserole dish, cover, and bake for 45 minutes.

Kale-Rice Casserole

Preheat oven to 325°F.

    2 cups cooked brown rice or other grain

    1 bunch raw kale, washed and chopped

    ½ cup shredded cheddar cheese

    ¼ cup fresh parsley

    2 beaten eggs

Mix above ingredients and press into greased baking dish. Top with this mixture:

    ¼ cup whole wheat bread crumbs

    ¼ cup wheat germ

    3 tablespoons melted butter/oil

    ¼ cup Parmesan cheese

Bake, uncovered 40 minutes.

Sweet Potato Loaf

Preheat oven to 350°F. Mix the following ingredients in one bowl.

    5 tablespoons melted butter/oil

    ½ cup orange juice

    ¾ cup cooked mashed sweet potatoes

    1 beaten egg

    1 cup ground oatmeal

    ¼ cup wheat germ

    1 teaspoon pumpkin pie spice

    ½ teaspoon baking powder

    1 teaspoon vanilla

    2 tablespoons blackstrap molasses

    ½ cup ground or chopped nuts

Add a little more orange juice if your loaf is too thick. Pour mixture into greased loaf pan. Bake for 40-45 minutes, until cake tester or toothpick comes out clean.

Easy Cheese Strata

Preheat oven to 350°F. Butter a 9 x 13-inch pan and arrange 6 slices of whole grain bread in bottom of pan. Cover with cheese slices or sprinkle with about 2 cups of shredded cheese. Layer another 6 slices of bread over cheese. In bowl, beat 3 eggs and mix in 3 cups milk. Pour egg mixture over bread/cheese layers. Bake uncovered for 45-50 minutes or until lightly browned.

Variation: Add leftover chopped cooked veggies as a layer. Sauté first.

Sweet Potato Casserole

Preheat oven to 350°F. Place cooked purée from two sweet potatoes into a large bowl. Add 1 beaten egg and ½ cup yogurt. Mix well with mixer or potato masher; don't use a blender or food processor. Stir in 2 tablespoons fresh parsley. Optionally add *Healthy Extras*. Place into greased baking dish and bake in preheated 350°F oven for 35 to 40 minutes until browned. You can make the casserole ahead and refrigerate—but add about 12 minutes to baking time.

Eggplant Parmesan

Preheat oven to 350°F. In a shallow bowl, mix these dry ingredients which will make approximately ½ cup:

¼ cup Super Flour
1 tablespoon Parmesan cheese
1 tablespoon wheat germ
1 tablespoon whole wheat bread crumbs
1 teaspoon parsley

In another bowl, mix wet ingredients:

a tablespoon of milk
1 beaten egg

Slice one raw eggplant into ¼-½ inch slices. Wet both sides of each slice by dipping in wet ingredients. Then dip into bowl of dry ingredients to coat each side with flour mixture.

Grease a large baking pan. Layer coated slices into the pan. Cover each layer with tomato sauce and sprinkle with Parmesan cheese. Cover the pan tightly and bake 35-45 minutes until eggplant is tender when pierced with fork. Turn off the oven. Sprinkle top with shredded mozzarella cheese and return pan to oven. Let sit for 5 to 10 minutes until mozzarella is nicely melted.

Serve or freeze in individual TV dinners using the *Phantom Container Freezing Method*.

Quiche

Grain Quiche Crust

Preheat oven to 350°F. Beat 2 eggs in a bowl. Add 3 cups total of cooked brown rice, millet, or other whole grain. Grease a 9-inch pie plate (preferably glass). Press grain/egg mixture into pie plate to that it covers the bottom and up the sides. Bake 15 minutes. It will bake further when you put in the quiche filling and bake in the oven. (If you're going to use this crust for a pie that does not require baking, bake it for 25 minutes instead of 15.)

Potato Quiche Crust

Preheat oven to 425°F. Grate 3 cups of raw potato. Mix with a tablespoon or two of oil. Press into 9-inch pie pan and bake for 15 minutes until it just starts to brown. Add quiche filling and bake according to directions. Because of this thick crust, you can reduce the number of eggs to three.

Rice and Cheese Crust

Preheat oven to 425°F. Mix 2 cups cooked brown rice, 1½ ounces of grated cheese, and 1 beaten egg. Pat into greased pie tin. Bake for 15 minutes.

Broccoli Cheese Rice Quiche

Prepare crust, above. Preheat oven to 350°F. Arrange in bottom of crust:
  1 cup cooked chopped broccoli florets
  1 cup shredded natural cheese (Swiss and mozzarella are good)
In separate bowl, mix:
  4 beaten eggs
  1½ cups milk
Pour over broccoli and bake in preheated 350°F oven until firm. Let stand 15 minutes before serving.

Tomato Quiche

Prepare crust (see above). Preheat oven to 375°F. Arrange 1 large or two small sliced tomatoes in bottom of crust. Sprinkle on tomato slices:
  1 teaspoon oregano
  ½ cup chopped onion
  1 cup shredded cheese
Mix in separate bowl:
  2 beaten eggs
  2 tablespoons wheat germ
  1 cup evaporated milk
Pour over tomatoes and bake for 45 minutes or until set. Let stand for 10 minutes before serving.

Frozen Treats

Tip: Popsicles can be very messy. Poke the stick through a small paper plate, a plastic lid, or a coffee filter to catch the drips. Or, for a deeper drip catcher, use a paper cup cut short. Wrap a napkin around the stick under the plate or cup to absorb the liquid that will seep through the hole.

Healthy Sundae Topping

Thaw one of your frozen baby fruit cubes to use as a topping on ice cream. Or use a jar of baby prunes, pineapples, or some other sweet fruit.

Creamsicle

Mix frozen vanilla yogurt or ice cream mixed with thawed frozen orange juice concentrate.

No-Added Sugar Popsicles

Just try to find popsicles made from 100% real fruit or fruit juice at a reasonable price in the supermarket or natural foods store. It's so easy and cheap to make your own! You can buy popsicle molds, use ice cube trays, or buy little paper cups. They have 3-ounce or 5-ounce paper cups with cute designs that are sold as disposable bathroom cups. For sticks, use wooden popsicle sticks—recycled (boil to sterilize) or purchased or buy small plastic spoons. Making popsicles could not be easier—just fill the cups, place the sticks in, and freeze! To make sticks stand centered and upright, place them into popsicles after about an hour of freezing, when they are partially frozen. If using paper cups, you can unmold using that tip or just rip them off.

Use plain fruit juice or concentrated fruit juice mixed into plain yogurt or vanilla flavored yogurt. Fresh fruit pieces (or even cooked veggie pieces) mixed into fruit juice or yogurt makes a popsicle more interesting. Be careful—watch little ones for choking! Or make layered popsicles by pouring small amounts of fruit juice/yogurt into molds and letting it freeze before another layer of a different color is added on top. Insert fruit pieces between the layers. Have your child decide on the layers and flavors.

Framed Personalized Picture Popsicles

Use a small, flat, shallow, freezable container for each popsicle. (I sometimes use small paper boxes lined with freezer wrap.) Fill halfway with plain yogurt sweetened with honey or maple syrup and a little lemon juice.

Freeze until semi-solid, but still mushy. Remove from freezer and push small berry pieces or other *Decorative Touches* into the yogurt to "draw" a design or a name. For really detailed pictures or words (that require higher resolution), you can use dried fruit chopped well in the blender.

Insert a popsicle stick into the yogurt without ruining the picture (this takes skill). Place into freezer and let freeze solid.

Remove and cover design with a clear fruit juice, such as white grape or apple juice or even plain water. Make the juice layer as thin as possible, so it won't become cloudy and hide the picture. Freeze again until solid.

The opaque yogurt acts as the background and frame for the picture, the juice acts as a clear glassy cover. If you need the containers, remove the popsicle and place in a freezer bag, as in the *Phantom Container Freezing Method*.

Tip: To make a young (or not so young) house guest feel special, make a personalized popsicle before their arrival. Make one for each guest at a birthday party.

Homemade Frozen Yogurt

Freeze plain yogurt in a flat shallow container, well covered, until mushy (about one or two hours). Remove from freezer and mix well with whisk or fork. Add flavoring: about ¼ cup of sweetener and ½-1 cup mashed fruit for each cup of yogurt. Try fork-mashed strawberries and/or bananas. (You need a lot of flavoring because sweetness is hard to taste in frozen foods.) Mix well and return to the freezer until firm.

Variation: For us chocoholics, not our babies, add as flavoring ¼ cup chocolate syrup to a cup of yogurt. After adding flavoring, freeze in popsicle molds or in paper cups with popsicle sticks for individual servings.

Frozen Yogurt Loaf

Mix yogurt with flavorings and freeze in a plastic-lined loaf pan. When solid, transfer to a freezer bag. For a quick snack, cut off a slice, let stand at room temperature for about 10 minutes to soften a bit before eating.

Yogurt Milkshake

Add 1 cup milk to at least ½ cup frozen yogurt. Fork mix or use blender and serve immediately.

Variations: Add frozen fruit for an extra sweet taste. Add an ice cube or two to make it super cold.

Mock Ice Cream

Purée frozen bananas in blender or food processor. Add orange juice, honey, and/or vanilla to taste.

Ring Around the Ice Cream

Place a bit of *Mock Ice Cream* in the middle of a canned pineapple ring. Use *Decorative Touches* to make a smiley face or other picture.

Variation: Instead of a pineapple ring, use a ring of cantaloupe or honeydew. Slice melon in half and remove seeds. Use sharp knife to cut all the way around the inside, very close to rind. Slice to make rings.

Fruit Freeze Pops

1 6-ounce can frozen orange juice concentrate
¾ cup strawberries or bananas
⅓ cup water

Mix in blender. Pour into paper cups with popsicle sticks. Freeze.

Push-Up Pops

My son discovered squeeze pops at a friend's house and now insists on eating "the cold, long, long lollipops." So I bought a box of the commercial unhealthy, artificially colored and flavored sugar water push-up pops, making sure they were pasteurized. This was solely for the purpose of obtaining the plastic containers. You, too, can buy and reuse these containers for healthy freeze pops for your child.

Cut the tops off them, pour out their contents, rinse them out with very hot water, and use a tiny funnel to pour natural, no-sugar added pasteurized fruit juice into them. The natural foods store has a great selection—try watermelon or pina colada!

If your child complains that they don't taste as good as the commercial brands, make them just a bit sweeter by adding a little honey or maple syrup.

After filling the containers, I considered taping them shut, but was concerned about my son eating that glue on the tape, so I just leave the containers opened.

Place the filled pops into a very tall plastic cup to keep them upright and prevent spillage. Keep the filled freeze pops in the cup and place into the freezer for a few hours until they freeze solid. Then transfer them to a large air-tight freezer bag. You can reuse the containers over and over again if you wash them between each use with very hot water and antibacterial dish soap. Rinse well to get every last trace of soap out!

Fruit Ice Milk

In blender, blend 1 cup fruit (blueberries, peaches, strawberries, or other fruit) with 2 cups of milk (cow or soy). Pour into shallow tray, cover tightly, and freeze until mushy. Remove from freezer and mix with electric mixer, fork, or whisk until smooth. Optionally, add more fruit chunks or *Healthy Extras*. Place back in the freezer until frozen.

Frozen Fruit Cream

Blend in processor until smooth.
> ½ cup evaporated milk
> package of frozen fruit

Freeze in paper cups with popsicle sticks.

Homemade Ice Cream Sandwiches

Make your own ice cream sandwiches by placing *Mock Ice Cream*, frozen ice cream, or yogurt between two large, flat homemade cookies. Freeze until solid using the *Nested Plastic Bag Method*.

Ice Cream Soda

Place a scoop or two of ice cream in a bowl or cup. Pour some *Mock Soda Pop* over the ice cream. Serve immediately. Optionally cover with *Mock Whipped Cream*.

Variation: In place of ice cream, use Mock Ice Cream or frozen yogurt or any frozen sweet food, such as frozen fruit chunks.

Watermelon Alphabet or Artwork Popsicles

From a whole watermelon, slice a circular piece about 1 inch thick from the center of the melon where the circumference is greatest. With a sharp knife, cut out shapes or your child's initials. Insert a popsicle stick up through the bottom. Freeze using the *Tray-Freeze Method*. These popsicles are very drippy and are best eaten while wearing a bathing suit!

Real Fruit Sherbet

This is too easy. Simply blend frozen fruit (store-bought or your own frozen fruits) in the food processor or blender until smooth. Frozen melon balls are great for this. So are frozen strawberries and blueberries. Optionally add into blender some frozen fruit juice concentrate (about 1 tablespoon for each cup of fruit), or a little orange and/or lemon juice. The mixture is very thick and it may be necessary to open a stir a few times and add a little juice or water. Sprinkle *Healthy Extras* on top. Or you can freeze the fruit in individual cups to have Italian Ice.

Fruit Slushy

In blender, mix fresh fruit with ice cubes. Add ice cubes gradually until desired consistency.

"Creamy" Fruit Slushy

Blend together:
  ½ cup unsweetened apple juice or any fruit juice
  ½ cup low-fat plain yogurt
  1 teaspoon maple syrup or blackstrap molasses
  2 ice cubes
Blend very well, adding more ice or water to desired consistency.

Variation: Instead of juice, you can add fruit pieces, such as strawberries, bananas, or blueberries. Or you can add re-hydrated dried fruit, such as papaya and apricots.

Strawberry Fruit Ice

In blender, mix 1 cup water or juice with 1 cup fresh strawberries or other fruit until smooth. Optionally add a teaspoon of lemon juice. Freeze using the *Food Cube Method*. Take what you need, chop until smooth in blender or food processor. Serve in shallow bowls. Sprinkle *Healthy Extras* on top.

Lunch Box Slushy

Freeze strawberry fruit ice or any fruit ice in small lidded containers or empty single serving yogurt containers. Cover well before freezing. In the morning, put in lunch box (next to a food or drink that should be kept cold). By lunchtime, your child has slush!

Fruit Juice Snowballs

Crush ice in blender to make snow. Use ice cream scoop to shape like snowballs and place in bowls or shallow glasses. Pour (very cold) fruit juice over snowballs.

Variation: For a sweeter, thicker topping, use frozen juice concentrate diluted with a little water. Use paper cups instead of glass for a refreshing outside summer snack.

Quick Vanilla Ice Cream

Mix 2 tablespoons cream or milk with 2-3 tablespoons honey and ⅓ teaspoon vanilla. Stir into 2 cups crushed ice from blender. Eat immediately.

Frozen Fruit Crunch

In a blender, mix ⅓ cup milk with 2 tablespoons frozen fruit concentrate. Add 2-4 ice cubes gradually until desired consistency.

Non-Dairy Ice Cream

8-12 ounces of tofu
1 frozen sliced banana
1 tablespoon honey
¼-½ cup fruit juice or water

Mix in blender for about a minute until creamy. Place in freezer container and optionally stir in frozen fruit pieces, such as strawberries, blueberries, etc. Freeze for 30 minutes before serving.

Variation: Make your own recipe. Add ground nuts, a tablespoon of tahini, and/or other *Healthy Extras*. This is a good way to use up leftovers.

Frozen Banana Pops

Cut bananas in half lengthwise and then width-wise to make 4 banana quarters. Stick popsicle sticks in the widest end. Roll in honey, maple syrup, fruit juice concentrate, or fruit juice to coat. Then roll in a mixture of dry ingredients, such as chopped or ground nuts, wheat germ, finely chopped dried fruit, unsweetened coconut, or mini chocolate chips. Freeze using the *Tray-Freeze Method*.

Tofutti

Mix 1 box tofu with ½ cup fruit juice concentrate or to taste. Freeze in plastic cups.

Desserts and Dessert Toppings

Tip: Freeze leftover whipped topping by glopping it onto cookie sheets and using the *Tray-Freeze Method*.

Parfait Buffet

Allow your child to be "in charge" by having him make his own parfait. Or you can make it under his direction; it's quicker and much less messy. The choices in the buffet could include yogurt; sliced, diced, or puréed fresh fruits and veggies or thawed food cubes; ground nuts and seeds, soft peanut butter and other nut or seed butters; grated cheeses; wheat germ; cooked grains and legumes; raisins and other dried fruits; and *Mock Whipped Cream*. You certainly don't need all of these!

Your child will feel just as special if you allow him to direct your parfait construction with only two or three ingredients— "Which one do you want on the bottom? Is that enough?" You should, of course, use a tall transparent plastic (or glass if you are brave enough) container so that your child can see the layers he created. A *Parfait Buffet* is a good way to use leftovers.

Instant Blender Whole Grain Bread Pudding

1 cup whole grain bread crumbs

¼ cup cream or milk

1 teaspoon lemon juice

2 tablespoons raw apple, diced

2 tablespoons diced dried apricots or raisins

Grind in blender and serve. Add a little more milk if too thick.

Baked Whole Grain Bread Pudding

Preheat oven to 350°F. Combine in 2 quart casserole dish:

8 slices whole grain bread, crusts removed and cubed

1 can evaporated skim milk (12 ounces)

Let stand for 10-15 minutes until milk is absorbed. Meanwhile, combine in a small bowl:

2 extra large eggs

1 egg white

1 cup milk

½ cup honey

1 teaspoon vanilla

½ teaspoon cinnamon

Stir ½ cup plumped raisins or other dried fruit into bread and milk mixture. Pour egg mixture from small bowl into casserole. Bake 45 minutes or until set. Serve warm with *Mock Whipped Cream*.

Edible Play Dough

2 tablespoons creamy peanut butter

2 tablespoons honey

Approx. 4 tablespoons instant powdered milk (do not mix with water)

Mix and knead until dough-like consistency. Add a little water to thin or milk powder to thicken. Roll into balls, shape into snakes, make your child's initials, flatten and cut into any shape you want. Use *Decorative Touches* to decorate. And then EAT! Make each guest at your child's birthday party feel special: Place her edible initials on her party plate to mark her place at the table.

Play Dough Cookies *(Marizipan Cookies)*

These cookies can be shaped (as you would play dough) and then baked and eaten. Preheat oven to 300°F. Mix:

1 cup butter or margarine

½ cup sugar

¼ teaspoon almond paste

2½ cups Super Flour (use mostly white flour)

Cream first three ingredients and add flour. Divide into several batches and color. Let children mold into shapes using *Decorative Touches*. Bake for 25-35 minutes depending on size of shapes. Watch very carefully so they don't burn. Remove smaller shapes if they are done, leaving larger shapes to continue baking.

Oatmeal Raisin Cookies

Preheat oven to 375°F. Grease two cookie sheets. In large bowl combine:

    1 cup whole wheat flour or Super Flour
    ¾ cup wheat germ
    ½ cup rolled oats
    1 tablespoon baking powder
    2 teaspoons cinnamon

In blender/processor, process at medium or low speed until dried fruit is finely chopped:

    1 cup apple juice concentrate
    ¼ cup oil
    1 egg
    ¾ cup dried fruit (raisins, apricots, prunes, etc.)

Pour blender mixture into bowl of dry ingredients. Stir together. Drop by heaping teaspoons onto cookie sheets one inch apart. Flatten with back of fork. Bake 8-10 minutes, watching carefully to prevent cookies from becoming crispy and brown. Let cool slightly and place in plastic bag to prevent cookies from becoming hard. Cool completely before closing bag.

Crunchy Apple Crisp

Apple mixture: Wash, peel, core and slice thinly 8 large apples. Mix with:

    3 tablespoons honey
    3 teaspoons lemon juice
    1 teaspoon of cinnamon

Place apple mixture into a 9-inch square baking dish. The apples will really fill the dish, but will shrink during cooking.

    Preheat oven to 350°F.

Oat topping: Combine:

    1 cup rolled oats
    ¼ cup Super Flour
    ¼ cup wheat germ
    ¾ cup chopped walnuts
    1 teaspoon cinnamon

Then combine ¼ cup melted butter or oil with 6 tablespoons of maple syrup or honey and mix with oat topping mixture.

Sprinkle oat mixture over apples. Bake 45-50 minutes until top is lightly browned and apples are soft. If oat topping begins to burn before apples are cooked, shield with aluminum foil. Serve topped with *Mock Whipped Cream* or *Mock Ice Cream*.

Variation: Replace apple mixture with this peach mixture:
    2 pounds of sliced frozen peaches
    2½ tablespoons of lemon juice
    3 tablespoons honey
    ¼ cup of melted butter or oil
Oat topping remains the same as above.

Cheesecake

Preheat oven to 375°F. Make a graham cracker pie shell by whizzing whole grain honey graham crackers from the natural foods store in the blender to make 1 ½ cups crumbs. Mix crumbs with 2 tablespoons of melted butter/oil and 3-4 melted concentrated fruit juice. Press into 9 inch pie pan and bake for 7-8 minutes. Meanwhile, combine:
    2 beaten eggs
    1 cup (8 ounces) combination of cream cheese and/or cottage cheese
    ½ cup honey
    ¼ cup nonfat dry milk powder
    2 teaspoons vanilla
    2 tablespoons lemon juice
Pour mixture into crust and bake at 375°F for 30 minutes. Refrigerate for at least 45 minutes before eating. Top with fresh strawberries or other fruit.
Variation: Add to filling ground nuts or a small can of crushed pineapple.

Peanut Butter Pudding

Mix in blender:
    1 small mashed banana
    ½ cup yogurt or tofu
    ½ cup natural peanut butter
    1 teaspoon maple syrup or honey
    ¼ teaspoon vanilla
Process until smooth, pour into individual cups, and refrigerate until cold.
Variation: Replace all or part of the peanut butter or tofu with tahini, almond butter, or other nut/seed butters.

Mocked Whipped Cream

Here are healthy alternatives to the expensive supermarket whipped cream products, which have lots of sugar and preservatives.

Tip: Poke beaters through a sheet of wax paper before inserting into mixer base. The wax paper covering the bowl will help prevent messy splatters.

Tip: To whip a small amount of cream, use a sturdy cup and only one beater of your electric mixer. As always, make sure the ingredients, cup, and beater all very cold for better whipping. For sweetened topping, confectioners' sugar makes more fluff than granulated. Evaporated milk will whip, but with more work than heavy cream with its high fat content. For best results, freeze milk in ice cube tray until ice crystals just begin to form. Using an ice cube tray will allow the center of the milk to get colder then a bowl would.

Tip: For a special touch that requires only a few seconds, sprinkle whipped topping on desserts with a little powder that has color: cinnamon, carob or cocoa powder, nutmeg, powdered kelp, etc.

Mock Whipped Cream I

Process at high speed until peaks form:
> 1 cup cottage cheese
> 1 tablespoons unsweetened pineapple concentrate
> 1 tablespoon lemon concentrate

Serve immediately.

Mock Whipped Cream II

Add equivalent of one pasteurized egg white to a thoroughly mashed banana. Use an electric mixer and beat until mixture stands in peaks. Add ½ teaspoon vanilla and 1 tablespoon honey or other sweetener. If you wish, add coloring.

Mock Whipped Cream III

Put one cup ice water in your blender. Slowly mix in one cup nonfat dry milk and blend until consistency of whipped cream—about 5 minutes. Serve immediately.

No-Cook Brown Rice Pudding

Mix together:
> 2 cups cooked brown rice or other cooked whole grain
> 1 cup chopped pineapple, drained
> ¼ cup dried fruit, chopped (raisins, dates, prunes, apricots, etc.)
> ½-¾ cup yogurt, plain
> ¼ cup ground nuts (optional)
> grated coconut (optional)

Mix together and refrigerate at least 2 hours before serving.

Brown Rice Pudding

In a saucepan over medium heat, heat to boiling:
- 1 cup cooked brown rice or other cooked whole grain
- 1 cup milk
- 1 cup applesauce
- ½ cup raisins

Reduce heat to low and add:
- ½ cup chopped nuts
- 2 teaspoons tahini

Cook over low heat for 20 minutes. Remove from heat and stir in:
- 1 tablespoon vanilla

Serve with yogurt topping:
- 1 cup yogurt mixed with
- 2 tablespoons honey or maple syrup

Sprinkle with a dash of cinnamon and/or nutmeg.

Tofu Icing

In blender, mix:
- 1 pound of tofu
- ½ cup maple syrup or other sweetener
- 1-2 tablespoons tahini
- 1 tablespoon vanilla
- 2-3 drops almond extract
- ⅛ teaspoon nutmeg
- ¼ teaspoon kelp or salt

Yogurt Icing

Mix thick yogurt cheese with honey, maple syrup, puréed fruit, or concentrated fruit juice to make a healthy alternative to sugary cake icings.

Powdered Milk Icing

- ½ cup softened butter or oil
- ½ cup honey
- ¼ cup maple syrup
- 1 teaspoon vanilla
- 1 cup nonfat dry milk powder
- 1-3 tablespoons water

Mix first three ingredients and slowly add milk powder while mixing. Add water, a small amount at a time, until desired consistency.

Pineapple Cream Cheese Icing

Mix in blender/processor:
    1 package (8 oz) cream cheese
    ¼ cup frozen pineapple juice concentrate or canned crushed pineapple
    ¼ cup ground cashews and/or other nuts
Variation: Use any fruit juice concentrate.

Apple Juice - Cream Cheese Frosting

1½-2 teaspoons unflavored gelatin or agar
½ cup apple juice concentrate divided into 2 tablespoons and
    6 tablespoons
16 ounces cream cheese
2 teaspoons vanilla
½ cup finely chopped dried fruit (raising, apricots, prunes, etc.)

In small saucepan, stir 2 tablespoons of thawed juice concentrate into gelatin and let stand two minutes. Heat to boiling and stir to dissolve. Meanwhile, in blender or processor, mix the rest of the ingredients until smooth. Beat gelatin mixture into cream cheese mixture until well-blended. Refrigerator for 30-60 minutes until frosting begins to set, and use to frost the cake.

Mock Cream Cheese Frosting

2 cups ricotta cheese
3 tablespoons honey
1 teaspoon vanilla

Whip until smooth in blender and chill in refrigerator immediately. When cold, use as frosting.
Variation: Replace part of ricotta cheese with yogurt cheese or tofu.

Cream Cheese Frosting

Blend equal parts of butter, cream cheese, and honey. Add a touch of vanilla.

The Easiest Cream Cheese Icing

Mix cream cheese and honey together. Use about 2½ tablespoons of honey for each 4 ounces of cream cheese.

Lemon Sugar Drizzle

Mix the juice of one lemon with ¼ cup of sugar/honey and drizzle immediately over cake.

No-Fail Party Cake Frosting

In large bowl, mix with an electric mixer:

    6 ounces cream cheese
    4 tablespoons butter
    1 teaspoon vanilla

When smooth, gradually beat in:

    4 cups sifted confectioners' sugar

Sifting prevents lumps. If you don't have a sifter, sift by shaking sugar in a strainer or sieve over bowl while adding to mix. Tint with food coloring. Enough for one 9-inch round double layer cake or one 9 x 13 sheet cake.

Nut Frosting

    ½ cup ground nuts (almonds are good)
    ¼ cup olive oil or melted butter
    ¼ cup honey

In saucepan, heat oil and honey until they almost boil. Remove from heat and stir in nuts. Spread on cake (good for carrot cake) and place under oven broiler for a minute.

King Lion's Milk Bars

Here is a homemade version of one of the expensive health food store candy bars:

    ¾ cup peanut butter
    1 tablespoon nutritional yeast
    1 teaspoon honey
    3 tablespoons sugar
    1 cup instant nonfat dry milk

Mix ingredients above with your hands (because it is so thick and dry). Shape into candy bars or balls. Dip bars into about ½ cup of melted sweetened carob chips plus 1 teaspoon canola oil. Dry on waxed paper.

Variation: Add raisins or other dried fruit, ground nuts and seeds, or coconut.

Dried Fruit Bars

Preheat oven to 375°F.

    1 beaten egg
    ½ cup melted butter/oil
    ¼ cup honey
    ¼ cup orange juice
    1½ cup Super Flour
    1 tablespoon wheat germ

1¼ teaspoon baking powder

· 1 cup dried fruit (dates are good)

Mix ingredients in bowl in the order above, adding dried fruit last. Press into square pan. Bake 25 minutes or until lightly browned.

Bunny Birthday Cake

In medium saucepan, bring to a boil:

2½ cups grated raw carrots

1 cup plus 2 tablespoons of frozen apple juice concentrate, thawed

Lower to simmer, cover, and cook 15-20 minutes or until carrots are tender. Purée in blender or processor until smooth. Add:

1½ cups dried fruit (raisins, apricots, prunes, etc.)

Process until fruit is finely chopped. Let cool. Preheat oven to 350°F. Grease two 9-inch square cake pan and line with wax paper. In large bowl, combine dry ingredients:

2 cups Super Flour or whole wheat flour

½ cup wheat germ

2 tablespoons baking soda

1 tablespoon ground cinnamon

Combine wet ingredients:

2 eggs

4 egg whites

1 tablespoon vanilla

1¼ cup apple juice concentrate

Add wet ingredients into dry ingredients and beat until well mixed but don't overbeat. Fold in carrot purée from blender and ¾ cup unsweetened applesauce.

Bake 35-40 minutes. Cool before frost with cream cheese icing.

Bunny Cake

Grease and flour a 9x13 baking pan. Preheat oven to 325°F. Use whisk to beat until foamy (about 1 minute) in a large bowl:

4 eggs

½ cup melted butter/oil

¾ cup pineapple juice concentrate

½ cup orange juice concentrate

Add to bowl:

1½ teaspoons cinnamon

1¼ cups grated carrot

2 cups Super Flour

Hand beat for 3 minutes. Sprinkle 1 tablespoon baking soda into the mixture and mix by hand for exactly 30 strokes. Immediately pour into readied baking pan. The mixture will seem like it's foaming. Bake for 30 minutes until toothpick or cake tester comes out clean.

Tip: For more nutrition, dust a cake pan with wheat germ instead of white flour.

Easy Carrot Cake

Preheat oven to 350°F. Grease and flour a 9 x 13 baking pan. In large bowl, mix ingredients in this order:

2 beaten eggs
½ cup olive oil
½ cup honey
½ teaspoon cinnamon
1¼ cup grated carrots
½ cup ground nuts
1¼ cups Super Flour
2 teaspoons baking powder

Bake 25-30 minutes. Good with Nut Frosting or any cream cheese frosting.

Healthy Honey Cake

Preheat oven to 325°F. Grease a flour a loaf pan. Mix together in this order:

1 beaten egg
3 tablespoons melted butter/oil
¾ cup honey
½ cup milk
1½ cup Super Flour
½ teaspoon baking soda
¾ cup ground almonds

Bake for 45 minutes until loaf begins to pull away from sides of pan.

No-Egg Dried Fruit Squares

On stove top or in microwave oven on low power, melt:

1 cup frozen apple juice concentrate
¼ cup butter/oil

Stir in:

½ cup raisins and ½ cup dried apricots

Let sit for 10 minutes. Meanwhile, in large bowl, combine dry ingredients:

1¼ cups Super Flour
¼ cup ground nuts
1½ tablespoons baking powder

Slowly stir juice-butter mixture into dry ingredients, until just blended. Pour into greased 8-inch square pan. Bake in a preheated 325°F oven for 30 minutes, until a cake tester/toothpick comes out clean. Slice into 16 squares.

Nutty Rattle Snake

Grind 1 cup nuts (almonds, cashews, filberts, walnuts, etc.). Mix with:
   ½ cup honey
   4 tablespoons softened butter
   1 teaspoon vanilla

Roll dough into a snake shape. Place two small nut pieces for the snake's eyes. Wrap in waxed paper and refrigerate overnight. Place chilled roll on ungreased baking sheet. Shape chilled dough into wavy snake with raised "head" and "rattler tail." Bake in preheated 350°F oven for 8-10 minutes or until browned. Place on white paper towels to absorb excess oil and allow to cool before serving. Refrigerate.

Slithery Snake Snacks

Mix together in this order:
   2 cups ground nuts
   1 cup ground pitted prunes
   1 beaten egg
   1 cup of honey

Shape into slithery slimy snakes. Bake in a preheated 375°F oven on a buttered cookie sheet for about 10 minutes. Refrigerate.

Dairy-Free Pumpkin Pie

Preheat oven to 350°F.
   16 ounces of tofu (Silken, Firm, or Extra Firm)
   2 cups canned or cooked pumpkin
   ⅔ cup honey
   1 teaspoon vanilla
   1 teaspoon pumpkin pie spice
   1 unbacked 9-inch pastry crust

Mix tofu in blender or processor until smooth. Add other ingredients and blend well. Pour into a 9-inch deep dish pie shell. Bake for about one hour. Filling will be soft, but will firm up as it chills. Chill and serve.

Almond Cupcakes

Preheat oven to 325°F.

½ cup almond butter/oil
1½ teaspoons almond extract
1 teaspoon vanilla
¾ cup honey
1 cup milk
2 beaten eggs
1 cup Super Flour
2 teaspoons baking powder
½ cup ground almonds

Mix ingredients in a bowl in the order given, reserving 2 tablespoons of ground almonds. Pour into 12 greased or lined muffin tins. Sprinkle reserved almonds on top for garnish. Bake 25-30 minutes until toothpick comes out clean and tops are a golden brown.

Tip: Instead of frosting cupcakes on top, slice them in half and frost the cut edges making a cupcake "sandwich." Use in lunch boxes to prevent icing from sticking to wrap.

Easy, Healthy Pie Crust

Mix in a pie pan:

1½ cups Super Flour
⅓ cup oil
6 tablespoons ice water

Prick with fork and bake 10-12 minutes.

Granola Pie Crust

Pulverize 2 cups granola in blender or food processor. Mix with 3 tablespoons apple juice. Press into pie pan and bake at 350°F for about 10 minutes.

Variations: Instead of granola, pulverize whole grain honey graham crackers, breakfast flake cereal, or whole grain cookies. Instead of apple juice, mix with no-sugar added jam or preserves, concentrated frozen fruit juice, or jam-flavored or honey-flavored yogurt.

No-Bake Mini-Cream Pies

You can make a few of these mini-pies and refrigerate for up to one week, or make lots and freeze them for up to two months. These make great little healthy lunches or snacks. Thaw them overnight in the refrigerator before serving.

Containers: Butter or oil-spray 24 mini muffin tins.

Crusts: Mix:
- ½ cup wheat germ
- ½ cup ground nuts (almonds or walnuts are good)
- ¼ cup melted butter/oil

Press crust mixture into containers to form crusts that go ¾ up the sides.

Filling: Mix:
- ½ cup of mashed avocado
- ½ cup of yogurt cheese
- 1 teaspoon lemon juice
- ¼ cup honey or maple syrup

Spoon mixture into crusts.

Topping: Sprinkle top with ground nuts and/or wheat germ. Or place a small dollop of jelly or jam or a fresh strawberry or other berry on top. Or, make a happy face or other design with *Decorative Touches*.

After mini pies are assembled, cover well and freeze until solid. When frozen, remove pies and place in freezer bags.

Filling Variation: Instead of avocado, use all yogurt cheese, or use all cream cheese, or use a mixture of cream cheese and yogurt cheese and mashed avocado.

Peanut Butter Fudge

- 4 tablespoons honey
- ½ cup peanut butter
- 1 cup nonfat powdered milk (not instant)
- ¼ teaspoon vanilla

Mix well and press into pan lined with waxed paper. Refrigerate until firm and cut into squares.

Peanut Butter Carob Fudge

Make peanut butter fudge as in previous recipe, replacing ½ cup of powdered milk with carob powder (or, for adults, cocoa powder or a mixture of both).

Nut Banana Bites

- 3-4 ripe bananas
- ½ cup crushed wheat squares cereal
- 1 tablespoon peanut butter or other nut butter
- 1 tablespoon honey
- 1 teaspoon carob powder

Mash all together and roll into bite-sized balls.

Peanut Butter Cookies

Preheat oven to 375°F. Mix these ingredients in this order:

   2 beaten eggs
   1 mashed ripe banana
   2 tablespoons melted butter/oil
   1 teaspoon vanilla
   ½ cup natural creamy peanut butter
   1 cup Super Flour
   ½ teaspoon baking powder
   ½ teaspoon nutmeg
   1 cup chopped peanuts or other nuts

Mix well. Drop by teaspoonfuls onto greased cookie sheets. Flatten by making crisscross perpendicular lines with a fork . (Let your toddler help by making the lines.) Bake 6-8 minutes until lightly browned. Cool on rack. Makes at least 2 dozen.

Tip: For an easy cookie topping that gives a nice taste and glaze, spread a thin layer of jelly over the cookies before baking.

Tip: If you're short on cookie sheets, use a broiler pan or other large shallow baking pan. Flip upside down and use the bottom.

Tip: Remove a baked cookie stuck to the pan by sliding dental floss under it.

Tip: Roll cookie dough into a sausage shape for easy cutting of uniformly shaped cookies. Or freeze dough in large juice can. Thaw at room temperature 15 minutes before pushing up and slicing, using the can's edge as a cutting guide.

Oatmeal Cookies

Preheat oven to 325°F. Mix in this order:

   2 beaten eggs
   ½ cup oil
   ¾ cup honey
   ¼ cup blackstrap molasses
   1 teaspoon vanilla or almond extract
   2 tablespoons wheat germ
   1 cup nonfat dry milk
   3 cups rolled oats

Drop teaspoon-sized amounts two inches apart on buttered or oil-sprayed cookie sheet. Bake 10-12 minutes or until browning begins around edges.

Tip: You may enjoy the flavor of oatmeal cookies more if you bake the oatmeal before you start. Sprinkle oatmeal evenly on a cookie sheet and bake at 300°F for about 10 minutes. Use as ingredients for cookies and other recipes.

Pear Date Sandwich Bars

Preheat oven to 350°F. Mix together:
- 1 cup puréed pears (or baby food pears)
- 2 eggs
- ⅓ cup melted butter/oil
- 1½ cups Super Flour
- 1 cup rolled oats
- 2 teaspoons baking powder

Spread into two buttered 8-inch square baking pans or one 9 x 13 pan. Bake 20 minutes until lightly browned. Cool on wire racks. Cut cake into bar-sized pieces. Make sandwiches by spreading date filling between two pieces.

Date Filling: Process pitted dates in blender or food processor, adding enough water to make spreadable consistency.

Variation: Instead of pears, you can use applesauce or other puréed fruit. Instead of date filling you can use Prune Butter.

Orange Topping

Place ¼ cup orange juice in the freezer to make it ice cold. Mix in blender the cold orange juice, 1 teaspoon frozen orange juice concentrate until smooth. Add ½ cup nonfat dry milk powder and blend until stiff. Add *Healthy Extras*. Yields about 1 cup. Serve immediately over muffins or cake and keep refrigerated or freeze.

Maplenut Yogurt Topping

- 2 tablespoons maple syrup
- 2 tablespoons ground walnuts or other nuts or seeds

Stir ingredients and serve immediately. Good on pancakes.

Watermelon Pudding

- 2 cups puréed watermelon, seeds removed
- 1 tablespoon arrowroot
- 1 tablespoon frozen orange juice concentrate
- ½ teaspoon vanilla
- 3-4 tablespoons honey or maple syrup

In saucepan, heat all ingredients to almost boiling. Turn down heat to low and stir until thick. Refrigerate and serve cold.

Applesauce Pudding

In saucepan over low heat stir 1 cup applesauce with 1 tablespoon arrowroot or cornstarch. Stir constantly until pudding-like consistency.

Gelatin/Agar Agar

Healthy Juice Gelatin

Make gelatin from fruit juice, not the commercial stuff which is sugar and chemicals. Save money by buying unflavored gelatin in bulk—it keeps indefinitely. One tablespoon of gelatin (equal to one packet) will gel two cups of liquid. For juice gelatin, mix one tablespoon (one packet) of dry gelatin into one cup of cold juice and let sit for one minute. Add one cup of boiling juice and stir until dissolved. Pour into mold or individual cups and refrigerate until gelled.

Gelatin Tips

If you are not using a colorful juice (such as apple juice which makes brown gelatin), you may want to add food coloring for a brighter color.

To prevent lumping, always mix gelatin first with cool liquid and let stand one minute to let the granules separate (even though a recipe may say to add boiling water directly to the dry gelatin.)

For a sweeter gelatin, replace one quarter cup of fruit juice with 2 tablespoons of concentrated fruit juice.

When serving pudding or gelatin at a child's birthday party, pour into muffin tins double-lined with paper muffin cups. Then serve by placing on the child's paper plate.

Baby food jars are a nice size for a single serving of gelatin.

Speed the gelling process by placing gelatin in the freezer for 30 minutes and then placing in the refrigerator.

Freeze individual gelatin servings in yogurt containers and place in your child's lunch box. Gelatin will be thawed by lunchtime.

Before turning a gelatin mold out onto a plate, wet the plate with cold water so that it will be easy to move the mold and center it on the plate.

Unmold by sliding a knife between the gelatin and the container to break the vacuum. Then submerge the mold up to its edge into a bowl of hot water for about 5 seconds. Hold the wet plate upside down firmly over the mold, flip, and jerk once. The mold should fall onto the plate.

Basic Vegetarian Gelatin

Gelatin is made from animal products, agar agar is made from seaweed. One tablespoon of agar agar will gel 1-2 cups of liquid, depending on the brand. Follow the directions on the label or mix two tablespoons of dry agar agar into two cups fruit juice. Bring to a boil, reduce heat, and simmer for 5 minutes. Refrigerate until set in individual containers or mold.

Juicy Vegan Cloud

Stir two tablespoons agar agar into ½ cup orange juice in a medium bowl and let sit for 1-2 minutes. Meanwhile, bring ½ cup juice to a boil and stir until dissolved. Stir in one cup of cold soy milk. Refrigerate until set.

Juice Blocks

To make jiggly gelatin blocks, simply add twice as much gelatin (one tablespoon per cup of liquid) for a more firm gelling. To make a 9 x 13 mold, sprinkle four tablespoons (four packets) dry unflavored gelatin into one cup of cold juice. Wait 1-2 minutes. Add three cups of boiling juice and stir until dissolved. Pour into 9 x 13 pan and refrigerate until firm. Cut into blocks, use cookie cutters, or cut freehand into *Simple Shapes*.

Dinosaur DNA

If you've seen the movie *Jurassic Park*, you may remember the mosquito fossilized in sap. Make gelatin bars with raisin or prune pieces inside, which could be cut and shaped to look like flying insects. Place a "mosquito" in each gelatin block. For a less creepy dessert, place a piece of candy or a small non-toxic plastic toy favor into each block.

Jiggling Jelly Worms

Make recipe for *Juice Blocks* in a shallow baking dish. Submerge large straws in the mixture so that they fill with the gelatin. (Place jars on top of the straws if they float to keep them submerged.) Refrigerate overnight or for 6-8 hours to let gelatin become very solid. Remove straws, and use a rolling pin from the end of each straw to push out the worms.

Gelled Orange Slices

Wash an orange and cut a small hole in one end. Hollow out the orange thoroughly. Prepare *Juice Blocks* recipe with orange juice and pour into orange shell. Refrigerate until very solid. Use a sharp serrated knife dipped in very hot water to cut orange into slices and serve. These slices make a hit at birthday parties.

Fruit Yogurt Mold

Dissolve 1 tablespoon gelatin into ½ cup orange juice in a saucepan. Wait one minute and heat over low heat or in the microwave for 30 seconds. Add two tablespoons honey. Stir an additional ½ cup cold orange juice into gelatin-juice mixture. Into one cup yogurt, mix ¼ cup all-fruit jelly. Add yogurt and jelly to orange juice mixture and stir well with fork or whisk. Pour into mold and let set in refrigerator.

Fruit Frappé

Dissolve 1 tablespoon gelatin in ¼ cup cold water and heat water until hot. Let cool in freezer for a few minutes. Place 1 cup fruit in blender with 1 tablespoon of lemon juice. Add a 6-ounce can of frozen orange juice concentrate and keep blending. Add ice cubes one at a time while blending until good consistency. Serve immediately.

Cantaloupe Gelatin Planet

Wash uncut whole cantaloupe (or honeydew). Cut off a circular slice of rind from the stem end of the cantaloupe to use as a lid. Discard seeds. Use melon baller to hollow out cantaloupe and make melon balls. Invert melon and let drain.

Make gelatin using agar or by following directions on box of unflavored gelatin using orange juice instead of water.

Fill hollowed out cantaloupe. Pour any extra gelatin into another container. Refrigerate.

After gelatin is slightly thickened, add melon balls. Return to refrigerator to finish gelling.

Replace "lid" on cantaloupe planet and serve. If the bowls are rolling around and unstable, slice a little piece off the bottom to make it flatter. Let your kids eat the oceans, lava, rock layers (the melon balls are big rocks and they have teeth as strong as lions, or their mouth is a front loader or other construction machine).

Orange Peel Moons

For smaller servings of planet innards, use hollowed out oranges or lemons instead of melons in the *Cantaloupe Gelatin Planet* recipe above.

Condiments, Sauces, Seasonings, and Dips

Tip: If you are using dried herbs in these sauces, place them in hot water for just a moment and drain, and they'll be fresher, greener, and have more flavor. Before using dried herbs in any recipe, roll them with the palms of your hands to crumble them and this will bring out more flavor.

Tip: To get stubborn ketchup flowing from the bottle, release the vacuum by sticking a drinking straw, knife, etc. into the center.

Mustard Mayonnaise

Don't buy mustard mayonnaise—make your own by mixing mustard and tofu mayo in a proportion that suits you. Begin with 1 tablespoon mustard to ½ cup mayo and experiment from there.

Mustard Butter

As with mustard mayo, you can save money by making your own mustard butter. Blend about a tablespoon of prepared mustard with ½ cup of softened butter. Melt over cooked veggies or use to fry scrambled eggs.

The Easiest Cheese Sauce

Place a slice of cheese or shredded cheese pieces over vegetables and either microwave for 30 seconds, or place in 450°F oven, or under the broiler until the cheese has melted. Another easy cheese sauce is a can of condensed cheese soap from the natural foods store mixed with ¼ cup milk. Pour over cooked vegetable pieces such as broccoli or cauliflower.

Cheese Driz Sauce

Mix in your blender/processor in this order:

½ cup warm water

1 teaspoon liquid lecithin

¼ teaspoon powdered kelp

12-ounce package of shredded natural cheese at room temperature (sharp cheddar is good)

Gradually add a small amount of instant nonfat powdered milk until consistency is similar to commercial Cheese Whiz®. Refrigerate in airtight glass jar.

Fruit Sauces

Instead of the very common applesauce, make sauces from bananas, blueberries, cherries, strawberries, mangos, papayas, peaches, pears, pineapples, and plums. Simply purée the peeled, cored, fresh fruit in the blender. Or you can use frozen fruit. Fruit sauces are used in some recipes in this book. For the easiest fruit sauce of all, use baby food fruit in jars.

Thickened Fruit Sauce

½ cup frozen concentrated fruit juice

2 tablespoons water

1 tablespoon arrowroot

1 tablespoon lemon juice

Cook above ingredients in saucepan, stirring constantly with fork, over medium heat until arrowroot dissolves and mixture begins to thicken.

Add 2 cups chopped fresh or thawed frozen fruit. Stir and continue cooking over low heat for 10 minutes. Use over ice cream, in yogurt, and in cottage cheese.

Nut Sauce

Blend in processor until smooth:
    ½ cup nuts
    ¼ cup water or more
    1 teaspoon maple syrup
    ¼ teaspoon vanilla
Use in yogurt, cottage cheese, and *Super Porridge*, and mixed with cooked, puréed veggies.

Mock Cream Sauce

Blend equal amounts of cottage cheese and vanilla flavored yogurt. Use over fruit pieces or as fruit dip.

Tofu Sauce

Saute in 2 tablespoons of butter/oil:
    1 medium onion, chopped
    1 block tofu, cubed
Add:
    2 cups well-cooked mashed beans
    2 tablespoons parsley
    ¼-¾ cups water to make a sauce
Serve over cooked grains. Freeze leftovers.

Shake It Up Baby Salad Dressing

Place into clean baby food jar:
    3 tablespoons olive oil
    1 tablespoon apple cider vinegar
    1/4 teaspoon prepared mustard
    herbs (parsley, basil, dill, etc.)
Place lid tightly on jar and shake well.

Cottage Cheese Dressing

Blend until smooth:
    3 tablespoons cottage cheese
    3 teaspoons olive oil
    3 teaspoons apple cider vinegar
    1 teaspoon lemon juice
    ¼ teaspoon oregano or dill
    pinch of garlic powder

Lemon Tahini Dressing

1 teaspoon olive oil
¼ cup lemon juice
¼ cup tahini
½ teaspoon dry parsley or 2 teaspoons fresh parsley
½ teaspoon dry oregano or 2 teaspoons fresh oregano
1 clove minced garlic (optional)

Mix well and store in covered jar in refrigerator. Refrigerate until cool before serving.

Yogurt Dip

In blender, mix:
6 walnut halves, ground
1 tablespoon olive oil
1 clove garlic
1 cup yogurt
2 teaspoons lemon juice

Avocado Dip

Mix mashed avocado with an equal amount of cottage cheese or tofu. Optionally add *Healthy Extras*. The avocado skins can be used as cups to hold this dip. Use it for dipping anything from whole-grain bread sticks to carrot sticks. Or use as a spread in sandwiches, on whole-grain crackers, celery sticks, or fruit pieces.

Guacamole

Mash together a ripe avocado and 1 teaspoon mayonnaise, ½ teaspoon salsa, and 1 teaspoon lemon juice. Optionally add a pinch of kelp or tamari/soy sauce or maple syrup. Mix well. Use chilled as a dip for fresh vegetables or whole-grain crackers or bread sticks, or as a sandwich or cracker spread.

Tofu Dip I

Mix in blender until smooth:
8 ounces tofu (first press between clean towels to remove as much moisture as possible)
1 tablespoon lemon juice
¼ teaspoon dry mustard

Tofu Dip II

Mix in blender until smooth:

½ pound tofu
4 tablespoons apple cider vinegar
3 tablespoons olive oil
1-2 teaspoons tamari

Variation: Add a few teaspoons of minced onion and/or grated cheese and/or parsley, basil, chives, dill, Italian herbs, onion powder, paprika, garlic powder.

Cream Cheese Dip

4 ounces softened cream cheese
½ teaspoon vanilla
2 tablespoons honey or maple syrup
water

Mix first three ingredients in processor or by hand and slowly add water, a tablespoon at a time, until desired consistency.

Pineapple Cottage Cheese

Drain ½ cup canned shredded pineapple and mix it into an 8-ounce container of cottage cheese. Refrigerate.

Tofu Mayonnaise

Mix in blender until smooth:

8 ounces tofu
1½ tablespoons lemon juice
2 tablespoons apple cider vinegar
1 teaspoon tamari/soy sauce
4 teaspoons safflower oil
½ teaspoon dry mustard
2 cloves pressed fresh garlic

Mock Ricotta Cheese

1 pound firm tofu
5 teaspoons sugar
½ teaspoon salt or kelp
2 tablespoons lemon juice or 1 frozen cube

Mix until consistency resembles cottage cheese. Use in stuffed shells, manicotti, and lasagna or other layered casseroles.

Mock Sour Cream I

Mix recipe above for mock ricotta cheese in blender until very smooth.

Mock Sour Cream II

In blender mix:
½ cup yogurt
1 tablespoon fresh lemon juice
Slowly blend in 1 cup cottage cheese.

Mock Sour Cream III

¾ cup low-fat or nonfat cottage cheese
⅓ cup yogurt cheese
¼-½ cup plain low-fat yogurt
1 teaspoon lemon juice
minced fresh chives or other herbs

Blend cottage cheese in blender until smooth. Gently fold in yogurt cheese and enough plain yogurt until desired consistency is reached. Add herbs.

Easy Mock Sour Cream

Blend until smooth.
1 cup cottage cheese
1 tablespoon milk or yogurt
2 tablespoons lemon juice

Pizza Seasoning

Combine well:
2 tablespoons dried oregano
1 tablespoon dried basil
1 teaspoon onion powder
¾ teaspoon garlic powder

Add about a teaspoon of mixture to each cup of tomato sauce or next pizza sauce recipe.

Economical Pizza Sauce

Mix a 15-ounce can of tomato sauce with a 5-ounce can of tomato paste and add flavorings above.

Pumpkin Pie Spice

Mix in proportions that suit your own taste buds. If you don't know where to start, try:
2 parts cinnamon
1 part nutmeg and/or allspice
½ to 1 part cloves
½ to 1 part cinnamon (optional)

Homemade Vanilla Extract

NEVER buy imitation vanilla, which is made of artificial flavorings, or vanilla flavoring, which is a combination of real vanilla and imitation vanilla. Real or pure vanilla extract is more expensive, but it's worth it. You can save money by making your own. Vanilla and some other flavorings are mostly alcohol—read the ingredients list and you'll see.

Soak vanilla beans from the natural foods store in vodka (or brandy). Use anywhere from 2 to 4 vanilla beans—whatever size package the health food store sells. The more beans, the stronger the vanilla flavor, of course.

Split the beans with a sharp knife vertically without cutting in half, making sure that any small seeds are captured on wax paper. Place beans and seeds into a small glass jar with about ¾ cup of vodka. A 6-ounce baby food jar is the perfect size.

Chop the beans lengthwise so that they'll fit in the jar. Let age in a dark cabinet for at least two weeks, shaking occasionally—at least every few days. The longer it sits, the stronger the vanilla flavor, of course.

As you use your vanilla, keep replenishing the jar with more vodka. This homemade vanilla will not be as dark as store-bought.

Vanilla beans should be replaced every 6 months.

Beverages

For any of these drinks, add a bendable straw and a garnish on the side of the cup, such as a triangular pineapple piece or a citrus fruit circle or wedge. For older children, use as a beverage stirrer a short celery stick with its top leaves or a cucumber stick. (Strings in celery are choking hazards.) Your kids will think it's fancy. Garnishes (not celery) can be cut and frozen using the *Tray-Freeze Method*. Cut slits in garnishes before freezing to easily slip on cup. Many of these beverage recipes call for fruit juice. Your local natural foods store has a smorgasbord of natural fruit juices, from coconut to kiwi juice. Try them all and use any of them in these recipes.

Sweeteners: Many of these beverage recipes call for sweetener. Use honey, maple syrup, rice syrup (available at natural foods stores), or frozen apple juice concentrate or frozen concentrate for pineapple juice or grape juice or any no-sugar added fruit juice.

Add thickness: Any of the drink recipes below can be made thicker by adding a tablespoon or two of nonfat dry milk powder.

Tip: Here's a tip to keep beverages cold in the lunch box without diluting them with melted ice. The night before day care or school, place your child's plastic drink container in the freezer with ½-1 inch of fruit juice in the bottom. It will freeze overnight into a big ice cube that will keep your child's juice cold until lunchtime. As it melts, it will not dilute the juice. You can, of course, do this with milk or other beverage. If the plastic container has a straw that can't fit into the container because of the block of ice on the bottom, try freezing the container on its side, so that the block of ice doesn't shorten the length of the inside space of the container.

Tip: To prevent juice or other beverage from getting diluted from melting ice cubes, enclose ice cubes in a plastic bag and place in pitcher so that melted water won't dilute the juice. Or forget the plastic bag and make ice cubes out of the juice itself.

Mineral Water

In a quart jar, place:

½ cup organically-grown raw almonds with skins
¼ cup organically-grown rolled oats
¼ cup organically-grown raisins
1 tablespoon blackstrap molasses (optional)

Let soak in the refrigerator. Strain and keep refrigerated. Discard after 2-3 days.

The water absorbs minerals and iron from the food. The almond skins contain an enzyme that will help protect babies/toddlers from getting worms. Use the strained out almonds, etc. for older family members' cereals and salads.

Lemonade or Limeade

Squeeze the juice of one lemon or lime into a glass. Add 1½ tablespoons sweetener. Fill with water and ice. Drink immediately for maximum vitamin C. Or use lemon/lime ice cubes instead of fresh fruit. Thaw by microwaving 1 2 minutes on high first before adding to honey, water, and ice. Or better yet, let the lemon ice cubes thaw naturally in the water. Or, for real convenience, freeze ice cubes made of 2 tablespoons lemon juice plus 1½ tablespoons honey for "instant lemonade" cubes.

Tip: To keep pesky bugs out of kids' outside drinks, prevent spilling, and keep drinks colder, use a lidded cup with a straw.

Purple Barney Milk

Mix 2 parts milk or yogurt with 1 part purple grape juice.

Fruit Soy Milk

Blend all ingredients.
    1 cup soy milk
    1 banana
    ½ cup orange juice
    ½ cup pineapple juice
    1 tablespoon honey
    1 tablespoon wheat germ
    dash of kelp

Easy Orange Whip

Mix on high speed in blender equal parts orange juice and milk (soy or cow's) and serve immediately.

Mock Soda Pop

Mix 1-2 tablespoons of frozen fruit juice concentrate into 1 cup no sodium seltzer water or club soda. Add a few ice cubes.

Variation: Mix 1 part fruit juice to 2 parts seltzer water/club soda.

Variation: Mix equal parts fruit juice and no sodium seltzer water.

Tip: Run water over ice cubes before placing into carbonated beverages to reduce foam.

Mock Cream Soda

Mix 1 teaspoon honey and ½ teaspoon vanilla into 1 cup of club soda.

Yahoo Yogurt Fruit Drink

Here's a delicious way to get yogurt into your toddler. Mix equal parts plain yogurt and apple or other fruit juice. Optionally add a little lemon or orange juice.

Variation: For a thicker, creamier shake, add some fresh fruit or use yogurt cheese and use blender to mix.

Banana Yogurt Shake

Mix ½ cup of yogurt or milk (try soy milk) and frozen banana chunks (about ½ banana) in blender. Optionally add any of these:
    1 teaspoon lemon juice
    chunks of other frozen fruit (strawberry is great)
    a dash of vanilla
    a little sweetener
    Add milk if too thick.

Tofu Yogurt Smoothie

In blender, mix:
  ½ cup silken tofu
  1 small banana
  2 teaspoons lemon juice
  ½ cup yogurt
  1 tablespoon sweetener
  Add water or fruit juice if too thick.

Apricot Prune Smoothie

Soak in refrigerator overnight:
  2 tablespoons dried apricots
  1 cup prune juice
In morning, mix in blender with:
  1 cup yogurt:
  1 teaspoon lemon juice
  1 tablespoon sweetener

Any Fruit Milkshake

Blend in blender:
  1 cup cold milk (cow or soy)
  ¼ cup nonfat powdered milk
  1 cup frozen fruit (strawberries, blueberries, peaches, or other fruit)

Melon Juice

  1 cup cold melon pieces (cantaloupe, watermelon, honeydew)
  1 teaspoon lemon juice or lemon juice ice cube
  1 tablespoon sweetener (optional)
  2 ice cubes
  approximately ¼ cup of water

Mix all in blender. Slowly add more water, a tablespoon at a time, until desired thickness is achieved.

Watermelon Crush

Mix in blender ½ cup watermelon pieces with seeds removed, ½ cup strawberries, and a few ice cubes.

Variation: Replace fruits with (or add) pineapple or cantaloupe chunks.

Thick Fruit Drinks

Mix part applesauce or any fruit sauce and fruit juice. Try applesauce and pear juice, pineapple sauce and grapefruit juice, and pear sauce and papaya juice.

Carotene Cocktail

This drink is high in beta carotene.

¼ cup of sweet potato purée (or two thawed food cubes)

1 tablespoon of frozen orange juice concentrate

½ cup milk or mixture of milk and yogurt

Mix all in blender. Slowly add more milk, a tablespoon at a time, until desired thickness.

Variation: Instead of sweet potato, use carrot purée or canned pumpkin or a mixture of all three.

Fruit and Veggie Shake

In blender, mix orange juice with chunks of carrots, broccoli, and/or other raw vegetables.

Veggie Beverage

Mix in blender:

1 cup nut/seed milk

2-3 carrot cubes

Fancy Fruit Party Punch

Open a 10 or 16 ounce package frozen strawberries, remove about half of them, and replace the other half in the freezer. To make fancy ice cubes, mix in blender:

1 cup cold water

¼ of a 6-ounce can orange juice concentrate (3 tablespoons)

¼ of a 6-ounce can pineapple juice concentrate

Pour mixture into 12 muffin tins or popsicle molds. Drop strawberries into the tins and freeze until mushy. Place mint sprigs, orange slices, or celery leaves into the mushy ice cubes as garnishes so that they stand vertically and partially stick out of the cubes. Return to freezer and let freeze solid. These are the ice cubes for the punch. You may also use food coloring to make different colored fancy ice cubes.

Mix in the blender:

the other ¾ of the orange juice and pineapple juice concentrates

the other ½ of the frozen strawberries from the freezer

1½ cups of cold water

Pour blender mixture into punch bowl and add:

2 more cups of cold water

the fancy ice cubes

orange slices and whole strawberries as garnishes

32 ounce (quart) bottle of chilled ginger ale

Makes about 12 6-ounce servings before the ice cubes melt. If you need a few more servings, add more ginger ale.

Variation: Use a loaf pan, a small rectangular pan, or bundt cake pan to freeze one big ice cube instead of 12 little ones. With the larger surface area, you can spell a child's name with *Decorative Touches* or make some interesting design. Partially freeze until mushy, place designs into the mush, then freeze solid. Or wash and freeze a cluster of grapes still on the vine and use as a garnish in the punch bowl. Or fill very clean balloons with water, freeze, and float in the punch bowl. Put colored water in the balloons and use rubber bands to shape like a teddy bear or mouse ears and freeze on cookie sheet. Cut off balloons with knife. Be careful and discard balloon parts—they are choking hazards for young children.

Healthier Hot Chocolate

The commercial mixes are made up of mostly sugar! Make your own mix by combining 4 parts nonfat dry milk powder to 1 part unsweetened carob powder or cocoa powder. To serve, mix 3 tablespoons into heated water and add 1 teaspoon of honey or other sweetener or to taste. Mix with whisk or fork to remove lumps. And a marshmallow melting on top now and then will not hurt too much!

Non-Dairy Hot Chocolate

1 cup soy milk heated slowly in a saucepan or microwave oven
1 teaspoon cocoa
1 teaspoon honey or to taste

Mix with whisk or fork to remove lumps.

Variation: Use almond milk, oat milk, or other non-dairy milks. Or use your own super milk from the recipes that follow.

Super Milks

The Super Milks here are super nutritious, but should not decrease your baby's intake of breast milk, formula, or cow's milk, which is your baby/toddler's main source of calcium, vitamin D, and protein. Make sure your baby is getting the recommended amounts of milks. Use Super Milks in addition to regular milk.

Straining Nut Milks: A fine strainer is needed to remove the powdery pulp in blended nut milks so they will not clog bottle nipples. A yogurt strainer works great to remove the pulp.

Nut/Seed Milk

⅓ cup organic nuts or seeds (cashews, almonds, sesame seeds, are good)
1 cup water

Rinse nuts and seeds and let soak in water overnight before blending. This will begin the sprouting process, increase the nutrients in the water, and soften the seeds/nuts for better blenderizing. In the morning, liquify in blender. Shake well before each use. You can strain this milk, but don't discard the pulp—it's full of nutrients. Use it in adult family members' cereals and salads. The milk will keep in the refrigerator for up to 3 days.

Nut Milk

Grind in blender ⅓-½ cup organic nuts to fine powder. Slowly add 1 cup cold water. Good nuts to use are raw cashews and blanched almonds. (Blanch almonds by pouring boiling water over almonds, let stand for two minutes, and drain. Remove skins by pressing each almond between your thumb and index finger and popping the nut out of its skin.)

Warm Super Milk

Boil 1 cup water. Place in blender with:
    1 tablespoon nuts
    1 teaspoon flaxseed
    1 teaspoon pumpkin seeds
    1 tablespoon blackstrap molasses or other sweetener

All ingredients should be organic. Blend until smooth. Shake or stir before sipping and drink immediately.

Variation: Optionally add one or more of the following:
    1 teaspoon carob or cocoa powder
    1 teaspoon peanut butter
    1 tablespoon strawberry jam or other fruit jam
    1 teaspoon tahini
    pinch of cinnamon

Super Easy Soy Milk

In blender, combine
   ½ cup silken tofu
   1½ cups milk or water
Homemade soy milk made with water has little calcium and vitamin D and no vitamin K. You can buy soy milks at your natural foods store. Make sure you get a brand that is enriched with calcium and vitamin D.

Tahini Milk

Liquify in blender:
   3 tablespoons tahini
   1 cup water
   1 drop almond flavoring (optional)
   1 tablespoon honey or other sweetener to taste (optional)

Raisin Sweetened Milk

Place organic raisins in milk and let soak for 2-3 days in the refrigerator. Use about ½ cup raisins for each cup of milk. Strain. You can use the raisins in cereal, but they will have lost of lot of their taste.

Warm Oat Milk

   1 cup cold water
   1 tablespoon organic rolled oats
   1 tablespoon organic sunflower seeds
Mix ingredients and place over medium heat for 5 10 minutes. Then turn heat down to low and let simmer for another 15 minutes. Liquify in blender. Add 1 tablespoon sweetener (honey, blackstrap molasses, maple syrup) or to taste.

Toddler Hors d'oeuvres

Toddler Hors d'oeuvres are my favorite kids' snacks, because they are so nutritious and easy to make. Kids love them. They are actually more than snacks—serve them with a fruit and/or a vegetable and they make a meal. You can make a whole batch and refrigerate or freeze them. Each of the hors d'oeuvres recipes can be refrigerated for up to one week or frozen for up to two months. Use the *Tray-Freeze Method* and the *Nested Plastic Bag Method*. To make hors d'oeuvres, mix the ingredients and form into balls. Some need cooking and some don't.

TIP: Wetting your hands to roll the sticky mixture into balls makes rolling easier. Or use a small melon baller to make uniform-sized ball shapes. Flatten balls for a cookie shape.

How To Cook Hors d'oeuvres

Cook by baking on greased baking sheet in pre heated 350°F oven for 10-15 minutes. Or you can sauté hors d'oeuvres in a frying pan on the stove top for a few minutes, turning to cook all sides. Drain on paper towels to absorb some of the butter. Refrigerate or freeze.

Variation: Instead of balls, press the mixture into a baking pan, bake in preheated 350°F oven for 15-20 minutes, let cool, cut into bars, and refrigerate or freeze.

TIP: A pizza cutter speeds the job of cutting out bars. Be careful that pieces are not windpipe size so they are not a choking hazard.

Variation: Instead of bars/balls, make other shapes, such as triangles, stars, hearts, snakes, etc. Or flatten the mixture with your hands or a rolling pin, and use a knife to make Simple Shapes or use cookie cutters. You may wish to refrigerate before cutting for a firmer mixture that will cut more easily.

Make Your Own Toddler Hors d'oeuvres Recipes

Recipes for *Toddler Hors d'oeuvres* follow, but you can see how easy it is to make up recipes of your own. Just mix together a few foods until you have a consistency that will form little cohesive balls. Refrigerate or freeze until snack time. *Toddler Hors d'oeuvres* are a great way to use up leftovers!

Granola Hors d'oeuvres

> 1½ cups rolled oats
> ¼ cup wheat germ
> ¼ cup ground nuts
> ¼ cup nonfat dry milk
> ¼ cup melted butter or oil
> 5 tablespoons honey
> 1 beaten egg
> ¼ teaspoon vanilla
> ¼ teaspoon cinnamon
> ½ cup dried fruit

Mix all dry ingredients. Mix honey, oil, and vanilla into dry mixture. Add more honey moisten or dried oats to dry if necessary. Form into small balls. Bake or fry, making sure that egg gets thoroughly cooked.

Variation: To make granola bars instead of balls, press mixture into 8 x 8 baking pan. Bake at 350°F for 15-20 minutes, cool, and cut into bars.

Nut Butter Hors d'oeuvres

¾ cup creamy natural peanut butter
¼ cup mashed cooked beans
2 tablespoons tahini or soft butter
¼ cup wheat germ
¾ cup crumbled shredded wheat cereal

Mix peanut butter, beans, and tahini in saucepan and warm over low heat until soft and melted. Mix in wheat germ and cereal. Don't cook these balls. Drop mixture by tablespoons onto plate, aluminum foil, or waxed paper. Cover with plastic wrap and refrigerate until firm. Or freeze.

Variations: You can use almond butter or any nut butter in place of some of the peanut butter. In fact these balls are a good way to vary nut butters in your child's diet. The dry ingredients (the germ and cereal) can be mixed half and half or in any proportion as long as they add up to one cup. (Actually, you can use any quantity as long as you can form cohesive balls.) You can substitute part of the dry ingredients with ground oatmeal or ground whole germ corn flakes. Ground seeds can replace some dry ingredients, too, but remember that ground seeds may get rancid in as soon as a few hours. The balls must be eaten immediately if they contain ground seeds. Make some with the seeds and eat right away and make the rest without and refrigerate or freeze.

Cheese Hors d'oeuvres

1 cup grated natural cheese
½-1 cup Super Flour or wheat germ
2 tablespoons olive oil (optional)
water or milk

Mix, adding enough water or milk to make a good consistency. Bake at 350°F for 15-20 minutes.

Variation: Replace some Super Flour with ground nuts or wheat germ.

Cream Cheese Hors d'oeuvres

In large bowl, mix thoroughly:
1 8-ounce package of cream cheese, softened at room temperature for an hour
1 teaspoon vanilla
2 tablespoons nonfat dry milk powder
1 tablespoon frozen orange juice concentrate, thawed

Form into 16 one-inch balls. Place about one cup of wheat germ in shallow ball and roll each ball until covered with the germ. Do not cook these. Keep refrigerated.

Tofu Hors d'oeuvres

Drain one silken tofu packet (10½ ounces). Mash with:
  ½ cup whole wheat breadcrumbs ¼ cup ground nuts
  1 tablespoon tamari
Eat uncooked or bake at 350°F for 15-20 minutes.

Whole Grain Neatballs

  1 cup whole grains (rice or bulgur is good)
  12 ounces of tofu, soft
  ½ cup whole grain bread crumbs
  ½ teaspoon kelp powder or salt
  1 teaspoon tamari
Mix all ingredients and bake as directed above.

Dried Fruit Hors d'oeuvres

Chop 1 cup of dried fruit (pears or prunes are good) in processor. Soak in ½ cup frozen juice concentrate overnight in refrigerator to soften. Mix with ¼ ½ cup of ground nuts/seeds until you can roll into balls. Don't cook these. If you use ground seeds, eat immediately. I mix a few balls with ground seeds and serve right away. Then I make the rest with ground nuts and refrigerate or freeze.

Variation: Use wheat germ or ground oatmeal for all or part of the ground nuts/seeds.

Easier Dried Fruit Hors d'oeuvres

Mix ½ cup of finely chopped dried apricots or other dried fruit with 1 cup of peanut butter and ½ cup of chopped nuts/seeds. Don't cook these. Form balls and optionally roll to coat in shredded coconut.

Variation: Add a few tablespoons of wheat germ to the mixture.

Fresh Fruit Hors d'oeuvres

  1 ripe mashed banana, or some avocado or other mashed fruit
  ½ cup nuts
  2 teaspoons honey
Do not cook. Form into balls and refrigerate or freeze.

Sweet Potato Hors d'oeuvres

Mix together:
  flesh from 2 cooked sweet potatoes
  1 beaten egg
  2 tablespoons milk

Form balls and roll in ½ cup of whole wheat bread crumbs (or wheat germ) mixed with ½ teaspoon fresh finely minced parsley. Bake or fry, making sure that egg gets thoroughly cooked.

Variation: Use 1 cup canned pumpkin or cooked carrot purée instead of puréed sweet potato.

Super Green Veggie Hors d'oeuvres

Follow recipe above for Sweet Potato Hors d'oeuvres replacing sweet potatoes with puréed cooked Super Green Veggie.

Raw Grated Carrot Hors d'oeuvres

Mix finely grated raw carrot with cottage cheese, tofu, or yogurt cheese until good consistency. Form into balls. Do not cook.

Variation: Use raw broccoli instead of carrots, or any other raw vegetable.

Red Lentil Hors d'oeuvres

Cook 1 cup of split red lentils (or other lentils) to yield 2 cups of cooked lentils. Fry 1 finely chopped onion in about 1 tablespoon butter on stove top until soft. Mix onions to lentils and add ¼ cup wheat germ. Form into balls (will be very sticky) and bake.

Variation: Shape into patties or cutlets instead of balls, and fry. You can also use ground oatmeal instead of wheat germ.

Latke Hors d'oeuvres

Coarsely grate in food processor 1½ pounds white potatoes and 2 medium onions. Add 2 beaten eggs, ¼ cup wheat germ, ¼ cup fresh chopped parsley. Mixture will be wet. Bake, making sure that egg gets thoroughly cooked.

Bean Balls

    1 cup mashed cooked beans
    ½ cup ground nuts
    whole wheat bread crumbs

Mix ingredients above, using enough crumbs to make a mixture cohesive enough to be rolled into balls. You can cook these, but you don't have to.

Honey Wheat Germ Balls

    1 cup Super Flour
    ½ cup toasted wheat germ
    ½ cup vegetable oil
    ⅓ cup honey
    1 beaten egg
    1 teaspoon vanilla

Mix all ingredients well and roll into balls. Cover balls with wheat germ by rolling balls in shallow dish with about ½ cup of additional wheat germ. Bake at 350°F for 15 minutes, watching so they don't burn.

Honey Milk Balls

½ cup honey
½ cup creamy peanut butter
1 cup nonfat dry milk powder
1 cup ground rolled oat flakes

Mix all ingredients and shape into balls. Don't cook these.

"I Love You" Hearts

Mash a banana with 1 tablespoon lemon juice to help prevent discoloring and to add flavor. Color with red food coloring (beet juice is good). Add enough dry *Healthy Extras* (ground nuts/seeds, wheat germ) to make a fairly stiff mixture. Divide into several parts and shape into hearts—use cookie cutters to make it easier. Don't cook these. Serve immediately or freeze. Tell your child that they are "I will love you forever, no matter what you do" hearts.

Monster or Cat Eyes

On a circular whole grain cracker, place a round slice of banana, and top with an olive slice.

Egg Burgers or Mini-Balls

3 hard-cooked eggs, mashed
½ cup cooked brown rice or other whole grain
4 tablespoons mayonnaise
1 teaspoon finely diced onion
½ cup whole grain cornflakes, pulverized in blender

Mix first 4 ingredients and shape into 4 burgers or other shapes, or make mini balls. Roll in cornflakes to coat. Bake in pre-heated 425°F oven on greased cookie sheet for 10 15 minutes until browned. Burger shapes can be served on whole grain buns or bread.

Muffin Man Buffet

Make a meal more fun by serving it to your toddler in a muffin pan: cheese bits in one tin, Cheerios in another, fruit pieces in another, etc. A small drink in another tin gives it some support and makes it less likely to be spilled. A well-washed Styrofoam egg carton also can be used for a small buffet of snacks.

37

Decorative Touches

Toddlers think it's lots of fun when you make playful, decorative food. Decorating takes only seconds, but it makes your child feel very special. Some recipes in this chapter, such as Apple Smiley Face, Stuffed Froggy, Pineapple Sailing Ship, Mr./Ms. Sweet Potato Head, and Personalized Picture Pancakes call for eyes, noses, legs, and other body parts.

> WARNING: All Decorative Touches should be age appropriate; for example, babies younger than one year should not eat honey.

For eyes: use cooked sliced eggs—the whites can be the whites of the eyes, add olive slices for irises, or try sliced kiwi fruit, cooked beans, peas, halved grapes, or anything round or oval.

For nose: use raisins, strawberries or other berries, small round carrot or cucumber slices, mushroom pieces, pumpkin seeds, or carob chips.

For mouth: use softened rehydrated dried fruit pieces, an orange section, tomato wedge or semi-circular green pepper slice, a line of raisins, a crescent-shaped apple section or ½ cucumber slice with rectangular teeth cut out jack-o-lantern style.

For hair: use millet grains, corn kernels, mashed beans, or cooked crumbled egg yolk for blonde hair; tomato pieces and curly carrot peelings for red hair. To make curly carrot peelings, peel large strings from carrot and place in ice water—they will curl in a few minutes. Or peel strings with a vegetable peeler from a block of cheese. Try cooked brown rice, wheat germ, or ground raisins for dark hair, or use a vegetable peeler to peel strings of chocolate/carob from a candy bar. For green hair, use sprouts and broccoli florets. A regular garlic press or a tubular garlic press is great for making hair: squish colored tofu, colorful veggies, or other food through the holes and you will get spaghetti-like strands that can be hair, a beard, a mustache, animal fur, etc.

For arms and legs: use whole wheat pretzel pieces, small celery or carrot sticks, long slices of other veggies or fruits, pasta pieces, or thin long pieces of whole wheat bread or crusts.

For deer antlers, dog legs, cat whiskers, elephant tusks: use pieces of curved whole wheat pretzels or elbow macaroni.

For sails on sailboats and geometric designs: use cheese slices or fruit leather cut into triangles and other shapes.

For cement: use mashed bananas, mashed beans, and cream cheese make good glues for holding decorative food pieces together.

Glaze: use honey for a glaze that looks like windows or stars.

Pasta (whole grain) is a great *Decorative Touch*, with its multitude of sizes and shapes. Elbow macaroni can be used for eyebrows, nose, or mouth. Spaghetti or fettuccine can be used to draw lines, circles, and other shapes. Soak them in water with food coloring to tint them.

Cooked grains, such as brown rice, can be molded before serving. Place rice in a well-buttered mold and cover the top with plastic or foil. Place a weight (a full unopened can or other heavy item) on top and store in refrigerator for at least one hour before unmolding and serving.

Tofu and cheese slices can be cut with cookie cutters into fun shapes. Or use a sharp knife to make your child's initials or other favorite shapes. Create snow people, "molecules," and silly creatures from tofu and cheese chunks and marshmallows. Give your child small cheese cubes to drop into his soup to watch them melt.

Whole grain bread pieces or crusts, toasted or untoasted, can be shaped into just about anything. Use scissors instead of a knife for easier cutting, or cut with cookie cutters.

The ultimate food for making *Decorative Touches* is fruit leather. See page 226 for recipes.

TIP: Use old mustard squeeze bottles for more control when decorating food. Strawberry jelly in a squeeze bottle is my favorite. It takes only seconds to write a child's name on an open-faced peanut butter sandwich. And toddlers love to decorate their own sandwiches!

Special Days

Make Valentine's Day special by adding red food coloring to milk, or to batter for making heart-shaped pancakes. Make green milk and clover-shaped green pancakes on St. Patrick's Day. Alternate red and green pancakes in a stack of Christmas morning pancakes. Use your child's favorite color on his birthday or on any day to make your child feel special.

Special Dishes

Serve food to your toddler on "special" dishes, such as leftover party plates or plain paper plates cut into fun shapes, disposable containers from TV dinners or fast food meals, and rarely-used specialty dishes, such as those for corn on the cob. Serve a glob of flavored tofu, cottage cheese, yogurt cheese, super sandwich spreads, etc. in an ice cream cone just for fun! Or in a hollowed-out orange half or cantaloupe half. Or roll up a spread in some romaine lettuce or in a whole grain tortilla.

Picnics

Your child will love a picnic—indoors or outdoors. For indoor picnics, make a big fuss and lay a tablecloth on the living room carpet. Pack a basket or cooler with everything including napkins and utensils. Outdoor picnics can be as close as your porch or back yard. If the ground is damp, place a tarp, shower curtain, or ripped flat plastic bag under a blanket.

Buy a sale-priced leftover twin-fitted sheet with a colorful pattern to use as a picnic tablecloth; the fitted ends can be stretched over a picnic table to prevent blowing in the wind. Or make a regular tablecloth blow-away-proof by sewing pockets in the corners and placing rocks or other heavy objects in the pockets to weigh it down.

Bring damp wipe-up towels in a plastic freezer bag for easy clean-up.

Instead of packing six condiment bottles, use a muffin tin or a clean egg carton to hold ketchup, mustard, mayonnaise, pickles, relish, sliced onions, etc. and seal with foil.

Use a clean egg carton to hold plums, apricots, and other easily bruised small items.

Instead of bowls that must be cleaned and carried back home, use scooped out melon halves, orange halves, coconut halves, etc.

Line food bowls with wax paper so you won't have to wash them.

Protect your drinks from insects by using cups with tops.

Pack charcoal briquettes in cardboard (not Styrofoam) egg cartons. Light the cardboard carton with the briquettes still inside for no-mess charcoal cooking.

No need to buy blue ice packs if you wet large sponges, freeze until solid, and place them into water-tight small freezer bags in your cooler. When the picnic is over, use them to clean up.

Instead of blue ice, fill clean paper milk cartons with water or juice and freeze, and drink when melted.

Or freeze water in plastic containers, pop out these huge ice cubes (the larger the ice cube, the longer it takes to melt), and place in large freezer bags and into the cooler.

The more full the cooler and the less you open the lid, the longer it will stay cold. Cover the cooler with a light blanket and place it in the shade.

Food Coloring

For tinting anything from mashed potatoes to yogurt or cream cheese, and for "painting" pictures on flat foods used as canvases, such as bread and pancakes, use these foods for colorings:

Blue: mashed blueberries, red cabbage leaves, sunflower seed hulls.

Red and Pink: tomato sauce, ketchup, mashed strawberries, cherries, cranberries, red cooking water from beets (reduce by boiling for a really concentrated red color), food cubes of puréed beets. Be careful, beet stains are impossible to get out of clothing, plastic containers, wood, etc.

Green: green water from cooking kale, spinach, and other greens (reduce by boiling), mashed honeydew for light green.

Orange: mashed sweet potatoes, cantaloupe, orange pulp and peels.

Yellow: mashed millet, acorn squash, corn, orange peels, pomegranate rinds, onion skins.

Purple: blackberries, elderberries, mixed mashed blueberries and strawberries (as in imaginary dinosaurs). See more about color mixing on the next page.

Brown: walnuts, filberts, and other brown nuts, almond skins. For projects that will not be eaten, instant coffee makes a nice brown color.

A convenient food coloring is jelly or jam. Orange marmalade, red strawberry jam, purple grape jelly, just take your pick from the shelf.

In a pinch, drink mixes, such as Kool-Aid®, sweetened or unsweetened, can be used to color cake icing and other food.

TIP: When cooking, reserve a few tablespoons of "food colorings." Freeze them in ice cubes and have a special food coloring freezer bag.

Commercial Food Colors

Instead of using natural food colors, you can always buy commercial food coloring! I suggest using the paste food colors, because they are much more economical than the drops. They are very concentrated and last forever because you need so little—use a toothpick to scoop out the tiniest bit of paste to color a large batch. The pastes also make colors that are much darker and brighter than the food coloring drops. They can be found in kitchen stores and arts and crafts stores. Look for the 2-ounce Wilton® Primary Colors pack with four ½-ounce jars of these colors: lemon yellow, Christmas red, sky blue, and brown. It's all you need if you use color mixing.

Color Mixing
green = yellow + blue
pink = red + white
orange = red + yellow
gray = black + white
purple/violet = red + blue
navy blue = blue + black
turquoise = blue + a little yellow
black = brown + blue
brown = orange + green
For black icing, mix chocolate icing and blue food coloring.

WARNING: Be very careful with food colorings! Some make stains that are impossible to get out of clothing, furniture, carpets, etc.

A Little Decorative Color Goes a Long Way

Some children need just a little coaxing to eat their food. If your child won't drink his cow's or soy milk or mashed potatoes, try adding a drop of food coloring. Purple dinosaurs and blue dogs often eat foods like this.

Let your child "paint" his sandwich with a small bowl of milk with added food coloring. Give him a sterile toothbrush, new paintbrush, or cotton swab to dip in the colored milk and paint his sandwich, pancake, waffle, etc.

TIP: Make colored ice cubes with water and food coloring. Put 2 primary colored cubes in a little bowl, let them melt, mix into a secondary color.

TIP: Teach your children about mixing primary colors by using food colored water. Mix red water and yellow water to make orange, etc. Don't leave the room to answer the phone, as I did, or when you come back all of the water in the glasses will be black! Mix on a cookie sheet to minimize the mess, or in the bathtub.

Gross and Disgusting

Some kids love gross and disgusting. Make insects out of raisins, dates, and dried prune pieces. Use scissors to cut slits, separate, and you have insect heads and wings. Rub a little butter or use oil spray on scissors to prevent sticking. Raisins are the perfect size for black houseflies and carpenter ants, prunes are good for large crawling insects, like scorpions. Place a slit raisin in gelatin to make the fossil in Jurassic Park. Earthworms can be rolled out of mashed beans or softened cheese. Other gory things can be bought at the supermarket, like those candy worms.

TIP: Whenever you are cooking, keep toddler food decorating in mind, and put aside in the freezer any food pieces that would be good *Decorative Touches*. For instance, when chopping fresh fruit or cooking elbow macaroni, freeze a small amount for use in future food decorating. Use the *Nested Plastic Bag Method* and have a special freezer bag just for *Decorative Touches*.

Simple Shapes

It is obvious by the way I drew the simple shapes on the next two pages that you do not have to be a professional artist to create patterns for decorating your child's food. I made them by simply tracing the edges of pictures in children's books and coloring books. Details, such as faces and inside lines, can be added into the shapes by copying them from the pictures (see the lines drawn in the barn shape on the next page). Simple shapes also can be taken from the hundreds of cookie cutter shapes available in kitchen stores, and from pictures printable from the Internet at children's websites. Another source for simple shapes is scroll saw pattern books. Look for them at hardware stores and at your local library. Children's books, cookie cutters, and scroll saw pattern books also contain special patterns you can use for the holidays.

As long as your child recognizes a shape, she won't care how perfectly you drew it. She'll think it's great fun!

Part VII

Going Green
For Your Super Baby

38

Organic is Best

Only organic foods should be fed to your precious baby. "Certified" organic means that the food has been grown and handled according to strict uniform guidelines, and that the farm fields and food-processing facilities have been inspected to assure that all organic standards are being met.

Pesticides kill living things. Let me repeat that. Pesticides kill living things. Pesticides came about after chemical warfare tactics were used in World War II. During the war, toxic chemicals were used to kill human beings, and it was decided that dilutions of these toxic chemicals could be used to kill bugs on crops. Who knows what long-term effects these supposedly safe levels of pesticides used on our nation's crops will have on your baby (or you for that matter), especially since "safe" pesticide levels on our nation's crops are set according to tolerances by adults and not babies!

Pesticides are tested individually–one at a time. The United States Department of Agriculture (USDA) has found many instances of multiple pesticide residues (as much as 60 different pesticides!) on some foods. The synergistic effects of many combinations of pesticides mixed together have not been examined! It's like mixing drugs with alcohol–the combined effects are worse than twice the effects from each individually.

Another problem with pesticides and your baby is this: Your baby eats much more food per pound of body weight than adults do, so pesticides get more concentrated in her little body. Babies are especially vulnerable to pesticides because their immune system, their organs, and their developing brains are so immature.

Organically-grown foods usually cost more than conventionally-grown foods, but they are well worth the extra expense. Foods grown using conventional methods are typically cheaper than foods grown organically, because weeding and pest control are accomplished by spraying lots of weed killers and toxic pesticides onto crops. Organic farming uses human labor instead of toxic chemicals to keep weeds and pests in check, which is more expensive than spraying crops. These toxins are unhealthy for farm workers, consumers, and for our Earth and its animals and wildlife.

If you feel that your food budget will not allow you to purchase ALL organic foods for your family meals, please know that some foods have much higher pesticide levels than others. In general, foods with thick peels and foods that grow higher off the ground and away from the soil have less pesticides than foods with soft peels and foods that grow close to the ground. The twelve foods most contaminated with many different pesticides, referred to as the *Dirty Dozen*, are: peaches, apples, sweet bell peppers, celery, nectarines, strawberries, cherries, pears, grapes (imported), spinach, lettuce, potatoes. The fifteen least contaminated and most "clean" foods (*The Clean 15*) are onions, avocado, sweet corn (frozen), pineapples, mango, asparagus, sweet peas (frozen), kiwi fruit, bananas, cabbage, broccoli, papaya, cantaloupe, mushrooms and eggplant. If you are on a tight food budget and cannot buy all organic foods for your family, please still try to buy organic versions of the *Dirty Dozen*, and save money by buying the cheaper, non-organic versions of the cleaner foods.

Whether or not you have bought organic fruits and vegetables, please wash them very well before you feed them to your baby. You never know who was touching these foods and what was on their possibly unwashed hands. Eeewww! First soak the foods in water for at least two minutes and then spray them with an organic vegetable wash. Scrub well and rinse thoroughly. (Make your own homemade inexpensive vegetable wash by mixing one cup water with one cup white distilled vinegar. Add one or two tablespoons of baking soda and the juice of one organic lemon, strained well to remove pulp and seeds. Mix well and use a funnel to pour the mixture into a clean, empty spray bottle.)

To peel or not to peel your fruits and vegetables. After carefully washing and rinsing conventionally-raised fruits and vegetables, there may still be some pesticide residues left on the peel, so peel them before feeding to your children. Be sure to peel conventionally-grown apples and other produce that have wax coatings on them—wax often contains fungicides.

Edible peels on fruits and vegetables are very nutritious and have lots of fiber, so eat the peels of organic fruits and vegetables after you have washed them well.

> **WARNING: Never feed your baby homegrown foods unless you are sure the soil contains no lead or other dangerous components.**

Some health professionals believe that any health risk from high-nitrate vegetables in babies is so small that restriction is not really necessary. But I recommend that no matter how small the risk, do not take the chance. Wait until at least 7-9 months before feeding your baby these homemade foods.

> WARNING: The American Academy of Pediatrics (AAP) recommends that you wait until your baby is between 7-9 months old before you introduce homemade carrots, beets, turnips, spinach, or collard greens. In some parts of the country, these crops contain nitrates and may cause a type of anemia (methemoglobinemia) in young infants, also known as "blue-baby" syndrome. These nitrates, deposited on foods from some conventional fertilizers, can form cancer-causing nitrosamines. It is important to note that even organically-grown foods can contain some of these nitrates, so don't feed your baby homemade baby foods from these vegetables even if you purchased organic. Commercial baby food manufacturers can test for nitrates, but we parents can't, so don't make baby food from these vegetables for your baby if your baby is younger than 7-9 months old.

For eye-opening and surprising information about organic food, read Cindy Burke's book *To Buy or Not to Buy Organic: What You Need to Know to Choose the Healthiest, Safest, Most Earth-Friendly Food.*

Support your Local Farmer
Buy Local
Buy local food as often as possible. Foods grown locally are fresher than foods that have traveled a long way, and therefore do not need waxing or other unnatural processing to keep them looking good after their long journey. In general, the longer it has been since a fresh fruit or vegetable has been picked, the more nutrients have been lost. Locally grown foods are usually more nutritious, fresher, tastier, and good for your local economy. Buy directly from your local family farmers to help them stay in business. Visit your farmers' market and stop at road-side stands.

> TIP: *Food, Inc.* is a must see! Borrow it from your local library. Go to www.FoodIncMovie.com for more info.

Support Sustainable Farming

Sustainable farming also helps support your local small-time farmers. Unlike conventional farming methods used by the huge food manufacturers, sustainable agriculture is healthy for farmers, workers, consumers, farm animals, wildlife, and our Earth.

"Sustainable" indicates that the resources used to grow foods, including soil and water, are used no faster than their rate of recovery in the Earth. Sustainable farming "sustains" our Earth. The land and environment are protected. The soil is not stripped of its nutrients and later sown with synthetic fertilizers to replace them. Soil fertility is maintained and improved in an eco-friendly manner. Water sources are protected. Energy and waste are within the Earth's capacity to re-create and absorb them. Farmers make livable incomes and workers are treated kindly and paid fairly. Animals are treated with respect and wildlife is protected. Try to buy only organically grown foods using sustainable farming methods.

Food Coops

Community Supported Agriculture (CSA) is yet another way to help support your local farmers. Join a CSA and you will build a relationship with your local farmer, purchase a share of his or her crop or agree to work a number of hours on the farm, and receive a weekly basket of produce.

A food co-op is a buying club in which a group of people buy foods in bulk at discounted prices, as retail stores do. The bulk foods are then divided into smaller quantities and distributed to members, thereby costing them less money than if the foods were purchased at retail prices. Some food coops have retail stores.

TIP: Go online to search for CSAs and food co-ops in your local community.

Local Grocery Produce Aisles

As demand increases for organic foods, mainstream grocery stores are adding more organic and/or local foods to their shelves. It is now possible to buy organic foods from your conventional mega-supermarket instead of having to make an extra trip to a special natural foods store. But please, though, continue to support your small local "mom and pop" natural foods stores by buying your organic, sustainably-grown foods from them. Without regular customers, they will be driven out of business.

39

Frugal Living is Green Living

Easy Ways to Live Green for Cheap
Reduce, Reuse, Recycle
Be thrifty by buying used items, by making your own products, or by using a smaller amount per use of a purchased product. Being frugal is part of Going Green!

Buy Used
Find a friend with children a little older than yours and offer to buy their outgrown clothes, toys, and baby items. Shop at your local thrift shops and garage sales for used items.

Used or Older Baby Items Create a Safety Concern
Be sure to research all items purchased for your baby to be sure they have not been recalled or are old and unsafe, such as old cribs with slats that are too wide to be safe for your baby.

Don't Buy . . . Borrow or Share
Borrow books from the library instead of buying them. Or buy one book and share it with a bunch of friends. Your local library is a treasure trove of free books and videos for your child. Why buy when you can borrow!

Protect for Long Use
Always have on hand some clear two-inch wide shipping tape. Use it to repair books, "laminate" artwork, and to tape the corners of new toy/game boxes to reinforce them and keep them looking new.

Stretch Your Hair Detanglers and Your Dollars
Commercial spray detanglers and conditioners that you buy for your baby's hair are nothing more than very dilute solutions of hair conditioner. Make your own by adding one or two tablespoons of organic hair conditioner into a pump or spray bottle and fill with water. Shake well before each use. Spray into hair after shampooing and towel drying. Use it on your baby and yourself.

Another way to save money on hair conditioners is to take a tiny dollop (about ½ teaspoon), spread it on the palms of your hands, and massage it through your hair after a shampoo and towel dry. This "leave-in conditioner" will make hair as soft and tangle free as when you use a lot of conditioner in the bath or shower and rinse it out. This method makes a bottle of conditioner last for months. As a bonus, you also save time and water in the shower because you don't have to rinse.

Homemade Hairspray

Don't spray commercial hairspray around your baby and allow him or yourself to inhale it! Make your own hairspray by mixing a little of any of the following sticky ingredients into water: lemon juice, honey, corn syrup, or even Elmer's® glue! This may sound strange, but it's better than using commercial hair sprays—who knows what chemicals go into them! Organic products are expensive. Save money by making your own and you will feel safe using homemade spray to hold down baby's stubborn hairs for those posed baby pictures. Boil the water before adding the sticky stuff.

Use an empty, well-cleaned, commercial hair spray pump bottle. For your first batch, try adding two tablespoons of corn syrup to ½ cup of boiling water. Stir until dissolved, let cool, and pour into pump spray bottle. Or try this homemade citrus hair spray: Peel and chop one lemon (or for dry hair, one orange). Place in a pot and cover with two cups of water. Bring to a boil and keep boiling until liquid is reduced to one cup. Let cool, strain, and keep refrigerated in a spray bottle. It smells absolutely delicious and works well as a hairspray!

> **MONEY SAVER:** If you use non-aerosol commercial hairspray in a pump bottle, try diluting the liquid with an equal amount of water. You have just reduced your price by half and you will probably find that it works just as well. Use an empty pump bottle and mix half hair spray, half water. Try this with just a little hair spray first, not half of a bottle, in case you don't like it.

Hair Gel

Dissolve ½-1 teaspoon of unflavored gelatin in one cup of warm water. Keep refrigerated and use as you would a commercial hair gel—it works just as well. If you use commercial hair gel, try diluting it with water. You may find that it actually works better because it's less stiff and easier to smooth into your hair.

Mom's and Dad's Deodorant

If you are breastfeeding or even if you are not, it's probably a good idea to prevent your baby from inhaling deodorant when you are holding her close. I believe that deodorant isn't necessary at all, except maybe on hot sticky days. Plain baking soda will keep you dry and comfortable. Sprinkle about ½ teaspoon onto the palm of your hand and smooth it under your arm.

Oatmeal Bath

Adding oatmeal to your bathwater is soothing to baby's and your skin. Place a handful of organic oatmeal into a clean stocking and tie it shut. Let water from the tap flow through the sock or swish through the bath water.

Soap

Organic soaps, either bar or liquids, are now available at natural food stores and online. Stretch your dollar by using only small amounts on baby. Or just use plain water to bathe your baby. You don't need to smear large amounts of soap all over your baby's body; soaps can be drying to baby's skin and your baby is just not that dirty!

First-Aid for Your Home

Resolve right now that you will not become upset or angry when (not if) your child writes with crayon on the good wallpaper, jumps on the couch with her shoes and breaks the springs, and spills boxed cereal all over the kitchen counter and floor while picking out just the raisins to eat. Here are a few fixes for some of the damage your little angel might cause to your unimportant home and material possessions.

Wood Scratches and Rings

Use your child's brown crayons to fix scratches in wood furniture. Walnut or pecan meat rubbed into scratches in wood furniture or wood floors helps erase them. Repeat several times for best results. Or, try mixing one teaspoon instant coffee or tea with two teaspoons water and applying with a cotton ball. Or, use equal parts of lemon juice and salad oil. For large holes, mix instant coffee with white toothpaste, Elmer's glue, or spackling paste to match the color of the wood, fill holes, and smooth with a damp paper towel. For white rings on wood furniture, try mixing cigarette/cigar ashes into corn oil and rub into the ring with the grain. Or try gently rubbing the ring with equal parts toothpaste and baking soda on a soft cloth, or with just plain toothpaste.

Loose Knobs

Kids love to unscrew dresser-drawer handles and knobs, making them too loose to stay securely in their holes. To create a snug fit again, coat screw with Elmer's glue or clear nail polish, screw into hole, and let dry thoroughly before touching.

Crayon Marks

From most flat surfaces (washable painted wall, washable wallpaper, table top, blackboard, etc.), remove crayons marks with one of these methods: rub with toothpaste on an old toothbrush and rinse well; spray on WD 40®, let sit 10 minutes, and blot with a paper towel; gently scrub with steel wool; apply rubber cement, let dry partially, and roll off; warm with hair dryer and wipe off; place paper towel over crayon mark and apply warm iron to absorb wax. Toothpaste will not work well on porous surfaces or wallpaper. Always test method on inconspicuous spot first in case damage results.

Melted Crayon Wax in the Carpet

Crayon wax melted into your carpet or car's cloth interior via the greenhouse effect can be removed. First ice the wax down until it is very cold. Pick off wax pieces with your fingernails, being careful not to pull the fibers. Spread a few layers of paper toweling or a brown grocery bag over the spot and apply a warm (not hot) iron. Some of the wax will be absorbed by the paper. Remove and replace with fresh paper and iron again. Repeat until all wax is gone. Be very careful with some car interiors and synthetic carpet which may melt—test on an inconspicuous spot first. (Newspaper can also be used but the ink may cause a spot problem.) A color stain may remain if the crayon was a dark color or one in contrast to the rug. Sorry.

Ink

To remove ink from hands or clothing, rub toothpaste into the spot, scrub, and rinse thoroughly. Or try squirting the ink stain with commercial hair spray.

Stickers, Adhesive-backed Paper, Chewing Gum, Silly Putty, Bathtub Decals, Price Tags, Stick-on Hooks

Remember to test on inconspicuous spot first before trying any of these methods: Rub full-strength hot white vinegar or saturate a cloth with the vinegar and place over the sticker. Squeeze the liquid so it gets on the glue behind the sticker. Give the vinegar time to soak in before rubbing off. Instead of vinegar, try vegetable oil (or spray WD-40®).

Another method: Apply a warm iron directly to the sticker, or on a paper towel placed over the sticker, to melt the adhesive. Or hold a hair dryer over the spot until the adhesive melts. To remove chewing gum from hair, harden it by placing ice on it and pick it out of the hair, or try rubbing the gum with peanut butter.

Stains and Odors

When baby spits up, remove as much as possible, and then rub dry baking soda/washing soda into the spot to remove odor and prevent stain from setting. Let it dry and brush off. Keep a small container of baking soda in the diaper bag for this purpose. Or, fill a spray bottle with equal parts baking soda and water to spray on spit up on furniture or clothes.

Urine Stain and Odor Remover

Get to that stain immediately. Rinse repeatedly with warm water, then apply a solution of 3 tablespoons white vinegar and 1 teaspoon liquid soap. (Test on inconspicuous spot first.) Leave on for 15 minutes, rinse, and rub dry.

Blood Stains

One day I walked into my twins' room and there was blood all over—on the walls, the cribs, the carpet, everywhere! It looked like a murder scene! I almost lost it when I looked at their little hands and they were all blood! They had somehow knocked a picture with glass off the wall, and they had been playing with the pieces of broken glass! I spent a long time finding all the pieces and putting them back together like a puzzle to be sure I found every last sliver.

To remove blood stains, you probably know to treat the stain immediately by soaking in COLD water (never hot water or it will set the stain) and scrubbing with a mild soap. Perhaps you didn't know that hydrogen peroxide is great for removing blood stains. I poured it directly on the blood stains on the carpet and they came right out! It was like magic! Club soda also works on some blood stains.

Those of you with twins (or more!) have a bit more to worry about in terms of your babies' safety. They can get into so much more trouble together! For example, one day my twins used the drawers as steps to climb up their high dresser and their combined weight made the dresser fall on them, pinning them to the floor. The adrenaline kicked in and I was able to lift the dresser, holding the drawers closed at the same time.

Twins are a blessing for a million reasons, and one is that they can watch out for each other. I was outside when one of my twins came running out of the house to tell me something. He was scared and I didn't wait to understand what he was trying to tell me—I knew something had happened. When I ran into the house, I found his brother pinned under our large game-room-sized video game, which had fallen on him! I don't know how, but I lifted that heavy machine as if it were light as a feather, just enough so that Freddy could crawl out from under it. I was expecting broken bones or worse, but fortunately he didn't have a scratch on him.

I've tried to lift that machine many times since then, but couldn't budge it one inch. I believe the story about the grandmother who lifted a car to save her grandchild!

Another incident happened when they were older and Freddy had gotten himself stuck in the snow at the playground. He was really stuck! His twin brother John, the only other person there, "saved" him by running to get me to shovel him out! Having twins is the greatest!!

40

Homemade Baby Products

Homemade Diaper Ointments and Wipes
For Diaper Rash

Use plain white solid shortening (Crisco® or generic brand) as a preventative barrier to wetness and acidity as soon as you see your baby developing a diaper rash. If baby cries when you touch his bottom, smooth the shortening on the diaper instead of his skin and it will be applied painlessly when you put the diaper on.

> **TIP:** Use your pinky and ring finger to spread diaper cream and your other three fingers will remain clean and dry to tape the diaper.

Breast milk applied directly to baby's skin will soothe and help clear up a diaper rash. No kidding! Squeeze some liquid from your aloe house plant and smooth on baby's bottom to help soothe diaper rash. Put a few tablespoons of baking soda in baby's bath water to neutralize the acidity of a diaper rash and to soothe baby's skin. Or while changing a diaper and during potty training, rinse a wash cloth in a sink half filled with comfortably warm water and a few tablespoons of baking soda. Squeeze out excess water and wipe your little one clean to alleviate urine odor and soothe the rash.

Homemade Organic Diaper Wipes

Save money by making your own organic wipes, especially good for babies with sensitive skin who are prone to rashes or allergies. Use the liquid recipe below in a spray bottle to spray on baby's butt before wiping or to dampen soft paper or cloth. For the liquid part of the diaper wipes, mix:
- 2 cups water
- 2 tablespoons of organic baby oil
- 2 tablespoons of either organic baby shampoo or baby wash
- 1-2 tablespoons of aloe gel from a houseplant (optional)
- 7-8 drops of essential lavender oil for a great fragrance that will also help kill bacteria—optional for babies with sensitive skin

TIP: 100% essential lavender oil is very baby-friendly and unlikely to cause skin reactions. Find it at your local natural foods store or in an arts and crafts store, or online. Buy the real stuff and not the synthetic, chemical fragrance liquid.

A Simpler Liquid Recipe: Instead of the previous recipe, mix a little baking soda into water. The soda will neutralize the acidity of a diaper rash and soothe baby's skin. About a tablespoon of baking soda, more or less, to a cup of water is fine. (You can also sprinkle a little baking soda in your baby's bath water, which will act as soothing bath salt.)

Put the liquid recipes or plain water into a spray bottle to wet washable, reusable organic cotton wash cloths before cleaning up baby.

Some parents claim that their babies get reactions from any wipe solutions. You can use just plain water to clean up your baby.

Homemade Disposable Organic Baby Wipes

Many moms have e-mailed to say that this recipe has saved them lots of money while being gentler to baby's skin than the commercial organic wipes.

Buy a roll of chemical-free paper towels. Choose a brand that is reusable or microwaveable because they tend to be the strongest and most like cloth. Cut the roll in half by using an electric knife or a sharp non-serrated knife (serrated causes small bits of toweling).

Remove the inside tube core—use a pair of pliers to pull it out and it will be easy. Place the half roll in a cylindrical container (an old baby circular wipe container or a cylindrical food storage container). Save the other half of the roll for the next batch or make up two containers to keep in different parts of your home.

Make 2 cups of one of the liquids on the previous page. Pour the liquid into the container, cover, and turn the container upside down. Let sit for 15 minutes to allow the liquid to be absorbed.

Open the container and pull out the first towel from the inside of the roll and pull it through the hole in the top. If you are not reusing a commercial baby wipes container and your container has no hole in the lid, take a sharp utility knife and cut an X in the lid. Cut off a little of the plastic from the four inside corners of the X to make a small hole. The hole will allow the paper towels to be pulled out without shredding.

Disposable organic wipes can be made more easily with individual paper towels in stacks. Use the kind that pull out of dispensers in public restrooms, not the brown stuff that's as stiff as grocery bags. The softer white towels may be difficult to find—try a restaurant supply or medical supply store. Place the wipes into an empty baby wipe container or a similar rectangular container and add enough liquid to keep the wipes wet.

Disposable cotton squares—the ones used for makeup removal—can also be used as soft baby wipes. Spray with or dip in the homemade liquid above before wiping.

You may prefer to use plain dry tissues as baby wipes because they are so easy and convenient and so soft. Use a good eco-friendly brand of tissue that is extra strength—they are still much cheaper than paper towels or commercial baby wipes. Keep the liquid recipe above in a spray bottle and shake well before use. Spritz baby's fanny with the liquid or spritz the tissue before wiping.

TIP: If the wipes turn out too dry, add more water. If they are too wet, leave the top of the container off to allow some of the water to evaporate. Make a note on how much you had to adjust the water in the liquid recipe above so you will remember for next time.

For homemade machine washable baby wipes, use pieces of old cloth diapers cut to size. Or use pieces of terry cloth washcloths or an old towel. You can buy packs of cheap washcloths in department stores and cut them in halves or quarters. I found 50 all-cotton, soft washcloths at Sam's Club for about $10. These homemade cloth baby wipes can be washed with cloth diapers, if you use them.

Diaper Powder

The days of powder made from talc are gone, since it was discovered that talc can be inhaled into baby's lungs. Never let baby play with powder—some babies have actually died while playing with talc baby powder. If you do wish to use powder to keep baby dry, use a little cornstarch on an old powder puff or smooth it on baby directly with your hand. If using a commercial powder, save money and use less by taping most of the holes closed.

Diapers

I got tired of paying big bucks for the overnight diapers. Before my in-toilet-training son went to bed, I put on him my own cloth diaper contraption: I folded and placed two or three wipe-up towels, washcloths, or a cotton diaper between his legs inside his underpants, over which I put rubber training pants. Worked just fine for those nights when my son had an accident, and I figure I saved the better part of a dollar each time. By the way, I had to put this contraption on him after he had fallen fast asleep.

Diaper Mat

In an emergency, a large plastic storage bag or a sheet of wax paper can be used as a diaper changing mat. Keep one folded up in the diaper bag.

Bath Accessories

Bathtub Toy Bag

Instead of buying the net bag for holding your child's toys in the tub, why not use a large nylon net from oranges or onions or a waterproof net laundry bag. Hang them with suction cups where the water will drain back into the tub. A plastic garbage bag with holes poked in the bottom for drainage works well, but remember that it is a suffocation hazard so hang it high out of baby's reach on the shower faucet. (The same can be used at the beach—fill it with toys and dunk to rinse off all of that sand.) I use a large laundry basket by the side of the tub. My little one can then take and return his toys by himself. When the basket needs a cleaning, I dip in into the tub when the baby is done and use the bath water to wash it.

Non-Slip Holders

Use a white cotton glove when bathing baby and you can keep a better grip on her. If you use bar soap, tie it inside part of an old pair of pantyhose. No more dropping slippery soap!

Bath Bottles

Buy the fancy bottles shaped like your child's favorite cartoon characters only once (when they are on sale and you have a coupon). Then keep refilling them with the cheaper bottles of baby shampoos, conditioners, baby washes, and soaps. If they get gooey, wash the bottles in the bathtub water with an old toothbrush.

Shampoo

It is less clumsy if you use a squeeze bottle for applying shampoo—you also use less and save money.

Dilute baby shampoo with water (at least one part water to three parts shampoo) to use less and save more money.

Make shampooing fun by forming your child's hair full of shampoo into spikes and other shapes and letting him look in a mirror. Kids usually hate to get their hair shampooed because water and soap get in their eyes and ears.

Rub a slanted line of petroleum jelly on your child's forehead just over the eyebrows so shampoo will run off to the side instead of into his eyes. Give your child a small hand towel to hold over his eyes and ears while you shampoo.

If your child will not lie down in the bathtub water, rinse the shampoo out by pouring water over his hair. Place your one hand over your child's eyes sun-visor style to help prevent water from running down his face. Use your second hand to pour rinse water down the back of his head while he holds his head way back. A lightweight pitcher filled one time for rinsing is easier and much faster than a small cup filled several times.

Distract and relax him by asking him to "quack" at a rubber duck held over his head with your third hand. Those of us with only two hands can hang the rubber duck from the shower curtain rod or shower head. Another possibility is some type of waterproof inclined plane that your child can lie back on while you wash his hair.

Hair Detanglers

The commercial spray detanglers and conditioners that you buy for your baby's hair are nothing more than very dilute solutions of hair conditioner.

Make your own by adding one or two tablespoons of baby-safe hair conditioner into a pump or spray bottle and fill with water. Shake well before each use.

I sometimes use this for my own hair after shampooing and towel drying. But most times, while I'm still in the shower and after shampooing, I take a tiny dollop (about ½ teaspoon) of regular hair conditioner, spread it on the palms of my hands, and massage it through my hair. I don't rinse and this "leave-in conditioner" makes my hair as soft and tangle-free as when I use a lot of conditioner and rinse it out. This method makes a bottle of conditioner last for years. As a bonus, you also save time and water in the shower because you don't have to rinse.

More bath tips

Let your child's towel double as a big bib for you to help keep you dry—use a large diaper pin to keep it around your neck. When bath time is over, you can hug your child dry!

Don't discard those leftover slivers of bar soap. Wet and stick them to a new bar of soap. They'll become one with the new bar.

At the end of your shower, place a little baby oil on a wet washcloth and rub it all over your skin. Unlike applying it with your hands, the washcloth prevents the shower floor from getting slippery and saves money because you use so little.

Unwrap bar soap and let it open to the air; it will freshen your cabinet and become harder and last longer.

Help your boy toddler-in-training improve his aim by floating a Cheerio® or a square of toilet paper in the toilet as a target.

Baby Clothes

Don't discard baby clothes with minor damage which can be fixed. Use fabric markers to color in bleach spots. Or use paint, food coloring, or matching color crayon. Heat the spot with an iron, color with crayon, and set the color by placing a sheet of wax paper over the spot and ironing the spot again. Protect your iron from wax paper by placing a piece of brown paper from a grocery bag between the iron and the wax paper.

Spit-up stains are impossible to get out of used baby clothing. Try applying Dawn® dishwashing liquid directly to the stain. If nothing works, dye the entire item a darker color. Onsies® are cute when tie-dyed.

Camouflage tears or stains in clothing with a patch cut from a matching or contrasting fabric in a *Simple Shape*. Sew it over the damage to make it look like it was a decoration originally designed into the clothes item. Add more patches for symmetry or a continuous pattern. Or use colored iron-on patches cut into *Simple Shapes*. Place aluminum foil on the ironing board under the hole, so that the glue doesn't melt onto the ironing board cover.

Baby clothes with stains can still be worn if they are under another clothes item. For example, who cares if a baby's t-shirt has a stain if it's under a new-looking shirt and cannot be seen.

Sew or iron patches to the inside or outside of a crawling baby's pants to strengthen the knees or to hide worn knees. For an expensive look, sew a corduroy, vinyl, or leather patch over the knees. (Cut the vinyl/leather patch from an old purse or boot.) Cut the patch into a *Simple Shape* for a cute touch. Knee pads can be made from sweatbands or the cuffs from an old pair of thick adult socks (cut the foot off). Fold to reduce to a few inches in length and to thicken, then zig-zag stitch. These can be used on your crawling baby's bare knees or over his pants. Be sure they are not too tight around the knees. Make yourself a similar pair of knee pads with old socks and sponges or shoulder pads. Sure makes kneeling to clean floors easier!

Use the cuffs from white or colored socks as pony-tail holders or wrist sweat bands. Long cuffs from adult cotton socks can be used to protect children's sleeves from getting dirty while eating or painting.

Homemade Bibs

Cloth pullover bibs with—the ones that cost $4-5—can be homemade from an old sweatshirt, dickey style. Cut the neck and chest parts out of the sweatshirt. To prevent fraying, cut with pinking sheers or zig-zag the edges. Fold up the bottom to form a food-catcher pocket.

A waterproof bib for baby or yourself can be made from an old sterile shower curtain (machine wash in hot water and bleach). Use duct tape, your sewing machine, and Velcro® tabs (available at craft and sewing stores) to finish. Don't use string to tie a bib around baby's neck; it's a strangulation hazard.

A large men's shirt worn backwards will also work as a bib for you; a smaller boy's/girl's shirt will work for baby.

Use the tops of old socks to protect your child's sleeves.

Socks and Shoes

Rings from milk jugs make good sock holders.

Buy many identical socks. All pairs will be a match and if you lose two socks, you've only lost one pair.

Make non-slip socks by putting non-toxic fabric puff paint on the bottom of baby's plain socks. (You can often find puff paint in undesirable colors on sale at fabric stores.) Follow washing instructions for puff paint.

Check often to make sure pieces have not come off—they are choking hazards. Or sew on pieces of self-sticking bathtub appliques. Puff paint and appliques can also be used to prevent throw rugs from slipping. Be careful about ruining the floor underneath.

Sew non-slip patches to the bottom of a child's pajama feet to help prevent falls. Stick small bits of non-slip bath appliques to the bottom of new shoes to make them less slippery.

Fix a shoe lace that is frayed on the end with a dab of nail polish, white glue, a piece of clear tape, or some melted crayon/candle wax to make it stiff again. (Use this same idea on a string that is difficult to thread. Dip it in a bottle of nail polish, let it dry, and thread away.)

Don't pay a fortune for fancy shoe laces. Decorate plain shoelaces with colorful permanent markers. Or use fancy or glittery ribbons as shoelaces. Strengthen the ribbon, if necessary, by folding and sewing around a plain shoelace. Or use colorful pipe cleaners as shoelaces.

Use a dab of petroleum jelly to polish baby's patent leather shoes and make them shine, and to protect them from snow and rain. Apply olive oil or a nut oil to leather with a chamois cloth.

If boots spring a leak, place plastic bags over your child's socks before putting on the boots. Your child's socks and feet will be kept dry and warm.

If over-the-shoe boots are too difficult to get on and off, try placing a plastic bag over the shoe before putting on the boot. Store the bag in the boot until it's time to go home.

When shoes and boots get wet inside, place a hand-held hair dryer into them part way and set the dryer on low heat. They will be dry in minutes. Watch very carefully for over-heating.

In my opinion, it was too expensive to buy snow boots for my twins when they were very young. They rarely used them, and when they did, it would be for only a few minutes outside and then they'd want to come back in the house. They grew out of them in one year, so I decided not to buy them boots until they were much older. Until then, for playing in the snow, first I put on their regular socks and shoes, second I put plastic freezer bags over their shoes, and third I put an old pair of adult thick socks over the bags to hold them in place. This worked just fine—it kept their feet and ankles dry and warm.

Gloves

For gloves, I placed a cheap pair of baby gloves or a pair of cotton socks on their little hands. Then I placed over the gloves/socks a thick pair of adult wool socks. The socks went up to their elbows and prevented snow from getting on their wrists and up their sleeves.

To prevent the loss of gloves, sew buttons on them. Your child can then button them into the front buttonholes of her coat. Two matching buttons on the knuckles will look like eyes if you add a nose and smile with yarn.

Other Baby Clothes Tips

For snow pants, I sprayed a cheap pair of a size-too-big sweat pants with Scotchguard® protector for fabric that repels spills. The directions will tell you how to do this. (Spray outside so kids don't inhale it.) The twins wore these pants over a regular pair of sweat pants, winter pajama bottoms, or long winter underwear. The two pairs of pants kept them warm, and snow and water rolled off the outer Scotchguarded pair.

A missing zipper pull tab can be replaced with a paper clip. Sew matching fabric over the paper clip to camouflage it and to contain sharp wire ends. Zippers will slide more easily if you rub them with wax paper, a bar of soap, or a bit of petroleum jelly.

Pulled threads on sweaters or other clothing can be fixed by using a crochet needle to pull them through the fabric to the inside of the garment. Knot them to prevent the strings from catching and pulling, causing more damage.

Lace collars on baby's clothes (or doll clothes) can be freshened by ironing them between two sheets of wax paper. Protect your iron and ironing board by placing paper from a brown grocery bag between the wax paper and the iron and ironing board.

Use a damp sponge to remove hair and lint from clothing.

Bend the outer ends of wire hangers down to make baby clothes-sized hangers.

Instead of using thread, use dental floss to sew buttons on your child's clothes, stuffed toys, or doll clothes. It is much stronger than thread and it can be touched up with marker to match the color of the garment.

Baby Linens

If you sew, even just a little, you can save money by buying baby sheets on sale and making a matching comforter, crib ruffle, and curtains for baby's windows. Buy a pattern that has bright primary colors, not pastels, for baby's room. A matching stretchy fabric can be folded into a triangle to make a stuffed toy hammock. Tie ends tightly around three large metal rings and place on three hooks on a wall in a corner of the room. Make an infant head support by stuffing a sleeve from an old sweatshirt and sewing it around a piece of semi-circular fabric. Use a friend's commercial head support as a pattern, to make sure that your design is safe.

Personalize Blankets
Use non-toxic fabric paints to decorate and personalize blankets.

Baby Furniture
Rub wax paper or petroleum jelly on your baby's high chair if the tray begins to stick. Or on your baby's crib runners to make them glide smoothly.

King size pillow cases will fit some baby changing table pads and infant beds.

Place an old sterile shower curtain (machine wash in hot water and bleach) between the mattress and bed covers to protect the mattress from a bed wetter.

Homemade Lap Table
Serve meals to sick children in bed on a cookie sheet on top of a homemade bed table. The pan's lip helps keep food and spills from getting onto the bed. Place a damp paper towel between the pan and dishes and glasses to prevent slipping, and then use the towel for face and hand cleanup at meal's end. To make the homemade bed table, find a sturdy cardboard box and cut semi-circular holes in the bottom to fit over your child's legs.

Storage
For more organization and storage space, make shelves and cubby holes by hot-gluing cardboard boxes together. Or use large juice cans with no jagged edges. Decorate with wallpaper, decorative self-adhesive paper, fabric, or non-toxic paint. Hang smaller shelves on the wall above the changing table. Larger shelves on the floor can hold your toddler's toys.

Make your own modular toy holders with an old bookshelf unit (pick one up at a garage sale), or buy several plastic storage crates at the local hardware store. Place several kitchen dishpans on the shelves to hold toys. Note how much these modular units sell for in baby stores and toy catalogs!

Line baby's drawers with pretty baby gift wrapping paper. Iron the wrong side to remove wrinkles in used gift paper.

Use clean egg cartons as drawer organizers to hold baby's socks and other small items. Keep out of baby's reach—bitten pieces of the carton are choking hazards.

A lower rod can be added to baby's closet with a shower curtain rod cut to size, swing chains, and metal self-closing shower curtain rings.

Make your child her own personal coat hanger from a piece of wood and golf tees. Paint it her favorite color and personalize it with her name.

An old dish drainer will hold children's books and records upright. Crayons and markers fit nicely in the silverware holder.

Use the playpen (that your child refuses to use) as a large toy chest.

Homemade Toys

You don't have to buy expensive, foreign and cheaply made, plastic toys from mega-toy stores to entertain your baby and toddler. Make these toys for your very young child and your child will love them and they will cost you next to nothing.

Babies and toddlers are not yet aware of copyrighted or trademarked TV/movie icons or cartoon characters. (If they are, you can print pictures from the internet to decorate homemade toys.) Very young children are happy with just about any toys, purchased or homemade, as long as they come with your time and attention. Anything is fun at this age!

These toys can be made by older children as homemade, personalized gifts for their new baby brother or sister. Homemade gifts are so much more meaningful than purchased gifts.

Mobiles

Mobiles can be expensive. Make your own personalized crib mobiles by hot-gluing or taping two triangular plastic hangers together at right angles. Suspend colorful small toys and pictures of human faces from your family from the hangers using short pieces of dental floss (not more than 4 inches to prevent strings that can be strangulation hazards) and hang on the crib so that your baby can see it. Make sure you design the mobile from your baby's point of view and not that of a standing adult's viewpoint. A mobile should be about one foot from your baby's face. Change the toys and pictures periodically. Be sure to suspend the mobile in your baby's crib very securely, so it will not fall into the crib.

> **WARNING:** Mobiles are dangerous to older babies. For safety, mobiles should be removed from cribs as soon as your baby begins to reach for the objects with her hands. Your baby will get frustrated if she is trying to grab something she cannot reach.

Tactile Stimulation

Stuff a clean sock with beans and tie it shut. Baby will love to squeeze it and shake it. Or make a safe ball for throwing inside the home by stuffing a sock with old pantyhose and tying it shut.

Homemade Blocks

Make a big toy block by cutting the tops off two clean half-gallon milk cartons. Push the open ends together by placing one inside the other; this closes the ends and adds strength to the block.

Make several of these blocks in different sizes by cutting off more or less of the cartons. Your child can stack them and build high walls of castles or forts.

These blocks cost you nothing but a little time and your child will have fun with them! Write your child's name on heavy paper with white glue or glue colored with food coloring or puffy paint and let dry thoroughly.

Cardboard Village

Make a child-size neighborhood with houses made from large appliance boxes. (If you have no new appliances, ask your local major appliance store for donations.) Cut out swinging doors and windows with shutters. Use packaging tape to strengthen. Don't forget a large garage for your child's riding toy and smaller garages for those big toy dump trucks.

Practice interior decorating with white glue and wallpaper remnants, fabric scraps from old blankets and clothing, and decorative contact paper. Tell your child it's OK to color on these walls.

Buy cheap leftover remnant self-stick floor tiles for your child's floors. This personalized toddler-sized village would be very expensive to buy. Homemade doll houses could be made with smaller cardboard boxes.

41

Homemade Household Products

Economical, Safe, and Environment-Friendly Cleaning Products

If you can't eat it . . .

There simply is no need to use products made from dangerous chemicals to clean and maintain our bodies and our homes. If you can't eat it, you should not put it on your baby's skin or your skin! Skin is very porous and absorbs any skin care products you put on it. Blood tests have been found to have traces of the toxic chemicals used in skin care and household cleaning products.

As people become more aware of the unnecessary toxic ingredients and fragrances used as ingredients in the thousands of household products currently on the market, they are demanding more natural and safer products. Be aware that some words on labels, such as "natural," mean absolutely nothing.

> WARNING: Be careful not to mix hazardous cleaning solutions together. Especially, do not mix products containing ammonia with products containing chlorine bleach, because a dangerous gas will form. For example, don't use a product with ammonia to clean a bathroom mirror over a toilet cleaned with a product containing bleach—the ammonia may drip and mix with the bleach.

Cleaner for Baby's Toys

Don't use poisonous disinfectants to wash your baby's things. Mix a little baking soda into a cup of warm water and wipe down baby's crib railing, car seats, playpens, etc. Also, plain white vinegar can be used as a mild disinfectant. Mix with water and clean baby's things, but first test on an inconspicuous spot for color fastness and to prevent other possible damage. Plain hot water will wash away and kill some of the germs.

Clean stuffed toys by sprinkling liberally with baking soda or cornstarch. (Put in a large plastic bag first for less mess.) Let remain for at least 15 minutes and then shake it off or vacuum or brush it off.

Sprinkle baking soda into plastic storage bags along with the summer toys before storing to keep mildew from forming: pool toys, beach toys, small blow-up children's pools (sprinkle inside before rolling up), canteens, picnic coolers, etc.

Place an old shower curtain under an inflatable children's pool to protect it from sharp rocks and keep it clean.

All Purpose Cleaner

For general heavy-duty cleaning around the home, try this solution: Into a warm gallon of water, stir one tablespoon of borax and one tablespoon of liquid soap (not detergent). For grease cutting purposes, also include a tablespoon or more of vinegar. See warning about babies drowning in the box below. For all-purpose cleaning, mix ½ cup vinegar and ¼ cup baking soda into a gallon of warm water.

WARNING: Never leave a bucket of water around your home. Babies can drown in a bucket or toilet very easily, because they are head-heavy and can easily fall upside down in this type of container. Clean with spray bottles only and never buckets. Even if your baby squirts your homemade cleaning solutions into her mouth, no problem because most of the recipes here are edible!

Bathroom Cleaners

Use plain white vinegar to clean your bathroom—it disinfects and gets rid of soap scum buildup. In a spray bottle, mix equal parts vinegar and water and use to clean bathroom fixtures, floor, bathtub, tile, and shower curtain. Rinse with water. To remove soap scum, mildew, and bathtub grime, wipe with undiluted white vinegar and then scrub with baking soda on a damp sponge. Rinse with water.

Clean the toilet bowl by pouring in one cup of white vinegar, let soak for five minutes, brush, and flush. A sprinkle of baking soda can be used in combination with the vinegar to remove a stubborn toilet bowl ring.

Never mix vinegar with bleach.

For a very stubborn toilet bowl ring, make a paste of borax and lemon juice. Flush to get sides of bowl wet, rub on the paste, let sit for two hours, and scrub.

Instead of using cleanser to scour a bathtub, try baking soda or salt or borax on a damp sponge as an abrasive cleanser. When kids leave a glop of toothpaste in the sink, take a washcloth and use the glop to scrub up the sink and fixtures. Bon Ami Cleaning Powder or Bon Ami Polishing Cleanser are also safe scouring cleansers. Check your natural foods store for others.

Prevent mold and mildew in your bathroom by keeping things as dry as possible. Heat will kill mold/mildew. If you can afford the utility bill, try leaving a portable electric heater running for several hours in your bathroom with windows and door closed, but do this while you remain at home and are awake, so you check it periodically for overheating and prevent a fire. For a small mold/mildew spot, hold a portable hair dryer on the spot to bake away those germies.

Remove hard lime deposits around faucets by covering with vinegar soaked paper towels. Let sit for an hour before cleaning. Chrome will be clean and shiny. Soak a clogged shower head in vinegar and water to remove deposits.

Don't use soap to clean ceramic tile, it leaves a film. Use a mixture of ¼-½ cup vinegar in one gallon water.

In the Kitchen

As with the bathroom, baking soda and vinegar can be used on kitchen sinks and faucets. To make your counter tops sparkle, pour club soda on them, clean with a wipe-up towel, rinse with water, and wipe dry.

Dishwasher Detergent

Commercial dishwasher detergents are toxic and most release low levels of chlorine fumes into the air when mixed with water. The levels are considered "safe." A minute film of detergent remains on the dishes.

An alternative homemade detergent for your dishwasher is equal parts borax and baking soda. Use about a quarter cup of this mixture (two tablespoons borax plus two tablespoons baking soda) per dishwasher load. I put one tablespoon of each in both the open and closed detergent compartments. This mixture may not work quite as well as commercial detergents and some pre-rinsing may be necessary.

Oven Cleaner

If you do not have a self-cleaning oven, it's probably better to have a dirty oven than to use commercial oven cleaners. Like drain cleaners, they contain lye, ammonia, and other poisons. Avoid them as you would avoid plutonium, especially the aerosol sprays which disperse tiny droplets of the poison into the air and maybe into your lungs, on your skin, and into your eyes.

Here's a safer method of cleaning that oven, which I found in Debra Lynn Dadd's wonderful book *Home Safe Home*. In a spray bottle, mix 2 tablespoons liquid soap (not detergent), 2 teaspoons borax, and fill to the top with warm water. Shake well until completely dissolved to prevent squirt device from clogging.

With rubber gloves and safety glasses, spray very close to the inside surface of the oven so solution does not disperse into the air. Let sit for 20 minutes and scrub with plain steel wool and non chlorine scouring powder. If necessary, use pumice (buy in hardware department) to scour off black spots.

Prevent oven stains on your oven by lining the oven floor with aluminum foil. Place foil under the burner, but don't let the foil touch the burner.

Air Fresheners

On your stove top, simmer a small saucepan of water with natural aromatic food stuffs. Try a mixture of lemon/orange/tangerine peels, apple peels, cloves, cinnamon, allspice, and pine needles. What a delicious and homey smell! To rid the house of cabbage, cauliflower, and other cooking smells, mix a little vanilla flavoring into plain simmering water.

As an air freshener, place vanilla on a cotton ball and place in a saucer out of children's reach. (Vanilla contains alcohol.) Use in your home, the refrigerator, or even in your car.

For a homemade spray air freshener, place one teaspoon of baking soda into a trigger spray bottle and add about a cup of water. Spray a fine mist to remove odors from the air. Or spray plain white vinegar full strength.

Refrigerator Odors

Keep an opened box of baking soda in the back of your refrigerator to absorb odors and then pour it down a drain to freshen the drain too. Place a few drops of vanilla on a cotton ball in a custard cup and your refrigerator will soon smell great.

Drain Cleaners

Drain cleaners are lethal to your child, any living thing, and to the environment. Their main ingredient is lye, and one drop of it will cause severe skin damage and blindness. Do not have any drain cleaners in your home, Grandma's house, your babysitter's house, and any place where your child will be.

Prevent clogs before they happen by inserting a little nylon netting or a lint catcher under the drain cap to catch hair and soap gook. Use rubber gloves to replace often—yuck! Never pour grease or any other drain clogging materials down your drains.

I used to have trouble with my kitchen and bathroom drains clogging often. Now I flush them at least once a month with just plain boiling water (being careful that my children are out of the way) and the problem is gone. Be very careful not to burn yourself: hold the water container as close to drain as possible and pour slowly and directly into drain. We eat whole grain pasta frequently and I save energy by draining the boiling water from the cooked pasta down the bathroom sinks alternately with the kitchen sink.

If you have a slow-running drain, and plain boiling water doesn't help, try this: Into the drain, pour ½ cup of baking soda/washing soda. Then pour in about one cup of white vinegar. If you wish, first heat the vinegar in the microwave until it's fairly hot. It should break down fat and soap scum. If possible, cover or close the drain tightly. Wait several minutes until the bubbling stops—this fizzing creates pressure to dislodge the clog. Then flush with lots of very hot or boiling water. Repeat if necessary. Do this regularly to keep your drains clear. Use baking soda and vinegar in your garbage disposal to keep it clean and sweet-smelling.

> WARNING: Do not use baking or washing soda in drains which are blocked, because they may harden and cause the block to get worse. Use only in slow running drains or in clear drains to keep them clear.

For blocked drains or really tough clogs, use a small plumber's helper (a plunger). They are cheap and you can buy them in any hardware department. Cover the plunger's rubber cap with water before plunging and it will work better, but first drape an old bath towel around it before plunging to prevent splatters. It may take several plunges to clear the drain.

> WARNING: Do not use a plunger after any commercial drain cleaner has been used in the drain or if commercial drain cleaner is present in the standing water.

If the above methods did not clear the drain, try pouring ¼ cup of 3% hydrogen peroxide into the drain, wait ten minutes, and plunge, being careful not to splatter the peroxide, especially into your eyes. Keep peroxide out of children's reach.

There are also garden hose pressure devices and mechanical snakes that you can buy to unclog drains. Or try carefully fishing down your drain pipes with an unbent wire hanger.

Window Cleaner

In a spray bottle (either a purchased spray bottle or a used, empty thoroughly-cleaned bottle), mix a solution of plain distilled white vinegar and water. Try a few tablespoons of vinegar for every cup of water or mix half vinegar and half water. Spray on windows and wipe clean with a lint-free cloth. Or use newspaper instead of a cloth to wipe windows clean. You'll find that this recipe cleans windows as well as or better than the expensive commercial window cleaning solutions that you purchase at the grocery store.

In the winter, coat your car's windows with a mixture of one part water and three parts vinegar to keep them frost- and ice-free.

TIP: Do your windows or drawers stick? Try "painting" their inside moldings or glides with petroleum jelly by using a small paint brush. Or rub them with soap.

NOTE: If vinegar and water cause your windows to look streaky, there is probably a wax buildup on your windows from previous commercial window cleaners. Remove the wax with rubbing alcohol. Vinegar and water will then work just beautifully.

Furniture and Floor Polish

The main ingredient in most commercial furniture polishes is mineral oil, which gets absorbed into the wood. You can mix your own by adding a little lemon oil to mineral oil, but it is better with a baby around the house to use an edible oil.

Mineral oil is not safe for a baby to drink. Any oil can be used to polish wood furniture: olive oil, corn oil, any vegetable oil, and even mayonnaise. Any smells will dissipate and the oil will not become rancid on your furniture. Be careful not to stain cloth, furniture, or rugs.

Another recipe: Mix one part vinegar with two parts olive oil. (Use white vinegar for light furniture and cider vinegar for dark wood furniture.)

Or, mix one part lemon juice to two parts olive or other vegetable oil in a spray bottle, shake well, and have fun dusting! Keep refrigerated.

Clean mahogany with equal parts vinegar and water.

Another more economical recipe for furniture polish: Add ½-1 tablespoon olive oil and ½-1 teaspoon vinegar to 1 cup warm tap water in a spray bottle. Mix it fresh each time because it should be warm while you are using it.

Use a mixture of equal parts white vinegar and vegetable oil on wood floors. Apply a thin coat of this mixture and rub in well.

> **WARNING:** Be careful not to stain cloth, furniture, or rugs with oils. And never put a cloth with vegetable oil in the washing machine or dryer, as it will turn rancid, smell terribly, and possibly permanently make your washer and dryer smell also.

Linoleum Floor Cleaners

You don't want your baby crawling on a poisonous floor cleaner, especially when she puts her wet fingers into her mouth while she's crawling. To clean, mop no-wax linoleum floors with plain water or water with a little mild detergent. Pour a cup of white vinegar into a gallon of warm water and go over the floor again to add luster. Instead of floor wax, mop your floor with water into which has been added one capful of baby oil. Or add some skim milk to the mop water for a shine. Keep water away from linoleum seams and edges to prevent loosening.

Carpets and Rugs

To deodorize, don't use the commercial powder. You don't want your baby crawling on chemicals. Instead, sprinkle baking soda or half baking soda/half cornstarch into your rugs. Let sit overnight and vacuum. No need for artificial fragrance if you add a pinch of cinnamon for a nice scent. First test on an inconspicuous spot if you have light-colored rugs. Instead of buying those vacuum scent inserts, put a cotton ball soaked with lemon juice or vanilla into your vacuum cleaner bag to freshen the air while you vacuum. Let the juice/vanilla dry before inserting.

To remove wet mud from your carpet, sprinkle liberally with cornstarch, wait 15 minutes, and vacuum.

When carpeting has an absolutely unremovable stain, it's time to cut and paste. Use a utility knife or razor blade widget to cut out the rectangular or circular piece of carpet with the stain. Do not cut out the underpadding.

Cut a matching piece of carpet from a closet floor or from under a piece of furniture that will never be moved. Use the cut piece of stained carpet to get the correct size and shape. (You may want to cut the unstained carpet piece a little bit bigger so you can trim it to fit exactly.) Then do the switch. Place the unstained carpet piece where the stained piece was. Use a glue gun to hot glue into place. Use plenty of glue so your vacuum cleaner won't pull up the carpet piece.

If the carpet has a stain that is lighter than the color of the carpet, try painting it back to its original color. Use a few shades of fabric paint close to the color of the carpet. Place paint globs on a paper plate, get down on the carpet, and mix the paints together until the color matches the carpet perfectly. Paint that stain away. More than one paint application may be necessary.

In the Laundry Room
Super Dirt Placer

Insert child into center of shallow puddle. Let soak five minutes. Move child over dirt pile and lower gently into sitting position. Spin.

Laundry Soap and Detergent

Detergents, which were invented to clean synthetic fabrics, are very different from natural soaps, which have been used to clean natural fabrics (cotton, silk, wool, linen) for hundreds of years. Detergents are made from petrochemicals, synthetic whiteners, artificial fragrances, and other chemicals. Soaps are made from natural minerals and fats. As you know from your bathroom, soaps have the problem of leaving scum. Buy laundry soaps at your natural food store.

> WARNING: Do not use soap on clothing that is flame retardant, as are children's sleepwear. Follow the manufacturer's instructions on the label for cleaning flame retardant garments.

If you run out of laundry soap/detergent, here's a recipe you can use in a pinch: Mix one tablespoon of baking soda/washing soda plus ½ tablespoon of borax into one cup of water. Add to washing machine at the beginning of the wash, as you would laundry detergent.

> WARNING: Dryer lint is very flammable and should not be used to stuff homemade toys. Remember to clean out the lint trap of your dryer after every load and the lint trap on your washing machine.

Washing machines and clothes dryers should be taken apart to clean the lint out of their workings on a regular basis. Besides preventing a fire, this will cause them to work more efficiently and will save money on energy bills.

Take Advantage of Your Machines

Get away with any manual washing that you can! Run plastic toys through the dishwasher on the top shelf. I have done entire loads with only toys. Clean hair combs, toys, and other items by running them through the clothes washing machine, but be careful not to wash them with clothing that may be easily damaged. I wash them with a load of wipe-up towels.

Wash large items in the bathtub with the shower massage and an old vegetable brush. First line the bathtub with a towel to prevent scratches. Save water by re-using your baby's bath water, if the item doesn't need to be sterile. I often do this with my son's fully submersible plastic potty chair or the toy wagon he plays with outside.

Fabric Softener

Fabric softeners are just another chemical to keep away from your baby. They leave a film on clothing to prevent or reduce the static cling that develops on synthetic fabrics and often contain heavy perfumes and fragrances. Natural fibers (cotton, silk, wool, linen) do not need static reduction. Fabric softeners may irritate baby's sensitive skin and cause reactions in allergic persons. They may also make clothing more flammable. Instead, use ¼ cup of baking soda/washing soda in the rinse cycle of your clothes washing machine. Mix soda into water before adding to remove white clumps.

Plain white vinegar is another non-irritating fabric softener. Add ½-1 cup vinegar to the final rinse water, but do not pour it directly on clothing or it may damage the color. Clothes will not smell vinegar-y when they are dry. Vinegar will help eliminate soap residue—it is mild on fabrics but strong enough to dissolve the alkalies in soaps and detergents. Vinegar breaks down uric acid, so it's especially good for your baby's clothes. Be sure that the manufacturer's instructions say that vinegar is OK to use in your washing machine. Or call the manufacturer to be sure that vinegar will not damage the machine. Do NOT use vinegar in your rinse water if you've used chlorine bleach during the wash cycle!

If you absolutely need a static reducer, the best commercial type to use is the unscented sheets, not the liquids. Bounce Free® is an example of such a fabric softener sheet, or use a brand from your natural foods store. Save money by cutting each sheet in half or in quarters. I've found that part of a sheet works just as well as a full sheet.

MONEY SAVER: If you do choose to use scented fabric softener sheets, save money by using them for more than one dryer load. Save the used sheets, wet them with a little liquid fabric softener, let them air dry, and use them as you would the original new sheets. Or buy some cheap sponges and cut them up into small pieces. Soak the sponge pieces in liquid fabric softener. Squeeze out excess softener, and toss into the dryer as you would use a fabric softener sheet. Keep reusing.

MONEY SAVER: No need to buy commercial spray starches, which are nothing more than cornstarch, chemicals, and water. Make your own by measuring one or two tablespoons of cornstarch into a spray bottle and filling with about one cup cold water. The more starch, the stiffer the result. Shake frequently during use and clean spritzer well after use to prevent clogging.

Bleach

Hydrogen peroxide can be used as a gentle bleach. It may also remove mildew from colored fabrics without bleaching them out. Always spot test first.

Super Clothing Stain Remover

This remover is not safe for you, the environment, or your clothes. It is to be used only in desperate stain situations when you are ready to throw the hopelessly-stained item out. Fill your washing machine to the low water level with hot water. Add one cup powdered Cascade® dishwasher detergent and one cup laundry bleach for whites (or Clorox II® for colored fabrics) and let your washing machine begin agitating in order to stir the detergent until all powder has dissolved. Then stop the machine, add clothing, let agitate a few minutes, and stop the machine to let soak for a few hours or overnight. Then let the machine finish the entire wash and spin cycles. Hope it works for you!

Dry Cleaner's Secret

I heard from a friend that dry cleaning is not really necessary, except in very rare cases. Do your pocketbook and the environment a favor by hand washing almost any article of *Dry Clean Only* clothing in mild soap and water. Use a true soap such as Ivory® Soap Flakes (not Woolite® or Dawn®), to prevent damage to fibers. Ironing the clothing is no fun, but you can take difficult items to the dry cleaner for a professional pressing. It's less expensive than a cleaning and pressing.

Use a baby gate over the bathtub to dry sweaters and other hand washables.

Irons and Babies Don't Mix

Ironing is too dangerous to do around a small child. Besides the possibility of serious burns, even a cold iron can cause serious injury if a baby pulls it off the ironing board by the cord. If you absolutely must iron when your child is in the house, keep your child in a playpen where he is in full view across the room from you. If your child won't stay in the playpen, get into it yourself with a small tabletop ironing board (here's my phobia of burns again!). Do this whenever you are working with any dangerous items, such as sharp scissors.

Making Clothing Flame-Retardant

Some children's clothing, such as sleepwear, has a flame-retardant film on it by law. This film can be washed off with soaps, so be careful to use the type of detergent recommended on the label of these flame-retardant clothes.

I appreciated flame retardancy the time my son's shirt caught fire from a sparkler at a Fourth of July party. The flame fizzled out immediately. (I discovered that there are some situations where you immediately and willingly place your naked hand on an open flame.)

If you suspect that your children's old pajamas are no longer flame-retardant, or when members of your family will be near an open flame, you may want to make their clothing flame-retardant. They'll be much safer as they toast marshmallows and sing around that campfire.

I was all ready to print a recipe here with instructions on how to make clothing flame-retardant, but I was strongly advised not to, due to the litigious society in which we now live. I suggest that you call your local fire department for the information. Sorry for the inconvenience.

Miscellaneous Tips

Human hair is extremely flammable. When children are around any type of fire, keep their long hair tied in a tight bun behind their necks.

Hot Water Bottle

For cold toes, use a spill-proof plastic bottle as a hot water bottle.

Ice Melt and Traction

Sprinkle plain baking soda on your sidewalks to prevent slipping on ice and to melt the ice. If the baking soda comes in on people's shoes, your crawling baby will be safe with it. Soda will not damage your rugs, sidewalks, or shoes. For more traction, sprinkle some of your child's play sand.

42

Your Kitchen Window is a Green Mine

Food plants grown in your own kitchen give you delicious fresh organic food. This chapter has directions on how to grow herbs. Herbs are easy to grow in your kitchen for actual food. Directions are also given in this chapter for other food plants, which will not really supply very much food, but are fun and educational nonetheless. Watching them grow is a good lesson for your children, who will learn that food is alive and comes from the Earth, not from cans and boxes in the supermarket.

How to Grow Herbs on Your Windowsill

There's nothing like fresh herbs picked from a plant growing right in your own kitchen (or backyard). I've got pots of parsley and other herbs growing on my windowsill, from which I frequently pick leaves for healthy little snacks. Kids think it's really neat (and so do adults).

> WARNING: Make sure your children know what is safe to eat and what is not. After seeing your kitchen herb garden, they may think it's OK to eat ANY green plant. Keep poisonous houseplants at a friend's house until your toddler gets older. Watch her carefully when she is outside, where green plants are everywhere.

Plants are dormant during the winter, so plan on planting indoor plants in the spring. If you plant herbs from seeds, you will be able to start eating leaves from the plants after several weeks, depending on the plant (read the seed package). Included here are the basics of growing herbs from seeds. If you find that you're really getting into indoor gardening, there are dozens of books at your local library that will give you all the details you need.

The Pots

Clay pots are best for growing herbs. Ready NEW clay pots by soaking them in plain water for at least one hour and allowing them to dry, so they won't absorb moisture from the soil. Wash old pots or those acquired from friends or yard sales thoroughly in soap and water.

You can use plastic pots, but clay is porous and lets the soil "breath." All pots should have drainage holes in the bottom.

> **MONEY SAVER:** Instead of buying pots, you can use milk cartons cut about 6 inches up from the bottom. Wash out the milk cartons thoroughly with hot water and soap. Poke a few small holes in the bottom for drainage.

The Soil

For the soil, mix together 1 part vermiculite, 1 part pearlite, and 2 parts sterilized potting soil. To know how much to buy, figure that a typical 4-inch (diagonal of the rim) pot takes about 2 cups. Or plug and fill your pots with water to figure the amount needed. If you're not sure how sterile your soil is, sterilize it yourself.

Line shallow baking pans with aluminum foil. Spread soil very thinly on pans and bake in pre-heated 180°F oven for at least 30 minutes. Cool before using. **DISCLAIMER:** The author is not responsible for any strong odors emanating from the oven during or after the baking procedure.

Place screening, nylon net, flat rocks, nut shells, sponge pieces, pantyhose pieces, cheesecloth layers, coffee filter pieces, or pieces of broken clay pot in the bottom of the pots to prevent the soil from falling out the drainage holes. Then place a layer of small pebbles or gravel on the bottom of the pot.

Fill each pot with the soil mixture to one inch from top. Place filled pots on the drip saucers that came with the pot to protect your windowsill from dirt and water.

Or use an old tray, plastic tops or containers, an old baking pan, Styrofoam trays, or whatever. I have one of my plants on a Frisbee, which is borrowed occasionally by my kids.

TIP: Chlorine from tap water will evaporate in a day or two. After watering your plants, fill the watering can with tap water immediately and let sit until the next watering. Chlorine will be gone and the water will be at room temperature. Chlorine causes brown tips on plants. Brown tips are also caused by bottom roots remaining too wet.

Parsley, Sage, Rosemary, and Thyme

You can buy seeds from mail order seed catalogs, your local garden store, or online. Common herbs that will grow well indoors are parsley (Extra Curly), basil (Green Ruffles Italian), and chives. You can also try anise, bay (bay leaves), chamomile (for tea), chervil, fennel, mint, mustard, oregano, rosemary, sage, and savory. Dill is my favorite.

I usually wait to buy seeds at the end of the season when they are on sale for use the next summer. They germinate just fine even though they are a year old, if you store them in a cool dry place or in an airtight jar in the refrigerator.

Soak the soil in the pots until it is thoroughly wet before you plant the seeds. Plant a few seeds into each pot until they are ¼-½ inch deep in the soil. (A good rule of thumb to follow when planting any seeds is to plant them as deep as they are long.)

You may wish to sprinkle a thin layer of sterile play sand on the top of the soil, which will help to keep it moist. The soil must be keep wet until the seeds germinate (sprout into little plants); however, don't water the seeds as you would houseplants or you'll flood and displace them. Keep the soil wet by misting it at least once a day, or use an old dropper from your baby's vitamins to gently drip water onto the soil.

Caring for Herb Plants

Herb plants should be kept warm (about 70°F) and in a sunny window. However, when the seeds are first sprouting, they are very delicate and must be protected from direct sunlight. Move them away from the window or cover them with cheesecloth so they don't burn up and die. In the winter, move them back from cold windows and make sure no leaves touch the cold window glass.

After a few weeks, sprouts will appear. When they are about 3 inches high, thin them. This means to remove the small, scrawny ones to leave room for the healthy, larger ones to grow. (Survival of the fittest.)

Keep the soil moist—you may have to water as often as once a day. Always have non-chlorinated water handy for your plants. See tip on previous page.

To help keep the air around your plants humid, place a layer of pebbles in a large shallow pan. Fill partway with water and place your plants in their pots on the pebbles and over the water.

Occasionally, spray your plants with the sink hose or soak them with a mister until they are dripping wet in order to rinse off any accumulated dirt and dust on the leaves.

Harvesting Herbs

When the plants grow to more than 4 inches high, you can pick off the largest leaves every few days. Take the outside leaves or the largest leaves from the top. Or, when taller, use sharp scissors to cut 2 or 3 inches off the top for eating or cooking. Always leave some leaves so you don't kill the plant, and leave the plants so that they are at least 4 inches high in the pot. If the plants grow into 3 sections, such as parsley, clip off the middle leaves.

Keep the picked leaves cool and eat them within 2-3 days, or freeze or dry them.

TIP: Add fresh chopped parsley or dill to cream cheese or butter and use as a spread for crackers or baked potatoes. Or sprinkle fresh herbs into scrambled eggs or pasta sauces.

Aroma Therapy for You

Grow some English lavender in your bedroom. Anytime you need a quick pampering, take in the fragrance of this wonderful smelling plant. Other fragrant herbs are scented geraniums, lemon verbena, patchouli, and tansy. Place mint leaves in your bath water for a wonderful scent.

Plant Tips

There's no need to buy special pots for plants—recycle containers you already have around the house: plastic containers of all sizes from small laundry detergent cups to large wastebaskets, old mugs, cups, bowls, etc.

- Make a small greenhouse out of one of those plastic bottles with the dark saucer bottoms. Remove the dark saucer and put soil and plants in it. Cut off top of clear bottle, turn upside down over saucer, and punch air holes in the top. Keep out of direct sunlight. Water but don't drown your plants. If moisture builds up within the greenhouse, remove the top and let it dry out a bit

- If you have an old aquarium that you no longer use for fish, use it for growing plants.

- Change a plain plant container into a fancy one by covering completely with small pebbles or by gluing on other textured art materials.

- Use an old bubble umbrella as a greenhouse.

- Germinate seeds indoors on top of the refrigerator, where they will be warm and cuddly.

- Wipe leaves with a mixture of half skim milk and half water to make them glossy. Or use mayonnaise or olive oil. Or use glycerin, which will not collect dust.

- Re-pot a plant into a large pot that is two inches larger.

- Mark each plant by placing a popsicle stick with its name and date written on it. Cover with transparent tape or clear nail polish to protect the writing. Or make plant markers by writing with permanent marker pen on white plastic spoons.

- A bent wire hanger will act as a trellis for a climbing houseplant. Bend into a heart or other shape and insert hook end in soil.

- Splint a bent houseplant with some clear tape and a toothpick or popsicle stick.

- Seal pruned stems and branches with Elmer's® Glue-All to prevent moisture loss and damage by insects.

- Fix cracks in a flowerpot with chewing gum.

- Keep egg shell halves and use as miniature planters. Paint a face on the front of the shells and the plants will look like hair growing out the top of the face.

- Make live potato heads: Cut raw potatoes in half and scoop out part of flesh. Plant grass seed in soil in the hollow. Growing grass looks like silly hair. Paint a face on the front of the potato.

- A layer of gravel on top of the soil in window boxes prevents dirt from splattering on windows during a rain.

- Free fertilizer! Feed your plants by watering them with nutrient-containing gray water: the soak water from your sprouts, the cooled water in which you boiled eggs or corn on the cob, water which contained cut flowers, weak tea (either orange pekoe and pekoe cut black tea, such as Lipton®), melted snow (minerals), flat club soda (minerals). To the soil, add a little wood ashes (controls pH), coffee grounds (adds acid), or egg shells that have been dried and pulverized in the blender (bone meal). Occasionally water them with skim milk.

- A good nutrition lesson for your child: Grow two plants side-by-side. Fertilize one and not the other and ask your child which one is healthier.

- Let your toddler water houseplants with squeeze bottles, for more control.

- Can plants spell!? Punch holes in the bottom of an aluminum baking sheet for drainage. Cover holes with nylon stocking or cheesecloth to prevent soil from falling out. Fill sheet with soil and trace your child's name into the soil with your finger. Plant small seeds along the soil lines. The small shoots will spell out your child's name. Write your child's name with small flowers in an outdoor garden.

- Cut black paper in the shape of your child's initial and glue it on the leaf of a tree outside or on a fruit before it ripens. Wait several weeks. Soak leaf in water to remove paper and let your child see her initial.

- Soak raw onions and garlic in some water for a week. Place in spray bottle and use as a natural insecticide for plants.

- My dog used to love to "dig" in the soil of my houseplants and eject soil all over the floor. I stopped her by covering the soil with plastic mesh, cut to fit around the plant like a big collar.

Fun Fruit Plants

Grow Citrus Plants

Take several plump-looking seeds from an orange (or grapefruit or lemon) and gently rinse them under cold water and dry them. Let them dry for 3-4 days.

In a 4-inch pot, place several (in case some don't germinate) orange seeds one inch apart and ½-1 inch deep into the soil. Place the fat, rounded end of the seed down.

Keep the soil moist (but not soaked) and in a sunny window, but not in direct sunlight.

In 3-6 weeks (the seeds are slow to germinate), a plant will come up. Because it takes so long to germinate, you may wish to enclose the pot in a large plastic bag for a greenhouse effect and to keep moisture in. Or cut the top off a clear plastic two liter bottle and place over plants—punch some air holes in the top.

Remove from plastic bag or bottle after germination. Keep in a sunny window and water when soil begins to dry.

Johnny Appleseed

Start an apple tree by following the directions above for citrus fruits.

Grow A Grape Vine

Take a few grape seeds and soak them in water overnight. Plant ¼-inch deep. Follow directions for citrus plants.

Grow a Pineapple Plant

Buy a whole pineapple with healthy, unbroken, symmetrical, green (no brown) leaves. Slice off the top green leafy part of a whole pineapple, leaving about an inch of flesh. Gently pull off the lower row of green leaves. Place it in a jar of water out of direct sunlight.

In a week or two, roots will appear. Transplant to a 6-inch pot, covering brown skin and flesh with soil and keeping leaves above the soil. Keep in a sunny spot and water once a week, pouring water into the middle of the leaves.

Take care of it and in a few years (good things take time), a little pineapple may appear.

Grow an Avocado Plant

Take the huge seed from the avocado, rinse off the green flesh, and remove the thin brown skin. Insert three toothpicks or nails equal distance around the middle of the seed. The toothpicks will support the seed in the top of a glass of water, larger flat side down. The glass's perimeter should be larger than the seed, to allow air to circulate around the seed.

Keep the glass in a warm place out of direct sunlight. Each day or two, replace evaporated water so that the lower third of the seed remains under water. Change the water every week or so.

In a few weeks, roots will grow underwater and the seed will split to allow a small green stalk to emerge.

When the roots are several inches long and the stalk is 6 inches high, replant into a 6-inch clay pot, so that half the seed is exposed above the soil. To do this, make a hole in the soil large enough so that you can put in the seed, root side down, without damaging the delicate roots.

Give it plenty of water and sun and watch it grow! When it is about a foot tall, cut 2 inches off the tip of the shoot, which will cause it to branch and get bushy. Periodically prune your avocado plant.

Grow a Sweet Potato Plant

Buy an unwaxed sweet potato (if you can find one). Grow using the same method as with an avocado seed above. Buds will appear on the top and roots will sprout under the water. In about a month, your windowsill will be crawling with potato vines.

Grow a Peanut Plant

Plant 5 raw shelled peanuts 1 inch deep into the soil of a clay pot, placing as far apart as possible from each other and the sides of the pot. Keep moist and in a sunny spot.

Grow a Carrot, Beet, Turnip, or Parsnip Plant

Unlike the boy in Ruth Krauss's book, *The Carrot Seed*, who started a carrot plant with a seed, have your child start with a whole, fully grown carrot with greens still attached. From carrot (or other veggie), slice the greens off the top so that ½-1 inch of orange flesh remains. Place orange part of carrot halfway into a saucer with water or into wet sterile sand or pearlite. Keep wet, and leaves will grow in a week or two.

Forest Plants

Take a nature walk and gather wild outdoor plants: moss from the side of a tree, small ferns, tiny plants. Make a forest terrarium with your gatherings.

Flowers

Collect seeds from yours or a friend's annual flowering plants for next year. Place a plastic bag over a dried up blossom and wait several days for seeds to fall into bag. Shake occasionally to help the process. Place seeds in an envelope labeled with the name of the flower. Store the envelope in a cool dry place.

Collect several different types of seeds and give as gifts along with gardening accessories: a trowel, gardening gloves, a planter, etc. Include instructions.

When you spouse brings you flowers and they slump in the vase, stretch lengths of clear tape from one edge of the vase to another and perpendicular to each other. Place flowers between crisscrossed tape to "straighten them up."

For flower stems that are damaged or too short, lengthen by inserting into plastic straws cut to the length you need. Cut stems at an angle with sharp scissors. Remove leaves below water line—they'll decay and poison the water.

To keep cut flowers fresher longer, refrigerate them overnight and as much as possible. Preserve cut flowers by placing them in water mixed with a little white vinegar (antibacterial) and cane sugar (food). Use about one tablespoon each of vinegar and sugar per pint of water.

Appendices

Measures and Metric Equivalents

Common Cookbook Abbreviations

t = tsp = teaspoon	oz = ounce
T = tbsp = tablespoon	lb = pound
c = cups	L = liters
pt = pint	ml = milliliters
qt = quart	g = grams
gal = gallon	kg = kilograms

Common Equivalent Measures

3 tsps = 1 tbsp = ½ fluid oz
2 tbsps = 1 fluid oz
3 tbsps = 1½ fluid ounces = 1 jigger
4 tbsps = ¼ cup = 2 fluid ounces
8 tbsps = ½ cup = 4 fluid ounces
12 tbsps = ¾ cup = 6 fluid ounces
16 tbsps = 1 cup = 8 fluid ounces
¼ cup = 5 tbsps + 1 tsp
½ cup = 10 tbsps + 2 tsps
2 cups = 16 fluid ozs = 1 pint
4 cups = 32 fluid oz = 2 pints = 1 qt
4 quarts = 1 gallon
pinch = less than ¼ tsp
1 food cube = 2-3 tbsps
1 stick butter = ½ c = ¼ lb = 8 tbsps
1 liter = 1000 milliliters
1 milliliter = 0.001 liter
1 kilogram = 1000 grams
1 gram = .001 kilograms

Metric Equivalents Common Approximate Measures

1 teaspoon ≈ 5 milliliters
1 tablespoon ≈ 15 milliliters
¼ cup ≈ 60 milliliters
⅓ cup ≈ 80 milliliters
½ cup ≈ 120 milliliters
⅔ cup ≈ 140 milliliters
¾ cup ≈ 180 milliliters
1 cup ≈ 240 milliliters
1 ounce ≈ 30 milliliters
1 teaspoon ≈ 5 grams
1 tablespoon ≈ 15 grams
1 ounce ≈ 30 grams
1 pound ≈ 454 grams
1 quart ≈ 0.95 liter
1 gallon ≈ 3.8 liters
1 gram = 0.035 ounces
1 kilogram = 2.21 pounds
1 liter = 1.06 quarts

Note: ≈ means almost equal to

Metric Equivalents

Liquid Measure

⅛ teaspoon = 0.61 milliliters
¼ teaspoon = 1.23 milliliters
½ teaspoon = 2.47 milliliters
¾ teaspoon = 3.70 milliliters
1 teaspoon = 4.94 milliliters
**Multiply teaspoons by 4.94
to get milliliters.**

⅛ tablespoon = 1.84 milliliters
¼ tablespoon = 3.69 milliliters
½ tablespoon = 7.39 milliliters
¾ tablespoon = 11.08 milliliters
1 tablespoon = 14.78 milliliters
**Multiply tablespoons by 14.79
to get milliliters.**

1 ounce = 29.57 milliliters
**Multiply fluid ounces by 29.57
to get milliliters.**

⅛ cup = 29.57 milliliters
¼ cup = 59.14 milliliters
½ cup = 118.28 milliliters
¾ cup = 177.42 milliliters
1 cup = 236.56 milliliters
**Multiply cups by 236.56
to get milliliters.
Multiply cups by 2.37
to get liters.**

1 pint = 473.18 milliliters
**Multiply pints by 473.18
to get milliliters.
Multiply pints by .473
to get liters.**

1 quart = 946.00 milliliters
½ gallon = 1.89 liters
¾ gallon = 2.83 liters
1 gallon = 3.78 liters

Dry Measure

⅛ teaspoon = 0.54 grams
¼ teaspoon = 1.09 grams
½ teaspoon = 2.19 grams
¾ teaspoon = 3.28 grams
1 teaspoon = 4.38 grams
**Multiply teaspoons by 4.38
to get grams.**

⅛ tablespoon = 1.77 grams
¼ tablespoon = 3.54 grams
½ tablespoon = 7.09 grams
¾ tablespoon = 10.63 grams
1 tablespoon = 14.18 grams
**Multiply tablespoons by 14.18
to get grams.**

⅛ ounce = 3.59 grams
¼ ounce = 7.39 grams
½ ounce = 14.18 grams
¾ ounce = 21.34 grams
1 ounce = 28.35 grams
**Multiply ounces by 28.35
to get grams.**

2 ounces ≈ 60 grams
4 ounces = ¼ pound ≈ 115 grams
8 ounces = ½ pound ≈ 225 grams
16 ounces = 1 pound = 453.59 grams
**Multiply pounds by 454
to get grams.**

Note: ≈ means almost equal to

Metric Equivalents - Temperature

To convert Fahrenheit to Centigrade, subtract 32° from Fahrenheit temperature and multiply the difference by 5/9 (or .5556).

$$
\begin{array}{rcl}
0°F &=& -18°C \\
32°F &=& 0°C \\
40°F &=& 4°C \\
60°F &=& 16°C \\
120°F &=& 49°C \\
140°F &=& 60°C \\
165°F &=& 74°C \\
200°F &=& 93°C \\
212°F &=& 100°C \\
225°F &=& 107°C \\
250°F &=& 121°C \\
275°F &=& 135°C \\
300°F &=& 149°C \\
325°F &=& 163°C \\
350°F &=& 177°C \\
375°F &=& 191°C \\
400°F &=& 204°C \\
425°F &=& 218°C \\
450°F &=& 232°C
\end{array}
$$

Metric Equivalents - Growth Charts

For the height and weight growth charts on pages 391-392:

Multiply pounds by 0.454 to get kilograms.

Multiply pounds by 454 to get grams.

Multiply inches by 2.54 to get centimeters.

Resources

Books

You will find many of these books on the shelves in your local library. If your library does not have a book that you want, ask your librarian for assistance with an interlibrary loan. These loans are usually free.

American Academy of Pediatrics. *Caring for Your Baby and Young Child.* New York: Bantam Books, 2009.

American Academy of Pediatrics. *Pediatric nutrition handbook (6th ed.).* Elk Grove Village, IL: American Academy of Pediatrics, 2008.

American Academy of Pediatrics, & Remer, Tanya Altmann. The wonder years: helping your baby and young child successfully negotiate the major developmental milestones. New York : Bantam, 2006.

Berman, Dr. Jenn. *SuperBaby: 12 Ways to Give Your Child a Head Start in the First 3 Years.* New York: Sterling, 2011.

Berthold Bond, Annie. *Home Enlightenment: Create a Nurturing, Healthy, and Toxin Free Home.* Emmaus, PA: Rodale, 2005.

Brazelton, T. Berry, M.D. *Touchpoints.* Reading, MA: Da Capo Press, 2006.

Burke, Cindy. *To Buy or Not to Buy Organic: What You Need to Know to Choose the Healthiest, Safest, Most Earth-Friendly Food.* Reading, MA: Da Capo Press, 2007.

Butte, Nancy, Cobb, Kathleen, Dwyer, Johanna, Graney, Laura, Heird, William, & Rickard, Karyl. *The start healthy feeding guidelines for infants and toddlers. Journal of the American Dietetic Association.* (Vol. 104, Issue 3). 2004

Caplan, Theresa. *The First Twelve Months of Life, Rev. Ed.* New York: Bantam, 1995.

Carruth BR, Skinner, JD. *Feeding behaviors and other motor development in healthy children (2-24 months).* American College of Nutrition. (Vol. 21, Issue 2), 2002.

Collins, Lisa Cipriano. *Caring for your child with severe food allergies: emotional support and practical advice from a parent who's been there*. New York: Wiley, 2000.

Costenbader, Carol W. *The Big Book of Preserving the Harvest, Rev. Ed.* Pownal, Vermont: Storey Communications, 2002.

Dadd, Debra Lynn. *Home Safe Home*. New York: Penguin Putnam, 1997.

DeLong, Deanna. *How to Dry Foods*. Tucson, Arizona: HP Trade, 2006.

Duyff, Roberta Larson, & American Dietetic Association. *Complete food and nutrition guide,3rd Ed*. Hoboken, NJ: John Wiley & Sons, 2006.

Eiger, Marvin S., M.D. and Sally Wendkos Olds. *The Complete Book of Breastfeeding, 4th Ed.* New York: Workman Publishing Company, 2010.

Eisenberg, Arlene, Heidi E. Murkoff, and Sandee E. Hathaway. *What to Expect the First Year*. New York: Workman Publishing Company, 2003.

Fassa, Lynda. *Green babies, sage moms: the ultimate guide to raising your organic baby*. New York: New American Library, 2008.

Gavigan, Christopher. *Healthy child, healthy world: creating a cleaner, greener, safer home*. New York: Dutton, 2008.

General Mills, Inc. *Betty Crocker's Vegetarian Cooking, 3rd Ed*. New York: Betty Crocker, 2012.

Greene, Alan R. *Raising baby green : the earth friendly guide to pregnancy, childbirth, and baby care*. San Francisco: Jossey Bass, 2007.

Fomon, Samuel J. *Feeding Normal Infants: Rationale for Recommendations*. Journal of the American Dietetic Association. (Vol. 101, Issue 9), 2001.

Hertzberg, Ruth, Beatrice Vaughan, and Janet Greene. *Putting Food By; Revised edition*. Brattleboro, VT: Plume, 2010.

Hollender, Jeffrey, Davis, Geoff, Hollender, Meika, & Reed Doyle. *Naturally clean: the Seventh Generation guide to safe & healthy, non toxic cleaning*. Gabriola Island, BC, Canada: New Society, 2006.

Holtzman, Debra Smiley. *The safe baby: a do it yourself guide to home safety*. Boulder, CO: Sentient Publications, 2005.

Hood, Joan, compiler for *Home and Freezer Digest. Will It Freeze?* New York: Scribner, 2002.

Jensen, Bernard. *Foods that Heal.* New York: Avery Publishing Group, 1993.

Johnston, Ingeborg M., and James R. Johnston. *Flaxseed (Linseed) Oil and the Power of Omega-3.* New York, McGraw-Hill, 1995.

Joneja, J.V. *Dealing with food allergies: a practical guide to detecting culprit foods and eating a healthy, enjoyable diet.* Boulder, CO: Bull Publishing Company, 2003.

Karmel, Annabel. T*he Healthy Baby Meal Planner.* New York: Atria Books, 2009.

Kimmel, Martha, David Kimmel, and Suzanne Goldenson. *Mommy Made Home Cooking for a Healthy Baby & Toddler, Revised edition.* New York: Bantam Books, 2000.

La Leche League International. *The Womanly Art of Breastfeeding, Rev. Edition.* New York: Ballantine Books, 2010.

Lansky, Vicki. *Baby Proofing Basics: How to Keep Your Child Safe, 2nd Ed.* The Book Peddlers, 2002.

Lappé, Frances Moore. *Diet for a Small Planet, 20 Ann. edition.* New York: Ballantine Books, 1991.

Lipsitt, L, Crook, C, & Booth, C. *The transitional infant: Behavioral development and feeding.* American Journal of Clinical Nutrition, Vol. 41, Issue 2, 1985.

Mahan, L. Kathleen & Escott-Stump, Sylvia. *Krause's Food & Nutrition Therapy (12th ed.).* St. Louis, MO: Saunders, 2008.

Malkan, Stacy. *Not just a pretty face : the ugly side of the beauty industry.* Gabriola, B.C.: New Society, 2007.

McDonald, Libby. *The toxic sandbox : the truth about environmental toxins and our children's health.* New York: Penguin, 2007.

National Research Council. *Recommended Dietary Allowances 10th edition.* Washington, D.C.: National Academy Press, 1999.

Ojakangas, Beatrice. *Great Whole Grain Breads*. Univ. Of Minnesota Press; 2002.

Olds, Sally B., Marcia L. London, and Patricia A. Ladewig. *Maternal Newborn Nursing, 9th Ed*. New York: Prentice Hall, 2012.

Pantley, Elizabeth. *The No-Cry Picky Eater Solution: Gentle Ways to Encourage Your Child to Eat-and Eat Healthy*. New York: McGraw-Hill, 2011.

Prince, Francine and Harold Prince. *Feed Your Kids Bright*. New York: Simon and Schuster, 1987; iUniverse, 2000.

Robertson, Laurel, Carol Flinders, and Bronwen Godfrey. *The Laurel's Kitchen Bread Book A Guide to Whole-Grain Breadmaking*. New York: Random House, 2003.

Robertson, Laurel, Carol Flinders, and Brian Ruppenthal. *The New Laurel's Kitchen: A Handbook for Vegetarian Cookery and Nutrition*. Berkeley, California: Ten Speed Press, 1986.

Rombauer, Irma S., and Marion Rombauer Becker. *Joy of Cooking, anniversary edition*. New York: Scribner, 2006.

Samour, Patricia Queen & King, Kathy. *Handbook of Pediatric Nutrition (3rd ed.)*. Boston, MA: Jones & Bartlett, 2005.

Sandbeck, Ellen. *Green housekeeping*. New York: Simon & Schuster, 2006.

Sicherer, S. H. *Understanding and managing your child's food allergies*. Baltimore, MD: The Johns Hopkins University Press, 2006.

Spock, Benjamin, M.D., and Michael B. Rothenberg, M.D. *Dr. Spock's Baby and Child Care*. New York: Dutton, 1992.

Stanfield, Peggy. *Nutrition and Diet Therapy*. Boston: Jones and Bartlett Publishers, 2009.

Stang, Jamie. *Improving the Eating Patterns of Infants and Toddlers*. Journal of the American Dietetic Association. (Vol. 106, Issue 1), 2006.

Steinman, David. *Safe trip to Eden: 10 steps to save planet Earth from the global warming meltdown*. New York: Thunder's Mouth Press, 2007.

O.R. Sweet, O. Robin Sweet, and Thomas Bloom. *The Well-Fed Baby, 2nd Ed*. New York: William Morrow Cookbooks, 2000.

White, Burton L. *The First Three Years of Life*. New York: Fireside Books, 1995.

Whitney, Eleanor Noss, and Eva May Nunnelley Hamilton. *Understanding Nutrition,* 13 edition. Wadsworth Publishing, 2012.

Wolverton, B.C. *How to grow fresh air: 50 houseplants that purify your home or office*. New York: Penguin, 1997.

Yntema, Sharon. *Vegetarian Baby*. Ithaca, New York: McBooks Press, 1999.

Internet References
Connect with Ruth Yaron

Super Baby Food Web Site
http://www.superbabyfood.com

Ruth Yaron's Blog
http://www.superbabyfood.com/blog

Super Baby Food Facebook Page
http://www.facebook.com/SuperBabyFood

Super Baby Food Twitter Page
http://twitter.com/Super_Baby_Food
@Super_Baby_Food

Super Baby Food Pinterest Page
http://pinterest.com/SuperBabyFood

Connect with Others to Chat About Super Baby Food

BabyCenter.com Super Baby Food Community Board: Super Baby Food
http://community.babycenter.com/groups/a6690395/super_baby_food

The Bump's Community Board for feeding Baby
http://pregnant.thebump.com/new-mom-new-dad/feeding-baby.aspx

CaféMom has hundreds of Community boards for you to choose from
http://www.cafemom.com/parenting/

Parents.com talks all baby feeding all the time!
http://www.parents.com/advice/babies/feeding/

Fantastic website and Community Boards on feeding baby
http://www.justmommies.com/babies/feeding-baby

Informational Web Sites

Easy Homemade Baby Food Recipes & Solid Food Tips
http://wholesomebabyfood.momtastic.com

This Livestrong Site is chock-full of healthy information for Mom & Baby
http://www.livestrong.com/baby

American Academy of Pediatrics Website
http://www.aap.org

National Institute of Allergy and Infectious Diseases
http://www.niaid.nih.gov

Food Allergy and Anaphylaxis Network
http://foodallergy.org

American Academy of Allergy, Asthma and Immunology
http://www.aaaai.org

United States Department of Agriculture Guidelines
http://choosemyplate.gov

La Leche League
http://www.llli.org

Juvenile Products Manufacturers Association (JPMA)
http://www.jpma.org

Consumer Product Safety Commission (CPSC)
http://www.cpsc.gov

Food and Drug Administration (FDA)
http://www.fda.gov

Organic Trade Association
http://www.ota.com

National Pesticide Information Center
http://npic.orst.edu

Beyond Pesticides
http://www.beyondpesticides.org

Retail Web Sites

The Bread Beckers
http://www.BreadBeckers.com

True Foods Market
http://www.truefoodsmarket.com

Organic Kingdom
http://www.organickingdom.com

Organic Direct
http://www.organicdirect.com

Papa's Organic
http://www.papasorganic.com

shopOrganic and shopGMOfree
http://www.shoporganic.com

Mountain Rose Herbs
http://www.mountainroseherbs.com

Starwest Botanicals
http://www.starwest-botanicals.com

Seventh Generation
http://www.seventhgeneration.com

* Ruth Yaron is not compensated in any way for suggesting these web sites.

Recipe Index

Index

About the Author

When Ruth Yaron's twin boys were born premature and very sick, she knew the most important thing she could do for them was to feed them the healthiest diet possible. Unhappy with the information that was available to her, Ruth decided to do her own exhaustive research on nutrition and health food. Although she an inexperienced cook, she used dozens of natural cookbooks to learn her way around a kitchen, experimenting with tofu, carob and wheat germ, much to the surprise of friends and family.

A determined mother is a great motivator. She utilized her skills, developed writing technical manuals for the everyday reader, to diligently record her research of homemade, mostly organic, whole grain cereals, fruits, and home-cooked vegetables, as well as the best storing and freezing methods. The result was a remarkably easy and complete system of baby food preparation: *Super Baby Food*.

Ruth continues her research and to share *Super Baby Food* tips with her audience through her blog at www.SuperBabyFood.com, her active Facebook page and Twitter account (@Super_Baby_Food). She loves to interact AND hear feedback from new parents and will answer any of the energetic, insightful questions they have.

Ruth graduated from East Stroudsburg University in Pennsylvania with degrees in Mathematics and Computer Science. She worked at the GE Space Division and programmed satellites for NASA before writing *Super Baby Food*. She has three sons and lives with her husband in Scranton, Pennsylvania.

Please visit Ruth's websites:

SuperBabyFood.com for additions, corrections, and updates to this book.

RuthYaron.com for Ruth's book with special recipes for food pouches.

RuthOnAmazon.com for a list of Ruth's Kindle books.

RuthRecommends.com for products Ruth recommends to her readers.